D1482478

Envision In Depth

READING, WRITING, AND RESEARCHING ARGUMENTS

Envision In Depth

READING, WRITING, AND RESEARCHING ARGUMENTS

Christine L. Alfano and Alyssa J. O'Brien

PEARSON
Longman

New York • San Francisco • Boston
London • Toronto • Sydney • Tokyo • Singapore • Madrid
Mexico City • Munich • Paris • Cape Town • Hong Kong • Montreal

Executive Editor: Lynn M. Huddon
Senior Marketing Manager: Sandra McGuire
Development Editor: Michael Greer
Production Manager: Stacey Kulig
Project Coordination, Text Design, and Electronic Page Makeup: Pre-Press PMG
Cover Designer/Manager: Wendy Ann Fredericks
Cover Images: *left to right* Rob Crandall/The Image Works; Benno de Wilde/Punchstock.com; and Patrick
    Broderick/ModernHumorist.com
Photo Researcher: PhotoSearch
Manufacturing Buyer: Lucy Hebard
Printer and Binder: Quebecor World Taunton
Cover Printer: Coral Graphics

For permission to use copyrighted material, grateful acknowledgment is made to the copyright holders on
pp. 661–664, which are hereby made part of this copyright page.

Library of Congress Cataloging-in-Publication Data
Alfano, Christine L.
    Envision in Depth / Christine L. Alfano, Alyssa J. O'Brien. — 1st ed.
        p. cm.
    Includes bibliographical references and index.
    ISBN-13: 978-0-321-35571-3
    ISBN-10: 0-321-35571-7
    1. English language—Rhetoric. 2. Persuasion (Rhetoric) 3. College readers. 4. Report writing. 5. Visual
communication. 6. Visual perception. I. O'Brien, Alyssa J. II. Title.
    PE1431.E56 2008
    808'.0427—dc22

                                                                                            2007020811

Copyright © 2008 by Pearson Education, Inc.

All rights reserved. No part of this publication may be reproduced, stored in a retrieval system, or
transmitted, in any form or by any means, electronic, mechanical, photocopying, recording, or otherwise,
without the prior written permission of the publisher. Printed in the United States.

Please visit us at www.ablongman.com

ISBN 13: 978-0-321-35571-3
ISBN 10: 0-321-35571-7

2 3 4 5 6 7 8 9 10—QWT—10 09 08

Contents

Preface   *xvi*

PART III: DESIGN, DELIVERY, AND DOCUMENTATION   177

Chapter 14

Representing Reality   529

Snapshots of the Ordinary   531

Images of Crisis   560

Preface

Students today are surrounded by words and images that try to persuade them to see the world in a certain way, buy particular products, play specific video games, and understand political realities from diverse perspectives. This textbook offers instruction in *how* to understand such texts while also teaching students to make a written contribution of their own.

Our purpose with *Envision in Depth* is to provide a sound base in writing pedagogy while leading students through the steps in analyzing and researching verbal and visual compositions such as images, ads, films, speeches, and multimedia displays. To develop students' understanding of texts of all kinds, we instruct students in the writing process from **analysis** to complex tasks such as **argumentation**, **research writing**, and **presentation**. To do so, we walk students through interactive lessons on crafting thesis statements, structuring argumentative essays, developing research topics, evaluating sources, integrating quotations, revising papers, and, finally, designing and presenting effective presentations and writing projects. At the same time, students learn key **rhetorical concepts** for effective communication, such as attending to audience, understanding rhetorical appeals and fallacies, practicing the canons of rhetoric, differentiating levels of decorum, and using the branches of oratory.

While we provide instruction in writing about visual and multimedia texts, most chapters begin by focusing on words (print materials and articles) and then expand out to include writing about images and other contemporary texts (ads, photographs, films, video games, and even graffiti art). The annotated student writing examples and print articles in the book serve both to demonstrate the writing lessons presented in each chapter and to show students how to accomplish specific writing tasks and successfully implement rhetorical strategies in their own texts.

Envision in Depth also offers a selection of readings about visual culture, gaming, photography, body image, copyright issues, and globalization so that students can explore issues in more depth, sharpen their skills of analysis, and study models of research and writing. With the wide variety of readings in Part IV, students can examine controversies on subjects such as downloading music or violent video games, learn about customs and dress of people across the globe, or understand the impact of McDonald's fast-food restaurants in various countries. The "Reflect and Write" questions about the readings help sharpen students' analytical abilities, provide opportunities for written composition, and even launch research projects on topics that interest students today.

It is our hope that this book will accomplish two goals: that it will give teachers everywhere the confidence and resources to lead students in an engaging and rhetorically sound pedagogy focused on accessible writing instruction; and that it will interest students while empowering them to become knowledgeable and skilled writers, researchers, and producers of well-composed rhetorical texts for a range of audiences.

Preview of the Readings in Part IV

In classes using *Envision* (a shorter version of this book, without readings), we heard constantly from our students that they wanted to study more articles like the one by Nora Ephron in Chapter 3. To that end, we explored many possible topic areas that corresponded to crucial issues in the world today. We developed a set of chapters based on current concerns that intrigue and matter to students. These include issues about body image, and in the chapter "Marked Bodies" we explore how the media shapes our notions of the ideal body as well as what this means for visual representations of gender and cultural identity. We also look at how people seek to control the way society looks at them through making a fashion statement with body art, tattoos, religious clothing or jewelry, and other signs of a self-crafted identity.

As many students hold a deep interest in sports, we offer three components to our chapter of readings on "Sports and Media," including controversies over engineered athletes, trends in the globalization of sports, and an exploration of stereotypes in media coverage of sports.

Two chapters subsequently tackle problems emerging from digital advances in how to produce and share texts. In "Copyright and Creativity" we look at copyright controversies such as file sharing, creative commons, and remixing culture. Turning from idea generation, borrowing, and distribution of digital products to contemporary arguments about video games, in "Gaming Culture" we explore how gender is constructed and we analyze debates on videogame violence. We then turn to consider "persuasive games" that are designed with a specific agenda intended to mobilize change in users.

While video games offer one interpretation of our lived experience, photographs provide even more compelling images of our contemporary world. In "Representing Reality," we examine the power of persuasion in photos, both of local "normal" life in America and of difficult times experienced around the world, as explored in the section on "Images of Crisis." This chapter wrestles with the ethics of photojournalism, embedded journalists in war, and the recent appearance of "citizen journalists" who take photos with cell phone cameras.

Finally, Part IV ends with a chapter on "Globalization" in which we take a careful look at current trends in corporate franchises potentially overwhelming aspects of traditional cultures, as many claim McDonald's has done. We expand out, however, to consider how Eastern cultures and practices have in turn influenced popular activities and trends in the West, such as is shown by the impact of Bollywood films, anime, and even martial arts or meditation. The last section on "Outsourcing and Global Communities" provides economic and political perspectives on our changing multimedia world linked by Internet communication and an increasing interconnectedness of people writing in various mediums. As with the previous chapters, "Globalization" asks students to analyze the arguments of each article, ad, or photograph and provides writing prompts, activities for collaborative work, and ideas for developed research projects.

While our mission with this book is to teach students how to understand, analyze, conduct research on, and compose arguments about all kinds of texts, both throughout the book and in this new fourth section we seek to capture and sustain student interest by using contemporary examples. We hope to enable students to develop the skills, confidence, and enthusiasm for writing, research, and effective communication about issues that matter to them.

Structure and Sequence of Assignments

Students of *Envision in Depth* will develop the skills to become confident, competent, and effective writers through following the book's four-part structure. At the same time, teachers can use chapters and assignments in any order.

Part I: Analysis and Argument

This section aims to train students in analysis and argument. Students work through exercises to become proficient, careful readers of rhetorical texts and to learn practical strategies for writing thesis statements, rhetorical analysis essays, and synthesis essays incorporating different perspectives. Students learn how to analyze the forms of persuasion in verbal and visual texts—from short articles to political cartoons, ads, and photos. Chapters 1–3 focus on writing, from drafting thesis statements to understanding formal strategies of argument. These pages examine both conventional academic essays and contemporary popular articles.

Part II: Research Arguments

Chapters 4–6 focus on strategies of research argument for sustained writing projects. The writing lessons in this section of the book take students through the research proposal, techniques for keeping a research log, how to locate sources, how to include charts and graphs, methods of outlining, drafting, and revising, and best practices for integrating sources in writing. We spend time learning how to gather and evaluate sources, conduct library and field research, and work collaboratively on a draft. Students can consult sample writing in the form of proposals, outlines, and drafts while they examine textual examples such as articles, propaganda posters, and film trailers.

Part III: Design, Delivery, and Documentation

The chapters in Part III offer students an opportunity to polish their writing. Students learn about document design—both for academic papers and for visual arguments such as op-ads and photo essays. We offer a chapter on translating written work into effective oral and multimedia presentations, with attention to drafting a script, designing a PowerPoint slideshow, and practicing delivery of arguments. Students learn how to design memorable and compelling writing projects for a range of academic and professional purposes, including service-learning courses, and we conclude the section with a chapter on plagiarism and MLA documentation.

Part IV: Readings

Chapters 10–15 offer readings for analysis, discussion, and writing prompts. We ask students to think critically about each text in "Reflect and Write" boxes at the end of each reading, and we offer synthesis questions at the end of each chapter in which students might conduct a comparative analysis or use the readings as a springboard for a larger research project.

Sequence of Assignments

Throughout the book, we've delineated examples of steps in the writing process: Chapter 1 shows students how to construct a thesis statement; Chapter 3 focuses on introductions and conclusions; Chapter 4 spends time on writing a proposal; and Chapter 6 includes two outlines, a draft, and a revised paper. In this way, *Envision* takes students through all the necessary components for effective writing—from generating an idea, to implementing rhetorical appeals and evidence, to crafting effective transitions, to acknowledging sources using proper MLA style and without risking plagiarism, to conventions of document design. Since the way a paper is formatted represents a type of visual rhetoric, we've also taken time to instruct students in both academic conventions (from papers and abstracts) and in innovative forms (for service-learning projects and visual arguments such as op-ads, photo essays, and Websites).

We base our writing assignments for all these learning goals on lessons from classical rhetoric but we offer a media theme for each chapter—such that we teach students to analyze a range of texts from cartoons, ads, and news photos to propaganda posters, film trailers, and student presentations. To meet our goal of teaching writing skills in analysis, research, and argument through use of verbal, visual, and multimedia examples, we've devised our assignments to meet specific learning objectives delineated by WPA, as shown in the accompanying table.

MAJOR ASSIGNMENTS AND LEARNING OBJECTIVES

Chapter Title	Chapter Learning Goals	Major Assignments	Media Focus
1: Analyzing Texts	■ Understanding the rhetorical situation ■ Considering relationship between audience, text, and purpose ■ Textual analysis ■ Developing thesis statements	■ Personal narrative essay ■ Rhetorical analysis essay	Cartoons, comic strips, and editorial cartoons
2: Understanding Strategies of Persuasion	■ Strategies of argumentation ■ Understanding rhetorical appeals: logos, pathos, ethos ■ Abuses or exaggerated uses of rhetorical appeals ■ Importance of context and *kairos*	■ Contextual analysis essay ■ Analysis of rhetorical appeals and fallacies ■ Comparison/contrast essay	Advertisements
3: Composing Arguments	■ Introductions and conclusions ■ Arrangement and structure of argument ■ Considering various perspectives on argument ■ Developing persona and rhetorical stance ■ Addressing opposing opinion in an argument ■ Effective titles	■ Position paper ■ Multiple sides of argument assignment ■ Argumentative essay incorporating diverse viewpoints	Photographs, photo essays

(Continued)

Chapter Title	Chapter Learning Goals	Major Assignments	Media Focus
4: Planning and Proposing Research Arguments	■ Generating and narrowing research topics ■ Prewriting strategies ■ Developing a research plan ■ Drafting a formal proposal	■ Research log ■ Informal research plan ■ Research proposal	Propaganda posters
5: Finding and Evaluating Research Sources	■ Research strategies ■ Evaluating sources ■ Distinguishing between primary and secondary sources ■ Locating sources ■ Conducting field research ■ Best practices for note taking	■ Critical evaluation of sources ■ Annotated bibliography ■ Field research contact assignment	Magazine and journal covers, Websites
6: Organizing and Writing Research Arguments	■ Organizing and outlining arguments ■ Importance of multiple drafts and revision ■ Writing and peer response ■ Quoting from sources	■ Formal outline ■ Peer review and response ■ Using visual evidence ■ Research argument	Film and movie trailers
7: Designing Arguments	■ Understanding the conventions of academic writing ■ Writing abstracts ■ Adopting appropriate voice and tone ■ Considering different genres of argument ■ Relationship between rhetorical situation and types of argument ■ Formatting and genre considerations	■ Writing an abstract ■ Visual argument—opinion advertisement or photo essay ■ Creating electronic arguments using multimedia (audio and visual)	Op-ads, photo essays, Websites, and multiple media
8: Delivering Presentations	■ Using technology to address a range of audiences ■ Transforming written arguments into visual or spoken texts ■ Strategies of design and delivery ■ Conducting field research	■ Conversion assignment—written to oral discourse ■ Fieldwork assignment ■ Multimedia presentation ■ Collaborative conference presentation	Presentations, poster sessions, PowerPoint
9: Documentation and Plagiarism	■ Best practices in documenting sources ■ MLA style rules ■ Avoiding plagiarism	■ Ethical note-taking exercises ■ Citation practice	

Envision **Companion Website**

In addition to the exercises and major assignments contained within the pages of the book, we've also designed a comprehensive and multilayered Companion Website to provide further resources to help students learn to be effective writers, researchers, and rhetoricians through an *active learning* model. From John Dewey to Cynthia Selfe, researchers in rhetoric and composition have shown the advantages of student-centered classrooms and student-focused pedagogy. Moreover, the well-known Learning Pyramid depicting student retention rates demonstrates clearly the efficacy of active student engagement in the learning process (see Figure 1). *Envision in Depth* has been designed around the pedagogical philosophy that students learn more when they interact with the course material and when they are challenged to teach each other than when they simply implement the lessons taught to them.

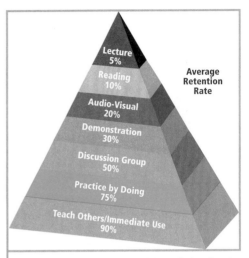

FIGURE 1. The Learning Pyramid shows the benefits of interactive pedagogy.

Accordingly, we supplemented the material in *Envision in Depth* with a Companion Website that contains a wide variety of links and materials designed to facilitate learning as an interactive experience. On the Website, students will find

- links to writing, research, and rhetoric resources
- supplemental readings designed to complement those in the book
- detailed assignment sheets and additional interactive writing activities
- more than 250 student writing projects to serve as models

We aim to maximize student engagement and retention through a variety of interactive, student-centered exercises and assignments. This methodology eschews the "banking model" disparaged by educational theorist Paolo Freire and positions students as experts in their own learning.

Instructors will also find invaluable resources available on the Companion Website, designed to help with everyday practical instruction in the classroom; with facilitating learning about ways of writing and methods of analysis; and with leading students to becoming adept researchers and confident producers of arguments across a range of media. These include

- pedagogical resources, including lesson plans and classroom activities
- sample syllabi and annotated bibliographies for research projects
- expanded assignment guidelines and assignments for added challenge
- supplemental classroom readings to use in building topical lessons
- advice for working with students of varying abilities and learning styles

We hope you will use the *Envision* Companion Website to contribute ideas, suggestions, feedback, and even writing projects of your own. Working on this book has been a collaborative process from the beginning, and we hope that you, too, will join the conversation. Thanks for using *Envision in Depth*; we hope you find the book as helpful to your teaching as it has been for us to use in our own classes.

A Note of Thanks

The appearance of *Envision in Depth* as a reader, with chapters offering students perspectives on issues in our contemporary multimedia world, signifies the result of much hard work and encouragement from those people who continue to support us in this writing venture.

First, again, we extend our greatest appreciation to our families and friends whose love and understanding sustains us through much hard work and sacrifice. Second, we thank our students for providing the impetus and the encouragement that this labor would benefit them as writers and learners. Third, we thank our professional colleagues at Stanford University and across the discipline for sharing conversations about writing, research, and understanding the world through a rhetorical lens. We'd like to thank our reviewers for their helpful suggestions at both early and late stages of this project: Steve Adkison, Idaho State University; Cora Agatucci, Central Oregon Community College; Scott Earle, Tacoma Community College; Christopher Eisenhart, University of Massachusetts-Dartmouth; Catherine Gouge, West Virginia University; Sibylle Gruber, Northern Arizona University; Dan Holt, Lansing Community College; Brooke Hessler, Oklahoma City University; Rebecca Ingalls, University of Tampa; Dawnelle Jager, SUNY ESF, Syracuse University; Joseph Jones, University of Memphis; Rachela Permenter, Slippery Rock University; Sarah Quirk, Waubonsee Community College; Andrew Scott, Ball State University; Julie Wakeman-Linn, Montgomery College; and Lynda Walsh, New Mexico Tech.

Finally, we thank our team at Longman, who support the *Envision in Depth* project in its many manifestations—from the first and second editions of the shorter book to the Instructor's Manual and now finally to the publication of this reader. To our editor and prime mover, Lynn Huddon, who made this reader a reality. To Lai Moi, who helped develop the book in its beginning stages and came up with the title *Envision in Depth*, and to Michael Greer, our development editor and strongest supporter, whose grace under pressure is unmatched in the field. We thank Joe Opiela for his wisdom and faith in our authorial team, and Nicole Solano for her assistance throughout the project. We extend warm appreciation to the entire sales and English team who have long awaited this reader, especially Andy Draa, Mike Coons, Rick Perez, Katherine Bell, Doug Day, and Megan Galvin-Fak. To all those working in permissions and production—to Shaie Dively, Warren Drabek, and Caroline Gloodt for securing image and text permissions, to copy editor Mark Mayell, and to Katy Faria in her leadership at an expert publication house—we are grateful for excellent work under uncompromising deadlines. We dedicate this reader to Michael Greer, our development editor, who returned to us after finishing other books: he is the reason we signed on to *Envision in Depth* in the first place, and there would be no books at all without him.

Christine L. Alfano and Alyssa J. O'Brien
May 2007

Part I

ANALYSIS AND ARGUMENT

Rhetoric's classic definition as the art of persuasion suggests a power. So much of what we receive from others—from family and friends to 30-second blurbs on TV—is intended to persuade. Recognizing how this is done gives greater power to choose.

—Victor Villanueva, Jr.

CHAPTER 1
Analyzing Texts

CHAPTER 2
Understanding Strategies of Persuasion

CHAPTER 3
Composing Arguments

CHAPTER 1

Analyzing Texts

FIGURE 1.1 Nick Anderson's cartoon from *The Courier-Journal* uses color and exaggerated form to argue that steroid-using baseball players are popping the dreams of young children.

Source: Copyright 2004 Nick Anderson. All rights reserved. Reprinted with permission of Nick Anderson in conjunction with Washington Post Writers Group and the Cartoonist Group.

Chapter Preview Questions

- How do we read and analyze texts rhetorically?
- How do we write about visual texts?
- How do thesis statements help us make arguments?
- How can we compose titles and draft analysis essays?

Everywhere around us, words and images try to persuade us to think about the world in certain ways. From "Got Milk?" ads to political campaign posters, words and images combine to move us, convince us to buy something, shape our opinions, or just make us laugh. Living in such a world requires us to pay attention and to think critically and analytically about all the texts we encounter every day. We can see this persuasive power especially in visual texts, such as the political cartoons and comics you might find on your favorite Weblog or in the campus newspaper.

Consider the political cartoon shown in Figure 1.1. How do the words and the images work together to persuade audiences to think, feel, or act a certain way?

Nick Anderson's cartoon conveys a powerful message about how steroid use has damaged the relationship between young fans and their baseball-star role models. Notice how when the athlete's steroid needle literally "pops" the child's balloon—and thus, implicitly, the child's admiration for the athlete—the written words "Oh, sorry kid" show a lack of true contrition; the font, selection, and arrangement of words make the player seem anything but sincere. Rather, the brightly colored muscular back takes over the entire space of the cartoon, showing the audience (baseball-loving fans) how steroids not only hurt the players but also hurt the game, the fans, and even perhaps our country's future by demoralizing children.

We can understand how this cartoon works by asking questions about its argument, audience, and author. When we ask questions like these, we are analyzing how texts can be **rhetorical,** how they aim at persuading specific audiences through the careful choices made by the writer in composing the text.

We've chosen to focus on comics and political cartoons in this chapter; by studying these texts, you'll develop skills as both a reader and a writer, learn how to analyze rhetoric, and create powerful arguments about the texts you encounter every day. In the process, you'll come to appreciate how writing as we know it is changing, causing us to approach it with a new set of eyes and rhetorical tools.

Seeing Connections
Compare this argument made by Nick Anderson in Figure 1.1 to that found in other cartoons about steroid use on page 329.

Understanding Texts Rhetorically

To approach texts rhetorically means to ask questions about how the text conveys a persuasive message or *argument*, how the text addresses a specific *audience*, and how the writer operates within a *specific context* or *rhetorical situation*.

You encounter many kinds of texts every day, even in just walking across campus. Once you recognize how these texts function *rhetorically*, you'll see that, as rhetoric scholar Victor Villanueva writes, "So much of what we receive from others—from family and friends to 30-second blurbs on TV—is intended to persuade. Recognizing how this is done gives greater power to choose." In other words, once you see how texts try to shape your mind about the world, then you can decide whether or not to agree with the many messages you encounter on a regular basis.

To grasp this concept, let's follow one hypothetical student—we'll call her Alex—as she walks to class and note the rhetorical texts she sees along the way. First stop: the dorm room, your average institutional room, which Alex and her roommate have decorated with Altoids ads they've ripped from magazines. There's also a large poster for the women's basketball team on one wall and a small Snoopy comic taped above the computer screen. As Alex turns off her computer, we notice what's on the screen: the Website for Slate.com, complete with an animated ad for an online dating service and an annoying pop-up telling Alex she'll win $50 if she clicks now. But Alex doesn't click; she shuts the machine down, piles her glossy-covered textbooks in her backpack, and slams the door shut on her way out.

Alex walks down the hall, past the rooms of other students in the dorm who have photos and graffiti on their doors, pausing in the lounge where several of her friends are watching a rerun of Jon Stewart on a large flat-screen TV. She watches until the show breaks for a commercial for Nike shoes, then she continues, down the stairwell decorated with student event flyers—a charity dance for the victims of Hurricane Katrina, a rally against immigration laws, a dorm meeting to plan the ski trip—and she pushes her way out into the cool autumn air. She only has two minutes to get to class, so she walks briskly past the student union with its event bulletin boards and its large hand-painted sign, "Café, open 6 a.m.–midnight, best crisps on campus." Two students at a small card table have painted their faces blue, and they hand her a small blue card with the cartoon of a surfer on it. "Come to our Hawaiian luau at the fraternity Saturday night!" they call to her as she crosses the quad and heads toward the statue of the university founder on his horse.

Alex then walks over the school crest embedded in the center of the walkway and past a group of students congregated outside the administration building, waving signs that protest the conditions of university janitorial workers. She turns left, weaving along the back of a cluster of gleaming steel and brick buildings that constitute the engineering quad. To her right, she passes a thin metal sculpture called *Knowledge and Life* that guards the entrance to the library. Finally, she reaches her destination: the English department. As Alex jogs up the stone steps, she stops momentarily to pick up the campus newspaper and scan the photos and headlines on the front page before folding the newspaper under her arm. Down the hall and into the classroom she rushes, but she's late. The professor has started the PowerPoint lecture already. Alex picks up the day's handout from the TA and sits down in the back row.

Now that we've seen Alex safely to her seat, how many rhetorical texts did you notice along the way? Ads, posters, cartoons, Websites, textbooks, television shows, flyers, statues, signs, newspapers, PowerPoint slides, even architectural design: each can be seen as an example of rhetoric. Once you begin to look at the world rhetorically, you'll see that just about everywhere you are being persuaded to agree, act, buy, attend, or accept an argument: rhetoric permeates our cultural landscape. Recognizing the power of rhetoric to persuade is an important part of learning to engage in contemporary society. Learning how to read texts rhetorically is the first step in thinking critically about the world.

CREATIVE PRACTICE

The next time you walk to class, pay attention to the rhetoric that you find along the way; take notes as you walk to catalog the various types of persuasion you encounter. Then, write up your reflections on your observations into a *personal narrative essay*. Discuss which types of rhetoric were most evident, which were most subtle, and which you found the most persuasive.

Understanding Rhetoric

In one of the earliest definitions, ancient Greek philosopher Aristotle characterized **rhetoric** as *the ability to discern the available means of persuasion in any given situation*. Essentially, this means knowing what strategies will work to convince your audience to accept your message. As shown in Figure 1.2, this involves assessing and attending to the **rhetorical situation**—that is, to the relationship between writer, text, and audience. Think of the politician who might argue the same political platform but in strikingly different ways depending on what part of his constituency he's addressing; of the various ways mothers, students, or police officers might convey the same antidrug message to a group of middle school students; of how clothing retailers adapt their marketing message to suit the media in which they're advertising—magazines, radio, or television. In each case the *argument* has been determined by the unique relationship between the writer, the audience, and the text.

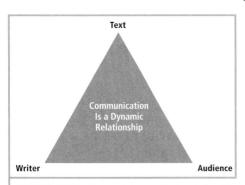

FIGURE 1.2 The rhetorical situation is the relationship between writer, text, and audience.

In constructing your own arguments every day, you undoubtedly also, consciously or not, evaluate your rhetorical situations. When you want to persuade your coach to let practice out early, you probably make your case face to face, rather than through a formal letter. When you ask for an extension on a paper, you most likely do so in a well-crafted email rather than a hasty after-class appeal. When you apply for a job or internship, you send a formal résumé and cover letter to indicate the seriousness of your interest. Here again we see that the success of your argument depends at least in part on your choice of text (verbal plea, written email, cover letter) in relation to the audience (coach, professor, potential employer) that you're addressing. All these examples are rhetorical acts in the form of oral and written arguments.

Student Writing
Read Esmeralda Fuentes's short narrative about the visual rhetoric she observes during the course of one day.
www.ablongman.com/envision/201

Seeing Connections
Consider how Michael Eisner, former CEO of Disney, took his rhetorical situation into account in his Address Before Members of the United States Congress on the dangers of copyright infringement (p. 439).

Understanding Visual Rhetoric

Yet persuasion happens through visual means as well: how you stand and make eye contact, how you format your professional documents, even how you capitalize or spell words in an email. Moreover, when you insert an image in an essay, create a poster to advertise a club sport, or draw a cartoon spoofing university policy, you are moving into the realm of **visual persuasion**— "writing" with images. From photographs to Websites, political cartoons to advertisements, these visual texts use rhetorical means to persuade an audience. Although some images may be more aesthetic than argumentative, many convey either inherent or explicit persuasive messages. Think about brochures, movie trailers, flyers, commercial Websites, and even comics; these are all created as arguments to convince audiences.

Since such strategies of persuasion occur through images—either alone or combined with words—rather than merely through words, they are called **visual rhetoric**. A documentary is produced and edited specifically to suggest a particular point of view; the illustration in a children's book provides a way to read a story; the sequential cartoons of a comic strip offer powerful commentary on American society. In each example, the writer chooses the best visual representation for the message of the text. The study of visual rhetoric provides you with the means to understand how and why such choices are made, and what the significance of these decisions is in the larger culture in which we live.

Analyzing Texts Rhetorically

Think of your favorite comic strips or political cartoons. Although they may seem purely aesthetic, merely informative about current events, or just plain funny, they do serve as an important mode of communicating ideas. For example, the comic antics of Dilbert or of Pig and Rat from *Pearls Before Swine* may not appear to carry any strong arguments about our society, human nature, or social relations. However, if you look closely at the details—the choice of words, the composition of the image, the particular colors, layout, character placement, and design—then you can gain a deeper understanding of the cartoon's message. This is what we mean by analyzing texts rhetorically.

Consider the following argument, made by cultural critic Scott McCloud as part of his book, *Understanding Comics:*

> When pictures are more abstracted from "reality," they require greater levels of perception, more like words. When words are bolder, more direct, they require lower levels of perception and are received faster, more like pictures.

What's significant about this quote is not only *what* McCloud says about the relationship between words and images but also *how* he says it. In effect, we can look to this brief passage as an example of a persuasive use of rhetoric, in which McCloud makes very deliberate choices to strengthen his point. Notice how he uses comparison-contrast (pictures versus words), qualified language ("reality"), and parallel structure (both sentences move from "When" to a final phrase beginning with "more like") to persuade his audience of the way pictures and words can operate in similar ways. Such attention to detail is the first step in rhetorical analysis—looking at the way the writer chooses the most effective means of persuasion to make a point.

To fully appreciate McCloud's rhetorical decisions, however, we need to consider the passage in its original context. As you can see in Figure 1.3, McCloud amplifies his argument by creating what we call a **hybrid text**—a strategic combination of words and images.

This complex diagram relies on the visual-verbal relationship itself to map out the complicated nature of how we understand both written text and pictures. The repetition and echoes that we found in the quoted passage are graphically represented in Figure 1.3; in fact, translated into comic book form, the division between word and image breaks down. It becomes a visual continuum that strongly suggests McCloud's vision of the interrelationship between these rhetorical elements. The power of this argument comes from McCloud's strategic assessment of the rhetorical situation: he, the **author,** recognizes that his **audience** (people interested in visual media) would find a **text** that relies on both visual and verbal elements to be highly persuasive.

McCloud's example is also instructive for demonstrating the way word and image can collaborate in modern arguments. Today more than ever, rhetoric operates not just through word choice, but also through choice of multimedia elements—images in a TV commercial, sounds accompanying a radio program, the font and color of a Website or flyer, even the layout strategies of this book. So we need to develop skills of analysis for all rhetorical texts. We need to envision argument as writing across diverse media and in turn develop **multimedia literacy,** or a careful way of reading, analyzing, and understanding media (visual, verbal, and other rhetorical texts).

Seeing Connections
For examples of graphic novels that function as powerful, rhetorical texts, see "Bound By Law?" on page 393 and an excerpt from Marjan Satrapi's *Persepolis* on page 318.

FIGURE 1.3 Scott McCloud writes in the medium of cartoons to explain comics.

Source: Courtesy of Scott McCloud

Analyzing a Comic Strip

Comic strips are a productive starting point for examining how an understanding of the rhetorical situation and compositional strategies work together to produce powerful texts. We can begin with the cartoon in Figure 1.4, looking closely at its detail and composition. Focusing first on the central, circular frame in the middle of the strip, we can see even within this single frame the power of rhetoric at work. When you look at the circular panel, what do you see?

You may see a split screen with two boys and two alien creatures; if you are more familiar with comic strips, you may identify the boy as Calvin from the cartoon *Calvin and Hobbes.* What is the *rhetorical function* of this image? The cartoon provides a dramatic enactment of a moment of crisis in this boy's life. The left side portrays the "real" Calvin, cast in green liquid, an expression of alarm on his face. The white air bubbles surrounding him suggest his panic and amplify the impression of fear. In contrast, the right side of the cartoon features a different Calvin, his head opened up to reveal a mechanical brain, his eyes wide and staring like a boy possessed.

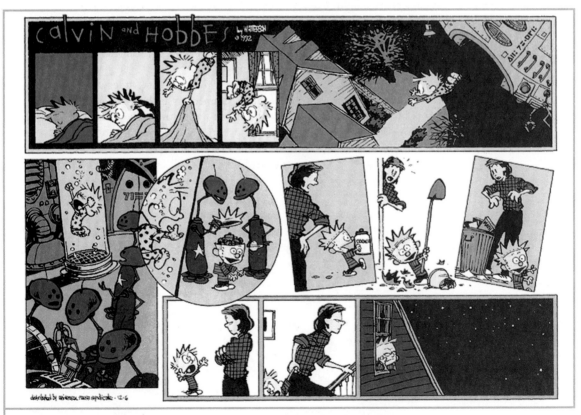

FIGURE 1.4 This *Calvin and Hobbes* cartoon conveys meaning through its colorful combination of sequential images.

Source: CALVIN AND HOBBES © 1992 Watterson. Reprinted with permission of UNIVERSAL PRESS SYNDICATE. All rights reserved.

Student Writing

Read Jack Chung's interpretation of a *Calvin and Hobbes* cartoon strip.

www.ablongman.com/envision/202

It seems a standard body-snatcher science fiction scenario, complete with a pair of aliens preparing to refasten Calvin's spiky blonde hair on top of this new brain. As an individual image, this panel taps into a message of fear and childhood imagining, with the aliens readying Robot Calvin to take over the functions of the real Calvin's life.

Let's think about how the meaning of a cartoon changes when it is integrated into a full strip. When we view still frames in succession, we find that meaning becomes more complex in a wonderful array of possible interpretations. When read in conjunction with images of a stolen cookie jar, broken lamp, and discarded math book, Calvin's crisis takes on a slightly different meaning. As we arrive at the frame of Calvin gesticulating to his mother, her eyes narrowed with skepticism, we realize that the cartoon itself represents a moment of storytelling; the strip in effect juxtaposes Calvin's version of reality with his mother's. The final frame reveals the end of the tale, with Calvin banished to his room, staring out at the stars. These new elements add levels of meaning to the comic, as we are invited to ponder versions of reality, the power of childhood imagination, and the force of visual detail.

Watterson is hardly alone in the strategy of using his comic strip as a means of producing an argument or cultural critique. For instance, Aaron McGruder's *Boondocks* and Gary Trudeau's *Doonesbury* offer sharper, more critical messages about society through a combination of words and images.

In the *Boondocks* comic strip shown in Figure 1.5, McGruder argues for the power of political cartoons as a form of social commentary by having his protagonist, Huey, draw his own cartoon to comment on electoral politics. The irony in his line "Well, that's the key—not beating the reader over the head with your point" reveals the very way in which *Boondocks* does, in fact, make its point explicit for readers of the strip.

Significantly, McGruder subtitled his 2000 collection *The Boondocks: Because I Know You Don't Read the Newspapers.* In choosing these words for the title of his book,

FIGURE 1.5 Cartoonist Aaron McGruder emphasizes the power of visual rhetoric in this comic strip.

Source: THE BOONDOCKS © 2002 Aaron McGruder. Dist. by UNIVERSAL PRESS SYNDICATE. Reprinted with permission. All rights reserved.

he presents his *cartoon* as a means of communicating information and arguments that we might see as equivalent to the news; that is, his comics persuade us to see current events, political controversies, and key issues concerning race in America in a certain light. This is shown in the second frame of Figure 1.5, where the main character, Huey, turns to cartooning itself as a way to craft a persuasive political message. He makes a rhetorical statement with his visual image and accompanying word choice; the drawing here is much more than merely an aesthetic, humorous, or informative text. It is a powerful rhetorical act.

To analyze *Boondocks*, we needed to assess the cartoon's *rhetorical situation* in drawing conclusions; we had to understand the way the writer (Aaron McGruder) took the audience (contemporary Americans) into consideration when creating the text (a comic strip, combining images and words). We can interpret McGruder's cartoon as offering a striking example of a rhetorical situation: although the Universal Press Syndicate had anticipated that this edgy strip would appear in between 30 and 50 newspapers, *Boondocks* was published in 160 newspapers for its first run in April 1999 and was eventually carried by more than 200 daily papers, and by 2005 it had been converted into an animated television series. McGruder's effective use of visual and verbal rhetoric to engage the topic of American race relations made his strip the most successful debut comic in the Universal Press Syndicate's history.

To apply this understanding of the rhetorical situation yourself, complete the following "Creative Practice." What is your analysis of these texts?

CREATIVE PRACTICE

Look at the *Penny Arcade* comic in Figure 1.6. Jot down your analysis of the elements of the cartoon: color, composition, characters, and action. Pay attention to facial expression, the use of symbols, and the changes

FIGURE 1.6 *The Hipness Threshold* cartoon depicts the adventures of Gabe and Tycho as they accompany their friend Charles into an Apple Computer store, while in a blog entry, the cartoonist Jerry Holkins addresses Apple culture more broadly.

Source: Penny Arcade, Inc. www.penny-arcade.com

between the panels. Then ask yourself: What persuasive statement does the cartoon convey? What is its argument? What is the message for readers?

Having done so, now read the following excerpt from one of the cartoonists' blog posts that accompanied the online publication of this comic. In it, Jerry Holkins makes a very similar argument—but in words. In what ways does this different rhetorical situation (blog versus Web comic) influence the way he makes his argument?

> The way Apple projects its brand, however, has nothing to do with the underlying technology. It could not be more divorced from it. So if they want to create largely empty stores staffed exclusively by young hardbodies in ill-fitting t-shirts, it's open season. It's possible that each manifestation of this chain does not resemble the others, that each one is not populated with the scrubbed, tousled young things of the sort one sees in serious teen dramas. You'll forgive me if I don't believe that. I'd say it's far more likely that there is a single Apple Store, connected by a series of geographically distinct portals.
>
> I don't put this out there to imply that the places I have to go to get technology or software are somehow superior, because they aren't. They're horrid. But at least I never feel underdressed.

As these examples demonstrate, we can gather a tremendous amount of information from a seemingly simple comic strip. Indeed, different readers will make different interpretations. This is what we mean by **visual arguments:** each viewer makes a separate interpretation of the image. As we learn to develop our *visual literacy,* we can make more and better-informed interpretations of such intriguing visual texts. And, as we will soon see, these skills of visual analysis will help you approach other kinds of texts rhetorically: political speeches, scholarly articles, letters to the editor about timely issues, even instant messaging and—as we just learned—blog posts.

Strategies for Analyzing Persuasive Texts

We've learned that rhetoric works as a means of persuading an audience to embrace the argument of the author. This is also true for the arguments *you make* about a text. In other words, rhetoric also applies to the texts you craft to persuade someone to accept your interpretation of a specific cultural or political artifact.

Why is it important for you to hone your skills in analyzing texts? Well, as we've seen, a single text visual can yield multiple interpretations. Your task is to argue convincingly—and persuade your audience—to see the text the way you see it. Your challenge as a student of writing and rhetoric is not only to identify the argument contained by a text but also to craft your own interpretation of that text. This involves a careful assessment of the ways in which the elements of the rhetorical situation work together to produce meaning in a text. In many cases your analysis will also address the interplay of words and images. Your analysis can take many forms: a written essay, an oral report, a visual argument, or a combination of these. Practice in analyzing the arguments of others is one of the best ways to develop your own persuasive skills.

Analyzing Editorial Cartoons

We can look at political cartoons—or **editorial cartoons** as they are also called—for another set of visual arguments to help us further develop effective strategies for analysis and interpretation. Editorial cartoons offer a rich resource for this sort of work since, as culture critic Matthew Diamond asserts, they "provide alternative perspectives at a glance because they are visual and vivid and often seem to communicate a clear or obvious message" (270). From the densely symbolic eighteenth-century plates of William Hogarth, to the biting social satire of *Punch*'s illustrators, to the edgy work of political cartoonists such as Ann Telnaes and Mike Luckovich in this century, the editorial cartoon has emerged as a succinct, powerful tool for writers to contribute to public dialogue on contemporary issues.

FIGURE 1.7 This cartoon by Daryl Cagle uses a striking symbol to make its argument.
Source: Daryl Cagle, Cagle Cartoons, Inc.

In the drawing by Daryl Cagle, for instance (see Figure 1.7), the particular face is recognizable to most twenty-first-century readers: the impish smile, the circular, black-frame glasses, and the prep-school tie identify this figure almost immediately as the young actor who plays Harry Potter in the film series. However, through one strategic substitution, Cagle transforms this image from illustration into commentary; he replaces the famous lightning bolt scar on Potter's forehead with a dollar sign. Cagle's Potter has been branded not by his encounter with a nearly omnipotent wizard but by his face-off with American capitalism. In this way, Cagle uses visual elements in his editorial cartoon to comment on the way this children's book hero has become a lucrative pop culture franchise.

For a more politically charged example, let's look at a powerful cartoon created by Pulitzer Prize-winning artist Mike Luckovich, depicting the Statue of Liberty crying in the aftermath of the attacks on the World Trade Center on September 11, 2001. As you examine Figure 1.8, ask yourself: What is the persuasive message of this political cartoon? Write down your interpretation, and be sure to consider the elements of the rhetorical situation as well as specific details that you observe.

FIGURE 1.8 Mike Luckovich's "Statue of Liberty" circulated widely in newspapers and on the Internet after September 11, 2001.
Source: By permission of Mike Luckovich and Creators Syndicate, Inc.

Seeing Connections
See page 422 for examples of cartoons that make powerful visual arguments about file sharing.

Perhaps, in your attempts to write a rhetorical analysis of this cartoon's meaning, you commented on the statue's childlike features, suggestive of innocence or vulnerability. You might have remarked on the nose and hair as seeming particularly Caucasian and asked: What message does this send about who is American? You might also have integrated the history associated with this statue into your interpretation. Is Luckovich offering an argument about how America's role as a haven for the oppressed and as a steward of peace and goodwill was attacked on September 11?

Some students reading this cartoon have argued that it casts an ironic eye on the history of America; they read the Statue of Liberty as crying about the abuses of civil rights in the wake of the attacks. Others claim that the composition of the cartoon—the visual details of the crying eye and childish face—suggests that this country is more vulnerable than previously thought. As you consider the rhetorical situation for the cartoon (the way in which it was written in the wake of the attacks), reflect on how different audiences might respond to its power.

Practicing Rhetorical Analysis

Before choosing your own text for rhetorical analysis, let's look closely at the strategies you can use to analyze a text and arrive at your own interpretation.

In Figure 1.9, for instance, you will find a hybrid argument on the national debate over the Pledge of Allegiance. To get started composing an interpretation of this text, first notice which specific verbal and visual elements stand out as you look at the cartoon.

The drawing itself suggests a generic classroom in America: several elementary school students, diverse in terms of gender and race, face the flag in the standard, patriotic pose, their teacher looking on. The flag, as you might expect, is center stage—but it is significantly limp and uninspiring. This strategic rendering of the flag becomes complicated by the words that accompany the image: "one nation, under nothing in particular." Not only has "God" been removed from the pledge, but with the clever substitution of "under nothing in particular," cartoonist Gary Markstein seems to speaks to the fear of raising a generation of Americans—and a future America—with no faith. His drawing of the disgusted teacher appears to embody the argument of the cartoon. Her mental thought, "God help us," voices an older generation's frustration and worry in the face of these young nihilists. In this way, you might argue, the cartoonist has taken the controversy over the use of "God" in the Pledge of Allegiance to an extreme; he has strategically used both word and image to create a powerful argument about this issue, as powerful as any written article found in a *Wall Street Journal* op-ed piece.

Like Markstein's editorial cartoon, the following excerpt from an editorial by Samuel P. Huntington comments on the debate over the Pledge of Allegiance. This debate was ignited by Michael Newdow, who filed a lawsuit against his daughter's school district, arguing that the words "under God" in the Pledge amounted to an unconstitutional endorsement of religion. A federal court ruled in favor of Newdow, but the Supreme

FIGURE 1.9 Gary Markstein conveys the controversy over the constitutionality of including the phrase "under God" in the Pledge of Allegiance.

Source: Gary Markstein and Copley News Service

Court reversed that decision in June 2004. No final decision has been made on the issue of whether or not the words "under God" violate the Constitution's provisions against the endorsement of religion by the government. As you read the excerpt, consider how Huntington's argument compares to Markstein's cartoon. Are they both making the same argument in different ways? Or is there a difference in what each text argues?

"Under God"
Michael Newdow is right. Atheists are outsiders in America.

Samuel P. Huntington

The battle over the Pledge of Allegiance has stimulated vigorous controversy on an issue central to America's identity. Opponents of "under God" (which was added to the pledge in 1954) argue that the United States is a secular country, that the First Amendment prohibits rhetorical or material state support for religion, and that people should be able to pledge allegiance to their country without implicitly also affirming a belief in God. Supporters point out that the phrase is perfectly consonant with the views of the framers of the Constitution, that Lincoln had used these words in the Gettysburg Address, and that the Supreme Court—which on Monday sidestepped a challenge to the Pledge of Allegiance—has long held that no one could be compelled to say the pledge.

    The atheist who brought the court challenge, Michael Newdow, asked this question: "Why should I be made to feel like an outsider?" Earlier, the Court of Appeals in San Francisco had agreed that the words "under God" sent "a message to unbelievers that they are outsiders, not full members of the political community."

    Although the Supreme Court did not address the question directly, Mr. Newdow got it right: Atheists are "outsiders" in the American community. Americans are one of the most religious people in the world, particularly compared with the peoples of other highly industrialized democracies. But they nonetheless tolerate and respect the rights of atheists and nonbelievers. Unbelievers do not have to recite the pledge, or engage in any religiously tainted practice of which they disapprove. They also, however, do not have the right to impose their atheism on all those Americans whose beliefs now and historically have defined America as a religious nation.

In composing your analysis of this text, you would need to follow a familiar process: First, look carefully at all the elements in the text. You might create a list of your observations or use the prewriting checklist at the end of this chapter to help you read the text more closely. Then, speculate about the meaning of each element. How does it contribute to the whole? Finally, complete the rhetorical triangle (see Figure 1.2) for the text, assessing who the author is, who the intended audience is, and what the argument of the text is, based on your observations of the details.

CREATIVE PRACTICE

Using the political cartoon shown in Figure 1.10, create your own hybrid text. First, jot down your observations about the cartoon; think about its rhetorical situation (its audience, author, and message) and determine a context (when and where you think it appeared). Next, develop an interpretation of the cartoon's meaning. Finally, fill in the blank tablet to clarify that argument for future readers. When you are done, move into a small group and share your work—both your written analysis and your hybrid text. Discuss what you have learned in producing oral, written, and cartoon texts, and how each text conveys your argument.

FIGURE 1.10 In this modified version of John Deering's cartoon, the words on the tablet have been removed, opening up many possibilities for alternative meanings.

Source: By permission of John Deering and Creators Syndicate, Inc.

As you completed your work for the "Creative Practice," you probably found that your additions to the blank tablet altered the cartoon's meaning in fundamental ways. Perhaps you inserted words that referred to religion, September 11, the war with Iraq, or the 2006 Danish cartoon controversy—in this way, you practiced the art of rhetoric that, through the combination of word and image, contributed a very specific political message or strong social commentary. Or perhaps you drew something in the tablet instead, using *visual persuasion* as your means of practicing rhetoric.

Student Writing

See Jeff Enquist's analysis of a cartoonist's commentary on the media representation of Catholic priests as part of a larger social issue dealing with the place of religion in American culture.

www.ablongman.com/envision/203

When we gave this exercise to our students, some offered the words "We support the USA" or "Women for equal rights" while others suggested filling in the blank with a visual text—a photo of Hillary Clinton or a drawing of a Muslim woman lifting her burka to expose her heels. In the actual published version from the 2001 *Arkansas Democrat Gazette*, cartoonist John Deering made the tablet present the ironic words "To the Taliban: Give us Osama Bin Laden or we'll send your women to college." Thus, Deering used the ongoing search for Osama Bin Laden as a springboard for lampooning cultural differences in gender roles; his words suggest international and cultural differences among countries. His cartoon practiced visual and verbal means of persuasion, both of which are important to consider when we are analyzing and writing about a text.

COLLABORATIVE CHALLENGE

To begin writing about cartoons as powerful rhetorical acts, get into groups of three and turn to the Internet, a vast resource for finding visual rhetoric, to locate political cartoons that address the same issue from diverse national perspectives. Go to the Chapter 1 resource page of the *Envision* Website, and select two or three cartoons from Daryl Cagle's Professional Cartoonist Index. Compare how different countries craft persuasive visual arguments about the same issue with remarkably divergent messages. Working collaboratively, write an analysis of each cartoon, and prepare to share your interpretations with the rest of the class. Be sure to describe elements of the visual text in detail and discuss how each contributes to the rhetorical force of the image.
www.ablongman.com/envision/204

What we can learn from this practice with rhetoric is that the relationship between interpretation and argument is a complex one. Although the author might intend to produce a certain argument, at times the audience may offer a slightly different interpretation. Our task as readers and writers is both to study a text carefully and to learn how to persuade others to see the text as we see it.

One powerful example of how texts can be read in multiple ways occurred in 2002 when Pulitzer Prize-winning cartoonist Doug Marlette created a political cartoon following the 9/11 attacks (see Figure 1.11). The title of the cartoon, "What Would Mohammed Drive?" makes a clear link between the Muslim religion and terrorism, as depicted by the nuclear warhead in the Ryder truck.

FIGURE 1.11 Doug Marlette received death threats after publishing this cartoon.
Source: Courtesy of Doug Marlette

The cartoon caused a firestorm of protest from the Muslim community in America, including death threats on the cartoonist. Marlette responded by asserting that "the objective of political cartooning 'is not to soothe and tend sensitive psyches, but to jab and poke in an attempt to get at deeper truths, popular or otherwise'" (quoted in Moore). Marlette's own words reveal that cartoons are not merely humorous texts but rather, as we have seen, they are rhetorical—they intend to persuade.

Look again at the cartoon and ask yourself *how* it attempts to jab or poke. What elements of composition, framing, shading, and layout suggest to you the target of Marlette's jab? How does the title set up or shape possible readings of the cartoon? How might this cartoon be read differently by an American audience, an Arab audience, and an Arab-American audience? How might it be interpreted in the United States or in the Middle East as conveying a different persuasive message?

Some might argue that the cartoon takes the announced threat of terrorists potentially using trucks to carry out nuclear attacks and reproduces it without irony. Another reader analyzing the cartoon could say that it mocks the government issuing the warning about post-September 11 terrorists. A third reader could point to the caricature of the driver and state that the cartoon makes fun of people of Arab descent. These varied ways of reading and responding to the text depend on both *audience* and *context*, bringing to light the importance of the rhetorical situation. They also reveal the importance of learning effective means of persuading others to see the text through a certain interpretative lens or way of reading the cartoon.

Let's turn now to Doug Marlette's writing to see how he used the art of rhetoric to persuade his many readers to see the cartoon from his perspective. Marlette's article stands as another persuasive text for us to analyze. As you read this article, originally published in the *Columbia Journalism Review*, use some of the same strategies of analysis that we've used on comics and cartoons throughout the chapter. Ask yourself: Who is his audience? How does he position himself as author? What is his argument? What evidence does he use to support that argument? Which parts are the most persuasive? Which are the least persuasive? What visual images does he convey with words? Are you persuaded by his argument?

Marlette uses a provocative title to capture his readers' attention.

Marlette begins his article by establishing the context behind it. Notice how he implicitly defends the cartoon by describing how it was intended not just to poke fun at Mohammed but at Christian evangelicals as well. The play on words at the end of this paragraph gives the readers their first taste of the humorous, slightly irreverent tone and the close attention to style that characterize this piece.

In the second paragraph, Marlette uses specific examples of the threats he received to construct a rather unfavorable image of the people offended by his cartoon.

I Was a Tool of Satan

Doug Marlette

Last year, I drew a cartoon that showed a man in Middle Eastern apparel at the wheel of a Ryder truck hauling a nuclear warhead. The caption read, "What Would Mohammed Drive?" Besides referring to the vehicle that Timothy McVeigh rode into Oklahoma City, the drawing was a takeoff on the "What Would Jesus Drive?" campaign created by Christian evangelicals to challenge the morality of owning gas-guzzling SUVs. The cartoon's main target, of course, was the faith-based politics of a different denomination. Predictably, the Shiite hit the fan.

Can you say "fatwa"? My newspaper, *The Tallahassee Democrat,* and I received more than 20,000 e-mails demanding an apology for misrepresenting the peace-loving religion of the Prophet Mohammed—or else. Some spelled out the "else": death, mutilation, Internet spam. . . . "What you did, Mr. Dog, will cost you your life. Soon you will join the dogs . . . hahaha in hell." "Just wait . . . we will see you in hell with all jews. . . ." The onslaught was orchestrated by an organization called the Council on American-Islamic Relations. CAIR bills itself as an "advocacy group." I was to discover that among the followers of Islam it advocated for were the men convicted of the 1993 bombing of the World Trade Center. At any rate, its campaign against me included flash-floods of e-mail intended to shut down servers at my newspaper and my syndicate, as well as viruses aimed at my home computer. The controversy became a subject of newspaper editorials, columns, Web logs, talk radio, and CNN. I was condemned on the front page of the Saudi publication *Arab News* by the secretary general of the Muslim World League.

My answer to the criticism was published in the *Democrat* (and reprinted around the country) under the headline *With All Due Respect, an Apology Is Not in Order.* I almost felt that I could have written the response in my sleep. In my thirty-year career, I have regularly drawn cartoons that offended religious fundamentalists and true believers of every stripe, a fact that I tend to list in the "Accomplishments" column of my résumé. I have outraged Christians by skewering Jerry Falwell, Catholics by needling the pope, and Jews by criticizing Israel. Those who rise up against the expression of ideas are strikingly similar. No one is less tolerant than those demanding tolerance. Despite differences of culture and creed, they all seem to share the notion that there is only one way of looking at things, their way. What I have learned from years of this is one of the great lessons of all the world's religions: we are all one in our humanness.

In my response, I reminded readers that my "What Would Mohammed Drive?" drawing was an assault not upon Islam but on the distortion of the Muslim religion by murderous fanatics—the followers of Mohammed who flew those planes into our buildings, to be sure, but also the Taliban killers of noncompliant women and destroyers of great art, the true believers who decapitated an American reporter, the young Palestinian suicide bombers taking out patrons of pizza parlors in the name of the Prophet Mohammed.

Then I gave my Journalism 101 lecture on the First Amendment, explaining that in this country we do not apologize for our opinions. Free speech is the linchpin of our republic. All other freedoms flow from it. After all, we don't need a First Amendment to allow us to run boring, inoffensive cartoons. We need constitutional protection for our right to express unpopular views. If we can't discuss the great issues of the day on the pages of our newspapers fearlessly, and without apology, where can we discuss them? In the streets with guns? In cafes with strapped-on bombs?

Although my initial reaction to the "Mohammed" hostilities was that I had been there before, gradually I began to feel that there was something new, something darker afoot. The repressive impulses of that old-time religion were now being fed by the subtler inhibitions of mammon and the marketplace. Ignorance and bigotry were reinventing themselves in the post-Christian age by dressing up as "sensitivity" and masquerading as a public virtue that may be as destructive to our rights as religious zealotry. We seem to be entering a Techno Dark Age, in which the machines that were designed to serve the free flow of information have fallen into the hands of an anti-intellectual mobocracy.

Twenty-five years ago, I began inciting the wrath of the faithful by caricaturing the grotesque disparity between Jim and Tammy Faye Bakker's televangelism scam and the Christian piety they used to justify it. I was then working at *The Charlotte Observer,* in the hometown of the Bakkers' PTL Club, which instigated a full-bore attack on me. The issues I was cartooning were substantial enough that I won the Pulitzer Prize for my PTL work. But looking back on that fundamentalist religious campaign, even though my hate mail included some death threats, I am struck by the relative innocence of the times and how ominous the world has since become—how high the stakes, even for purveyors of incendiary doodles.

He recounts his response to the protests and comes to one of the most important points of his essay: that he is an equal opportunity offender, having penned cartoons that had enraged many different groups. By moving the question away from an issue of Islam to a larger issue of tolerance, Marlette sets up the issues of censorship and freedom of speech that are the real subjects of this essay.

Notice the way that Marlette also condemns the "murderous fanatics" he describes based on an ongoing pattern of behavior—a rhetorical decision that makes his critique seem less reactionary and more thoughtful.

In this paragraph, he evokes the First Amendment and ends with an implicit comparison between America, with its civil liberties, and more militaristic and war-torn countries. Notice the power of the rhetorical questions that he uses at the end of the paragraph, asking readers to consider the alternatives to American freedom of speech.

At this point, he returns to describing his career as an equal opportunity offender, shifting the focus off Islam and instead discussing his troubles with evangelical Christians. By mentioning the death threats he received for his cartoons about the PTL Club (a televangelist show hosted by Jim and Tammy Bakker in the 1980s), he draws an implicit comparison here between Christian fundamentalists and what he calls Islamic "fanatics."

Although he doesn't reproduce his 1978 cartoon here, he offers a clear description to his readers.

One of the first cartoons I ever drew on PTL was in 1978, when Jim Bakker's financial mismanagement forced him to lay off a significant portion of his staff. The drawing showed the TV preacher sitting at the center of Leonardo Da Vinci's *Last Supper* informing his disciples, "I'm going to have to let some of you go!" Bakker's aides told reporters that he was so upset by the drawing that he fell to his knees in his office, weeping into the gold shag carpet. Once he staggered to his feet, he and Tammy Faye went on the air and, displaying my cartoons, encouraged viewers to phone in complaints to the *Observer* and cancel their subscriptions.

Jim Bakker finally resigned in disgrace from his PTL ministry, and I drew a cartoon of the televangelist who replaced him, Jerry Falwell, as a serpent slithering into PTL paradise: "Jim and Tammy were expelled from paradise and left me in charge."

This exchange brings humor back into the piece and demonstrates Marlette's seemingly flippant response to his critics.

One of the many angry readers who called me at the newspaper said, "You're a tool of Satan."

"Excuse me?"

"You're a tool of Satan for that cartoon you drew."

"That's impossible," I said. "I couldn't be a tool of Satan. *The Charlotte Observer*'s personnel department tests for that sort of thing."

Confused silence on the other end.

"They try to screen for tools of Satan," I explained. "Knight Ridder human resources has a strict policy against hiring tools of Satan."

Click.

Again, Marlette takes time to implicitly defend himself against claims of targeting Islam by describing how he has offended other religious groups as well.

Until "What Would Mohammed Drive?" most of the flak I caught was from the other side of the Middle East conflict. Jewish groups complained that my cartoons critical of Israel's invasion of Lebanon were anti-Semitic because I had drawn Prime Minister Menachem Begin with a big nose. My editors took the strategic position that I drew everyone's nose big. At one point, editorial pages were spread out on the floor for editors to measure with a ruler the noses of various Jewish and non-Jewish figures in my cartoons.

Here Marlette cleverly plays on the idea of cartooning by pausing to assert that the reaction of his critics is "cartoonish" and exaggerated.

After I moved to the Northeast, it was Catholics I offended. At *New York Newsday*, I drew a close-up of the pope wearing a button that read " No Women Priests." There was an arrow pointing to his forehead and the inscription from Matthew 16:18: "Upon This Rock I Will Build My Church." The *Newsday* switchboard lit up like a Vegas wedding chapel. *Newsday* ran an apology for the cartoon, a first in my career, and offered me a chance to respond in a column. The result—though the paper published it in full—got me put on probation for a year by the publisher. That experience inspired the opening scene of my first novel, *The Bridge*.

* * *

But how do you cartoon a cartoon? It's a problem of redundancy in this hyperbolic age to caricature an already extravagantly distorted culture. When writers try to censor other writers, we're in Toontown. We are in deep trouble when victimhood becomes a sacrament, personal injury a point of pride, when irreverence is seen as a hate crime, when the true values of art and religion are distorted and debased by fanatics and zealots, whether in the name of the God of Abraham, Isaac, and Jacob, the Prophet Mohammed, or a literary Cult of Narcissus.

It was the cynically outrageous charge of homophobia against my book that brought me around to the similarities between the true believers I was used to dealing with and the post-modern secular humanist Church Ladies wagging their fingers at me. The threads that connect the CAIR and the literary fat-was, besides technological sabotage, are entreaties to "sensitivity," appeals to institutional guilt, and faith in a corporate culture of controversy avoidance. Niceness is the new face of censorship in this country.

The censors no longer come to us in jackboots with torches and baying dogs in the middle of the night. They arrive now in broad daylight with marketing surveys and focus-group findings. They come as teams, not armies, trained in effectiveness, certified in sensitivity, and wielding degrees from the Columbia journalism school. They're known not for their bravery but for their efficiency. They show gallantry only when they genuflect to apologize. The most disturbing thing about the "Mohammed" experience was that a laptop Luftwaffe was able to blitz editors into not running the cartoon in my own newspaper. "WWMD" ran briefly on the Tallahassee Democrat Web site, but once an outcry was raised, the editors pulled it and banned it from the newspaper altogether.

The cyberprotest by CAIR showed a sophisticated understanding of what motivates newsroom managers these days—bottom-line concerns, a wish for the machinery to run smoothly, and the human-resources mandate not to offend. Many of my e-mail detractors appeared to be well-educated, recent emigres. Even if their English sometimes faltered, they were fluent in the language of victimhood. Presumably, victimization was one of their motives for leaving their native countries, yet the subtext of many of their letters was that this country should be more like the ones they emigrated from. They had the American know-how without the know-why. In the name of tolerance, in the name of their peaceful God, they threatened violence against someone they accused of falsely accusing them of violence.

With the rise of the bottom-line culture and the corporatization of news gathering, tolerance itself has become commodified and denuded of its original purpose. Consequently, the best part of the American character—our generous spirit, our sense of fair play—has been turned against us.

Tolerance has become a tool of coercion, of institutional inhibition, of bureaucratic self-preservation. We all should take pride in how this country for the most part curbed the instinct to lash out at Arab-Americans in the wake of 9/11. One of the great strengths of this nation is our sensitivity to the tyranny of the majority, our sense of justice for all. But the First Amendment, the miracle of our

Marlette now comes to one of the focal points of his discussion: the way censorship is enforced not by angry critics but by a culture of "niceness" that is afraid to offend.

The reference to the Columbia journalism school would have extra force considering that this piece was originally published in the *Columbia Journalism Review*. Here, also, he clearly articulates the central point of his extended Mohammed story: that the most "disturbing thing" was that critics were able to influence his editors into refusing to run the cartoon.

Having begun his argument applauding American principles—namely, freedom of speech—he now demonstrates the way that corporate structure and an ideology of tolerance (both hallmarks of American culture) are actually operating in conflict with First Amendment rights.

He ends this paragraph by clarifying his interpretation of the First Amendment, specifically with relation to journalism. He then uses a cliché to emphasize his point.

Notice the analogy he makes between political cartoonists and bald eagles. It operates on two levels, on the one hand emphasizing that they are endangered and on the other hand suggesting that cartoonists represent America's freedoms.

His references on this page to important political cartoonists (Herbert Block, Jeff MacNelly, Paul Conrad) underscore his message about the decline of political cartooning as a genre.

In the next paragraph he returns to his metaphor of the bald eagle, developing it into a richer analogy.

As he moves toward his conclusion, Marlette draws his essay together by echoing and slightly revising the title of the cartoon that started the controversy and demonstrating the way that images carry symbolic weight.

Marlette solidifies his connection to great contributors to American culture by referring to great American writers and trailblazers, from novelist John Steinbeck (the Joads are the family from *The Grapes of Wrath*) to cultural icon Ken Kesey and astronaut Neil Armstrong.

In his final paragraph, Marlette repeats his new catch phrase and uses it to provide a final comment on his vision of America and its inherent freedoms.

system, is not just a passive shield of protection. In order to maintain our true, nationally defining diversity, it obligates journalists to be bold, writers to be full-throated and uninhibited, and those blunt instruments of the free press, cartoonists like me, not to self-censor. We must use it or lose it.

Political cartoonists daily push the limits of free speech. They were once the embodiment of journalism's independent voice. Today they are as endangered a species as bald eagles. The professional troublemaker has become a luxury that offends the bottom-line sensibilities of corporate journalism. Twenty years ago, there were two hundred of us working on daily newspapers. Now there are only ninety. Herblock is dead. Jeff MacNelly is dead. And most of the rest of us might as well be. Just as resume hounds have replaced newshounds in today's newsrooms, ambition has replaced talent at the drawing boards. Passion has yielded to careerism, Thomas Nast to Eddie Haskell. With the retirement of Paul Conrad at the *Los Angeles Times*, a rolling blackout from California has engulfed the country, dimming the pilot lights on many American editorial pages. Most editorial cartoons now look as bland as B-roll and as impenetrable as a 1040 form.

We know what happens to the bald eagle when it's not allowed to reproduce and its habitat is contaminated. As the species is thinned, the eco-balance is imperiled.

Why should we care about the obsolescence of the editorial cartoonist?

Because cartoons can't say "on the other hand," because they strain reason and logic, because they are hard to defend and thus are the acid test of the First Amendment, and that is why they must be preserved.

What would Marlette drive? Forget SUVs and armored cars. It would be an all-terrain vehicle you don't need a license for. Not a foreign import, but American-made. It would be built with the same grit and gumption my grandmother showed when she faced down government soldiers in the struggle for economic justice, and the courage my father displayed as a twenty-year-old when he waded ashore in the predawn darkness of Salerno and Anzio. It would be fueled by the freedom spirit that both grows out of our Constitution and is protected by it—fiercer than any fatwa, tougher than all the tanks in the army, and more powerful than any bunker-buster.

If I drew you a picture it might look like the broken-down jalopy driven by the Joads from Oklahoma to California. Or like the Cadillac that Jack Kerouac took on the road in his search for nirvana. Or the pickup Woody Guthrie hitched a ride in on that ribbon of highway, bound for glory. Or the International Harvester Day-Glo school bus driven cross-country by Ken Kesey and his Merry Pranksters. Or the Trailways and Greyhound buses the Freedom Riders boarded to face the deadly backroads of Mississippi and Alabama. Or the moon-buggy Neil Armstrong commanded on that first miraculous trip to the final frontier.

What would Marlette drive? The self-evident, unalienable American model of democracy that we as a young nation discovered and road-tested for the entire world: the freedom to be ourselves, to speak the truth as we see it, and to drive it home.

In his written argument, Marlette describes the observations he has made about the public's response to his cartoons. This process parallels the work you have done in walking across campus and observing rhetoric or in listing your observations of the visual detail found in the *Calvin and Hobbes* cartoon. Notice how specific Marlette is in describing the reactions to his cartoons and how concretely he conjures up American identity through the imagery of the bald eagle and the driven vehicle. These are *rhetorical moves,* strategic choices he has made as a writer in deciding how best to persuade his readers (especially those outraged by the cartoons) to see his drawing from a different point of view. Just as Markstein picked the most appropriate words and images for inside his Pledge of Allegiance cartoon, Marlette picked the most appropriate words and metaphors to use in his article.

Writing a Rhetorical Analysis

As you turn now to write a longer, more sustained rhetorical analysis of a text, you'll be putting into practice all the skills you've learned so far in this chapter. You'll need to write down your observations of the text; spend time discussing them in detail, as we have done with the many examples we've worked on so far; and use these observations as evidence to make an argument that will persuade others to see the text the way you see it.

It's crucial to remember that when you write a rhetorical analysis, you perform a rhetorical act of persuasion yourself. Accordingly, you need to include the key elements of analytical writing that we've learned so far: (1) have a point of interpretation to share with your readers, (2) take time to walk readers through concrete details to prove your point, and (3) lead your readers through the essay in an engaging and convincing way. But of all these, the most important is your argument, your "take" or interpretation of the text—your **thesis.**

Developing a Thesis Statement

Perhaps the single most important part of your writing will be your **thesis statement,** the concise statement of your interpretation of your chosen text. To understand thesis statements, let's work through an example. Imagine, for instance, that you want to write an argument about the editorial cartoons in Figures 1.12 and 1.13. Both cartoons comment on recent debates about immigration policy. How might you develop a thesis statement that persuasively conveys your interpretation of how these cartoons contribute to the debate surrounding the status of undocumented immigrants?

Start by jotting down what you see; make close observations about these cartoons. Then use questions

AT A GLANCE

Selecting a Visual Rhetoric Image

When choosing a visual text for analysis, ask yourself the following questions:

- Does the image attempt to persuade the audience?
- Are there sufficient elements in the image to analyze?
- What do you know about the author or the intended audience?
- What's your own interpretation of this image?

FIGURE 1.12 Cartoon by Daryl Cagle about the immigration debate.
Source: Daryl Cagle, Cagle Cartoons, Inc.

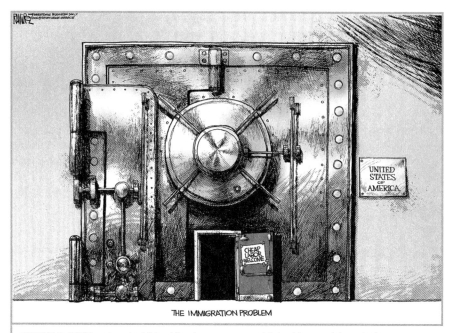

FIGURE 1.13 This cartoon by Michael Ramirez uses a powerful visual image of the United States.
Source: Michael Ramirez and Copley News Service

to bring your argument into focus and to make a specific claim about the images. The end product will be a *working thesis.* The process of developing your thesis might look like this:

1. **Write down your observations.**

   Close observations: Both pictures focus, literally or symbolically, on the border between the United States and Mexico and on the way that we set up fences (or vault doors) to keep illegal immigrants out. Both also show holes in those barriers: one focuses on people running through a hole in the fence; the other shows a small door in the vault that looks as if it's been propped open from the inside. The words are interesting, too. In the Cagle cartoon, the big sign says "Keep out," while the smaller signs are designed to draw people in. In the Ramirez cartoon, the small sign says "Cheap labor welcome," contradicting the message of the large, high-security door that blocks access to the United States.

2. **Work with your observations to construct a preliminary thesis statement.**

   First statement: Both cartoons focus on the contradiction in American border policy.

3. **Refine your argument by asking questions that make your statement less general.**

   Ask yourself: How? What contradictions? To what effect? How do I know this?

4. **Revise your preliminary thesis statement to be more specific; perhaps include specific evidence that drives your claim.**

   Revised statement: The cartoons in Figures 1.12 and 1.13 focus on the contradictions in American border policy by showing that on the one hand, the American government wants to keep illegal immigrants out, but on the other hand, economic forces encourage them to enter the United States illegally.

5. **Further polish your thesis by refining your language and asking questions about the implications of your working thesis statement.**

   Ask yourself: What do you find interesting about this observation? How does it tap into larger social or cultural issues?

6. **Write your working thesis to include a sense of the implications of your claim. Sometimes we call this the "So What?" of your claim.**

   Working thesis: The political cartoons in Figures 1.12 and 1.13 offer a pointed commentary on the recent immigration debate, suggesting ways the official government stance against illegal immigration is undermined by economic forces that tolerate, if not welcome, the entry of undocumented workers into the United States.

This activity should show you that a strong, argumentative thesis does more than state a topic: it makes a claim about that topic that you will develop in the rest of your paper. Let's look at one more example to further consider ways to produce sharp, clear, and persuasive thesis statements. The examples that follow are a series of thesis statements about Mike Thompson's cartoon in Figure 1.14, published in 2006 in reaction to rising gas prices.

FIGURE 1.14 Mike Thompson's cartoon uses visual and verbal arguments to make a powerful statement about rising gas prices.
Source: Mike Thompson and Copley News Service

Thesis #1: Mike Thompson's cartoon is very powerful.

> *Assessment: This thesis relies too heavily on subjective opinion; the author offers no criteria for evaluating the cartoon or a context for understanding the statement.*

Thesis #2: Mike Thompson's drawing shows his opinion about SUVs.

> *Assessment: This thesis statement rests too much on a broad generalization rather than specific analysis.*

Thesis #3: In response to rising gas prices, Mike Thompson draws a powerful editorial cartoon about the relationship between driving SUVs and consuming fossil fuels.

> *Assessment: This thesis statement merely states a fact and makes a broad claim rather than offering a focused interpretation of the cartoon. It needs to explain how the cartoon was powerful.*

Thesis #4: In his 2006 editorial cartoon "Aptly Named," Mike Thompson persuasively plays with the term *fossil fuel* to suggest that SUVs and the "wanton consumption" of gasoline represent an outdated approach to transportation that needs to recognize its own imminent extinction.

> *Assessment: Of the four examples, this thesis provides the most provocative and specific articulation of the author's interpretation of the significance of Thompson's cartoon.*

A strong argument, driven by a strong thesis statement, is at the heart of any successful essay.

Let's look at how one student, Jason Benhaim, combines effective strategies of analysis with a carefully crafted thesis statement to compose his own rhetorical analysis of a recent editorial cartoon.

AT A GLANCE

Testing Your Thesis

Do you have a specific and interesting angle on your topic?

- **Does it offer a statement of significance about your topic?**
- **Is the thesis sharp enough (not too obvious)?**
- **Could someone argue against it (or is it just an observation)?**
- **Is it not too dense (trying to compact the entire paper) or too simplistic (not developing your point thoroughly)?**

Notice the way Jason begins his essay with a series of evocative questions that directly engage readers.

Tapping into the American Psyche:

Using Bird Flu to Critique the American Government

What comes to mind when you hear the phrase "Hurricane Katrina"? Does it conjure up pitiful images of human suffering or evoke a sense of anger at the American government's failure to respond? What about the phrases "war in Iraq" or "obesity epidemic"? "Enron scandal"? "Global warming"? "Monica Lewinsky"? Indeed, the media has ground these key phrases so deeply into the American psyche that their mere mention triggers a particular emotional response in even the most socially unaware audience. The fact that all audiences automatically associate these key phrases with certain images, ideas, and feelings makes their invocation a powerful tool for all varieties of social commentators, especially political cartoonists. Certainly, political cartoonists employ several readily apparent methods of condensing as much meaning as possible into a single frame, including the use of symbols, such as having an eagle represent an entire country, or simple artistic decisions, such as portraying Uncle Sam as aging and frail instead of youthful and muscular. However, the cartoonist's ability to take advantage of the associations the public already has concerning certain current events is often overlooked. A recent cartoon by Eric Devericks provides a powerful example of the way in which cartoonists can combine manipulation of classic symbols

Source: Eric Devericks/The Seattle Times

with allusion to a current event, in this case the imminent bird flu epidemic, in order to construct a visual-verbal argument speaking to issues that extend beyond the current event in question.

The central image of the Devericks cartoon is a crotchety old Uncle Sam staring intently through a pair of binoculars, his rifle at the ready. Because he faces to the right, the direction in which Americans read, Uncle Sam appears forward-looking and vigilant. However, the details of Uncle Sam's figure hint at his shortcomings. Though armed, Uncle Sam's frail and thin limbs betray his weakness. In the context of the cartoon, his white hair only serves to emphasize his old age, and even his characteristic bowtie contributes to his appearing old-fashioned. His antique rifle, so outdated to be equipped with a bayonet, most directly conveys a sense of his being behind the times. The scowl on Uncle Sam's face indicates a certain stubbornness, as though he is obstinately clinging to obsolete means of combating dangerous adversaries.

In his first paragraph, he carefully sets up the context for his argument—that cartoonists tend to work with symbols or issues that automatically provoke a ready-made response in their audience.

By the end of the paragraph, Jason has moved from the context to his thesis statement, which refers to the specific cartoon he will be discussing.

The placement of the cartoon here is quite strategic: by including it in his first paragraph, he presents it as visual evidence to readers, making a much more powerful argument than if he had simply appended it to the end of his paper.

Jason spends his first main body paragraph describing the cartoon, drawing readers' attention to key details. Notice how, as the paragraph progresses, Jason moves from description to analysis.

Jason argues persuasively by using concrete details from his careful analysis of the cartoon.

Jason includes a strong transition here to move readers'
attention from the Uncle
Sam figure to that of the
bird perched on the end of
his rifle.

Notice the way Jason revises
his own initial description of
Uncle Sam to sharpen his argument about how the in-
clusion of the bird influences
the way we read the cartoon
as a whole.

In his penultimate paragraph,
Jason strengthens his argument by speculating about alternative ways the cartoon
might have been drawn.
The summation sentence at
the end of this paragraph is
a key moment when Jason
firmly articulates his interpretation of the cartoon.

Notice the way Jason carefully offers a summary of his
argument here without
sounding repetitive.
He ends his essay with a
provocative question that
points readers back to his interpretation of this cartoon:
that it is ultimately less a
commentary on bird flu than
a critique of the government.

Uncle Sam's presentation alone constitutes an argument regarding the American government's outdated militaristic obsession and could potentially stand alone as a complete political cartoon. However, when coupled with the image of the sickly bird labeled with the cartoon's only words, "bird flu," the danger for America in focusing solely on military endeavors becomes immediately apparent. The bird's mere presence indicates that the specter of disease is wholly capable of bypassing America's military defense. Indeed, the bird's highly significant position atop the rifle further suggests that America's military might is not only ineffective against disease but actually supports its presence—without the rifle, the disease-carrier would have no place to perch! In light of the bird's position atop his weapon, Uncle Sam's binoculars become useless and even detrimental. His focus on enemy attackers blinds him to the possibility of other dangers. The presence of this sickly bird, representative of an impending costly and potentially life-threatening epidemic, wholly undermines Uncle Sam's vigilant appearance. Despite its simplicity and scarcity of words, the Devericks cartoon makes a clear statement: the American government's focus on its military endeavors results in a dangerous ignorance regarding other critical issues.

Though bird flu provides an excellent example of an issue potentially ignored by the American government in favor of war, the bird perched on the end of Uncle Sam's rifle could easily be replaced by a symbol of a different issue facing America. For example, Devericks could just as easily have argued that America's militaristic attitude detracts from its focus on a crumbling educational system or its president's plummeting polls. The bird's tired and sickly appearance indicates that it bypassed Uncle Sam's defenses without much effort, suggesting that America's military defenses are equally susceptible to infiltration by other nonmilitary dangers.

Merely noting America's recent infatuation with war efforts constitutes a mildly effective statement, but using bird flu as a tangible example of why such an attitude is detrimental to the health of the United States brings the message home. Portraying the American eagle as weakened and sickly might make for a startling image, but captioning such an image with a modern phrase forces people to consider bird flu in a different light. Allusion to bird flu adds extra punch to this political cartoon. Even if its audience knows nothing about the details of bird flu, Devericks can at least count on their associating the phrase with a sense of helplessness, panic, or fear. Certainly the mere thought of an epidemic is frightening, but for Devericks bird flu merely shines light on what ought to be the American public's main fear—will their government be able to handle it?

AT A GLANCE

Visual Rhetoric Analysis Essays

- Do you have a sharp point or thesis to make about the visual text?
- Have you selected key visual details to discuss in support of your main point?
- Do you lead readers through your analysis of the text by discussing important details in sequence? These include:
    Visual composition, layout, and imagery
    Verbal elements in the text
    Color, shading, and arrangement of items
    Caption or title of the image
- Do you have an effective title, main point, introduction, body, and conclusion?
- Have you included the image in the essay?

Turning to Texts of Your Choice

As you turn now to selecting your own texts for rhetorical analysis, consider the ways the lessons you've learned in this chapter can help you approach the task. Keep in mind the need to begin with observations—whether it is of rhetorical texts all around your campus or the most provocative texts in the newspapers or online. As you select a text for analysis, think back to the cartoons or comics you found most striking in this chapter—perhaps the steroids cartoon, the *Boondocks* strip, or the Pledge of Allegiance cartoon. Each of these texts conveys a powerful message through words and images, verbal and visual rhetoric. Spend some time working on your thesis before composing the entire draft. Make sure your angle is sharp and your interpretation is complex. Consider working through a counterargument as well.

When you choose your own text for rhetorical analysis, make sure you pick one that offers a persuasive point. Also, in your own writing, avoid simply describing the elements you see in the work that you're analyzing. Instead, zoom in on specific details and comment on their meaning. Make a persuasive argument by using *specific* evidence to support your analysis of how the text succeeds at convincing an audience to see an issue in a particular way. This is key to crafting a persuasive and effective rhetorical analysis.

PREWRITING CHECKLIST
Comics and Cartoons

❏ **Topic:** What key issue is the comic or cartoon addressing?

❏ **Story:** On the most basic level, what is happening in the cartoon?

❏ **Audience:** In what country and in what historical moment was the cartoon produced? In what type of text did it first appear? A journal? A newspaper? Online? Was this text conservative? liberal? radical? feminist? How does it speak to this audience?

❏ **Author:** What do you know about the artist? What kinds of cartoons does he or she regularly produce? Where does he or she live and publish? What kinds of other writing does this person do?

❏ **Argument:** What is the cartoon's message about the issue? Is there irony involved (does the cartoon advocate one point of view, but the cartoonist wants you to take the opposite view)?

❏ **Composition:** Is this political cartoon a single frame or a series of sequential frames? If the latter, how does the argument evolve over the series?

❏ **Word and image:** Does the cartoon rely exclusively on the visual? Or are word and image both used? What is the relationship between the two? Is one given priority over the other? How does this influence the cartoon's overall persuasiveness?

❏ **Imagery:** What choices of imagery and content does the artist make? Are the drawings realistic? Do they rely on caricatures? Does the artist include allusions or references to past or present events or ideas?

❏ **Tone:** Is the cartoon primarily comic or serious in tone? How does this choice of tone create a powerful rhetorical impact on readers?

❏ **Character and setting:** What components are featured by the cartoon? A person? An object? A scene? Think about how character and setting are portrayed. What are the ethnicity, age, socioeconomic class, and gender of the characters? Do they represent actual people? Are they fictional creations? How are these choices rhetorical strategies designed to tailor the cartoon and its argument to its intended audience?

❏ **Cultural resonance:** Does the cartoon implicitly or explicitly refer to any actual people, events, or pop culture icons? What sort of symbolism is used in the cartoon? Would the symbols speak to a broad or narrow audience? How does the cultural resonance function as a rhetorical strategy in making the argument?

WRITING PROJECTS

1. **Personal Narrative:** Complete the "Creative Practice" on page 4. Recall Alex's observations of rhetoric on her way to class; conduct a similar study of the rhetoric in your world. Write your reflections into a *personal narrative essay.* Discuss which types of visual, verbal, bodily, or architectural rhetoric were most evident, which were most subtle, and which you found the most persuasive.

2. **Rhetorical Analysis:** Choose a political cartoon on a current issue and write a *rhetorical analysis.* You might find an appropriate cartoon in a recent issue of *Newsweek,* in a collection such as Charles Brooks's *Best Editorial Cartoons of the Year,* or online through the *Envision* Website resource page for Chapter 1 (www.ablongman.com/ envision/200). Use the prewriting checklist to help you write a rhetorical analysis of the cartoon. If you choose to analyze more than one cartoon on the same issue, introduce all your texts in the opening paragraph, and spend some time analyzing each one in detail. Make sure that your argument raises a larger point about rhetorical attributes of all the texts you are comparing.

3. **Comparative Rhetorical Analysis of Text and Image:** After you've begun project 2, search through recent newspapers, newsmagazines, or a news database like LexisNexis to find an article that addresses the same issue. Write a *comparative analysis* of the text and the political cartoon. What is each one's argument, and what rhetorical strategies does each one use to effectively make that argument? You may want to use the prewriting checklist in looking at the political cartoon. If you want to take a historical approach to this assignment, choose both a political cartoon and an article that span across the historical spectrum but focus on one issue, such as racial profiling, immigrant workers, or what's "hip" in the entertainment industry. You might consult articles and cartoons from *The Onion*'s "Our Dumb Century" or from online archives available through the *Envision* Website. For whatever texts you choose, write a *comparative historical analysis essay* in which you analyze how the cartoon and article use rhetoric to address a pressing issue of the time. Be sure to include specific details about each text, shape your observations into a thesis using the process on pages 22 and 23, and don't forget a title.

 Visit www.ablongman.com/envision for expanded assignment guidelines and student projects.

CHAPTER 2

Understanding Strategies of Persuasion

FIGURE 2.1 This eye-catching iPod ad from Stockholm, Sweden, draws the audience immediately into its argument.
Source: © Alyssa J. O'Brien, 2006

Chapter Preview Questions

- What specific strategies of argumentation work as persuasion?
- What role do the rhetorical appeals of logos, pathos, and ethos play in persuasion?
- What is the effect of exaggeration in these appeals?
- How does an awareness of context work to create a persuasive argument?
- How can you incorporate strategies of persuasion in your own writing?

What convinced you to buy that new pair of cross-trainers, to try that new sports drink, to purchase that new cell phone calling plan, or even to decide which college to attend? Chances are some sort of text combining words and images—whether it was a printed advertisement, television or radio commercial, billboard, or brochure—influenced your decision. Consider the street scene in Figure 2.1. What strategies of persuasion does the striking iPod banner ad use? Notice the simple design, the contrast between the bright background color and the dark silhouette, and the strategic use of white that draws your eye from the iPod in the figure's hand to the logo and slogan at the top of the image. How does this ad appeal to you? Does it appeal to your own enthusiasm for music that allows you to identify with the dancer? Or does it draw you in logically, asking you to identify yourself with one type of iPod because of its technical features?

Think now about other advertisements you have seen. How does the look of an ad make you pause and pay attention? Does a magazine ad show someone famous, a good-looking model, or characters you can identify with emotionally? Does a television spot tell a compelling story? Does a brochure offer startling statistics or evidence? Perhaps it was not one but a combination of factors that you found persuasive. Often we are moved to action through persuasive effects that are so subtle we may not recognize them at first; we call these effects **rhetorical strategies**—techniques used to move and convince an audience.

Ads offer us a productive means of analyzing rhetorical strategies because they represent arguments in compact forms. An ad has little room to spare; persuasion must be locked into a single frame or into a brief 30-second spot. Advertisements represent one of the most ubiquitous forms of persuasion. The average adult encounters 3000 of these compact, powerful arguments—that is, advertisements—every day (Twitchell, *Adcult* 2). Consider all the places ads appear nowadays: not just in magazines or on the television or radio but also on billboards and computer screens; on the sides of buses, trains, and buildings; in sports stadiums and movie theaters; and even spray-painted on sidewalks.

You probably can think of other places you've seen advertisements lately, places that may have surprised you: in a restroom, on the back of a soda can, on your roommate's T-shirt. As citizens of what cultural critic James Twitchell calls "Adcult USA," we are constantly exposed to texts that appeal to us on many levels. In this chapter, you'll gain a working vocabulary and concrete strategies of rhetorical persuasion that you can use when you turn to craft your own persuasive texts. The work you do here not only will make you a savvy reader of advertisements but also will equip you with skills you can use to become a sharper, more strategic writer of your own arguments.

Analyzing Ads as Arguments

By analyzing advertisements, we can detect the rhetorical choices writers and artists select to make their points and convince their audiences. In this way we realize that advertisers are rhetoricians, careful to attend to the *rhetorical situation.* We can find in advertisements specific strategies of argumentation that you can use to make your case in your own writing:

- Advertisers might use **narration** to sell their product—using their ad to tell a story.
- They might employ **comparison-contrast** to encourage the consumer to buy their product rather than their competitor's.
- They might rely upon **example** or **illustration** to show how their product can be used or how it can impact a person's life.
- They might use **cause and effect** to demonstrate the benefits of using their product.
- They might utilize **definition** to clarify their product's purpose or function.
- They might create an **analogy** to help make a difficult selling point or product—like fragrance—more accessible to their audience.
- They might structure their ad around **process** to demonstrate the way a product can be used.
- They might focus solely on **description** to show you the specifications of a desktop system or a new SUV.
- They might use **classification and division** to help the reader conceptualize how the product fits into a larger scheme.

These strategies are equally effective in both visual and written texts. Moreover, they can be used effectively to structure both a small unit (part of an ad or, in a more academic

FIGURE 2.2 This problem-solution ad for Rusk hairspray uses several strategies of argumentation.

text, a paragraph or section of an essay) and a larger one (the entire ad or, in an academic paper, the argument as a whole).

Even a single commercial can be structured around multiple strategies. The famous "This Is Your Brain on Drugs" commercial from the late 1980s used *analogy* (a comparison to something else—in this case comparing using drugs and frying an egg) and *process* (reliance on a sequence of events—here, how taking drugs affects the user's brain) to warn its audience away from drug use. In this 30-second spot, the spokesperson holds up an egg, saying, "This is your brain." In the next shot, the camera focuses on an ordinary frying pan as he states, "This is drugs." We as the audience begin to slowly add up parts A and B, almost anticipating his next move. As the ad moves to the visual crescendo, we hear the words, "This is your brain on drugs" and the image of the egg sizzling in the frying pan fills the screen. The final words seem almost anticlimactic after this powerful image: "Any questions?"

These strategies function just as persuasively in print ads as well. For example, look at the advertisement for Rusk hair spray in Figure 2.2, an ad designed to draw the viewer's eye through the visual argument. What the reader notices first are the striking pictures of the golden-haired model, somewhat flat hair on one side and voluminous curls on the other, exemplifying the powerful *comparison-contrast* strategy that is echoed in many levels of the ad. The entire ad is bisected to reflect this structure, opposing "problem" to "solution" and literally dividing the main caption—"Go from ordinary . . . to Extraordinary"—in half. What bridges the divide, both literally and figuratively, is the strategically positioned can of hairspray, tilted slighted toward the right to reinforce emphasis on the *example/ illustration* of a satisfied Rusk-user. By centralizing the red-capped canister in this way, the ad therefore also establishes a persuasive *cause and effect* argument, implicitly suggesting that using this hairspray allowed this girl to overcome the perceived challenges of limp hair.

Within written texts, the use of such strategies provides a similar foundation for a persuasive argument. As you read the following online article from Slate.com, look carefully to see which strategies author Seth Stevenson utilizes to make his argument about recent iPod commercials.

Seeing Connections
Read Clive Thompson's "The Making of an X Box Warrior" on page 508 for an example of the effective use of argumentative strategies such as narration and example.

You and Your Shadow

The iPod ads are mesmerizing. But does your iPod think it's better than you?

Seth Stevenson

The Spot: Silhouetted shadow-people dance in a strenuous manner. Behind them is a wall of solid color that flashes in neon shades of orange, pink, blue, and green. In each shadow-person's hand is an Apple iPod.

I myself own an iPod, but rarely dance around with it. In part because the earbuds would fall out (Does this happen to you? I think I may have narrow auditory canals) and in part because I'm just not all that prone to solitary rump-shaking. It's a failing on my part. Maybe if I were a silhouette I might dance more.

All that said, these are very catchy ads. I don't get sick of watching them. And yet I also sort of resent them, as I'll later explain.

First, let's talk about what the ads get right. For one, the songs (from groups like Jet and Black Eyed Peas) are extremely well-chosen. Just indie enough so that not everybody knows them; just mainstream enough so that almost everybody likes them. But as good as the music is, the visual concept is even better. It's incredibly simple: never more than three distinct colors on the screen at any one time, and black and white are two of them. What makes it so bold are those vast swaths of neon monochrome.

This simplicity highlights the dance moves, but also—and more importantly—it highlights the iPod. The key to it all is the silhouettes. What a brilliant way to showcase a product. Almost everything that might distract us—not just background scenery, but even the actors' faces and clothes—has been eliminated. All we're left to focus on is that iconic gizmo. What's more, the dark black silhouettes of the dancers perfectly offset the iPod's gleaming white cord, earbuds, and body.

This all sounds great, so far. So what's not to like?

For the longest time, I couldn't put my finger on it. And then I realized where I'd seen this trick before. It's the mid-1990s campaign for DeBeers diamonds—the one where the people are shadows, but the jewelry is real. In them, a shadow-man would slip a diamond ring over a shadow-finger, or clasp a pendant necklace around a ghostly throat. These ads used to be on television all the time. You may recall the stirring string music of their soundtrack, or the still-running tagline: "A Diamond Is Forever."

Like the iPod ads, these DeBeers ads used shadow-people to perfect effect. The product—in this case, diamonds—sparkles and shines on a dusky background. But what bothered me about the spots was the underlying message. They seem to say that we are all just transient shadows, not long for this world—it's our diamonds that are forever. In the end, that necklace is no overpriced bauble. It's a ticket to immortality!

My distaste for these ads stems in part from the fact that, with both the iPod and the diamonds, the marketing gives me a sneaking sense that the product thinks it's better than me. More attractive, far more timeless, and

As part of his online series "Ad Reportcard," Stevenson uses a format not usually associated with academic writing—notice here he sets up the commercial under discussion in a separate section before even starting his essay.

Stevenson's chatty voice is very appropriate for his online audience

Notice the way Stevenson defers his thesis, although he gives us a sense of his approach toward the ads (resentment).

In this section, Stevenson relies on **description** to set up the foundation for his discussion of the ads; yet, notice that he is somewhat selective, emphasizing the elements that are most important for his analysis—namely, the way the use of silhouettes emphasizes the product.

The rhetorical question here points to the turn in his piece from description to analysis, the point where the reader will come closer to understanding his resentment.

At this point in the article, Stevenson moves to **description** and **example** to set up the powerful **comparison-contrast** strategy that he develops further in the next paragraphs.

By **comparing** the iPod commercials to the DeBeers campaign, Stevenson can clearly articulate his ambivalent feelings about Apple's ads. In his semihumorous interjection, Stevenson returns to the **contrast** between himself and the Apple silhouettes with which he started the article.

Notice how he builds on his **comparison** by opening his concluding paragraph with an **analogy**, using a simile ("like diamond jewelry") that reminds the reader of the connection he has established between the two campaigns.

frankly more interesting, too. I feel I'm being told that, without this particular merchandise, I will have no tangible presence in the world. And that hurts. I'm a person, dammit, not a featureless shadow-being! If you prick me, do I not write resentful columns?

Like diamond jewelry, the iPod is designed and marketed to draw attention to itself, and I think (I realize I'm in a minority here) I prefer my consumer goods to know their place. If I did it over, I might opt for an equally functional but slightly more anonymous MP3 player. One that deflects attention instead of attracting it. Because I'm the one with the eternal soul here—it's my stuff that's just transient junk.

Grade: B–. Perfectly executed. Mildly insulting message.

Slate.com and Washingtonpost. Newsweek Interactive. All rights reserved.

COLLABORATIVE CHALLENGE

Visit an online repository of commercials, such as those linked through the *Envision* Website. With a partner, browse through several commercials, selecting two or three in particular that you find persuasive. Discuss what strategies of argumentation you see at work in these visual rhetoric texts. Try to find an example of each approach listed earlier in the chapter. Write a short paragraph analyzing one of the commercials; compare your interpretation with a partner. Then share your work with the rest of the class.

www.ablongman.com/envision/205

Understanding the Rhetorical Appeals

The rhetorical strategies we've examined so far can be filtered through the lens of classical modes of persuasion dating back to 500 BCE. The formal terms are ***logos, pathos,*** and ***ethos.***

Seeing Connections
To see how pathos, logos and ethos factor into the development of an advertising campaign, read Susie Orbach's "Fat is an Advertising Issue" on page 268.

Each type of rhetorical appeal represents a mode of persuasion that can be used by itself or in combination. As you might imagine, a text may employ a combined mode of persuasion, such as "passionate logic"—a rational argument written with highly charged prose, "goodwilled pathos"—an emotional statement that relies on the character of the speaker to be believed, or "logical ethos"—a strong line of reasoning employed by a speaker to build authority. Moreover, a text may use rhetorical appeals in a combination that produces an *overarching effect,* such as irony or humor. You might think of humor as one of the most effective forms of persuasion. Jokes and other forms of humor are basically appeals to pathos because they put the audience in the right emotional state to be receptive to an argument, but they can also involve reasoning or the use of the writer's authority to sway an audience.

Since they appear so frequently in combination, you might find that conceptualizing logos, pathos, and ethos through a visual representation helps you to

AT A GLANCE

Rhetorical Appeals

- **Logos** entails rational argument: appeals to reason and an attempt to persuade the audience through clear reasoning and philosophy. Statistics, facts, definitions, and formal proofs, as well as interpretations such as syllogisms or deductively reasoned arguments, are all examples of means of persuasion we call "the logical appeal."

- **Pathos,** or "the pathetic appeal," generally refers to an appeal to the emotions: the speaker attempts to put the audience into a particular emotional state so that the audience will be receptive to and ultimately convinced by the speaker's message. Inflammatory language, sad stories, appeals to nationalist sentiments, and jokes are all examples of pathos.

- **Ethos** is an appeal to authority or character; according to Aristotle, *ethos* means the character or goodwill of the speaker. Today we also consider the speaker's reliance on authority, credibility, or benevolence when discussing strategies of ethos. Although we call this third mode of persuasion the "ethical appeal," it does not strictly mean the use of ethics or ethical reasoning. Keep in mind that ethos is the deliberate use of the *speaker's character* as a mode of persuasion.

understand how they relate to one another (see Figure 2.3).

As you read this chapter, consider how each text relies upon various rhetorical appeals to construct its message.

Appeals to Reason

Logos entails strategies of logical argument. As a writer, you use logos when you construct an essay around facts and reason; in general, an argument based on logos will favor the use of logic, statistical evidence, quotations from authorities, and proven

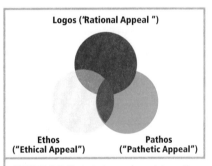

FIGURE 2.3 Rhetorical appeals are intersecting strategies of persuasion.

facts. In the opening pages of this chapter, for instance, we used logos—quotations and statistics about advertising—to persuade you about the omnipresence of advertising in today's culture. Scholars often rely on logos in this way to make persuasive academic arguments. Consider, for instance, the way Laurence Bowen and Jill Schmid use *logos* as a strategy of persuasion in this passage from "Minority Presence and Portrayal in Mainstream Magazine Advertising: An Update":

> Some might argue that the small number of minorities featured in mainstream magazine advertising may be due to a very deliberate media strategy that successfully targets minorities in specialized and minority media. However, each of the magazines analyzed does have a minority readership and, in some cases, that readership is quite substantial. For example, according to *Simmons 1993 Study of Media and Markets,* the Hispanic readership of *Life* is 9.9%, yet the inclusion of Hispanics in *Life*'s advertisements was only .8%. *Cosmopolitan* has a 11.3% Black readership, yet only 4.3% of the advertisements included Blacks; 13.3% of the magazines' readership is Hispanic and only .5% of the advertisements use Hispanics.

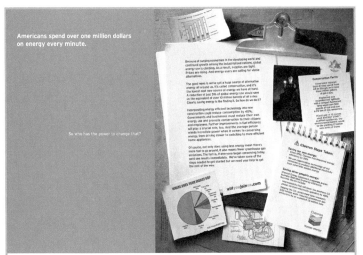

On the left side, the written text, set in relief against a vivid green background, sets up the problem using a striking statistic and poses the key question ("so who has the power to change that?") that governs the rest of the ad.

The right side provides the answer to the question, using a variety of research-based evidence including a memo, a fact sheet, a pie chart, a schematic, and a bar chart. Note that even the very abundance of materials is persuasive, suggesting that the ad's argument is based in fact rather than simply option.

FIGURE 2.4 The Chevron ad relies on a logical argument to persuade the reader.

Notice how the authors drive their point home through reference to their research with mainstream magazines as well as to statistical data that they have both uncovered and analyzed. The inclusion of this concrete information and examples makes their argument much more convincing than had they provided a more general rebuttal to the statement that begins their paragraph. In this way, appeals to logic can take on many forms, including interpretations of "hard evidence," such as found in syllogisms (formal, structured arguments), reasoned arguments, closing statements in law, inferences in the form of statistical models, and appeals to "common sense" or cultural assumptions.

In advertising, the mode of persuasion we call logos often operates through the written text; significantly, the Greek word *logos* can be translated as "word," indicating the way in which we, culturally, often look to words as repositories of fact and reason. Let's see how the Chevron ad featured in Figure 2.4 presents a reasoned argument.

The type of logos-based reasoning found in the Chevron ad appears in many ads that you may also be familiar with: think, for instance, of a computer ad that juxtaposes a striking photo of a laptop with a chart detailing its processor type, memory capacity, screen size, and graphics features; a car ad that offsets a glossy showroom photo with safety ratings and positive reviews from *Car & Driver* and *Motor Trend;* or a commercial for a bank that features a smiling agent listing the reasons to open a checking account at that branch. In each case, the advertisement drives its point through facts, evidence, and reason.

In fact, some might argue that logos as an appeal underlies almost all advertising, specifically because most advertising uses an implicit *causal argument:* if you buy this product, then you or your life will be like the one featured in the ad. Sometimes the associations are explicit: if you use Pantene shampoo, then your hair will be shinier; if you buy Tide detergent, then your clothes will be cleaner; if you buy a Volvo sedan, then your family will be safer driving on the road. Sometimes the *cause-and-effect* argument is more subtle: buying Sure deodorant will make you more confident; drinking Coke will make you happier; wearing Nikes will make you perform better on the court. In each case, logos, or the use of logical reasoning, is the tool of persuasion responsible for the ad's argumentative force.

Student Writing

Fred Chang analyzes Apple Computer's reliance on logos in its advertising battle with Intel.

www.ablongman.com/envision/206

FIGURE 2.5 In this Crest Whitening Strips advertisement, inset images offer visual evidence for the ad's argument.

The ad for Crest Whitening Strips in Figure 2.5 offers us a useful example of how logos can operate in more subtle ways in an ad—through visual as well as verbal argumentation. When we first look at the ad, our eyes are drawn immediately to the model's white smile, positioned near the center of the two-page spread. Our gaze next moves up to her eyes and then down again to the two juxtaposed close-up shots of her teeth.

These two close-ups carry the force of the argument. They are before-and-after stills, demonstrating, in brilliant color, the whitening power of Crest. The contrast between the two images makes a deliberate logos appeal by constructing a *cause-and-effect* argument. The captions for these two close-ups confirm the message imparted by the images and solidify the visual promise of the ad. The final small box insert is our last visual stop; it shows the product and suggests the solution to the logical equation at work in this ad. The fact that the ad's words, "Your new smile," appear beneath the photo of the product—as the conclusion of the logical argument—reinforces the persuasive message that Crest indeed will give its users such white teeth. To put the logic plainly: if people brush with this product, then they too will achieve this result. In this way, the ad relies on logos to attract and convince its audience.

Seeing Connections
For an effective use of logos to drive an argument, see Harrison Pope's "Evolving Ideals of Male Body Image as Seen Through Action Toys" on page 284.

Logical Fallacies

When crafting your own written analysis of advertisements, be careful not to rely on mistaken or misleading uses of logos, commonly called **logical fallacies.** The causal

AT A GLANCE

Logical Fallacies

- **The post hoc fallacy:** confusing cause and effect
- **The cum hoc fallacy:** interpreting correlation as causation
- **The hasty generalization:** drawing a conclusion too quickly without providing enough supporting evidence
- **The either-or argument:** reducing an argument to a choice between two diametrically opposed choices, ignoring other possible scenarios
- **Stacking the evidence:** offering evidence for only one side of the issue
- **Begging the question:** using an argument as evidence for itself
- **The red herring:** distracting the audience rather than focusing on the argument

strategy underlying most advertising can be seen as an example of faulty logic, for surely it is fraudulent to suggest that wearing a certain brand of clothing will make you popular or that drinking a certain beer will make you attractive to the opposite sex. In classical rhetoric, this fallacy of causality is called a ***post hoc ergo propter hoc* fallacy**—namely, the idea that because something happened first (showering with an aloe-enhanced body gel), it is the direct cause of something that happened afterward (getting great grades on your midterms). A similar effect can be produced by the ***cum hoc ergo propter hoc* fallacy**, often called a *correlation-causation* fallacy. According to this model, because two unrelated events happen at the same time (are correlated), they are interpreted as cause and effect. For instance, the following is an example of a *cum hoc* fallacy: (1) a teenager plays his varsity basketball game wearing his new Air Jordans; (2) the teenager makes many key rebounds and jump shots while playing the game; (3) the Air Jordans caused his success in the game. You can probably think of many commercials that rely on these two particular logical fallacies.

However, in those same commercials, we see more and more cases of advertisers guarding themselves against claims of false causality. For instance, consider the typical weight-loss advertisement. "I lost 31 pounds in 3 months using this nutritional plan!" one happy dieter exclaims on camera. The camera shows an old video clip of the subject at her previous weight, and then it moves to the newly trimmed-down version, usually with a trendy hairstyle and tight-fitting clothes—a clear before-and-after strategy. However, more and more often, you now find these images captioned with one telling phrase: "These results not typical." This disclaimer points to advertisers' recognition that they, like other rhetoricians, need to be careful in their use of logos as an argumentative appeal.

Appeals to Emotion

Roughly defined as "suffering" or "feeling" in its original Greek, the term *pathos* actually means to put the audience in a particular mood or frame of mind. Modern derivations of the word *pathos* include *pathology* and *pathetic,* and indeed we speak of pathos as "the pathetic appeal." But pathos is more a technique than a state: writers use it as a tool of persuasion to establish an intimate connection with the audience by soliciting powerful emotions. For instance, consider the way the following paragraphs foster an emotional reaction from the reader:

> Dorsey Hoskins' father Bryan felt a tingling in his arm. The diagnosis—an inoperable brain tumor. Six months later, he died at the age of 33, leaving his wife to raise Dorsey and sister Hattie.
>
> Fortunately, Bryan bought life insurance when he married, and again when his daughters were born. Thanks to Bryan's foresight, Dorsey, Hattie, and their mom are taken care of.
>
> Are you prepared should the very worst happen?

This passage relies on a pathos appeal on many levels. Clearly, the very premise of the piece—moving from tragedy, to a sense of tempered relief, to personal identification—is designed to evoke a sympathetic response. Looking more closely, however, suggests that even the more subtle stylistic choices also contribute to the emotional appeal. Notice, for example, the power of word choice: the author initially introduces Bryan as "Dorsey Hoskins' father," establishing him from the first in terms of his daughter and, ultimately, her loss; the author withholds Bryan's age for three sentences, at which point he can disclose it to accentuate the tragedy of his early death; finally, after the powerful, opening anecdote, the author uses the second person to draw the audience itself into the piece through the pointed rhetorical question.

It shouldn't be a surprise to discover that this passage is in fact taken from an advertisement for life insurance or that the pathos of the text is echoed by the emotional charge of a close-up photograph of 5-year-old Dorsey, which serves as the background for the advertisement. We encounter ads that rely on pathos all the time, and indeed, the visual composition of an ad often taps our emotions in ways we barely recognize.

Let's look closely at another advertisement that relies on creating an emotional connection with the audience to sell its product. In the spring of 2006 Volkswagen launched a new marketing campaign aimed at pitching safety rather than sportiness; the "Safe Happens" commercials revolve around an unexpected moment of collision and its surprisingly reassuring aftermath (Figure 2.6). In this particular commercial, the viewer finds herself transported into the interior of an automobile. At this point, there is no clue as to the car's make or model; the camera shots are all of the car's occupants, a group of friends in their late twenties or early thirties. The camera focuses on each face in turn, identifying them as the points of identification and creating a bond between the characters and the viewer. We encounter them in the middle of a friendly, light-hearted conversation, the women gently teasing the men about crying at the end of the movie they have just watched. The exchange is informal and comfortable, the mood light.

In a second, everything changes. Replicating in real-time the experience of a car accident, the commercial cuts the characters off midsentence with a screech of brakes, blinding headlights, and the sound of a collision. The viewer, an invisible passenger in the car, feels the same surprise and horror as the main characters. The camera focus abruptly changes and moves us outside the vehicle; we become bystanders, watching a nondescript SUV plow into the white sedan that we identify as *our* car, the

Government star ratings are part of the National Highway Traffic Safety Administration's (NHTSA's) New Car Assessment Program.(www.safercar.gov) All crashes are different and severe injuries can occur. Airbags do not deploy in all accidents. Always use safety belts and seat children in rear using appropriate restraint systems.

FIGURE 2.6 The final frame from a Volkswagen commercial reinforces the audience's identification with the occupants of the damaged vehicle and extends the pathos appeal of the ad's narrative.

power of the collision captured with harsh accuracy. As the screen goes black, suddenly silence prevails, except for the uneven clatter of a rolling hubcap.

After a couple of seconds, the image reappears, and we see our former companions, unharmed, standing outside the battered vehicle. This first moment of product identification is captioned by an unusual voice-over; the camera zooms in on one of the female passengers, who looks with disbelief at the wreck and whispers, "Holy . . . ." The implied expletive is silenced by a quick cut to a more traditional car-commercial shot: the Jetta, in a spotless white showroom, slowly revolving on a turntable. Even here, beyond the end of the commercial's central narrative, the pathos appeal is reinforced. The rotating car is clearly not a showroom model; the dented driver's side door identifies it once again as *our* car, the one that kept the main characters safe. The written caption reinforces this association, proclaiming "Safe Happens" (playing with the female character's final words) and then announcing that Jetta has received the government's highest safety rating. This moment of logos appeal becomes doubly persuasive because of the viewer's emotional engagement with the commercial: we feel that we ourselves have survived the crash and we look to the Jetta as the reason.

Pathos does not only operate through triggering the highs and lows of emotion in its audience; sometimes the appeals, though still speaking to the visceral more than the rational, are more subtle. Patriotism, indignation, excitement—all these effects can be linked to the pathos appeal. Consider the Porsche commercial showing a sleek red car speeding along a windy mountain road, the Ford Escape TV spot featuring the rugged SUV plowing through a muddy off-road trail, or the Cooper Mini ad using uniqueness as a selling point for the little car. Each of these ads uses pathos to produce a specific feeling in viewers: I want to drive fast, wind in my hair; I want to get off the beaten path, forge a new frontier; I want to stand out in a crowd, make a statement.

You are probably even more familiar with another type of pathos appeal—the appeal to sexuality. Clearly, "sex sells." Look at Victoria's Secret models posed in near nudity or recent Abercrombie and Fitch catalogs featuring models more likely to show off their toned abs than a pair of jeans, and you can see how in many cases advertisers tend to appeal more to nonrational impulses than to our powers of logical reasoning. Perfume and cologne advertisers in particular often use the rhetoric of sexuality to sell their fragrances, whether it be Calvin Klein's Obsession or Armani's Acqua Di Gio. Such ads work cleverly to sell perfume, not on the merits of the scent or on its chemical composition but through the visual rhetoric of sexuality and our emotional responses to it.

Student Writing

Cyrus Chee's rhetorical analysis reads the appeals to pathos in two poster ads for contemporary films about the Holocaust.

www.ablongman.com/envision/207

Seeing Connections
See Jane Juffer's effective use of pathos in the introduction of "Who's the Man?" on page 362.

COLLABORATIVE CHALLENGE

Find five advertisements from recent magazines—for instance, *Cosmo, Vogue, Seventeen, GQ, Details, Esquire*—that use sexuality to sell their products. In your group compare the use of pathos in these ads. When is this appeal an effective marketing strategy? When does it seem ineffectual or inappropriate?

One final—and perhaps most pervasive—pathos appeal deserves mention at the close of this section. Looking at Figure 2.7, we can see yet another typical use of pathos to drive an argument.

Humor underlies the visual argument of this ad; by depicting a monk wearing sunglasses and enjoying a game of golf at a new resort, this advertisement from Beijing, China, provides a particularly amusing rendering of how consumer goods and services can transform life. If you think about it, as a culture we tend to be quite persuaded by humor; against our more rational impulses, the ads that make us laugh are usually the ones we remember. To prove this point, you need only think back to last year's Superbowl ads: Which ads do you remember? Which ads did you talk over with your friends during and after the game? Probably most of those memorable commercials relied on humor—or "humos" as one of our students, David Baron, named it. The arguments made by these ads may not always be the most logically sound, but the way they foster a connection with the audience makes them persuasive nonetheless.

FIGURE 2.7 This Chinese ad for a new resort uses incongruous elements for visual humor.

Exaggerated Uses of Pathos

Although these strategies of persuasion successfully move their audience, sometimes advertisers exaggerate the appeal to emotion for more dramatic effect.

Consider the case of exaggerated pathos found in the Listerine campaign from the early twentieth century. In the 1920s, Gerard Lambert introduced the term *halitosis* into the popular vocabulary as a marketing strategy; he used it to convince Americans that Listerine was their only alternative to public embarrassment from bad breath (Twitchell, *Adcult* 144). Regardless of the fact that Listerine's primary use at the time was as a hospital disinfectant, Lambert transformed American culture through his successful use of **false needs.**

In Figure 2.8, we see an example from the 1950s of this famous ad campaign. The words of the headline, spoken by the two women in the upper-right corner ("He's Hanging Himself Right Now!"), are a bit cryptic so that the reader has to look to the image in the center of the ad to understand its message. The drawing of the man and woman dancing makes a direct correlation between personal hygiene and romantic relationships, creating a sense of *false need* in the consumer for the product. In this case, the woman's averted head suggests her rejection of the suitor. Moreover, as you can see, the ad also uses the **scare tactic;** the disapproval on the faces of the women at the side table arouses in viewers a fear of rejection. The way the dancing woman's body turns away from the man augments this pathos appeal. Having deciphered the meaning of the ad

AT A GLANCE

Exaggerated Uses of Pathos

- *Over-sentimentalization:* distracting the audience from evidence or issues
- *The scare tactic:* capitalizing on the audience's fears to make a pitch
- *The false need:* amplifying a perceived need or creating a completely new one
- *The slippery slope fallacy:* suggesting that an event or action will send the audience spiraling down a "slippery slope" to a serious consequence

FIGURE 2.8 This Listerine ad uses appeals to pathos to persuade readers to use its product.

from the image, the words now seem to confirm the idea in the headline that the man stands little chance of a romantic encounter. Image and text collaborate here to produce a powerful emotional reaction in the audience. Moreover, the threat of impending loss signifies a successful use of the **slippery slope,** an argument asserting that one thing leads to a chain of events that results in an undesirable conclusion: in this case, bad breath leads to solitude and loneliness.

Many contemporary advertising campaigns also operate in a similar fashion, defining a problem and then offering up their product as a solution: think, for instance, of Clearasil's acne cream or Ban Invisible Solid deodorant. Take a moment now to think about times in your life when you may have been motivated to purchase a product through *false need:* have you ever bought a man's or woman's razor? pump-up basketball shoes? an angled toothbrush? curl-enhancing mascara? a transparent band-aid? What other examples of false needs or exaggerated pathos can you recall?

CREATIVE PRACTICE

The written copy that follows is from the Listerine print ad featured in Figure 2.8. As we've seen, the more prominent visual and verbal elements rely primarily on pathos to drive their arguments. Read the copy from the ad over carefully and analyze the rhetorical strategies at work there. Does it also rely on pathos? At which parts? What other strategies or appeals do you see at work in the text? Why do you think the copywriter chose to employ those rhetorical strategies at those points in the argument?

"Mark my words," Edith went on, "by the time they've gone twice around the dance floor, he'll get the complete brush-off from her."

"But why?" Polly queried. "He's so attractive . . . seems so attentive . . ."

"Indeed he is. And he's been wangling this date for weeks. Poor guy . . . he's through before he even starts . . . and he'll never know why*."

This sort of thing can happen, and usually does, when people are careless about halitosis* (unpleasant breath).

How About You?

Are you guilty? The insidious thing about halitosis is that you, yourself, may not realize it is present. So at the very moment you want to be at your best, you may be at your worst . . . offending needlessly.

Sometimes, of course, halitosis comes from some systemic disorder. But usually—and fortunately—it is only a local condition that yields to the regular use of Listerine Antiseptic as a mouth wash and gargle.

Why Run Such a Risk?

Don't risk offending others. And don't trust to makeshifts. Put your faith in Listerine Antiseptic which millions have found to be an *extra-careful* precaution against halitosis. Really fastidious people look up to Listerine Antiseptic as a part of their passport to popularity. It's so easy, so delightful to use, so lasting in effect.

Sweetness for Hours

Listerine Antiseptic is the *extra-careful* precaution because it sweetens and freshens the breath, *not for seconds or minutes . . . but for hours, usually.* Your breath, indeed your entire mouth, feels wonderfully fresh and clean.

Never, never omit Listerine Antiseptic before any date where you want to be at your best. Better still, get in the habit of using it night and morning for that clean, fresh feeling.

Appeals to Character and Authority

The last of the three appeals that we'll look at in this chapter is *ethos*, "character." Perhaps you have used ethos in other disciplines to mean an argument based on ethical principles. But the *rhetorical* meaning of the term is slightly different: according to Aristotle, ethos works as a rhetorical strategy by establishing the goodwill or credibility of the writer or speaker. In fact, as a writer you use ethos every time you pick up a pen or proofread your essay—that is, you construct an argument in which your power to persuade depends on credibility, your word choice, your tone, your choice of examples, the quality of your research, your grammar and punctuation. All these factors contribute to your ethos as an author.

Let's look to one of the articles we've already encountered in this chapter to see the subtle ways in which an author can create ethos. Below are the opening lines of Seth Stevenson's "Me and My Shadow":

> I myself own an iPod, but rarely dance around with it. In part because the earbuds would fall out (Does this happen to you? I think I may have narrow auditory canals) and in part because I'm just not all that prone to solitary rump-shaking. It's a failing on my part. Maybe if I were a silhouette I might dance more.

Seeing Connections
See how Paul Mitchell uses ethos or an appeal to character to drive his argument in "Faith and Fashion" on page 323.

Notice the way in which Stevenson immediately establishes why he feels authorized to talk about iPods: "I myself own an iPod." He is not an uninformed critic; from the first, he sets himself up as an iPod owner, someone familiar with the product—and by extension with the advertising. He also goes to lengths to establish a connection with his audience and gain their trust. By confessing that he rarely dances around with his iPod and then using this as an excuse to draw in his audience ("Does this happen to you?"), he more firmly ingratiates himself with his readers, many of whom have probably had the same experience. In this way, he deliberately constructs his ethos from the opening lines of his essay so that he can then launch into his analysis with the full confidence of his audience.

Clearly, ethos can be a very powerful tool for establishing trust and therefore facilitating the persuasiveness of an argument. Companies have long recognized the persuasive power of ethos. In fact, a brand logo is in essence ethos distilled into a single symbol: it transmits in a single icon the entire reputation of a company, organization, or brand identity. From the Nike swoosh to McDonald's golden arches, the NBC peacock, or the Apple computer apple, symbols serve to mark (or brand) products with ethos.

Yet the power of the brand logo as a seat of ethos relies on the company's overall reputation with the consumer—a reputation that the company carefully cultivates through advertising campaigns. Many companies, for instance, trade on ethos by using celebrity endorsements in their advertising campaigns. Although a rational appeal is at work behind some endorsements—having basketball superstar LeBron James sell basketball shoes, for instance, makes sense—many campaigns rely not only on the celebrity's suitability for selling a product but also on the person's star appeal, character, and goodwill. Consider the power of the famous "Got Milk?" campaign. Here's the argument: if this celebrity likes milk, shouldn't we? Indeed, when we see Kelly Clarkson—or others, such as Serena Williams, Nelly, Ben Roethlisberger, or Jackie Chan—sporting the famous milk moustache, we find the ad persuasive because these celebrities are vouching for the product. We look to their goodwill as public figures, to their character as famous people putting their reputation on the line.

While the impact of a famous spokesperson can be a powerful use of ethos, celebrity endorsement is only one way to create this sort of appeal. Sometimes the *lack* of fame can be a strategic tool of the trade. Consider the Apple "Switch" ad campaign that featured everyday people stepping into the role of spokesperson for the Apple computer system. These ads featured everymen or everywomen of various ages, nationalities, and professions speaking directly into the camera about their reasons for changing from PCs to Apple computers. The combination of an unknown spokesperson, a clear example, a simple white background, and a slightly choppy film style—designed to seem edited and somewhat amateur—brought an ethos to the campaign based not on star power but on no-nonsense use and everyday application. In assessing the rhetorical situation for creating its ads, Apple recognized an important fact: for a large part of its audience, ethos would derive not from the flash of a celebrity smile but from identification with real-life Apple users.

Sometimes an ad features a corporate ethos to establish the credibility of the company. Microsoft's "We See" campaign, for instance, sells not software but a company image. One representative ad from this campaign depicts young children at work in a classroom. What makes the ad visually interesting is that the image includes white shadowy sketches that transform the children into successful future versions of themselves. Complemented by the header, "We see new skills, tomorrow's inventions," and the closing tagline, "Your potential. Our passion," the ad becomes a window into the future, Microsoft's image of the new generation. The message of the ad relies heavily on ethos: Microsoft cares about America's youth and wants to help them realize their dreams.

In contrast to the Microsoft ad that promotes its corporate ethos rather than a particular product, many ads sell products directly through appeals to character. In Figure 2.9, for example, a Longines watch ad makes its pitch through words and images: the line, "Elegance is an Attitude" suggests that both the company and the wearer of the company's product can share in elevated ethos. The visual image reinforces this idea through the representation of a well-dressed man standing confidently in a black jacket and pinstriped shirt. He looks directly out at the viewer, potentially catching the eye of possible viewers and literally standing in for corporate ethos.

FIGURE 2.9 This Longines ad from Beijing, China, uses corporate ethos to market its watch through the image of the man's character and the words "Elegance is an Attitude."

COLLABORATIVE CHALLENGE

With a partner, look at the car advertisements in Figures 2.10 and 2.11. How does each use specific argumentative strategies and rhetorical appeals to make its argument? Choose one of the ads and brainstorm with your partner a way in which the company might market the same car through an ad that relies primarily on a different strategy or appeal. Sketch out your hypothetical ad—including both image and copy—and share it with the class, discussing how the shift in appeal affected your understanding of the rhetorical situation and the effectiveness of the ad.

FIGURE 2.10 An advertisement for a Saab.

FIGURE 2.11 An advertisement for the Ford Escape hybrid.

Misuses of Ethos

One consequence of relying on ethos-driven arguments is that sometimes we come to trust symbols of ethos rather than looking to the character of the product itself. This tendency points us to the concept of **authority over evidence**—namely, the practice of overemphasizing authority or ethos rather than focusing on the merits of the evidence itself, a strategic exaggeration of ethos that helps entice audiences and sell products.

The most prominent examples of *authority over evidence* can be found in celebrity endorsements; in many commercials, the spokesperson sells the product not based on its merits but based on the argument, "Believe what I say because you know me, and would I steer you wrong?" However, the American public has become increasingly skeptical of such arguments. Living in a world where rumors of Pepsi-spokesperson Britney Spears's preference for Coke circulate on the Internet, Tiger Woods's $100 million deal with Nike makes front page news, and a star like former Sprite spokesperson Macaulay Culkin publicly announces, "I'm not crazy about the stuff [Sprite]. But money is money" (Twitchell, *Twenty* 214), the credibility of celebrity endorsements is often questionable.

AT A GLANCE

Misuses of Ethos

- *Authority over evidence:* placing more emphasis on ethos than on the actual validity of the evidence
- *Ad hominem:* criticizing an opponent's character (or ethos) rather than the argument itself

Often, companies deliberately attempt to undermine the ethos of their competition as a way of promoting their own products. You probably have seen ads of this sort: Burger King arguing that their flame-broiled hamburgers are better than McDonald's fried hamburgers; Coke claiming its soda tastes better than Pepsi's; Visa asserting its card's versatility by reminding consumers how many companies "don't take American Express." The deliberate *comparison-contrast* builds up one company's ethos at another's expense. At times, however, this technique can be taken to an extreme, producing an *ad hominem* argument—that is, an argument that attempts to persuade by attacking an opponent's ethos or character. We see *ad hominem* at work most often in campaign advertisements, where candidates end up focusing less on the issues at hand than on their opponents' moral weaknesses, or in commercials where companies attack each other for the way they run their businesses rather than the quality of their products. In other words, this strategy attempts to persuade by reducing the credibility of opposing arguments.

Exaggerated Ethos Through Parody

Another strategy of persuasion is attacking ethos through **parody,** or the deliberate mocking of a text or convention. Parody has long been recognized as an effective rhetorical strategy for making a powerful argument. To see how this happens, let's turn to an ad designed by TheTruth.com, an innovative anti-tobacco organization (see Figure 2.12). Through the strategic use of setting, character, font, and layout, this ad deliberately evokes and then parodies traditional cigarette advertising to make its claim for the dangers of smoking.

Student Writing

Amanda Johnson, in her analysis of a Barbie parody ad, and Georgia Duan, in her reading of cigarette advertising, explore the construction of body image in the media and the use of parody in ads.
www.ablongman.com/envision/208

Even if you are not familiar with the Masters Settlement Act, you probably have seen some of the Marlboro Country ads, often showing the lone cowboy or groups of cowboys riding across a beautiful, sunlit western American landscape. During the early part of its campaign, TheTruth.com recognized the impact of the long tradition of cigarette advertising on the public and decided to turn this tradition to its advantage. In the TheTruth.com parody version, however, the cowboy's companions do not ride proudly beside him. Instead, they are zipped up into body bags—an image that relies on exaggerated ethos and employs pathos to provoke a strong reaction in the audience. By producing an ad that builds on and yet revises the logic of Philip Morris's ad campaign, TheTruth.com could get past false images (the happy cowboy) to get at its idea of the "truth": that by

FIGURE 2.12 This TheTruth.com antismoking ad attacks ethos through parody.

smoking cigarettes "You Too Can Be an Independent, Rugged, Macho-Looking Dead Guy." The visual complexity of the image (and the combination of appeals) resonates powerfully by evoking the audience's familiarity with cigarette advertisements to pack some of its punch.

Considering Context

As you can tell from examining ads in this chapter, a successful argument must take into account not only the *rhetorical situation* but also the context, or the right time and place. That is why promotional trailers for the ABC series *Invasion*—featuring big-budget scenes of a Florida hurricane—could captivate audiences in the early summer of 2005 but horrify and outrage that same audience two months later in the wake of hurricanes Katrina and Rita. In ancient Greece rhetoricians called this aspect of the rhetorical situation **kairos**—namely, the contingencies of time and place for an argument.

In your own writing, you should consider *kairos* along with the other aspects of the rhetorical situation: audience, text, and writer. As a student of rhetoric, it is important to recognize the *kairos*—the opportune historical, ideological, or cultural moment—of a text when analyzing its rhetorical force. You undoubtedly already consider the context for persuasive communication in your everyday life. For instance, whether you are asking a friend to dinner or a professor for a recommendation, your assessment of the timeliness and the appropriate strategies for that time probably determines the shape your argument takes. You pick the right moment and place to make your case. In other words, the rhetorical situation involves interaction between audience, text, and writer *within* the context or *kairos*.

Consider, for instance, Coca-Cola's ad campaigns. Coke has exerted a powerful presence in the advertising industry for many years, in part because of its strategic advertising. During World War II, Coke ran a series of ads that built its beverage campaign around the contemporary nationalistic sentiment. What you find featured in these ads are servicemen, international landscapes, and inspiring slices of Americana—all designed to respond to that specific cultural moment.

Look at Figure 2.13, an advertisement for Coke from the 1940s. This picture uses pathos to appeal to the audience's sense of patriotism by featuring a row of seemingly carefree servicemen, leaning from the windows of a military bus, the refreshing Cokes in their hands producing smiles even far away from home. The picture draws in the audience by reassuring them on two fronts. On the one hand, it builds on the nationalistic pride in the young, handsome servicemen who so happily serve their country. On the

FIGURE 2.13 This Coca-Cola ad used *kairos* to create a powerful argument for its World War II audience.

other, it is designed to appease fears about the hostile climate abroad: as both the picture and the accompanying text assure us, Coca-Cola (and the servicemen) "goes along" and "gets a hearty welcome."

The power of this message relates directly to its context. An ad such as this one, premised on patriotism and pride in military service, would be most persuasive during wartime when many more people tend to support the spirit of nationalism and therefore would be moved by the image of the young serviceman shipping off to war. It is through understanding the *kairos* of this advertisement that you can appreciate the strength of the ad's rhetorical appeal.

Using Strategies of Persuasion

As you can tell from our work in this chapter, ads convey complex cultural meanings. Recognizing their persuasive presence everywhere, we realize the need to develop our ability to make better-informed interpretations of ads around us. You can pursue your study of ads by conducting your own careful rhetorical analyses of these visual-verbal texts. You'll find over and over again that ads are a microcosm of many of the techniques of persuasion. From billboards to pop-ups on the Internet, ads employ logos, pathos, and ethos to convey strong messages to specific audiences. We've learned how compact and sophisticated these texts are. Now it's time to apply those insights in your own writing.

As you begin to perform your individual analyses of advertisements, consider the way your own writing, like the ads we've discussed, can "sell" your argument to the reader. Consider the rhetorical situation and the specific *kairos* of your argument. What *strategies of argumentation* and *rhetorical appeals* would be most effective in reaching your target audience? Do you want to use narration, a humorous analogy, or a stirring example to forge a connection with your readers based on pathos? Or is your analysis better suited to logos, following a step-by-step process of reading an ad, drawing on empirical evidence, or looking at cause and effect? Perhaps you will decide to enrich your discussion through cultivating your ethos as a writer, establishing your own authority on a subject or citing reputable work done by other scholars. It is probable that in your essay you will use many strategies and a combination of appeals; as we saw in the advertisements presented earlier, from the Crest Whitening Strips ad to the Coca-Cola campaign, a successful argument uses various rhetorical strategies to persuade its audience.

While focusing on the individual strategies, don't forget to keep an eye on the composition of your argument as a whole. Just as an ad is designed with attention to layout and design, so you should look at the larger organization of your essay as key to the success of your argument. As you approach the organization of elements in your essay to maximize your persuasiveness, even a question like "Where should I insert my images?" has profound implications for your argument. Consider the difference between an essay in which the image is embedded in the text, next to the paragraph that analyzes it, and one with the image attached as an appendix. In your writing, use the persuasive power of visual rhetoric more effectively by allowing the reader to analyze the images alongside the written explanations. Use similar careful attention to organization, placement, and purpose as you begin your own analysis and craft your own rhetorical argument.

PREWRITING CHECKLIST

Analyzing Advertisements

❑ **Content:** What exactly is the ad selling? an object? an idea? both?

❑ **Message:** How is the ad selling the product? What is the persuasive message that the ad is sending to the audience?

❏ **Character and setting:** What is featured by the ad? An object? a scene? a person? How are these elements portrayed? What are the ethnicity, age, socioeconomic class, and gender of any people in the advertisement? How do these choices relate to the ad's intended audience and reflect deliberate rhetorical choices?

❏ **Story:** On the most basic level, what is happening in the advertisement?

❏ **Theme:** What is the underlying message of the ad (beyond "buy our product")?

❏ **Medium:** What medium was the advertisement produced in? television? print? radio? How did this choice suit the rhetorical purpose of the ad and accommodate the needs of a particular audience?

❏ **Historical context:** In what country and at what historical moment was the advertisement produced? How do the demands of context shape the persuasive appeals at work in the ad? How does the ad reflect, comment on, challenge, or reinforce contemporary political, economic, or gender ideology? How does this commentary situate it in terms of a larger trend or argument?

❏ **Word and image:** What is the relationship between the word (written or spoken) and the imagery in the ad? Which is given priority? How does this relationship affect the persuasiveness of the advertisement?

❏ **Layout:** How are the elements of the ad arranged—on a page (for a print ad) or in sequence (for a television commercial)? What is the purpose behind this arrangement? How does the ad's organization lead the reader through—and facilitate—its argument?

❏ **Design:** What typeface is used? What size? What color? How do these decisions reflect attention to the ad's rhetorical situation? How do they function in relation to the ad's rhetorical appeals?

❏ **Voice:** What voice does the text use to reach its audience? Is the language technical, informal, personal, authoritative? Is the voice comic or serious?

❏ **Imagery:** What choices did the advertiser make in selecting imagery for this ad? If it is a static print ad, does the ad feature a line drawing or a photograph? Is the photograph black and white? a close-up? a panoramic shot? If the advertisement is drawn from television, what are the pace and sequence of the images? Where does the camera zoom in? What does it focus on? Does the ad feature a close-up or a long shot? Is the image centered? completely captured in the frame? Is it cut off? If so, how? Does it feature a head-on shot? a three-quarter shot? Whose point of view, if any, is the viewer supposed to assume?

❏ **Rhetorical appeals:** How does the advertiser use the images to work in conjunction with rhetorical appeals? For instance, does the image reinforce an appeal to reason? Is it designed to produce an emotional effect on the audience? Does the use of a certain style, such as black-and-white authority, contribute to the ethos of the ad?

❏ **Strategy of development:** What strategy of development does the ad rely on? narration? definition? comparison-contrast? example or illustration? classification and division? How do these strategies contribute to the ad's persuasive appeal?

❏ **Cultural resonance:** Does the ad use ethos—in the form of celebrities, famous events or places, or recognizable symbols—to increase its persuasiveness? If so, how does that establish audience or a particular relationship to a cultural moment?

WRITING PROJECTS

1. **Rhetorical Analysis:** Choose two or three ads for the same product and analyze the strategies of persuasion these ads use to reach specific audiences. To find your ads, you might visit an ad archive such as those linked through the Chapter 2 resources on the *Envision* Website, or look at old magazines in your school library. Alternatively, you can use current print or television advertisements as your sources and select ads that showcase an exaggeration of rhetorical appeals, such as logical fallacies, exaggeration of pathos, misuse of ethos, parody, or self-referential ads. Use the prewriting checklist to help you analyze the appeals at work in the ads and to help you develop your argument about the persuasion in these texts. Be sure to address how *strategies of argumentation* operate and what the effects are on the audience as well as a description of context: where and when was the ad published and to whom? Refer back to the rhetorical triangle in Chapter 1 to help you.

2. **Contextual Analysis:** Write a contextual analysis on the *kairos* of the Coca-Cola campaign. Examine, for instance, another Coke ad from the 1940s through the Adflip link on the *Envision* Website. Do some preliminary research and read about this era: explore the time, place, and culture in which the ad appeared. Ask yourself: How do the rhetorical choices of the ad you selected reflect an awareness of this context? How does the ad use the particular tools of logos, pathos, and ethos to comment upon or criticize this cultural moment?

3. **Historical Analysis:** Working in groups, look at several ads from different time periods produced by the same company. Some possible topics include ads for cigarettes, cars, hygiene products, and personal computers. Each member of your group should choose a single ad and prepare a rhetorical analysis of its persuasive appeals. Share your analyses and collaborate to explore how this company has modified its rhetorical approach over time. As you synthesize your argument, be sure to consider in each case how the different rhetorical situations inform the strategies used by the ads to reach their target audience. Collaborate to write a paper in which you chart the evolution of the company's persuasive strategies and how that evolution was informed by *kairos.*

4. **Cultural Analysis:** Write a paper in which you compare two ad campaigns and examine the ideology behind specific constructions of our culture. Does one campaign portray gender- or race-specific ideas? How do the tools of persuasion work to produce each message? What larger message is conveyed by the reliance on such cultural ideals or notions of identity? What representations of sexuality, gender roles, or class are presented by these ads? Write up your findings and then present them to the class, holding up examples of the ads to discuss in support of your analysis.

 Visit www.ablongman.com/envision for expanded assignment guidelines and student projects.

CHAPTER 3

Composing Arguments

Chapter Preview Questions

- What are the canons of rhetoric, and how do they help us to understand arguments?
- How can you create strong introductions and conclusions?
- What roles do persona and rhetorical stance play in arguments?
- How do photographs function as both visual evidence in arguments and as visual arguments themselves?
- How do writers synthesize multiple perspectives on an issue in an argument?

FIGURE 3.1 A photograph of supplies being dropped to New Orleans survivors of Hurricane Katrina.

Imagine that it is September 2005, and the United States is still reeling from the aftermath of Hurricane Katrina. As you visit the newsstand to purchase a paper, you pause to reflect on the various front pages before you. Each showcases a different photograph to comment on the tragedy. One features a striking photo of a military helicopter dropping supplies to the citizens of New Orleans (see Figure 3.1). Another shows an African-American mother clutching two small children to her chest and wading through waist-deep water. Yet another displays the image of a mob of angry people, packed together and arguing as they try to evacuate the city. A final front page uses the picture of a child's dirt-smeared doll, swept into a pile of debris on the road, as its poignant commentary on natural disaster.

Based on these images, which newspaper would you buy? How does each photo make a different argument about exactly what happened? How might the words of the caption or title shape the kind of interpretation you might make about the visual texts? How does the choice of a particular visual-verbal combination present a specific point of view?

Photographs and captions in newspapers work through the tools of persuasion that we examined in earlier chapters. In this chapter, we'll look at photographs to continue our exploration of how visual rhetoric shapes our reality in particular ways. We will also move forward in our understanding of analysis and argument by learning effective ways to create arguments. We'll become acquainted with the canons of rhetoric—five classifications of argument from ancient Greece—and we'll work through coming up with ideas, structuring those ideas, and developing a style for your own compositions.

Understanding the Canons of Rhetoric

In ancient Greece, all communicative acts were classified into five categories, or what scholars call the **canons of rhetoric.** These are the principles by which all writing, speaking, or visual arguments operate: **invention** (coming up with ideas), **arrangement** (organizing ideas in effective ways), **style** (expressing those ideas in an appropriate manner), **memory** (accessing learned materials), and **delivery** (presenting crafted ideas to an audience).

AT A GLANCE

Canons of Rhetoric
- *Invention:* generating ideas
- *Arrangement:* ordering and laying out ideas effectively
- *Style:* developing the appropriate expression for those ideas
- *Memory:* retaining invented ideas, recalling additional supporting ideas, and facilitating memory in the audience
- *Delivery:* presenting or performing ideas with the aim of persuading

Each of these canons is necessary for persuasive communication, whether that be through spoken word, written discourse, or more recently devised visual/multimedia/hybrid forms of communication. For our discussion of composing arguments in this chapter, we'll focus on the first three canons (you can look to Chapter 8 for discussion of the last two canons).

Invention in Argument

When you craft language with the purpose of persuading your audience, you are **inventing** an argument. That is, you are generating ideas about a topic. The classical Roman rhetorician Cicero defined invention as the "discovery of valid or seemingly valid arguments to render one's cause probable" (*De Inventione*, I.vii). To develop ideas, you can use a range of rhetorical strategies: invoking pathos, using ethos or good character, or employing logos to reason calmly with your readers or listeners. Your task as a writer is to forge a powerful text that argues a point, to convince others to see a particular perspective, usually your own. In composing arguments you can look not only to writing but also to verbal-visual texts all around you as examples of arguments.

When we look at a photograph, we might think that it provides a window on another person's reality. But in fact photographs, like written texts, are artifacts of rhetorical invention. They are created by a writer or artist. Therefore, the "reality" that photographs display is actually a *version* of reality created by a photographer's rhetorical and artistic decisions: whether to use color or black-and-white film; what sort of lighting to use; how to position the subject of the photograph; whether to opt for a panorama or close-up shot; what backdrop to use; how to crop, or trim, the image once it is printed. In effect, when we see photographs in a newspaper or art gallery, we are looking at the product of deliberate *strategies of invention.* In photography, these strategies include key elements of composition, such as selection, placement, perspective, and framing. In written texts, the same elements—selection, placement, perspective, and framing—are critical to making an argument.

Look at Figure 3.2, an image captured by photojournalist Margaret Bourke-White, showing a line of homeless African Americans, displaced by the 1937 Louisville flood, waiting on line to receive food and clothing from a local Red Cross center. Does the photo merely document a moment in the history of Kentucky? Or have the choice of subject, the cropping, the angle, the background, and the elements within the frame all been selected by the photographer to make a specific argument about race and American culture during the first half of the twentieth century?

In your own writing, you could look to this photograph as inspiration for invention. You could use this image to support a historically focused argument, perhaps one that examined the catastrophic 1937 Louisville flood and its impact on the local community. Or, you could refer to this photograph as visual evidence in a paper that examined the link between social status, race, and disaster relief. Either argument could draw on the power of photographs like this one, a power created by the invention strategies of the artist.

FIGURE 3.2 Margaret Bourke-White, "At the Time of the Louisville Flood," 1937.

CREATIVE PRACTICE

Examine the picture in Figure 3.3, taken by photographer Todd Heisler, of a soldier's coffin returning home on a civilian flight into Reno, Nevada, being draped with the American flag prior to being unloaded from the plane. What argument is Heisler making about Americans' response to the Iraq war and casualties? Now consider this image as the foundation for your own process of invention: What types of arguments might you construct that would use this image as visual evidence? What other sorts of images or evidence would you use to develop your argument?

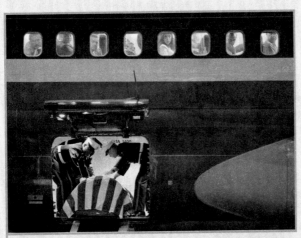

FIGURE 3.3 Photograph of the arrival of a soldier's coffin in Reno, Nevada.

FIGURE 3.4 Dorothea Lange's wide shot gives a stark sense of the experience of migrant farmers.

FIGURE 3.5 The close-up focuses on the struggles of the migrant mother.

Let's look more closely at how invention factors into the way photographers and writers compose arguments. Consider two famous photographs by Dorothea Lange (see Figures 3.4 and 3.5), which offer very different representations of migrant workers during the Great Depression. In each case, we see a migrant family huddled inside a tent. The subjects seem to be poor, hungry, and struggling to make a living. Their material conditions are bleak.

But notice the effects of the different perspectives. In Figure 3.5, we get an intimate look inside this woman's eyes, where we can see her concern. The lines on her face, visible in this close-up, are evidence of her hard life and worries. The photograph in Figure 3.4 has a wider frame that encompasses the tent and the barren ground. This perspective makes a different kind of argument, one that addresses the condition of the soil, the landscape, the living quarters. We can hardly make out the woman huddled in the darkness of the tent. When we look for visual evidence of the living conditions of migrant workers in the American West during the 1930s, each photograph offers different angles on our argument. Which one would we use to support a thesis about the labor conditions of migrant workers? Which one would we use to argue that the human body is scarred by hardship? Depending on our purpose, we would choose one photograph over the other. Each one makes an argument that we can in turn select as evidence for our claims about the Great Depression. Each photograph uses a particular strategy of invention, creating and constructing ideas in visual form about the "reality" of life for migrant workers. We can, in turn, invent different arguments based on our starting point: which photo do we use as evidence for our thesis?

Seeing Connections
For other examples of how photographers utilize careful composition and arrangement in creating powerful photographs, see Gideon Mendel's" Heads-up Move" photographs on page 357 and the photographs from "America 24/7" on pages 535–536.

In written documents, different perspectives on the same topic can yield diverse arguments. Commentary on Lange's *Migrant Mother* photographs exposes the variety of perspectives not only on the photographs' status as "documentary" evidence from the Great Depression, but also on the way our historical understanding of that period itself is constructed by the invention or arguments of others. For instance, the following excerpt from historian James Curtis's article "Dorothea Lange, Migrant Mother, and the Culture of the Great Depression" demonstrates the way in which Lange's photos are often interpreted as windows into that period:

> In addition to being a timeless work of art, *Migrant Mother* is a vital reflection of the times. Examined in its original context, the series reveals powerful cultural forces of the 1930s: the impact of the increasing centralization and bureaucratization of American life; the anxiety about the status and solidarity of the family in an era of urbanization and modernization; a need to atone for the guilt induced by the destruction of cherished ideals, and a craving for reassurance that democratic traditions would stand the test of modern times.

For Curtis, the images function both as what he calls elsewhere in the article "a timeless and universal symbol of suffering in the face of adversity" (1) as well as the key to understanding Lange's relationship to the evolving genre of documentary photography. For journalist Geoffrey Dunn, however, Lange's series prompts a different response:

> The photographs taken by Lange and her colleagues at the Resettlement Administration (later to become better known as the Farm Security Administration) have been widely heralded as the epitome of documentary photography. The eminent photographer and curator Edward Steichen called them "the most remarkable human documents ever rendered in pictures."
>
> In recent years, however, the FSA photographs have come under a growing criticism. Many view them as manipulative and condescending, to the point of assuming a "colonialistic" attitude toward their subjects. Still others have argued that they are misleading and disingenuous, and in some instances, fabricated.
>
> In a compelling essay entitled "The Historian and the Icon," University of California at Berkeley professor Lawrence Levine has argued that the FSA photographers focused their lenses on "perfect victims," and in so doing, rendered a caricatured portrait of the era.
>
> "Americans suffered, materially and physically, during the years of the Great Depression to an extent which we still do not fully fathom," Levine asserted. "But they also continued, as people always must, the business of living. They ate and they laughed, they loved and they fought, they worried and they hoped . . . they filled their days, as we fill ours, with the essentials of everyday living."
>
> With the notable exception of FSA photographer Russell Lee, and later, Marion Post Wolcott, whose largely overlooked bodies of work actually capture the dimensions of "everyday living," Lange and her colleagues focused almost exclusively on human suffering. That is most certainly the reason that people like Florence Owens Thompson—and many others who appeared in FSA images—resented their photographic portrayal.
>
> "Mother was a woman who loved to enjoy life, who loved her children," says Thompson's youngest daughter, Norma Rydlewski, who appears as a young child in Lange's classic photograph. "She loved music and she loved to dance. When I look at that photo of mother, it saddens me. That's not how I like to remember her."
>
> Rydlewski noted that while the Depression was hard on her family, it was not all suffering. "Mama and daddy would take us to the movies a lot. We'd go to the carnival whenever it was in town, little things like that. We listened to the radio. If they had any money

at all, they'd get us ice cream. In Shafter, we had friends and relatives visiting. We also had our fun."

Troy Owens echoed his sister's sentiments: "They were tough, tough times, but they were the best times we ever had."

Like Curtis, Dunn uses the photographs as the basis for an argument about Lange's practice of documentary photography; however, Dunn's process of invention led him to a different argument, one that prompted him to widen his perspective and consider first-person accounts from other witnesses of that historical moment. The conclusion he reaches through this broader view is that the series exemplifies not reflection but misrepresentation.

All texts—whether written accounts or photographs—are actually shaped by individual perspective and point of view. Texts are "invented" for a specific audience. Your own writing is a text informed by your invention strategies, your purpose, and your point of view. In your writing, you are like a photographer, making important compositional decisions: What will be the subject of your text: an individual, a group, an institution? How will you pose that subject to best convey your own perspective? Should you zoom in, focusing on one particular example as a way of addressing a larger concern? Or should you take a step back, situating your argument in relation to the broader context that surrounds the issue? The choices you make will determine the ultimate impact of your argument: like photographs, effective writing persuades the viewer to look at a topic through the lens of the author's interpretation.

COLLABORATIVE CHALLENGE

In groups of two or three, visit the Collection Highlights of "Suffering Under a Great Injustice: Ansel Adams's Photographs of Japanese-American Internment at Manzanar" through the Chapter 3 resources on the *Envision* Website. Browse through the contents and analyze the framing, cropping, and composition strategies of a selection of the photographs. In some cases clicking on an image will pull up a page comparing the print with the original negative so that you can better understand how Adams cropped his photographs to sharpen the argument conveyed by the images. Working from a comparison of photographs, or of photos and their negatives, make an argument about the perspective offered by each visual text on the experience of Japanese Americans interned during World War II.

www.ablongman.com/envision/209

Arrangement in Argument

After invention, **arrangement** becomes your key consideration because the way in which you present material on the page will shape a reader's response to the ideas. In many cases, attention to arrangement takes the form of the way you order elements in your argument—whether that be the layout of images and text on a newspaper front page or the way you structure a written argument in a more academic paper. It is the arrangement of an argument that gives it structure or that separates a free-form reaction from a carefully developed and proven argument.

Therefore, when we refer to "arrangement" in a written argument, we often are referring to the underlying structure of the essay itself. Although unifying an essay with a smooth flow of ideas is important, it is just as important that the structure of the essay not be completely associational—that is, that it not simply move from one idea to the next through the process of free association. Here are some common organizational strategies you might choose in composing your own arguments:

- **Chronological structure:** Chronology is perhaps the most intuitive strategy for any paper that contains examples across time, such as the transformation in the Apple computer marketing campaign from Macintosh to iPod.
- **Cause-effect:** An essay confronting the issue of sexist imagery in rap music videos might start by exploring how women are represented in popular rap videos (*cause*) and then conclude by discussing the impact of this representation on the self-esteem of young girls (*effect*).
- **Problem-solution:** A paper about violence and video games might devote the first half of the paper to exploring the *problem* of desensitization and then focus in the second half of the paper on proposing a possible *solution*.
- **Block structure:** Work your way through a series of examples or case studies— such as individual James Bond films in a paper about the relationship between real-world political climates and spy narrative—progressing systematically through each example before moving on to the next one.
- **Thematic structure:** Organize by theme rather than example. A paper on reality TV might include sections on voyeurism, capitalism, and Darwinism (*the themes*), integrating examples from *Survivor*, *American Idol*, and *America's Next Top Model* as evidence in each section.
- **Deferred thesis:** As you become more comfortable with strategies of argumentation, you might choose to substitute a thesis question for a thesis statement at the beginning of your essay. For instance, rather than announcing your argument at the beginning of your paper ask a question such as "How did images featured in the news define our understanding of the impact of hurricanes Katrina and Rita?" Your thesis would then appear at the end of your paper as a way of synthesizing the evidence explored in the paper itself.

Let's look to photography to see the way a successful argument relies on strategies of arrangement. Figures 3.6 through Figure 3.9 offer a selection of photographs from Jane Gottesman's photo essay *Game Face*, a work devoted to redefining the concept of the modern female athlete. A veteran sports writer, Gottesman spent years accumulating photographs of amateur and professional women athletes of all ages, races, and socio-economic backgrounds, a collection that was a museum exhibit and both a print and online photo essay. It is not surprising to find that she gave extra care to strategies of arrangement in composing her visual argument.

Looking at this version of *Game Face*, we can see from the top menu bar that it is divided into four sections: "Prepare," "Compete," "Finish," and "Achieve." Clearly, this is an example of an argument *organized by theme*. This arrangement gives a logical structure to the text: the argument moves along a continuum, from pre-game, to game play, to post-game. Within each of these sections (which roughly approximate the sections of a book or written essay), Gottesman includes several examples (which we might correlate to

Seeing Connections
For an innovative example of essay structure, see Richard Cobbett's "Writing a 'Girls in Gaming' Article" on page 489.

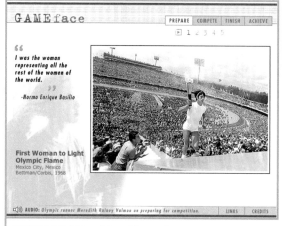

FIGURE 3.6 Picture 1 from "Prepare."

FIGURE 3.7 Picture 1 from "Compete."

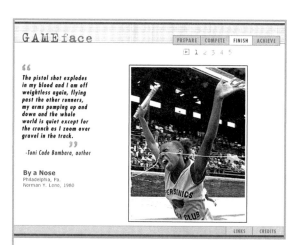

FIGURE 3.8 Picture 1 from "Finish."

FIGURE 3.9 Final picture from the photo essay.

paragraphs in traditional academic writing). Looking at the individual images, we can see how arrangement plays a strong role in constructing an argument; each page makes its commentary on women's athletics by juxtaposing a powerful photo with a descriptive caption and a relevant quotation from a female athlete. The recurring structure gives the overall photo essay coherence and consistency, despite its variety of examples.

Let's take a closer look at the way the pictures reinforce the underlying structure produced by the section headers; we can do so by carefully examining the lead images for the various sections. The lead image, for instance (Figure 3.6), centers on an inspirational event: the moment in 1968 when a woman, for the first time, lit the Olympic flame. As the first image in the photo essay, this picture of Norma Basilio symbolizes accomplishment, possibilities, a global perspective, and even more importantly, an auspicious beginning to the argument, the same way in which the lighting of the flame itself marks the beginning of an auspicious event. The next image (Figure 3.7), which heads the "Compete" section, offers a similarly strong statement but shifts perspective from the international to the local, capturing the first moments in a 1994 Pennsylvania triathlon. In this image, as much as we see individual competitors, we also see community—a theme that reappears at many different points in that particular section. The next photograph (Figure 3.8), from the "Finish" section, moves us from the start of competition to its conclusion, focusing on the victory of the female athlete. The series of photographs in this section, from the victorious track star to the weary but triumphant soccer team, celebrate the rewards that come from following through on one's dreams. In the last section, "Achieve," the images escalate in strength, culminating with the inspirational picture of a young girl swinging powerfully toward the stars (Figure 3.9).

COLLABORATIVE CHALLENGE

When we discuss arrangement in reference to photographs like Dorothea Lange's and Jane Gottesman's, we usually refer to the way the photographer stages a shot or orders a series of images. However, in the age of digital photo editing, the canon of arrangement is often used in producing striking arguments in the form of photo illustrations, such as the one shown in Figure 3.10, a hoax photo circulated on dorm chat lists that offers a rather humorous version of photo manipula-

FIGURE 3.10 Snowball the monster cat fools many viewers with his huge size.

tion. Discuss this image with your group: how were the elements in the photograph altered and arranged to produce the visual joke? Now break into small groups and visit the following sites, linked through the *Envision* Website:

- The Hoax Photo Gallery: a collection of doctored photographs from the online Museum of Hoaxes.
- Frank Van Riper's "Manipulating Truth, Losing Credibility": article from the *Washington Post* about the Brian Walski photo scandal.
- Floyd's Website: before-and-after images that demonstrate the dramatic effects of photo editing.
- "The Case of the Missing Limb": an article from *The Digital Journalist* about how newspaper editors altered a photograph to make it less offensive to readers.

Look through these sites and consider how the canon of arrangement functions in these cases in relation to the ethics of argument. Which altered images are the most convincing? the most disturbing? Why? How do you distinguish between creativity and manipulation? Are there times when photographic manipulation is justified? How can we apply these observations about ethics and arrangement to our consideration of written texts?

Student Writing
See Tiffany Yun's and Chris Mathakul's projects about photo manipulation.
www.ablongman.com/envision/211

Style in Argument

Inventing a thesis or main idea and arranging the elements of your writing are two steps in completing your task of written persuasion. You need also to spend some time considering how you are going to present that idea to your audience. This is where **style**—the third canon of rhetoric—enters the scene. Style concerns choosing the appropriate expression for the ideas of your argument; these choices relate to language, tone, syntax, rhetorical appeals, metaphors, imagery, quotations, level of emphasis, and nuance.

We often translate *style* into *voice* to indicate a writer's unique persona and rhetorical stance as it is manifested in word choice, syntax, pacing, and tone. To construct a successful argument, you need to be able to employ the voice or style that best meets the needs of your rhetorical situation. If you are writing a feature article for *Time* magazine, for instance, you will most likely use accessible language, common expressions, and references to contemporary events. Your paragraphs may be only one or two sentences long, and you may use wit, humor, or pathos to try to move your audience. You might also include a color photograph or even clip art to convey your point to your readers. Such writing choices are all part of your persona as a popular writer. You would make very different composition choices if you were writing for an academic journal that would be read by scholars in the field. In that case, you might use disciplinary jargon or diction, longer paragraph structures, and references to other researchers. Those rhetorical choices would distinguish your persona from that conveyed in the popular article. In both cases, your persona and your stylistic choices contribute to building your ethos and persuading your audience.

How do you move from the thesis as a promise of your argument to fostering a strong relationship with your readers so that they will be most inclined to entertain your perspective? The answer lies in careful attention to developing *persona* and *rhetorical stance* in your writing.

Constructing Persona

When you select a certain image, a set of words, or a written phrase to shape your argument and try to persuade your audience, you are constructing a **persona** for yourself as a writer and rhetorician. Your persona is *a deliberately crafted version of yourself as writer.* A public figure will often use *persona* as a purposeful rhetorical tool. President George W. Bush might choose to give a speech about war dressed in army fatigues and flanked by a group of soldiers, but when addressing the state of the economy, he's more likely to hold his press conference from his ranch, wearing a casual shirt and blue jeans. In each case, he constructs a different *persona* designed to be the most appropriate and persuasive for his given rhetorical situation.

The same principle governs the writing process. When you compose a text (written, verbal, or visual), you decide how to use language to present a particular persona to the audience you wish to address. You create a portrait of yourself as the author of your argument through tone (formal or informal, humorous or serious); word choice (academic, colloquial); sentence structures (complex or simple and direct); use of rhetorical appeals (pathos, logos, ethos); and strategies of persuasion (narration, example, cause and effect, analogy, process, classification, or definition). Creating a persona requires care. A well-designed one can facilitate a strong connection with your readers and therefore make your argument more persuasive. However, a poorly constructed persona—one that is, for instance, biased, inconsistent, or underdeveloped—can have the opposite effect, alienating readers and undercutting your text's overall effectiveness.

COLLABORATIVE CHALLENGE

Bring to class a selection of photographs of yourself, including both informal and formal shots (such as your school yearbook photo). In a group, examine each other's photographs and discuss the differences in *persona* evident in each one. Be sure to take into account the details that construct the persona (expression, posture, pose, clothing, background scene, people of various professions in the photo, etc.) as well the composition of the image (color, layout, perspective, angle, lighting). Which picture would you want printed in the newspaper alongside an article describing a prestigious scholarship that you have won? Which photo would you include on the dust jacket of your first published novel? Which photo would you submit to your dorm newsletter? Which would you use on your MySpace or Facebook Webpage? Discuss your decisions and how your assessment of the different rhetorical situations influenced the *argument* you want to make through constructing your persona.

Choosing a Rhetorical Stance

To be persuasive, you must assume a persona that responds appropriately to your specific rhetorical situation. Wayne Booth, one of the most important twentieth-century revivalists of classical rhetoric, defined the writer's position in relation to the rhetorical triangle as the **rhetorical stance** and claimed that it is the most essential aspect of effective communication. He argued that communication failed between people (or a text failed to persuade a reader) if the writer assumed a position that ignored the necessary balance of the rhetorical triangle.

We see examples of inappropriate rhetorical stances constantly: the TV evangelist who moves his congregation with a polished sermon that completely distracts them from flaws in his moral character; the used-car salesman who pads his sales pitch with offers of free gifts, rebate specials, and low percentage rates; the actor who uses her celebrity status to drive a product endorsement, rather than clearly articulating the merits of that product itself. In each case, the *rhetorical triangle*—the relationship between author, audience, and text—is out of balance, and the argument itself, ultimately, is rendered less persuasive. In your own writing, therefore, you need to pay special attention not only to the persona you create but also to the stance you assume in relation to your specific rhetorical situation.

AT A GLANCE

Three Rhetorical Stances That Lead to Communication Failure

- *The pedant or preacherly stance:* the text is paramount and both the audience's needs and the speaker's character are ignored.

- *The advertiser's stance:* the effect on the audience is valued above all, ignoring the quality of the text and the credibility of the speaker.

- *The entertainer's stance:* the character of the speaker is elevated above the text and the audience.

Titles, Introductions, and Conclusions

In writing, you signal your persona and rhetorical stance through your word choice, sentence structure, tone, and strategies of persuasion. Let's zoom in for a moment on three key elements of the written argument to see the way each operates as an important site for these stylistic choices.

Your reader's first encounter with your topic and argument comes through your title; in this way, the title itself operates as a rhetorical act that provides a frame and sets up the argument. Let's return for a moment to Figure 3.1. Many newspapers featured this image on their front pages on September 2, 2005—but with different headlines. Figures 3.11 and 3.12 are two examples. Consider how each paper signals its rhetorical stance through the visual-verbal arguments contained on its front page.

FIGURE 3.11 Front page of the *Fresno Bee*, September 2, 2005.
Source: © THE FRESNO BEE, 2006

FIGURE 3.12 Front page of the *Deseret Morning News*, September 2, 2005.

How does the headline "City desperate for help" read in combination with the helicopter image suggest a different argument than "Rising rage: Descent into anarchy" coupled with the same image? The difference in tone, perspective, and rhetorical stance apparent from these contrasting examples underscores the role a headline—and, relatedly, a title—plays in forming a reader's expectations for the argument that follows. In effect, a title is often the first step in writing an interpretation or making an argument.

In writing your own papers, you should spend some time brainstorming your titles. Some writers find constructing a powerful title to be a useful brainstorming activity to start their composition process and help them with invention; others construct the title only after completing the first draft of their paper, as a way of synthesizing the argument by bringing it into sharper focus. As you work with a title, think about its role in setting up your stance on your topic, indicating to your readers not only the scope of your analysis but also your angle on it. Try to play with language, linking the title to your main point, to a key image you discuss, to an underlying metaphor or motif, or to the larger issue raised by your argument. Test your working title by sharing it with a partner in class.

Like your title, your introduction offers your readers insight into the persona and rhetorical stance that will characterize your essay as a whole. In these opening paragraphs (an introduction may be more than one paragraph), you establish your voice (informal? formal?), your tone (measured? firm? angry? cautious?), your persona, and your topic through careful attention to word choice, sentence structure, and strategies of development. Most introductions also provide the first articulation of your argument as well, moving from a general statement of topic to a more focused statement of your thesis.

However, perhaps even more importantly, the introduction is the moment in which you capture the attention and interest of your reader, often through a device that we call a rhetorical "hook." For instance, looking back at Jane Gottesman's photo essay, we can see how she hooks her online readers in her opening image (Figure 3.6) by framing the 1968 Olympics as a landmark event for women athletes. The reader is drawn in by the ethos of the Olympics and intrigued by the fact that it was only as recently as the late 1960s that women first participated in the torch-lighting ceremony. This hook prompts readers to wonder what other "firsts" they might not be aware of, what other facts about women athletes Gottesman might reveal. This is the hook that gets readers interested—and prompts readers to continue reading.

In written texts, you can use your introduction to hook your readers through one of several methods:

- Defining your terms (especially if you're writing on a subject that not everyone may be familiar with)
- Including a significant quotation or a startling statistic or fact
- Presenting an overview of the issue you're discussing
- Using an anecdote or narration
- Incorporating a vivid example
- Drawing on a relevant analogy or metaphor
- Using the second-person pronoun (*you*) to invite readers to make personal connections

Your choice of hook will depend to a large extent on your broader stylistic decisions about your essay and the way in which you want to develop your argument.

Let's look at how one student, Michael Zeligs, took the canon of style into consideration while composing his introduction to a rhetorical analysis of Robert Frank's photography:

> "Robert Frank, Swiss, unobtrusive, nice, with that little camera that he raises and snaps with one hand he sucked a sad poem right out of America onto film, taking rank among the tragic poets of the world."
>
> In his introduction to Robert Frank's *The Americans,* Jack Kerouac captures the photographer's responsible position as a concerned observer of his time, as the first person to sweep away dominating prejudice and expose what post–World War II America really represented. In his book, Frank pushes the limits of traditional art photography—limits that required clear foregrounds and backgrounds, clear subject and exposure and level tilt—and this enables him to focus more on scenes that dominate his eye and inspire emotional arguments. The America that Frank addresses, however, is not one of fulfilled dreams and two-car garages. It is a struggling foreground for change, founded in the two beautifully conflicting scenes of "Charleston, South Carolina," and "Trolley," where unique photographic elements merge to advance a critique of racial inequality during America's postwar crisis of identity.

What hooks the reader first is the quotation, or epigraph, that heads the introduction: an abstract, lyrical statement that refuses to sacrifice its vision by adhering to conventional punctuation. Commenting on the subject of the paper—the photography of Robert Frank—this quote announces the essay's topic at the same time that it provides a sharp contrast for the writing style of the main body of the introduction that follows. By comparison, Michael's voice seems crisp, focused, and academic, establishing a persona that is both informed on his subject (he clearly not only has analyzed Frank's photographs but has read the introduction to the book as well) and is also able to discuss it articulately. Notice the way that Michael fashions his first sentence to serve as a bridge between his opening hook and the rest of the paragraph. Rather than using the epigraph simply as a snappy device to capture the reader's attention and then abandoning it, Michael creates an ethos appeal by identifying the quotation's author (Jack Kerouac, an iconic critic of American culture) and then restates the meaning of the quote in a way that pulls it in line with his own argument about Robert Frank's photography. The rest of the paragraph moves from general (a description of the project of Frank's larger book, *The Americans,* and a definition of traditional photographic methods) to specific (clarification of the two images Michael is most interested in), ending ultimately with a clear articulation of Michael's rhetorical stance and thesis statement.

Seeing Connections
Look at Steve Shapin's engaging introduction and conclusion for "Clean Up Hitters" on page 330.

If the introduction offers the writer the opportunity to hook the audience's readers' while articulating a personal stance on a subject, the conclusion provides the final opportunity to reinforce an essay's argument while making a lasting impact on readers. For this reason, although a conclusion by its nature should include some elements of summary (synthesizing the key points from the essay), it should also have a rhetorical power of its own. Let's look at how Michael concluded his essay on Frank's photographs:

> Robert Frank, in his images from *The Americans*, takes compelling pictures of a socially conflicted south to expose the growing struggle of race in 1950's America. His images spark from a new ideology of the photographer—a lack of concern for absolute photographic

perfection allows him to document situations that really *mean* something. He chooses conflicting lives, black and white together on the page but unequal, his film subtly showing sympathy for the downtrodden worker and the weary traveler. Careful lines and deliberate tones show two opposing worlds where skin color can change the appearance of an entire backdrop, where stark white prison bars show us the walls we have erected within ourselves. These are not simple pictures of ordinary people. They are an artist's whisper about the elusiveness of equality, how in the war against bigotry, we are not done yet.

While offering a summary of his evidence, Michael resists the temptation to center his conclusion on a simple paragraph-by-paragraph reiteration of his argument. Instead he takes care to make his conclusion as stylistically sophisticated as his introduction. Notice his careful use of word choice ("takes compelling pictures," "expose") that works in tandem with the subject of his essay; his return to the task of redefining American photography that he began in his introduction; his implicit reference to his analysis of the images themselves in the main body of his paper ("downtrodden worker and weary traveler," references to "lines" and "tones"); and, finally, the way he broadens his topic to touch on larger, ongoing issues of race relations. His conclusion leaves readers with more than a simple summary of points, prompting them to reflect on the ongoing state of race relations in America.

Consider ways to make your own conclusion a powerful part of your argument. You might use a key quote, example, or reference that either epitomizes or summarizes your points. You might return to an opening example or analogy, offering a slightly different, perhaps more informed perspective on it to connect introduction and conclusion as a frame for your argument. Along similar lines, if you use a chronological structure, you might move from the past to recent times, perhaps ending with a projection into the future. Or, like Michael, you might use your conclusion to suggest broader implications that could increase the reader's sense of personal connection to the topic or its urgency. No matter which strategy you choose, remember to maximize the persuasive potential of your conclusion as a means of reaffirming the strength of your argument with your readers.

Crafting a Position Paper

One way to experiment and put into practice these concepts—invention, arrangement, and style—is to draft a position paper on your topic. By definition, a **position paper** presents one side of an issue, allowing you the opportunity to construct a strong thesis statement and actively argue your main points. A position paper also can be an ideal medium for developing your own particular style, persona, and rhetorical stance. Angela Rastegar, for instance, experimented with persona during a project on photographic coverage of the war in Iraq. She tried out two very different ways of writing. First she composed an argument about the issue from the perspective of an unnamed academic or journalistic commentator. Then she revised the argument by writing a short paper representing an extreme position on the toppling of a Saddam Hussein statue by U.S. troops. Her first "position" offers the academic voice with an ostensibly objective perspective. Notice that there is no obvious "I" speaking, and yet an argument about the power of the media clearly emerges.

Angela Rastegar

Academic Position Paper

Imagine a chaotic world in which you cannot trust the media—newspapers, television reports, and magazines are full of lies about the world and politics. Picture trying to decipher current events or important situations without knowing whom to turn to or what to believe. Sounds far-fetched? Unfortunately, this is not far from the truth. Current newspapers are filled with subtle, clever methods used to deceive the public.

As you look at photographic images in widely respected newspaper articles, consider the techniques used to deceive the public. Concerning one incident—the April 9th destruction of Saddam Hussein's monument in Baghdad—the actual events of this day have been carefully concealed from the public. Although the media portrayed a "heroic" destruction of Saddam's symbol by American forces and mobs of Iraqi supporters, this event was essentially staged by the media.

We must use a cautious eye when viewing news stories and alert ourselves to subtle biases. The media has been called the "fourth branch of the government" because of the undeniable power it yields over the American public. No other source of information is so readily and unquestionably accepted. The government realizes this, and it often takes great measures to work with the media to create effective, captivating stories that not only portray Americans in a positive light but will also sell papers. Examples of the media's influence are not by any means limited to this single event; however, wars provide the perfect opportunity for the media to influence the public. They open wounds in all Americans, leaving viewers vulnerable, easily influenced, and starving for more information. As a result, studying the media's influence on any war opens a vast field of controversy. In this time of crisis, we must read the news with a wary eye.

Finding this voice to offer too much of the "advertiser's stance," Angela then experimented with first person to shape her argument into an analysis of a specific photograph (see Figure 1 in her letter to the editor). She developed this position paper as an examination of the image and named her persona "Elizabeth Grant," a concerned media activist.

Angela Rastegar

Writing a Letter to the Editor as "Elizabeth Grant,"

Left-Wing Media Watchdog

I am writing in response to the astonishing display of deceit attempted by President G. W. Bush and the American government on Thursday, April 10th. President Bush's public address began with the words, "Iraqi citizens support overthrowing Saddam," which was illustrated by the enclosed photograph. It depicts an American marine tying the Iraqi flag around the neck of Saddam Hussein's 15-foot monument. Seconds later, U.S. troops connected the ropes and cables to the statue's neck and brought it crashing to the ground.

The photograph, which contains a brightly colored red and white Iraqi flag in the center, focuses the viewer's attention on this emblem. Did the Iraqi citizens request to use this flag? We don't know, but we can see how the government attempted to appeal to those watching by having a soldier tie Iraq's own flag to the chains.

Figure 3.1 Laurent Rebours, Associated Press. *The New York Times: On the Web.* "Scenes from Baghdad." Online Posting. 9 April 2003. *The New York Times Company.* 14 April 2003.

The flag falsely suggests that the Iraqi people were behind the destruction of the monument and that America can work in harmony with the people of Iraq to overthrow Saddam. This message drastically distorts the truth; in fact, the soldier originally held an American flag, but his commanding officers ordered him to tie this particular flag to the chains. Thus, the government's use of logos in this photo subtly attempts to convince the public that Iraq wanted to bring down Saddam's statue—when, in reality, the citizens there had nothing to do with it.

Rastegar 2

In this photograph, the picture also appeals to the viewers' emotions by placing a rope and chains around the neck of Saddam's image. In this sense, it evokes the American hatred for Saddam and creates a clear, understandable aim. The military is able to put a noose around the neck of a symbolic Saddam, displaying the government's ability to destroy him. The government draws on these emotions from the viewers to increase patriotism. Bush applies these same tactics to his public speeches, focusing on American strength to justify our intervention.

In addition, the photo strategically includes a U.S. marine to add to the photo's visual credibility. This symbol of America—a solider in uniform—forces the viewers to place more trust in the photographer and what we see here. My greatest fear is that the average American will hear Bush speak and see this photo without realizing that their goal is to convince the world of Iraqi support for American intervention. They claim that they are fighting to "free Iraq," but in reality, our government simply ties Iraq's fate to Saddam and destroys them both.

In her first position paper, Angela writes about the power of photographs from a generalized, academic perspective, the voice of analytical assessment. But in her subsequent paper, she explores a specific point of view about media coverage of international politics. The persona of Elizabeth Grant—whose style Angela develops through careful attention to word choice, rhetorical appeals, and prose style—relies on the use of "I" and repeated use of strong language. As you can tell, the experimentation with *voice* itself was the most important product of her revisions: it allowed her both to reach into her topic and to examine differences in *style* and *rhetorical stance,* in particularly powerful ways. As she moved into the final stages of her project, she brought the power of this writing to bear on her longer researched argument; although she wrote the final paper from her own perspective, working with the pro and con points of view enabled her to construct a sharper thesis statement and a more persuasive approach to the photographs she was discussing.

Seeing Connections
Read "Copying Isn't Cool" on page 415 and "File Sharing Must Be Made Legal" on page 419 for examples of two position papers on the subject of music downloading.

Writing Multiple Sides of an Argument

Angela Rastegar's project opens up some interesting possibilities for developing your own persuasive arguments. Sometimes when we write from our own points of view, we get so locked into our individual perspectives that we fail to take into account the diverse or multiple sides of our topics. Such limited vision can weaken our persuasiveness; if we fail to consider or acknowledge alternative positions on our topics, we produce one-sided arguments that lack complexity or credibility with our readers. Recall our earlier discussion of photographs: each photograph suggests a different angle, a unique "version" of an event, and the perspective of a particular persona. When we bring these different sides to light, we find that suddenly an incident or issue that seems polarized—or "black and white"—is actually much more complex. The same holds true for the issues we confront every day as writers and rhetoricians: it is only through exploring the multiple sides of our argument that we can engage it persuasively and effectively.

Begin experimenting with inventing diverse perspectives to achieve a thorough understanding of a complex situation. Although you may be tempted to think of these various perspectives in oppositional terms—as the "pro" or "con" of an issue—such a point of view closes off the richer complexity of the issue. Try to think of arguments not in terms of right or wrong but rather as a spectrum of differing perspectives. As you turn to write your own arguments, consider how you can explore different viewpoints by trying out personas; by inventing diverse responses to your own point of view; and by exploring various writing strategies through experimentation with diction, syntax, style, image selection, arrangement of argument, and voice.

When writing arguments, you might choose to explore more than one *persona* or *rhetorical stance* to see different sides of an issue. Student Aisha Ali, for instance, developed her project on the conflict in the Middle East by creating three articles, or sides, around a single photograph (see Figure 3.13). Using the image as the foundation for each article, she assumed the personas of an African photo journalist, an Israeli soldier, and a Palestinian boy. Aisha's contrasting personas offered a series of riveting snapshots of the Palestinian conflict. To create this effect, she took extra care with word choice, sentence structure, and the development of her arguments. In her first side, she opens the piece by exploring the context of the Middle Eastern situation and then moves with fluid and articulate language to the central narrative: the freeing of the doves in front of an oncoming tank. Her second side adopts a different approach: using direct, informal speech, and biased language suitable to a soldier hardened by armed conflict, this persona launches immediately into the narrative itself. The last side also presents the story of the doves' release; however, as the excerpt from her work shows, the voice is clearly that of a child. Using simple sentence structures and word choices to build a narrative with an underlying pathos appeal, Aisha has brought to life the perspective of the young boy forced to free his doves in the shadow of military occupation.

Student Writing
See persuasive position papers by Katie Jones about photography depicting the civil rights era, and by Ryan Kissick on media depictions of baseball star Pete Rose.
www.ablongman.com/envision/212

Student Writing
Read Aisha Ali's complete project and other student Multiple Sides projects.
www.ablongman.com/envision/213

FIGURE 3.13 The powerful image of doves in front of a tank in the Middle East offers multiple interpretations.

Mohammed al-Durra

Occupation: Elementary School Student

Age: 8

My birds are gone. I had to let them go. I didn't want to, but we had to leave the house and I couldn't carry them. Mommy told me this morning that we would go to my Aunt Fatema's house in Jenin. I didn't want to go, but she made me. And today, in school, we were going to have Show and Tell, and I told her that, but she said that I could bring in Ali another time. Now I won't get to. Because I had to let him and Nayla and Hassan go free. They were my three doves, and every day I gave them food and talked to them. I knew that sometimes they were scared because of the loud noises that came from town, but I would talk to them in their cage and let them know that it was okay. Mommy said that nothing bad would happen to us because we didn't do anything bad—but Daddy had to leave us, and now I lost my three best friends.

Together, the variety of perspectives in Aisha's writing enabled her to avoid producing a simplistic argument about the violence in the Middle East, and instead to demonstrate its complexity. Although the photograph Aisha used in her series of articles constitutes a powerful visual argument in itself through its striking juxtaposition of fluttering doves (a symbol of peace) and military tanks (a symbol of war), she was able to convey the meaning of the image for diverse viewers through powerful writing. You can try this strategy of writing multiple sides of an argument in your own compositions.

COLLABORATIVE CHALLENGE

Download two to three images from MSNBC.com's "Week in Pictures," accessible through the Chapter 3 resources on the *Envision* Website. As a group, select photos that convey different sides of a situation or event. Come up with three personas—the voice of the person in the photo, the voice of the photographer, and the voice of an observer. Now develop a thesis for each side and write a brief description of your imagined persona. Allow each person in the group to contribute a new perspective. Write up each of these sides; format them into a feature article or cover story for a newspaper or magazine, and, when you are done, present your work as a group to the class.

www.ablongman.com/envision/214

Synthesizing Multiple Perspectives

Although experimenting with writing in different styles from the perspectives of different personas, incorporating diverse strategies of arrangement for each piece, and inventing opposing arguments allow you to develop a deeper understanding of the complexity of an issue, in many academic contexts you will be asked to **synthesize** these perspectives into a single, thesis-driven text. The task then is to incorporate discussion of multiple perspectives (including positions you might find through research) in a way that reveals the complexity of the issue but ultimately advances your own, final rhetorical stance on the topic at hand.

FIGURE 3.14 The *Boston Herald American* chose to print the most sensational photograph on its cover.

We find an outstanding example of successfully balancing multiple perspectives with a clear, authorial thesis in Nora Ephron's article "The Boston Photographs," published in *Scribble, Scribble: Notes on the Media* (1978). This essay offers a useful model of the canons of rhetoric we've been discussing so far—invention, arrangement, and style.

Ephron provides insight into the constant struggles that newspaper editors face in selecting photographs for publication—in this case, deciding whether or not to print the "sensationalist" images of a woman and child falling from a fire escape during a 1976 apartment fire (Figure 3.14). Ephron brings into her article at least three perspectives, each embodying a unique rhetorical stance: from her own perspective to those of Stanley Forman, photographer, and Charles Seib, the *Washington Post* ombudsman (the editor who monitors the content of the paper to ensure that it is not offensive to readers). She also represents in miniature other points of view through a series of brief quotations from letters to the editor that appeared shortly after the publication of the controversial photographs. The writers of these letters each get a turn to argue their unique points from the basis of their own rhetorical stance. However, the argument that ultimately is most persuasive is Ephron's own; in this way, she *synthesizes* the arguments to arrive at her own, persuasive conclusion.

The Boston Photographs
Nora Ephron

"I made all kinds of pictures because I thought it would be a good rescue shot over the ladder . . . never dreamed it would be anything else. . . . I kept having to move around because of the light set. The sky was bright and they were in deep shadow. I was making pictures with a motor drive and he, the firefighter, was reaching up and, I don't know, everything started falling. I followed the

Ephron begins with the voice of the photographer, Stanley Forman, using a direct quote to present his perspective. Her next two paragraphs provide background for Forman's recollections.

girl down taking pictures. . . . I made three or four frames. I realized what was going on and I completely turned around, because I didn't want to see her hit."

Notice Ephron's use of the second person to establish a rapport with her reader built on a sense of shared cultural experience.

Although this section is ostensibly description, look closely at her stylistic choices—especially word choice—to see the way she is setting up her stance on the topic.

You probably saw the photographs. In most newspapers, there were three of them. The first showed some people on a fire escape—a fireman, a woman, and a child. The fireman had a nice strong jaw and looked very brave. The woman was holding the child. Smoke was pouring from the building behind them. A rescue ladder was approaching, just a few feet away, and the fireman had one arm around the woman and one arm reaching out toward the ladder. The second picture showed the fire escape slipping off the building. The child had fallen on the escape and seemed about to slide off the edge. The woman was grasping desperately at the legs of the fireman, who had managed to grab the ladder. The third picture showed the woman and child in midair, falling to the ground. Their arms and legs were outstretched, horribly distended. A potted plant was falling too. The caption said that the woman, Diana Bryant, nineteen, died in the fall. The child landed on the woman's body and lived.

She establishes her ethos in the beginning of this paragraph by demonstrating her knowledge of photography.

The pictures were taken by Stanley Forman, thirty, of the *Boston Herald American*. He used a motor-driven Nikon F set at 1/250, f5.6-S. Because of the motor, the camera can click off three frames a second. More than four hundred newspapers in the United States alone carried the photographs: The tear sheets from overseas are still coming in. The *New York Times* ran them on the first page of its second section; a paper in south Georgia gave them nineteen columns; the *Chicago Tribune,* the *Washington Post* and the *Washington Star* filled almost half their front pages, the *Star* under a somewhat redundant headline that read: Sensational Photos of Rescue Attempt That Failed.

While here Ephron finally gives her own assessment of the images (that they "are indeed sensational"), she refrains from a definitive thesis statement at this point.

Word choice once again hints at her argument: Notice how the term "sensational" (with slight negative connotations) has become "spectacular," which suggests awe and appreciation.

She focuses here on audience reaction to the photographs. The accumulation of quotations increases her those as a researcher and also gives weight to their outrage, even though it is a reaction that Ephron does not share.

The photographs are indeed sensational. They are pictures of death in action, of that split second when luck runs out, and it is impossible to look at them without feeling their extraordinary impact and remembering, in an almost subconscious way, the morbid fantasy of falling, falling off a building, falling to one's death. Beyond that, the pictures are classics, old-fashioned but perfect examples of photo journalism at its most spectacular. They're throwbacks, really, fire pictures, 1930s tabloid shots; at the same time they're technically superb and thoroughly modern—the sequence could not have been taken at all until the development of the motor-driven camera some sixteen years ago.

Most newspaper editors anticipate some reader reaction to photographs like Forman's; even so, the response around the country was enormous, and almost all of it was negative. I have read hundreds of the letters that were printed in letters-to-the-editor sections, and they repeat the same points. "Invading the privacy of death." "Cheap sensationalism." "I thought I was reading the *National Enquirer.*" "Assigning the agony of a human being in terror of imminent death to the status of a side-show act." "A tawdry way to sell newspapers." The *Seattle Times* received sixty letters and calls; its managing editor even got a couple of them at home. A reader wrote the *Philadelphia Inquirer:* "*Jaws* and *Towering Inferno* are playing downtown; don't take business away from people who pay good money to advertise in your own paper." Another reader wrote the *Chicago Sun-Times:* "I shall try to hide my disappointment that Miss Bryant wasn't wearing a skirt when she fell to her death. You could have had some award-winning photographs of her underpants as her skirt billowed over her head, you voyeurs." Several newspaper editors wrote columns defending the pictures: Thomas Keevil of the *Costa Mesa* (California) *Daily Pilot* printed a ballot for readers to vote on whether they would have printed the pictures; Marshall L. Stone of Maine's *Bangor Daily News,* which refused to print the famous assassination picture of the Vietcong prisoner in Saigon, claimed that the Boston pictures showed the dangers of fire escapes and raised questions about slumlords. (The burning building was a five-story brick apartment house on Marlborough Street in the Back Bay section of Boston.)

For the last five years, the *Washington Post* has employed various journalists as ombudsmen, whose job is to monitor the paper on behalf of the public. The *Post's* current ombudsman is Charles Seib, former managing editor of the *Washington Star;* the day the Boston photographs appeared, the paper received over seventy calls in protest. As Seib later wrote in a column about the pictures, it was "the largest reaction to a published item that I have experienced in eight months as the *Post's* ombudsman. . . .

"In the *Post's* newsroom, on the other hand, I found no doubts, no second thoughts . . . the question was not whether they should be printed but how they should be displayed. When I talked to editors . . . they used words like 'interesting' and 'riveting' and 'gripping' to describe them. The pictures told of something about life in the ghetto, they said (although the neighborhood where the tragedy occurred is not a ghetto, I am told). They dramatized the need to check on the safety of fire escapes. They dramatically conveyed something that had happened, and that is the business we're in. They were news. . . .

"Was publication of that [third] picture a bow to the same taste for the morbidly sensational that makes gold mines of disaster movies? Most papers will not print the picture of a dead body except in the most unusual circumstances. Does the fact that the final picture was taken a millisecond before the young woman died make a difference? Most papers will not print a picture of a bare female breast. Is that a more inappropriate subject for display than the picture of a human being's last agonized instant of life?" Seib offered no answers to the questions he raised, but he went on to say that although as an editor he would probably have run the pictures, as a reader he was revolted by them.

In conclusion, Seib wrote: "Any editor who decided to print those pictures without giving at least a moment's thought to what purpose they served and what their effect was likely to be on the reader should ask another question: Have I become so preoccupied with manufacturing a product according to professional traditions and standards that I have forgotten about the consumer, the reader?"

It should be clear that the phone calls and letters and Seib's own reaction were occasioned by one factor alone: the death of the woman. Obviously, had

---

Consider the order in which she arranges the quotes: the last two are the most colorful and memorable.

Her final parenthetical aside slightly undermines the power of this perspective by pointing out an inaccuracy.

At this point in the essay, she features the *Washington Post* editor who decided to run the photographs in that newspaper. The fact that she follows the reader-response with Seib's reaction is clearly strategic because her own stance most closely resembles his.

She gently qualifies Seib's argument, asserting the side or perspective while at the same time suggesting her own interpretation of the issue.

It is only now, after showcasing these many voices on the issue, that Ephron moves to her own argument.

she survived the fall, no one would have protested; the pictures would have had a completely different impact. Equally obviously, had the child died as well—or instead—Seib would undoubtedly have received ten times the phone calls he did. In each case, the pictures would have been exactly the same—only the captions, and thus the responses, would have been different.

But the questions Seib raises are worth discussing—though not exactly for the reasons he mentions. For it may be that the real lesson of the Boston photographs is not the danger that editors will be forgetful of reader reaction, but that they will continue to censor pictures of death precisely because of that reaction. The protests Seib fielded were really a variation on an old theme—and we saw plenty of it during the Nixon-Agnew years—the "Why doesn't the press print the good news?" argument. In this case, of course, the objections were all dressed up and cleverly disguised as righteous indignation about the privacy of death. This is a form of puritanism that is often justifiable; just as often it is merely puritanical.

Seib takes it for granted that the widespread though fairly recent newspaper policy against printing pictures of dead bodies is a sound one; I don't know that it makes any sense at all. I recognize that printing pictures of corpses raises all sorts of problems about taste and titillation and sensationalism; the fact is, however, that people die. Death happens to be one of life's main events. And it is irresponsible—and more than that, inaccurate—for newspapers to fail to show it, or to show it only when an astonishing set of photos comes in over the Associated Press wire. Most papers covering fatal automobile accidents will print pictures of mangled cars. But the significance of fatal automobile accidents is not that a great deal of steel is twisted but that people die. Why not show it? That's what accidents are about. Throughout the Vietnam war, editors were reluctant to print atrocity pictures. Why *not* print them? That's what that was about. Murder victims are almost never photographed; they are granted their privacy. But their relatives are relentlessly pictured on their way in and out of hospitals and morgues and funerals.

I'm not advocating that newspapers print these things in order to teach their readers a lesson. The *Post* editors justified their printing of the Boston pictures with several arguments in that direction; every one of them is irrelevant. The pictures don't show anything about slum life; the incident could have happened anywhere, and it did. It is extremely unlikely that anyone who saw them rushed out and had his fire escape strengthened. And the pictures were not news—at least they were not national news. It is not news in Washington, or New York, or Los Angeles that a woman was killed in a Boston fire. The only newsworthy thing about the pictures is that they were taken. They deserve to be printed because they are great pictures, breathtaking pictures of something that happened. That they disturb readers is exactly as it should be: that's why photojournalism is often more powerful than written journalism.

By using the phrases "all dressed up and cleverly disguised," Ephron exposes her own impatience with some of the reactions elicited by the publication of the photos.

Her clever play on words (puritanism/puritanical) further clarifies her stance.

Look at her use of rhetorical questions to make her point and to throw the issue back at her readers.

The use of the first person here marks a moment where Ephron begins to clearly assert her own opinion, rather than reporting on the perspectives of others.

In her conclusion, Ephron ends with a concession to those who were offended and then a strong articulation of her position on the topic that links to larger issues in photojournalism.

How does Ephron present her own argument despite allowing so many voices in her piece? How does she achieve the synthesis of multiple sides while developing her own argument through invention, arrangement, and style?

Let's first determine her main idea, the *invention* in her thesis statement. Where is her thesis? What new perspective on the issue of representing death in photographs has she invented in this essay in order to share it with her reading audience? Look at the final paragraph for the answer.

Now let's analyze the *arrangement* of her essay. As we read through the essay, we see that Ephron strategically allows the multiple viewpoints on the issue to play themselves out in the early part of her article, providing the reader with a firm grounding in the debate, before concluding with her own very strong point of view. By arranging her essay in this way, Ephron focuses the audience reaction to the images and to the editor's decisions to run them through the lens of her own argument. However, Ephron's strategy is just one of many patterns of arrangement that take into account incorporating counterarguments while producing a persuasive text. You have multiple options available to you when dealing with opposing viewpoints. You can follow the classical method of arrangement (see table) or select a modified version, depending on your purpose.

Seeing Connections

See "The Photo Felt Around the World" on page 567 for another article that talks about the editorial decisions that go into running or not running a photo.

AT A GLANCE

The Arrangement of Ephron's Argument

1. Quotation from photographer (1 paragraph)
2. Background (2 paragraphs)
3. Ephron's general assessment of images (1 paragraph)
4. Reader reaction to photos (1 paragraph)
5. Editor's point of view (4 paragraphs)
6. Qualification of Seib's point of view (1 paragraph)
7. Her own argument (final 3 paragraphs)

Strategies of Arrangement

A Classical Speech or Oration

1. Introduction
2. Statement of facts
3. Division
4. Proof
5. Refutation
6. Conclusion

Option A

Use when you want to ground the reader in your argument before bringing up opposing perspectives.

1. Introduction, identification of rhetorical stance
2. Thesis
3. Statement of background, definition, or context
4. Evidence and development of argument
5. Opposing opinion, concession, qualification, refutation
6. Conclusion

Option B

Establish opposing opinion up front so that the entire piece functions as an extended rebuttal or refutation of that line of argument.

1. Introduction and opposing viewpoint
2. Thesis and identification of rhetorical stance
3. Evidence and development of argument
4. Conclusion

Option C

Treat diverse viewpoints as appropriate during the development of your argument and presentation of your evidence.

1. Introduction, identification of rhetorical stance
2. Thesis
3. Statement of background, definition, or context
4. Evidence, opposing opinion, concession, qualification, refutation
5. Conclusion

The models of arrangement in the table are not designed to be rigid parameters. Instead, they should suggest possibilities and potentially productive strategies of arrangement; in your own writing, you will have to select the most productive way to lay out your topic and the diverse opinions that surround it.

You'll need to consider first the strength of the other perspectives on the issue. Do they corroborate your argument? Then you could include them as supporting evidence. Do they offer points of view that you can disprove? Then you might present the opinion and provide a **rebuttal,** or refutation of the points, demonstrating why they are not valid. Do they offer points of view that you can't disprove? Then you might *concede* the validity of their argument but go on to *qualify* their points by showing why your own argument is nonetheless persuasive. The key is to treat these other voices with respect; always represent their points of view fairly and without bias, even if you disagree with them. In a sense, when you are dealing with multiple perspectives, some of which may run counter to your own argument, you face a question of ethics quite similar to that the editors faced with the Boston photographs: How do you present possibly volatile material in a way that is both fair and yet advances your persuasive purpose?

We can see how Ephron herself answered that question by assessing her use of the canon of *style,* specifically in the persona and rhetorical stance she developed in her essay. As a careful analysis of her essay demonstrates, Ephron presents the background on the issue as if through an objective lens; however, her word choice, her selections of quotations, and even the sentence structures themselves collaborate to produce a rhetorical stance that seems all the more persuasive for its earlier objectivity when she moves to the strong statement at the end of her essay. For this reason, when her voice becomes more clearly argumentative in her conclusion, the reader does not automatically resist her argument. Instead, because of Ephron's stylistic choices, readers are more likely to be persuaded by her thesis, "That they [the photographs] disturb readers is exactly as it should be," and to welcome Ephron's fundamental redefinition of the purpose and characteristics of good photojournalism.

AT A GLANCE

Dealing with Multiple Perspectives in Your Arguments

When incorporating other viewpoints into your writing, you can use them in one of three ways:

- *Evidence:* you can use the diverse viewpoints to support your own thesis statement.
- *Concession/Qualification:* you can admit that the person has a strong point but then explain why it doesn't diminish the persuasiveness or validity of your argument.
- *Rebuttal:* you can present an opposing opinion, fairly and respectfully, and then demonstrate why it is not a valid argument in this case.

CREATIVE PRACTICE

Rewrite the Nora Ephron piece from the perspective of one of the personas that she mentions in her text: the editor, the photographer, or a disgruntled reader. As you do, incorporate the other perspectives into your argument, experimenting with arrangement and style to produce a piece that synthesizes diverse viewpoints while still making its own strong argument.

Constructing Your Own Argument

In this chapter, you've learned to harness the canons of rhetoric—invention, arrangement, and style—to compose effective arguments of your own. You've developed strategies for crafting titles, introductions, and conclusions; you've explored the importance of persona and rhetorical stance in argument. You've experimented with developing a position paper, crafting multiple sides of an argument, and then integrating diverse perspectives through a synthesis paper. Now it's time to implement these skills. Practice inventing a position on an issue, arranging claims and evidence for your argument (including working with images as evidence for your points), developing a rhetorical stance, and working on persona through style by crafting your prose with care. You might want to brainstorm first with the help of the prewriting checklist and then try out the longer writing projects described below.

PREWRITING CHECKLIST
Analyzing Photographs

❏ **Content:** What, literally, does the photograph depict? Who or what is the subject of the photo? What is the setting?

❏ **Cultural context:** What is the historical context of the photograph? If it "documents" a particular event, person, or historical moment, how prominently does this photograph factor into our understanding of this event, person, or place? (For instance, is it the only known photograph of an event, or is it one of a series of pictures taken of the same subject?)

❏ **Material context:** Where was this photograph reproduced or displayed (an art gallery, the cover of a magazine, the front page of a newspaper)? If it was published elsewhere originally, does this source credit the original?

❏ **Argument:** What, thematically, does the photograph depict? What is its message to the audience? For instance, while the photo might *show* a group of people standing together, its argument might be about love, family unity across generations, or a promise for the future.

❏ **Photographer:** Who took this photograph? What was the person's purpose?

❏ **Genre:** Is this a news photo? a self-portrait? a piece of art? How does it fulfill or confound the expectations of this genre? (For example, the expectation for a news photo is that it clearly captures a person, moment, event; the expectation for a self-portrait is that it evokes an artist's sense of his or her own persona.)

❏ **Audience:** Was the photograph intended to persuade a larger audience or to function as a more personalized expression of a point of view?

❏ **Purpose:** What is the photograph's purpose? Is it intended to be overtly argumentative and to move its audience to action? Or is the argument more subtle, even to the point of "seeming" objective or representational?   *(continued)*

❏ **Rhetorical stance:** How does the composition of the photo convey a sense of the rhetorical stance or point of view of the photographer? Pay attention to issues of focus (what is "in focus"? This may differ from the ostensible "focus" of the picture); cropping (what is "in" the picture, and what has been left "out"?); color (is the picture in black and white? color? sepia?); setting (what backdrop has the photographer chosen?); and perspective (are we looking down? up?).

❏ **Representation versus reality:** Does this photograph aspire to represent reality, or is it an overtly abstract piece? Is there any indication of photo manipulation, editing, or other alteration? If so, what rhetorical purpose does this serve—what argument does this alteration make?

❏ **Word and image:** Does the photo have a caption? Does it accompany an article, essay, or other lengthy text? How does the image function in dialogue with this verbal text? Does it offer visual evidence? Does it argue an independent point? Does it provide a counterargument to the print text?

WRITING PROJECTS

1. **Written Argument:** Write an argument about an issue that moves you; base your argument on your analysis of a powerful image, and include your interpretation of the image as part of your writing. Invent a strong thesis, pick your persona, decide on your strategy of arrangement, and write with particular attention to style. You might choose to write a popular article, such as a letter to the editor of the campus newspaper, a Weblog entry, or a newspaper column such as *Newsweek*'s "My Turn."

2. **Three Position Papers:** Write three position papers or articles, with each one commenting on the previous one so that the project forms a coherent whole. Give each persona a name, an occupation, a geographic location, and a strong perspective to argue in words. Each position can offer a new point of view on one image or can develop complexity about an issue by bringing in a new image as visual evidence. You might choose to format your project as a feature article for a specific magazine or reading audience. To do so, first conduct a rhetorical analysis on the features of a chosen publication (*The New Yorker, The Economist,* a national newspaper, or a campus journal) and then format your three arguments as part of that publication. Include a cover page with an introduction by the editor and a closing assessment page, perhaps by a staff writer. You could also format your project as a Website or multimedia text (a bound book, a flash montage, or photo essay).

3. **Multiple Sides Collaboration:** Collaborate on composing multiple position papers by assigning the writing of each argument to a different member of your group. You might, for instance, write about the conflict between your college campus and the surrounding town: have someone interview locals, the sheriff, the administrators, and the students. Provide a series of arguments from each perspective and images to function as argumentative texts for each side. Be sure to include concession and refutation. Collaborate in the writing of the introduction and the conclusion as well as in the design, arrangement, and style of the project as a whole. The last writer in the group should compose a synthesis paper, incorporating the positions of everyone and providing a closing argument.

4. Argument Presentation: As a class, present your arguments in a conference format; set up the day as a showcase of arguments. Each speaker can project his or her argument and images on a screen and deliver the words of the argument in a powerful voice. You might pursue this option either individually, by having each person present the project in turn, or collaboratively, by having each member of a team present an argument and the images that inform and direct that point of view. Decide if you want to provide written feedback for each person, and award a prize to the most effective use of visual rhetoric, the most persuasive argument, and the best style.

 Visit www.ablongman.com/envision for expanded assignment guidelines and student projects.

Part II

RESEARCH ARGUMENTS

Research is never completed. . . . Around the corner lurks another possibility of interview, another book to read, a courthouse to explore, a document to verify.
—Catherine Drinker Bowen

CHAPTER 4

Planning and Proposing
Research Arguments

CHAPTER 5

Finding and Evaluating
Research Sources

CHAPTER 6

Organizing and Writing
Research Arguments

Planning and Proposing Research Arguments

FIGURE 4.1 How does this parody propaganda poster use visual elements to undermine the RIAA's stance on file sharing?

Chapter Preview Questions

- How do I generate a productive topic for a research paper?
- What prewriting techniques can I use to develop ideas and focus my topic?
- How do I keep a research log?
- What are the steps for conducting a research inquiry and writing a strong research plan?
- How do I transform my plan into a formal research proposal?

What's going on in the poster shown in Figure 4.1? Why the juxtaposition of a menacing Soviet officer with a contemporary college student listening to downloaded music? Why the deep red background color and the placement of characters with the officer looking over the student's shoulder? Why is *Communism* so large and visually echoed by the hammer and sickle? At some point, you begin to realize that this poster is intended as a parody and that it pokes fun at recent publicity campaigns by the Recording Industry Association of America (RIAA) to combat file sharing and unauthorized music downloading. These observations will help you begin to make an argument about the poster, but in order to back up or substantiate your claims about its meaning, you would need to do some research. That is, you would need to place the rhetorical elements of the poster in their historical and critical contexts.

One important point of reference for this poster is the 1950s cold-war era, in which anti-Communist propaganda posters originated. You would need to study the history and culture of that period to support your claims about this contemporary visual parody. A second is the current debate about music downloading and copyright law. As you try to grasp the significance of representing the RIAA's position through a parody of anti-Soviet propaganda, you would need to investigate the political and legal controversies surrounding file sharing.

Research is one way to gain access to a specific period of time or set of issues. You can also conduct research to find out how other writers have approached and analyzed texts such as these. Your research might entail interviews with experts about your topic area or a survey of your peers.

Doing research lends depth and complexity to your interpretation of a given text and positions your argument within a larger discussion on an issue. Such research involves more than going to the library and gathering sources. It's an inquiry that you pursue by exploring a variety of sources: online, in libraries, and through fieldwork. In this chapter, you will learn the first steps of becoming an active participant in a research community and begin to develop the skills for turning a research topic into an effective research plan and a solid research proposal.

Asking Research Questions

The discussion in this chapter focuses on a specific subset of persuasive images—propaganda posters—because such texts make very powerful public statements and because, for many of us, to understand the motivations behind a propaganda poster, we have to perform a certain amount of research. Often this research involves pursuing answers to questions we have formulated about the poster. In fact, most research papers begin with the act of asking questions.

One way you can get started on your research is to pick a text that moves you and start brainstorming questions about it. Let's say that you came across the 1917 American enlistment poster shown in Figure 4.2 in an exhibit on campus or as part of a class discussion about World War I posters. Approaching it for the first time, you and your peers probably will start to analyze the visual rhetoric, much as we did in the earlier chapters of *Envision*.

What are your eyes drawn to first, the words or the image? Maybe you look first at the simian figure in the middle, roaring menacingly at you, and then at the swooning, seminaked woman in his arms. In contrast, maybe the person next to you explains that her eyes first are attracted to the bold yellow text at the top and then move to the bottom, where the words "U.S. Army" in black are superimposed on the imperative "Enlist." In synthesizing various responses to the text, you most likely would find yourself with more questions than answers. This is actually good, for those questions can be the beginning of your research inquiry.

You might ask, Is that gorilla King Kong? Following up on that question through research, you could confidently answer, No, since you would discover that the poster was made decades before the movie was released. During that same research, you might find several books that discuss the wartime practice of casting enemies as subhuman creatures, offering a possible explanation for why the enemy nation is portrayed as a menacing gorilla in this poster. Adding to that your observation that "*culture*" is spelled "Kultur" (on

FIGURE 4.2 This World War I propaganda poster offers a wealth of detail for historical analysis.

the club the gorilla is holding), you probably would realize that the enemy symbolized here is in fact Germany.

Then you might ask: What is the significance of that bloody club? Why is the woman unconscious and partly naked? More research might provide insight on how bestiality emerged as a wartime theme in World War I enlistment posters. The idea was that if a nation's women were threatened with potential attack by such "monsters," then the men would surely step up to save and protect their wives, daughters, sisters, and mothers.

These very specific observations and questions about the posters should lead you to look up sources that will provide compelling answers and, eventually, to acquire new knowledge. In other words, by asking questions about your text, you can move beyond an initial response and into the realm of intellectual discovery.

In fact, your first questions about a text will lead you to ask more pointed questions about the context, political environment, key players, and social trends informing your text. For the propaganda poster in Figure 4.2, such questions might include: What conflicts was America involved in during 1917? What was the meaning of the word on the gorilla's hat, "Militarism," at that time? How would an appeal to enlist factor into that historical situation? Who is the audience for this poster, and how is this poster part of a series of wartime propaganda images? If you were to work through these questions, you might begin to develop ideas for a feasible research topic—one that could yield an interesting paper on war propaganda and the relationship between America and Germany in 1917.

As you investigate your research topic, your questions will likely become more specific: Do other posters of the same historical period use similar imagery and rhetorical strategies? How do the techniques used in early twentieth-century posters differ from those used during World War II? How are the rhetorical strategies used in this poster similar to or different from enlistment posters you might encounter today? In what ways have enlistment posters changed over time?

To answer these questions, you might perform an online search to yield useful information. Perhaps you might visit the library, talk with a history professor, or visit a museum. In all cases, what these questions lead to is a focused *research topic* and, ultimately, a written project that draws on and contributes to the arguments that others have made about such texts. Generating a range of interesting and productive questions is the first step in any research project; the process of inquiry itself helps you to define a project and make it your own.

Constructing a Research Log

As you move from asking questions about a text to producing a feasible research topic for your paper, keep track of your ideas in a **research log**. This log will help you organize your ideas, chart your progress, and assemble the different pieces of your research.

It can contain primarily written text, or it can include images as well, as does the example in Figure 4.3. The log itself can take many forms, from a handwritten journal, to a series of word processing documents, to an online Weblog. The key lies not in what form you choose, but in the way you use your chosen form to help you develop your topic into an interesting and provocative research project.

This is a brainstorm for my research paper on homeless people. The arguments that I brainstormed here are basically the arguments I used.

Brainstorm for research paper

The homeless are portrayed negatively in the media
They are portrayed as being bums, drug addicts, alcoholics
They are often seen putting around shopping carts with bags, old bottles their miniscule possessions
They often look ugly as they are portrayed as dirty, smelling, having beards being old middle aged men with gray hair
- pigeons are always around them
- they are always mumbling or begging people for money
- there are no real movies or tv shows where the homeless are the main characters
- there might be a few instances where they are the main character, but it is very rare and I cannot remember one
- people often avoid them in television and movies or they are juxtaposed next to this really likeable, affluent character
- they are often portrayed as crazy – mumbling to themselves or trying to hurt someone
- no news on the good of the homeless or true statistics such as how many of them are families and children
- people don't have sympathy for the homeless
- there have been stories about how people are losing sympathy
- influences people
- it is an endless circle
why does the media do this?
- American dream, protestant work ethic – says that people have to work hard to earn money and/or please God
- Says that anyone can succeed if they want to and put the effort
- If that is the truth than how can a person who is homeless be good
- The homeless person must be to blame for their state because they are not working hard enough if they do not have success
- The media shows the American dream in a positive light, so people believe that
- Don't consider that homeless might not be to blame or some unforeseen consequences could have hurt them
Money being taken away from the homeless recently maybe this is why
When I walk on the streets with some friends they always make negative comments about the homeless – I wonder if the media and the American dream has something to do with it – they always talk about how it is the homeless people's fault that they can get work – they do not realize how hard it is to get work especially in this economy and if you have not gone through college
In my area there are many people who have gone through college and are homeless

FIGURE 4.3 Felicia Cote uses a preliminary brainstorm generated from a news photograph of a homeless man to develop a topic in her research log.

AT A GLANCE

Constructing a Research Log

To start your research log, include a variety of entries related to the initial stages of the research process:

- Write freely on possible topic ideas.
- Insert and annotate clippings from newspaper or magazine sources that offer interesting potential topics.
- Paste in and respond to provocative images related to potential topics.
- Write a reaction to ideas brought up during class discussion.
- Insert and annotate printouts from emails or other collaborative work on research ideas.
- Track preliminary searches on the Internet and in your library catalog.
- Develop your research plan.
- Vent anxieties over your topic.

Generating Topics

One of the most crucial aspects of starting a research project is selecting a viable and engaging **topic**. The word *topic,* in fact, comes from the ancient Greek word *topos,* translated literally as "place." The earliest students of rhetoric used the physical space of the papyrus page—given to them by their teachers—to locate their topics for writing. Similarly, your teacher may suggest certain guidelines or parameters for you to follow when it comes to your topic; for instance, you may be given a specific topic (such as representations of race in Dr. Seuss cartoons) or you may be limited to a theme (the rhetoric of political advertisements on television, radio, and the Internet).

Seeing Connections
See Scott Matthews, "Copying Isn't Cool" on page 415 for an example of an essay that takes its topic from a poster campaign.

In some cases, you may not have any restrictions at all. But regardless of the degree to which your topic has been mapped out for you, you still can—and should—make it your own. You do this partly by generating your own range of questions and path of inquiry and partly by responding to the rhetorical situation provided by your assignment. Even if your whole class is writing on the same topic, each person will present a different argument or approach to the issue. Some will use a different stance or persona, some will rely on different sources, some will use different rhetorical appeals, and all will argue different positions about the topic.

To see how this works, let's look at one student's project on propaganda posters to see how he moved from a series of images to a more fully developed research topic. When asked to choose a topic for a research paper, student Tommy Tsai found he was interested in propaganda posters from World War II. Looking at selection of images (see Figures 4.4 through 4.6), Tommy started by asking some questions, such as the ones that follow:

- Who is depicted in these posters? Are these depictions positive or negative?
- What is the purpose of each poster?
- What strategies are these posters using to persuade their audiences?
- How do these posters reveal cultural prejudices?

FIGURE 4.4 This Uncle Sam poster from 1917 was reissued for World War II.

FIGURE 4.5 Anti-Nazi propaganda relied on religiously charged rhetoric.

FIGURE 4.6 American war efforts employed extreme visual messages to galvanize support.

COLLABORATIVE CHALLENGE

Get into groups of three or four and look at the series of posters in Figures 4.7 through 4.10, which fall under the broad topic of World War I enlistment posters. As a group, come up with a list of three research questions that you might explore based on two to four of the posters. Now exchange your list with another small group and discuss the differences in your questions. By the end of the session, come up with three or four concrete research topics you might pursue.

Seeing Connections
To see how two authors develop the same topic (soccer's international impact) in different ways, see Thomas Jones's "Ode to Maradona" and Courtney Angela Brkic's "Group Therapy" on page 354.

FIGURE 4.7 An American woman wears a Navy man's suit in Christy's propaganda poster.

FIGURE 4.8 A group of British women watch male soldiers leave for battle in Kealey's 1915 poster.

FIGURE 4.9 This 1917 U.S. poster presents a direct message from a woman dressed for war.

FIGURE 4.10 Great Britain's John Bull points straight at the viewer in this 1915 poster.

Through the process of asking such questions, Tommy was able to identify his preliminary topic as "the rhetoric of World War II propaganda" and began to frame it more formally in his research log notes. He wrote in one research log entry that he wanted to analyze these posters in their historical contexts: "In particular, I plan to focus on the propaganda posters that appeared in the three most active countries in that time period: the United States, Germany, and Japan. My research paper will report my findings from the comparison of the different rhetorical strategies employed by the three nations." By generating a set of preliminary research questions, he was able to focus more clearly on the dialogue between those posters and his interest in them. In this way he was able to turn an overly broad initial topic into one that was more specific and workable.

As you completed the "Collaborative Challenge," your responses to the posters undoubtedly varied. Perhaps you generated some of these topics:

- Women in World War I recruitment posters
- Cross-dressing and enlistment posters
- The use of sexuality in Navy propaganda
- The differences in portrayals of men and women

No matter what topics you and your collaboration partners wrote down, you all probably have one thing in common: you were drawn to themes that interested you. This is key: successful research topics need to interest you, inspire you, or even anger you. Even with assigned topics, you should be able to find some aspect of the assignment that speaks to you. In general, there needs to be a *connection* between you and your topic to motivate you to follow through and transform it into a successful argument.

In addition, while selecting your topic, you might consider the type of research you'll need to do to pursue it; in fact, you might select your topic based mostly on the sorts of research it allows you to do. For instance, a student writing on propaganda of the Prohibition era will work extensively with paper sources, which might involve archival work with original letters, posters, or government documents from that time period. A student writing on visual advertising for ethnic-theme dorms on campus will be more likely to complement paper sources with interviews with the university housing staff, student surveys, and first-person observations. A student writing on sexualized rhetoric in student campaign materials might take a poll,

AT A GLANCE

Looking for the "Perfect" Topic

1. **Look inward.** Ask questions about yourself: What issues, events, or ideas interest you? Are there any hot-button topics you find yourself drawn to again and again? What topic is compelling enough that you would watch a news program, television special, film, or relevant lecture on it?

2. **Look outward.** Ask questions about the people, structures, and issues you encounter every day. Walk through campus or your neighborhood and look around: What are the central issues of student life on campus? Do you walk by a technology-enhanced classroom and see the students busy writing on laptops or using plasma screens? Topic: technology and education. Do you see a fraternity's poster about a "dry" party? Topic: alcohol on campus. Do you see workers outside the food service building on strike? Topic: labor relations at the college.

3. **Use creative visualization.** Imagine that you are at a party; you are chatting casually with a friend when you overhear someone nearby talking about something. Suddenly, you feel so interested—or so angry—that you excuse yourself from your companion to go over and participate in the conversation. What would move you so strongly?

4. **Use the materials of the moment.** Perhaps the *topos* might be closer to the classical Greek model; although not a roll of papyrus, your class reading list or a single issue of a newspaper can house many topics. Scan the front page and opinion section of your school or community newspaper to see what events or issues people are talking about. Be sure to look at the pictures as well for hot issues or events. You might shift your perspective from local to global and pick up a national or international newspaper or a newsmagazine; what is gripping the community at large?

gather concrete examples, and research the newspaper's written coverage of past and present elections. Think broadly and creatively about what kinds of research you might use and what types of research (archival work versus fieldwork involving interviews and survey taking) appeals most to you. A final important consideration is whether you can actually get your hands on the source material you need to construct a persuasive argument.

CREATIVE PRACTICE

Examine a copy of a school, local, or national newspaper for compelling stories or images that might offer interesting topics for research. Which have you seen in the news for several days? Which focus on issues you've discussed before? Which seem to be workable topics that you can explore through a sustained research inquiry? What type of research would each one entail? Select two or three of these issues, and for each one ask yourself the screening questions listed in the "At a Glance" box. Finally, look over your answers and consider: Which topic would you be most likely to pursue and develop into a full research paper? Why? Write these ideas down in your research log.

AT A GLANCE

Screening Questions for Topics

1. *Am I interested in the topic?* We write best about ideas, events, and issues that touch us somehow—through curiosity, passion, or intellectual interest.

2. *Can I argue a position on this topic?* At this stage, you may not have developed a stand on the issue, but you should see promise for advancing a new perspective on the topic.

3. *Will I be able to find enough research material on this topic?* Brainstorm some possible sources you might use to write this paper.

4. *Does this sort of research appeal to me?* Since you will be working with this topic for an extended period of time, it is best to have a genuine interest in it and in the type of research that it will require (archival work or fieldwork).

Bringing Your Topic into Focus

Once you have settled on a topic, the next step in the research project involves exploring your knowledge—and the limitations of your knowledge—about it. A productive way to do this is through **prewriting**. Defined literally, prewriting is writing that precedes the official drafting of the paper, but, practically speaking, it can take many forms. Lists, scribbled notes, informal outlines, drawings—all different types of prewriting serve the same goal: to help you explore and focus a topic.

Graphic Brainstorming

The practice of **graphic brainstorming** provides writers with a great way to develop topics. This technique transforms traditional **brainstorming**—jotting down a series of related words and phrases on a topic—into a more visible process. Also called *webbing, clustering,* or *mapping,* the goal of *graphic brainstorming* is to help you develop your topic by exploring relationships among ideas. You can brainstorm by hand or on a computer; in either mode, begin by writing a topic in a circle (or square or rectangle, if you prefer). Figure 4.11 shows the first step you might take in brainstorming for a paper generated from the World War I posters discussed earlier (Figures 4.7 through 4.10).

Next, brainstorm ideas and questions about that topic, and then arrange them in groups around your main circle to indicate the relationships among them. As you answer each question and pose more developed ones in response, you begin to bring your topic into focus. You'll notice that in Figure 4.12, we show how you might start to do this by writing questions that differentiate between various posters and by grouping them by gender issues. In addition, in our brainstorm, we use various types of notations—including words, phrases, and questions—and insert lines and arrows to indicate the relationship between the concepts. We even use color to further emphasize these associations. These techniques help us develop the argument and eventually can lead to a more narrowed topic and perhaps even a preliminary thesis.

As we continue to brainstorm—whether for an hour or over several sessions—it becomes clear why some people call this technique **webbing**. As Figure 4.13 shows, our graphic turns into a web of ideas. By using this technique, in fact, we have done more than simply develop our topic: we have made it visually apparent that our topic is too broad for a standard research paper assignment. Our web now offers enough ideas for an entire book on the subject. But our diagram also provides us with clues about the direction in which to take our project. We can pick a *subsection* of ideas to focus on in our writing.

FIGURE 4.11

Zooming in on a Topic

Let's zoom in on one part of our diagram—the part, color-coded yellow, that asks key questions about representations of women in military posters. Working with this part of the web, we could write a focused paper that examines the implications of the way women are depicted in these texts.

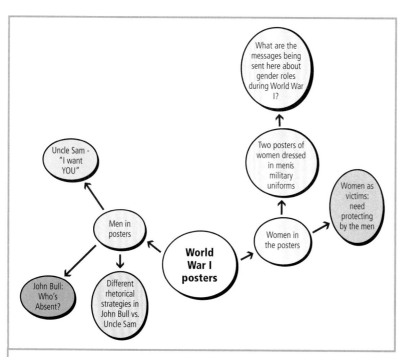

FIGURE 4.12

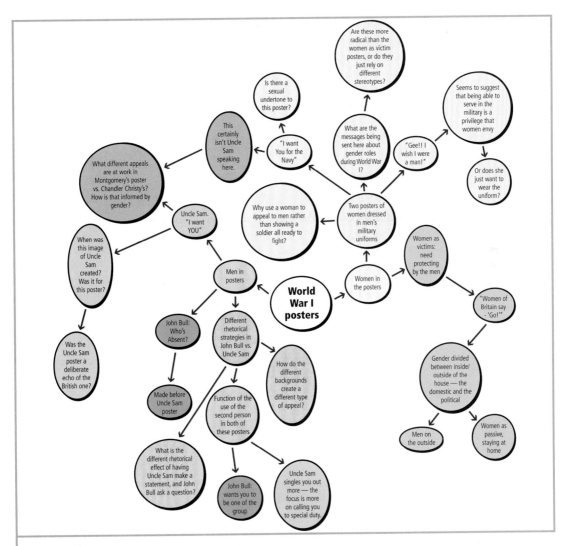

FIGURE 4.13

We could write about how cross-dressing is used as a deliberate appeal to the audience, or about how military posters evoke the image of wife and mother to mobilize troops. However, to narrow our topic, we should sharpen questions about these images.

Focusing Questions for a Research Topic

1. **Write down your topic.**

   Topic formulation: Gender Roles in World War I.

2. **Work with that topic by asking a pointed question based on close analysis of the text at hand.**

   First question: Is there a sexual undertone to the posters?

3. **Refine the topic by answering that question.**

   Topic narrowing: Yes, in one of the posters, the woman is standing in a provocative pose, looking at the audience in a sexual manner, but in another, the women seem more identified with family (mother, daughter) than with sexuality.

4. **Revise the narrowed topic to be more specific.**

   Revised topic formulation: the different constructions of femininity in World War I propaganda posters.

5. **Identify significant aspects of that topic to explore.**

   Second question: How so? In what way? What is the significance?

6. **Use the answers to these questions to focus the topic.**

   Final topic focus: the use of the Madonna-whore stereotype as a persuasive strategy in World War I recruitment posters.

In working with the webbing process and then asking key questions in this way, we have just completed one of the most important steps in developing a viable research topic: **narrowing** a large subject to a more manageable one. By asking such questions—and we could come up with many others along different lines of inquiry (such as race, sexuality, international representations, and nationalism)—we begin to develop a *focused* topic that will offer us the opportunity for close analysis, rigorous research, and a sharp argumentative stance. That is, we can move from "World War I posters" to "changing gender norms reflected in World War I posters." With this focused and narrowed topic, we'll be able to contribute a new opinion about war posters and add to the ongoing dialogue that we find in our secondary sources.

CREATIVE PRACTICE

Try out this practice of *narrowing a topic* with a pair of early twenty-first-century posters that protest the U.S. war with Iraq. Examine the posters shown in Figures 4.14 through 4.17, and then complete a *graphic brainstorm* to develop a feasible topic for your essay. Be sure that you narrow your topic from "anti-war propaganda posters" to a more focused one that you might pursue in a research paper. You might decide during your graphic brainstorm to focus your topic by identifying which images you'd like to write about or by generating key questions to ask about particular texts: What is the significance of the style that is used in the posters? How do the words and images work together in these posters? How do they work against each other? What is the significance of showing people who have been wounded? How does symbolism operate in these posters? The more specific the questions you ask, the more focused your topic will be.

FIGURE 4.14 This recent anti-war poster uses strong language to catch the reader's attention.

FIGURE 4.15 This striking poster implies a connection between the war with Iraq and the oil trade.

FIGURE 4.16 This poster solidifies the visual agument through a caption.

FIGURE 4.17 Originally composed to protest the Vietnam war, this poster recently re-emerged in reference to the Iraq war.

AT A GLANCE

The Research Freewrite

- Write your ideas in full sentences.
- Use a three-paragraph model to focus your answers:
  - Paragraph 1: Announce the topic and state your thesis.
  - Paragraph 2: Identify key sources.
  - Paragraph 3: Anticipate problems.

Planning Your Research Through Writing

In completing the "Creative Practice" you most likely constructed a set of web diagrams that, like those in Figures 4.12 and 4.13, alternated between asking and answering questions. This process will narrow your focus and provide you with a direction for your research inquiry. But did you find yourself concerned that you don't have the knowledge necessary to write this essay? Are you worried that the gaps in your own knowledge will prevent you from answering those questions in a satisfactory way? If so, then you are in good company. All researchers and scholars fear the limitations of their knowledge. The key is to use that lack of knowledge as a motivation to put ideas on paper—the first step in the writing process for your research argument. We'll discuss three ways of putting ideas on paper: freewriting about your topic, drafting a formal research proposal, and developing a research hypothesis.

Freewriting about Your Research Topic

One way to start planning your research process is to freewrite about your ideas in your research log. Testing out your research plan in this way will move you from the work you did in narrowing your topic to the work you need to do in gathering sources and developing a research outline. This method also will provide an informal structure for your research, giving it shape and sharper focus as you move deeper into the research process.

Student Writing

See Joseph Yoon's research freewrite on the Vietnam War Memorials in the United States and in Vietnam.

www.ablongman.com/envision/215

In completing your freewrite, you may find it helpful to follow a **three-paragraph model:** in the *first paragraph,* announce your topic and state a preliminary thesis so that you can begin the project with a critical and focused perspective; in the *second paragraph,* identify the sources you plan to use to investigate this topic; in the *third paragraph,* speculate on obstacles or problems you might encounter in your research and how you might avoid or solve these problems. Let's look at a freewrite from student Bries Deerrose, who shaped his research inquiry around questions concerning a piece of contemporary propaganda: a leaflet dropped in Afghanistan by the U.S. military in the 2002–2003 campaign there.

This freewriting process allowed Bries the opportunity to work through his topic, his sources, and his methodology as a way of moving to a concrete research plan.

This first paragraph introduces the research topic and describes what Bries thinks the main focus of his paper might be. At the end of the paragraph, he includes a tentative thesis to help him focus his interest and argument as he begins researching this topic.

Research Freewrite

America's image has come increasingly under the scrutiny of our allies and enemies alike. In response, President George W. Bush established the Office of Global Communications, the stated purpose of which is "to

advise . . . on utilization of the most effective means for the United
States Government to ensure consistency in messages that will promote
the interests of the United States abroad, prevent misunderstanding,
build support for and among coalition partners of the United States, and
inform international audiences." In this paper, I will examine how this
office has gone about this, especially through visual rhetoric. I will
examine how the world has responded to such propaganda, especially the
Middle East, and I will examine what image the office portrays, whether
this is an accurate image of America or an example of political rhetoric.
Finally, I will discuss whether such marketing is beneficial or
detrimental, from both a foreign and American perspective. ***Tentative
thesis:*** America is actively projecting an image of itself using various
forms of visual rhetoric; this image is both accurate and necessary for
the dissemination of various liberal perspectives, in the hopes of
providing more choice for the public and private lives of individuals
worldwide, as well as ensuring meaningful, peaceful dialogue between
America and the world.

In the second paragraph, Bries discusses the sources he intends to use. Notice the broad range of possibilities he considers: flyers, television commercials, radio broadcasts, and both American and international sources.

   To research this topic, I hope to examine firsthand government-
generated materials: flyers, commercials, radio broadcasts, publications,
etc. I will also attempt to find any commentaries on this effort as well as
on domestic conceptions of what America is and what its image should
be. I will compare this with foreign opinions regarding America's image
and reactions to the American marketing techniques. To do this, I will
need to find foreign commentaries, including visual rhetoric responding to
our own visual rhetoric. I will need secondhand sources concerning
foreign opinions.

   The most difficult part of this assignment will be determining foreign
opinion, since I am not fluent in other languages. I will also need to form
my own opinion about the effectiveness, morality, and accuracy of these
rhetorical tactics (are we really projecting the objective truth, what is
the objective truth, and should we really market ourselves at all?). Such

In the third paragraph, Bries anticipates the difficulties he might face and how he can solve them.

philosophical issues are always sticky, and will require much thought and a wide array of perspectives.

Bries concludes with a concrete example of the visual
rhetoric he will use in his research paper, a leaflet
dropped in Afghanistan by
the United States in the
2002-2003 campaign.

Office of Global Communications leaflet air-dropped in Afghanistan.
http://www.psywarrior.com/afghanleaf08.html.

Drafting a Research Proposal

In many academic contexts, you will be asked to move beyond freewriting and formalize your research plan through composing a full-length **research proposal**. This type of text is common in many disciplines and professions and is used by writers to develop agendas for research communities, secure funding for a study, publicize plans for inquiry and field research, and test the interest of potential audiences for a given project. In the writing classroom, the research proposal provides a similar formal structure for developing a project, but it also serves another purpose: it is a more structured means of organizing your thoughts to help you solidify your topic and move into the next stages of the research process. For these reasons, the *genre, organization,* and *content* of the research proposal differ in important ways from other kinds of popular and academic writing that you might do. In drafting out your proposal, include the following elements:

- *Background:* What do I already know about my topic? What do I need to find out more about?
- *Methods:* How am I going to research this topic? What research questions are driving my inquiry?
- *Timeline:* What are my goals for the different stages of research and how can I schedule my work to most effectively meet these milestones?

AT A GLANCE

Key Functions of the Research Proposal

- It introduces the narrowed *topic.*
- It presents the *rhetorical stance* or *thesis* that the writer will develop.
- It explains the *significance* of the research project.
- It lists possible *sources* for investigation.
- It outlines your research *methods* or planned approach to the research.
- It delineates a detailed *timeline* for investigating the topic.
- It often anticipates any *difficulties* that might arise in pursuing this topic.
- It often includes a brief *biography* of the researcher (usually a one-paragraph description of the writer's credentials, interests, and motivations).
- It includes, if appropriate, a carefully chosen and analyzed visual rhetoric text as a case study or concrete example of the topic.

- *Ultimate goal and significance:* What do I hope to accomplish in my research? What are the broader issues or implications of my research?

As this list suggests, in your proposal it is important to explain your interest in your chosen subject and establish a set of questions to guide your inquiry. You should also use the proposal to delineate the timeline for your research and writing process. Although this part may seem obvious, it is crucial for time management. Some proposals may require you to have done some preliminary work with sources, while others may be designed to facilitate the very earliest stages of the research process.

As the last item on the "At a Glance" list indicates, you should incorporate an appropriate visual text—a sample propaganda poster to be analyzed or an editorial cartoon that introduces the issue—into your proposal to show readers an example of the materials about which you'll be conducting your research. If your research project focuses on visual texts, you might incorporate an appropriate image to introduce an issue, present the context, captivate your audience, provide a rhetorical stance, or offer insight into the complexity of your topic.

As you craft your research proposal, realize that while it serves to clarify your research intentions, it should also *persuade* an audience of the feasibility and significance of your project. In fact, perhaps the most important step in launching your research inquiry is to address the issue of your project's significance or, as some writing instructors call it, the "So What?" part of the project. It is the "So What?"—an awareness of the significance of the topic you're addressing and the questions you're asking—that moves the proposal from being a routine academic exercise to a powerful piece of persuasive writing. When addressing the "So What?" question, consider why anyone else would care enough to read a paper on your topic. Ask yourself:

- What is at stake in your topic?
- Why does it matter?
- What contribution will your project make to a wider community?

These are difficult questions to answer, and they may be ones that you defer until later in your research when you have gathered evidence and developed your argument to support your thesis. However, the sooner you clarify the significance of your work, the faster you will move toward producing a rigorous and interesting piece of writing. Keep notes in your research log on how the answers to these questions change as you proceed with your research and your thinking about the topic.

Let's look at an example: a research proposal Susan Zhang developed on digital manipulation.

Susan Zhang

Little Photoshop of Horrors?: Digital Manipulation of Media Images

When O. J. Simpson was arrested in the summer of 1994, Newsweek and Time magazines featured his mugshot on their covers. But while Newsweek's

Susan begins with a specific example to hook the audience and to set up the context for her proposal.

In the proposal she turned in for class, Susan also embedded images from the *Newsweek* and *Time* covers in her introduction as visual evidence for her claims. She uses questions to identify common assumptions that her audience might hold about her topic.

photo was unaltered, Time had darkened the color of his skin and reduced the size of his prisoner ID number. To anyone who saw the two magazines on the news rack, the difference was obvious. To some it was even unethical: minority groups protested that the digital manipulation made O. J. look darker and more menacing, thereby presuming his guilt. The Time illustrator who altered the image later claimed that he only "wanted to make it more artful, more compelling." The impartiality of the photography was widely contested.

You can't always believe what you read in the news, but a photograph doesn't lie, right? Because the photographer and the camera are perceived to be mere vehicles for converting reality into image, people are more apt to trust a photo, believing it to be the product of a machine rather than a human, and consequently free of bias. But with the advent of digital imaging, that credibility has been compromised. Image-editing programs such as Photoshop make it possible to perform cosmetic touch-ups, graft parts of pictures onto others, even construct a picture entirely from scratch. In many ways, digital imaging has redefined the field of photography. With words like "composograph" and "photoillustration" being coined to describe altered images indistinguishable from the real thing, people have grown wary of deeming the photograph a purveyor of truth.

She then clearly states her research goals. She suggests some key research questions and then ends with a declarative sentence that underscores her intentions as a researcher. Notice how she mentions the significance—or importance—of the project early on in the proposal.

For my research project, I want to explore how the capacity of image manipulation has affected the way we perceive photos in the news and media. Has it led to a permanent loss of faith? Or, on the flip side, to the establishment of stricter standards for allowable alterations? By examining past incidences of digital manipulation and current guidelines for photographs in the media, and the contexts in which they apply, I hope to gain a better understanding of the credibility of news and media imagery in the digital age.

Methods

First, I want to approach my topic through its historical context. I will start with the pre-digital era and look at whether photo manipulation existed then. Surely there were tricked, staged, and doctored photos also? To what extent were photos altered using darkroom techniques? What kind of ethical considerations governed the editing of media images then? By comparing past precedents with the types of digital manipulations commonly used today, I can determine whether digital imaging really has made photo manipulation a bigger and more prevalent problem.

Next, I will look at digital manipulation from the public's point of view. In the past when a digital image was altered, how did the public respond? For example, if a photograph is altered in an obvious or humorous manner, it could be perceived as satire or social commentary, but if it is altered subtly and the change not announced, it could be perceived as deception. How easily can people recognize an altered photo? And when a magazine or newspaper is exposed for digitally manipulating a photo, does this automatically discredit it in the public eye?

I will also consider the photographer's point of view. Do photographers consider photo manipulation a recent development stemming from digital imaging? What are the moral and ethical justifications for manipulated photographs? What kinds of standards exist in the field of photojournalism and media photography? How do these standards regulate the integrity of digital photojournalism?

Sources

To begin my research, I will look at books on the ethics of photojournalism. So far I have checked out Paul Lester's *Photojournalism: An Ethical Approach* and Julianne Newton's *The Burden of Visual Truth: The Role of Photojournalism in Mediating Reality*. These books will help me understand the history of ethical photojournalism, the ways in which a photograph conveys a message, and the public's response to photographs.

Then, moving toward the digital side of media images, I will turn to books such as Thomas Wheeler's *Phototruth or Photofiction?: Ethics and*

Susan writes her "Methods" section by using her research questions: the historical perspective, the audience's perspective, and the photographer's perspective. She carefully thinks through each line of inquiry.

Although this was written before she began serious research, Susan increased her proposal's persuasiveness (and her own ethos as a researcher) by including the titles of specific texts she located through a computer search of her library's holdings. She carefully groups her intended sources and also explains briefly why these types of sources would be useful for her research.

Media Imagery in the Digital Age and Larry Gross's *Image Ethics in the Digital Age*. The first book examines specific examples of photo manipulation and later provides an ethical framework for considering image manipulation in photojournalism. The second book is a collection of articles on aspects of digital image ethics.

I will also search online databases such as EBSCO and LexisNexis for articles on digital manipulation and recent controversies over digital manipulation. Search terms I might use include "photo manipulation," "digital photojournalism," and "digital image ethics." Through these databases I hope to find authoritative opinions from photojournalists as well as public reactions to altered images in magazines and the news.

As a primary source, I will look at photojournalism Websites. I will visit large news and magazine sites and smaller photojournalism communities, browsing their photographs to see if they use digital manipulation, and if so, how it is addressed. Also, there are many web resources that explain the guidelines that have been development by photojournalists. For example, the National Press Photographers Association's Website features a digital code of ethics. These sites will clarify the guidelines of digital photojournalism and how closely they are being followed.

Timeline

1/20 Research proposal due

1/20–1/22 Search for articles on photojournalism and digital manipulation using online databases

1/22–1/27 In-depth research using books

Primary research using photojournalism sites

1/27–1/31 Review notes and write a thesis

Talk with classmates and instructor for advice on my thesis

Evaluate which sources to use

2/1–2/5 Outline paper: decide on the major arguments, draft topic sentences, and choose support for each argument

By including search terms and specific database names, Susan shows that she is ready to move to actual research.

Susan finishes her discussion of sources with attention to primary sources—the actual photographs themselves—that she intends to find to use in her paper.

In her timeline, Susan lists not only deadlines imposed by her instructor but also key steps in the research process: finding books, evaluating sources, taking notes, constructing a thesis, peer review, a second round of research, drafting, and revising.

With this detailed timeline, Susan shows her careful time management and builds her ethos by demonstrating her understanding of the research process; she even uses colored font for due dates to highlight their importance.

2/5–2/12 Write first draft of paper

2/12 Research paper draft due

2/15–2/28 Obtain and reflect on feedback

Additional research and revision as necessary

3/3–3/6 Review second draft for polish, errors

3/6 Revision of research paper due

Significance

With advancements in technology, photography has moved from the darkroom to the computer lab, making it possible to alter photographs beyond what is considered ethical. The abuse of this technology has resulted in manipulated photos being passed off as real in the media, and a resulting public skepticism over the reliability of all media images. A closer look at the occurrences of digital manipulation today, as regulated by the evolving guidelines of photojournalism, could reveal to what extent such skepticism is warranted.

In her conclusion, Susan reasserts the importance of her project, broadening to address the "So What?" that she needs to answer as she enters into her research.

Drafting the Research Hypothesis

In reading Bries's freewrite and Susan's proposal, you might have noticed that as they developed their topics, they were simultaneously trying their hands at formulating their arguments. For instance, in Bries's first paragraph, he moves from the open-ended language of a proposal ("I will examine," "I will discuss") to a restatement of his subject in terms of a tentative thesis statement at the end of the paragraph. Many times as you draft your research plan, you will find that you enter into your project relying on broad questions ("What do the leaflets that Americans dropped on Afghanistan in 2003 say about our country and our international policy?") or on statements of intention (i.e., "In this paper, I will explore how . . . image manipulation has affected the way we perceive photos in the news"). However, as we see in the examples from Bries and Susan, it is also useful to use your research plan as an opportunity to try to define your rhetorical stance in relation to that topic.

So how do you make a claim about a topic that you have not yet researched completely? This is a key question, and it is often a frustrating one for many writers. Realize, however, that you've already taken the first step just by asking pointed questions about your topic. From these questions, you can develop a working thesis that makes an argumentative claim that you'll attempt to prove. At this point, you might

Student Writing
See many examples of research proposals.
www.ablongman.com/envision/216

call it a **hypothesis,** rather than a *thesis,* to suggest its tentativeness. It is crucial for you to try to formulate a working hypothesis for your research plan as a way of looking at your project with an analytical eye. Of course, you may revise your hypothesis—and maybe your entire approach to the subject—several times over the course of your research. Indeed, most writers do modify their thesis statements, and this revision process is a natural part of what happens when you actually begin to read your sources and take notes about them in the research log. Nevertheless, trying to state your thesis or hypothesis is an important first step in focusing your argument and making the most out of the timeline available to you for research.

Student Writing

Examine Anastasia Nevin's research proposal on the historical mystery of the Romanov assassination, a study of archival photographs and artifacts.

www.ablongman.com/envision/217

Seeing Connections

To see how one writer's stance on her topic continued to evolve during her research, see Zoe Flower's "Getting the Girl" on page 472.

One way to develop your detailed hypothesis is to rewrite one of your more narrowed questions from the research proposal as a polished declarative statement that you intend to prove. For example, if you asked yourself, "How were representations of race used in World War II propaganda?" then you might turn that question into a potential thesis: "Representations of race deployed in World War II propaganda functioned as a way to justify the internment of innocent civilians." As you continue your research, you may come to disagree with that statement, but at least beginning with a tentative thesis gives you somewhere to start your research.

Let's consider how this process might play out for a research argument on propaganda posters. We're going to follow Tommy Tsai's research process as he developed his paper on propaganda posters entitled, "This is the Enemy': Depravation and Deceitfulness of America's World War II Political Art."

To develop his research hypothesis, Tommy worked his way through a series of questions:

1. **First, he clarified his familiarity with the topic, even prior to doing any research**.

   Question: What do I already know about my topic?

   Tommy: The different styles of propaganda posters of three countries during World War II. The United States exploited the nationalist feelings of Americans with their posters by using images like the American flag to represent the glory associated with "fighting for your own country." Germany also exploited nationalist feelings among its citizens; the German government did so by using the *ethos* appeal associated with its political leader Adolf Hitler. Japan used a more logical approach; many of their posters show images of Japanese soldiers as victors of a battle.

2. **His next question moved him toward a specific argument.**

   Question: What do I want to know more about?

   Tommy: The people who designed the posters and the work that went into the design process. Also, I would like to know more about the historical context (basic information about the war would be really helpful).

3. With the last question, he began to create his hypothesis for the project.

Question: What are the specific aspects of this topic I hope to explore?

Tommy: The specific rhetorical strategies employed by each country. I also want to look at how these rhetorical strategies affected people, and how effective each country's propaganda was.

Notice that at this point Tommy's hypothesis relies more on his intentions than any firm conclusions; however, by refining his writing in this way, he could approach his research with clearer goals in mind. Accordingly, he was soon able to craft a more polished working hypothesis.

Working Hypothesis

I have conjectured that German propaganda made use of the *ethos* appeal of its fascist leader Adolf Hitler; that Japanese propaganda utilized the *logos* appeal by continually portraying images of a victorious Japanese army; and that American propaganda for the most part employed the *pathos* appeal by evoking nationalistic feelings and associating war with glory and patriotism (see Figure 1). These conjectures coalesce into my argument that the government of each nation is able to bring its political messages across effectively by employing the appropriate rhetorical appeal in its propaganda posters.

Figure 1. Uncle Sam poster.

Working with this hypothesis, Tommy launched his research project, and he eventually wrote a compelling paper that examined U.S. propaganda posters against both the German and Japanese nations. Some of this material was rather disturbing (see Figures 4.4 through 4.6), but Tommy felt compelled to work with these images. In his final reflection on the research paper, Tommy looked back at the development of his argument and even proposed ideas for future study. His reflection letter should show you that a research paper is only the beginning of your engagement with the issues that matter to you.

Student Writing
See Tommy Tsai's complete research plan and proposal.
www.ablongman.com/envision/218

Final Reflection Letter, Tommy Tsai

The final paper turned out to be very different from what I envisioned it to be at the beginning. First of all, my topic changed from World War II propaganda posters in general to a criticism of America's portrayals of their World War II enemies. Also, for my final draft, I had to cut out an entire section from my paper (the one about how America portrayed the political leaders of other nations) since it did not work well with my thesis. Instead, I concentrated on the two remaining sections in order to give my paper more focus. . . . I have also developed an interest in the topic. Perhaps the world wars will make another appearance in one of the many other research papers I will have to write in my four years at the university.

Planning Your Own Research Project

Now that you've learned about the process of generating a topic, focusing the research questions for your topic, developing a hypothesis, and then writing up your plans for research in a structured freewrite or a formal proposal, what can you argue about the first propaganda poster of this chapter (Figure 4.1)?

In answering this prompt, you might start to work through the projects related to the research process. You might develop a research focus that begins with questions and ends with a "So What?" statement of significance. You might try to incorporate visual images into a proposal that will conclude with a clear statement of your future authority on this topic as a researcher. Try the strategies for keeping track of your ideas and work in progress in a research log, a key tool that you'll be using in the next chapter as we turn to gathering and evaluating sources for your topic. It's time to get started on the research process for writing a persuasive argument about an issue that matters to you.

Seeing Connections
For examples of more modern posters that might likewise provide a basis for a researched argument, see the "Think Ink, Not Mink" poster page 313 and the 2004 Get Real Campaign poster on page 280.

PREWRITING CHECKLIST
Analyzing Propaganda Posters

❏ What is the underlying message of this poster? What idea is it trying to convey to its audience?

❏ What are the specifics of the rhetorical situation informing this piece of propaganda? Who produced the poster? Who was its intended audience?

❏ What is the historical context for this poster? What country was it produced in, and what was the social and political situation of the time? How does an understanding of its context affect our understanding of its message?

❏ What type of rhetorical appeal does the poster feature? Does it rely primarily on logos, pathos, or ethos to make its point? How does attention to this appeal manifest itself visually in the poster?

❏ What is the relationship between word and image in the poster? How does this relationship contribute to its rhetorical appeal?

❏ How do design elements such as color, font, layout, and image selection (photograph or illustration) work as persuasive elements in this text?

❏ What strategies of argumentation does the poster use? Does it feature narration? comparison–contrast? example?

❏ Recalling the discussion of exaggerated use of appeals from Chapter 2, does the poster rely on any logical fallacies? any exaggerated use of pathos? If so, how do these work to persuade the audience?

❏ Does the poster use stereotypes to convey its message? How do stereotypes figure as rhetorical devices in this situation? How does the stereotype place the poster in the context of a larger cultural discussion?

❏ What research questions can you develop about this poster?

❏ What kinds of sources might you look at to understand better what's going on with this propaganda poster?

WRITING PROJECTS

1. **Research Freewrite:** Freewrite about your *research ideas* by first writing out answers to the questions provided in the "Prewriting Checklist" and then developing them into a three-paragraph freewrite. In the first paragraph, introduce your research paper topic and describe what you think the main focus of the paper might be. Include a tentative thesis in this paragraph. In the second paragraph, discuss the sources that you intend to use. In the third paragraph, speculate on what obstacles you foresee in this project and/or what you anticipate to be the most difficult part of the assignment. If appropriate, use an image to complement your written text. Show your answers to your instructor or your peers for feedback.

2. **Research Proposal:** Write a detailed research *proposal* that discusses your topic, planned method, and purpose in depth. Be sure to cover your topic, your hypothesis, your potential sources and problems, your method, timeline, and, most importantly, the significance of the proposed project. For more specific instruction consult the Writing Guidelines on the *Envision* Website. When you are done with the writing, present your proposal at a roundtable of research with other members of your class. Answer questions from your classmates to help you fine-tune your topic and troubleshoot your future research.

3. Peer Review: Collaboratively peer review your research proposals. Assume that you are on the review board granting approval and funding to the best *two* proposals of each group. Complete research proposal review letters for each member of your group. When you are done, discuss your letters and what changes you can recommend. Then revise your proposals to make them stronger, better written, and more persuasive. For more specific instructions and for **peer review forms** for the research proposal, consult the *Envision* Website.

 Visit www.ablongman.com/envision for expanded assignment guidelines and student projects.

CHAPTER 5

Finding and Evaluating Research Sources

Chapter Preview Questions

- What is the best way to locate research sources?
- What is the difference between a primary and a secondary source?
- How do I critically evaluate both print and electronic sources?
- How do I pursue field research for my project?
- What is an annotated bibliography, and how can it help me?
- How should I take notes while researching?

As you move from planning to conducting research, you'll need to investigate resources of all kinds and evaluate them for use in your project. You can use your analytical skills to make important distinctions when locating, evaluating, and using sources for your research project. Look, for instance, at the magazine covers in Figures 5.1 and 5.2. Although they focus on the same topic—global warming—the visual rhetoric of the covers suggests that the content of each journal will be quite different. The audience for *Time* magazine differs from that of *Science*, and, consequently, the writing styles within the articles will be different as well. The cover of each magazine previews the distinct content inside.

Specifically, the cover of *Time* in Figure 5.1 conveys how the editors chose to represent global warming to their audience. Ask yourself: What is the argument conveyed by the visual rhetoric of the cover? What is the significance of the choice to use a polar bear as the main character in their image? How is color used strategically? How does the "spotlighting" of the polar bear and the positioning of the image in relation to the words contribute to the rhetorical effect? What kind of stance toward the dangers of global warming does the cover suggest?

In contrast, the *Science* cover (Figure 5.2) features a photograph of an ice-covered lake. The photo appears to have been taken with a "fish-eye" lens, bringing several ice fragments into prominence in the foreground. How do such different rhetorical strategies appeal to the journal's very scientifically informed audience?

Clearly, the editors deliberately located, evaluated, and used materials for the covers that would reflect their magazine's contents. As a researcher, you can use your skills in rhetorical analysis to help you evaluate sources

FIGURE 5.1 Cover of *Time*, April 3, 2006.

FIGURE 5.2 Cover of *Science*, March 24, 2006.

for your own research project, looking to the different elements of a text—from the cover design, to the table of contents, to the index—to better understand the text's perspective on your topic and its usefulness for your project.

COLLABORATIVE CHALLENGE

Working in small groups, compare Figures 5.1 and 5.2 to another image depicting the topic of global warming, the one on the cover of the August 26, 2002 issue of *Time* (see Figure 5.3). What similarities and differences are clear from the use of visual and verbal rhetoric? What stance does the cover suggest that *Time* will take on the topic? How is that stance represented in the cover design?

Through the *Envision* Website, look at other *Time* covers that have addressed the issue of global warming and climate change over several years (the April 9, 2001 cover; the February 17, 1992 cover; the October 19, 1987 cover). How do these covers take different approaches to this issue? How does context seem to inform this approach? Look in the table of contents for each issue; do the article titles seem to support the position suggested by the covers? Finally, as a group, develop your own stance on this issue. Together, sketch a design for a new cover for an upcoming issue of *Science, The Economist*, or *Time*. Use the cover to suggest an argument for a specific perspective on global warming and to provide a visual preview for the contents inside. Share your design and argument with the class.

 www.ablongman.com/envision/219

FIGURE 5.3 Cover of *Time*, August 26, 2002.

Your task as a researcher will be quite similar to that of the editors of *Science* and *The Economist*. As you begin gathering and evaluating sources for your own research-based argument, keep in mind that you will need to shape the argument into a paper addressed to a particular audience: your writing class, a group of scientists, a lobbying organization, an advertising firm, or browsers on the Web. To take part in any of these conversations, a researcher needs to learn what is being talked about (the *topic*), how it is being discussed (the *discourse*), and what the different positions are (*research context*). But your conversation about your research project also will extend beyond your audience; you will, in fact, be engaged in a discussion with the sources themselves.

Visualizing Research

When you think of the act of research, what comes to mind? Surfing the Web? Looking through a library? Interviewing experts in the field? All these images represent different research scenarios. The material you gather in each situation will compose the foundation for your research; this body of knowledge will inform your essay, but not all of it will find its way into your final paper. Nevertheless, you need to research widely and thoroughly to be fully informed about your topic and write a compelling research-based argument. One helpful way of visualizing the relationship between the *process* and the *product* of research is through the metaphor of the **iceberg of research** (see Figure 5.4). In essence, your topic represents only a starting point for your research project; beneath it lie the many different sources you should explore to lend depth and body to your argument. Published books, journal articles, Websites, and field research all constitute the materials of your potential research. As you move beyond a surface knowledge of your topic, you will gather, assess, keep, throw out, and ultimately use a variety of sources. Moving into the depths of your project can therefore be quite exciting as you encounter a rich array of voices, knowledge, and opinions on your topic.

Sometimes, however, this process can be a bit overwhelming. We all share anxieties about writing a research argument. Many times we think of brilliant words penned by minds of genius and fear that we will have nothing new to add to the conversation. Or we worry that we won't find anything interesting to say despite the richness of our sources. Both of these views are extremes. It is more helpful to think of research sources as texts written by people who were once, like yourself, struggling to add substance to their research ideas and seeking to fulfill the plan of their research proposals. In this way, you might consider the process of gathering and assessing sources as a very social one, a process in which you respect and acknowledge the ideas of others and then seek to add your own voice to an ongoing conversation. One way to begin that conversation is to discover what others before you have said, thought, written, and published and to keep track of that process in your research log.

FIGURE 5.4 The iceberg of research.

AT A GLANCE

Using Your Research Log

As you begin gathering sources, follow the crucial steps below.

1. Note where and when you find new ideas.
2. Keep a detailed and careful record.
3. List all the search terms you try and note how helpful each is.
4. Write a short paragraph on your discovery of source leads.
5. Keep notes on your developing ideas about this argument.
6. Jot down quotes from sources, including page numbers and direct quotes.
7. List your sources in full, including author, title, place of publication, and date.
8. Copy down complete URLs for Web articles and image sources online.
9. Feel free to brainstorm new ideas and ways you could develop your argument or change your research direction.

This chapter addresses the fears and anxieties that can be obstacles on the research path. We'll use the metaphor of the *conversation* to accentuate the point that the research process is an act of *composing a response to an ongoing dialogue about a topic*. By gathering, synthesizing, and sorting the perspectives of others, you begin to shape your own stance on a research topic. By adding your voice as a writer, you are responding to others. Research is a *relationship* that you develop with the source material and the writers you encounter along the way.

Developing Search Terms

The first step in the research process lies in locating relevant and interesting sources to draw into your conversation. This involves finding the best **search terms** to use in looking for sources on your topic. Your search terms will change depending on whether you are searching the Web, a library catalog, or an academic database. You will need to identify the most productive keywords for searching in each of these situations.

Let's take as our example a project about Internet advertising. In a preliminary Web search, you would find that specific terms such as "pop-up ads," "banner ads," and "ethics & advertising online" would yield more results than generic terms like "Internet advertising" and "Internet advertisements." Moving to your library catalog, you would likely find that a successful search requires *different terms* than you used in your broader Web search. That is, you might instead use academic terminology, such as "electronic commerce" or "Internet marketing," because those phrases appear in scholarly book titles. However, if you search a database such as LexisNexis (a resource for news articles as well as legal, medical, and business articles), your keywords might change again to be closer to your preliminary Internet search. In this case, searching a database using the term "Internet advertising" would provide you with more than 90 citations in popular magazines and journals, while "pop-up ads" would yield only 16 hits, an inverse amount from your Internet search. As you can see, experimenting with a range of terms can help you narrow your sources by finding materials relevant to your topic.

AT A GLANCE

Tips for Using Search Terms

- **Web:** Use popular or colloquial terminology in your Internet searches because search engines pick up actual terms from pages as they crawl across the Web.

- **Library:** The Library of Congress has created a set of terms used by librarians to catalog information. These Library of Congress Subject Headings (LCSHs), as they are called, may not be obvious to you. (For example, the Library of Congress calls the Vietnam War the "Vietnamese Conflict, 1961–1975," so you won't find anything if you put "Vietnam War" into a subject heading search in a library catalog.) You can find the LCSH terms in two ways: by looking at a library record online or by consulting the print index. By plugging the terms into your library catalog, you can access information for your project more efficiently.

- **Databases:** Since databases can house a wide range of materials, from academic publications to popular articles, you will have to customize your language based on the database you have selected. Match your search terms in diction and formality to suit the type of resource you are exploring.

For instance, you might use the more specific term "Internet advertising & law" to narrow your search and focus on the legal aspect of the issue if that interests you. Through such experimentation you will find the search term that yields the most productive results.

CREATIVE PRACTICE

Perform a search on your topic, first on the Web, then in your library catalog, and then in a database. Experiment with your search terms and record your results in your research log. Now locate the Library of Congress Subject Headings for your topic (often located in library citations under the "subject" header), and use those terms in another catalog search. Do you achieve different results? Are your results more tailored to your needs or more general? In your research log, assess which search terms function best.

Primary and Secondary Sources

Your initial searches will yield a range of sources—from magazine articles to books, video recordings, and perhaps even manuscripts or a photograph collection. Each of these sources can play a vital role in your research. Scholars divide research into primary and secondary research, and sources, likewise, into **primary sources** (original texts you analyze in your research paper) and **secondary sources** (sources that provide commentary on your primary material or on your topic in general).

Consider, for instance, Tommy Tsai's project, examined in detail in Chapter 4. Propaganda posters were Tommy's *primary sources,* and the articles, books, and transcribed interviews providing analysis of those posters were his *secondary sources.* His paper is now *another* secondary source, one that contributes to an ongoing intellectual discussion about the meaning and power of the posters.

AT A GLANCE

Primary and Secondary Sources

- *Primary sources:* materials that you will analyze for your paper, including speech scripts, advertisements, photographs, historical documents, film, artwork, audio files, and writing on Websites. Primary sources can also include testimonies by people with firsthand knowledge or direct quotations you will analyze. Whatever is under the lens of your analysis constitutes a *primary source.*

- *Secondary sources:* the additional materials that help you analyze your primary sources by providing a perspective on those primary materials; these include scholarly articles, popular commentaries, background materials (in print, video, or interview format), and survey data reinforcing your analysis. Whatever sources you can use as a lens to look at or understand the subject of your analysis constitutes a *secondary source.*

But as you search for your research materials, keep in mind that no sources are *inherently* primary or secondary; those terms refer to *how you use them* in your paper. For instance, if you were working with the topic of Internet advertising, you might use actual banner ads and Flash animations as your primary sources, as well as press releases and advertising Websites. For secondary sources you might turn to articles that discuss innovations in on-line marketing, a Website on the history of digital advertising, and perhaps even a book by a famous economist about the impact of technology on corporate marketing strategies. However, imagine that you shift your topic slightly, making your new focus the economist's theories about the corruption of traditional advertising by multimedia technology. Now, that same book you looked at before as a *secondary* source becomes a *primary* source for this new topic.

As you can see, your inquiry will determine which sources will be primary and which will be secondary for your argument. In most cases, you will need to use a combination of primary and secondary materials to make a persuasive argument. The primary sources allow you to perform your own analysis, whereas the secondary sources offer you critical viewpoints that you need to take into account in your analysis and integrate into your argument to build up your ethos. How you respond to and combine your primary and secondary sources is a matter of choice, careful design, and rhetorical strategy.

Finding Primary Sources

Searching for **primary sources** can sometimes be challenging; they come in many forms but can also be some of the most exciting sources to work with in your research process. Consider, for instance, the sources that student James Caputo used in his project on the media representations of the early years of the NASA space program. James had many fascinating primary resources to work with: John F. Kennedy's inspirational speeches about the formation of the space program; front pages of both American and Russian newspapers detailing the successful completion of the first Apollo mission; publicity shots of the astronauts; the first images—both still and moving—from the moon's surface; and advertisements published after the first moon landing that showed the space program's attempts to win public support through publicity. He chose to focus on multiple magazine covers and images from magazine articles for his primary source materials (see Figures 5.5 and 5.6).

The image in Figure 5.5 originally appeared in an article published in *Collier's* magazine on October 23, 1948, concerning the military applications of space travel. James analyzed it and found that it was intended to warn American readers of the consequences of falling behind in the "space race" with the Russians. Similarly, Figure 5.6, a cover shot from *Time*'s July 25, 1969 issue, relied on pathos to persuade the American readers to view the U.S. space program in a certain light. James found that the image,

FIGURE 5.5 James used this illustration, "The Rocket Blitz from the Moon," which originally accompanied a 1948 *Collier's* magazine article, as a powerful primary source for his research paper.

FIGURE 5.6 James also analyzed other primary sources, including magazine covers like this one from a 1969 issue of *Time*.

Seeing Connections
For more examples of the argumentative function of primary sources like magazine covers, see the Sports Illustrated covers featured on pages 372–373.

with its strong nationalistic overtones, cast the successful Apollo 11 mission once again in terms of the Cold War and the American-Soviet space race. He placed these primary sources at the center of his research argument, and then he turned to secondary sources to substantiate his own claims about them.

Primary materials like the one James found are more accessible than you might think. They can be found in your library—whether in the general stacks, archives, or multimedia collections—or at community centers such as library exhibits, museums, and city hall. Many public libraries have special collections and archives with particularly rich primary source materials, including the following:

- Original documents (perhaps a handwritten letter by Mahatma Gandhi, the design sketches of a propaganda poster artist, or Charles Lindbergh's journals)
- Rare books and manuscripts (such as an illustrated first edition of William Blake's *Songs of Innocence and Experience* or Roger Manvell's manuscripts on the history of the Third Reich)
- Portfolios of photographs (photos of Japanese American internment camps or of Black Panther demonstrations from the 1960s)
- Other one-of-a-kind texts (for example, AIDS prevention posters from South Africa, a noted artist's sketchbook, or a series of leaflets produced by the U.S. Psychological Warfare Department, distributed to the Vietnamese during the Vietnam War)
- Government documents (including U.S. censuses and surveys, reports from the Department of Agriculture, or even congressional papers).

Seeing Connections
For effective discussion of primary sources, see Susan Sontag's "America Seen Through Photographs Darkly" on page 537.

In many cases, you can work directly with these materials so you can perform your own first-hand analysis of that piece of cultural history.

While the best way to determine the holdings of your college library or community museum may be to search a catalog or contact a reference librarian, an increasing number of academic institutions and organizations digitize their collections to make them widely available to an international community of researchers. Your school's electronic access to primary sources might be as simple as a list on the library Website of holdings you can explore at the library itself. Alternatively, it might be as extensive as a complete set of digital reproductions or links to Internet archives of primary materials that you can analyze.

Searching for Secondary Sources

Just as important as your primary materials are your **secondary sources**—texts that provide commentary on your topic and often analyze the texts you have chosen as primary sources. The writers of these texts offer the voices with which you will engage in scholarly conversation as you develop the substance of your argument.

Your first stop in your search for secondary sources should be your library's reference area, the home of dictionaries, guides, encyclopedias, bibliographies, and other resource materials. These storehouses of important information can be invaluable in providing you with the *foundational information* for your project, including basic definitions, historical background, and brief bibliographies. Yet, while such "background" materials are necessary to help you construct a framework for your research argument, they represent only one part of your *iceberg of research*. For more rigorous analysis, you should turn to books and articles that provide critical analysis and arguments about your specific research subject. To locate these more specific secondary sources, you might search your library catalog for relevant books and films and other published materials. However, you also have another valuable type of resource available to you: databases and indexes.

You'll find databases and indexes indispensable to your research because they provide you with bibliographic citations for academic articles on your topic of interest. Keep in mind that databases can come in many forms: they can be housed on CD-ROMs, online, or as collections of electronic journals. Additionally, although some databases provide only a bibliographic citation that you can use to locate the source in your library catalog, many include a detailed abstract summarizing a source's argument, and others link you to full-text electronic copies of the articles you are searching for.

As you continue to search for sources, remember that the best strategy for keeping

AT A GLANCE

Using One Source to Locate Additional Sources

Here's the process for finding sources:

1. Locate one relevant source through the library catalog.
2. Retrieve it from the library stacks.
3. Spend some time looking over books in the same area to discover additional books on the same topic.
4. Assess briefly the applicability of each text to your project, and check out the ones most valuable to you.
5. Look at the bibliographies in the backs of your most useful books to locate sources that were helpful to the authors and may be of use to you.
6. Repeat the process often to build your iceberg of research.

careful track of your research process entails recording the dates, details, and relevance of your searches in your *research log;* you might also want to keep a running list of your sources by call number and title, or include printouts of relevant articles or database entries, as Vivian Chang did for her research log on a project discussing the fantasy world of *The Lord of the Rings.* (See Figure 5.7)

Although databases, catalogs, and search engines provide indispensable tools for conducting your research, don't overlook the resource you have in your peers. As colleagues in the research journey, your peers will have discovered helpful print sources, databases, and indexes. Ask others who are working on

Finding Secondary Sources

You can use the following library resources to locate secondary material:

- *Dictionaries, guides, encyclopedias:* Such foundational texts provide helpful background information for your topic.
- *Library catalog:* This engine allows you to search the library holdings for relevant books or documentaries.
- *CD-ROM indexes and bibliographies:* These CDs contain vast amounts of bibliographic information, but often they can be used only in the reference section of the library.
- *Electronic databases and indexes:* These databases are available on the Internet through subscription only; many provide access to full-text versions of articles from a range of sources.
- *Electronic journals:* Many libraries offer access to the full digital versions of academic journals for a range of disciplines.

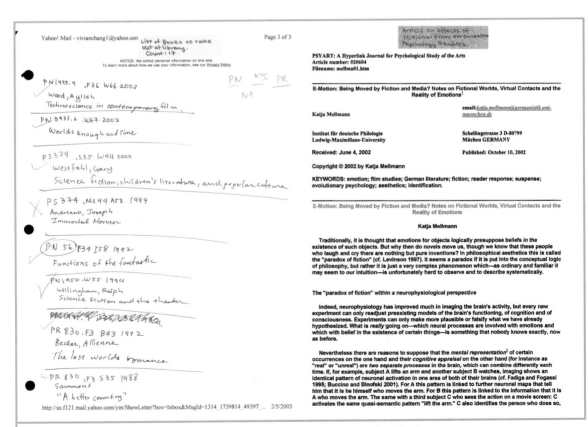

FIGURE 5.7 Vivian Chang's research log includes both handwritten notes and annotated article printouts.

Seeing Connections
For an example of how secondary sources can enrich your argument, see Helen Kennedy, "Lara Croft: Feminist Icon or Cyberbimbo?" on page 479.

AT A GLANCE

Recording Searches in Your Research Log

- Date each entry in your log to keep track of your progress and show the evolution of your ideas.
- Write down complete identifying information for any source you consult, including images on the Web, articles online, journals or magazines in the library, articles from library databases, and chapters in books.
- Double-check transcribed quotations for accuracy while you still have the source before you, and include page numbers (or paragraph numbers for Website articles).
- Annotate the entry by including an evaluation of the source and an indication of how you might use it as part of your final paper.
- If you are using Web sources, be aware that Websites tend to be updated or to simply disappear. To avoid losing important source material, print out significant Webpages and insert them into your log or download them to your hard drive and include them on a CD-ROM with your research log.

similar topics to share their research logs, and help each other along the route of your research. This is particularly true for the stage in your research when you produce a *preliminary bibliography*—a working list of the sources for your iceberg of research.

COLLABORATIVE CHALLENGE

Form groups of three or four and share your preliminary bibliographies. To prepare, each person should practice locating and evaluating sources. First, each person should come up with three to six keywords as well as Library of Congress Subject Heading about the topic, and then perform a search for both primary and secondary sources. Make sure each person explores print sources through the library catalog as well as online texts through databases and e-journals. Then, each person should produce a preliminary bibliography —a list of eight to ten potential sources. Next, get into your groups and share your preliminary bibliographies. Each person in the group should spend five minutes presenting a narrative of his or her research process: What sources have you found so far? Which databases were unexpectedly fruitful to your search? What journals hold the most helpful secondary sources? How are you formatting your research log? Then, have each person in the group lend another person a particularly useful source. Broaden the base of your research argument by incorporating more sources.

Evaluating Your Sources

Implementing these research strategies to locate primary and secondary materials will provide you with access to many interesting sources, but how do you discriminate among them to find those that will be the best for your argument? The key rests in understanding the argumentative perspective, or *rhetorical stance,* of each source. At times, the source's stance may be self-evident: you may automatically gravitate toward experts in the field, well known for their opinions and affiliations. It is just as likely, however, that you may not be familiar with the names or ideas of your sources. In either case, it is essential to develop a method for evaluating the sources you encounter.

Evaluating Websites

For many of us, when we hear the words "research paper," our first impulse is to log onto the Internet and plug our topic into a search engine such as Google (http://www.google.com). However, because you are likely to encounter a vast number of hits, you will need a method for assessing the credibility and usefulness of your findings.

To understand effective methods of evaluating different types of sources, let's take the example of a research paper on the stem cell debate. What would be the best way to evaluate sources for this project? For instance, if you search the term "stem cells," you are likely to generate close to a million results. On the one hand, such a plentiful search gives you ample means to "eavesdrop" on the ongoing conversation about your topic; on the other hand, the sheer magnitude of hits can be overwhelming. Faced with such a massive amount of material, how do you begin to sort through them to identify those most helpful to your research?

Your best resource in this situation is your skill as a rhetorician. While opening various Webpages, consider how their visual and verbal elements suggest the sites' rhetorical stances and points of view on topic. The CNN.com "In-Depth Special" on the stem cell debate provides a good example of how rhetorical analysis factors into the research process (see Figure 5.8 on the following page). As you study this page, three prominent aspects of the site probably stand out: the large CNN.com logo in the upper-right corner, which establishes the ethos of the site; the topic header, "The Stem Cell Debate," which identifies the focus and approach of the page; and the picture of the scientist at work. From here you can perform a more careful analysis of the way this homepage suggests CNN's approach to the stem cell issue, including the written words categorizing this debate into "issues," "science," "politics," and "analysis."

The writing is very scientific and logos based in tone, providing a credible source for your project. You can even analyze the words of the opening blurb:

> A year after President Bush's decision on stem cell research, scientists say they are being hindered by federal rules governing the use of embryonic stem cells because access to stem cell lines approved for research is limited. But the director of the National Institutes of Health said the agency is "diligently working" to make more cell lines available.

Notice how the paragraph begins with an appeal to an authority, President Bush, and then uses strong language to convey its stance on the issue—that scientists are "hindered by federal rules." These words give you a clue to the stance of the article: it is pro-science, anti-government. The words work together with the image of the scientist to provide one side on the issue of stem cell research.

Consider how this works for another example from your Google search. A quick glance at the stem cell page for the American Association for the Advancement of

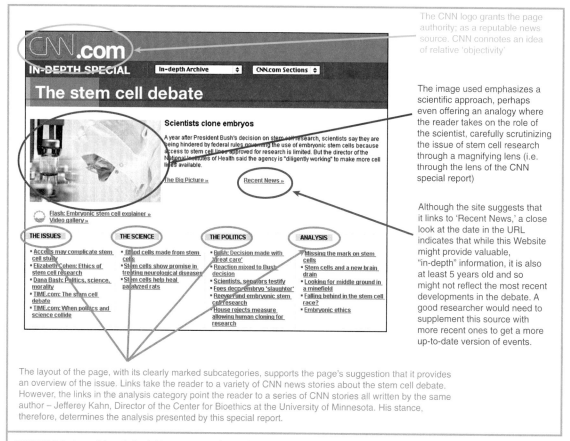

The CNN logo grants the page authority; as a reputable news source. CNN connotes an idea of relative 'objectivity'

The image used emphasizes a scientific approach, perhaps even offering an analogy where the reader takes on the role of the scientist, carefully scrutinizing the issue of stem cell research through a magnifying lens (i.e. through the lens of the CNN special report)

Although the site suggests that it links to 'Recent News,' a close look at the date in the URL indicates that while this Website might provide valuable, "in-depth" information, it is also at least 5 years old and so might not reflect the most recent developments in the debate. A good researcher would need to supplement this source with more recent ones to get a more up-to-date version of events.

The layout of the page, with its clearly marked subcategories, supports the page's suggestion that it provides an overview of the issue. Links take the reader to a variety of CNN news stories about the stem cell debate. However, the links in the analysis category point the reader to a series of CNN stories all written by the same author – Jefferey Kahn, Director of the Center for Bioethics at the University of Minnesota. His stance, therefore, determines the analysis presented by this special report.

FIGURE 5.8 A careful analysis of this CNN.com Webpage demonstrates its rhetorical stance on the issue of stem cell research; notice the words of the title bars.

Science, shown in Figure 5.9, might indicate that it is also a prime candidate for your work. It is directly related to your topic, it showcases a comprehensive report on the topic, and it even offers links to other sources on stem cell research. However, more careful scrutiny of the site is necessary to fully gauge the organization's stance on the issue. Through rhetorical analysis, you can evaluate this source for your project.

Specifically, assess the written language. The header—*Scientific Freedom, Responsibility and Law*—encapsulates the tensions inherent in the stem cell debate between the desire to maintain the researcher's freedom to conduct research as he sees fit with questions of moral responsibility and legality; in this way, the page suggests that it provides a balanced approach to the issue. Yet phrases in the central paragraph, such as *extraordinary advances* and *unprecedented opportunities,* indicate a stronger position on the topic. The question is not whether stem cell research should continue (a question that might concern other organizations), but how to carry on stem cell research "in an ethical manner." Having identified the stance, your task as a researcher is not only to

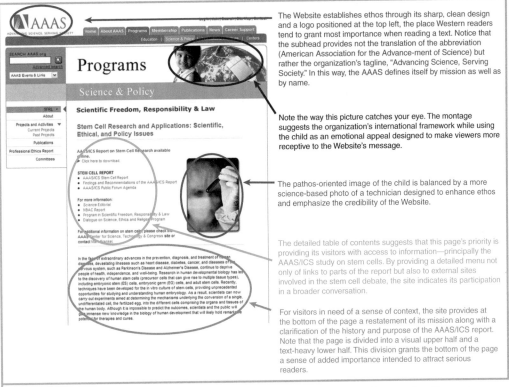

The Website establishes ethos through its sharp, clean design and a logo positioned at the top left, the place Western readers tend to grant most importance when reading a text. Notice that the subhead provides not the translation of the abbreviation (American Association for the Advance-ment of Science) but rather the organization's tagline, "Advancing Science, Serving Society." In this way, the AAAS defines itself by mission as well as by name.

Note the way this picture catches your eye. The montage suggests the organization's international framework while using the child as an emotional appeal designed to make viewers more receptive to the Website's message.

The pathos-oriented image of the child is balanced by a more science-based photo of a technician designed to enhance ethos and emphasize the credibility of the Website.

The detailed table of contents suggests that this page's priority is providing its visitors with access to information—principally the AAAS/ICS study on stem cells. By providing a detailed menu not only of links to parts of the report but also to external sites involved in the stem cell debate, the site indicates its participation in a broader conversation.

For visitors in need of a sense of context, the site provides at the bottom of the page a restatement of its mission along with a clarification of the history and purpose of the AAAS/ICS report. Note that the page is divided into a visual upper half and a text-heavy lower half. This division grants the bottom of the page a sense of added importance intended to attract serious readers.

FIGURE 5.9 The American Association for the Advancement of Science stem cell page combines words and images to encourage readers to access—and trust—its report on the issue.

Source: Screenshot of AAAS science & Policy webpage: http://www.aaas.org/spp/sfri/projects/stem/index.shtml. Reprinted with permission from AAAS.

take this position into account while reading, but also to broaden your research to include many different perspectives on the issue.

As you can see, you need to take special care in evaluating Webpages since the reliability varies widely across the Internet. Attention to the visual and verbal rhetoric of a site's homepage—its "cover"—is essential to understanding its argument and therefore its suitability as a research source. After assessing the "cover" pages of each Website, the next step is to move deeper into the site to analyze its content and argument.

CREATIVE PRACTICE

Compare the Websites shown in Figures 5.8 and 5.9 with two others generated from searching "stem cell" on Google: the Stem Cell Research Foundation site and the DoNoHarm site (see Figures 5.10 and 5.11 on the following page).

What rhetorical decisions are apparent from each site's homepage design? How do the images suggest different approaches to the stem cell issue? How does the organization of information, the menu, and the written text contribute to this impression? Follow the site links to explore how the rhetorical stance suggested by the "cover" is reflected in the site's contents. Evaluate these two pages as sources for a paper on stem cell research. Develop a list of criteria for evaluating Webpages, and share it with the class.

FIGURE 5.10 Homepage for the Stem Cell Research Foundation.

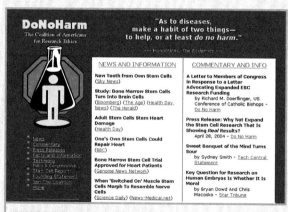

FIGURE 5.11 Homepage for the Do No Harm site.

The list of criteria generated by the "Creative Practice" may have varied from person to person, but most likely everyone focused on issues of authority, accessibility, and suitability in assessing the Webpages. After your preliminary rhetorical analysis, you might have looked at the URL to establish the author or host of a Website, or you might have examined the selection of images or the word choice for indications of bias or sensationalism. Perhaps you looked for the "last updated" note to check the currency of the site or for the "contact" link to evaluate the author's sense of accountability for his or her work. You may have followed the links to see if the site was self-contained, linking only to its own materials, or whether it contained external links, connecting it to the broader conversation on the topic. In addition, you most likely evaluated the *type* of material the site contained: primary documents or secondary commentary. Each of these steps inevitably took you beyond the cover, deeper into the contents of the site and closer to assessing its appropriateness as a source for your own research.

Evaluating Library and Database Sources

Clearly, popular Websites provided a multitude of sources for your project on stem cells. However, it's important to remember that no matter how productive a Google search may be, for almost all college research papers, you will need to seek out sources through library shelves and databases since they host scholarly materials that will be more useful for your project.

Let's see how you might evaluate library and database sources for your stem cell research paper. Your first stop would be the library's reference area, where you look up foundational information in the *Encyclopedia of Bioethics*. Then you would search the library catalog for book-length sources, generating a long list of citations. You then decide to track down some journal articles that, you reason, will provide balance to your research because they often represent the most current discussions on a topic. To find relevant articles, you begin searching the electronic databases that most closely suit the specific focus of your project: SciSearch, MEDLINE, LegalPeriodical, BIOSIS. You produce an impressive list of citations and even retrieve a few full-text articles. You also search some sources that are more news related, including LexisNexis and ProQuest, to

AT A GLANCE

Evaluating Websites

- Who is the author of the Website? Is it a personal Website or is it institutionally affiliated? What sort of authority does it draw on?
- Does the author take responsibility for the page by offering a place for comments or an email link for feedback?
- Who is the audience?
- What is the purpose?
- What is the rhetorical stance of this Website? Does it deal with both sides of the issue or only one side?
- Does it offer links to other sites on the Web?
- How timely is the page? Does it have a date? Does someone maintain the Website? Are there broken links?
- Is it an archive of primary material? If so, does it cite the original sources in a correct and complete manner?
- Is it easy to navigate? Does it have a search engine?

find a selection of references to popular newspaper and magazine articles that will balance the scholarly sources. Finally, armed with your list of citations, you head into the library stacks, returning shortly after with a rather heavy collection of books and bound periodicals.

Your first search complete, you can now retreat to a quiet space and assess the significance and value of your findings. You can be relatively confident in the quality of the texts you've accumulated because library holdings and scholarly databases tend to contain materials that have been more rigorously screened than those found through an Internet search engine. However, keep in mind that you'll still need to apply the same evaluation criteria to these texts as you would to Web sources.

You can start by assessing the visual rhetoric of some of the journal covers spread across your desk, beginning the process of assessing topic, stance, and reliability. You might, for instance, have come across the two covers found in Figures 5.12 and 5.13. A rhetorical analysis reveals differences in purpose, audience, and focus. *Stem Cells,* by using an actual image of embryonic cells, signals its focus on cellular biology and scientific applications; in addition, by listing its table of contents—complete with authors and article titles—on the front cover, it privileges ethos as an appeal. *Yale Scientific*

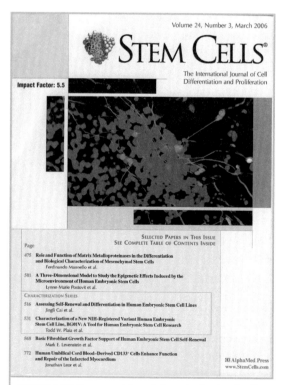

FIGURE 5.12 The cover of *Stem Cells* emphasizes its scientific approach in choices in cover image and text.

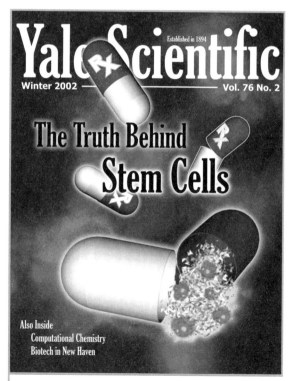

FIGURE 5.13 The cover of *Yale Scientific* zooms in on the debate rather than on the science of stem cells.

chooses a different approach, using a powerful visual metaphor coupled with the term "Truth" to suggest its engagement with the debate surrounding stem cell research.

However, in many cases you may not be able to use a cover image as a guide to evaluation; many scholarly journals and books have been re-covered in plain library bindings. In that case, what steps should you take to select those that would be most productive for your research?

First, assess the **author.** Perhaps your teacher recommended the author to you or you notice that the author has written many books and articles on the topic. You can look this person up in a bibliography index or on the Web to assess the ethos of the writer. If the author turns out to be disreputable or affiliated with an extreme organization, would the source still be an important one to consider? Would the exaggerated stance help you argue for the existence of extremist positions on your topic?

Check out the **place of publication.** Is it a university press (suggesting peer-reviewed scholarship) or a trade press (suggesting a commercial venture)? Is it published by a foundation or organization (suggesting a political agenda) or self-published (suggesting the author's struggle to have his or her views accepted for publication)?

Look also at the **date.** Is it a recent contribution or an older study? An older source can provide historical context, but sometimes it can be too outdated to be useful. Usually, you should pick the more recent sources to engage the most timely perspectives on your topic.

Next, go beneath the cover of the book or journal. Open it and turn to the **table of contents** and the **index** to see exactly what the book contains. Is it a collection of articles by different authors, or does it reflect the viewpoint of a single author?

Now flip through the pages, looking for interesting arguments and judging the quality or complexity of the writing. You may note its **voice** or **tone:** Is it written for specialists in the field or for a popular audience? Does it focus on issues relevant to your research?

This rhetorical attention to the writing—the language, tone, date, context, and stance of the author—even at this early stage, is crucial to successful assessment of each of your sources. For the articles you collected for your stem cell research project, you might come across Gretchen Vogel's "Can Old Cells Learn New Tricks?" from the February 25, 2000 issue of *Science* (see Figure 5.14 on the following page). Opening to the first page, you can perform a quick rhetorical analysis of its visual and verbal elements to evaluate its usefulness.

The first things that probably catch your eye are the colorful images of stem cells, as close up as if they were being viewed through the lens of a microscope. This imagery suggests that the article will have a scientific focus, and yet the arrows leading to each of the images suggest that it will teach a popular audience something new about stem cells.

AT A GLANCE

Evaluating Academic Sources

- **Author:** Is the author an expert in his or her field? What professional or personal affiliations or experiences has this author had that might have influenced his or her argument or ethos?

- **Date:** When was the text published? If not recently, might it be outdated? Is it a text that sets a certain framework for discussion that other writers have since built on? Or does it offer a new perspective to an ongoing discussion?

- **Publisher:** Is the publisher an academic or popular press? Which would be most appropriate for your topic? Does the publisher have any connection to the topic under discussion?

- **Rhetorical stance:** What is the author's point of view on the topic? Is it moderate or extreme? How does that affect his or her treatment of the issue?

- **Audience:** For whom was this work intended: an academic or a popular audience? What level of specialized knowledge does the author assume that the audience has?

- **Relevance to your project:** How does this text relate to your argument? Does it provide background material? an opposing opinion? a supporting argument?

Can Old Cells Learn New Tricks?

Stem cells found in adults show surprising versatility. But it's not yet clear whether they can match the power of cells from embryos

Stem cell biologist Margaret Goodell has never seen her work on muscle and blood development as particularly political, so she was surprised when last month the Coalition of Americans for Research Ethics (CARE), a group that opposes the use of embryos in research, invited her to speak at a congressional briefing in Washington, D.C. She was even more astonished to find herself quoted by conservative columnist George Will a few weeks later.

Goodell gained this sudden notoriety because her work, and that of other teams around the world, just might provide a way around the moral and political quagmire that has engulfed stem cell research to date. Since their discovery in 1998, human embryonic stem cells have been

says bioethicist and CARE member Kevin Fitzgerald of Loyola University Medical Center in Chicago.

But can adult stem cells really fulfill the same potential as embryonic stem cells can? At this stage, the answer is by no means clear. Indeed, scientists caution that it is too early to know if even ES cells will produce the cornucopia of new tissues and organs that some envision. "It is still early days in the human embryonic stem cell world," says stem cell biologist Daniel Marshak of Osiris Therapeutics in Baltimore, which works with adult-derived stem cells.

From a scientific standpoint, adult and embryonic stem cells both have distinct benefits and drawbacks. And harnessing either one will be tough. Although scientists have

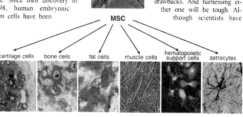

Multitalented. Mesenchymal stem cells (MSC) from adult bone marrow can become bone, cartilage, and even brain cells in lab culture.

one of the hottest scientific properties around. Because these cells can theoretically be coaxed to differentiate into any type of cell in the body, they open up tantalizing possibilities, such as lab-grown tissues or even replacement organs to treat a variety of human ills, from diabetes to Alzheimer's. Politically, however, human stem cells have been a much tougher sell, as they are derived from embryos or fetuses. Indeed, most research is on hold as policy-makers grapple with the ethics of human embryo research.

Enter Goodell, whose work suggests that stem cells derived from *adults*, in this case, from mouse muscle biopsies, can perform many of the same tricks as embryonic stem (ES) cells can—but without the ethical baggage. Both CARE and George Will seized upon her work as an indication that research on ES cells could remain on hold with no appreciable loss to medicine. "There's a lot less moral ambiguity about the adult stem cells."

been working with mouse ES cells for 2 decades, most work has focused on creating transgenic mice rather than creating lab-grown tissues. Only a handful of groups around the world have discovered how to nudge the cells toward certain desired fates. But that work gained new prominence in late 1998, when two independent teams, led by James Thomson of the University of Wisconsin, Madison, and John Gearhart of The Johns Hopkins University, announced they could grow human stem cells in culture. Suddenly the work in mouse cells could be applied to human cells—in the hope of curing disease.

The beauty of embryonic stem cells lies in their malleability. One of their defining characteristics is their ability to differentiate into any cell type. Indeed, researchers have shown that they can get mouse ES cells to differentiate in lab culture into various tissues, including brain cells and pancreatic cells.

Studies with rodents also indicated that cells derived from ES cells could restore certain missing nerve functions, suggesting the possibility of treating neurological disorders. Last summer, Oliver Brüstle of the University of Bonn Medical Center and Ronald McKay of the U.S. National Institute of Neurological Disorders and Stroke and their colleagues reported that they could coax mouse ES cells to become glial cells, a type of neuronal support cell that produces the neuron-protecting myelin sheath. When the team then injected these cells into the brains of mice that lacked myelin, the transplants produced normal-looking myelin (*Science*, 30 July 1999, p. 754). And in December, a team led by Dennis Choi and John McDonald at Washington University School of Medicine in St. Louis showed that immature nerve cells that were generated from mouse ES cells and transplanted into the damaged spinal cords of rats partially restored the animals' spinal cord function (*Science*, 3 December 1999, p. 1826). Although no one has yet published evidence that human ES cells can achieve similar feats, Gearhart says he is working with several groups at Johns Hopkins to test the abilities of his cells in animal models of spinal cord injury and neurodegenerative diseases, including amyotrophic lateral sclerosis and Parkinson's disease.

While Gearhart and his colleagues were grappling with ES cells, Goodell and others were concentrating on adult stem cells. Conventional wisdom had assumed that once a cell had been programmed to produce a particular tissue, its fate was sealed, and it could not reprogram itself to make another tissue. But in the last year, a number of studies have surprised scientists by showing that stem cells from one tissue, such as brain, could change into another, such as blood (*Science*, 22 January 1999, p. 534). Evidence is mounting that the findings are not aberrations but may signal the unexpected power of adult stem cells. For example, Goodell and her colleagues, prompted by the discovery of blood-forming brain cells, found that cells from mouse muscle could repopulate the bloodstream and rescue mice that had received an otherwise lethal dose of radiation.

Bone marrow stem cells may be even more versatile. At the American Society of Hematology meeting in December, hematologist Catherine Verfaillie of the University of Minnesota, Minneapolis, reported that she has isolated cells from the bone marrow of children and adults that seem to have an amazing range of abilities. For instance, Verfaillie and graduate student Morayma

FIGURE 5.14 The first page of Vogel's article on her innovations in stem cell research.

The first paragraph confirms the more popular focus of the piece; rather than starting with detail about the characteristics or applications of stem cells, the introduction zooms in on an individual biologist and her own reluctant participation in the ethical debate. By skimming, you see that the writing is clear and engaging, even when it is describing technical issues. Furthermore, you find that the rest of the article both explores some of the more recent scientific discoveries and, true to its introductory frame, continues to position that science in relation to the ethical debate. Since you are concerned as much with the debate as with the mechanics of stem cells, you can quickly ascertain that this article will be very helpful in your formulating your own analysis of the issue.

As our analysis of Vogel's article reveals, the most important assessment question is how *useful* a source will be for your project and your potential argument. Then you are on your way to knowing *how* you will use that text from your iceberg of research to craft your own research-based argument on the issue. Depending on your project, you might decide that you want to use not only print and electronic sources but also **field research** in the form of interviews or surveys. Collecting these sources often involves fieldwork, gathering and collecting your own evidence and data. For instance, one student, Megan Nesland, used fieldwork prominently in her research project about elevated asbestos levels at a local reservoir. In her preliminary research, she found many articles by community activists, geologists, and environmental experts on the extent and dangers of the contamination. However, she soon realized that her argument would be much more powerful if it drew on her own first-hand impressions. Consequently, she took an afternoon to visit the reservoir, where she interviewed hikers about their awareness of the asbestos issue, took a tour with a local geologist who pointed out key rock formations to her, and even took photographs that highlighted the incipient asbestos problem to use as visual evidence in her paper (see Figure 5.15).

FIGURE 5.15 Megan's photo and caption: "A large serpentinite outcrop alongside the Crystal Springs Reservoir, already showing signs of its hidden asbestos."

This field research added depth to her argument by allowing her to uncover her own evidence to support her argument. Not all fieldwork involves trips to local sites. Sometimes you gather your own primary data about a topic from carefully determined sample groups or individuals. If you were interested in studying grade inflation at your campus, for instance, you might do a survey of a sample of students and professors. If you were studying the layout and impact of a new proposed park in your community, you might interview a city planner or the landscape architect involved in the project. One student, Sean Bruich, writing on visual rhetoric marketing strategies used by the Oakland Athletics baseball team, wrote a letter to the team's marketing coordinator. Consult his letter to learn how to begin your field research.

Sean writes a formal letter to the contact he has found for his field research.

April 7, 2003

Lynne Tibbet

Sales & Marketing Coordinator

Oakland Athletics

Dear Ms. Tibbet,

He introduces himself and his project fully, relying on ethos and stating the purpose of his letter early.

My name is Sean Bruich and I am a freshman at Stanford University. As part of Stanford's required courses in writing, I am enrolled in Dr. Alyssa O'Brien's course on Visual Rhetoric. Writing a sizable research paper that focuses on visual rhetoric is a required portion of this class. As a long-time fan of the Oakland Athletics, I was hoping to write my paper on the marketing strategies employed by the Athletics over the course of the last few years (specifically, I'm hoping to focus on the "Baseball Country" and "Baseball: A's Style" ads since they are so memorable).

At this point I'd like to request some materials from the Athletics. Specifically, if the A's could send me, by either email or by mail, the print materials from these campaigns, I would be really appreciative. In addition, if possible, I would love to also get copies of some of the commercial spots

He makes his request specific and feasible, taking into account any potential obstacles.

that are shown on TV. I will reimburse your office for any and all expenses incurred, including materials and mailing costs.

At some point, I'd like also to discuss with you or one of your colleagues how the A's create and direct their marketing campaigns, if you have the time available.

I only need ads that are now or have been in the marketplace—I'm not in any way requesting unpublished work. I will talk to my professor to ensure that none of these materials extend beyond this project, and are not republished or retransmitted in any way without prior permissions from the Athletics. In addition, if the A's need me to sign any confidentiality agreements, I would be happy to do so.

  Basically, I'm going to start working on this term paper in the course of the next week or so, although I do have several smaller writing assignments that could be aided greatly by these materials if I can get hold of them sooner.

  Please do not hesitate to contact me if you have questions or want to discuss this situation further.

Thank you very much for your time!

Regards,

Sean

Sean Bruich
P.O. Box 12345
Stanford, CA 54321
(650) 555-1878 (dorm)
(650) 555-7694 (cell)
seanstudent@university.edu

He offers to sign a confidentiality agreement, a rhetorical strategy to convince his audience to send him field research materials.

He ends politely, with an invitation for the person to contact him. He lists his full contact information, including an email address.

You also can take advantage of resources closer to home by interviewing faculty members from your university who have written or lectured on subjects related to your topic. This is a great way to make contacts and develop your iceberg of research because, in addition to interviewing the faculty member as another secondary source, you can usually ask him or her to recommend two or three key books in the field that you might consult as you continue on your research journey.

Evaluating Fieldwork and Statistics

When you conduct interviews and surveys, you are looking for materials to use in your paper as supporting arguments, evidence, or statistical data. But as you pursue your interviews and surveys, keep in mind the need to evaluate your field research sources as carefully as you assess your print and electronic sources. If you interview a professor, a marketing executive, a witness, or a roommate, consider the rhetorical stance of that

AT A GLANCE

Conducting Interviews and Surveys

1. *Target your population:* Identify the best sources for your field research: a professor at your college who is expert in this area? a professional from the community? peers in your class, dorm, athletic team, or town?

2. *Develop questions:* Compose a list of questions to ask in your interview or survey. Review them with a peer or show them to your instructor. For interviews, avoid general questions; design your questions to elicit quotations you can use in your paper. For surveys, you want to balance short, multiple choice questions (that yield primarily statistical data) with some short answer question that will produced more nuanced responses. Keep your survey short; the longer your form, the fewer completed surveys will probably be returned to you.

3. *Prepare:* For interviews, look up the biography of the interviewee online or in the paper. Read any publications by the person so you can show you already know a little about the person's stance on the issue. Also, be ready to talk about your background knowledge in this area. For surveys, prepare by getting to know the population's stance on the issue and by researching the best mode of distribution for that population (for instance, an electronic form might not be the best choice when surveying populations with limited Internet access).

4. *Make contact:* For interviews, make initial contact by email, mail, or phone. Explain clearly your purpose, your identity, and your goal for the field research. Offer two or three concrete times that might work for the interviewee (check a professor's office hours or a professional's working hours); also offer to interview over the phone or by email. If your interviewee does not reply at first, send a polite follow-up email, asking for just 15 minutes of time, or requesting the name of someone who would be available instead. Don't hesitate to persist, but do so respectfully. For surveys, find a reliable means of distribution—in person or electronic—and, just as importantly, make clear on the survey a deadline and where/how the forms should be returned if you're not going to collect them immediately yourself.

5. *Record and document:* Ask permission from interviewees and survey subjects for you to use their words in your paper. If you record an interview with a tape recorder or cell phone device, be sure to ask permission first and to create a transcript as soon as possible after the interview. Document all uses of the interview with quotation marks in your paper.

6. *Follow-up:* If you do complete your field research successfully, send a thank you note to any interviewees and even offer a copy of your completed paper. Although it is more difficult to follow up with survey subjects, consider sharing your findings with them through a local newsletter or college newspaper article.

person. What kind of bias does the person have concerning the topic of your project? Similarly, if you conduct a survey of your peers or in your dorm, remember to assess the value and credibility of your results as rigorously as you would evaluate the data of a published study. It's easy to fall into the trap of misusing statistics when making claims if you haven't taken into account the need for **statistical significance,** or to paraphrase the social psychologist Philip Zimbardo, the measure by which a number obtains meaning in scientific fields. To reach this number, you need to design the survey carefully, conduct what's called a *random sample,* interview a *large enough* number of people, and ask a *range of different* people. These are complex parameters to follow, but you will need to learn about them to conduct survey research that has reliable and credible results. It's easy to draw improper conclusions without a clear understanding of statistics. Your teacher—or a psychology professor who is familiar with these concepts—can help you to design effective surveys and incorporate statistical evidence accurately into your research paper.

Let's turn again to Professor Zimbardo's explanation of statistics to understand how careful you need to be when using scientific data—whether your own surveys or a secondary source that relies on scientific studies and statistics—as evidence in your paper: "Statistics are the backbone of research. They are used to understand observations and to determine whether findings are, in fact, correct and significant. . . . But, statistics can also be used poorly or deceptively, misleading those who do not understand them" (595). The point is that statistics—though we often think of them as Truth—actually function rhetorically. Like words and images, numbers are a mode of persuasion that can mislead readers. Thus, you need to be especially vigilant when using a survey or statistics as a supposedly "objective" part of your iceberg of research, particularly if you plan to depend on such materials in your argument.

For example, the information graphic "Estimated number of new cancer cases, 1997-2006" provides an example of the argument that charts can be misleading in the way that it mixes and matches the years it samples. Clearly, you need to take as much care with how you convey information visually as you do with how you convey it in writing. We see this in David Pinner's writing project about grade inflation at the university level. David accumulated enough quantitative information through fieldwork and primary research to compose his own charts. He discovered a wealth of information in archived faculty senate minutes, which he sorted through during his research. From that work, he came across important statistical data that reflected the change in grade distribution at Stanford over the course of 25 years. In addition to including the numbers in his written text, he created two powerful pie charts (see Figure 5.17), using a visual comparison of

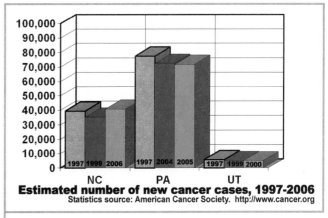

FIGURE 5.16 The bar graphs here might be based on figures from the American Cancer Society, but the random sampling of years produces a misleading argument about the rise of cancer rates in these states.

Seeing Connections
For examples of different approaches to using statistical data in chart form, see Harrison Pope's "Evolving Ideals of Male Body Image as Seen Through Action Toys" on page 287 and CBS News Chart on Drug Testing on page 338.

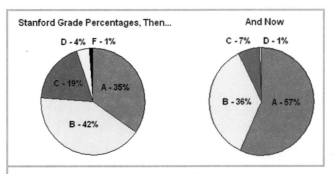

FIGURE 5.17 Student David Pinner created these information graphics from his research data to suggest the difference in grade distribution between 1968 and 1992.

statistics to underscore his point. His argument was more powerful not just because of his impressive primary research but also because of how he represented it in his paper through responsible use of statistics.

Creating a Dialogue with Your Sources

Throughout this chapter we have emphasized the point that research is social, a relationship with the people whose ideas and writing came before yours. You are contributing to this conversation, building on the work of others, and adding a new perspective. Indeed, this notion of writing as communal is the reason why you need to use the author's name when citing a quotation or an idea; remember that all your sources are authored sources. From the DoNoHarm Website shown in Figure 5.11, to Gretchen Vogel's article depicted in Figure 5.14, each source mentioned in this chapter was composed by a person or a group of people. If you think of these texts as written *by people like you,* you will have an easier time remembering to acknowledge their ideas and integrate their quotations into your essay. You can begin this process through an exercise we call a **dialogue of sources**—a fictional conversation among the primary and secondary sources of your research paper designed to help you identify each one's central argument and main idea.

You can find a visual equivalent for the dialogue of sources in comedian Jon Stewart's video sketch from *The Daily Show,* "Bush v. Bush," in which he moderated a "debate" between President George W. Bush and his younger self, Texas governor George W. Bush, on matters of foreign policy (see Figure 5.18). In reality, the debate was composed of carefully edited excerpts from speeches from different points in Bush's career; the result was a provocative look into his changing opinion on U.S. foreign intervention. Although the video dialogue was comic, the premise was a sound one: many news commentary shows feature "roundtable" discussions among a diverse group of people, with the idea of promoting a conversation about a relevant social or political topic.

FIGURE 5.18 Screen shot from "Bush v. Bush," a debate staged by Jon Stewart on *The Daily Show.* Still courtesy of Comedy Central.

Student Writing
See the dialogues of sources by Andrew Timmons on PetCo Park and by Amanda Johnson on tobacco advertisements.
www.ablongman.com/envision/220

You may find it helpful to create your own *dialogue of sources* in which you write out the diverse opinions you've encountered in your research:

- First, identify the key players from your research log. Which ones have the most influential or important arguments?
- Then, create a cast of characters list in which you create a short "bio" for each speaker, including yourself, describing

each person's credentials and rhetorical stance—their ethos and argument. You may even want to create identifying pictures to give "faces" to the participants.

- Now, draft the script. Begin by writing key questions to ask your sources about your topic. As they articulate their positions, use quotes from your sources where possible, and include page numbers.
- Next, consider what your sources would say in response to each other. Write their fictional conversation by using quotes from your sources.
- Don't just play the "objective" moderator. Respond to the sources and, in the process, start to develop your own argument.

Seeing Connections
For an example of how sources can be brought in dialogue with one another, see "Playing Unfair" on page 379.

To prepare for her research paper on tobacco advertisements, Amanda Johnson (AJ) wrote this dialogue between several sources she had found: RJ Reynolds Tobacco Co. (RJRT); Larry C. White, author of *Merchants of Death* (LW); and Hugh High, a professor of Economics, Finance, and Law who published a collection of tobacco studies titled *Does Advertising Increase Smoking?* (HH), among others.

Dialogue of Sources

AJ: I would like to thank the panel for joining us this afternoon. We have quite a diverse group of writers, researchers, spokespeople, and a professor here to discuss the focus and objectives of current tobacco advertising. Since I know your comments on this subject vary widely, I suppose I will start off by asking you to talk about what you believe to be the focus of tobacco advertising as it exists today.

RJRT: RJ Reynolds tobacco products are among the best advertised in the industry, and we take pride in our commitment to maintaining honest advertising to the public. We do not intend for our advertising to manipulate nonsmokers into trying our products, nor do we choose to target these audiences. Advertising is simply a method by which we are able to maintain our share of the market and compete with other tobacco manufacturers.

LW: How can you possibly claim to avoid targeting specific audiences and replenishing your older dwindling population with new younger smokers!?! The whole point of advertising is to get more people to buy your

Amanda's complete dialogue begins with a list of speakers and their bios. Then she introduces the topic of her research project. She reproduces the argument of each source, both print and interview, through paraphrase.

By allowing debate to evolve, Amanda begins to see how she might use quotations from these sources in her paper.

Most importantly, she begins to develop her own argument for her research paper in the context of these other perspectives.

product, and, since market shares don't change all that much for large companies like yours, the best way to get more people to buy your product is to increase the number of overall smokers. Youth are your best option because if you can get them hooked now, you will have a steady flow of income for several decades to come.

HH: Mr. White, you make a good point about general economic objectives. However, studies show that advertising does very little to change the number of new smokers. Countries that have banned advertising for tobacco-related products have seen very little decline in the number of consumers that buy their product. As RJRT stated previously, advertising is only successful at making adjustments within the market concerning the relative amounts each company is able to sell.

AJ: I recently reviewed a chart concerning the prevalence of smoking among U.S. adults and found that over the past 40 years since the surgeon general first warned about cigarettes' cancerous effects, the steady decline in smokers has slowed to rest around 25 percent of the population over the age of 18. With the number of people dying each day, it is surprising that this number does not continue to go down. How would you account for the slowed change?

She does this by questioning the responses, adding facts from her research, and moving the argument forward as she will need to do in her paper.

As you can tell, the dialogue of sources is a process of literally responding to the main arguments in your texts. It can produce a helpful interchange about the research topic and move you toward refining your own argument.

Note Taking and Annotated Bibliographies

You can use the dialogue of sources as a note-taking strategy while you work through your research sources. Indeed, many students find this approach to note taking to be the best way to create thorough research logs for their projects, one that keeps their own thesis evident. However, there are many methods of note taking, and at this point in your research process, you probably have developed some techniques of your own: taking notes right in your research log or on note cards, on loose-leaf paper, in a spiral notebook, or on your laptop.

As you move further into your research, you might want to synthesize your notes in what researchers call an **annotated bibliography**—a list of research sources that provides informational notes about each source and how you might use it as you turn to drafting your paper.

Realize that composing entries in the annotated bibliography involves much more than merely recording information: it is a way for you to synthesize arguments and add your response to what the source has to say about your research topic. Be sure to name the sources in your notes so you start to create the same type of interactive dialogue with your sources as you might have with faculty members or interviewees. Moreover, if you quote from textual passages either in your notes or in your annotated bibliography, include name prompts, use quotation marks, and show clearly the distinction between direct quotes from your source and your own summaries or commentaries. In this way, you can avoid potentially misquoting or plagiarizing sources later.

Seeing Connections
To understand how a critical perspective on your sources can inform your use of them in your research paper, see Margo DeMello's treatment of her source material in "Not Just for Bikers Anymore" on page 300.

AT A GLANCE

Note-Taking Strategies

As you read your sources, take notes on materials you could use in your paper:

- Particularly memorable quotations
- Background information you can summarize
- A well-written passage providing context or a perspective useful to your argument

Be sure to double-check your notes for accuracy and to include complete source information and page numbers.

AT A GLANCE

Composing an Annotated Bibliography

1. Put your sources into alphabetical order; you can also categorize them by of primary and secondary sources.

2. Provide complete identifying information for each source, including author's name, title, publication, date, page numbers, URLs for Websites, and database information for online sources.

3. Compose a three- to five-sentence annotation for each source:

   - First, summarize the main argument or point of the source; use concrete language. Include quotations if you wish.
   - Next, indicate the writer's stance. How credible or biased is this source?
   - Finally, and most importantly, describe the relevance of this source to your research argument. Will the source be used as background for the opening part of your paper? Does it offer a key counterargument? Will it provide the main authority to back up your claims?

AT A GLANCE

Constructing a Visual Annotated Bibliography

List your sources in alphabetical order; you can separate your list into primary and secondary sources or provide one complete list.

- Include images for your primary sources and the covers or Website images of secondary sources to show each source's stance through visual rhetoric.

- For each source, include all identifying information.

- Briefly state the argument of each source, the possible audience, and the bias or slant of the writer and include any specific passages of particular interest.

- Most importantly, explain the relevance of this source to your own research project and even where and how you might use it in your paper.

Student Writing

See samples of visual annotated bibliographies on a wide range of topics.
www.ablongman.com/envision/221

As you compose your annotated bibliography, consider including images that you might use as primary or secondary sources as well. In this way, you are crafting a **visual annotated bibliography**—a working list of potential sources in which you include images. This is very helpful if you plan to analyze images in your paper or if your rhetorical analysis covers visual and multimedia texts, such as James Caputo's project on the government's space program.

Consider, for instance, Carly Geehr's visual annotated bibliography for her research project on the representations of swimming as a gendered sport in the American media throughout history (see Figure 5.19).

Both the image of a swimmer from the early 1920s in the secondary source by Douglas Booth and Colin Tatz, as well as the more recent advertising from *U.S.A. Swimming* were key images that Carly analyzed in her paper to make an argument about the feminization of swimming in American sports culture.

Carly Geehr   Dr. Alyssa O'Brien
Visually Annotated Bibliography   May 13, 2003

The American Media and Swimming: Investigating the "Uphill Battle"

Booth, Douglas and Colin Tatz. *One Eyed: a View of Australian Sport.* Allen and Unwin 2000.

In order to make my argument that swimming could be a more popular sport in the United States, I will need to present strong evidence: this book provides it to me. Booth and Tatz chronicle the history of Australian sports in both society and in the media. From their descriptions of media coverage and the role of gender in sports, I can find out why, culturally and historically, swimming has been able to achieve such a high level of popularity in Australia. Of particular interest to me so far has been their focus on the traditional, accepted role of women in sports-it is drastically different in US history. By comparison to my sources about American sports culture, I will find out the key differences between the two countries and hopefully draw some concrete conclusions as to why swimming is not as popular in the United States as it is in Australia. This photo is the image of a female Australian swimmer whose look and demeanor demand respect, unlike her beautified American counterparts (212). I will be able to compare the Australian images of swimmers with the American images of swimmers, hopefully noting some key differences in visual rhetoric techniques employed—preliminarily, I suspect that the American images will focus much more on aesthetics while Australian images will focus on intensity and ruggedness (more pertinent to the sport itself).

"Duel in the Pool Advertisement." 3 Apr 2003. http://www.usaswimming.org/Duel.

[A little background: USA Swimming recently staged its first "made-for-TV" dual meet versus the Australian national team. The goal was to attract network attention and draw the people who would normally be watching sports on weekend afternoons into watching swimming for a change. According to Mary Wagner, the ratings were good but not exceptional.] This image is one of the advertisements put out by USA Swimming before the event to attract its target audience of teenagers and others (particularly males) who would be watching television on Saturday and Sunday afternoons. It appeals mostly to ethos, citing Michael Phelps as a world record holder, but also appeals more subtly to pathos in using the national colors and the national flag to create a sense of nationalism and passion for the event. However, this image helps me support my claim that USA Swimming's promotions have fallen short of successful in that it is not an exciting image—if the intent was to attract teenagers and adults who typically watch traditional, exciting American sports, then this image fails to create sufficient energy to generate interest or a desire to deviate from watching normal weekend sports on TV.

FIGURE 5.19 Well-chosen images and detailed annotations show Carly Geehr's progress on her research project.

Implementing Your Research Skills

As you begin to articulate your contribution to the research dialogue about your topic, use the strategies that you've learned in this chapter. These include visualizing research as a conversation that you are joining and understanding the process of researching your argument as a movement from surface to depth. As you learn to search and locate both primary and secondary sources, you can engage in critical evaluation of these texts in your research log. You can also engage in innovative fieldwork of your own to generate original resource material to use in your argument. In writing your own annotated bibliography, remember that effective annotations and note-taking practices can help you develop the strategies of an academic writer and that these practices will move you toward finalizing your own argument about the topic. By moving from covers to contents, you will watch your iceberg take shape, and you will begin to let your own voice be heard.

PREWRITING CHECKLIST

Focus on Evaluating Websites, Magazines, and Journals

❏ What images are featured on the cover? Do the images lend themselves to an appeal to logic? to an appeal to emotion? to an appeal to authority?

❏ Do the words included as headings and subheads on the cover contribute to any of these appeals?

❏ What do the cover images suggest about the contents of the larger text? Do they suggest a specific rhetorical stance or point of view? What is the effect of each visual choice?

❏ How do the words on the cover or homepage work in conjunction with the image to suggest the entire text's rhetorical stance? Do the words complement the image? Do they offer a contrast to the image?

WRITING PROJECTS

1. **Research Log Entries:** Continue to write in your *research log*; keep a running commentary/assessment of potential research sources for your project. Realize that careful research notes are a crucial part of the process and will help you avoid unintentional plagiarism of material (see Chapter 9 for more tips on avoiding plagiarism). Include in your log a combination of typed notes, highlighted photocopies, emails to yourself, a CD-ROM of sources from databases, note cards, scanned images, and other means of processing all the information you encounter.

2. **Working with your Preliminary Bibliography:** Create a *dialogue of sources* or an *annotated bibliography* to showcase the primary and secondary sources you'll employ in the major paper. Be sure that your writing provides a range of primary and secondary sources. Include both print and electronic sources and, if appropriate, include images to demonstrate the kinds of materials you'll be analyzing in the project.

3. **Collaborative Peer Review:** In groups of three or four, present your annotated bibliographies to one another. Pull the "greatest hits" from your research log, create a multimedia annotated bibliography, and tell the class about how your research is going. In other words, *present a discussion of your work in progress.* You should identify your thesis, key points, obstacles, and successes so far. You'll get feedback from the class about your developing research project.

 Visit www.ablongman.com/envision for expanded assignment guidelines and student projects.

CHAPTER 6

Organizing and Writing Research Arguments

Chapter Preview Questions

- What strategies of organization work best for my paper?
- What are the best ways to get started writing a full draft?
- How do I know when to quote, paraphrase, or summarize?
- How can collaboration and peer review help me revise?

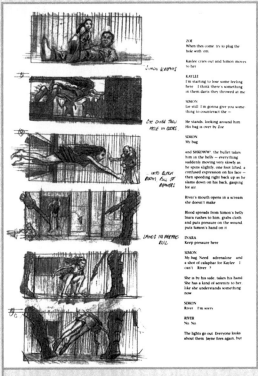

FIGURE 6.1 This storyboard for Joss Whedon's film *Serenity* shows an initial draft for one of the film's climactic action scenes.

As you've seen, constructing a research argument is a complex and ongoing process. From selecting a topic to locating and evaluating sources and taking notes, it involves a series of interrelated steps. This is true of the *drafting* stage as well. In fact, organizing, drafting, and revising information are prominent parts of the process of creating any text, whether it be an academic essay, a television commercial, a radio essay, or even a film. Figure 6.1, for instance, offers us a rare glimpse at the drafting process behind a major motion picture—in this case, *Serenity* (2005). You might have watched this exciting scene in the theaters or on DVD; in it, one of the main characters, River, single-handedly fights an entire roomful of Reavers—the cannibalistic bad guys of the film—to protect her brother and friends. What you see in Figure 6.1 are the storyboards for this scene—an artist's draft that lays out the action in chronological increments, mapping out not only the movement of the characters but also the camera angles and thus the audience's experience of the events depicted. Notice the way it captures a sense of motion by rapidly changing perspectives and how it creates a narrative tension in the last panel with the close-up of the Reavers grabbing River to drag her back during her attempted escape. Storyboards like this one clearly operate as a visual outline, a type of organizational strategy that underlies most films. The polished final version seen in the theater is actually made possible by drafting steps like this one.

In many ways, the process of writing is like film production: both have many small steps that support a grounding vision or main idea, both have a carefully planned structure, and both involve rigorous editing. Because producing a film and producing a research argument share such rich similarities, we'll use the medium of film throughout this chapter to explore various aspects of the process of writing a research paper: from constructing a visual map and formal outline to integrating sources, key quotations, and evidence. We'll talk about incorporating sources responsibly in a way that sustains the conversation you began in the previous chapter, and we'll walk through the drafting and revision process. Just as filmmakers leave many scenes on the cutting room floor, you too will write, edit, cut, and rearrange much of the first draft of your research paper before it reaches its final form. You'll find that the process of completing your research argument is as collaborative as film production. Additionally, both film and writing involve parameters of length, cost, and time that you need to contend with to produce the best possible text. No matter what your topic, you can think of the way in which film works to help you visualize the final product and move from notes to writing the completed paper.

Of course, you have been writing all along: conducting analysis and forming arguments, drafting the proposal, completing the research log, and building an annotated bibliography. These are all ways to develop your argument through writing. Recognizing the connection between these shorter writing activities and the supposedly all-consuming task of "writing the research paper" can help the process seem more enjoyable and productive; it can help you avoid "writer's block" as you see that you've been making progress all along.

Organizing Your Draft in Visual Form

It can be quite challenging to turn on the computer and try to crank out a complete draft without first arranging materials into some kind of order. Using storyboards like those shown in Figure 6.1, or the bubble webs or graphic flowcharts described in this section, can be productive ways to prewrite through visual means. In fact, filmmakers and screenwriters often begin the production process by visually mapping out movie ideas, key scenes, and plot progressions. Similarly, you can use various forms of visual mapping to organize your research notes and argumentative points in order to sort, arrange, and make connections between ideas.

The most basic way to get organized is to physically stack your research books and materials and then write labels for each pile. This organizational strategy functions as a concrete way of categorizing the resources you have and figuring out, visually, how they relate to one another. Next, you can produce a visual map of these sources by using colored pens and paper or by cutting out shapes and constructing a three-dimensional model for your paper's organization.

If you have access to a computer, you can turn your handwritten visual map into a **bubble web,** in which you arrange your ideas into categories using shapes and colors. Figure 6.2 shows Lee-Ming Zen's visual map for his project on the video game Lara Croft: Tomb Raider titled "Finding the Woman Who Never Was: Gender Exploration Through Lara Croft." As Lee's legend for the visual map explains, each color represents his categorizing process for the many points he wishes to cover in his paper. By grouping his research and his ideas into categories contained within colored circles and then drawing

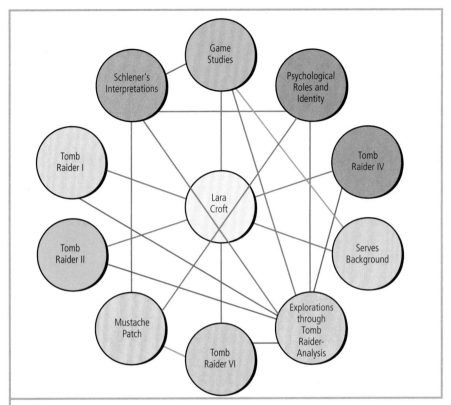

FIGURE 6.2 The bubble web by Lee-Ming Zen helped him organize the ideas of his argument into categories and, ultimately, sections he wanted tocover in his written paper. His categories include content- (or detail-) related materials for rhetorical analysis, idea or broad concept-related materials from his research, and material that requires Lee's own synthesis of ideas of analysis.

relationships between these categories using colored lines, Lee can sort through the sources he has read, the ideas he has encountered, and the many points and sections he wishes to cover in his written research paper. Ultimately, Lee turned this visual map into a formal written outline (see page 176). But it was crucial for him to make sense first of the research he had gathered. Through this map, he began to see how he could articulate his argument about gender roles played out in the video game.

In addition to such free-form visual maps, you could try more hierarchical or linear graphic flowcharts as a means of organizing your materials. In **graphic flowcharts,** you list one idea and then draw an arrow to suggest cause and effect and to show relationships among items. Figure 6.3, for example, presents Ye Yuan's graphic flowchart of his ideas about war photography, arranged in a tree structure. This visual hierarchy helped him assess his project by asking questions:

- Is each point developed thoroughly?
- Do I have a balance among the sections?
- Is there a coherent whole?

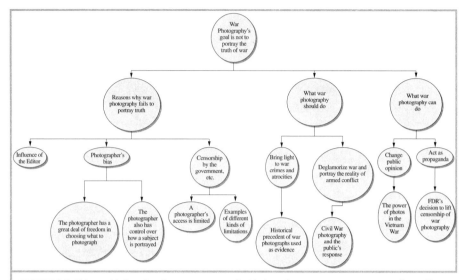

FIGURE 6.3 This graphic flowchart by Ye Yuan, created with the software program Inspiration, allowed him to visualize the sections of his written paper.

COLLABORATIVE CHALLENGE

Using the visual-mapping technique of your choice, begin to arrange your ideas for the research paper. Create a bubble web of ideas or make a graphic flowchart of concepts. When you are done constructing your visual map, explain your organizational plan to your peer review partners. Ask for feedback on what areas seem under-developed, isolated, or extraneous. Use this feedback to think about the balance of materials and arrangement of sections in your written essay.

Learning Outline Strategies

Visual maps can help you sort out your materials and prepare you for the next step: the detailed, written outline. For a longer, more complex paper, such as a research-based argument, an outline is an extremely useful method of arranging ideas and expediting the drafting process. Outlines offer a plan for your paper and should show the relationships among the various sections in your argument. If your outline simply consists of a list of topics, you won't be able to see the argument of the whole paper, nor will you be able to check for connections and progression between your individual points. In other words, the secret to producing a successful outline—and by extension a successful paper—is to pay special attention to the flow or development of ideas.

It's often hard to know for certain what the best way of organizing your paper will be without some trial and error. We can learn a lot from films about the ways in which various texts are organized. Consider how a film's **trailer**, or short prerelease video, provides a brief outline of the key scenes, the main conflict, the crucial characters, and the message of the movie. Figure 6.4 shows still shots from the theatrical trailer of *Kill Bill: Volume 1.*

FIGURE 6.4 Still shots from the trailer for *Kill Bill: Volume 1*.

Structured loosely as a narrative, this segment of the trailer suggests an outline of the film, moving from an identification of conflict, to defining the main character's central nemesis, to a scene of confrontation and physical combat. In doing so, the trailer reproduces one of the central themes of the *Kill Bill* series: the identification of evil and the quest for revenge through violence. But there are many ways to arrange these elements, each of which suggests a different argument for the film. The power of the trailer as an organizational tool is that it allows the filmmakers to experiment with order and meaning.

COLLABORATIVE CHALLENGE

In groups of three or four, visit the movie trailers site on Apple.com through the *Envision* Website and view two or three trailers, either for the same film or different ones. Write down the main features of each trailer. How does each one function as an outline of the film's key scenes, characters, conflict, and message? What tone or style is conveyed through the selection of imagery, the choice of music, and the emphasis on a particular plot or character? What can you apply to your own outline strategies of arrangement?
www.ablongman.com/envision/222

Keeping the idea of the trailer in mind, take your ideas from the visual map you have created and craft them into a **formal outline,** a detailed list that uses numbers and letters to indicate subsections of your argument. Rather than list three sections only—such as *Introduction, Body,* and *Conclusion*—create several points within the body to show the development of your argument. Lee-Ming Zen, for example, developed a formal outline from his visual map on video game character Lara Croft. He broke the body of his paper into several points he wished to cover, taking readers through the history of Lara Croft, various interpretations of gender roles in the game, and then a close analysis of the games in chronological order, from earliest to most recent.

Lee drafted a working title on his outline to help him focus the argument.

Lee-Ming Zen

Research Paper Outline

April 23, 2003

Dr. Alyssa O'Brien

Finding the Woman Who Never Was: Gender Role Exploration Through

Lara Croft

   I. Introduction

       A. "Hook" line

       B. Background

C. Thesis: By examining the various expressions of Lara Croft and the evolution of her aesthetic character, we are offered a chance to explore the various cultural and sociological aspects of our understanding of gender, especially in relation to videogames. In particular, her evolution parallels the different stages of gender exploration that adolescents experience and struggle through. Yet, at the same time, Lara Croft is a paradox acting as an objectification of women that both stereotypes and empowers women by allowing anyone to explore gender through her body.

D. Organizational hints

II. The Woman Who Never Was

A. Origins of Lara Croft

1. concept

2. reasons

B. *Tomb Raider* Series

1. general information

2. statistics to show the import and impact

C. Schleiner's role interpretations of Lara Croft

1. female Frankenstein

2. drag queen

3. dominatrix/femme fatale

4. female role model

5. lesbian idol

D. University of Michigan's proposed stages of gender-role development

E. Ideas and concepts of masculinity/femininity

1. Girls

2. Boys

III. Evolution of Lara Croft

A. Version 1.0

1. *Tomb Raider* box cover

2. Lara Croft's features

Lee includes a complete, detailed statement of his working thesis to guide and shape his outline.

Lee lists his argument points briefly in the body sections of his outline. If you prepare a more detailed outline, you may want to identify sources you will use to support your claims. Include quotations and page numbers.

       3. Schleiner's analysis's applications to this image

       4. Relation to Stage I in Parsons and Bryan

  B. Version 2.0

       1. Mustache patch image

       2. Mustache patch background and information

       3. Schleiner's analysis's applications to this image

       4. Relation to Stage II and especially Stage III in Parsons
         and Bryan

  C. Explorative Analysis

       1. Flanagan's take

       2. Gender role exploration in Stages I-III through Lara Croft versions
         1 and 2

       3. Game concept relation in gender exploration

         a) Game immersion

         b) Character identity

  D. Version 4.0

       1. Version 3.0 is the same as the 2.0 engine but tweaked

         a) brief explanation of game engines

         b) lack of major change in her image

       2. A sexier Lara Croft – image analysis

       3. Analysis of changes in her image since versions 1 and 2

       4. Schleiner's analysis's applications to this image

       5. Relation to Stage III and IV in Parsons and Bryan

  E. Version 6.0

       1. Concept art and the new 'realistic' look

         a) The new 'Gen-X' Lara Croft

       2. Changes since versions 1, 2, and 4

       3. Comparative analysis in regards to Schleiner and
         Flanagan (hopefully in order to begin tying everything
         back together)

       4. Relation to Stage IV and V in Parsons and Bryan

F. Explorative Analysis

  1. Gender role exploration in Stages III–V through Lara Croft versions 4 and 6

  2. Change in the trend of Lara as a parallel to the adolescent development

    a) Significance of this trend

    b) Applications of this trend to other research on gender identity, roles

  3. Game concept relation in gender exploration

  a) Game spaces

    b) Gender difference in technology use

IV. Conclusion

  A. Quick look back

  B. Overall import of these findings

  C. Further reaching impacts of this study

Indicate where your argument will lead to in your conclusion. Rather than just restate your thesis and summarize your argument, discuss the significance of your points.

As you can tell from Lee's example, formal outlines can help you work step by step through the process of arguing your position. Additionally, they can save you a lot of time as you approach the writing process itself. Consider using full sentences to most clearly articulate your thoughts or inserting sources right into the outline; these techniques can help you troubleshoot areas where you might need to do supplemental research or expand your argument.

One benefit of outlining as a prewriting practice is that it allows you to experiment with different organizational structures to discover which one works best for your paper. Depending on your topic, you can try several approaches, just as filmmakers rearrange a film to create a variety of trailers. Do you want to start your paper with a question, move through evidence, and then arrive at a declarative thesis statement? Or do you feel that your argument is best served by a firm thesis statement up front, followed by an accumulation of supporting evidence that ultimately touches upon larger related issues? The key in organizing your paper is to consider the relationship between *form* and *content,* or the way your structure can facilitate your argument.

AT A GLANCE

Useful Organization Strategies

- *Chronological:* relevant for historical discussions
- *Thematic:* helps with diverse case studies
- *Cause and effect:* focuses on consequences
- *Problem-solution:* useful for social issues papers
- *Illustrative:* emphasizes examples of a pattern
- *Macro to micro:* moves from the general to the specific
- *Micro to macro:* moves from the specific to the general
- *Narrative:* employs the personal experience

Lee centered his argument principally on a **chronological** model, but as the "At a Glance" box demonstrates, that is only one of many strategies available to you. Let's look again to film for an organizational example you may wish to follow. If you visit the PBS Frontline Website to view the documentary *The Merchants of Cool*, you would find the film chunked into thematic "chapters." The first chapter, "hunting for cool," establishes a definition and sets up the research problem: how do advertisers successfully market products to teens? The next segment, "under-the-radar marketing," shifts the thematic focus from advertising to company image; and "the mtv machine" chapter narrows to examine MTV as a marketing tool. In its sixth and final chapter, "teen rebellion: just another product," the documentary reinforces its thesis, using the band Limp Bizkit to demonstrate how extreme materials can be successfully marketed to a mass audience. In this way, the organization functions as part of the film's argument. Structure (*form*) fits argument (*content*).

CREATIVE PRACTICE

Watch Frontline's *The Merchant of Cool* (available through the *Envision* Website), paying close attention to how the argument as a whole is organized. Notice that when you roll your mouse over the image, a one-sentence summary of each segment appears. Explore the way the film addresses its target audience, incorporates sources and evidence, and arranges its argument into subthemes. Write a detailed outline that reveals the organizational structure of this documentary. What can you learn and apply to the research paper you will be writing?

 www.ablongman.com/envision/223

Outlines with Subheads and Transitions

Outlines can also help you develop the complexity of your research argument if you incorporate subheads and transitions into your writing. **Subheads,** or labeled headings for each subsection of your outline, are a terrific way to structure your ideas into discrete units to show the progression of your argument and help your readers make sense of a complex argument. Subheads work particularly well for longer, research-based essays. You can transform the key parts of your outline into a short list of argumentative subheads.

If you were writing a detailed outline, you might insert into the body of your paper subheads that indicate specific parts of your argument. For a paper on film marketing, a subhead could be "A Look at Website Marketing of Films." You can feel free to get creative by connecting your subheads thematically or by using a single metaphor to add a rich layer of vivid words to your essay. For a film-marketing paper, the body might include the following subheads: "Movies Online are a Big Splash," "Surfing for Movies," and "The Next Wave in Viral Marketing." After you write a list of working subheads, exchange them with a partner. Suggest modifications and new ideas to each other; keep focused on using subheads to advance the argument of the essay. Let's take a look at how Dexian Cai met this challenge by incorporating argumentative subheads into his outline.

Seeing Connections
For examples of how to use subheads effectively to help structure a long, researched argument, see Margo DeMello's "Not Just for Biker's Anymore" on page 300, David Leonard's "Yo, Yao!" on page 359, Helen W. Kennedy's "Lara Croft" on page 479, and Mike Milliard's "I Like to Watch" on page 552.

Dexian Cai

PWR1 H-1

Dr. Alyssa O'Brien

Research Paper—Outline

November 12, 2003

I. Introduction

    1. Hook: A brief description of a current McDonald's advertisement

        for 2003. While ostensibly American and Western, the interesting

        aspect is that this ad is in fact for an Asian market.

    2. Thesis: McDonald's advertising in East Asia has evolved over time,

        adapting to trends and changes in Asian societal values. The paper

        will argue that McDonald's both shapes and is shaped by these

        evolving trends, creating a dynamic relationship between the

        restaurant and consumers.

    3. Implications: What are the effects of McDonald's influence

        on Asian values and societal evolution? Is this is a healthy

        trend or merely a restaurant moving with the times? Are

        accusations of cultural imperialism or degradation of morals

        justified?

II. Background

    • A brief history of McDonald's entry into the various East Asian

       markets. In particular, research will center on Japan, Hong Kong,

       Korea, Taiwan, China, and Singapore.

    • A summary of McDonald's image and ethos in the

       United States.

III. McDonald's: From Homely to Hip

    Then

    • Rhetorical analysis of ads from the 1970s and 1980s, when

       McDonald's first broke into the Asian markets.

    • Argument that McDonald's was attempting to portray itself as a

       family restaurant that made children feel special. Highlight the fact

Notice how Dex includes the opening line for his paper, the hook, right in the outline, setting the tone for the paper.

His thesis comprises two sentences since this argument is complex.

He ends the intro with questions to engage the reader.

After a brief background section, Dex moves on to the heart of his argument. The subhead "From Homely to Hip" reflects in words the point Dex will make in this section, namely, that McDonald's has changed its brand image from conservative to trendy. The play on words in the subhead helps keep Dex on track and to interest the reader.

that the campaigns differed across the various countries because McDonald's tailored each campaign to the specific market's characteristics and perceived needs.

- Compare and contrast with contemporary American campaigns. Family vs. fast food.

- Sources: McDonald's Corporation. (Pending the approval of a request sent via e-mail.)

- Secondary Source: Watson, James L. Golden Arches East: McDonald's in East Asia. Palo Alto, CA: Stanford University Press, 1997.

Now

- Rhetorical analysis of ads for 2003.

- Argument that McDonald's marketing strategy has evolved to embrace East Asia as an "assimilated market," as the campaign and slogan are standardized the world over. There is no longer a uniquely Asian campaign; instead it is replaced by the homogeneous American set of ads.

- Image of fun and relaxation is interspersed with images of McDonald's products. Using youth to drive the campaign is a clear signal of the target audience and the aim of creating a "cool" and "hip" image for the franchise. This contrasts the familial tone of ads from the "early days."

- Sources: McDonald's Country Websites

IV. Getting Behind the Arches

- Key Question: What has brought about this evolution in advertising strategies in East Asia? Why the shift in image?

- Argument: The dynamics of influence are mutual and interactive. Although McDonald's largely responds to perceived societal trends, it also seeks to influence attitudes and sell its version of "hip" or "cool," especially to Asian youth.

Note that he includes his sources right in his outline so he'll be sure to weave them into his paper.

Since his paper focuses on the visual rhetoric of McDonald's advertising in Asia, it is appropriate for Dex to include images in his outline. These images will serve as evidence for his argument. [Images were removed for copyright purposes but appeared in Dex's original outline.]

He includes a key research question as a transition into this section. His next sub-head again uses language to convey this point in the progression of his argument; with such argumentative subheads, he can be certain that his argument is building in significance.

- Analyze how the Asian case is reflective of McDonald's marketing strategy internationally. Discuss the moral/ethical implications of such strategies.
- Consider the McDonald's "Culture of Power" argument in Kincheloe's book. Are the claims leveled against the franchise valid?
- Source: Kincheloe, Joe L. The Sign of the Burger: McDonald's and the Culture of Power. Philadelphia: Temple University Press, 2002.

V. Amer-Asia? A Peek at the Future of Asia
- Summarize/recap the arguments of the paper.

Larger Questions
- Given the trend of increasing global integration, is homogenization under American leadership an inevitable end of modern civilization?
- Discuss ways in which this is not so ("dissenting opinion"). Asia's cultures continue to greatly influence McDonald's, causing wide variations between McDonald's image in Asia and in America.
- What are the implications of changing societal trends for Asian youth? How does McDonald's advertising affect and influence these trends? Do the ads exacerbate/speed up the "Americanization" of Asian youth? or merely reflect what is already present?

He is still working on points of the argument, even in the outline, as shown in his question whether to bring in Joe Kincheloe's argument as a secondary source here.

The final section is not titled "Conclusion" but instead uses an argumentative subhead to transition into the closing argument of the paper, namely that the presence of McDonald's is potentially changing distinctions between nations, blurring cultures into a combined identity Dex calls "Amer-Asia."

As you can see from Dex's example, using an appropriate metaphor in a subhead provides consistency in language that in turn can help the flow of your essay. Similarly, you can enhance the flow of your writing with careful attention to **transitions**— phrases that provide the connections between the paragraphs or sections in your paper. When creating transitions, even during your outlining phase, think about how you can signal the next idea, build on the previous idea, or reiterate the key terms of your thesis as you advance your argument. Many students like to think of the game of dominoes when composing transitions: each domino can only touch another domino with a matching number; two connects with two, three with three. Using this notion of progressive, connecting terms, you can incorporate transitions within sections of your outline to give it overall structure and flow. Then, when you turn to writing the paper, you will avoid big jumps in logic. Instead, by incorporating the transitions from your outline, you will produce a polished piece of written work.

Seeing Connections
Read the transcript of the NPR audio essay "Cultural Differences Seen in Male Perceptions of Body Image" on page 293 and Michael Eisner's Address Before Members of the United States Congress on pages 430–438.

COLLABORATIVE CHALLENGE

Using scissors, cut your outline into pieces so that each main subject heading (with its related subcategories) is on a separate piece of paper. For example, for a five-paragraph essay, you would end up with five pieces: an introduction, a piece for your first section, a piece for your second section, a piece for your third section, and a conclusion; for a research outline, you should have at least eight pieces. Be sure to cut *off* the heading numbers from each piece of paper to eliminate any sense of the way the headings were originally arranged on your outline. Now shuffle your pieces so they are out of order, and give them to your collaborative partners. Have your partners reassemble the pieces in the order they feel is most appropriate for your argument and then explain their reasons. Now discuss your original organization, and the rationale behind it.

Spotlight on Your Argument

As you turn now from writing an outline to fleshing out the full draft, consider the decision before you concerning what kind of voice or rhetorical stance to take in the language of your prose. Again, we can learn a lot from filmmakers as they face similar decisions.

AT A GLANCE

Assessing Outlines

- *Thesis:* Is it complex, contentious, and interesting?
- *Argument:* Is there a fluid progression of ideas? Does each one relate back to the thesis? Is there extraneous information that you can cut? Do more points need to be developed?
- *Sources:* Are primary sources identified for analysis in the paper? Are secondary sources listed to provide support and authority for the argument? Are there sufficient sources listed for each point? Are visual texts included as argumentative evidence?
- *Format:* Are there argumentative and interesting subheads?

In *Fahrenheit 9/11,* Michael Moore is careful to introduce and acknowledge his sources, but even while he includes many other voices in his film, he ultimately emphasizes his own argument. Of course, the film relies on research as background material, offering the narrator's comments as interview segments, in which a primary or secondary authority speaks directly to the audience, and as quoted material spoken directly by the narrator or through voice-over. But, as the promotional movie poster in Figure 6.5 suggests, Moore's opinion provides the foundation for everything disclosed in the film, making his rhetorical stance a prominent part of the text.

As you approach writing your paper, consider diverse ways to present your argument. Think of the power of a casting director on a film set. In a film such as Franco Zeffirelli's version of *Hamlet* (1990), for instance, the entire sexual politics of the narrative was influenced by the decision to cast Glenn Close (age 43 at the time) as Queen Gertrude, mother to Mel Gibson's Hamlet (Gibson was 34). Their close proximity in age set in relief an incest plot at which Shakespeare himself had only hinted. In essence, what audiences watched in the movie theater was less Shakespeare's *Hamlet* and more Zeffirelli's interpretation of it. In your own writing, you have a comparable power; the way you "cast" your sources can influence your reader's understanding of your argument.

In fact, your treatment of your sources will define your approach to your topic. Consider the "objectivity" of a celebrity biography shown on TV: although the text purports to offer no explicit argument, the selection of quotations used, the identities of people interviewed, and the emphasis given to certain stages of the artist's career collaborate to produce not some objective *truth* but a single *version* of that artist's life. Or think about Oliver Stone's *JFK* (1991) and the controversy it stirred. The film was in fact an argument: Stone used primary and secondary evidence to create his own interpretation of the events surrounding President John Kennedy's assassination. Even years after its release, *JFK* sparks heated debate; many of the film's most vocal critics continue to argue about the validity of Stone's version of events.

As seen in the examples presented here, sometimes you want to put your sources center stage and direct from behind the scenes, and sometimes you will want to step out of the shadows and articulate your argument more explicitly to the audience. Whichever way you go, you should decide what role you, the writer, will play in your paper. The key is to choose the role that will produce the most effective argument on your topic, one that fits the needs of your rhetorical situation. Your voice is your spotlight on your argument; it should have rhetorical purpose and complement the content of your project.

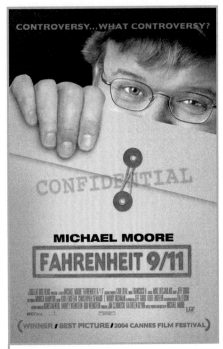

FIGURE 6.5 The promotional poster for *Fahrenheit 9/11* reveals the way Michael Moore emphasizes his own argument in the film.

CREATIVE PRACTICE

Watch "Protesting the Protesters" through the link on the *Envision* Website. How does the filmmaker convey his opinion about the war protest? How does he direct the interplay between image and spoken word to reproduce his argument? How does his voice-over commentary function as a spotlight developing his research argument?
www.ablongman.com/envision/224

Working with Sources

After you decide on your approach to working with sources—as a strong explicit narrator or as the synthesizer of information—you need to start turning your outline into a rough draft. But how will you introduce and weave these other voices—your sources—into your written prose?

As you work on the balance between your sources and your own argument, you will need to include your sources not only appropriately (to avoid plagiarism) and strategically (to decide on how much of a presence you will have in the paper) but also purposefully (to provide a range of quotations and supporting evidence for your paper).

AT A GLANCE

Reasons to Use Direct Quotation

- *Evidence:* The quotation provides tangible evidence for part of your argument.
- *Ethos:* The original author is a primary source or an expert on the subject, and including a direct quotation would increase the ethos of your argument.
- *Language:* The original author used memorable phrasing or has a particular voice that would be lost in paraphrase.

We call this process **integrating sources,** and it's a complex process that occurs in three basic ways:

- **Summary:** synthesizing a great deal of information from a source
- **Paraphrase:** putting a source quotation into your own words
- **Direct quotation:** excerpting a specific passage from a source, enclosing it in quotation marks

You'll want to alternate between methods while incorporating your sources with stylistic variety. This means knowing your options as a writer and selecting the best method for each rhetorical situation within your research essay. There is no single "correct" way to integrate sources. Instead, to accomplish the goal of purposeful citation with variation, you'll need to make some important choices. When should you paraphrase? insert a direct quote? summarize material? Your decisions will be dictated by the specific needs of each part of your argument, but there are some guidelines that you should follow.

If a quotation does not fit into any of the categories listed in the "At a Glance" box, consider paraphrasing or summarizing it. What you want to avoid is a paper dominated by unnecessary quotations; in such a case, your voice—what readers expect most in your paper—gets buried. It's similar to what happens in film when the filmmaker splices together too many different scenes; the audience becomes lost in the montage and can no longer follow the narrative. If you're worried that you have integrated too many sources (and lost your own voice), spend some time reviewing the draft and ask yourself:

- Am I still the moderator of this conversation?
- Is my voice clear, compelling, and original?
- Do I allow my own argument to emerge as foremost in this piece?

Source material should *support* your argument, not supplant it.

Integrating, Not Inserting, Quotations

Seeing Connections
For effective use of paraphrase and integration of quotations, see Jane Juffer's "Who's the Man?" on page 362.

But how, practically, do you go about integrating sources appropriately and effectively rather than simply inserting them? To work successfully with quotations, try using the three R's: ***read***, ***record***, ***relate*** (see At a Glance box on next page).

Although a direct splice may be a successful film technique, in argumentative writing, we need clearer signposts of transition and context. Consider the stylistic options available to you to integrate sources by reading through the quotation examples from a paper on Al Gore's 2006 film about global warming, *An Inconvenient Truth.*

- **Using an introductory clause/phrase:** With this technique, the writer formally introduces the quote with a clause or phrase—one that often, but not always, refers to the author and/or the original text title. For example:

  Reacting strongly to the environmentalist message, online columnist Joseph Blast argues, "'An Inconvenient Truth' contains very little truth, and a big helping of propaganda."

AT A GLANCE

How to Integrate Sources Appropriately and Effectively

- *Read.* Read a text carefully and actively, underlining passages that move you or suggest moments of deep meaning, or passages that might contribute to your argument/interpretation. If you are working with online texts, cut and paste the citation into a computer document, noting the paragraph number (for Websites) or page number (for regular texts) in parentheses. Always keep track of the page number and source information if you transcribe citations as you read.

You'll need this part in order to provide the citation in your writing.

- *Record.* Keep a notebook or an annotated computer file of quotes in which you *record* your reactions to a particular passage you've read. Does this passage move you? How so? Does it reveal the theme of the text, the climax of the scene, the point of the argument, the purpose of the passage? Always engage critically with a citation, developing your reason for including it later.

You'll need this part in order to provide your interpretation of the citation.

- *Relate.* Place the citation and your interpretation in an appropriate place in your essay. Where in the paragraph should the quotation and the comment appear? What is around it? above it? after it? Make sure that you *relate* the inserted text to the material that precedes and follows your citation and interpretation. Never just "stick in a quote" without explanation and strategic placement.

You'll need this part in order to achieve the most successful quotation integration.

- **Using an incorporated structure:** Using this strategy, the writer seamlessly melds the quotation into a sentence of the essay so that it flows smoothly with the rest of the prose. For example:

  > Joseph Blast articulated one of the most common critiques of Al Gore's global warming film in a June 2006 online editorial when he claimed that "'An Inconvenient Truth' contains very little truth, and a big helping of propaganda."

- **Using an interrupted structure:** In this variation, the writer breaks the quote into two halves, embedding information regarding the author and/or the original text in the middle of the quotation itself. For example:

  > "In the style of a previous generation of propaganda films," Joseph Blast argues in his June 2006 editorial, "Gore substitutes vivid images of the alleged effects of global warming for an accurate account of the scientific debate."

- **Using an end comment:** In this technique, the writer inserts the quotation and then provides an interpretation, or closing comment, that importantly advances the argument. For example:

  > Joseph Blast's claim that "'An Inconvenient Truth' contains very little truth, and a big helping of propaganda" exemplifies the critical tendency to undermine the legitimacy of an opposing point of view by categorizing it as "propaganda."

Final Check for Integrating Sources

- Did you **introduce the quote** in various ways?
- Did you **link the reference** to your argument to show the relevance?
- Did you **comment** on it afterward to advance your argument?
- Did you **cite** it properly using the appropriate documentation style for your subject area?

Experiment with these strategies in your own writing to determine which best serves your rhetorical purpose. For instance, if you want to draw attention to the *author* of a quotation to add ethos to your argument, you might opt to integrate using an introductory clause; however, if you want to emphasize *information* rather than authorship, an incorporated structure might be more effective. One key to remember is to avoid overusing any one type of integration strategy; otherwise, your writing style might become monotonous, like a film that relies too heavily on the same types of shots.

Documentation During Integration

As you incorporate sources into your draft, be sure to include citations for each quotation or paraphrase. This would also be a good time to begin drafting your works-cited list or bibliography, to save time later. The purpose of this is not only to provide a "list of credits" for your references but also to supply interested readers with the resources to continue learning about your topic. Just as you undoubtedly found certain articles inspiring while investigating your topic and used them as springboards for more focused research, so too might your paper serve as a means of leading your readers to intriguing ideas and articles. You can go back over the correct format for citations in your final edit, following the guidelines in Chapter 9 for documentation to do so.

COLLABORATIVE CHALLENGE

To check if you need to cite information you've paraphrased, or if you are worried about citing information that is "common knowledge," you can ask your roommate or your peer review partner to assess your outline or draft. Any passage that stands out as unfamiliar should be marked with a highlighter. Then return the favor by examining your reader's work in progress with highlighter in hand. You can help point out to your peers what knowledge is most probably not readily available to you (or other readers) without the help of sources. Your peer reviewers can also point out material that is "common knowledge" and doesn't need to be cited.

Drafting Your Research Argument

As you continue to forge ahead with your research argument, turning from an outline to a full draft or composing sections of your argument in separate time blocks, realize that there are many strategies for getting it done. For each of these ways of working, the key is to start and then just keep writing. Try out one of the many methods described in the "At a Glance" box on the next page.

Also realize that to write is to struggle with the process, as noted by Stanford psychologist David Rasch: "Almost all writers are familiar with the experience of feeling stuck, blocked, overwhelmed, or behind schedule in their writing." What can help? Staying motivated and relying on others.

Keeping Your Passion

As you move deeper into the writing process, integrating quotations and working out the flow of your argument, don't lose sight of your enthusiasm for your subject. Reread your earliest freewrites and your entries in your research log. What goals, what motivations prompted you to begin the project? What aspects of your topic excited you, angered you, or inspired you? What contribution did you imagine yourself making to this discussion? As you begin synthesizing your information and creating a unified argument, you are in effect realizing that initial vision.

AT A GLANCE

Strategies for Drafting

- *Following the linear path:* Start at the beginning, write the introduction, and then move sequentially through each point of argument.
- *Fleshing out the outline:* Gradually transform the outline into a full draft, moving from a keyword outline to a prose outline by systematically expanding each of the sections; as you add more detail, the keywords fall away, leaving behind drafted paragraphs.
- *Writing from the middle:* Start writing from a point of greatest strength or start with a section you can complete easily; then write around it and fill out sections as you go.
- *Freewrite and then reverse outline:* First, produce pages of freewriting; then compose a detailed **reverse outline** in which you record the point of every paragraph to assess the argument's flow and structure; and finally, reorder and rewrite the paper multiple times until it begins to take the proper form for the argument.

Remember, your audience will be reading your paper to learn *your* particular point of view on the subject. Your drafts are your shooting scripts, if you will—the versions of your paper that ultimately you will transform, through careful review, editing, and revision, into your "release" of the text into final form.

You should also allow yourself well-needed energy breaks. Brief periods away from the writing process can often recharge and reinvigorate your approach to the paper and help you think through difficult points in the argument. Ironically, a pause in drafting can also help you avoid writer's block by allowing you to remember what interested you about this project in the first place. Finally, if you are having trouble getting through the draft process, allow yourself to write what Anne Lamott, author of *Bird by Bird,* famously calls the "shitty first draft." In the words of Anne Lamott, "All good writers write them. This is how they end up with good second drafts and terrific third drafts." In other words, you should realize that the first version by no means has to be perfect or even close to what the final paper will look like. It is instead simply your first attempt at getting your ideas on paper. Freeing yourself to write something—anything—can help you escape from the weight of perfectionism or the fear of failure that often paralyzes writers. You will have plenty of opportunities to rework the material, show your draft to others, and move forward with the writing process.

Collaboration Through Peer Review

In addition, take advantage of the community of writers in your class to talk through your ideas and share work in progress. You might find your organizational plan confirmed by your peers, or you might be pleasantly surprised by their suggestions for alternative structures, ways of integrating sources, or images to include in the paper. Such discussions can help you get back your fire for your project as well as give you extremely useful advice to implement in the writing of the draft. Moreover, your peers' responses to your work in progress can help you determine if your writing is persuasive or not.

Consider how collaboration works in the film industry. Even though a film is generally recognized as a unified expression of a single idea, in reality it is the product of the collaborative effort of dozens of individuals, from the screenwriter and actors to the key grips and camera operators. But there is another, often less recognized collaborator: the audience. Think about how novels are adapted to the large screen: whether by adding a romantic subplot or substituting a "Hollywood ending" for a less palatable one, many scriptwriters deliberately revise original texts to accommodate the perceived desires of a mass audience. Sometimes an entire narrative is recast to make it more marketable; the 1995 hit, *Clueless,* and the 2001 teen film *O,* are good examples of films in which literary classics (Jane Austen's *Emma* and William Shakespeare's *Othello*) were updated to appeal to a mainstream modern audience.

Sometimes the audience's intervention is more direct. It is common practice for many filmmakers to hold "advance screenings" of major releases, designed to gauge audience reaction. In 1986, a preview audience's reaction to the ending of the film *Fatal Attraction* was so negative that director Adrian Lyne reshot the final scenes. When the film was released in the following year, it featured a markedly different conclusion. Similarly, the version of *BladeRunner* released in 1982 was significantly edited in an attempt to increase its box office appeal; however, director Ridley Scott changed the ending yet again years later, premiering his *BladeRunner—The Director's Cut* 11 years after the movie first appeared. In each case, collaboration shaped the final version and made evident the rhetorical triangle between audience, writer, and text. Similarly, writing needs to take into consideration the audience's expectations; we write to show an audience our work, so we need to respond to audience needs when we write and revise our texts.

As a writer you can benefit from "advance screenings" of your argument; the collaborative work you do on the structure and content of your outlines and drafts should guide you to a revised product that satisfies both you and your audience. But to do so, you need feedback from your audience in the form of peer review; then you will need to revise your draft to accommodate the suggestions you receive.

Consider the draft written by Sunthar Premakumar about the words within songs of Bollywood cinema, an Indian film genre that involves many long dancing numbers similar to Broadway musicals. Sunthar was curious about the messages in the song lyrics and the reasons the films are so popular (nearly twice as many are produced annually as Hollywood films) despite taxing demands of time and corniness on their audiences. He conducted a range of academic and field research, wrote a detailed outline, and then composed his first draft, keeping his passion in view. He would go on to revise the draft substantially by incorporating feedback from his teacher and his peers. But his first draft shows how you, too, can overcome your concerns and get your research argument down on paper.

Premakumar 1

Sunthar Premakumar

PWR2: Cross Cultural Rhetoric

Dr. Alyssa O'Brien

Research Paper—Draft

February 21, 2006

Bollywood Sing-Along

Introduction

I am sitting at the movie theatre in Sri Lanka with my family excited to watch the newly released Bollywood movie Yuva. The theatre is packed with people who have pledged the next three hours of their life to this movie, the latest hit film of the year. While everyone is busy eating their pop corn, the lights get dimmer in preparation for the screening of the movie. As the title is displayed the crowd starts cheering enthusiastically with young boys whistling as loud as they could. A five minute song follows the title by which time the crowd is already on its feet dancing to the upbeat tune. The crazy frenzy finally dies down as the crazy fans finally settle into their seats; a few minutes after the song had concluded. There is a long silence in the audience for a while as they are indulged in the intricate love story which involves six different characters. The whole love plot requires three hours to be developed effectively and intense concentration on the viewers' part for complete comprehension. However the random song and dance sequences that occur at frequent intervals absorb some of the tension accumulated through this intense plot. Twenty minutes into the movie the crowds go wild again. The hit number of the movie had just begun and in the spur of the moment the audience suddenly transforms into a giant chorus to start singing along with the song. Silence follows the song once again.

This procedure repeats many times over and finally the credits of the movie are displayed. As we walk out, my sister asked me what I thought of the movie and I respond with my usual 'the songs were amazing but the

Sunthar's draft title identifies his topic, but it does not yet indicate his argument. His revised paper addresses the "What about it?" question through a subtitle that reveals his sharper focus.

Sunthar chose an organizational strategy in which he opens with a personal narrative. He thereby enables his readers to understand the power of Bollywood movies on an audience.

The details in Sunthar's opening paragraph set up the key elements he'll explore in the research paper: the complicated plot lines, the long songs, and the magical allure of Bollywood films as a genre.

In this draft, Sunthar ends his introduction by posing one of his key research questions: why do people watch Bollywood films if the movies really aren't very good? He then states his hypothesis: that the music transforms an ordinary movie into an extraordinary one. During his final revision, he will develop this line into a substantial thesis paragraph, allowing readers to contemplate his argument in full and making them curious to read on and learn more about his claims.

Sunthar uses an argumentative subhead to set up his next section: providing background on Bollywood films.

Sunthar integrates his research effectively, not relying on sources too much. He introduces his source and gives a brief summary of the point before providing a direct quotation of statistical information that proves his point about the popularity of Bollywood cinema.

Sunthar has stated his thesis, though he has stated it at the end of the second section of his paper. However writing his thesis out is still a helpful first step in clarifying his argument; during revision, he can circle it and then, when he writes his next draft, he can move it up earlier into his introduction. When he does so, he'll also need to strengthen his transition to his next section.

movie wasn't good'. This would have been the two hundredth time that I had responded in this manner, but I would still go to watch more movies. Why? Well, the great songs would transform an ordinary movie into an extraordinary movie and thus making the time worth the while. However, I always wonder why these Bollywood film songs attract such fans like me and my friends time and time again.

Bollywood: An overview

Before we further explore the reasons behind the attractive force of these film songs, it is important to understand the nature of such songs. India is home to many 'ollywoods' such as Mollywood, Tollywood and Bollywood. The word Tollywood refers to the not-so- well know Telugu film industry in India. The word Mollywood is not used too much, however it refers to the Tamil film industry in South India.

Named after the Indian city renowned for movies, Bombay (now called Mumbai), Bollywood is the most prominent one of the three and is usually used to represent the entire Indian film industry. In his article titled "Bollywood", author Alex Ninian gives and overview of the Bollywood industry in a nutshell.

> On average, 800 films are produced and distributed every year, that is more than two per day, and shown to 11,000,000 people every day in 13,000 cinemas across India. To these statistics can be added the export of film to over a hundred countries where they are watched by millions of expatriate Indians, or NRIs (non resident Indians), mostly in Britain, the United States, and Europe. (235)

All these movies have many similarities such as abundant singing and dancing, cheesy love stories and unbelievable action sequences while catering towards the regional tastes. These elements differentiate the Indian movies from the ones made by its western counterparts, Hollywood. One might wonder why these songs have such an attractive impact on its audience and whether this attraction is used constructively to achieve something that transcends into ones daily life.

Premakumar 3

Indian film music has influential power on its Indian audience due its immense appeal to the public through the upbeat rhythms and classical tunes that are present in most of these songs. However, these film songs fail to make a revolutionary impact on the community since the public is more attracted to the entertaining dance numbers and don't pay much attention to the important message conveyed through the lyrics of the songs.

Religion and Music

It is interesting that music has such a power over the public in South Asia. The reason for this seems to be the importance given to religion and religious practices in this part of the world. Since the time I was born, music and religion have been integral parts of my life. My religion, Hinduism, has been instrumental in shaping my interest in music since from a young age I have been made to sing many spiritual songs during Hindu festivals. This is not just unique to me but rather something that I have in common with most of my friends in Sri Lanka, the country where I am from. The close relationship between music and religion is explained well by the famous Indian Sitar player, Pundit Ravi Shanker, in his book *"My Music, My Life"* asthe following:

> Many people have asked me if one must read, absorb, learn, and know about India's religions, philosophies, and spiritual atmosphere, or even come to India to visit and travel in order to understand our music, let alone play it. To this I would say yes, all this is necessary since our music is so closely connected to the complete unfolding of India's history and development. (Shanker 9)

In most Indian religions such as Hinduism, which is the most prominent religion in India, music one of the main tools that are used to promote spirituality and religious values. Most of the religious songs advocate love toward God and mankind while addressing importance social issues. It helps to guide the devotee towards nirvana by destroying his ungodly qualities, such as hatred, selfishness. Therefore there are numerous songs in Hinduism that focus on helping the follower to get rid of these bad qualities.

* * *

Integrating another key source, Sunthar opts for the block quote. He doesn't have the MLA format for block quotes down correctly yet, but it's crucial for him to integrate this source so he can continue to write in what we have been calling "a conversation" with his sources.

Sunthar forgets to comment on the quote after integrating it. That is, he needs to explain the evidence he has offered and then relate it to his argument before moving forward in his paper. He does a wonderful job revising this portion for his final paper, as you can see in the full version of his revision on the *Envision* website.

AT A GLANCE

Questions for Assessing Your Draft

- *Argument consistency:* Are your introduction and conclusion arguing the same points, or have you changed your argument by the end? Either revise the end to be consistent with your original thinking, or embrace your new vision and rework the beginning.

- *Organization and progression:* Does your paper flow logically, developing one idea seamlessly into the next? Do you provide important theoretical foundations, definitions, or background at the beginning of the paper to guide the audience through the rest of your argument?

- *Your voice versus sources:* Do you foreground your own argument in your paper or do you focus primarily on your sources' arguments, locating your point of view primarily in the conclusion? If the latter is true, bring your voice out more in commentaries on the quotations.

- *Information:* Are there any holes in your research? Do you need to supplement your evidence with additional research, interviews, surveys, or other source materials?

- *Opposition and concession:* Do you adequately address opposing arguments? Do you integrate your opposition into your argument (i.e., deal with them as they arise), or have you constructed a single paragraph that addresses opposing opinions?

As you notice from the draft excerpt here, Sunthar decided to use the pronoun "I" throughout his paper. His instructor suggested that he deploy the pronoun consistently, not to present unfounded opinion but to make a point based on his research or unique personal experience. The "I" has authority in these cases, but if you are not sure if you should use it in your paper, talk with your instructor about your options.

Revising Your Draft

As many professional writers can attest—and Sunthar would agree with this based on his drafting experience—a text goes through numerous drafts on its way to becoming a polished final product. Even filmmakers produce multiple drafts of their movies before they release their film, experimenting with different sequencing, camera shots, and pacing to create what they consider to be the fulfillment of their artistic vision. We've all seen the results of this process: deleted scenes or *outtakes* from popular film or television programs. What these segments represent are moments of work (writing, producing, and shooting) that, after review and editing, were removed to streamline the film.

As you might imagine, often it's difficult or even painful to reshape your work during revision; it's hard to leave some of your writing behind on the cutting room floor. However, as your project develops, its focus may change: sources or ideas that seemed important to you during the early stages of research may become less relevant, even tangential; a promising strategy of argumentation may turn out to be less suitable to your project; a key transition may be no longer necessary once you reorganize the argument. As you turn to your draft with a critical eye, what you should find is that in order to transform your paper into the best possible written product, you'll need to move beyond proofreading or editing and into the realm of macro changes, or **revision**.

That's not to suggest that proofreading is not a necessary part of the revision process; it is. Careless grammatical and punctuation errors and spelling mistakes can damage your ethos as an author, and they need to be corrected. It is very probable that you've been doing such microrevision throughout the drafting process—editing for style, grammar, punctuation, and spelling. However, sometimes it's difficult to do *broader revisions* until you have a substantial part of your paper written. It is only once your argument starts coming together that you can recognize the most productive ways to modify it. This is the key to successful revision: you have to be open to *both* microediting and large-scale, multiple revisions. Think of this process as **re-vision,** or seeing it again with new eyes, seeing it in a new light.

Let's look at decisions some students made during the revision process:

- **Draft:** Reading over her draft about the propagandistic elements in World War II films, Jennifer realized that she had gotten so caught up in presenting background information that her paper read more like a historical report than an argument.

  Revision: Jennifer sharpened her focus, cut down on some of the background information, and brought her own argument to the forefront.

- **Draft:** Miranda had the opposite problem; in her draft she made a compelling argument about the literary status of graphic novels but did not really quote from or mention any of her sources, so she wasn't showcasing her work as a researcher.

  Revision: She more prominently integrated her source material into her argument, both by referring to specific authors and articles she had read and by using additional direct quotations. In doing so, she greatly increased her ethos and the persuasiveness of her argument.

- **Draft:** After drafting her paper on hip-hop and gender identity, Sharita realized that her thesis was too broad and that in trying to cover both male and female imagery, she wasn't able to be specific enough to craft a really persuasive argument.

  Revision: Realizing that her interest really lay in exploring the conflicted stereotype of powerful, sexualized women in hip-hop videos, Sharita cut large sections of her paper revolving around the male imagery and focused on the female. The result was a provocative argument based on concrete, persuasive examples.

- **Draft:** Max, a dedicated Mac user, wrote his draft on the aesthetics of design in the Apple product line. The first version of his paper was visually stunning, detailed, and eloquently written. But it was so one sided that it read more like a marketing brochure than an academic argument.

  Revision: His task in revision was to provide a more balanced perspective on the Apple computer phenomenon. After further research, he incorporated a greater diversity of perspectives in his paper and softened some of his language to be less biased in favor of Apple products.

As these examples indicate, you need to enter into the research process looking not just for mistakes to "fix" but also for larger issues that might relate to your structure, your thesis, your scope, or the development of your ideas.

In addition to your own assessment of your writing, you should take into account **peer evaluations** of your drafts; consider your peer review sessions "advance screenings" with your audience. Sometimes you'll find that your peer reviewers vocalize ideas that echo your own concerns about your draft; other times you may be surprised by their reactions. Do keep in mind that their comments are informed *suggestions,* not mandates; your task, as the writer, is to assess the feedback you receive and implement those changes that seem to best address the needs of both your argument and your audience. Like the filmmaker looking to transform a creative vision into a box office hit, you want to reach your audience without sacrificing your own voice or argument in the process.

One way to facilitate a productive peer session is to use directed peer review questions for one-on-one discussions of your draft, rather than to rely exclusively on oral comments. When exchanging drafts with a peer group, you also may find it helpful to attach a cover memo that points your readers to specific questions you have about your draft so that they can customize their responses to address the particular issues that concern you as a writer.

COLLABORATIVE CHALLENGE

Form a peer review group to exchange the drafts of your research papers. Read your peer reviewers' papers carefully, annotating them with **constructive feedback**—positively framed suggestions about what might be changed and why. You might also complete the questions from the "Checklist for Peer Editing the First Draft" on the *Envision* Website. Then meet with your group and talk about both the strengths in the papers and suggestions for improvement. Next, go back to your computer and revise your paper. Bring a new version to class and exchange your second draft with a group composed of one new reader and one reader who was part of your group for the first draft. Again, read the drafts and write comments on them. This time, complete the questions on the *Envision* Website for the "Checklist for Peer Editing the Second Draft." Meet with your group and consider carefully the responses from both your new reader and your repeat reviewer. What do the suggestions have in common? How has your revision strengthened your argument? What further revisions do your peers suggest? Finally, discuss the extent to which audience feedback factors into your revision process.

 www.ablongman.com/envision/225

Let's return now to Sunthar's draft paper and see how he used the peer review suggestions he received to revise the sections we examined earlier.

Premakumar 1

Sunthar Premakumar

PWR2: Cross Cultural Rhetoric

Dr. Alyssa O'Brien

Research Paper—Final

March 8, 2006

Bollywood Sing-Along:

The significance of Music in the Indian Film Industry

Introduction

I am sitting at the movie theatre in Sri Lanka with my family, excited to watch the newly released Bollywood movie Yuva. The theater is packed with people who have pledged the next three hours of their lives to this movie, the latest hit film of the year. While everyone is busy eating their popcorn, the lights get dimmer in preparation for the screening of the movie. As the title is displayed, the crowd starts cheering enthusiastically, with young boys whistling as loud as they can. A five-minute song follows the title, by which time the crowd is already on its feet dancing to the upbeat tune. The crazy frenzy finally dies down as the fans finally settle into their seats, a few minutes after the song has concluded. There is a long silence in the audience for a while as they are indulged in the intricate love story that involves six different characters. The whole love plot requires three hours to be developed effectively and intense concentration on the viewers' part for complete comprehension. However, the random song and dance sequences that occur at frequent intervals absorb some of the tension accumulated through this intense plot. Twenty minutes into the movie the crowds go wild again. The hit number of the movie had just begun and in the spur of the moment the audience suddenly transforms into a giant chorus to start singing along with the song. Silence follows the song once again.

This procedure repeats many times over, until finally there is an intermission an hour and a half into the movie. As we walk out to buy a

First, Sunthar added a subtitle to indicate the focus of his research argument.

He made microedits to punctuate and still uses descriptive language that makes his writing vivid and memorable.

In this revision Sunthar incorporated advice from his peers and added several additional research questions. He also elevated his language, making it more academic in tone and word choice. In this way, he sets readers up for his argument by introducing his key argumentative terms right from the beginning.

Highlighted in yellow, the key terms of his argument revolve around his curiosity about the power of songs—words and music—to impact a community. He questions how song works as a form of persuasion. He wonders if the words can bring about change in listening audiences.

In this final revision, Sunthar expanded his one-line hypothesis into a thesis paragraph, a full articulation of argument. Notice how specific his thesis is: he lists how songs appeal through rhythm but then claims fail to make what he calls a "revolutionary" impact. Notice how he resists telling readers what the effect is— he keeps that surprise for his conclusion.

For his revision, he decided to move the background section about Bollywood to later in the paper to emphasize here instead his argument's focus on religion and music in history. In this way, his paper flows better from the previous paragraph, where his last point was about music and audiences.

drink, my sister asks me what I think of the movie, and I respond with my usual "the songs were amazing but the movie doesn't seem too good". This may be the two hundredth time that I have responded in this manner, but I will still go to watch more movies.

At this point, I began wondering about this strange mindset that I have about Indian film songs. I began wondering why these songs have such an impact on their audience. If they do have such a **strong influence** on their large audience, is it used constructively to make **an important impact** on the **Indian community**? Are the producers and music directors using this **music as a medium of persuasion** to bring about **a change in the society**? Do these songs serve a **purpose** greater than entertainment? These interesting questions motivated me to pursue the answer to these questions.

Even though Indian film music has influential power on its Indian audience due to its immense appeal to the public through the upbeat rhythms and classical tunes that are present in most of these songs, these film songs fail to make a revolutionary impact on the community because the public is more attracted to the entertaining dance numbers and do not pay much attention to the important message conveyed through the lyrics of the songs. However, these songs do fulfill their purpose as a source of entertainment that cheers up its audience by having a positive effect on their mindset.

Religion and Music

It is interesting that music has such a power over the public in South Asia. This is due to the importance given to religion and religious practices and the close connection between music and religion in this part of the world. Since the time I was born, music and religion have been integral parts of my life. My religion, Hinduism, has been instrumental in shaping my interest in music from a young age because I have been made to sing many spiritual songs during Hindu festivals throughout my life. This is not unique to me but rather something that I have in common with most of my friends in Sri Lanka. The close relationship between music and religion is

Premakumar 3

explained well by the famous Indian Sitar player Pundit Ravi Shankar in his
book *My Music, My Life:*

> Many people have asked me if one must read, absorb, learn, and know
> about India's religions, philosophies, and spiritual atmosphere, or even
> come to India to visit and travel in order to understand our music, let
> alone play it. To this I would say yes, all this is necessary since our music
> is so closely connected to the complete unfolding of India's history and
> development. (9)

Thus, Shanker explains how religion is an important component of
understanding Indian music, while at the same time music is an important
part of religion. In most Indian religions, such as Hinduism, music has been
one of the main tools used to promote spirituality and religious values.
Most of these religious songs advocate love toward God and mankind while
addressing importance social issues. These songs are composed to help
guide a follower toward nirvana by getting rid of his undesirable qualities,
such as hatred and selfishness. Therefore, these songs had the potential to
motivate a community to change for the better, a common quality found in
most Indian classical music songs.

Classical Music

Most classical songs, like their spiritual counterparts, have strong
messages embedded within them. The two eminent forms of classical music
found in India are Hindustani and Carnatic music forms. Both Hindustani
music, which is practiced in North India, and Carnatic music, which is
practiced in South India, include many inspirational songs in their
repertoires. All Indian dance forms are accompanied by one of the above-
mentioned types of classical music during performances. The combination of
music and dance in movies was inspired by these classical forms of dance
and music. The early movies included only the pure form of Indian classical
dance and music.

However, over the years the Western film industry has influenced
Bollywood, which was more than willing to adopt Western elements to
attract a larger audience. With the development of new technologies, the

Once again, Sunthar inte-
grates his research, this time
using proper MLA style: he
includes only the page
number since he has already
mentioned the author's
name above, and he elimi-
nates the unnecessary
quotation marks that he
included around the block
quotes in his draft.

Most importantly, Sunthar
paraphrases the point of this
quoted source so that readers understand the impor-
tance to the argument. He
then broadens his claim to
give more general information about the importance of
music in his community.

Sunthar sets up his next
section with a transition
word, (highlighted) foreshad-
owing his focus on "classical
music."

In this section, he provides
background research knowledge to instruct his readers
about the history of Indian
music and then transistions
into the background information on Bollywood as a
film genre that had been
located much closer to his
introduction in his final draft.
This new organization helps
him reinforce his emphasis
on the impact of the words
of Bollywood movie songs on
the audience—rather than
on the history of film itself.

Premakumar 4

music industry in India started shifting more toward a fusion path, incorporating Western and Eastern styles. Before talking about Bollywood in detail, it is important to have an overview of this industry and its imperial impact on the Indian community.

India is home to many "ollywoods," such as Mollywood, Tollywood, and Bollywood. The word Tollywood refers to the not-so-well-know Telugu film industry in India. The word Mollywood is not used too much; however, it refers to the Tamil film industry in South India. Named after the Indian city renowned for movies, Bombay (now called Mumbai), Bollywood is the most prominent term of the three and is usually used to represent the entire Indian film industry. In his article titled "Bollywood," author Alex Ninian gives an overview of the Bollywood industry in a nutshell:

> On average, 800 films are produced and distributed every year, that is more than two per day, and shown to 11,000,000 people every day in 13,000 cinemas across India. To these statistics can be added the export of film to over a hundred countries where they are watched by millions of expatriate Indians, or NRIs (non resident Indians), mostly in Britain, the United States, and Europe. (235)

Contemporary Film Music

The transformation of Indian film music into its present influential form started in 1993 with the introduction of the music director A. R. Rahman, who single-handedly changed the face of the Indian music industry with his amazing ability to fuse the two kinds of music with the aid of technology in a manner that attracted a huge audience in India. This was a major turning point in the Indian music industry.

Since 1993, this reformed version of film music has had a great impact on the general public in India. "Many people go for movies just to watch the wonderful upbeat songs included in them," said Arunan Skanthan, a film music lover in Sri Lanka, explaining the strong appeal these movies have on the public. In India music is played everywhere. From formalized concerts and shows to the songs played over the radio on the street corner, this music seems to flow into every Indian's ears

He relies on an important source he found during his research. This one presents a concise overview of the popularity of Bollywood films, so Sunthar includes a direct quote here.

Although the argument is flowing nicely here, Sunthar shows that he is having what we call "a dialogue with his sources" by weaving one into the next as evidence for his paper. He follows a quote by Arunan Skanthan with a passage from George Ruckert (see next page), placing the two sources in conversation.

Premakumar 5

most of the time. As George E. Ruckert states in his book Music in
North India:

> In India, one never gets too far from either tea or the sound of Lata's
> (Lata Mangeshkar is a famous India play-back singer) voice, although today
> it is mixed with other voices from the films, and popular selections from
> famous ghazal and bhajan singers, or the energetic qawwalalis of the late
> Nusrat Fateh Ali Khan. (2)

As Ruckert explains, music in India seems to be everywhere and one
cannot escape its influence.

With the emergence of film music, the focus on classical music has
somewhat diminished over the years, although it still attracts quite a few
music enthusiasts. However the reason why more and more people in
India prefer film music over the traditional forms is that an appreciation
of classical music requires formal training or prior knowledge, while film
music does not. The increasing popularity of film music encourages most
musicians to abandon their classical practice and pursue a career in play-
back singing for movies. Renowned classical singers such as Hariharan and
Unni Krishnan, who hail from Hinustani and Carnatic music traditions,
respectfully, are in the forefront of film music and rarely perform classical
music.

Most youngsters who start learning Indian classical music do not
intend to become professional classical singers but rather want to become
play-back singers for film songs. As a result of this mindset, film music is
gaining more influence on the Indian public than its classical predecessor.
However, film music does not use this influencing power to advocate social
values, something that classical music did effectively during its time as an
influential medium.

A Music Director's View on Film Songs

During my research I had the great honor of meeting the Indian music
director A. R. Rahman, who is considered to be the best music director in
India. During my interview with him I got the chance to obtain his
thoughts about the role played by these film songs. During the

Included in his research
iceberg were books, online
articles, journal articles, and
four interviews.

At this point, Sunthar introduces one of his key sources:
an interview with the famous
music director A. R. Rahman,
who happened to be visiting
the area and giving a talk
during the time of Sunthar's
research process. Sunthar was
able to conduct field research
with this authority and use
those quotes in his final
paper.

Premakumar 6

conversation with him I asked him whether he makes a conscious effort to include messages in his songs. He responded, "I try sometimes if the scope of the movie lets me to do it, but most of the times the producers want commercial dance numbers and that is what I have to deliver." He also mentioned that songs of such nature require a lot of time and attention to make, and in an industry for which he is expected to make many songs a month, it is nearly impossible to invest considerable time into one song.

This was a surprising reply to me since I was hoping that he would accept my view that some of the songs in the movies actually carry an important message regarding a social or ethnic issue. Although this is not completely false, it is interesting to see that movie producers and music directors don't try to include songs of this nature but rather prefer the dance numbers.

However, A. R. Rahman's first solo album, Vandae Mataram, which was not part of any movie but rather was like any other album, was a huge success in India. This album focused mainly on uniting the different provinces in India to bring about a love for the nation. Vandae Mataram, which means tribute to motherland, was made for the fiftieth anniversary of Indian independence and has sold many copies worldwide. When asked about this album and its effect on people, A. R. Rahman commented that it was made for such a purpose and thus a lot of time was put into making sure that it was "inspiring and powerful." Therefore, one can observe that it is not impossible to achieve this purpose but rather it is the thought and motivation that is required to make the film songs a powerful tool for social reform. Having listened to numerous film songs it was amazing to see the ratio between dance numbers and motivational songs that are prevalent in these movies. The motivational songs are highly outnumbered by the dance numbers.

The Appeal of Songs to the Bollywood Audience

Are the producers and the music directors the only ones to be blamed for the misuse of such a powerful medium of persuasion? It seems that the audience should share blame as well. During an interview with

---

Just as in his draft, Sunthar continues to use "I," allowing his readers to identify with his research discoveries and begin to be persuaded by his developing argument.

Sunthar draws logical conclusions from analyzing his evidence. He advances his argument by bringing in his own direct experience and analysis of films and songs, and then he leads readers to his preliminary conclusion, highlighted in yellow.

Using a question to signal a turn in his argument, he transitions to the next two sections of his paper, in which he will present the evidence of his extensive field research.

Premakumar 7

Stuti Goswamy, a junior at Stanford University majoring in economics,
I was able to get a good insight as to why so many Indians are crazy over
Bollywood songs. Stuti stated that she loves listening to Bollywood
songs, dancing to the beats, and singing along with the tunes. When
asked whether she feels that these songs carry a strong message, she
replied that she usually doesn't pay much attention to the lyrics because
most of the songs she listens to are dance numbers. When asked whether
she pays attention to motivational songs like "bharat hum ko" (a famous
motivational song from the movie Roja) she said that she is not fluent
enough in Hindi to actually understand the intricate details mentioned in
the song.

Specifically, Sunthar incorporates field research that he conducted on campus with some of his fellow students, as evidence for his argument about the impact of words and songs on an audience.

This is a common phenomenon in these Bollywood films, with both
dance numbers made up of simple lyrics and motivational songs using rare
words in Hindi that are rich in meaning but are not commonly used in
public. Therefore, these motivational songs are not easily accessible to
the common folk in India and to the second-generation Indians living
abroad. Ironically, these motivational songs are usually targeted toward
the common folk in India. For example, the song "malarodu malar," from
the famous movie Bombay, addresses the conflicts between religious
groups and advocates harmony between religions. However, the poet who
wrote the lyrics for this song uses complicated metaphors and deep words
to make the song sound pretty and thus makes it hard for the commoner
to comprehend it fully. Another example is the song "jana gana mana,"
from the movie Aayitha Ezhuthu, which is a song that inspires students to
get involved with government and social issues. Many who listen to this
song for its upbeat rhythm and amazing tune do not understand the
entire message embedded in the lyrics because the rhythm and tune
overshadow the lyrics.

These shortcomings and the huge demand for dance numbers force
most of the producers and music directors in India to abandon the idea of
including motivational songs, focusing instead on producing what the
audience demands.

Parallel Movie Industries in India

Second-year masters student Amritha Appaswami had some interesting insight regarding the other film industries in India that were not as popular as Bollywood: . . .

* * *

Roopa Mahadevan, a first-year masters student at Stanford University, mentioned that most of the "parallel cinemas" (movie industries that do not come under the classification of Bollywood) are based on some important social issue. However, since these movies, which are usually in English, only attract upper-class Indians, they remain underground most of the time and the general public rarely gets to know about them. Roopa commented that the reason for this occurrence was the mindset of most moviegoers in India. She said that most of the people who go to the theaters in India to watch movies are those who live under the poverty line, and the reason they watch these movies is to escape into an alternate reality where everyone is happy and miracles always occur. For them this is the relief after long days of struggles and worries. Therefore, Roopa argued, it is important that these movies are entertaining and have a lot of upbeat songs for the viewing pleasure of the audience. Echoing the nature of the audiences that view most of these movies, Roopa also stated that directors wouldn't concentrate too much on making a movie with a profound message when the majority of their audiences are uneducated.

Conclusion

As the crowd gets ready for the next part of the movie, I walk in slowly with a drink in one hand and popcorn in the other. My mind is still wondering about the purpose of these film songs as I look around to see whether I see any familiar faces in the audience. Even though I'm disappointed in not finding any, I notice many happy faces that are having a great time at the movie cinema after a long day at work. Then it

In this section Sunthar discusses parallel texts—other film industries—and presents more of his field research. Note that the asterisks here indicate that we have included only a portion of this section; the full paper is available online through the *Envision* Website.

Building off the field research, Sunthar advances his final argumentative point: that films serve as entertainment and even distraction, but the message of words in the music slips in nonetheless.

As he turns to the conclusion, Sunthar returns to the opening frame of his paper—the personal narrative. He embeds his final argument within this narrative, making it quite clear to readers that though the songs' revolutionary messages may not be discerned by the viewing audience, the films nevertheless give audiences a hopeful escape from the troubles they experience in their lives.

Premakumar 9

suddenly strikes me that this could be the purpose of these songs: happiness.

Even though these movies do not send out a message to the community, they do have some significance. While entertaining large masses of people who come to the cinemas to forget their sorrows, these movies also give audiences some hope in life, something to look forward to in the coming week. These movies often show miraculous events, such as someone poor becoming rich through hard work. For the common masses in India who are uneducated, these are small things that give them hope even through the numerous struggles they encounter in their daily lives. By picturing themselves in the context of the movie, they find joy in hoping that it would happen to them someday. With this new revelation, I go into the movie theater once again just to enjoy the songs, hoping that one day I will dance in the Alps with a beautiful lady dressed in a flashy costume, accompanied by numerous dancers who have a choreographed dance prepared just for this occasion.

In the final version, Sunthar developed his conclusion substantially, incorporating peer review suggestions to explain what the magical allure is for audiences. His tone becomes rhapsodic, and we can tell his argument is coming to a close.

The strong, developed ending of Sunthar's paper shows how careful revision can help you develop a compelling argument from beginning to end. Be sure to save some energy for your conclusion: you want your parting words to ring memorably in your reader's ears.

Revision as a Continual Process

Sometimes, when writing, we may continue to revise our papers even after we have "finished." Think back to the earlier *BladeRunner* example and how Ridley Scott revised the film for re-release years after its first showing. Similarly, while you may be satisfied with your final research product when you turn it in, it is possible that you have set the groundwork for a longer research project that you may return to later in your college career. Or you may decide to seek publication for your essay in a school newspaper, magazine, or a national journal. In such cases, you may need to modify or expand on your argument for this new rhetorical situation; you may produce your own "director's cut"—a paper identical in topic to the original but developed in a significantly different fashion. Keep in mind that revision is indeed "re-vision" and that *all writing is re-writing*.

AT A GLANCE

Revising Your Draft

1. *Read your essay out loud or have someone read it to you.* You can hear mistakes that you unknowingly skipped over when reading silently.

2. *Gain critical distance.* Put your essay away for a few hours, or even a few days, and then come back to it fresh.

3. *Answer peer review questions for your essay.*

4. *Don't be chained to your monitor.* Print out your draft, making revisions by hand. We conceptualize information differently on paper versus on a screen.

5. *Use your computer to help you look at your writing in different ways.* Take a paragraph and divide it into sentences, which you line up one under another. Look for patterns (for instance, is the repetition deliberate or accidental?), style issues (is sentence structure varied?), and fluidity of transitions between sentences.

6. *Take into account feedback.* You might not decide to act on the advice, but at least consider it before dismissing it.

7. *Revise out of order.* Choose paragraphs at random and look at them individually, or begin at the end. Sometimes our conclusions are the weakest simply because we always get to them last, when we're tired; start revision by looking at your conclusion first.

8. *Look at revision as a whole.* As you correct mistakes or prose problems, consider the impact that the revision makes on the rest of the essay. Sometimes it is possible just to add a missing comma or substitute a more precise verb, but often you need to revise more than just the isolated problem so that the sentence, paragraph, or essay as a whole continues to "fit" and flow together.

Focusing on Your Project

In this chapter, you have learned strategies for visual mapping, organizing, outlining, drafting, and revising your research paper. You have explored many ways of casting your argument and acquired concrete methods for integrating both written sources and visual texts as evidence for your argument. Chances are you have written the first full draft of your paper. Feel free to approach these writer's tasks creatively, such as creating a hypertext outline or packaging your research paper electronically on a CD-ROM with links to visual material such as film clips, advertisement videos, or audio files. Your work as a writer has only just started, and the "premiere" of your project awaits.

PREWRITING CHECKLIST
Focus on Analyzing Film and Documentary

❏ Assess the genre of the film (comedy? horror? drama? film noire? documentary?) and how this affects the audience's response to its content. Does the film combine elements of different genres? What is the rhetorical effect of this combination?

❏ What is the plot of the film? What is the organizational structure?

❏ Is this plot arranged chronologically? in parallel sequences? thematically? What is the rhetorical significance of arrangement?

❏ What is the message conveyed to readers? Is it persuasive or informative? Is this message conveyed through reliance on pathos, logos, or ethos?

❏ How is the ethos of the filmmaker conveyed to the audience?

❏ What notable types of shots does the filmmaker use? Jot down one or two instances where cinematic techniques (zoom-in, cuts between scenes, fade in/fade out, montage) are used for rhetorical effect.

❏ Is there a narrator in the film? voice-over? What is the effect on the audience?

❏ Is there any framing—a way of setting the beginning and end in context?

❏ How is time handled? Does the film move in chronological order? reverse chronological order? What is the significance of such rhetorical choices on the meaning and power of the film? Are flashbacks used in the film? What effect is achieved through the use of flashbacks?

❏ How are pathos, ethos, and logos produced by the different cinematic techniques? For instance, is pathos created through close-ups of characters? Is ethos created through allusions to famous films or filmmaking techniques? Is logos constructed through the insertion of a narrator's viewpoint?

❏ What is the audience's point of identification in the film? Is the audience supposed to identify with a single narrator? Does the film negotiate the audience's reaction in any specific ways? How?

❏ How is setting used to construct a specific mood that affects the impact of the message of the film?

❏ Is the film an adaptation of another work—a play or a novel? To the best of your knowledge, what modifications where made to customize the narrative for a cinematic audience? Does the text as film differ in content or message from the text in its original form? Can you see traces of revision and rewriting?

WRITING PROJECTS

1. **Visual Map or Outline:** Create a visual representation of your argument. This can be in the form of a bubble map, a flowchart, a hierarchal set of bubbles, or a handmade construction paper model. Give your ideas some kind of shape before turning to the outline. Try to write an annotation for each part of your drawing, model, or storyboard to help you move from mass of material to coherent research-based essay.

2. **Detailed Written Outline:** Working with your research materials and notes, create a written outline of your ideas, using numbers and letters to indicate subsections of your argument. Rather than simply calling the second section "II. Body," create several points within the body to show the development of your argument. You may want to start with a topic outline, but ideally you should aim for argumentative headings. Include your working thesis statement at an appropriate place in your outline, and include visuals that you will analyze in the essay itself. After you draft the outline once, go back and insert your primary source images in the outline to show how your research paper will analyze an issue through a rhetorical lens. Finally, add material from your sources at appropriate places: insert actual quotations (with page numbers) from your research sources where possible, and don't forget to cite your sources for both paraphrase and summary. Make sure you include the full names and page numbers for your sources wherever you can. This outline might easily turn into the paper itself. Use it to check the balance of sources, the progression of ideas, and the complexity of your argument.

3. **Research-Based Argument:** Write a 12- to 15-page argumentative research paper on a topic of your choice. If you wish to analyze and research visual rhetoric, consider the images that shape a debate, tell a certain history, or persuade an audience in a certain way. In other words, address an issue through a visual rhetoric lens. You should integrate research materials that can include articles, books, interviews, field research, surveys (either published or that you conduct yourself), TV programs, Internet texts, and other primary and secondary sources, including visuals. Keep in mind that, because this is a research paper, you need to balance primary and secondary materials. In addition, you should use both electronic and paper sources. Ultimately, your goal should be proving a thesis statement with apt evidence, using appropriate rhetorical and argumentative strategies.

4. **Reflection Essay:** After you have completed your essay, attach to the back of the essay a one-page reflection letter that serves as a self-evaluation. Reflect back on your research process and the development of your argument through research and revision. Include comments on the strengths of the essay, the types of revisions you made throughout your writing process, and how the collaborative process of peer review improved your essay. You might want to close by looking ahead to how you can continue to write about this issue in future projects and in future academic or professional situations.

 Visit www.ablongman.com/envision for expanded assignment guidelines and student projects.

Part III

DESIGN, DELIVERY, AND DOCUMENTATION

What a shift in the means of delivery does is bring invention and arrangement
into a new relationship with each other.

—Kathleen Yancey

CHAPTER 7
Designing Arguments

CHAPTER 8
Delivering presentations

CHAPTER 9
Documentation and Plagiarism

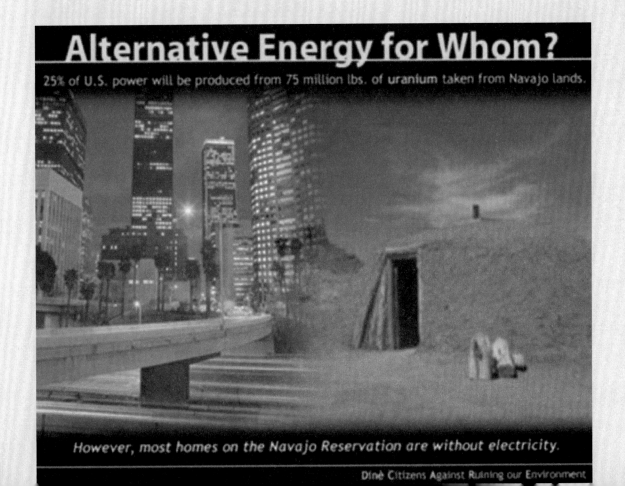

Alternative Energy for Whom?

25% of U.S. power will be produced from 75 million lbs. of uranium taken from Navajo lands.

However, most homes on the Navajo Reservation are without electricity.

Diné Citizens Against Ruining our Environment

CHAPTER 7

Designing Arguments

Chapter Preview Questions

- What are the best ways to design arguments for specific audiences?
- What purposes do abstracts, "bios," and cover letters serve?
- What is decorum and how does this rhetorical principle govern document design?
- What techniques can you learn for designing your writing in digital and multimedia formats?
- How do visual arguments work, such as opinion advertisements (or op-ads), photo essays, and Websites?

FIGURE 7.1 The cover of Michael Chaitkin's research essay offers a carefully designed visual argument.

This chapter will give you the expertise to design your work for diverse purposes and audiences. We'll provide specific guidelines for academic essays, including line-spacing, margin size, and other formatting considerations. You'll learn how to write an academic abstract, a short biography (bio), and a cover letter. Then we'll examine hybrid document design in the form of newsletters and brochures before turning to visual arguments, such as op-ads, photo essays, and multimedia projects.

Michael Chaitkin, for example, turned the cover of his research paper into a **visual argument**—a graphic representation of a written argument—that served as a compact visual depiction of his thesis (see Figure 7.1). For example, In his paper, Michael explored the significance of Michelle Bachelet becoming Chile's first elected female president; he contended that although she was the daughter of a convicted traitor who was tortured to death by Chilean dictator Augusto Pinochet, she offered the promise of "healing history's wounds" by bridging the political and cultural gap between fighting communities in Chile. Michael encapsulated this argument visually in many ways: by placing the photograph of Bachelet in the center of his collage; by using a picture of Pinochet as a somewhat oppressive top border for the page; by placing images of the Chilean communities on both sides of Bachelet; and by locating his central research question, in blue, between them. In this way, he carefully and deliberately employed the strategies of invention, arrangement, and style to produce a collage that served both as a cover for his written research paper and as an argument in its own right.

Understanding Document Design and Decorum

Let's return to Alex, our hypothetical student from Chapter 1. Her interest in a Health and Society major led her to write an analysis of antismoking advertisements and a research paper on the urban subculture of teenage runaways. She now needs to format her paper for her teacher, and she also is considering submitting it for publication in her college's undergraduate research journal. Moreover, her teacher wants her to convert her paper into a visual argument to appear in a class exhibit. Alex needs to learn appropriate document design for academic audiences, but she also needs to learn how to write an abstract and bio, and she wants to explore her choices of media for the visual argument. In each case, she has four key decisions to make: Alex must identify her *argument* (her main point), her *audience* (whom she intends to reach), her *medium* (printed article, abstract, advertisement, photo essay, or multimedia montage), and the specific *form* (the layout and design aspects) for her composition. What governs her choices in each case is a matter of document design strategy, or the choices writers make in formatting their work.

To use terms from classical rhetoric, the decisions you face for document design have to do with **decorum**—a word defined as "appropriateness." In everyday language, someone who exhibits decorum in speaking knows the right kinds of words and content to use given the circumstances and audience. For example, you might swear or whoop in joy at a baseball game, but not on a job interview when talking about how your team won the game. But decorum as a rhetorical principle extends beyond choosing the right words and phrases for the occasion.

In the Roman rhetorical tradition, Cicero separated decorum into three levels of style that he assigned to different argumentative purposes. Cicero defined the *grand style* as the most formal mode of discourse, employing sophisticated language, imagery, and rhetorical devices; its goal is to move the audience. He considered *middle style* less formal than grand style but not completely colloquial; although it uses some verbal ornamentation, it develops its argument more slowly in an attempt to persuade the audience by pleasing them. The final level, *plain style,* mimics conversation in its speech and rhythms, aiming to instruct the audience in a clear and straightforward way. By adding decorum to our rhetorical toolkit, we can make decisions about how to design documents. As demonstrated in the "Levels of Decorum" table below, we can attend to argument, audience, medium, and form by understanding the *level of style* for a particular occasion. Like our classical counterparts, we must understand our rhetorical situation and use a style that best suits the circumstance.

LEVELS OF DECORUM

Level	Characteristics	Example: Antismoking Campaign for a Written Argument	Example: Antismoking Campaign for Visual Argument
Grand or high style	Ornate language; formal structures; many rhetorical devices	Academic paper to be published in a scholarly journal	An antismoking advertisement in the *Journal of the American Medical Association*
Middle style	Some ornamentation; less formal language; argument is developed at a leisurely pace	Feature article or editorial column to be published in the campus newspaper	A photo essay or collage for a school exhibit about effects of smoking or lung cancer
Plain or low style	The least formal style; closest to spoken language; emphasis on clarity, simplicity, and directness	Weblog post on family experiences with cigarette's harmful effects	A Website devoted to the physiology and psychology of nicotine addiction

For the rest of this chapter, we'll look at various models for document design, examining the way in which we need to adjust our choice of style according to the formal and rhetorical demands of each situation.

Understanding Academic Writing Conventions

From the perspective of decorum, the conventional academic essay falls under either grand or middle style, depending on the preferences of your audience. If your instructor asks you to compose a formal written paper, you will definitely be writing in grand style.

In addition to mastering the content and using grand style for your word choices, you also need to follow the accepted format for designing your essay, as shown in the "At a Glance" box.

An entire scholarly community has reached consensus on format conventions for academic papers, so that everyone knows what information will be provided where. It's similar to the convention of every car in the United States having the steering wheel on the left; the convention fosters a set of shared expectations designed to promote consistency, order, and ease of use.

But there's a deeper *purpose* for these academic-writing conventions. Most have to do with a rhetorical relationship, the fact that people (your instructor and your peers) will be reading your paper, and these reviewers need ample space to provide written comments. By double-spacing your document and providing 1-inch margins on all sides, you leave room for reviewers to comment on lines or paragraphs. You put page numbers and your name in the upper-right corner to enable reviewers to keep track of whose paper it is and to easily refer to your writing by page number in closing comments. The rationale for stapling or clipping is to keep your pages from getting lost.

AT A GLANCE

Characteristics of Academic Writing in Grand Style

- Language should be be more sophisticated than ordinary speech
- Use formal structures to organize your paper, including:

  A complete introduction containing your thesis

  A transition paragraph predicting your argument

  Clear subsections for each part of your argument

  A substantial conclusion

AT A GLANCE

Key Elements of Academic Document Design

- Double-space all pages.
- Provide 1-inch margins on all sides.
- Number pages at the top right; include your last name.
- Use subheads to separate sections.
- Staple or clip the paper together.
- Use in-text citations to acknowledge research sources.
- Use endnotes or footnotes for additional information.
- Include a list of references at the end.
- For specific examples of documentation, see Chapter 9.

COLLABORATIVE CHALLENGE

Cut and paste a short paragraph from your research paper into a new document in your word processing program. Now copy it, and position the copied paragraph below the original on your screen. Change the font in the newly copied paragraph to one distinctly different from the original. Repeat this procedure twice more, so that you end up with four paragraphs, each with a markedly different font. Print out your paragraphs and exchange them with a partner. As you look at your partner's printout, consider the following questions: How does the font change the way that you understand what is being said in the paragraph? How do you form different expectations about the paper based on the font? How do you form a different perception of the author? Which font would you recommend the author use for the final research paper? Why? Discuss your answers with your partner.

Integrating Images in Academic Writing

There are many reasons you might want to include visuals in your research paper. If, for instance, your topic concerns hybrid cars, you might want to insert a technical diagram to explain the car's mechanics to readers. If you are analyzing advertisement campaigns for hybrid cars, your argument would benefit from showing readers an example through a strategically integrated image. But realize that randomly inserting a picture into your paper does not serve the *purpose* of using images rhetorically in an academic argument. Instead, you need to integrate visual texts into your document design in a rhetorically effective manner.

AT A GLANCE

Including Visuals in a Paper

- Does your paper focus on a visual topic, such as the analysis of ads or films? If so, you probably want to include images or screen shots as evidence and as primary materials to analyze in your writing.
- Does your paper rely on images, such as political campaigns from billboards or Websites, as supporting evidence for your thesis? If so, include image of these materials into your paper.
- If you simply insert an image without comment, a readers will skip over it. Make sure you describe its relevance in the text near the image.
- Include a caption with the figure number and a brief description.
- Provide the complete image source in your bibliography.

Carefully consider your strategy of arrangement and the *placement* of your images: Will you put them in an appendix? on your title page? on a separate page? on the same page as your written argument? Each decision is both a stylistic and rhetorical choice. An image placed in an appendix tends to be viewed as *supplementary,* not as integral to an argument; an image on a title page might act as an epigraph to set a mood for a paper, but it is less effective as a specific visual example. If you want to use your images as *argumentative evidence,* you need to show them to your readers as you analyze them; therefore, placing them beside the words of your argument will be most successful.

Once you have determined the placement that best serves your rhetorical purpose, you need to insert the image effectively. Like a quotation, an image cannot be dropped into a text without comment; it needs to be **signposted,** or connected to your argument through deliberate textual markers. You can accomplish this by making explicit **textual references** to the image—for example, "shown in the image at the right" or "(see Figure 3)"—and by taking the time to explain the rhetoric of the image for readers. Just like words quoted from a book or an interview that you might use as evidence, visual material needs *your interpretation* for readers to view it the way you do. Your analysis of its meaning will advance your argument by persuading readers to see the image as you do, and in the process, readers will pause to contemplate the evidence rather than skip over it.

Albert includes a still shot as visual evidence in case his readers haven't seen the film.

His caption includes a figure number, the name of the person and the text (the film), as well as a link to his argument: "Cassel's character . . . uses capoeira to evade this laser grid."

A less effective caption would have simply named the film.

Figure 1. Vincent Cassel's character in *Ocean's 12* uses capoeira to evade this laser grid.

Moreover, it is crucial to draft a **caption** for the image that reiterates the relationship between the point you are making in the paper and the visual evidence you include. In a paper Albert Thomas wrote about the popular sport of capoeira, a form of Brazilian martial arts that resembles dancing, he included a still image from the film *Ocean's 12* and wrote an effective caption.

Remember, however, that what is most important is the analysis of the image you include in the body of your paper; don't hide the meaning of the image in the caption. Captions should be concise but not do the work of the written argument.

Design of Academic Papers

A page from student Allison Woo's paper on Asian-American female stereotypes in contemporary cinema provides an example of *both* effective academic writing conventions and effective placement and captioning of visuals (see Figure 7.2). Since Allison's project analyzed female stereotypes in two films, *Tomorrow Never Dies* (1997) and *Payback* (1999), she decided to include two images as evidence. Rather than relegating these pictures to an appendix, Allison positioned them in the paper with text flowing around it, making the visuals an integral part of her arguments.

Woo 9

Meanwhile, the Dragon Lady images of sexuality are equally prevalent in film

today. In Tomorrow Never Dies (1997), Asian actress Michelle Yeoh plays a seductive

Chinese spy, who simultaneously flirts, manipulates, fights, and plays with her costar,

James Bond (played by Pierce Brosnan). Screenwriter and novelist Jessica Hagedorn

lists Yeoh's character as an archetypical Dragon Lady. Dressed in a tight jumpsuit in her

favorite color of corruptible black, Yeoh's character double-crosses, connives, and

seduces her way through the movie, and it is always unclear whether she is good or evil.

Figs. 8 and 9. Michelle Yeoh in
Tomorrow Never Dies, 1997 (left);
Lucy Liu in *Payback*, 2002 (right).
Their common characterization, dress,
hairstyle, weaponry, and "dangerous"
sexuality illustrate the way Hollywood
repackages the same stereotyped
characters in different movies.

Bond eventually conquers all, winning sexual access to the Asian woman. In Payback, Lucy Liu's character Pearl also double-crosses both sides.

Although she only appears in a few scenes, most of them show her seductively

whispering a few lines of sexual prompting. Achieving almost orgasmic pleasure from

sexually manipulating and dominating men, she thrives in her sexuality and moral

corruption. Even Caucasian movie critic Sam Adams recognizes Pearl as a stereotypical

"Dragon Lady," as she makes sexual advances on the hero (Mel Gibson) and the villains

in the movie. Her Asian heritage is distinguishable from the Caucasian prostitute in the

Allison's last name and the page number are in the upper-right corner.

She indents the first line and double-spaces the text.

By embedding the images in the paper, Allison makes readers pause to analyze them as evidence—the way readers would study a poem or a quoted line from a book.

She arranges the visuals so they are in dialogue, reproducing the comparison that is the purpose of her paragraph. In this way, the two figures function effectively as visual evidence for her argument: the striking similarity in pose, costume, and demeanor between actresses Lucy Liu and Michelle Yeoh substantiate Allison's points about the prominence of the "Dragon Lady" stereotype in popular American films.

FIGURE 7.2 Allison Woo, "Slaying the Dragon: The Struggle to Reconcile Modern Asian Identity with Depictions of Asian Women in Past and Present American Film," page 9, showcases visual and verbal arguments working together.

Allison's caption lists necessary information—figure numbers, descriptive titles, names of the actresses and films, and the years of release—as well as the sources for the images. Moreover, by paraphrasing the written argument, the caption paraphrases the central point of Allison's paragraph. Through this successful union of words and images, Allison constructs an academic argument effectively and persuasively.

Tools of Design for Academic Audiences

In addition to the research paper, you might choose to compose supplemental pages, such as a cover page containing an academic *abstract* and research *bio*—a brief biography of the author. We'll discuss these aspects now so you can add them to your toolkit of writing strategies.

AT A GLANCE

Writing an Abstract

- Plan to write 1 or 2 paragraphs about your paper, working through these questions:
- What level of decorum or style do you wish to use?
- How will the style predict the tone of your paper and establish your persona as a researcher?
- Do you want to you use "I"?
- How much specificity should you include from the paper?
    - Do you want to list the concrete examples you analyze in your writing?
    - Do you want to give an overview of your argument?
    - Should you name sources you use in making your argument?
- How can you be both brief and engaging?

Composing an Abstract

The **research abstract** is a professional academic genre designed not only to present the research topic but also to lay out the argument. There are many versions of abstracts depending on the disciplinary audience and the purpose of the writing. When applying to academic conferences in the humanities, for example, academics often must write a 500-word abstract that predicts the paper's argument, research contribution, and significance. Other times, especially for writers in the sciences or social sciences, abstracts are written *after* the paper has been completed to serve as a short summary of the article. You will undoubtedly encounter these abstracts when you begin searching for research articles; they often precede a published paper or accompany bibliographic citations in online databases.

Abstracts can range from a few sentences to a page in length, but they are usually no longer than two paragraphs. The key in writing an abstract is to explain your argument in one brief, coherent unit. As you compose your abstract, you will need to make several rhetorical decisions.

To understand how your answers to the questions listed in the "At a Glance" box will shape your writing, let's consider three student abstracts each correspond to a different level of decorum, use varying levels of specificity, and implement diverse means of constructing a research persona.

Seeing Connections
See an example of a scientific abstract at the beginning of Harrision Pope's "Evolving Ideals of Male Body Image as Seen Through Action Toys" on page 284.

- Molly Cunningham, for her abstract on her paper "Illuminating the Dark Continent: Hollywood Portrayals of Africa," writes in the *grand style* of decorum: she uses complex academic terms and a sophisticated vocabulary, including terminology from her discipline of postcolonial anthropology. In three complex sentences, she conveys her theoretical approach to analyzing film, names the films, and provides her thesis before ending with a statement of broader significance.
- Laura Hendrickson's abstract for her paper titled "Plastic Surgery Among Women in South Korea" uses the *middle style* of decorum by combining the use of "I" with specific terms from her research, such as "Neo-Confucian ideals."

She identifies her topic—observations about plastic surgery in Korean female role models—and makes a claim about it—that surgery represents a projected Western standard of beauty.

- David Pinner relies more heavily on *plain style* for his abstract on copyright and the Creative Commons movement:

> Since the rise of Napster and mp3s, the battle for intellectual property control of artistic works has exploded. Restrictive measures by the RIAA and MPAA threaten to take control of creative works away from both users and creators, to the point where people can't even control the data on their computer. However, a new alternative has emerged: Creative Commons, a copyright license designed for flexibility, readability and ease of use. In my project, I examine the way that Creative Commons is changing the nature of artistic collaboration in a world where art is increasingly created and distributed through electronic means.

Several elements of this abstract mark it as plain style: the use of the contraction *can't*; the use of the first person; and the concluding statement of purpose that resists providing a fully developed argument. The abstract avoids excessive display or ornamentation and instead is direct, clear, and accessible—all hallmarks of plain style.

Shaping Your Bio

While the abstract offers a concise statement of the argument, the **bio** is a concise paragraph that explains the persona of the writer to the intended audience. The bio functions to persuade readers of the writer's depth of knowledge or connection to the topic. Usually, the bio describes the writer's credentials, interests, and motivations for engaging in research work. Molly Cunningham's bio for her paper on Hollywood depictions of Africa follows this model, resembling the polished "About the Author" paragraph that you might find at the back of a book on the topic or in the headnote of an academic article:

> Molly Cunningham is a sophomore planning to double major in Cultural and Social Anthropology and English. After spending time in East Africa, she has become interested in exploring cultural definitions of the orphan within

Student Writing

See abstracts and students bios by Molly, Laura, and David.
www.ablongman.com/envision/226

the community and family in light of postcolonialism as well as the AIDS pandemic. She is currently planning a summer research project in Botswana to do ethnographic research on this topic. Cunningham is also interested in the politics of humanitarian aid and the interplay between community and international donors. Involved in fundraising for a Kenyan orphanage, she hopes to deconstruct the meanings and attitudes that shape the nature and determine the amount of foreign aid going into Africa. She has utilized this research project to expand her thinking on this topic while learning to convey her findings to wider audiences.

Notice how Molly names specific qualifications and experiences she has had that make her an authority in this area. Moreover, she ends the bio with her future plans in this area of research that suggest her pursuit of a "research line" or academic path of scholarly inquiry.

It is possible, however, that if you are writing a bio to accompany a research proposal you may feel that, at this point in your project, you have no authority on the topic. It is important to keep in mind that as you explore your sources, you will become more knowledgeable about your topic and be able to contribute to dialogue about your area of research. Thus even at an early stage of your research, you can use language, tone, and style to construct a sense of ethos. Look, for example, at David Pinner's bio and the way he establishes his authority even though he had just begun his research:

Seeing Connections
See the Frag Dolls' About Us Webpage on page 475 for an example of how to use a biographical profile to create a sense of authority and ethos.

David Pinner is a sophomore at Stanford University majoring in physics. His father came from a traditional copyrighted background, while his mother's family had long been in the public domain. Being raised in a multilicensed household was difficult, but thanks to the work of Creative Commons and other copyleft organizations, his situation is finally being recognized by the general public. He enjoys electronic media, sailing, playing music, and Stickin' it to The Man. He is a dues-paying member of the Electronic Frontier Foundation (www.eff.org) and releases his blog under an Attribution- NonCommerical-ShareAlike v2.0 Creative Commons license.

David creates a sense of his credibility as a researcher on this issue in several ways: by demonstrating his familiarity with the sides of the debate (*copyright* versus *public domain*); by using terminology relevant to the topic (*multilicensed, copyleft*); and by referring to some of the prominent organizations involved in the copyright debate (*Creative Commons, Electronic Frontier Foundation*). In addition, his humorous tone in the bio anticipates the approach he will use in his research paper.

When formatting your own bio, you might decide to include a photograph of yourself. Remember to select your picture carefully, with attention to its rhetorical impact. Many students who choose to write a traditional bio like Molly's opt for a formal photograph such as a school portrait; other students, like David, might choose a more candid or humorous picture to complement the tone of their bios. One student, when writing about online gaming communities, even created a Photoshopped portrait of herself standing next to her onscreen avatar identity to represent the two perspectives she was bringing to her research. As you can tell, the picture works in conjunction with the bio not only to construct a persona for the writer, but also to suggest that writer's rhetorical stance.

CREATIVE PRACTICE

Write a short bio of yourself using plain style, such as you might include on a Facebook profile or MySpace page; choose a picture to accompany your bio. Now translate the plain style bio into grand style and choose a new photo to accompany a hypothetical published version of your research paper. Reflect on this process. How does the level of decorum relate to audience, context, and purpose? How satisfied are you with the success of each version of your bio?

Combining Visual and Verbal Design Elements

So far, we've been talking about design in written arguments. But we also know that the visual rhetoric of a page matters to an audience: from the paragraph indents to the margins and double-spaced lines, to the rhetorical placement of images—all these design decisions are ways of conveying your level of decorum and your purpose to your specific audience. When we say "first impressions," we often mean how well a writer meets the conventions anticipated by the audience.

When your audience allows you to combine visual and verbal elements, you can produce *a hybrid composition* such as a feature article for a magazine, a newsletter aimed at a community audience, or an online article for diverse readers. Research has shown that in such texts, readers tend to focus on the visual part of a text first, before the words. Whether it's a news article, a traditional academic paper with a visual, or a multimedia collage, the visual grabs the attention first. Perhaps the images in this book engage your interest more immediately than the prose. Indeed, according to Adbusters, an organization devoted to cultural criticism and analysis, the visual part of any page is noticed significantly more than any text on the same page. Adbusters uses this finding to provide

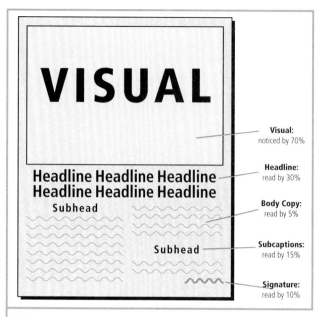

FIGURE 7.3 A graphic representation of what readers notice most on a page: visuals grab attention most.

advice for creating ads, but we can apply the insight to written compositions combining visual and verbal elements.

Figure 7.3 provides a useful diagram for understanding the way readers process information, showing that 70 percent of readers notice visuals and 30 percent pay attention to headlines; much farther down on the attention-grabbing scale are the body, subheads, and the signature. Knowing this, consider the importance of visual as you approach designing your own hybrid compositions. As for your headline—second in importance to viewers—follow a suggestion from Adbusters: "The most important thing to remember here is that your headline must be short, snappy and must touch the people that read it. Your headline must affect the readers emotionally, either by making them laugh, making them angry, making them curious or making them think." Clearly, headlines work through rhetorical appeals: you need to think carefully about which appeal—pathos, ethos, or logos—would provide the most effective way to engage your audience.

Let's look at the design decisions Ashley Mullen made in formatting her writing project on the topic of police brutality. She created a newsletter that featured a cover story in which she arranged words around a powerful image. In designing this text, Ashley took into account not only the argument she sought to make but also, as Figure 7.4 makes clear, the choices of layout, placement of images, font size, color, and overall design. Her painstaking care with the design of this text is evident in the power of her finished product. Inside the newsletter, Ashley selected several photographs—each functioning as an individual argument—as a graphic way of representing the additional points she wanted to make on the issue: each photo anchored her writing and complemented the diverse perspectives she crafted. We can see here how visual rhetoric functions as a powerful tool of argument for her hybrid composition; it complements her careful attention to style through her word choices, imagery, expressions, and argument for each position. You might do the same in your writing through formatting your work in newspaper columns or as a magazine feature article, Website, or personal letter.

Community-based writing—whether it is practical or academic—is *writing for real.* It engages tangible issues, uniting thought and action, and it calls for new approaches to writing.

—Carolyn Ross and Ardel Thomas, *Writing for Real*, 17

Designing Arguments for Public Audiences

Although Ashley Mullen designed her hybrid composition for an academic audience (her class), she could have easily decided to share this writing project with a community group, a public service organization, or a student group dedicated to social change. Often we call such projects **service-learning** or **community service** projects because they combine learning (or writing) with service to the community. The writing you do for this type of class project is likely to be produced for a nonacademic audience, including a nonprofit agency, a city council, or members of an outreach group.

FIGURE 7.4 Design of Ashley Mullen's hybrid composition.

For these writing projects, you might be asked to produce a grant letter, a newsletter article, a fact sheet, a brochure, or even a Website. Such projects benefit both the nonprofit organization and the members it serves; in addition, it provides you with experience producing the kinds of texts you'll be asked to write throughout your professional career.

Let's take a look at the design strategies employed in community service writing projects, which are often multilayered, just like many of the professional projects you might encounter outside the university setting. That is, you might be asked to develop not just one flyer, pamphlet, or poster but rather a series of interconnected texts; thus, design becomes a more complicated process of connecting diverse documents according to purpose and audience.

For example, as part of their service-learning project for the nonprofit organization Alternative Spring Break (ASB)—a program that offers college students an opportunity to use their spring break to help a community by working with the homeless, cleaning

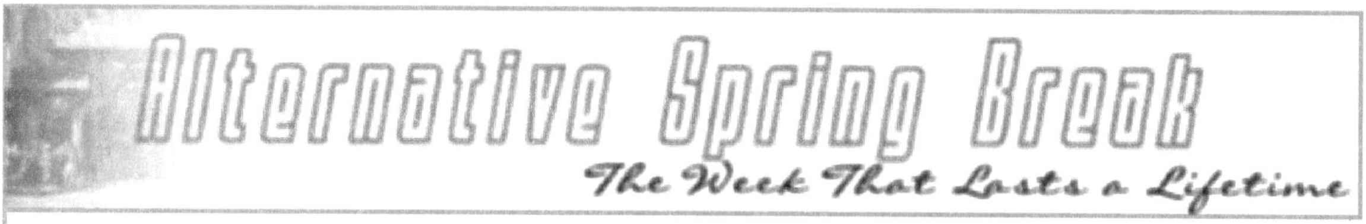

FIGURE 7.5 Gene Ma's redesigned logo for the ASB Website.

out land to grow plants, and building affordable housing—students Gene Ma and Chris Couvelier created an interview questionnaire, a formatted feature article for online publication, and as Figure 7.5 shows, designed a new logo as well as new content for the group's Website.

The logo features a sleek, minimalist approach to engaging prospective students: the red and white letters replicate the university's colors (in place of the blue and yellow used in the old logo); and the faint image of students in San Francisco's Chinatown conveys the location of one of ASB's most successful community programs that focuses on helping the Asian-American population.

The key to the design of this hybrid composition project, as with many nonacademic writing tasks, was collaboration. Here's how it worked: Gene and Chris divided the tasks. First, Chris contacted past participants of ASB through a written survey and follow-up telephone calls, and then he created a newsletter suitable for publication on the Webpage (see Figure 7.6).

After Chris completed his work, Gene analyzed the rhetoric of the organization's Website and found it dull and cluttered. He created a new logo, new content, different pictures, and 40 pages of updated materials (see Figure 7.7). Finally, he created a humorous PowerPoint presentation to convey to his colleagues in class the process of researching, designing, and producing this hybrid composition. The multiple layers of this service-learning project made it much more akin to the kind of work that you will find in the workforce, whether you work for a nonprofit or professional organization; in either case, the total needs of a specific community audience dictated the various steps along the way to completion of the project.

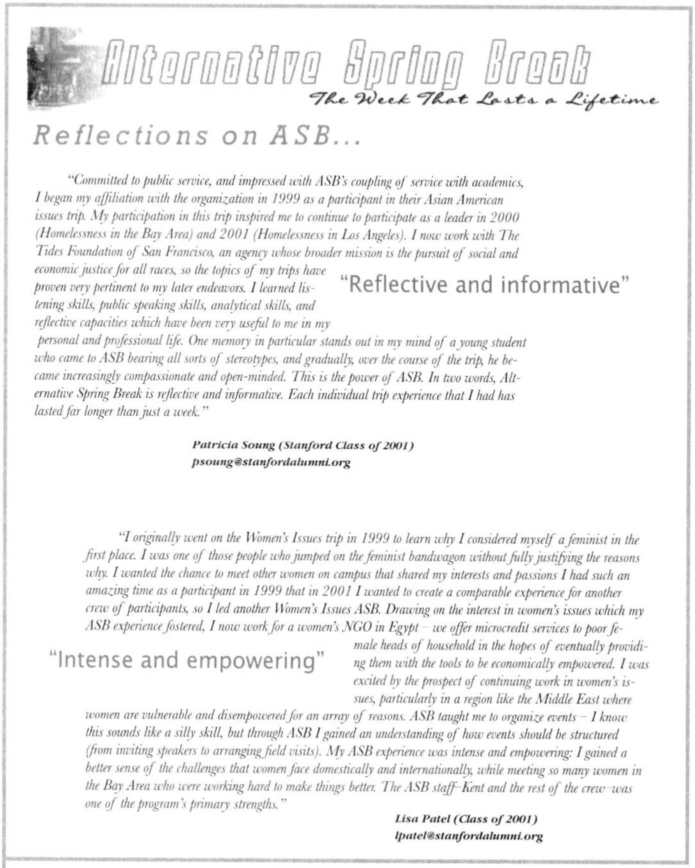
Alternative Spring Break
The Week That Lasts a Lifetime

Reflections on ASB...

"Committed to public service, and impressed with ASB's coupling of service with academics, I began my affiliation with the organization in 1999 as a participant in their Asian American issues trip. My participation in this trip inspired me to continue to participate as a leader in 2000 (Homelessness in the Bay Area) and 2001 (Homelessness in Los Angeles). I now work with The Tides Foundation of San Francisco, an agency whose broader mission is the pursuit of social and economic justice for all races, so the topics of my trips have proven very pertinent to my later endeavors. I learned listening skills, public speaking skills, analytical skills, and reflective capacities which have been very useful to me in my personal and professional life. One memory in particular stands out in my mind of a young student who came to ASB bearing all sorts of stereotypes, and gradually, over the course of the trip, he became increasingly compassionate and open-minded. This is the power of ASB. In two words, Alternative Spring Break is reflective and informative. Each individual trip experience that I had has lasted far longer than just a week."

"Reflective and informative"

Patricia Soung (Stanford Class of 2001)
psoung@stanfordalumni.org

"I originally went on the Women's Issues trip in 1999 to learn why I considered myself a feminist in the first place. I was one of those people who jumped on the feminist bandwagon without fully justifying the reasons why. I wanted the chance to meet other women on campus that shared my interests and passions I had such an amazing time as a participant in 1999 that in 2001 I wanted to create a comparable experience for another crew of participants, so I led another Women's Issues ASB. Drawing on the interest in women's issues which my ASB experience fostered, I now work for a women's NGO in Egypt – we offer microcredit services to poor female heads of household in the hopes of eventually providing them with the tools to be economically empowered. I was excited by the prospect of continuing work in women's issues, particularly in a region like the Middle East where women are vulnerable and disempowered for an array of reasons. ASB taught me to organize events – I know this sounds like a silly skill, but through ASB I gained an understanding of how events should be structured (from inviting speakers to arranging field visits). My ASB experience was intense and empowering: I gained a better sense of the challenges that women face domestically and internationally, while meeting so many women in the Bay Area who were working hard to make things better. The ASB staff–Kent and the rest of the crew–was one of the program's primary strengths."

"Intense and empowering"

Lisa Patel (Class of 2001)
lpatel@stanfordalumni.org

FIGURE 7.6 Chris Couvelier's newsletter design.

FIGURE 7.7 Screen shot from Gene Ma's newly designed Website for ASB.

Formatting Writing for Audiences

Let's look now at a purely verbal or written example of formatting writing for online audiences before we move to the visual arguments in the next section. In the following reading, the author employs many of the elements from the "At a Glance" box on document design that appeared earlier in the chapter. The selection includes a title, subheads, references, and a reference list at the end. But notice how the written argument has been changed or translated into a *hybrid composition* to meet the expectations of the online reading audience.

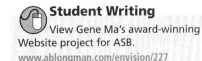
Student Writing
View Gene Ma's award-winning Website project for ASB.
www.ablongman.com/envision/227

What's Wrong With The Body Shop?
—a criticism of 'green' consumerism—

REFERENCED VERSION—all the facts and opinions in the London Greenpeace A5 'Body Shop' leaflet validated. Note: most references are given just by way of example.

The Body Shop have successfully manufactured an image of being a caring company that is helping to protect the environment [1] and indigenous

The title is in plain style and all capital letters, with the subtitle in lowercase. This font decision makes it appealing to online readers.

The numbers correspond to notes and sources at the end. These notes are *hyperlinked*, so readers can jump there easily while reading on the web.

peoples [2], and preventing the suffering of animals [3]—whilst selling 'natural' products [4]. But behind the green and cuddly image lies the reality—the Body Shop's operations, like those of all multinationals, have a detrimental effect on the environment [5] and the world's poor [6]. They do not help the plight of animals [7] or indigenous peoples [8] (and may be having a harmful effect), and their products are far from what they're cracked up to be [9]. They have put themselves on a pedestal in order to exploit people's idealism [10]—so this leaflet has been written as a necessary response.

Companies like the Body Shop continually hype their products through advertising and marketing, often creating a demand for something where a real need for it does not exist [11]. The message pushed is that the route to happiness is through buying more and more of their products. The increasing domination of multinationals and their standardised products is leading to global cultural conformity [12]. The world's problems will only be tackled by curbing such consumerism - one of the fundamental causes of world poverty, environmental destruction and social alienation [13].

FUELLING CONSUMPTION AT THE EARTH'S EXPENSE

The article uses argumentative subheads, as might an academic paper. They convey points of argument being made in the article. Moreover, they keep readers interested.

The Body Shop have over 1,500 stores in 47 countries [14], and aggressive expansion plans [15]. Their main purpose (like all multinationals) is making lots of money for their rich shareholders [16]. In other words, they are driven by power and greed. But the Body Shop try to conceal this reality by continually pushing the message that by shopping at their stores, rather than elsewhere, people will help solve some of the world's problems [17]. The truth is that nobody can make the world a better place by shopping.

20% of the world's population consume 80% of its resources [18]. A high standard of living for some people means gross social inequalities and poverty around the world [19]. Also, the mass production, packaging and transportation of huge quantities of goods is using up the world's resources faster than they can be renewed and filling the land, sea and air with dangerous pollution and waste [20]. Those who advocate an ever-increasing level of consumption, and equate such consumption with personal well-being, economic progress and social fulfillment, are creating a recipe for ecological disaster [21].

Rejecting consumerism does not mean also rejecting our basic needs, our stylishness, our real choices or our quality of life. It is about creating a just, stable and sustainable world, where resources are under the control of local communities and are distributed equally and sparingly—it's about improving everyone's quality of life. Consuming ever more things is an unsatisfying and harmful way to try to be happy and fulfilled. Human happiness is not related to what people buy, but to who we are and how we relate to each other. LET'S CONSUME LESS AND LIVE MORE!

MISLEADING THE PUBLIC

Notice how the article uses all CAPS to draw the online reader's attention and even begins a new section with a two word question.

Natural products? The Body Shop give the impression that their products are made from mostly natural ingredients [22]. In fact like all big cosmetic companies they make wide use of non-renewable petrochemicals, synthetic colours, fragrances and preservatives [23], and in many of their products they use only tiny amounts of botanical-based ingredients [24]. Some experts have warned about the potential adverse effects on the skin of some of the synthetic ingredients [25]. The Body Shop also regularly irradiate certain products to try to kill microbes - radiation is generated from dangerous non-renewable uranium which cannot be disposed of safely [26].

. . .

CENSORSHIP

As the Body Shop rely so heavily on their 'green', 'caring' image, they have threatened or brought legal action against some of those who have criticised them, trying to stifle legitimate public discussion [46]. It's vital to stand up to intimidation and to defend free speech.

WHAT YOU CAN DO

Together we can fight back against the institutions and the people in power who dominate our lives and our planet. Workers can and do organise together to fight for their rights and dignity. People are increasingly aware of the need to think seriously about the products we use, and to consume less. People in poor countries are organising themselves to stand up to multinationals and banks which dominate the world's economy. Environmental and animal rights protests and campaigns are growing everywhere. Why not join in the struggle for a better world? London Greenpeace calls on people to create an anarchist society - a society without oppression, exploitation and hierarchy, based on strong and free communities, the sharing of precious resources and respect for all life. Talk to friends and family, neighbours and workmates about these issues. Please copy and circulate this leaflet as widely as you can.

REFERENCES

1. See "Fuelling Consumption" paragraphs in the leaflet and associated references.
2. See "Exploiting Indigenous Peoples" paragraphs in the leaflet and associated references.
3. See "Helping Animals?" paragraph in the leaflet and associated references.
4. See "Natural products?" paragraph in the leaflet and associated references.
5. [Numerous publications, statements, advertisements, etc. by the *Body Shop*.] For example, the company's Mission Statement (1998) says that they are dedicating their business "to the pursuit of social and environmental change" and are trying to ensure that their business "is ecologically sustainable, meeting the needs of the present without compromising the future." "For us, animal protection, human rights, fair trade and environmentalism, are not just fads or marketing

Some sections are very short, a common feature in online writing, where information is "chunked" into accessible packages.

The article uses direct address, the pronoun *you*, to engage readers. This design strategy again indicates the use of the plain style.

For more information, contact:
London Greenpeace
5 Caledonian Road
London N1 9DX, UK.
Tel/Fax 0171 713 1269
Tel 0171 837 7557
E-mail: lgp@ envirolink.org

The "More Information" column above is an online design version of the bio; the contact information gives readers more knowledge of the persona while building ethos and authority.

Since these notes are positioned far down on the page, they can go into more detail because they assume that only very interested readers will be accessing this part of the composition.

gimmicks but fundamental components in our holistic approach to
life of which work and business are a part" [Gordon Roddick (Chairman)
quoted in 1996 *Body Shop* publication "Our Agenda".] "I'd rather promote
human rights, environmental concerns, indigenous rights, whatever, than
promote a bubble bath" said Anita Roddick (the *Body Shop* founder and
Chief Executive) [speech at 'Academy of Management', Vancouver
(Aug 95).]

Back to 'Beyond McDonald's—Retail' Section

London Greenpeace Press Release

WWW Body Shop FAQ

London Greenpeace reply to Body Shop statement

A5 version of 'What's Wrong With The Body Shop'

> From a design perspective, the final series of links for future reading signifies one of the great benefits of writing a hybrid composition in a digital environment.

As you can tell from this article, the same strategies of design that shape academic research papers also apply to other modes: what is most important in each is a consideration of *purpose, audience,* and *argument.* Think about how readers will interact with your writing—whether as a print copy handed in for comments (in which case you double-space and follow academic guidelines); as a newsletter (in which case you might open with a powerful image, lay out the writing in columns or boxes, and use an interesting page size); or as a hybrid piece to be read on the Web (in which case you include hyperlinks, single-space, create shorter chunks, and use font strategically).

Designing Visual Arguments

In essence, *visual arguments* are compact multimedia texts that exist as independent creations, such as op-ads, photo essays, Websites, and montages. We can understand these texts through the levels of decorum (outlined earlier in the chapter): someone surfing the Web might find the student Website dedicated to family members who died from smoking cigarettes (our plain-style example); a person browsing through departmental publications might encounter a student's photo essay about the effects of smoking (our middle-style example); or a visitor looking at an exhibit case in a library might see op-ads created by a Writing and Social Issues class and find in this work powerful pieces of visual rhetoric (our grand-style example).

When you construct a visual argument—whether generated for your research project, as a new argument about a issue, or as an assignment for your class—you have the opportunity to experiment with many forms of media to make a powerful argument. You can apply strategies for inventing, arranging, and producing the design of an innovative visual argument that will persuade viewers to agree with your message.

Keep in mind, however, that each medium structures information in a distinct way. A PowerPoint slide is set up differently than a Webpage, just as a Webpage is set up differently than a magazine advertisement. Therefore, part of creating a powerful visual argument lies in identifying your chosen medium's conventions of structure and style and adjusting the form of your argument—its layout, design, style, and organization of information—to be the most appropriate choice for your project.

Crafting an Op-Ad

The **op-ad,** or **opinion advertisement,** is one of the most concise forms of visual argument. Most op-ads promote an opinion rather than a consumer product. Many nonprofit organizations, special interest groups, and political parties find the op-ad a particularly effective way to reach their target audiences. Like all ads, the op-ad is a compact persuasive text, one that uses rhetorical appeals to convey its message. In addition, like other types of ads, an op-ad may rely partially on written text, but it tends to work through the visual components of its argument.

In Figure 7.8, for instance, the op-ad makes its point through a strategic combination of visual and verbal elements. The Body Shop has crafted an innovative image that communicates a powerful message: the realistically proportioned doll, set in a confident, casual pose against a natural background of ivy, produces a strong counterstatement against standards of body image in the mass media that promote exceptional thinness for feminine beauty. The words, "There are 3 billion women who don't look like supermodels and only 8 who do," are arranged to reinforce the visual argument of the non-supermodel-like body. The image creates an argument based on pathos, while the statistical words rely on logos. The design of the op-ad thus works through visual and verbal strategies to make people think twice about body image. The tiny words under the Body Shop name and logo accentuate and confirm the argument of the image: "Know your mind love your body." In this way, the op-ad uses the way readers attend to information on a page: image first, headline second, caption third.

In many ways, the figure of the heavyset Body Shop doll evokes Barbie; op-ads often rely on this rhetorical strategy—**parody,** or the use of one text's formal properties to subvert the meaning of the original and make an independent argument.

In Figure 7.9, a spoof ad from Adbusters, the iconic figure of Joe Camel has been transformed into Joe Chemo to dramatize the link between cigarettes and lung cancer. Even the mascot's trademark symbol of his "coolness"—his sunglasses—are transformed into a symbol of loss, as Joe gazes on them sorrowfully. Held away from his face, exposing his ravaged eyes, they are now a mere reminder of the ostensibly "cool" life he once had with his cigarette-smoking ways.

FIGURE 7.8 This Body Shop opinion advertisement relies on a powerful visual argument to shock readers into questioning concepts of beauty.

FIGURE 7.9 This Joe Chemo op-ad derives its power from its parody of the well-known Joe Camel character that appeared on cigarette boxes for years.

AT A GLANCE

Designing an Op-Ad

- Decide on your purpose (to inform, to persuade, to move to action).
- Identify your audience.
- Know your argument.
- Determine which appeals to use (pathos, logos, ethos).
- Select key images for your ad.
- Write your print text; decide how it will function in relation to your image(s).
- Draft a gripping headline to complement your image.
- Experiment with layout—arrangement, image size, organization of text—to arrive at the most effective design.

Seeing Connections
For an example of an OpAd poster, see the 2004 Get Real Campaign poster from the National Eating Disorders Association on p. 280.

To understand how to compose your own op-ad, let's look at the process by which one student, Carrie Tsosie, constructed her visual argument. After writing an effective research paper that presented the dangers of allowing uranium mining on or near Navajo reservations, Carrie decided to reformulate her argument as an op-ad to reach a larger audience. Her initial considerations were her visual format and her headline—two elements of her ad that underwent some revision. She explained:

> My first idea was to have an image of a deformed lamb because then the audience would see what radiation poisoning can do. I wanted to use the phrase "Stop mining before it starts," but it seemed like that phrase was overdone, and I don't think that my audience could really relate to the deformed lamb because they do not know how important it is to some Navajo people and their lives. (Tsosie, reflection letter)

As shown in her completed op-ad (Figure 7.10), Carrie decided against the pathos-based image of a sick animal.

She opted instead to feature different human environments through her strategic choices of images. In addition, rather than base her ad on a strong imperative such as "Stop Mining," she chose to soften her voice and reach her audience by asking them to question their assumptions about alternative energy. In her final op-ad, she composed a heading with the provocative question "Alternative Energy for Whom?" and then followed the words with a striking visual argument. It is here, in the image, that we find the main work of argumentation. Carrie combined an image from the urban landscape with a stereotypical image from the reservation to produce a striking effect, using what we call *visual juxtaposition,* or the combination of multiple images, as a rhetorical device to call attention to the discrepancy between these ways of life and inform readers about her critique.

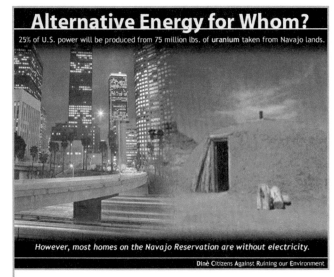

FIGURE 7.10 Carrie Tsosie's op-ad uses visual juxtaposition and a strong headline to make its argument against U.S. mining practices.

Producing a Photo Essay

Although op-ads offer a concise, forceful argument, you may wish to develop your points more thoroughly than one page allows or use visual space to show the range of material with which you've been working. If so, consider the **photo essay**—a text in which photographs, rather than print text, convey the central argument. In a word-based essay, verbal text takes priority, and images are typically used as supplements. In a photo essay, by contrast, the visual either collaborates with the verbal or becomes the *primary mode* of representation and persuasion.

As a genre, the photo essay first emerged in 1936 with the launching of *Life* magazine, whose mission statement was "to see life; to see the world." Over the 63 years it remained in print, *Life* hosted many of America's most famous photo essays, covering a range of topics from the space race to the Vietnam War, the civil rights movement, and rock and roll. But the photo essay can assume many different forms and use diverse media: it could be a series of documentary photographs and articles about southern sharecroppers published together in book form, such as Walker Evans's and James Agee's *Let Us Now Praise Famous Men* (1941); it could be a book-length photo essay that juxtaposes images with first-person narratives, such as Lauren Greenfield's *Girl Culture* (2002); it could be a striking 27-page color spread in a magazine, such as William Albert Allard's "Solace at Surprise Creek" in the June 2006 issue of *National Geographic;* or it could even be an online arrangement of captioned photos, such as *A Rescue Worker's Chronicle,* created by paramedic Matthew Levy. In each case, the photographs and written text work together, or the images themselves carry the primary weight of the argument.

Today electronic photo essays are essential conveyers of important events, a result of Internet news sources like CNN.com, Time.com, and MSNBC.com, which routinely publish photo essays as "picture stories" on their Websites. Such texts are composed of a series of images and words that work together to suggest an argument about a person, event, or story. Each electronic photo essay typically contains (1) a photo, (2) an accompanying caption, (3) an audio option, and (4) a table of contents toolbar that allows readers to navigate through the images. The result is an electronic text that maintains many structural similarities to print text: it offers readers a clear sense of progression from beginning to end while investing its argument with the rhetorical force of multiple media (word, image, sound).

COLLABORATIVE CHALLENGE

Perform an Internet search on the term "photo essay." In small groups, select one of the essays that results from the search and analyze how it creates an argument. What is the relationship between text and image? Which is given priority? What is the intended audience, and how does the design of the photo essay reflect attention to audience? How interactive is the experience? After assessing the properties of the photo essay as a group, together map out alternative strategies of design. Present the original and your plan for an alternative version to the class, clarifying the rationale behind the changes you would make and suggesting which project—yours or the original—you feel is the most rhetorically effective photo essay and why. Then, based on what you have learned, compose a photo essay about your university. First, decide on your thesis—that is, the main argument you wish to make about your school: is it an institution that prides itself on academic excellence? on student life? on tradition? on diversity? Then, using a digital camera, take appropriate photos, and design your photo essay, using captions or print text as appropriate, and present it to the class.

The Early Years	War photography has advanced much since its inception in 1848 during the Crimean War. However, in our media obsessed society it is easy to forget the reason why war photography is necessary. What good could possibly come from the images of death and destruction?	World War I
Despite the advantages of real time media, war photography can still profoundly touch us. Whether it be a picture of the bodies after Gettysburg, or of a haggard soldier half buried in a flooded trench, or of a German soldier taunting an elderly Jew, or of a Vietnamese girl running from her burning village, or of an emaciated POW in a Serbian concentration camp, these images etch deeply into our psyche. Their permanence is unmistakable.	1939–1945	In highly propagandized wars like the Civil War, World War I, and the Vietnam War images of suffering soldiers and civilians revealed to a naïve public what war is really about. These images show that glory, honor, truth, and valor do not exist in the savage frontlines.
The Vietnam War	Most importantly, however, war photography can reveal to us the crimes committed under the pretense of war. After World War II, horrifying images of the Holocaust insured that the world would never forget the crimes committed during war. And in the Balkans, the work of a few brave photojournalists would shed light on a hidden Holocaust.	The Balkans

FIGURE 7.11 Ye Yuan's "Looking Through the Lens" photo essay with the rollover graphic activated.

Documenting the Unspeakable

"The Final Solution" drawn out by the Nazis called for the total extermination of the Jews living in Germany and occupied Europe. This picture like most taken of the Holocaust were taken by German photographers employed by the Propaganden Kompanien. This picture shows a Jewish scholar about to be executed by a German SS officer.

1 2 3 4 5

FIGURE 7.12 One of Ye Yuan's linked pages in his photo essay. Each link contains a single photograph with an explanatory caption.

Let's now consider how one student, Ye Yuan, created an online photo essay that uses a dynamic format to give readers control over the way they view the information and the way the argument is assembled.

Figure 7.11 demonstrates this reader-oriented dynamic. The arrangement of information, though it follows a roughly left-to-right, top-to-bottom organization, also opens up the possibility of browsing this photo essay in a less rigidly determined fashion. As you might expect, clicking on a bolded title takes you to a series of sequential images from that time period, offering structure to this broad discussion of war photography. At first glance, this arrangement might seem to rely on a traditional hierarchy of image and word, with the pictures serving as a secondary layer to the word-based introduction. Yet as soon as the reader begins to interact with this photo essay, moving the mouse across the page, this illusion is dispelled. Each bolded title contains a rollover graphic, so that when the reader moves the mouse over the words, a representative image appears. This dynamic relationship between word and image suggests a conjunction of meaning between the two; cooperation between the visual and the verbal is designed to "hook" and move the reader to the next level of the photo essay.

At the subsection level (shown in Figure 7.12), the reader finds a carefully chosen image that represents war photography from that historical period. Here, the photographs function as the arguments, because the heading remains constant for each subsequent image; the pictures change, but the print remains the same.

The photo essay works best if you have a topic that can be effectively argued through an accumulation of visual evidence presented as a sequence of images. Keep in mind that designing a photo essay is like drafting a research paper: you may take pages of notes, but the task of crafting the argument involves sifting through information, deciding between relevant and irrelevant materials, and arranging the most powerful evidence in your finished product. Remember to shape your photo essay around your argument through carefully made rhetorical choices about purpose, audience, and medium.

Composing a Website

If you decide to move your project online and produce a Website, your readers will then encounter your visual argument as **hypertext,** or a series of interlinked Web pages. Hypertext authors construct a framework for an argument through the **homepage** (the site's introduction), the **navigation scheme** (the site's organizational structure), and the contents of individual pages, offering both internal and external links designed to guide readers through the various levels of argument and evidence. In effect, a *hypertext argument* is produced by the collaboration between the author's direction and the readers' participation; in this way, the rhetorical situation of a Website as a visual argument becomes literally interactive, with readers playing an active role in the construction of meaning.

AT A GLANCE

Designing a Photo Essay

1. Decide on the argument or thesis for your project.
2. Categorize your images, arranging them within the theme groups.
3. Organize them into different configurations: by chronology, theme, and subject.
4. Draft written text in the form of headings, captions, and paragraphs.
5. Determine your layout by experimenting with ways of formatting the words and images.

We see this dynamic determines the argumentative structure for a site such as the Truth.com's Crazyworld homepage, accessible through the Truth.com's archives of past pages (see Figure 7.13). The site's target audience might be young people inclined toward smoking. But by appearing on the Internet the site conveys its argument to the broader public, using the carnival motif to suggest what a "crazy world" we live in, where tobacco companies continue to sell—and consumers continue to buy and smoke—cigarettes that contain chemicals like arsenic, benzene, and cyanide. The site's primary *level of decorum* is plain style: through simple language, the carnival metaphor, and engaging visuals, the Website seeks to persuade viewers of the dangers of tobacco usage to both smokers and nonsmokers.

This draws readers into the site, where they encounter the more explicitly argumentative indictments of Big Tobacco in the site's subsidiary content pages that reveal statistics, interviews, and indictments of cigarette companies.

The power of this visual argument lies in the flexibility of its design, which allows the audience to explore its many features. Although it resists relying on the sort of linear development typically found in paper texts, it still offers readers a variety of structured and clearly delineated pathways into its central arguments against Big Tobacco. On the surface, the site presents striking graphics and a visual *menu bar,* consisting of links to different aspects of the site. However, its primary *navigation toolbar,* the list of links that

FIGURE 7.13 The Truth.com Crazyworld homepage demonstrates multiple strategies of effective Website composition.

provide direct access to the interior of the Website, is actually hidden beneath the clown image. The toolbar only appears when the viewer rolls the mouse over the word *Navigate,* placed beneath the curved arrow that points at the clown. This Website, then, has been composed as a highly interactive piece of digital writing. There is no "right way" to navigate this site, and the writers are able to reach a wide audience and convey a powerful argument about the dangers of smoking.

COLLABORATIVE CHALLENGE

Perform a rhetorical analysis of several Websites: first, using the link from the *Envision* Website, look at "Error 404," a parody Webpage created during the U.S. war with Iraq; then compare http://www.whitehouse.org, a parody site, with the official http://www.whitehouse.gov site. How does the parody site use rhetoric, organization, style, and decorum to produce an argument? Working collaboratively, draft a sample homepage that makes the same argument as the parody page but without using parody. What rhetorical choices did you make in designing your page?
www.ablongman.com/envision/228

AT A GLANCE

Essential Elements for Composing a Website

- Decide upon your target audience.
- Select your content and main argument.
- Determine your purpose (to teach, persuade, or move to action).
- Compose your level of decorum.
- Design your site organization, navigation, and layout.

The process of authoring your own Website may seem daunting at first. However, in many ways drafting text for the Web resembles drafting the complex argument of a long research paper: in both cases, you need to identify the necessary elements of your composition, and then you need to follow a process of careful planning and organization.

In designing your Website, you will need to account for three levels of information: a *homepage* at the **primary level** (which will serve as the introduction to your site); a *series of topic pages* at the **secondary level** (which will contain both content and, sometimes, links to further, more specialized sub topic pages); and the *subtopic pages* at the **deep level** (which will contain content and perhaps even more links). Although most sites contain only one homepage, some use a **splash page**—often featuring a single provocative quote, a flash animation, or gripping image—that functions as a hook or **gateway** to a more substantive introductory homepage. There is no limit on the number of topic and content pages you can include; you should determine the scope of your project and number of pages based on your assessment of how to make your argument most effectively.

In terms of design, composing a Website resembles the process of outlining a research paper. Yet there are important differences between digital writing and writing for print readers. First, you'll need to *chunk* your information—or divide it into manageable parts. Second, you'll want consistency of theme, font, and/or color throughout your site; avoid visual clutter and ineffectual use of images; think about the relationship between the words and images. Third, to achieve an effective design, you might want to create a *template,* or visual precedent, that establishes the key elements for the rest of the site, much as an introduction in a written paper often sets the style and conventions for the rest of the argument to follow.

Let's look at Sarah Douglas's research-based Website on Internet usage and isolation in forms such as instant messaging, online dating, and Weblogs. Her design challenge was to encourage her readers to explore each form of electronic communication in depth without losing perspective on the overall argument. Her solution entailed using design to structure her pages effectively (see Figure 7.14).

Her layers of navigation are embedded at the top of her site. First, in black, the title bar recurs from page to page. Beneath that, a navigation bar, also constant throughout the site, lists the major paths of her argument, color-coding each path with vivid, complementary colors. The third horizontal bar is the variable; it represents a secondary navigation bar for navigating within each node. Significantly, the color reproduces that of the major path from which it is derived. Therefore, at a glance, readers are oriented. In addition, in the blue box in the left margin, Sarah embedded key quotes that comment on the issues contained in that particular page. By choosing a color not otherwise used by the site and also by setting the quotation box next to the main frame, Sarah creates an argument in the digital medium that captures the dynamic nature of her research project.

As you compose your own Website as a visual argument, be sure to consider **usability**—how user friendly your hypertext is and how accessible to users with disabilities. Even a site with professional design and a state-of-the-art graphic interface is

FIGURE 7.14 Sarah Douglas's Website on isolation and the Internet uses color design for effective navigation.

AT A GLANCE

Designing a Website

- Draft a header; consider including an image in it.
- Map a logical organization for your site to help readers find information easily and understand your site's purpose and argument.
- Include a navigation tool, either at the top below the title or along the left margin.
- Develop clear content using words and images.
- Be consistent in using color, imagery, and font; avoid jarring color combinations or visual clutter.
- Resize images and locate them effectively on your pages.
- Create a series of links, either to subpages or to external sites.
- Provide a feedback link so users can email you comments.
- Include a "last updated" feature.
- Test your site for usability—both in terms of its general user friendliness and its accessibility to users with disabilities.

ultimately ineffective if the audience cannot navigate it. You can test your Website for usability through the resources available on the *Envision* Website. Learning to write with attention to diverse readers will make you a more rhetorically savvy and effective communicator.

Making a Multimedia Montage

In this last section, we'll introduce you to writing projects such as visual collages, multimedia mixes using audio and video, hand-painted murals, self-produced films, startup magazines, and more. We'll call these texts **multimedia montages** because they involve the combination of numerous media (images, sound, writing, digital elements, and more) and because they often consist of nonlinear collections of evidence; the argument occurs in the project as a whole. Although the term *montage* is taken from film studies and refers to a sequence of still images, we'll extend it to refer to any combination of diverse media elements. The key to designing multimedia montages lies in understanding not only your audience, argument, medium, and form but also the purpose for the project.

Consider Yang Shi's decision to construct a visual collage based on his purpose. He began his project with the goal of creating a print photo essay on the subject of Mao Zedong's political impact on China, but he soon found that the photo essay's linear structure seemed to suggest a single definitive interpretation of Mao's influence. Since Yang was interested in exploring the complexity and contradictions inherent to the issue, he found the graphic possibilities of a visual collage preferable since this format allowed for a dialogue between simultaneous, competing images. By juxtaposing and intertwining numerous images from 1960s China, Yang Shi created a powerful, complex argument about the causalities of Mao's Cultural Revolution. Yang recognized that in a collage he could not only exploit the power of numerous images but also crop and arrange those images for rhetorical purpose. Accordingly, he created an overtly chaotic layout, one that he felt reflected the lack of focus of the Chinese Cultural Revolution (see Figure 7.15).

Despite the initial impression of randomness, however, there is an underlying order to Yang's collage: from the portrait of Mao heading the page, to the patriotic children surrounding him, to the statistics at the bottom, and finally to the outline of China as a faint red background at the poster's center in front of the protestors, all the visual elements structure the text's visual argument. In one sense, China encompasses all these representations—struggles and tragedies, ideals and victories. Yet the collage's inclusion of Mao's choice of political imagery—the propaganda drawings of happy workers—suggests that Mao undermined his own anti-West stance by "marketing" himself along the same lines as traditional Western advertising. In this way, Yang's

FIGURE 7.15 Yang Shi's photo collage about Mao Zedong and the Chinese Cultural Revolution.

strategic use of the collage form produces a powerful statement through a careful arrangement of images and color.

Think carefully about your purpose, your argument, your audience's familiarity with the topic, and the organization of your materials as you design your own multimedia montage. You might decide to construct a dynamic text, using PowerPoint slide shows or film-editing software to produce a moving montage, slide show, or animation. KiYonna Carr, for example, in creating her visual argument on the enduring legacy of slavery on African-American women's self-image, paired a sequence of historical and contemporary photographs with her own voice-over commentary. Similarly, Derrick Jue chose a short-film format for his visual argument on protests over the war against Iraq. In what might be described as a photo essay set to music, Derrick developed his montage by carefully selecting images from the news that depicted scenes from the war, from protest demonstrations, and from footage of politicians speaking about the war, and then arranging them into a slide show set to the song "Wake Me Up," by Evanescence. Everything in the piece, from the order of images to their relationship to the accompanying sounds, serves a rhetorical purpose, working to convey Derrick's argument about the American public's sometimes angry, sometimes ambivalent reactions to the war against Iraq; the rapid succession of images paired with stirring music provokes an emotional reaction in its audience, without the need for written commentary.

Student Writing

Read Yang Shi's reflection letter concerning his design decisions.

www.ablongman.com/envision/230

Some of the most innovative multimedia montages convey their visual arguments not electronically but rather **tactilely,** using touch or physical form. Thus, when you think of *multimedia,* take it literally and don't rule out creating physical models, three-dimensional structures, and reproductions with material elements. You might follow Jessica Vun's example: she produced a hand-sewn manners book to give readers the "feel" for gender roles in the 1800s, the subject of her research paper. Or consider Allison Smith's project, in which she made drawings by hand and stained them with tea to suggest their age for a project on Margaret Sanger's political cartoons in her battle for legalized birth control. Perhaps Dexian Cai's work might inspire your invention strategies: for his visual argument against the globalization of McDonald's into Asian markets, Dex brought in traditional Chinese snacks as an alternative, food version of an op-ad. Finally, you might consider Lauren Dunagan's decision to transform her research argument about the visual rhetoric of graffiti into a 14-foot-long hand-painted mural that used graffiti itself to make an argument about the power of graffiti as a medium for social protest and self-expression. To paraphrase famous theorist Marshall McLuhan, in Lauren's project, the medium became the message.

In each of these cases, the student used the physical nature of the text itself (a model, a stained historical document, an edible artifact, and a mural) in a rhetorically purposeful manner. The range of possibilities for your visual argument suggests the ways writing has changed over time—and how it continues to evolve with the advent of new writing and composing technologies. From Weblogs to interactive multimedia exhibits and collaborative hypertext projects, the way we understand language, argument, and persuasion continues to evolve. With the ever-changing face of modern media, you have an increasing number of choices for designing arguments with purpose, power, and creativity.

Designing Your Own Arguments

In this chapter, you've learned how writing offers an opportunity to experiment with designing and producing your texts in ways that meet your purpose and match the expectations of your audience. Often this means knowing, understanding, and adhering to conventions set forth by a community of scholars, readers, or writers. This is the case for the document design of your research paper, cover page, abstract, and bio. At other times, this means exploring innovative approaches to design in multimedia contexts. It is also the case for the document design of hybrid compositions and visual arguments. All modes of design depend on your rhetorical expertise in choosing a level of decorum, in knowing what strategies best work for your situation, in deciding on your medium and your format, and then in having these choices support your purpose in designing your work. By examining academic essays, op-ads, photo essays, Websites, and multimedia montages, you have seen that the rhetorical principles of audience, argument, form, and purpose carry across diverse media. It's time now for you to make your contribution. Write out your brainstorming ideas, and begin to design your own argument.

PREWRITING CHECKLIST

Focus on Analyzing Design in Arguments

❏ **Argument:** What is the topic and the argument? What evidence is used to support the argument? What is the rhetorical stance and point of view on the topic? What role does verbal, visual, or multimedia play in persuasion in this text? Are words and images complementary or does the argument work primarily through one means?

❏ **Audience:** Whom is the argument intended to reach? What response seems to be anticipated from the audience? Sympathetic? Hostile? Concerned?

❏ **Medium:** Is the medium used appropriate for the argument and its target audience? What type of interaction does the medium create with its audience?

❏ **Form:** What are the specific characteristics of the medium? Consider layout, images, style, font. How are these elements organized?

❏ **Purpose:** What is the purpose in presenting the argument to the audience in this design? To move them to action? inform them? teach them? What type of decorum or style (grand, middle, or plain) is used to realize this purpose?

WRITING PROJECTS

1. **Design elements to accompany your final revision:** Write an abstract and bio for your final research paper. Check that you have adhered to proper academic document design. Now compose a one-page op-ad featuring the argument from your research project. The op-ad should combine both images and written elements. Keep in mind those elements important to successful advertising, including consideration of audience and purpose; use of space, color, and image; strategies of development; and an appropriate hook. Indicate in a written note the intended audience (who would read it) and context (what magazine or newspaper they would read it in) for your ad. Post all your documents online as a showcase of your work as a writer and researcher.

2. **Visual Argument:** Create a photo essay based on the argument from your research paper or as part of an independent project. The images you use in your photo essay may be from your paper, or you can use a completely new set, particularly if you did not use images in your paper. Your argument may mirror that in your research paper, or you may focus on a smaller portion of your overall argument. The style, arrangement, medium, and rhetorical strategies of your photo essay should match your audience and your purpose. Include written text in your photo essay strategically. Once you have finished, write a one-page reflection on the strategies you used in this project.

3. **Multimedia Argument:** Transform your written essay into an electronic format that uses audio strategically as part of the text's persuasive power. You can match your images to a recorded argument. Alternatively, combine visual images with a soundtrack. Pick your music carefully, and time each image to match a particular mood or moment in the music or select music to match the sequence of your images. If you are transforming a paper essay into an electronic audio version, feel free to modify your organization, arrangement, text selection, and even treatment of images to accommodate this shift in medium. Once you have finished, write a one-page reflection on how the shift in medium affected your argument.

 Visit www.ablongman.com/envision for expanded assignment guidelines and student projects.

CHAPTER 8

Delivering Presentations

FIGURE 8.1 Martin Luther King Jr. presents to a crowd at the Lincoln Memorial during his "I Have a Dream" speech in Washington DC, August 28, 1963.

Chapter Preview Questions

- How can I transform a written argument into a visual or oral presentation?
- When should I use a speech, a poster session, a PowerPoint show, or a live performance? What rhetorical choices shape my decision?
- What are the branches of oratory, and how do they shape my presentation options?
- How can the canons of memory and delivery help my presentation?

You've finished your written argument. You've submitted it to your instructor according to proper academic conventions as explained in Chapters 7 and 9, and maybe you have even translated it into a hybrid composition or visual argument. But sometimes you are asked to do more: to present your argument to an audience in the form of a "live" presentation. Both academic and public audiences call for oral or multimedia presentations on occasion, and you need to develop skills and strategies for designing and delivering presentations to take advantage of these opportunities. In this chapter, we'll learn from famous writers and speakers, such as Dr. Martin Luther King Jr., whose famous "I Have a Dream" speech offers one of the most powerful pieces of rhetoric in the English language. King's powerful presentation did not derive solely from the written script. As the image in Figure 8.1 captures, it was the convergence of well-crafted language, passionate delivery, and deliberate gesture that combined to produce that landmark articulation of the civil rights movement.

You might look to King and other orators as models for effective presentation strategies as you prepare to shape your writing for oral delivery. As you approach drafting your presentation, take time to explore the many possibilities available to you for this act of effective communication. You will need to base your decisions for picking certain presentation strategies on a solid rhetorical foundation, and to do so, you need to understand the *branches of oratory* as well as how to apply them to particular occasions. In this chapter, you'll learn effective strategies for selecting the appropriate branch of oratory for your rhetorical situation, for translating your written argument into a multimedia presentation, and for scripting and designing a memorable and effective delivery of your argument.

Understanding the Branches of Oratory

As you prepare to draft, design, and deliver a compelling presentation, it is helpful to turn to classical rhetoric for ways of understanding the needs of your specific writing situation—your own purpose, audience, and persona. For even though today we turn to rhetoric to shape any visual or verbal communication, originally rhetoric evolved as a technique in classical Greece for teaching people how to speak both eloquently and persuasively in public. Classical rhetoricians such as Aristotle divided oratory into three "branches" or causes based on time, purpose, and content. Let's explore the way the principles behind these **branches of oratory** can be applied to your goal of writing a presentation.

The first branch, **judicial** or **forensic discourse,** involves defending or accusing, and it usually deals with the past. Think of this as oratory about *right or wrong.* The second branch, **deliberative** or **legislative discourse,** concerns politics or policy and focuses most often on the future. You might think of this as oratory about what is beneficial or harmful. The purpose of such oratory is to argue for or against specific actions that might take place in the future. Finally, **epideictic** rhetoric deals with the present time. Also called *ceremonial* or *demonstrative* oratory, this discourse is all about praising or blaming, and the purpose is to revel in the moment.

Since the rhetorical branches may not be familiar concepts, let's look at some contexts for them that you might encounter in your own writing and speaking situations:

- For *judicial* or *forensic discourse,* you might present a position on a past action in debate team, moot court, or law school, using verbal arguments as well as charts, graphs, photos, and other visual evidence arranged and designed to persuade your audience.
- For *deliberative* or *legislative discourse,* you might exhort or dissuade an audience if you speak at a conference to promote the launching of your own business, the development of new software, or a plan for a cross-country fundraising trip; you would write a memo, a financial plan, and the specifications concerning the worthiness of the enterprise; you might also use PowerPoint slides, charts, images, prototypes, models, and animation to persuade your audience.
- For *epideictic* or *ceremonial discourse,* you might engage in a rhetoric of display in a senior thesis, company report, advertising campaign, or even a political party statement designed to praise (or blame) a candidate.

As you can tell, although the branches of oratory may be unfamiliar in theory, we see them in practice all the time, from the professor's PowerPoint lecture defending the inclusion of "intelligent design" in high school science courses (forensic) to a Kappa

BRANCHES OF ORATORY: CONTEMPORARY EXAMPLES

Judicial or forensic discourse—involves accusing or defending	Deliberative or legislative discourse—designed to argue for or against specific actions	Epideictic discourse—involves praise or blame
Johnny Cochran's 1995 defense of O. J. Simpson represented a notable instance of forensic discourse when Cochran used powerful visual and verbal rhetoric to clear O. J. Simpson of murder charges.	In his documentary film *An Inconvenient Truth* (2006), Al Gore employs deliberative discourse to advise the audience of the necessary steps for reducing the future impact of global warming.	Eulogies, such as the speech Maya Angelou gave at Coretta Scott King's funeral in February 2006, are a typical form of epideictic discourse in that they center on praising and celebrating people's lives.

Notice the way Cochran makes his point visually by slipping on gloves that had been used in the crime to underscore his point "If it doesn't fit, you must acquit."	*An Inconvenient Truth* features Gore giving a series of lectures, many of which are rendered more powerful by carefully chosen background images and striking photographs.	Although Maya Angelou's tone in speaking of Coretta Scott King was celebratory, her demeanor was somber and respectful.

Alpha Theta member's speech to her sorority sisters about the success of their community outreach program that year (epideictic). When you draft your presentations, you'll need to assess which branch of oratory best addresses the demands of your particular rhetorical situation.

Audience, Purpose, and Persona

The branches of oratory are only one of the resources from classical rhetoric that writers draw on in crafting successful presentations. Concepts such as attention to *audience, purpose,* and *persona,* which we've discussed in relation to written texts, are key elements for oral rhetoric as well. For instance, consider how attention to purpose, audience, and persona determines the presentations shown in Figures 8.2 and 8.3. What kind of audience might each of the speakers be facing? How does each one need to design a presentation, select words and visual material, and practice a form of delivery that is specific to the rhetorical situation? In each case, the speaker carefully constructed his or her presentation to be a powerful visual and verbal argument.

Consider the many kinds of presentations you encounter as part of your academic experience. Do you attend lectures on specific topics, with a single speaker standing at a podium and delivering a verbal argument? Have you been an audience member for a

FIGURE 8.3 Steve Jobs discusses Intel technology at the 2006 Mac World convention.

FIGURE 8.2 The Guerrilla Girls present at a symposium on the feminist role in contemporary performance art.

formal academic panel, where multiple speakers take turns presenting arguments, sometimes providing handouts to the audience or using a projection screen to convey their ideas? Or is your most frequent presentation experience the PowerPoint lecture, in which the speaker provides a point-by-point map of the material, includes images related to the subject matter, and sometimes posts a copy of the slides on a Website for future reading? Although these presentations might differ in format, they are similar in that all are designed to meet the needs of their particular audience and rhetorical situation.

CREATIVE PRACTICE

Keep a log of all the kinds of presentations you encounter in one week at your university. If possible, take a camera with you and document your observations about each kind of presentation. What are the differences between them? Write down as many details as you can and reflect on which type of presentation you would like to try. Write up your reflections in the form of a short narrative.

In your own work, you may find yourself presenting to your class, to a larger academic audience as part of a conference panel, to college administrators or a university forum, or even to a public audience. In each case, you'll have many choices to make. You can start determining the possibilities for your own presentation by using focusing questions such as those found in the "At a Glance" box, designed to help you identify your audience, purpose, and persona.

AT A GLANCE

Identifying Your Audience, Purpose, and Persona

1. What format will my presentation take (purely oral speech, multimedia slide show, interactive drama, etc.)?

2. Who is my audience? What do they know or not know about this topic already? How receptive will they be to my material?

3. What is my purpose? What do I hope to accomplish? What is my ultimate goal with this presentation?

4. What branch of oratory does my presentation represent? Is it designed to defend or accuse? To argue a position or policy? To celebrate or condemn?

5. What persona do I want to convey to my audience (knowledgeable, friendly, impassioned, concerned, expert, peer, etc.)? How do I visualize myself as a presenter?

6. What kind of tone do I want to use in my presentation (fun, serious, informative, sarcastic, concerned, alarmed, practical, etc.)?

7. What kinds of supporting materials do I plan to use in my presentation (quotes from research, photographs in a PowerPoint slide or on a handout, film or commercial clips, graphs, charts, posters, etc.)?

As the final point in the "At a Glance" box suggests, most presentations today include strategically chosen visual texts—what we used to call "visual aids"—that in fact perform a crucial rhetorical function: they collaborate with words to convey the speaker's argument. A photo of extensive crop damage can provide evidence in an environmental science lecture, and a chart can communicate economic trends to an audience quickly and effectively. Sometimes, moreover, visuals provide a stronger message than or even contradict the verbal component of the speech. A presenter might use a visual text ironically—for instance, showing a slide listing statistics that refute an opponent's argument or providing an emotional appeal while conveying information in a flat tone of voice. In these ways, visual texts communicate powerful arguments that you can use as part of your overall presentation.

Transforming Research into a Presentation

The process of transforming your research-based argument into a presentation can be quite challenging, for you need to take into account scope, content, and style. If you have 15 written pages of argument, this would probably take 40 minutes or more to read out loud. But of course, you would certainly not choose to simply read your written paper, for writing is often different when meant to be read silently versus when meant to be read out loud. Only in certain academic circles is there a preference for complex, written prose as a formal presentation style. In most cases, audiences desire clear, conversational speech that is easy to follow. To achieve this goal, you need to think about transforming your research argument from one kind of writing to another—from writing for readers to writing for listeners. You'll also need to cut down the sheer amount of material you can convey and think about ways to present it in an interesting, memorable way.

You can accomplish all these goals through a process of *selection, organization,* and *translation.*

Selection

Keep in mind that as you consider what materials to select, you should always plan for a shorter presentation time than what you actually have allotted. Most of us speak for longer than we realize; so if you are planning material for a 10-minute presentation, aim for 8; a 15-minute presentation, aim for 12; a 5-minute presentation, aim for 3. One way to keep your time frame manageable is to select a subset of material to present. That is, if your written argument comprises three main areas, plan to cover only one in your presentation. Also, if you plan on speaking extemporaneously (or improvising), be sure that you build this into your schedule for your presentation. Finally, remember to be as selective with your visual evidence as you are with your overall information; if your research relies heavily on images, charts, or graphs, be sure to carefully consider which to include in your presentation. You might opt to use only the most powerful images, or you might decide to center your presentation on a single case study or example and therefore feature only those materials relevant to that narrower focus.

You should find the focusing questions in the "At a Glance" box helpful for moving through the process of selection for your project. Question 1 will help you identify the crux of your presentation. This may be your thesis, but it may also *not* be your thesis. That is, in the course of writing your paper, you may have found that what really matters most is the need to raise awareness about an issue, the need to publicize potential solutions to a problem, or the need to advocate for a particular research agenda. Question 2 will help you narrow your project to a few points designed to convey your project's significance to the audience. Question 3 will help you confirm your purpose and begin to translate your main point into a medium that will persuade your audience: do you want to raise awareness, rally support, propose a change, offer new insights, or suggest avenues of future research? You need to select your materials with these goals in mind.

AT A GLANCE

Key Steps for Transforming Your Research Argument into a Presentation

- *Scope:* How do you convert 10, 15, or even 20 pages of argument into a 5-, 10- or 15-minute oral presentation?
  Answer: Selection
- *Content:* How do you reframe the content so that it makes sense to your audience?
  Answer: Organization
- *Style:* How do you change the written word to a spoken, visual, and digital medium?
  Answer: Translation

AT A GLANCE

Questions for Focusing Your Argument

1. What matters most about this project?
2. What two or three points can I make to convey my answer to the above question?
3. What do I want my audience to walk away thinking about when I am done?

Organization

As you move through the process of transforming your research into an oral presentation, you have an opportunity to **reorder** your written argument to meet the needs and expectations of a listening audience. You might, for instance, begin with your conclusion and then convey the narrative of your research. Or you might want to show your visual evidence first, ask questions, and then provide your thesis at the end. In other words, you don't need to create your presentation as a miniature version of

Slide 3

...the emergence of many technologically advanced weapons...

Slide 4

...and the deaths of a countless number of soldiers and innocent civilians.

Slide 5

But many people seem to neglect one important aspect of the war; namely, the wartime propaganda that emerged between the years 1939 and 1945. In the midst of its battles against the Axis Powers, the United States engaged in a propagandistic warfare with its rival nations in which political art played an indispensable role.

FIGURE 8.4 Tommy Tsai's presentation outline strategically juxtaposed the oral script with the visual evidence he would present in his slides. Note that he includes a blank slide so that his audience focuses exclusively on him as a speaker during this part of his presentation.

your written talk. Be innovative in your choice of organization; think about what structure would be the most effective for your audience.

To help with this process, create a flowchart, outline, or block graphic of each element of your presentation. Don't forget your opening "hook" and closing message as you work on organizing your presentation. Try matching each component to a minute-by-minute schedule to make sure that you are within time limits. And finally, consider creating a **visual outline** by drawing or pasting in images next to your verbal cues to show how and when you will use visual rhetoric as a part of your presentation. Looking at a section of Tommy Tsai's presentation outline (see Figure 8.4) for his oral presentation on World War II propaganda, we can see that he carefully paired the words he intended to speak (on the right) with the slides he would show to his audience (on the left). In this way, he could clearly map the relationship between the visual and verbal elements of his presentation, creating a strong underlying organization for his argument. The key here is to see the presentation as its own genre of writing and draft a text that meets the needs of both your audience and your purpose.

Translation

The final step of the transformation is to translate your writing from text meant to be read to text meant to be heard. This is more important than it may first appear. Think about presentations you've attended where the speaker read from a complicated, verbose script, without looking up or changing the inflection of his or her voice. It's possible that if you sat down and read that same speech, you might have found it interesting; however, listening to the material presented in that way, you probably found yourself bored, confused, or both. The point here is that there are important differences between these types of writing, and you need to carefully *translate* your research into a form accessible to your listening audience.

The extent to which you modify your writing as you draft your script depends on your audience and purpose; for instance, if you were trying to persuade your college

AT A GLANCE

Key Questions to Shape Your Organization

- How do I want to "hook" my audience? What would be an effective way to open my presentation? Should I appeal to emotion? to reason? Should I establish my authority as a researcher? What parts of my researcher would help me do so?

- What strategies do I want to use to organize my presentation? Narration? Example? Cause and effect? Problem-solution? Process? Definition? Which strategies would be most useful for conveying my argument clearly and leffectively to my audience?

- What main points do I want to use as the centerpiece of my presentation? Do I want to focus on a single case study or on multiple examples?

- At what point do I want to present my thesis? Do I want to start with a question or line of inquiry and then end with my argument in my conclusion? Or do I want to start strong with my thesis within the first moments of my talk and then prove it with evidence?

- How do I want to close my presentation? Do I want to conclude by summing up my points or by pointing to the future or further implications? Do I want to end with a call to action or with a provocative question? What strategy would create the greatest impact on my audience?

administrators to endorse a new recycling policy (an example of deliberative discourse), you would adopt a different style and mode of speaking than if you were accusing that same administration of inattention to the recycling issue at a student council meeting (an example of forensic discourse). However, in general, there are some steps you can take to facilitate the translation process. As you script your speech, examine the length of your sentences, the complexity of your prose, and the sophistication of your diction. Most listeners find shorter sentences, specific language, and clear transitions and prose structures important for understanding oral discourse. In addition, be sure to avoid jargon and to define any terms with which your audience might not be familiar. Consider adding to your script explicit **signposting**—verbal "signs" that indicate the steps of an argument or the structure of your presentation. More often than not, listeners need more explicit signposting than do readers of papers.

AT A GLANCE

Signposting

Help listeners by including these terms to structure your argument:

- First
- Second
- Third
- On one hand
- On the other hand
- For example
- Consider
- But
- Yet
- In conclusion

Listeners also respond to humor, direct address, concrete examples, and even questions. These strategies are designed to directly engage your audience's attention. As you write your script, annotate your written copy with places where you pause, emphasize words, look up, or laugh. Also include reminders of when to point to visuals or advance your slides.

CREATIVE PRACTICE

Compare the very different styles of two speeches, both given by women, both concerning human rights, but presented to very different audiences and by very different personas: Eleanor Roosevelt's speech entitled "Adoption of the Declaration of Human Rights," delivered December 9, 1948, in Paris, France; and a speech by Cher (played by Alicia Silverstone) from the movie *Clueless* (1995) on "Whether all oppressed people should be allowed refuge in America." Look at the written versions of their speeches as you listen to them talk. What characteristics of the spoken word does each piece of writing share? How are they different?

www.ablongman.com/envision/231

Transformation in Action

Let's take a close look at how one student transformed her written research paper into a multimedia research presentation. As we saw in Chapter 4, Susan Zhang wrote a research proposal on the photo manipulation of media images. After finishing the written proposal, she was asked to present her proposal orally to her class. What follows is the written script for her presentation; as you read through it, you may want to reference her original proposal (see pages 000–000) in order to appreciate the way she transformed her written argument into an oral presentation.

Note how Susan adds notes to herself about her slides into her script.

Her language is casual and low style. She even uses humor.

Hi everyone, my name is Susan, and before I begin, a little bit about me.

[cue slide: "About Me"]

Last summer I vacationed with my family in Australia, and that was the beginning of my interest in photography, as you can see. **[cue animation: Mom & me]** And I had a really great time taking pictures of wildlife there, including this one of a duck. **[cue animation: duck]** Well actually that was all a lie. I've never been south of the equator, and that picture of my mom and me is grafted onto the background of Sydney harbor, and that duck is a digital rendering of the animal.

This prompts some unusual questions. If I can pass off a digitally altered photograph as real, why can't others, such as the news and the media for example? Can we trust the pictures that we see in the news?

[cue slide: title slide]

And that brings us to the topic of my proposal, which is titled "Little Photoshop of Horrors? Digital Manipulation of Media Images."

Let's start by looking at some examples.

[cue slide: OJ] This photo is from 1994 when O. J. Simpson was arrested. *Newsweek* kept his mugshot unaltered, while *Time* darkened the color of his skin. Minority groups protested that this made him look darker and more menacing and therefore presumed his guilt. The photographer claimed that he was only going for a more artful, more compelling image.

[cue slide: Martha Stewart] This is the *Newsweek* cover released last year when Martha Stewart was released from prison. The caption is "Martha's Last Laugh: After Prison, She's Thinner, Wealthier and Ready for Primetime." This may be true, but the slim body pictured is not in fact hers.

[cue slide: Walinski]

This photo was taken in 1994, which is when a British soldier was photographed pointing a gun at an Iraqi citizen. It is actually a composite **[cue animation: original photos]** of these two photos. The photographer later apologized and was fired.

[cue slide: "Introduction"]

What happened? Before digital imaging, people trusted photography to be an honest medium. A photographer and his camera were deemed the unbiased purveyor of reality. How has the capacity for photo manipulation affected the credibility of photos in media? Some questions I have are: **[cue animation: point one]** has it led to a loss of credibility due to more powerful image-editing techniques, or **[cue animation: point two]** has it led to increased credibility due to the evolution of stricter standards?

[cue slide: "Perspectives"]

Some perspectives I plan to take are, number one, historical. **[cue animation: historical]** I intend to look at photo manipulation before

Her explicit signposting helps the audience follow her argument.

She uses rhetorical questions and cuts down the length and complexity of her prose in order to convey her argument effectively to her audience.

digital imaging to look at whether people doctored photos then and whether the guidelines are stricter then versus now. **[cue animation: public]** Also, I plan to look at the public response to digital manipulation. For example, where is the line drawn? Sometimes when the doctoring is obvious, it could be interpreted as social satire or commentary; however, if it's subtle, people could interpret this as perception. Also, how easily can people recognize altered images? **[cue animation: photographer]** And for the photographer's point of view, what are some of the reasons for our digitally manipulated photographs? Could it be out of respect for the privacy of the subject, or for the sensibilities of the audience? Also, what are the guidelines and the various contexts in which they may apply?

[cue slide: "Methods"]

Some of the sources I'll use for my research include books. **[cue animation: books]** I'll start with a kind of general approach to ethical photojournalism. Some books I have include *The Burden of Visual Truth: The Role of Photojournalism in Mediating Reality* and also some books on digital image ethics. I also plan at looking at **[cue animation: databases]** online databases to find some examples of digital image ethics and photo manipulation, some articles on recent controversies over altered photos, authoritative opinions by photojournalists and photographers, and some examples of how their public responded to the incidents.

[cue animation: Websites] And also I'll look at some other Websites such as news and media sites online and some smaller photojournalism sites to see how they address image authenticity and to see if they label their images as illustrations or as genuine photographs. And finally I'll look at online guidelines. The National Press Photography Association has a Website for a digital code of ethics, for example.

[cue slide: "Summary"]

In summary, we find digital imaging has made photo manipulation easier and perhaps more prevalent. For example, you could use aesthetic

The ample use of "I" works well in her presentation to convey a confident research persona.

She invokes specific examples in her script to make her talk persuasive.

Her strong and compelling conclusion provides an effective ending to her script.

touch-ups, graft parts of pictures onto others, and even construct a picture entirely from scratch. As a result, there's a lot of public skepticism over the reliability of the images. So my proposal is to explore to what extent this skepticism is really justified.

Reading through Susan's proposal, we can see the effective ways in which she transformed her proposal for oral delivery.

Selection: Although she focused on a single pair of images in her original proposal, Susan used a series of current, recognizable examples of photo manipulation to persuade her audience in her presentation, including some photographs she "altered" herself. She also condensed her sources section and eliminated her timeline altogether, taking into account what information would most interest her listeners.

Organization: Susan's organization in the latter half of her presentation resembles that found in her proposal in moving through methods, to sources, to conclusion. However, her introduction is completely reworked, designed to better capture the attention of a listening—and viewing—audience.

Translation: Throughout, Susan simplified her language and moved to a more colloquial tone that matched the very colloquial introduction she used to hook her audience. Compare, for instance, the final line of her oral presentation with this one, which served as the final sentence for her proposal: "A closer look at the occurrences of digital manipulation today, as regulated by the evolving guidelines of photojournalism, could reveal to what extent such skepticism is warranted." In her presentation, the language is much more direct, clear, and succinct. It is tailored to a listening audience.

Seeing Connections
Read Eugene F. provenzo Jr.'s "The Impact of inter active Violence on Children" for an example of the process of focusing and selection in moving from research to oral presentation.

CREATIVE PRACTICE

Visit the *Envision* Website to compare the writing in Martin Luther King Jr.'s "Letter from Birmingham Jail" with the transcript of his famous speech, "I've Been to the Mountaintop." How does each one indicate either a reader or a listener as the primary audience? Now work on writing for different audiences: translate the letter into a speech and the speech into a written argument. What did you change? What rhetorical techniques work best for each form of writing? What can you apply from this exercise to your own process of translation?
www.ablongman.com/envision/232

Considering Strategies of Design

As you can tell from Susan Zhang's presentation, careful translation can be the key to communicating your argument powerfully and persuasively. Her combination of personal example, a series of persuasive case studies, a strong voice, clear structure, and solid delivery all combined to create a compelling presentation. Let's discuss some other examples to get your ideas flowing about the possibilities available to you for your presentation. These designs include *oral delivery, media components,* and even *embodied rhetoric*—that is, the use of the body to communicate visual information.

- Jessica Luo, presenting on the media coverage of the Tiananmen Square incident in 1989, decided to center her talk on a significant number of photographs from both the Chinese and European presses. She organized them into pairs to demonstrate the different persuasive arguments made through the photos by each media organization. She wanted to move a mainly American student audience into caring about an incident that happened in China more than 15 years ago. Thus, she decided to transform her "objective" writer's voice into a personal narrative and used rhythmic, repetitive terms that explained the rhetorical significance of each image.

- For a project on land mines, Stewart Dorsey decided to show two PowerPoint presentations side by side on two large projection screens. He placed himself in the middle of the two screens to suggest that his argument offered a feasible compromise between polarized camps.

- Max Echtemendy used a hands-on approach to design his research presentation on fantasy violence. First, he set up a table showing horror novels, DVD boxes, articles in magazines, music videos, and many other examples of "fantasy violence all around us." Then he asked students to complete a brief questionnaire, and he worked with their answers as he discussed the key elements of his argument. He ended by showing a clip from *The Lord of the Rings* and asking for audience response.

- Tom Hurlbutt, exploring the implications of Internet surveillance, created a dynamic PowerPoint presentation that linked to Websites, asked students to log on to Amazon, and revealed code that showed their search history from previous class sessions. In this way, he integrated graphic effects in a rhetorically purposeful way.

- Eric Jung, for a presentation on art and technology, transformed the classroom into a twenty-second-century museum, complete with "exhibits" of technologically produced art. He assumed the role of museum guide and gave the class a "tour" of the exhibit, concluding with a "retrospective" lecture about the early twenty-first-century debate over how digital media changed popular conceptions of art.

As you can tell from these innovative projects, there are many effective ways to use strategies of selection, organization, and translation to design the most intriguing, powerful, and appropriate presentation for your purposes.

COLLABORATIVE CHALLENGE

Take 10 minutes to brainstorm the design possibilities for your presentation. Complete the following questions:

1. What format will your presentation take?
2. What materials do you plan to use in your presentation?
3. What might be a potential outline for your presentation?

Now peer review your responses with a partner. Have each person suggest changes, new ideas, and alternative ways of designing the presentation. You might also use this time to begin practicing the presentation. Finally, to get a sense of how your presentation will change according to your audience, consider how your answers would change depending on whether you presented to a class audience or a group of friends in the dorm, a review panel at a company, or a potential employer. Experiment to find the most effective ways to design your presentation.

Using Visuals Rhetorically

Presentations can vary greatly in their design and delivery. At times, you may be asked to deliver an exclusively *oral presentation,* in which you make your argument without the use of any visuals. This form of public speaking is the one most of us are quite familiar with: great civil rights leaders, peace activists, and political leaders rarely cue up a PowerPoint slide to make their points. Yet, more frequently, even the shortest talks are augmented by strategically chosen visual texts that enhance the persuasiveness of an argument. For your own assignments, it is likely that you will be given the option of using visuals in your presentations, so it is important that you develop strategies for doing so effectively—that is, with rhetorical purpose.

Writing for Poster Sessions

One mode of presentation that communicates an argument both verbally and visually is the **poster.** This presentation style is used most frequently in the sciences, where information is presented through the format of the poster session. At science conferences, visitors walk through giant halls show casing hundreds of posters, reading the ones of interest and often requesting a copy of the paper on which the poster is based. If you plan on pursuing a science major, you might want to use this presentation format to practice writing in that medium.

To write for a poster session, researchers take materials from their larger projects, select salient points, organize the material into shorter written summaries with complementary charts and illustrations, and attach the materials to a poster board. The goal of a poster session is that every contributor produces a visual-verbal display that conveys the research accurately, concisely, and in an engaging way. In Figure 8.5 and Figure 8.6, we can see examples of award-winning student posters produced for Stanford University's 2005 Symposium of Undergraduate Research in Progress.

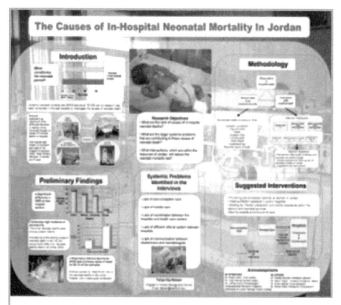

FIGURE 8.5 Tanja Haj-Hassan won awards for this poster, displayed at the 2005 Stanford Symposium for Undergraduate Research in Progress.

FIGURE 8.6 Co-researchers Carlos Ortiz and Jonathan Hwang transformed their research into this award-winning poster for the 2005 Stanford Symposium for Undergraduate Research in Progress.

Clearly, the authors of these posters designed them differently; however, we can see similarities in the strategies they used to create their visual arguments. In the words of the award committee, both demonstrate "visually exciting design" that conveys "intellectually compelling content" in a way that facilitates "overall excellent communication with a general audience." They accomplish these goals by signposting their posters with bold headers; structuring their information into a clear vertical hierarchy; pairing their concise, written content with powerful photographs and information graphics; and by presenting their visual-verbal argument in a way that effectively engages the interest and understanding of their audience.

When you turn to create your own poster, keep in mind the fundamental elements for writing this kind of presentation described in the "At a Glance" box. By following these guidelines, you can create effective visual-verbal texts that are consistent in format and easily understood by audience members.

Writing for PowerPoint or Slide-Based Presentations

In addition to poster sessions, PowerPoint presentations have become very popular in both academic and professional contexts. The software itself is just a tool, but it's an incredibly helpful and timesaving one that can organize and display your key points of argument and your visual materials into a series of slides. The more you become familiar with PowerPoint as a tool, the more you can use it effectively to offer a timed slide show of images, to emphasize points through visual design (highlighting text, blowing up images, sliding across a picture, engaging the audience by filling in blanks as you speak, and much more).

Alex Bleyleben, for instance, used Power-Point to project slides of endangered rhinos for a paper on global activism. In one dramatic move, he included a black slide to shift

AT A GLANCE

Guidelines for Creating Posters for a Poster Session

- Make sure your poster is readable from a distance; size your fonts accordingly.
- Put the poster's title, authors, and academic affiliation at the top.
- Avoid visual clutter; consider using white space to offset various elements, including tables, figures, and written texts.
- Arrange materials in columns not rows.
- Avoid long passages of texts; rely primarily on visual persuasion.
- Always check with the conference organizers for their specific guidelines.

For more detailed advice, go to the *Envision* Website.

the audience's attention from the gruesome images back to his own presence at the podium as he delivered the key points of his argument. He then concluded with an impressive image. Another student, Natalie Farrell, taught herself PowerPoint in one evening for her presentation on Yucca Mountain. She included slides with deliberate blanks left in the list of statistics to engage the class and ask them to calculate the projected environmental risk of a nuclear disaster (see Figures 8.7 and 8.8).

As Natalie clicked forward in her presentation, she elicited the class to guess at the power of radiation in Yucca Mountain before shocking the audience with the actual numbers. She succeeded in what cultural critic Stephen Shugart deems is the necessity of "transforming the concept of PowerPoint from 'presenting at' into 'a way of promoting discussion' or to use it in unconventional ways to create more effective learning situations." One way to think about writing with PowerPoint as a rhetorical tool is to return to our model of research as a conversation or dialogue. How can you

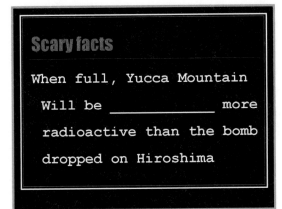

FIGURE 8.7 Natalie Farrell's presentation titled "Yucca Mountain and Nuclear Waste: Gambling with the Future of the Human Race, December 2002," slide 5.

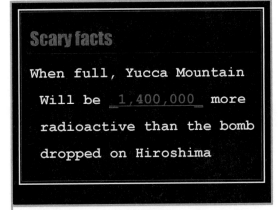

FIGURE 8.8 Natalie Farrell's presentation, slide 6, in which she dramatically fills in the blank

AT A GLANCE

Writing an Effective PowerPoint Presentation

- Use purposeful visuals not clip art.
- Plan to spend time discussing the images on each slide.
- Don't put too much text on each slide or rely too heavily on bullet lists.
- Keep fonts consistent in style, size, and color to avoid distracting the audience.
- Break complex ideas into multiple slides.
- Give a handout with full quotations as necessary.
- Include sound effects and animation rhetorically rather than for flair or flash.

Find more detailed advice on the *Envision* Website.

engage your audience, as Natalie did, rather than throw data at them or run through a list of ideas?

When writing for PowerPoint, keep in mind the way you want your audience to respond. Remember that before this software was developed, a speaker needed to use slides to share visual material. If you think of using PowerPoint the way you would use slides in a presentation, you might be less likely to fill each slide with bulleted lists of information or large amounts of writing. Consider exactly how you plan to use each slide and then craft your presentation around your answers:

- Do you want to show photographs, cartoons, or other visual images?
- Do you want to raise questions and then fill in answers?
- Do you want to show an interactive map or link to a Website?
- Do you want to embed a link to a movie clip or use animation?
- Do you want to include a blank slide for emphasis or use other creative methods of presentation?

These questions suggest many purposeful, rhetorical ways of writing for a Power-Point presentation. Again, begin with your purpose and your audience, and then design your presentation to meet your needs. The guidelines presented here cover some of the more common techniques you should incorporate in your presentation. But realize that you can modify these "rules" to suit your own needs. Some students have told us they find it helpful to use PowerPoint rather than create a poster session or present a purely oral speech because the program provides a structure that they can use to pace their presentations or keep them on track. This seems to be particularly true for students presenting in a second language or those who experience a great deal of anxiety when speaking. PowerPoint's timed slide function and ease for creating placeholders serve a *double rhetorical purpose* for such students: they actually find it helpful to read information off the slides, and in this way the presentation tool helps convey information and facilitate delivery. Consider your own needs as a speaker when you select your mode of presentation. Slide-based presentations in PowerPoint can be very compelling for an audience and very rewarding for you as a presenter.

Possibilities for PowerPoint

Seeing Connections
See Lawrence Lessig's "Free Culture" on pages 403–411 for examples of a well-structured speech and innovative PowerPoint slide design, including signposting and repetitive structure and an example of deliberative or legislative discourse.

Using a conventional PowerPoint format, Tracy Hadnott created five slides to serve as placeholders for her research-based presentation on the morality of stem cell research. As shown in Figure 8.9, she used a simple design, preventing the paper from being too cluttered. In the colored line on the left side of the slide, the mosaic colors replicate strands of DNA. Thus the slide design conveyed the content of her argument visually while she presented it orally.

Similarly, Sarah Trube designed her slides with careful attention to the visual argument made by the slide background. For her presentation on global warming, humorously titled

From Imagery of Greek Gods to the Garden of Eden
Pathos
- Religion
- Murder
Ethos
- Religious Figures
- GOD

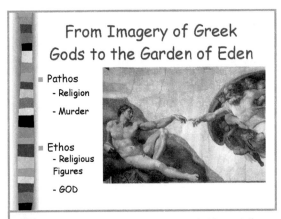

FIGURE 8.9 Tracy Hadnott's presentation titled "Stem Cell Research Through a Visual Lens," slide 2.

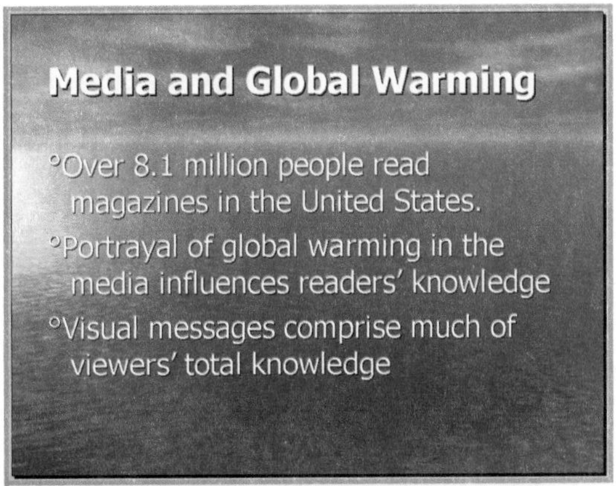

Media and Global Warming
°Over 8.1 million people read magazines in the United States.
°Portrayal of global warming in the media influences readers' knowledge
°Visual messages comprise much of viewers' total knowledge

FIGURE 8.10 Sarah Trube's presentation titled "Media and Global Warming," slide 9.

"Escaping the Frying Pan: The Media Fire and the Scrambled Egg of Global Climate Change," she used a background template that showed a watery image of the earth and sky to create the right mood (see Figure 8.10). She spent considerable time discussing each of the bullet points listed in her slide so that it served the rhetorical function of a brief outline.

In an unusual application of PowerPoint, Morgan Springer created a dynamic, animated map that colored red those countries experiencing political wars and military dictatorships (see Figure 8.11). He ended by circling the two countries that were the focus of his research paper on self-determination in Kosovo and East Timor.

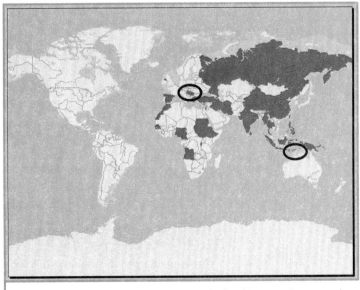

FIGURE 8.11 One of Morgan Springer's map slides from his PowerPoint presentation on self-determination in Kosovo and East Timor.

Using a more humorous and interactive approach for his presentation on the visual strategies of political campaigns, Kavi Vyas got the audience thinking about his argument by pretending to hold an election for the new governor of California. He announced the election in the first slide and then gave everyone a handout of his second slide that showed himself ostensibly dressed up as different candidates. After taking a class "vote," he delved into his argument that often voters respond to effective visual appeals

Student Writing

See Morgan Springer's map animation in action on his creative PowerPoint presentation.
www.ablongman.com/envision/233

AT A GLANCE

Delivery with PowerPoint Slides

- Practice your timing; experiment with advancing slides before or after you introduce them verbally.
- Make eye contact; look at the audience rather than the slides.
- Try not to read off the slides; prepare a separate script to create a dialogue with your audience.
- Always practice the slideshow at least once before giving it live, especially if you are using animation or film clips.

FIGURE 8.12 Kavi Vyas's slide announcing the election.

FIGURE 8.13 Kavi's slide showing the importance of embodied rhetoric for electorical candidates and public speakers.

rather than the substantive platforms of the candidates. Figures 8.12 and 8.13 show two consecutive slides from his presentation. The obvious use of humor made his presentation both quite engaging and effective in communicating his critique of the two-party system.

CREATIVE PRACTICE

Experiment with designing slides for your presentation, using either Power-Point or transparencies for overhead projection. First, create a title slide. Then try making slides that show only images, enlarged to fit the whole screen. Next, experiment with text slides. Should you use a bulleted list? a question followed by an answer? a blank to be filled in with the click of a mouse or an impromptu notation on a transparency? Finally, try some inter-active or dynamic features, such as links to Webpages, animation to make images cascade and change, or even audio or video clips. Avoid using sounds or images as mere decoration; make every slide a rhetorical part of your per-suasive presentation.

Choosing Methods of Delivery

As you can tell, the way you present your visual materials is just as crucial as how you draft content for that presentation. In other words, after *selection, arrangement,* and *design* of materials, you need to think about ways of *delivering* the presentation. But why is delivery so important? Won't the content carry the persuasiveness of the presentation? If the writing is good, won't the delivery be good? Indeed, the writing must be skillful; the selection, organization, and translation of your argument into an appropriate, audience-centered design are crucial for your success. But you also need to attend to *how* you communicate your argument to your audience. In other words, you need to involve those last two canons of rhetoric, *memory* and *delivery.* In brief, **memory** entails both memorizing one's argument to communicate it to the audience and evoking memorable phrases, while **delivery** concerns strategies of presenting your argument to an audience.

We know that memory was crucial for rhetoricians before the invention of the printing press. Speakers would memorize phrases, stories, and histories to pass down from generation to generation. Significantly, this process occurred through a form of visual organization called an **architectural mnemonic technique,** a method in which you associate a phrase to a location or part of a room so that as you look around during your presentation you receive visual clues to trigger your memory. Scholars William Covino and David Jolliffe explain that the rhetorician Cicero described this technique as "a set of visual images like the rooms of a house, which can be associated with the items in a long speech" (67). As you think about strategies of presentation, you might want to try memorizing key parts of your speech through this technique by creating a visual map of your script. Also, attend to the way your audience will remember your words, and choose your examples, your diction, and your pacing accordingly. In this way, memory leads naturally into delivery, the last canon of rhetoric.

When asked which three of the five canons of rhetoric he considered most significant, the Greek orator Demosthenes replied, "delivery, delivery, delivery." In other words, so crucial is this fifth canon that it can supersede the rest. One core aspect of the canon of delivery is the *sound* of the presentation: how speakers use tone of voice, pacing, strategic pauses, or changes in volume or inflection to make their arguments memorable and effective.

If you think of some of the most prominent speakers of recent history—Illinois Senator Barack Obama, former president Ronald Reagon, former Congresswoman Barbara Jordan—you probably can hear in your head the rhetorically powerful ways they used the sound of language itself. You can likewise prepare yourself for effective oral delivery by annotating your script to indicate places where you will pause,

---

AT A GLANCE

Some Fundamental Elements of Delivery

- *Stance or posture:* also called embodied rhetoric
- *Gesture:* use of hands to communicate information
- *Voice:* pitch, tone, loudness, softness, and enunciation
- *Pacing:* of words, visuals, and argument
- *Rhetorical appeals:* use of logos, pathos, ethos
- *Visuals:* slides, posters, graphics, handouts
- *Embodied visuals:* not only stance but dress, appearance, mannerisms
- *Style:* elements such as repetition, allusion, metaphor, stories, personal narrative, jokes, and pauses

---

Delivery, as one of the five canons of rhetoric, deals primarily with the effectiveness of a speech's presentation. Oral communication, combined with variations in the presenter's voice and body movements, comprises the delivery of speech. The speaker's ability to manipulate auditory and visual techniques enables him/her to effectively convey his/her argument to the audience.

—Kelly Ingleman

FIGURE 8.14 During her presentation on sexual assault on campus, Liz Kreiner opted against using multimedia, relying instead on her voice and embodied rhetoric to convey the seriousness of her subject.

Seeing Connections
Read Michael Eisner's Address Before Members of the United States Congress to examine the effective use of multimedia to enhance oral rhetoric.

emphasize a key word, or use the strength of your voice to underscore a point. Written cues like this can help you to deliver a memorable, moving, and convincing oral argument.

However, it is not just the *sound* of delivery that affects the persuasiveness of an oral presentation but the *look* of that presentation as well. How many times have you seen a talk in which the speaker dressed up to make a point or used the rhetoric of his or her body to persuade the audience? This form of presentation is a genre we call **embodied rhetoric,** a presentation in which the body becomes a visual means of communicating the message. Kavi Vyas, for instance, used embodied rhetoric prominently in his presentation, as seen in Figure 8.13. However, even in more traditional presentations, you employ the power of embodied rhetoric through the clothes you wear, how you stand, the voice you choose, and even how you hold the materials you use to convey your argument. When Liz Kreiner delivered her presentation on sexual assault on campus, for instance (see Figure 8.14), she made very strategic decisions about her embodied rhetoric: to emphasize the seriousness of her subject, she dressed conservatively and stood absolutely still at the podium as she recounted the disturbing stories of date rape that she had uncovered during her research. Her somber demeanor, reinforced by her serious tone of voice, produced an extremely powerful rhetorical moment.

However, in most cases, we see embodied rhetoric at work through gesture. Often, when we think about the term *gesture* in relation to public speaking, we think of very overt or intentional hand motions that public speakers make for emphasis, like that made by Jake Palinsky in Figure 8.15, in which he directs the audience's attention by gesturing to the diagram he is describing. Our eyes follow his finger to focus on the part of the diagram he is explaining at that moment.

The gesture is a careful rhetorical move: it has purpose and works effectively as a strategy of communication. sometimes gestures in public speaking seem less carefully composed, such as the one in Figure 8.16. Here we see the speaker in midsentence, her hands opened as if in an involuntary accompaniment to her words. But notice how the open palm, extended toward members of the audience, invites them to listen; it is tilted down to allow words to travel and open the space between the speaker and the audience. This subtle instance of embodied rhetoric invites the listeners into the argument and demonstrates a moment of explanation and connection.

Although we all use gestures without realizing that we do, it is in fact possible to train ourselves to use the rhetoric of the body more carefully, and even strategically, as an integral part of our overall presentation design. your purpose in using gestures as part of a presentation should be to harness the power of the body effectively to communicate ideas. Therefore, as you draft and deliver your presentation, remember that your *entire* body—from body language to clothes, posture, expression, and gestures—participates in communicating your ideas and information.

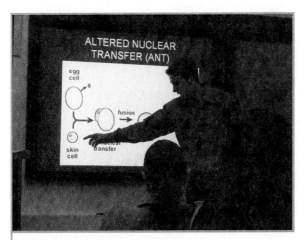

FIGURE 8.16 In a moment of explanation, Alina Lanesberg uses a subtle gesture to emphasize her point and draw her audience into her argument.

FIGURE 8.15 In his presentation on recent developments in stem cell research, Jake Palinsky used gesture deliberately to help his audience understand a scientific diagram.

CREATIVE PRACTICE

Analyze the gestures used by one of the most famous public speakers, Martin Luther King Jr. (see Figures 8.17 and Figures 8.18). Write a brief analysis of the suggested meaning and purpose of each gesture, describing each of the images as you make your argument. Then select the words you might match to the gesture. This exercise will help you explore strategies to use in your own presentations.

FIGURE 8.17 Martin Luther King Jr. gesturing at a press conference.

FIGURE 8.18 Martin Luther King Jr. emphasizes his point at a mass rally in Philadelphia, August 4, 1965.

COLLABORATIVE CHALLENGE

With a partner from class, conduct field research on the delivery strategies of three speakers. Write down your impressions using the fundamental elements of delivery listed in the "At a Glance" box. Then assess each speaker in terms of the effectiveness and appropriateness of delivery strategies based on the needs of the audience: Does a formal speaker put an entire lecture hall to sleep through monotone voice, lack of gestures, and a formal body language, or does the speaker use humor, vivid expressions, and clear pauses to keep the audience engaged? Does a teacher in a small seminar use direct eye contact and open body language to invite participation, or does the speaker stand towering over the group and silence others? Finally, identify key techniques that you can apply from each speaker in terms of excellent strategies of delivery and try to use them in your own presentation.

Practicing Your Presentation

Speakers like Martin Luther King Jr. dedicate much of their time to practicing their delivery. Similarly, two ideologically opposed political figures, Adolf Hitler and Winston Churchill, relied extensively on practice to develop their delivery. First-person testimonies about Hitler suggest that he incessantly recorded himself speaking and using hand gestures. Then, he would watch the films over and over again, selecting the motions that he felt were most powerful. Next, he would practice that form of delivery—the tone of voice, the pacing, the bodily stance, and the hand gestures— until he felt it was perfect. Finally, he would destroy the recordings so that no one would know how carefully he practiced. The practice made his delivery seem natural and his power seem real. At the opposite end of the spectrum, Winston Churchill used voice alone to persuade the British public to withstand the waves of Nazi attacks night after night in the bombing of Britain. Over the radio wires, his practiced and powerful words—delivered with the perfect amount of confidence and encouragement—helped the British persevere during those dark days. These examples reveal the power of practice in strengthening delivery and its capacity to persuade audiences.

Likewise, you should incorporate repeated practice into the process of drafting and revising your presentations. As with any assignment, your argument will benefit from peer review, so consider performing a "dress rehearsal" for a friend or roommate to get his or her feedback on the clarity of your ideas, your use of multimedia or visual aids, and the effectiveness of your delivery. Better yet, become your own peer reviewer by filming your "dress rehearsal" and then critiquing your performance. Sometimes, by becoming a member of the audience yourself, you can see how to revise your presentation into a truly powerful oral argument.

Winston Churchill could never have stirred the British public as he did were it not for the grave, serious, and controlled tone of voice that he employed in his radio speeches. His faith in the allied powers rang out in stentorian cadences that by their very vibrations instilled belief in the masses. His message was often cliché, but his delivery was never anything but spell-binding. Had he had a feeble voice, perhaps Germany would have fared better.

—Dr. Gideon Burton

COLLABORATIVE CHALLENGE

Have someone digitally record or film you while you practice your presentation to find out if you make any involuntary movements (such as rubbing your chin, clicking a pen, or twirling your hair) or verbal tics (such as repeating "umm" or "like"). Select two or three strong expressions, gestures, and verbal phrases that you can use with rhetorical purpose and effectiveness. Then practice these again on film until you feel completely confident. In addition to practicing your delivery, work on the canon of memory by trying to memorize some key points of your presentation to deliver them without having to look at your notes or script.

Anticipating Problems and the Question-and-Answer Session

As you practice your presentation, don't forget to consider problems that might arise, such as faulty technology, a bored or confused audience, or even hecklers. To troubleshoot technology, visit your room and test out your equipment in advance. Make sure you have backup for the technology: save your work on a CD or memory stick, or email it to yourself. But remember, even if your practice session goes smoothly, bring handouts in case your PowerPoint slides don't work, and be prepared to talk without technology if necessary. Also, be ready to cut down or extend the length of your talk by indicating on your speech places you might pause or points you might discuss in more detail. Realize that the more comfortable you are with your material, the more you can adapt on the spot to the needs of your audience.

Successful adaptation includes handling the question-and-answer session well; this part of a presentation, usually located at the end, serves as the final opportunity to clarify your argument and convince your audience. A successful presenter anticipates and, in some cases, even sets up the framework for the question-and-answer session. For instance, during his presentation on Marilyn Manson, Ben Rosenbrough realized he didn't have time to develop the link he saw between Elvis Presley and Manson in his formal presentation and so he made only a passing reference to the connection, hoping that the audience would be intrigued and ask about it after his talk. When they did, he advanced his PowerPoint beyond his conclusion slide to one documenting

Student Writing
Read Ben Rosenbrough's presentation script to see how he planned a "surprise slide" for the question-and-answer session.
www.ablongman.com/envision/234

these connections in a powerful way. His surprise preparation for the question-and-answer session made his presentation design exceptionally successful. Similarly, you can anticipate what questions your audience might have by delivering your presentation to a peer group member, seeing what questions your presentation generates and even practicing trial responses. Consider having some new evidence, a stunning visual, or even a handout prepared to answer a question that you hope might be asked after your presentation.

Documenting Your Presentation

Design. Delivery. Practice. What is left? After all your hard work on your presentation, you probably want to leave some kind of trace, a written artifact, or a form of textual memory of the presentation. **Documentation**—*some form of written or visual evidence of your presentation's argument*—is the answer. Documentation serves an important rhetorical function: to inform and persuade. This might take the form of a **handout** which provides additional information in the form of an annotated bibliography, a summary of your key points and thesis, visual rhetoric from your presentation, references for further reading, or a printout of your PowerPoint presentation. You should put your contact information on it so the audience can ask you further questions.

Documentation might also consist of a **text** or **script** for your presentation. This can either be the annotated printout of your PowerPoint presentation, a full speech, or a typed set of notes in outline form with placeholders for your slides or media aids such as shown in Tommy Tsai's visual outline (see Figure 8.4). More innovatively, you might document your presentation with a **creative take-away** that reflects a key aspect of your talk. Consider Wendy Hagenmaier's handout for her project on media coverage of the bombing of Hiroshima and Nagasaki (see Figure 8.19). The cover of the *New York Times* from August 1945 is attached to a small candle; Wendy's caption reads, "Light this candle in remembrance of how the August 1945 atomic bombings of Hiroshima and Nagasaki have been remembered by Japanese and American photojournalists. The 'flashes' of its flame will serve to remind you that photojournalistic coverage is often an attempt to shape collective national memory and that remembrance is subjective." Another student, Falco Pichler, presenting his research finding on Nike marketing strategies, created a "backstage pass" to what he called the "Nike Show" and invited students to read his paper online. Aaron Johnson, presenting his research on media representation of athletes who take performance-enhancing drugs, made a mock subscription card with the distorted title "Sports Exaggerated" as creative documentation for his presentation (see Figure 8.20).

Student Writing

See Courtney Smith's handout, designed to accompany her presentation on Palestinian female suicide bombers.
www.ablongman.com/envision/235

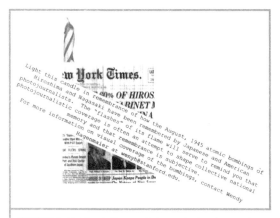

FIGURE 8.19 Wendy Hagenmaier's creative handout on the 1945 atomic bombings of Hiroshima and Nagasaki.

FIGURE 8.20 Aaron Johnson's creative presentation take-away for his research project on *Sports Illustrated*.

Using Photoshop, he embedded a cover of *Sports Illustrated* into the subscription card and listed the main points of his argument as "advertising points" for his presentation. Notice his complete contact information at the bottom of the card.

These examples begin to show the range of creative documentation strategies you might pursue as the final part of your presentation. Taking the lead from Aaron, you might even craft an interactive visual take-away such as a graphic montage, a minibook, or other forms of visual argument. The importance of such texts—whether conventional prose handouts or compelling visual creations—lies in their power to make your presentation memorable, convincing, and engaging. So consider your strategies for documentation as carefully as you design your entire presentation.

Creating Your Own Presentation

In this chapter, you have explored possibilities for presentations; learned how to convert a written argument into a spoken, visual, multimedia presentation or performance; and worked through the different ways of writing for oral, poster, and PowerPoint presentations. Recall the strategies of design, arrangement, and delivery you have learned, and keep in mind the importance of both gesture and embodied rhetoric as ways of communicating your message and your purpose to your particular audience. Finally, as you begin to craft your own presentation, remember the old adage, "practice makes perfect." Peer review and revision are as important to your presentation as collaboration on drafts and revision are to your written work. They enable you to anticipate problems and harness your creativity as you shape your ideas into a memorable, moving, and persuasive form of rhetorical communication.

PREWRITING CHECKLIST

Focus on Analyzing Presentations

❏ What is the presenter's purpose? To inform? persuade? instruct? motivate? initiate discussion? Did the presentation successfully accomplish that purpose?

❏ What is the presenter's relationship to the topic he or she discussed? Is the presenter an expert? a novice? fairly well informed?

❏ Was the presentation appropriate for the audience? Consider language, organization, and explanation of technical or specialized concepts.

❏ Did the speaker present him- or herself as an authority instructing the audience? as a peer sharing information? Did the presenter make eye contact (indicating a direct relationship with the audience) or simply read from a prepared text (indicating a focus on the material rather than the audience)? How did this affect the structure and style of the presentation?

❏ How was the presentation structured? Was an outline or summary provided for the audience to follow? Was this done orally, on the board, in a handout, or on a slide? Was the development of the argument clear? Did it follow the designated structure?

❏ Did the presenter take into account the audience's reaction? For instance, did he or she notice some confusion in the audience and pause to explain a difficult point?

❏ How did the presentation begin? Did the presenter use any effective oral or visual devices to "hook" the audience? Was there a clear conclusion? *(continued)*

❏ Were the main points clearly developed? How was the scope of the presentation? Was there too much information? too little?

❏ Did the presenter use word choices appropriate to the occasion, audience, and subject matter? Were the sentence structures too complex (as if to be read silently) or more colloquial (as if to be read aloud)? Did the presenter project his or her voice enough? Did he or she speak slowly and clearly or rush through the material?

❏ Did the presenter use any formal devices—figurative language, deliberate repetition, literary allusions?

❏ Consider the presenter's embodied rhetoric. Did he or she stand or sit? remain stationary, or move around? Did the presenter use gestures, facial expression, or even costume to add to the rhetorical effect of the argument?

❏ How did the presenter use visuals? Did he or she show slides, bring in posters, write on a blackboard, distribute handouts, engage in role-playing, pass around books, or bring in material evidence for the presentation? Were the visual components rhetorically purposeful or did they seem an afterthought?

❏ If the presenter used posters: Were they clear and accessible to the audience? Did they stand alone as arguments, or was their meaning only clear in conjunction with the oral presentation? Were the words large enough to read from a distance? Did the poster avoid visual clutter? Did it contain a clear title and use information graphics effectively?

❏ If the presenter used a slide program such as PowerPoint: Was the visual design of the slides effective? Did the slides have a unity of theme, color, and layout? Did the presenter avoid visual clutter on the slides? How much text was on each slide? Were placeholders used for emphasis or pacing? Were there innovations in the slideshow, such as using dual screens, animation, or embedded clips or Internet links? Were these effective or distracting? Did the presenter speak to the computer screen rather than the audience? Did the presenter's body block the screen, obscuring the slides?

❏ If the presenter used the blackboard or whiteboard: Did he or she write clearly and legibly? Were the notations on the board purposeful? Did the presenter block the board, making it difficult to read?

❏ If the presenter used technology: Were there any technical difficulties? Did the presenter overcome them smoothly (for instance, having a backup plan), or have a difficult time recovering from the glitch, perhaps because of relying more heavily on technology than on the force of argument?

❏ Did the presenter finish within the allotted time? How did he or she handle the question-and-answer session?

WRITING PROJECTS

1. **Field research:** As part of the necessary preparation for writing your own presentation, conduct field research in the form of observing three public speeches, presentations, or oral/ multimedia arguments, and type up a brief rhetorical analysis on the delivery, rhetorical strategies, and effectiveness of each one. These presentations can include lectures in any of your classes, speakers visiting

campus or your dorms, or the practice presentation of a member of your class. Find three speakers or presentations to expand the possibilities available to you. Write a brief analysis of each one; try to be as specific as possible in your observations and make sure that you indicate what strategies you plan to use in your own presentation.

2. **Formal presentation:** Create and deliver a timed presentation of your research argument for your class (ask your instructor for the precise time limit). You should include the appropriate media (visual rhetoric, PowerPoint slides, Websites, movie clips, performative or interactive aspects). In addition, the oral delivery of your presentation might include a handout that you distribute to the class to provide information—for example, an annotated bibliography, a summary of your key points and thesis, visual rhetoric from your presentation, references for further reading, or a printout of your Power-Point presentation—formatted in the proper manner (or in a creative way if that works for your presentation) with your complete contact information on it. Make sure that you compose a script for your presentation. This can either be the annotated printout of your PowerPoint presentation, a full speech, or notes in outline form (with placeholders for your slides or multimedia). Include references in the text or script of your presentation to any materials you use (handouts and printouts of multimedia).

3. **Collaborative Presentation:** Work in groups of two to four to design and deliver a presentation to the class. You might want to divide the tasks of selecting material, brainstorming strategies of presentation, and designing your visual materials. Will you take turns speaking throughout the presentation, or will each person be responsible for a distinct segment of the presentation? Will one person write the script, another person deliver it—perhaps from memory—while a third creates the slides? Choose the strategy that best suits your audience and your purpose. Don't forget to practice together, and when your group is presenting, look at the others who are speaking to keep the class's attention focused on your group presentation.

4. **Community Writing Presentation:** Either in groups or individually, design your presentation for a specific community audience. What happens if you present your research project on performance art to a group of politicians, to school administrators, to the theater department? Think about how your message can reach a broader audience in this way. What if your project is on the educational poster campaign to prevent the spread of AIDS? After you design one presentation for your writing class, rewrite it to meet the audience expectations of a not-for-profit organization, an international amnesty meeting, or an urban center continuing education class.

 Visit www.ablongman.com/envision for expanded assignment guidelines and student projects.

CHAPTER 9

Documentation and Plagiarism

FIGURE 9.1 Justin Cone's film, *Building on the Past*, remixes visuals and sound to emphasize how all our ideas rely on the works of those before us.

Chapter Preview Questions

- What is the difference between rhetorical imitation and stealing intellectual property?
- How can I avoid unintentional plagiarism?
- Why is it important to learn the conventions of a documentation style?
- What are the proper methods for in-text citations and bibliographies?

"Creativity always builds on the past." You probably learned the truth of this adage by basing your research paper on the many ideas you discovered through your extensive exploration of research sources or by composing a presentation of your research based on examples of effective delivery you noticed from your own classes. For many writers, the debt to those who have written before them is carefully acknowledged—whether through direct references, through parenthetical citations, or through a list of sources. Even visual artists and multimedia writers make their sources explicit to show that they belong to a larger community of writers and that they respect the work of others.

But Justin Cone, a designer and animator based in Austin, Texas, makes this point more emphatically through the multimedia montage shown in Figure 9.1, a short film called *Building on the Past*, which won first place in a Creative Commons contest. *Building on the Past* recycles and modifies public-domain film footage from the Prelinger Archive to make an argument about the relationship between creativity and legislation. The visuals, only a fraction of which you see here, are accompanied by a musical score and a voice-over that repeats the same sentence intermittently throughout the film: "Creativity always builds on the past." In this particular scene, which occurs at the opening of the film, Cone reedited the public-domain footage to run in reverse, showing the children running backward uphill instead of forward downhill. In this way, even in the first few minutes of his piece he offers a powerful argument about how we rely on others for our own creativity; he expresses that idea visually, through his strategy of organization, word choice, and design.

Your research project, too, draws its strength from previous work on the subject. It is a merger of your argument and the already existing dialogue on the topic. So even as you "re-edit it" to suit the purpose of your paper—by selecting passages to quote, paraphrase, summarize, or even argue against—it is crucial that you let your readers know *where* the ideas originated by providing what we call complete and ethical **source attribution,** or the acknowledgment and identification of your sources.

In this chapter, you'll learn how the rhetorical art of imitation—the process by which we all learn to write, compose, speak, and produce texts—differs from the theft of others' ideas, called plagiarism. We'll discuss intellectual property and why it is important to respect the work of others, and you'll acquire strategies for avoiding unintentional plagiarism. We'll provide a means of understanding the process of constructing in-text and end-of-paper citations, and we'll explain MLA, APA, CSE, and Chicago documentation styles.

Rhetorical Imitation and Intellectual Property

In ancient times, **rhetorical imitation,** or the practice of taking after others, was a celebrated form of instruction. Students would copy a speech out word by word, studying the word choice, organization, rhythm, and art of the work. Then they would write a rhetorical analysis (as you did in Chapter 1) of the speech to understand figures and tropes, strategies of argument, and organizational choices. Finally, they would use elements of the speeches they studied, including content (words) and form (arrangement), to draft their own speeches. Through this imitation, they learned to be great rhetors. Such imitative exercises helped students learn from models of excellence.

But, as Dr. Gideon Burton tells us, imitation signified only the beginning. It was "the bridge between one's reading and writing (or speaking). . . . Students moved from close imitations of their models to looser sorts, using these models increasingly as starting points for longer, more involved compositions of their own making." In other words, students started with imitation but soon moved on to create original texts.

This, too, is your task in the writing classroom. After analyzing articles and readings and emulating argumentative and organization strategies from samples of student writing, at some point you need to move on to create an original text. Yet, in the process, you may wish to refer back to those on whose work you are building. This is where **documentation** comes in—the responsible and correct acknowledgment of your sources and influences.

Seeing Connections
For a better understanding
of intellectual property and
copyright regulations, see
the readings in Chapter 12.

Today, it is common to talk about ideas, not just in terms of words and thoughts, but also in terms of **intellectual property,** that is, ideas that belong to someone as a form of property. People create patents and copyrights, go to court, and go to all sorts of extremes to protect their right to consider their ideas, inventions, and thoughts *as property.* In this increasingly litigious society, you need to understand when to stop imitation and when to start acknowledging your sources so that you preserve the rights of others and protect yourself as an emerging writer.

Understanding Plagiarism

Plagiarism means using another person's idea as your own. The etymological origin of *plagiarism,* according to scholars Peter Morgan and Glenn Reynolds, concerns stealing someone's work. In classical times, imitation was not a crime. But with the invention of printing technology, copyright law, and a cultural emphasis on intellectual property as profitable came a concern about taking someone else's ideas—and hence their earning potential—whether intentionally or unintentionally. The consequent demand for originality in writing, which continues in academic and professional circles today, is linked to profit margins and explains why plagiarism remains a punishable act.

In colleges and universities, plagiarism can often lead to suspension or even expulsion because the perpetrator is literally stealing the ideas and livelihood of someone else. Students and faculty members alike have been kicked out of universities on plagiarism charges pertaining to stolen words as well as stolen ideas, designs, and even computer code. In 2003, vice chancellor and physics professor B. S. Rajput of Kamaon University, along with his research assistant, was charged with replicating—word for word and equation for equation—sections of a published article by Professor Renata Kallosh of Stanford University's physics department. Both Rajput and his assistant were forced to leave their university, but, more importantly, the entire academic community felt that intellectual property had been stolen and a code of ethics broken.

As this example reveals, besides being aware of plagiarism for historical and economic reasons, there is another, even more compelling ethical reason for keeping the dialogue model of research in mind. As you work with sources, realize that the claims you are able to make are in fact based on the foundation provided by others. Identifying your sources thus becomes a writing strategy that you need to implement out of *respect* for those who have come before you. By acknowledging their names, ideas, and words, you contribute to a body of knowledge, graciously extending thanks to those who have paved the way. Therefore, while there are legal issues related to intellectual property, copyright law, and "fair use" that you need to know about, if you keep the *respect principle* in mind, it is unlikely that you'll fall into the trap of inadvertently "stealing" someone's work.

You can get started on including your sources by name in your research paper by listing them in your detailed outline at appropriate places. Include direct quotations whenever possible; don't forget to cite your sources for both paraphrase and quotations. Make sure you include the full names of your sources; cite them as people and put in page numbers to practice responsible and respectful writing strategies.

Avoiding Unintentional Plagiarism

To avoid accidentally taking someone else's ideas or words as your own, you might follow two practices. First, always keep in mind that you are contributing to a conversation with other writers interested in your topic. Think of each of your sources as an important participant in that conversation. When you are writing a research-based argument using a large number of texts, think of working with sources as responding to people whose works you **cite,** or quote, as a way of including them in the dialogue. Say to yourself, "I speak my part, I refer to another person's view, and I provide a citation of the statement." With research papers, you are having a conversation with an entire room of people, introducing each person in turn, and serving as the moderator.

Second, develop effective ways of note taking while reading through your sources. If you find an interesting quote, don't just underline or highlight it. Copy it into your research log with a notation about how you might use it. If you find an intriguing idea, write down the attribution in your research log.

Consider Michael Rothenberg's notations in his research log for a project on the design plans for the Twin Towers Memorial in New York City.

Safety: "there's no reason to believe the structures that replace the twin towers wouldn't also be targets." CNN? "they're a target forever"— Klemenic, president of an engineering firm Skilling Ward Magnusson Barkshire in Seattle.

Howard Decker, chief curator of the National Building Museum in Washington, DC said: the other target was the "squat pentagon." He said that shows terrorists choose targets because of their symbolism, not their height. "The desire to build tall buildings is an old one," he said. "The motivations for it are complicated. Commerce. Capitalism. Ego."

Michael lists his notes by category: safety. He then copies the source directly and writes down the full name and identifying information for the quote. He'll use this to build ethos in citing this authority within his paper.

Michael repeats this process for his second note. Here he puts the most interesting words in quotation marks and deliberately uses different words in composing his paraphrase of the source. (See Michael's completed paper on the *Envision* Website.)

This notion of considering your sources as people, as the cast of characters for your research paper, can help you avoid unintentional plagiarism, or the phenomenon that happens when we assimilate all the material we have read and then think that the ideas are our own. This can happen for many reasons: fatigue, oversaturation of information, poor memory, or sloppy note taking. Regardless, even the unintentional taking of others' ideas has very serious consequences, as we can learn from the plight of Doris Kearns Goodwin, a Pulitzer Prize–winning historian who was charged with stealing the words and ideas of others.

How I Caused That Story
A historian explains why someone else's writing wound up in her book

Doris Kearns Goodwin

I am a historian. With the exception of being a wife and mother, it is who I am. And there is nothing I take more seriously.

In recent days, questions have been raised about how historians go about crediting their sources, and I have been caught up in the swirl. Ironically, the more intensive and far-reaching a historian's research, the greater the difficulty of citation. As the mountain of material grows, so does the possibility of error.

Fourteen years ago, not long after the publication of my book *The Fitzgeralds and the Kennedys*, I received a communication from author Lynne McTaggart pointing out that material from her book on Kathleen Kennedy had not been properly attributed. I realized that she was right. Though my footnotes repeatedly cited Ms. McTaggart's work, I failed to provide quotation marks for phrases that I had taken verbatim, having assumed that these phrases, drawn from my notes, were my words, not hers. I made the corrections she requested, and the matter was completely laid to rest—until last week, when the *Weekly Standard* published an article reviving the issue. The larger question for those of us who write history is to understand how citation mistakes can happen.

The research and writing for this 900-page book, with its 3,500 footnotes, took place over 10 years. At that time, I wrote my books and took my notes in longhand, believing I could not think well on a keyboard. Most of my sources were drawn from a multitude of primary materials: manuscript collections, private letters, diaries, oral histories, newspapers, periodicals, personal interviews. After three years of research, I discovered more than 150 cartons of materials that had been previously stored in the attic of Joe Kennedy's Hyannis Port house. These materials were a treasure trove for a historian—old report cards, thousands of family letters, movie stubs and diaries, which allowed me to cross the boundaries of time and space. It took me two additional years to read, categorize and take notes on these documents.

During this same period, I took handwritten notes on perhaps 300 books. Passages I wanted to quote directly were noted along with general notes on the ideas and story lines of each book. Notes on all these sources were then arranged chronologically and kept in dozens of folders in 25 banker's boxes. Immersed in a flood of papers, I began to write the book. After each section and each chapter was completed, I returned the notes to the boxes along with notations for future footnoting. When the manuscript was finished, I went back to all these sources to check the accuracy of attributions. As a final protection, I revisited the 300 books themselves.

Somehow in this process, a few of the books were not fully rechecked. I relied instead on my notes, which combined direct quotes and paraphrased sentences. If I had had the books in front of me, rather than my notes, I would have caught mistakes in the first place and placed any borrowed phrases in direct quotes.

What made this incident particularly hard for me was the fact that I take great pride in the depth of my research and the extensiveness of my citations. The writing of history is a rich process of building on the work of the past with the hope that others will build on what you have done. Through footnotes you point the way to future historians.

The only protection as a historian is to institute a process of research and writing that minimizes the possibility of error. And that I have tried to do, aided by modern technology, which enables me, having long since moved beyond longhand, to use a computer for both organizing and taking notes. I now rely on a scanner, which reproduces the passages I want to cite, and then I keep my own comments on those books in a separate file so that I will never confuse the two again. But the real miracle occurred when my college-age son taught me how to use the mysterious footnote key on the computer, which makes it possible to insert the citations directly into the text while the sources are still in front of me, instead of shuffling through hundreds of folders four or five years down the line, trying desperately to remember from where I derived a particular statistic or quote. Still, there is no guarantee against error. Should one occur, all I can do, as I did 14 years ago, is to correct it as soon as I possibly can, for my own sake and the sake of history. In the end, I am still the same fallible person I was before I made the transition to the computer, and the process of building a lengthy work of history remains a complicated but honorable task.

Goodwin explains how she unintentionally plagiarized one of her 300 sources; her new technological approach to note taking offers a concrete strategy for preventing this disaster. As you develop effective practices for avoiding unintentional plagiarism, consider how you can include your sources more immediately (as Goodwin learned to do), develop a dialogue with them in your research log (as Michael Rothenberg does), and be particularly vigilant about checking and cross-checking to ensure that you've made proper attribution.

Understanding Documentation Style

As a writer, you have a rhetorical choice to make between documentation styles. Different styles are preferred by different communities of writers, as shown in the following table. The format guidelines for each style actually have a rhetorical purpose corresponding to the way that knowledge is constructed for that community.

Documenta- tion Style	Community of Writers	Defining Features	Purpose of Features	Example
MLA	Modern Language Association (language, literature, writing, philosophy, and humanities scholars and teachers)	Citation begins with author's name (last name first, full first name), then book title, then publication information, then date.	Knowledge advances based on individual author's contributions; thus, names are prioritized over dates; place of publication matters for building ethos	McCloud, Scott. Understanding Comics. New York: HarperPerennial, 1994.
APA	American Psychological Association (psychologists and social scientists)	Publication date immediately follows designation of author, multiple authors may be listed (last name and initials), titles are in sentence style (first word capitalized, rest lowercase)	Since knowledge advances based on dated contributions to the field, dates are prioritized; most writing is collaborative, so up to six authors are listed; titles, typically long and technical, are in lowercase.	Bruce, V., & Green, P. (1990). *Visual perception: physiology, psychology, andecology* (2nd ed.). London: Erlbaum.
CSE	Council of Science Editors (such as biology and physics)	Reference include last name and date; often superscript numbers are used	Like APA style, emphasis is on knowledge advancing through studies and scientific research; a heavily cited style of writing	[1]Goble, JL. Visual disorders in the handicapped child. New York: M. Dekker; 1984. p. 265.
Chicago	University of Chicago (business writers, professional writers, and those in fine arts)	Sources are listed as footnotes or endnotes and include page numbers	Knowledge is incremental, and readers like to check facts as a they go along	[2]Scott McCloud, *Understanding Comics* (New York: HarperPerennial, 1994), 33.

Seeing Connections
See the reference section of Harrison Pope's "Evolving Ideals of Male Body Image as Seen Through Action Toys" for an example of APA formatting.

For the purposes of this chapter, we focus on MLA style because the writing we've been discussing in this book belongs to disciplines in the humanities. The different styles, methods of organization, modes of argumentation, and conventions for writing in the social sciences, sciences, business, and fine arts communities are not covered in this book.

Documentation as Cross-Referencing

Documentation is not intended to be some surreptitious way to check up on you; rather, it is part of the research dialogue. The idea is that readers might be inspired enough by your research and your use of materials to want to read some of your sources themselves. In this way, documentation functions as a road map or signpost to your audience about how to locate the source—both in your bibliography and in the library or online. Accordingly, the central purpose of documentation is to point readers clearly and explicitly to the list of sources at the end of the paper.

Let's take a look at a citation in Michael Rothenberg's paper on the Twin Towers. We call this an **in-text citation** or **reference** because it occurs within the body of his paper. MLA style always places such references inside parentheses to set them off from the rest of the writing. Look at how the last name and page number of the citation in parentheses point the reader directly to the author's name in the "Works Cited" list.

. . . the Twin Towers were so enormous that together they encased a staggering 11 million square feet of commercial space (Czarnecki 31).

Works Cited

Bravman, John. Interview by Michael Rothenberg. 13 May 2003.

Bruno, Lisa D. "Studio Daniel Libeskind." 6 Nov. 2002. Sunspot.
1 June 2003 <http://www.sunspot.net/news/custom/attack/
ny-bzarch062993970nov06,0,2252478.story?coll=bal%2Dattack%
2Dstoryutil>.

Czarnecki, John E. "Architects at the Forefront as They Show Ground Zero
Aspirations." Architectural Record Nov. 2002: 31-50.

Notice that Michael has alphabetized the list by authors' last names, which corresponds to MLA style documentation placing author names as most important. Readers need only scan down the page to look for the last name of the source cited earlier. This makes it very easy, and once you understand that this **cross-referencing logic** governs all documentation rules, you can begin to understand how to document a wide range of sources—even new multi media sources for which there are no set rules of citation.

For instance, Michael needed to document several quotes he obtained from a temporary PDF document posted on the Website of a city review board. By understanding documentation as *cross-referencing*, here's what Michael wrote:

In particular, they required a memorial that would include both history and memory "such as the Libeskind's below-grade 'ground zero' space," as well as a proposal "that returns a much-lamented presence to the skyline" like Libeskind's tower, and finally, a plan that develops the site in the context of the community (Evaluation 3, 12).

Evaluation of Innovative Design Proposals. Ed. Ernest Hutton.
13 Jan. 2003. New York: New Visions. 25 May 2003
<http://www.nynv.aiga.org/NYNV20030113.pdf>.

As you can see, the word within the parenthetical documentation sets up a *cross-reference* to the first word listed in the "Works Cited" list at the end of the paper. This makes it easy to compose a very concise reference within the paper and easy to find that reference at the end of the paper.

Using Notes for Documentation

Although MLA style relies primarily on in-text citations and a final bibliography—unlike Chicago style, which uses primarily footnotes or endnotes—sometimes you might occasionally need to include a note. What situations allow for the use of footnotes or endnotes in MLA style? You'll use notes in MLA style when you want to include extra explanatory information but don't want to break the flow of your argument.

Following are two notes from Michael's paper. In the first case, he wanted to define some of the key terms of his argument, but he felt it would be intrusive to pause and explain his terms within the paper itself.

> [1] Those in the public who influenced the design of the new World Trade Center include all of those concerned with the project and not just New York citizens. However, even though the majority of these motivated individuals live in New York, they represent every state and many nations. Hence, the collective group of citizens in the worldwide community who are interested in this project are referred to as "the public" throughout this document, but this phrase should be understood to include primarily New York citizens.

In the second case, he wanted to add more information from his research log, but again he felt it would break the flow of his argument. In this case, he was able to include direct quotations and statistics from his research; this built his ethos and allowed interested readers to learn more about the subject. Notice that he included the source for his research again through the cross-referencing system. A reader would only have to scan down to the *O* section of his bibliography to find the full source for this citation.

> [2] Five thousand people from the New York area participated in a two-week in-depth discussion starting on July 20, 2002. According to their Website, "This historic gathering—called 'Listening to the City'—gave participants an opportunity to help shape the redevelopment of Lower Manhattan and the creation of a permanent memorial to the victims of 9/11." At this gathering, the 5,000 committed individuals responded to many questions and polls. Of the respondents, 60% thought that new towers should be built at least as tall as the originals, 71% thought that adding a "major element or icon" to the skyline was "very important," and 87% thought it was "important" or "very important" to add something unique to the skyline (Online Dialogues).

In addition to providing explanatory information, notes can also point readers to a list of sources you would discuss or include if you had space to do so. In Michael's case, he wanted to discuss mammoth architectural designs more broadly but did not have the space in his paper to do so. His solution was a note pointing the reader to a source on this topic, which happened to be another paper he had written. This note would also be the place for a list of sources about this tangential topic.

> [6] See my paper, "The Two Towers," on the Petronas Towers as the world's tallest, February 2003.

Typically, such notes are formatted as **endnotes,** appearing at the end of your paper, before the bibliography. **Footnotes,** which appear at the bottom or foot of the page, would again break the flow of the argument. But ask your teacher for specific guidance about your own paper.

MLA-Style Works Cited Lists

You've seen how documentation works as a *cross-referencing system*, in which the in-text citation within parentheses points the reader directly to the source in the bibliography. In MLA style, the bibliography is called a **Works Cited** list because it refers explicitly to the works (or sources) you have cited (or quoted) in your paper. Sometimes a Works Cited list is accompanied by another section called a **Works Consulted** list, which names all the other sources you may have read and studied but did not actually quote from in your final revision.

Realize that a reference page is a moment of ethos building as well: by listing both works *cited* and works *consulted,* you demonstrate your research process and new knowledge. You also invite your readers to explore the topic in depth with you.

If your instructor agrees, you can organize or format your bibliographic materials in different ways. You can either list all your sources alphabetically, or you can divide your sources into various categories—if you want to showcase your primary research, for example.

Consider Sunthar Premakumar's reference page from his paper discussed in chapter 6. Here, he loosely followed MLA form; he categorized his sources to show the range of his research and included some annotations, reminiscent of the annotated bibliography you learned about in Chapter 5.

Works Cited and Consulted

Books

- Devany, Arthur. <u>Hollywood Economics.</u> New York: Routledge, 2004.
- Ninian, Alex. <u>Bollywood.</u> Ipswich, MA: EBSCO, 2003.
- Ruckert, George E. <u>Music in North India.</u> New York: Oxford UP, 2004.
- Shankar, Ravi. <u>My Music, My Life.</u> New York: Simon, 1968.

Sunthar decides to categorize his sources according to his iceberg of research.

He includes both works he quotes and works he has consulted for background knowledge.

Sunthar uses a bulleted list instead of the conventional hanging indent shown in the following sample.

- Waterman, David. <u>Hollywood's Road to Success.</u> Cambridge, MA: Harvard UP, 2005.

Journal Articles

The journal articles Sunthar lists include volume and issue numbers as well as page numbers. Since Sunthar found them through a library database, he includes the name of the database at the end of the citation.

- Henry, Edward O. "The Rationalization of Intensity in Indian Music." <u>Ethnomusicology: Journal of the Society for Ethnomusicology.</u> 46.1 (Winter 2002): 33-56. <u>Expanded Academic ASAP.</u>
- Mayrhofer, C. M. "Media and the Transformation of Religion in South Asia." <u>Indo-Iranian Journal.</u> 43.1 (Annual 2000): 80(2). <u>Expanded Academic ASAP.</u>

Films

Sunthar also includes the films he analyzed providing a brief annotation for each one.

- <u>Kabhi Kushi Kabhi Gham</u>—A movie by the famous Bollywood director Karan Johar. This movie explores the simple dynamics that prevails in Indian families and advocates the important message of understanding within families. This is confirmed by the tag line of the movie, "It's all about loving your parents."
- <u>Kal Ho Na Ho</u>—With a tag line of "A Story of a Lifetime . . . in a Heartbeat," this movie depicts a story of a person who is willing to help everyone he meets. The movie calls out to the public to be less selfish. Filled with many glorious songs, it was one of the biggest hits of its time.
- <u>Lagaan</u>—This is an inspirational movie produced by the famous Bollywood actor Amir Khan, who also plays the lead in the movie. This movie is about how a group of villagers come together to fight against the British army, which ruled India at that time. This movie promotes the idea of unity and transcending social and cultural differences to build a strong bond with fellow countrymen.

Interviews

Amritha Appaswami

He also lists the interviewees, providing information to build the ethos of each person.

—a second-year master's student majoring in biological sciences at Stanford University. Having trained in Carnatic classical music, Amritha is an avid listener of Indian film music.

A. R. Rahman

—hailed by *Time* magazine as the "Mozart of Madras," Rahman is one of the most successful artists of all time and, according to a BBC estimate, is said to have sold between 100 million and 150 million albums. In India, Rahman is recognized as the artist who changed the face of music by successfully fusing traditional Indian classical strains with the elements of modern technology and evolving his own unique style.

Stuti Goswamy

—one of the biggest Bollywood fans on campus. I asked her about the influence of Bollywood songs on her. I also talked to her about the persuasiveness of these movies.

Roopa Mahadevan

—one of the well-known Carnatic music singers on campus, Roopa is a great admirer of Bollywood songs. She is a first-year master's student in biological sciences.

In contrast, Dexian Cai, whose outline appeared in Chapter 6, more strictly followed conventional MLA style for his works cited, alphabetizing his list and using hanging indentation format.

Works Cited

Kincheloe, Joe L. The Sign of the Burger: McDonald's and the Culture of Power. Philadelphia: Temple UP, 2002.

McSpotlight, 27 Oct. 2003 <http://www.mcspotlight.com>.

"The Merchants of Cool." Frontline. By Rachel Dretzin. Dir. Barak Goodman. 2001. PBS. 27 Feb. 2001 <http://www.pbs.org/wgbh/pages/frontline/shows/cool/>.

Ritzer, George. McDonaldization the Reader. Thousand Oaks, CA: Pine Forge, 2002.

Dex alphabetizes the list by last name.

If there is no author, as for "Merchants of Cool," the title is listed first. note that little words such as *the* are not considered for alphabetizing.

When an author's name
appears more than once,
three hyphens (–) stand in
for the name after the first
citation.

—. The McDonaldization of Society. Rev. ed. Thousand Oaks, CA: Pine Forge,
    1996.

Smart, Barry, ed. Resisting McDonaldization. London: Sage, 1999.

Vidal, John. Mclibel: Burger Culture on Trial. New York: New Press, 1997.

Watson, James L. Golden Arches East: McDonald's in East Asia. Palo Alto,
    CA: Stanford UP, 1997.

Each entry is formatted with
a hanging indent so readers
can skim the names more
easily.

Documentation for Print and Online Sources

MLA style follows a particular logic in ordering information for a citation. Consult the "At a Glance" box and the table below to begin to understand this system. You might also study the list of examples provided in this chapter, but realize that sometimes for less conventional sources (i.e. Facebook wall posts) you may need to improvise the format based on your understanding of MLA style.

AT A GLANCE

MLA Documentation for Print and Online Sources

For the Works Cited list, follow the order below in listing details about your source

1. Author or authors
2. Title of book or article
3. If an article, title of journal or book within which it is published
4. Place of publication
5. Publisher

6. Date of publication
7. If an online source, date you accessed it
8. If a printed or PDF article, page span
9. If online article from a database, the database or search engine
10. If online source, the full URL

LOGIC OF MLA STYLE

Satrapi, Marjane.	Persepolis: The Story of a Childhood	New York: Pantheon, 2004.
List the author's name first, by last name. If there are multiple authors, include them all, following the order listed on the publication. If there is no author, list the citation according to the title instead.	The title comes next. For books and films, underline or italicize the title. For shorter pieces (such as articles, TV shows, songs, etc.), put the title in quotation marks with the larger publication (the collection of essays, TV series, or album) underlined or italicized. If you need to refer to the title for in-text citations (and there is no author), use the first few keywords only.	Last comes publication information: place, publisher or company, and date. For shorter pieces, include the complete range of page numbers (for the article), and include URLs for online sources. Also include the date you accessed online sources.

Single-Author Book

> Satrapi, Marjane. Persepolis: The Story of a Childhood. New York: Pantheon,
>
> 2004.

Multiple-Author Book

> Andrews, Maggie, and Mary M. Talbot, eds. All the World and Her Husband:
>
> Women in Twentieth-Century Consumer Culture. London: Cassell, 2000.

Introduction, Preface, Foreword, or Afterword in a Book

> Gerbner, George. Foreword. Cultural Diversity and the U.S. Media. Eds. Yahya
>
> R. Kamalipour and Theresa Carillia. New York: State U of New York P,
>
> 1998. xv-xvi.

Article in an Anthology

> Boichel, Bill. "Batman: Commodity as Myth." The Many Lives of the Batman.
>
> Eds. Roberta Pearson and William Uricchio. New York: BFI, 1991. 4-17.

Article from a Journal

> Roberts, Garyn G. "Understanding the Sequential Art of Comic Strips and
>
> Comic Books and Their Descendants in the Early Years of the New
>
> Millenium." Journal of American Culture 27.2 (2004): 210-217.

Article from a Popular Magazine Published Monthly

> Maney, Kevin. "The New Face of IBM." Wired July 2005: 142-152.
>
> Sontag, Susan. "Looking at War." The New Yorker 3 Jan. 2003.
>
> 20 June 2006 <http://www.newyorker.com/printables/archive/
>
> 050119fr_archive04>.

Article from a Newspaper

> Cowell, Alan. "Book Buried in Irish Bog Is Called a Major Find." New York
>
> Times 27 July 2006. 31 July 2006 <http://www.nytimes.com/
>
> 2006/07/27/books/27psal.html?_r=1&ref=arts&oref=slogin>.

Article from a Database

> Chun, Alex. "Comic Strip's Plight Isn't Funny." Los Angeles Times 27 Apr.
>
> 2006, home ed.: E6. Lexis Nexis. Stanford University, Stanford, CA.
>
> 4 May 2006 <http://www.lexisnexis.com>.

Article from a Website

> Yagoda, Ben. "You Need to Read This: How Need to Vanquished Have To,
>
> Must and Should." Slate.com. 17 July 2006. 20 July 2006
>
> <http://www.slate.com/id/2145734>.

Anthology

Herndl, Carl G., and Stuart C. Brown, eds. Green Culture. Madison: U of
Wisconsin P, 1996.

Anonymous Article

"Hillary's American Dream." The Economist 29 July 2006: 32.

Definition

"Diversity." American Heritage Dictionary of the English Language. 4th ed.
Houghton, 2000.

"Greek Mythology." Wikipedia.com. 27 July 2006
<http://en.wikipedia.org/wiki/Greek_mythology>.

Letter to the Editor

Tucker, Rich Thompson. "High Cost of Cheap Coal." Letter. National
Geographic July 2006: 6-7.

Letter or Memo

Greer, Michael. Letter to the authors. 30 July 2006.

Dissertation

Li, Zhan. "The Potential of America's Army: The Video Game as Civilian-
Military Public Sphere." Diss. Massachusetts Institute of Technology,
2004.

Government Publication

United States. Census Bureau. Housing and Household Economic Statistics
Division. Poverty Thresholds 2005. 1 Feb. 2006. 20 May 2006
<http://www.census.gov/hhes/www/poverty/threhld/thresh05.html>.

Cover

Adams, Neil. "Deadman." Comics VF.com. 1978. 23 Oct. 2005
<http://www.comicsvf.com/fs/17164.php>.

Interview

Tullman, Geoffrey. Personal interview. 21 May 2006.

Cho, Ana. Telephone interview. 4 June 2005.

Email

Tisbury, Martha. "Re: Information Overload." E-mail to Max Anderson.
31 July 2006.

Online Posting

> Shelly, Ayla. "Visual Rhetoric, Girls, and Ads." Online posting. 5 Nov. 2005.
>
> > GrrlChatSpot. 2 March 2006. <http://groups.google.com/group/
> >
> > grrlchtspt/ExchangeDetail.asp?i+2234981>.

Chat Room Discussion or Real-time Communication

> Zhang, Zhihao. "Revision Suggestions." 25 May 2006. Cross- Cultural
>
> > Rhetoric Chat Room. 25 May 2006.> > ccrhet/chat>.

Documentation for Visual, Audio, and Multimedia Sources

Because many of the materials you may work with fall into the category of innovative text produced by new technologies—such as Webmovies, Flash animation, Weblogs, three-dimensional images, storyboards, sound clips, and more—you need to learn how to construct a citation that provides as much detail as possible about the text. Even citing interviews and surveys can be tricky for some because the format does not match conventional books or articles. Just follow the logical steps for citing print and online sources, developing a rubric that works to offer as much information as possible. The key is consistency and adhering as closely as possible to the logic of MLA style.

> **AT A GLANCE**
>
> ### MLA Documentation for Visual and Multimedia Sources
>
> For the "Works Cited" list, follow the order below in listing details about your source
>
> - Author or organization
> - Title of the image, film, ad, TV series, or document
> - If part of a collection, title of the collection
> - Place of publication and publisher
> - Date of publication
> - If an online source, date you accessed it
> - If online article from a database, the name of the database or search engine
> - If online source, the full URL (not just Google or the search engine name)

Photograph or Visual Image

> Golden Gate Bridge," San Francisco. Photograph by the author. 23 June
>
> > 2004.
>
> Goldin, Nan. Jimmy Paulette & Misty in a Taxi, NYC. 1991. San Francisco
>
> > Museum of Modern Art, San Francisco.
>
> Sherman, Cindy. Untitled Film Still #13. 1978. The Complete Untitled Film
>
> > Stills of Cindy Sherman. Museum of Modern Art. 7 July 2006
> >
> > <http://www.moma.org/exhibitions/1997/sherman/index.html>.

Advertisement

> Nike. "We Are All Witnesses." Advertisement. 3 Jan. 2006
>
> > <http://www.nikebasketball.com>.

Film or Film Clip

Beyond Killing Us Softly: The Impact of Media Images on Women and Girls. Dir./Prod. Margaret Lazarus, Renner Wunderlich. Cambridge Documentary Films, 2000.

"A Brief History of America." Bowling for Columbine. 2002. Dir. Michael Moore. 13 June 2006. <http://www.bowlingforcolumbine.com/media/clips/index.php>.

Comic Strip Online

Pastis, Stephen. "Pearls Before Swine." Comic strip. Comics.com 18 Apr. 2006. 16 May 2006 <http://www.comics.com/comics/pearls/archive/pearls-20060418.html>.

Entire Internet Site

Cartoonists Index. MSNBC. 4 Nov. 2005 <http://cagle.msnbc.com>.

Individual Webpage from an Internet Site

Stevenson, Seth. "Head Case: The Mesmerizing Ad for Headache Gel." Slate.com. 24 July 2006. 25 July 2006 <http://www.slate.com/id/2146382>.

Personal Homepage

Corrigan, Edna. Homepage. 31 Jan. 2005. 24 Oct. 2005 <http://www.ednarules.com>.

Television Program

"The Diet Wars." Frontline. PBS. 2004. 16 Aug. 2006 <http://www.pbs.org/wgbh/pages/frontline/shows/diet/view/>.

Computer Game

America's Army: Special Forces. CD-ROM. U.S. Army-Army Game Project, 2002.

Full Spectrum Warrior. XBOX disc. THQ and Pandemic Studios, 2004.

Computer Game Online

Second Life. Your World. Your Imagination. Linden Labs. 7 May 2006 <http://secondlife.com>.

Screen Shot

Star Wars Galaxies. Screen shot. Sony Online Entertainment. 5 Feb. 2005 <swg.stratics.com/content/news/images/jawa.jpg>

Radio Essay

"Book Marketing Goes to the Movies." <u>Morning Edition</u>. Narr. John Ydstie.

Natl. Public Radio. 18 July 2006. Transcript.

Sound Clip or Recording

Reagan, Ronald. "The Space Shuttle 'Challenger' Tragedy Address." 28 Jan.

1986. <u>American Rhetoric</u>. 5 Mar. 2006

<http://www.americanrhetoric.com/speeches/rreaganchallenger.htm>.

Class Lecture

Connors, Fiona. "Visual Literacy in Perspective." English 210B. Boston

University. 24 Oct. 2004.

Speech

Rheingold, Howard. "Technologies of Cooperation." The Annenberg Center

for Communication. University of Southern California, Los Angeles.

3 Apr. 2006.

Jobs, Steve. Commencement Address. Stanford University. 12 June 2005. 27

July 2006 <http://www.wiredatom.com/jobs_stanford_speech/>.

Painting

Warhol, Andy. <u>Self Portrait.</u> 1986. <u>The Warhol: Collections.</u> 3 Aug. 2006

<http://www.warhol.org/collections/index.html>.

Map

Hong Kong Disneyland Guide. Map. Disney, 2006.

Performance

<u>Phedre.</u> By Racine. Dir. Ileana Drinovan. Pigott Theater, Memorial Hall,

Stanford, CA. May 10–13, 2006.

Copyright and Citing Sources

When you decide to integrate visuals or multimedia in your writing, it's not enough to just include the source and provide the citation for it. You need to spend a few moments thinking about issues of copyright and permissions. Whether you are dealing with images or print quotations, you are using materials produced or prepared by another person, and you must give that person credit for the work. In some cases—particularly if you plan to publish your work—you also need to obtain permission to use it. As you browse through catalogs of images, you need to record the source of each image you decide to use. If you have copied an image from the Web (by right clicking and choosing "Save Picture As"), you need to include as much of the full source information as you can find: the Website author, the title, the sponsoring organization, the date. If you have found a visual (photograph, chart, ad) from a print source and scanned it into a computer so you can insert it into your essay, you need to list the print source in full as well as information about the original image (the name of the photographer, the image title, and the date). Listing Google as your source is not sufficient; take pains to find the original source and list it in full. Keep careful track as you locate images, give appropriate credit when you use them in your essay, and ask for permission if necessary.

Student Paper in MLA Style

Tanner Gardner's research paper focused on the influx of international sports stars into professional leagues, like the National Basketball Association (NBA). He included a wide range of sources and worked hard to meet proper documentation style.

Tanner includes complete identifying information in the upper-left corner. The whole paper is double-spaced for MLA style.

Tanner Gardner

Program in Writing and Rhetoric

Dr. Alyssa J. O'Brien

Final Research Paper

November 2, 2005

Tanner centers his title. he also uses an epigram to kick off the paper; the reader will look for McCallum in the "Works Cited" list.

Show Me the Money! The Globalization of the NBA

"Tomorrow the world: NBA will be international by the end

of the Century"

—Jack McCallum, *Sports Illustrated* Columnist, 1988

In a creative double opening, Tanner begins with a quote that builds off the epigram and introduces his theme of the economics of the NBA. The reader will look for Stern in the Works Cited list.

"With the 11th pick in the draft, the Orlando Magic select Fran Vazquez of Xantada, Spain." As David Stern, the NBA commissioner, made this announcement, representatives of the Orlando Magic couldn't help but smile. The team had just chosen a 6-foot-11 forward that would ideally return them to the glory days of the early 1990s. Like the Orlando Magic, other NBA teams have begun to increase their focus on players abroad and as a result, in the past decade the league has seen the proliferation of foreign-born players. Their impact has reached far beyond the court, altering the culture of the NBA. These players have caused a cultural overhaul in the league, creating a change of face in the NBA. Extending even further are the

Notice how Tanner links back to his epigram as he introduces his three-part thesis.

economic implications, as the NBA and large companies have benefited in enormous ways. Thus, Jack McCallum's prediction of an international NBA

Gardner 2

almost 20 years ago has become reality today. In the past fifteen years, foreign-born athletes have been lured by the rhetoric of competition, money, and advertising rhetoric to migrate to America where bright lights and bucks hopefully await them. In the process, they have brought their culture to America while also bringing economic perks to the countries involved.

Yao Ming, Manu Ginobili, and Peja Stojakovic are all players who fit this description and bring to mind the new global face of the NBA. These players from China, Argentina, and Serbia have led to a new trend of globalization in sports. Economics are often the focal point of globalization as the World Bank defines it as "the integration of growing economies and societies around the world" (World Bank). It is also important to look at the cultural side of globalization though, as another organization identifies it as "a rapid increase in cross-border social, cultural and technological exchange" (ASED). An economic view on globalization ignores the cultural benefit, shedding a negative light on globalization and even causing America to be viewed as imperialists for their part in it. However, there are situations in which globalization has benefited both America and more importantly the foreign country involved. This is particularly relevant to the globalization of sports, specifically in the NBA. While whether the NBA is a positive model of globalization remains to be seen, the past 15 years in the league provide a good example of how economies and cultures can come together in a positive way.

When David Stern was named commissioner of the NBA on February 1, 1984, the league was in turmoil. Financially, many teams were experiencing difficulties and close to bankruptcy. Culturally, the league reputation was sub par at best and plagued by "thugs and drugs." Relationally, the league and the players' association were constantly at each other's throats. Perhaps most significant to Stern, television ratings were at an all-time low, as the 1980 NBA finals were not even shown live on TV. The NBA had lost it luster and turned into a one-man show rather than the team game it had been. There was no doubt it was time for an overhaul in the league. Stern needed to implement a change to save the failing league and needed to do it quick.

Tanner composes an effective transition by moving from the macro to the micro and naming specific players.

Tanner puts the name of the organization as the author in this parenthetical citation.

Here he uses ASED; look for it in the Works Cited list.

The transition in the last line sets up the scope and purpose of his argument.

There's no need for source attribution for "thugs and drugs" because it is a common expression.

Gardner 3

Tanner's combination of narrative and research synthesis makes for quite an engaging style.

Stern, a brilliant marketer, quickly became allies with Boris Stankovic, head of FIBA, the worldwide governing body of basketball. Stern's relationship with Stankovic laid the groundwork for the NBA's interests in Europe, although the majority of the influx of foreign-born players would not take place until the middle to late 1990s. Although most NBA teams scouted in Europe by the late 1980s, the foreign players had not yet proven themselves in the competitive NBA. Nevertheless, Stern saw the economic potential in European markets for the NBA, specifically in television. At the time, a meager 20 foreign-born athletes were playing in the NBA, but this number would soon change.

Tanner introduces his graphic effectively, setting up the numbers with prose first and then using the information graphic as evidence.

If the numbers indicate anything, Stern's interest in Europe soon manifested itself. The 20 foreign-born athletes on NBA rosters in 1989 represented only 6% of the total players in the league. Fifteen years later, the 2004-2005 NBA season saw an unbelievable 81 international players, an increase of over 300% in only 15 years, as the graph below shows (see Figure 1). These international players now make up over 20% of the NBA.

Generating this chart from the research he completed, Tanner inserts it here.

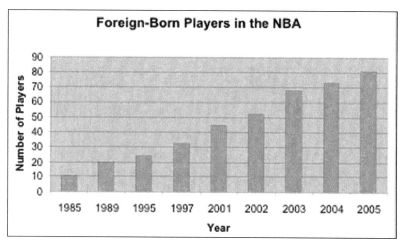

Figure 1. Statistics source NBA; chart created by Tanner Gardner.

Gardner 4

While the actual increase in numbers is important, the underlying impact of these numbers is much more striking. In addition to signing as free agents, foreign-born players have dominated the NBA draft in recent years, as they have been taken as the top pick in four of the last nine drafts. In the most recent draft, international players represented almost a third of total picks. Perhaps most important is the increase in diversity among players. In 1989, only 14 countries were represented in the NBA. 15 years later, 35 countries are now represented, integrating many new faces into the league. As Donn Nelson, president of basketball operations for the Dallas Mavericks comments, "You can't just label them foreign or international players any longer. They're just players who can do the same thing the other guys in the league can do" (qtd. in DuPree). Indeed these players are a norm in the NBA now. As the increase has occurred, NBA teams have reacted in an appropriate way, hiring new scouts focusing solely on players abroad.

A major factor that has contributed to the influx of foreign-born players in the NBA is foreign scouting. With the success of foreign players, developing contacts in the international markets is a must. The number of foreign-scouts employed by teams has increased drastically right along with the players. Today, most teams have numerous scouts focused on international talent. Europe tends to be the primary focus, but scouts in Asia and South America are also on the rise. Asia has been a recent target because of their abundance of big men, something the NBA has recently lacked. The point is clear though: foreign-scouting is essential. As Joe Ash, the Indiana Pacers' director of scouting notes, "Scouting foreign talent is a necessity, not an option. You have too" (Brunt). It is obvious the scouts have been pushing these foreign players to come over, but what exactly has been their prerogative for coming to America?

The main draw of foreign players to the NBA has been the intense and visible competition among the players. I call this phenomenon the rhetoric of competition. The 1992 Olympics was the turning point of this element.

Citing a source within a source, Tanner uses "qtd. in" to show that Nelson is quoted in DuPree's article.

Notice how the repetition of variations of the idea and word "scouting" (which we've highlighted here) advances Tanner's argument and forms an effective transition to focus on the next point: sports scouts in Asia and South America.

Gardner 5

On the previous page, Tanner ended the paragraph with a question to move the argument forward. He answers his own question and creates a new term: "the rhetoric of competition." He then turns to the example of the USA Olympic team in Barcelona to support his point.

The USA fielded perhaps their strongest team ever at the Olympics in Barcelona, showing the world the competitiveness of US basketball. Rick Welts, president of NBA Properties Inc. at the time, called this event "the most important in the history of the sport" (qtd. in Desens). International athletes, many of whom strive to be the best, took note and longed for the competition of the NBA. Simply put: they want to test their skills against the best. Consequently, there has been a steady flow of athletes to the NBA lured by the rhetoric of competition since. The competition has also been a medium for them to improve their skills both directly by playing and indirectly by watching. As it turns out, these foreign players are just as competitive as Americans. In addition, playing in front of large crowds breeds a more competitive atmosphere, as more people create a more electrifying environment. The NBA is the place to find this, as in 2002 the average attendance in the NBA (16,683) was more than double that of the premier European league, the Basketball Clubs Association of Spain (5,700).[1] With more fans and more support in America, there is inevitably more money.

Tanner includes an explanatory note here because he has drawn this data from several sources. The notes can either appear as footnotes or be placed at the end of the document.

While competition has been a large factor, there is no way to ignore the economics of the situation. There are enormous economic benefits to playing in the NBA. Take, for example, 2002 salary statistics: The average salary in the NBA was $3.95 million while the minimum salary was $350,000 compared to the average salary in the Basketball Clubs Association of Spain, $242,000.[2] Thus, foreign-born players are guaranteed a minimum salary in the NBA that is greater than the average salary in the best league in Europe or Asia. The money does not come only from playing in the NBA though, as the side benefits of endorsements by major companies provide these athletes substantial sums of money and visibility, increasing the financial benefit for the players

---

[1] Source: NBA and Eurobasket.com
[2] Source: NBA and Eurobasket.com

Gardner 6

Advertising rhetoric has been perhaps the most lucrative draw for athletes to come to America. These athletes have garnered multi-million dollar contracts from corporations, while simultaneously being the newest way for corporations to strike it rich abroad. There is no better example of this than Yao Ming. Ming has become the most prominent face of international advertising in sports. He has appeared in many commercials and advertisements for corporate giants like Apple Computers and Visa, projecting his face all over the world.

Photo not included for copyright reasons.

Figure 2.

Tanner introduces visual evidence not just as decoration. He spends time offering a rhetorical analysis of the elements of this image.

This advertisement shown on the right (see Figure 2) featuring Yao Ming and Verne Troyer, was released by Apple Computers in early 2003 as an international advertisement in the form of a commercial and a picture. In the picture, the face of Yao is cheerful and personable. By portraying him in this respect, it is obvious that Apple sees Yao as very marketable individual. Overall, the intent of Apple is clear: by using Ming in an international advertisement, they show that they feel international players can appeal to all audiences, regardless of race or ethnicity. This type of rhetoric is not unique to Apple, as other companies like Visa and MasterCard have also used this tactic in their advertisements. While the target audience of the advertisements is not the athletes, there is no doubt international athletes are noticing them.

Tanner includes this image in his paper here instead of in an appendix as a strategic choice to serve as evidence for his claims about the persona of Yao Ming.

Make sure you get permission to reproduce the image if you seek to post your paper online.

Seeing foreign athletes in advertisements is a direct economic appeal to other internationals looking to make it big in the US. The relationship is reciprocal: corporations like Apple and Nike tap into markets abroad by having these athletes wear there gear while the athletes themselves make a fortune simultaneously. Even in the midst of

Tanner provides supporting evidence through additional examples, but he does not need to spend time in the paper on these images since he is moving on to his next point: the economic benefit of ads to home countries.

Gardner 7

this, there are many other interests, namely the NBA, corporations, and the home countries of the foreign players, achieving substantial monetary returns.

While the financial benefit of international players coming to the NBA is no doubt substantial, the biggest financial winner in the scope of it all appears to be the NBA. Ironically, in 1989 Forbes' columnist Jeffrey Trachtenberg predicted in the future, "David Stern and his conquistadors in short pants will be making a lot of people a lot of money" taking the game international (Trachtenberg). Trachtenberg's prediction was, appropriately, right on the money. Between 1985 and 1990, the broadcast of NBA games overseas doubled to 70 countries. These broadcasts generated $5 million for the NBA. Almost ten years later, the NBA's revenue abroad had increased, but the NBA still took a loss of $25 million, prompting Business Week to label their approach to globalization "too conservative" (The NBA). The NBA must have taken the comment to heart, as by 2003 the NBA broadcasted games in a staggering 212 countries, earning the NBA $35 million dollars. In addition, 20% of NBA merchandise was sold overseas for a profit of $430 million (Eisenberg). Stern has even predicted that in the next decade, foreign broadcasts will reach 50% of US television revenue. Along the way corporations will continue to benefit too.

Corporations tapping into foreign markets have been a direct result of the influx of international athletes. Historian Walter LaFeber once observed, "aside from the illegal narcotics trade, sports have become the world's most globalized and lucrative business" (qtd. in Larmer). LaFeber couldn't have been more correct as corporations have quickly recognized the migration of foreign-born players as an opportunity to make millions. Spalding's eagerness to acclimate to foreign markets has come as a great benefit, increasing their sales by an astounding 44% in 2002. Nike, who had a mere 33% of sale internationally in 1993, increased this number by 53% in just

This secondary source offers a key point of argument for Tanner. Notice, though, how he builds on it to advance his own argument his by returning to the key terms of his title with "right on the money." He is emphasizing his own voice as a writer and researcher.

As Tanner turns to logos in his argumentation, Eisenberg's name is placed in parentheses, using the cross- referencing logic of MLA style.

Now Tanner turns to the historical sources in his iceberg of research.

Gardner 8

10 years.[3] The relationship between Nike and basketball is actually reciprocal, as their promotions actually promote basketball internationally by providing publicity for the sport ("The Yao"). Reebok, a partner of the NBA, derived 30% of its sales abroad in 2002, an increased of 10% in just two years (Eisenberg). 2002 also marked Rebooks commitment to long-term growth in Asia, as they signed their poster-boy, Yao Ming. Reebok is not the only one benefiting from Ming, though.

China is a perfect example of a foreign-country benefiting from globalization ("In the NBA"). The country has had a definite interest in Ming migrating to the NBA. Ming, who carried China's flag at the 2004 Olympics, is an economic benefit for China. China's government has a policy where players who come to the NBA must treat their salary as follows: 30% goes to the Chinese Basketball Association, 10% to the player's home city, and finally 10% to the State General Administration of Sports. This total represents 50% of Yao's salary, which was almost $4.5 million in 2005. As many consider Asia the world's fastest growing sports market, it seems China will continue to benefit financially from their policy on athletes playing internationally.

While money is a very important part in the equation of foreign-born players playing in the NBA, the non-monetary benefits to the league are more important. Foreign-born players in the NBA are a win-win situation for the league and the players. These players come from countries that stress the fundamentals of basketball and a team atmosphere. Rick Adelman, the coach of the Sacramento Kings, notes, "foreign players have added the skill factor back into the game" (qtd. in Eisenberg). Thus, the players not only improve their skills playing in the best league but also make the NBA more competitive. Along with this competitiveness comes a new exciting game.

---

[3] Locke, Richard M. "The Promise and Perils of Globalization: The Case of Nike." MIT's Sloan School of Business Website. 8 Oct 2005. <http://mitsloan.mit.edu/50th/nikepaper.pdf>.

Here Tanner refers to a Website, using the key words of the title.

Despite the ample use of sources in his paper, Tanner keeps the spotlight on his argument. His voice as a writer emerges as the one synthesizing all this research to construct his own original argument.

Tanner doesn't overload his paper with sources. He uses them rhetorically, turning to authority to support his claim about the character of the international NBA players.

Gardner 9

With the term "thugs and drugs," Tanner returns to a point made earlier in order to create coherence, complexity, and richness in his paper, even while he uses casual engaging language such as "talk trash."

The new and thrilling NBA has also been a result of a change in culture, which is perhaps the most significant effect of foreign-born players in the NBA. As stated earlier, "thugs and drugs" plagued the 1980's in the NBA. International players have helped change this image by bringing a more clean cut face to the NBA while at the same time bridging the cultural gap. These players don't talk trash: they simply play the game. Joe Davidson of the Sacramento Bee says it best: "They [foreign-born players] haven't been corrupted by ESPN highlights into thinking that dunking is the only way to succeed" (Davidson). The new culture and international element of the NBA has made it more fan friendly and accessible to all, providing an atmosphere in which almost any sports fan can be entertained regardless of ethnicity. Ultimately, the foreign-born players have brought fans back to the sport while simultaneously improving financial stability in the league. In this way, the change of face in the NBA has proven to be a success.

Tanner pauses to consider the counter-argument and uses conditional language to assert his own thesis one more time.

The influx of foreign-born players in the NBA has clearly benefited professional basketball on numerous levels: financially for the players, the league, various corporations and foreign countries, and culturally for the NBA in general. However, it is important to note that not all international players are bolting for the NBA. Fran Vazquez provides the perfect example. Although he initially thought he was ready to come to the NBA, "the timing, as it turned out, was just not right for him. More than anything, I think it was a cultural thing," said Dave Twardzik, assistant General Manager of the Orlando Magic (Povtak). Vazquez is just a rare exception though, as most players are ready to make the transition. While the money is important to the players, it appears the chance to compete at the highest level, fame from advertising, and the freedoms and excitement of America are what ultimately draw them over.

One last citation gives Tanner's argument authority before he moves to his conclusion.

In his conclusion, Tanner looks to the future, there by broadening out the scope and significance of his research-based argument.

Looking towards the future of the NBA, it does not appear like there is an end in sight to the trend. David Stern has even gone as far as to predict there will be a team in Europe in the next ten years. As international players continue to journey to America, the involved parties will continue to reap

Gardner 10

the benefits. Thus, the successful model of globalization in the NBA will continue. Overall, the trend towards globalization in the NBA is not unique: there is a search for global talent not only in other professional sports like the MLB and NHL, but also in all areas of society today. Yet, this has caused for some uneasiness. If other sectors of society use the NBA as a model for globalization, it may benefit all parties involved in a majority of situations and one day be viewed in a positive light.

Gardner 11

Works Cited

ASED. "Asia-Europe Dialogue on alternative political strategies." 2005.
ASED. 25 Oct. 2005 <http://www.ased.org>

Brunt, Cliff. "NBA Draft Gives Teams a Chance to Add International Flair."
Associated Press 23 June 2005.

Davidson, Joe. E-mail interview. 15 Oct. 2005.

Desens, Carl. "The NBA's Fast Break Overseas." BusinessWeek 5 Dec. 1994.
10 Oct. 2005 <http://www.businessweek.com/archives/1994/
b340279.arc.htm>

DuPree, David. "Foreign-Borns Aren't Unique." USA Today 14 Oct. 2004: 2C.

Eisenberg, Daniel. "The NBA's Global Game Plan." Time 17 Mar. 2003: 59+.

Larmer, Brook. "The Center of the World." Foreign Policy 15 Sept. 2005. 66.

McCallum, Jack. "Tomorrow the World." Sports Illustrated 7 Nov. 1988: 58.

"The NBA Needs to Do Some Globetrotting." Business Week 19 July 1999: 19.

Povtak, Tim. "Spanish Forward Reiterates He's Not Coming to NBA This
Season." Charlotte Observer 3 Aug. 2005. 8 Oct. 2005 <http://www.
charlotte.com/mld/charlotte/sports/basketball/12297039.htm>

Trachtenberg, Jeffrey A. "Playing the Global Game." Forbes 23 Jan. 1989: 90.

World Bank. "Globalization." 2001. 25 Oct. 2005 <http://www1.
worldbank.org/economicpolicy/globalization>

"The Yao Crowd." Economist 9 Aug. 2003: 55.

All sources are alphabetized. He includes articles and interviews.

He lists full information for online sources, but he doesn't just use online materials; Tanner uses many print texts as well.

Articles without authors are listed by title key words.

> Works Consulted
>
> Molina, Pablo Malo. "Spanish Basketball." Eurobasket.com. Feb. 2002. 8
>   Oct. 2005 <www.eurobasket.com/esp.intro.asp>
> "NBA Minimum Salary." InsideHoops.com. 10 Aug. 2005. 8 Oct. 2004
>   <http://www.insidehoops.com/minimum-nba-salary.shtml>

Tanner includes his works
consulted to show more of
his iceberg of research.

Documentation for Your Paper

Now that you've learned about the meaning of intellectual property, the dangers of plagiarism, the rhetorical purpose for documentation style, the cross-referencing logic of
in-text citations, and the guidelines for MLA Works Cited and Consulted lists, it is
time for you to review your own writing. Have you acknowledged all your sources in
full? Did you include proper and concise parenthetical attributions in the paper? Does
your bibliographic list provide an alphabetized reflection of your research? If so, then
you have accomplished a great deal as a writer.

WRITING PROJECTS

1. **Documentation Log:** Develop your own system of note taking to avoid the kind of plagiarism trap
   that writer Doris Kearns Goodwin fell into.
2. **Peer Review of Citations:** Share your draft paper with a group of peers, and have them check to
   see which sources need citation. Does your paper contain knowledge you must have obtained from
   a source? If so, you need to acknowledge the source of that knowledge. Do certain passages seem
   to be common knowledge? If so, you don't need to cite them. What paragraphs could go into
   notes? What aspects of your paper need more explanation and could use a note?
3. **Draft Works Cited List:** As you compose your paper and formulate your "Works Cited" list, visit
   the online tools available through the *Envision* Website to help you generate your list, double-check
   your entries, convert MLA to APA, or learn more about documentation style.
4. **Writing with Technology:** You might find it helpful to turn to one of the scholarly tools for producing a Work Cited list. These include *Ref Works, End Note,* and *TermPerfect*. You can find links to
   these tools on the Envision website. Many researchers and scholars depend on these tools—such
   writers will keep notes right in the program, insert all identifying information for a source, and then
   select the documentation format needed for their papers. The technology then produces a list in the
   proper documentation style. You need to double check the list, of course, but it can save you lots of
   time.

 Visit www.ablongman.com/envision for expanded assignment guidelines and student projects.

Part IV
READINGS

Photography takes an instant out of time, altering life by holding it still.
—Dorothea Lange

CHAPTER 10

Marked Bodies

FIGURE 10.1 A woman asserts her identity by marking her body with piercings and body art.

When you look at the photo of the woman in Figure 10.1, what do you see? What catches your eye? Is it her direct gaze? Her lip piercing? Her ornate tattooing? How does she choose to mark herself—and how does her body thereby operate as a rhetorical text? Finally, how did you begin to draw conclusions about her identity based on your reaction to or interpretation of the markings on her body?

When we look at bodies as visual texts in society, we often participate in a social process of reading people according to certain social categories: as male or female, young or old, rural or urban, and from a certain race, class, or culture.

But how much do people shape the way they are viewed in society by choosing certain ways to present themselves visually—how do they mark their bodies? What happens if someone walks into a job interview wearing sweatpants or gives a formal presentation in a three-piece suit? How is the choice of clothing or jewelry or tattoos a matter of claiming identity, trying to shape the way bodies are viewed by others?

In this chapter, we'll explore the rhetoric of bodies in society and how identity is shaped by the way people read visible signs and the way people use signs to construct identities. In other words, we will consider how bodies are both marked by culture and marked by their own choices (such as when people make rhetorical choices to change what society thinks of their identity through physical appearance, clothing, or adornment).

Marking in this way is linked to "looking." Often, we do not even have control over how we are looked at: others may interpret our bodies as markings that place us in a certain social group, race, age, or lifestyle choice. Many times in response, we—like the model in Figure 10.1—use our bodies purposefully to change the way we are looked at. We try to mark our bodies with signs of our identities, to announce who we are, our affiliation with a particular group or religion, our sexual orientation, and sometimes even our political stance. Hair-styles, piercings, clothing choices,

264

tattoos, toned abs, or even painted toenails: these choices all constitute ways we "mark" ourselves in relation to our culture—or try to change the way we are "looked at" by remaking the signs of our identities. In this way, we may deliberately mark our bodies to show our membership in certain communities, such as religious groups, sports groups, even groups determined through shared experiences, as we'll learn from looking at a group of firefighters who "marked" their bodies with similar tattoos commemorating lost ones.

In the pages that follow, we will examine different ways that bodies are marked in contemporary culture. In "Imagining the Ideal Body," we'll investigate the debate over body shape, race, and ideal beauty; in "Fashion Statements," we'll look at how people literally mark their bodies as a way of establishing their identity—such as when we write on an arm or leg with a beautiful ornate tattoo to signal membership in a certain community or just to change the way we are looked at, or when we wear a religious T-shirt or a head scarf in order to show the world our arguments about ourselves. In these instances, fashion works as argument; it changes the way we look and are looked at. It marks the body, and it makes a mark upon culture.

In all these examples, the body becomes a form of visual rhetoric, an argument about our identity: who we are, where we belong, and how others might read us. As you read the articles and write your own arguments about the marked bodies in this culture, you might begin to think more broadly about the way bodies function as visual rhetoric—in advertising, in places of worship, and in the ebb and flow of our daily lives.

IMAGING THE IDEAL BODY

What defines beauty? Who determines today's standards of "attractiveness"? How does the visual rhetoric of advertisements, films, television shows, and fashion magazines shape our notions of the "ideal body"? And how are our own bodies marked by the constructions of body image we see everywhere across cultures?

Consider the image in Figure 10.2. How does the woman's face and body both evoke and parody ideas about beauty that come from magazines such as *Vogue*, *Glamour*, *Cosmo*, or *Marie Claire*? If you were to flip through one of these magazines and locate a conventional beauty ad, what aspects would be similar? Perhaps you might comment on the model's direct gaze into the camera, her tussled hair, her makeup-covered eyes, or her arms raised in a seductive pose. But then why does this model have bandages? What sort of visual argument is Figure 10.2 making about the ideal body, especially in contrast with a standard beauty image from a fashion magazine?

FIGURE 10.2 Stylized to resemble a fashion magazine photo, this image captures the costs of cultural idealization of feminine beauty.

FIGURE 10.3 The words on this billboard from a poor neighborhood in Beijing, China, say "Illusion: Cosmetology Beauty Shop."

FIGURE 10.4 In this street scene in Beijing, China, women try to imitate the body image shown in billboards from their neighborhoods.

As you think about the typical fashion magazine ad consider also how contemporary images about men make equally powerful arguments about male beauty. Locate an ad from a men's magazine such as *GQ* or *Men's Health,* or look at how men are represented in a popular television show such as *Grey's Anatomy.* How, in each case, are we influenced by the images we see in the media? Your analysis of these images can help you begin to formulate your argument about how visual representations construct social notions that we come to accept as "natural."

The normalizing of these distorted images of ideal beauty becomes even more problematic if we shift to a broader, international context. The Beijing billboard shown in Figure 10.3 displays the white face and red hair of a Caucausian model but is situated in one of the poorest and oldest neighborhoods of the Chinese capital. How does this advertisement argue for a particular construction of "ideal beauty"? What visual and verbal elements contribute to the ad's argument about female beauty? Now compare the billboard to the photo of a street scene taken a few blocks away (see Figure 10.4). In the photo, Chinese women watch a demonstration on how to achieve the standard of beauty shown in the billboard. That is, they seek to color their hair red and fashion themselves after the body image shown in the advertisement. How does this photo show the cause-and-effect relationship of images of beauty in the media upon people in particular communities?

Advertisers within the past few years have become savvier about audiences' growing resistance to prescriptive representations of body image. A recent ad campaign by Dove, for instance, seems to celebrate a type of female physique that even five years ago would have been considered "too big," "heavy," or otherwise "out of proportion" with the ideal. According to their Website (http://www.campaignforrealbeauty.com), Dove's intention is to celebrate *realistic* body types. Notice how the company makes this argument through its Website:

> At Dove, we are proud to celebrate real women with real bodies and real curves. That's why our campaign for NEW Dove Firming features untouched photographs of six real women, not professional models, who are standing firm and celebrating their curves.

While this notion of nonprofessional models with realistically sized bodies seems a laudable solution to what Susie Orbach (in the article you will read in the pages that follow) calls the "Kate Moss generation," we'll learn that there's more complexity to the debate. Even with our increased awareness of the link between the media and body image, popular culture images, from ads for skin cream to toys such as Barbie and G.I. Joe—continue to shape our notions about ourselves, our physical appearances, and our self-esteem.

It is important to consider what happens to our sense of self when the body we are meant to strive for is represented by a model or doll that is overly thin, obviously Caucasian, or unrealistically sculpted. As the articles in this section suggest, these representations seem to affect people's attitudes toward eating disorders, drug abuse, self-esteem, and societal norms. In the pages that follow, we'll explore these issues and more as we look at body image across genders, races, and ages.

Reflect & Write

❏ How would you characterize the body image shown in Figure 10.2? Discuss the visual elements. What aspects evoke a more conventional fashion ad? Which aspects make you question fashion ads?
❏ Notice the visual elements of the billboard in Figure 10.3. How do these factors contribute to our notions of body image?
❏ Examine Figures 10.3 and 10.4. What elements are culturally or class specific? How is a particular standard of beauty created by the billboard?
❏ **Write:** Take a walk and look for billboards showing images of ideal beauty on your campus or in your community. Write a letter to your local newspaper analyzing the persuasive power of these images. Include photos of the billboards as evidence.

Psychotherapist and writer **Susie Orbach** *first became a leading participant in the discussion of women's body image issues with the publication of her 1978 book* Fat Is a Feminist Issue. *Since that time, she has both written and taught extensively on the issue of women's physical and emotional health and has appeared on numerous television and radio programs. This article recounts Orbach's involvement in the genesis of Dove's "Campaign for Real Beauty" and was originally published in the June 17, 2005 issue of* Campaign, *an online advertising, marketing, and public relations magazine.*

Fat Is an Advertising Issue

Susie Orbach

When O&M called Susie Orbach to ask her advice on Dove's campaign for real beauty, she jumped at the chance to turn advertising's often destructive relationship with women's body image on its head.

More than one million hits on the 'campaign for real beauty' website; pictures of women on billboards all over the UK that make you smile inside; a programme to deconstruct beauty ads going into secondary schools; a fund to raise girls' and women's self-esteem; mother-and-daughter workshops on self-image; a mission to change negative feelings women can have towards their bodies . . . and all this from a soap-cum-beauty company?

In January two years ago, Mel White of Ogilvy & Mather rang me. 'I'd like to book an hour of your time. Some of us working on the Dove brand have been worrying that beauty advertising has been damaging to women. We want to make sure we understand how, and what we might to do to change it.'

White was the global brand and category partner at O&M. She was part of a team spearheading an attempt to make a positive contribution to women's lives. 'We all—at Dove and the agency—are women of a certain seniority,' she said. 'We think we can make a difference, a positive impact on women's lives. Dove has never sold products on the basis of stoking up insecurity. But maybe we can go further. Can you help?'

5   Could I help? To hear that creative teams were now interested in investing their energy in strengthening women was extraordinary. Years of banging on the doors of clothing manufacturers, government, the food industry and advertising, to persuade them that by making fashion funkier and food more interesting they would increase sales, made this a dream meeting. I never thought the beauty industry would come asking. I was delighted. I was intrigued.

Could White be serious? Was this a bit of ethical window-dressing or a sincere endeavour? Could they change the grammar of beauty in an industry that had been so instrumental in promoting exclusivity? Was Dove really up for a genuinely radical transformation of the representation of women?

Would the creatives actually hear the dissatisfaction emanating from girls and women about the absolutely torturous standards of beauty they had either wittingly or unwittingly foisted on them? Could the art directors come up with some way to meet that dissatisfaction and make difference sexy, something the fashionistas could resonate with?

The first step was to persuade Unilever. Such a retool was going to take a lot of money and steady commitment. If the executives there could understand the difficulties their wives, mothers, lovers, sisters and daughters had with their own physical appearance, then maybe we had a chance. The change that the Dove team were advocating would require consciousness-raising throughout the agency and the business. The 400 or so people working on Dove would have to be behind it. This was not just a whoopee new campaign like any other.

On the advertising side, O&M assembled creative teams that knew the Dove brand and had done some of their best work on it. They also brought on board teams who did not know Dove, but who had previously done outstanding work on other accounts across the world.

10   The film O&M made for one of their first internal pitches featured the daughters of executives talking about their own bodies and the cute noses, freckles, hair and tummies they wanted to do away with or change. The poignancy of these little (and big) girls showing their dissatisfactions and their wish to be free of some of the most quintessentially adorable aspects of themselves was completely compelling. It's not possible to watch that three-minute DVD without reaching for a tissue. It was a testimony to the hurt and damage we were unintentionally doing to our daughters.

The film hinted at the longing these lovely girls had to be acceptable, to be pretty, to feel good about themselves.

That DVD and others made for internal Unilever and O&M purposes provided the opening through which I, as a psychotherapist, academic and political activist in the area of women's psychology, body image and eating problems, could now deliver the relevant clinical evidence. My writing, public speaking and research experience with thousands of women could provide the backbone to the Dove initiative, an initiative that had the potential to turn around the grief and distress that lurked inside so many girls' and women's physical experience of themselves.

I told Dove that the Harvard psychiatrist and anthropologist Anne Becker had found that three years after the introduction of TV into Fiji in 1995, 11.9% of adolescent girls were puking into the toilet bowl trying to change their Fijian build into one that resembled the Western images they were imbibing via their TV sets.

I told Unilever that just half-an-hour looking at a magazine could lower youngsters' self-esteem significantly. I told them that one in four college females has a serious eating problem and that most women wake up and feel their tummies to check how good or bad they've been the day before. Before they've even brushed their teeth, their critical selves are planning how punishing to be today.

15   I told them that without intending to, mums were passing on negative attitudes about their own bodies towards their infant girls, and that their daughters were now absorbing a shaky body sense that made them vulnerable to the blandishments of the market that purported to meet this distress while actually reinforcing it.

The women working on Dove knew how women's magazines had discreet cosmetic surgery ads in the back long before TV shows such as The Swan and Extreme Makeover came along. However expectant you felt before reading Vogue, Glamour, Cosmo or Marie Claire, you felt coshed by a mood depressant after it. And all the Dove women knew they weren't just victims of the image industries. In a sense, all of us women are complicit in these unrealistic representations of femaleness. In order not to feel entirely powerless inside a visually dominating landscape that represents beauty so narrowly, we play out our own beauty scripts inside it: not questioning it, but trying to meet it.

The psychoanalyst in me could try to explain how women's relationship to the beauty industry perfectly encapsulates the psychological essence of the abused. The victim, shunning that awful feeling of being exploited and to gain some self-respect, rejects the idea she is being used. Instead, she makes the job of appearing beautiful her own personal project. She is not being compelled to bind her feet, she does it willingly. It's the only way to be. She will involve herself in trying to look younger, skinnier, taller, bigger-breasted, smaller-breasted and making sure every surface is coiffed, painted, plucked, waxed, perfumed, moisturised, conditioned or dyed. Taking the job on for herself is her response to being targeted.

It is her refusal to, as it were, be done to.

That this can't bring women satisfaction works in the interest of the beauty industry. Having set up this relationship of insecurity, there is always another area to work on—and even if all enemies were banished, ageing would be waiting just around the corner.

20   Dove's mission was to reformulate this warped and damaging engagement with beauty and offer in its place something based not on impossibility, but on possibility. Daring and innovative, so far. But could they take the campaign through their company and into the public domain?

In May 1999, work coming out of the Women's Unit at the Cabinet Office showed eating problems and concern about the body was the number one issue for girls and women aged between 11 and 80. The UK Government held a Body Image Summit, under the leadership of Tessa Jowell and Margaret Jay. Research showed that the promotion of images of ever-skinnier, wan-looking but apparently need-free women who shoved attitude into the camera lens was creating serious (health and mental health) problems in the lives of girls and women.

The Body Image Summit included influential magazine editors, fashion designers and buyers who could have changed our narrow visual culture.

But the Summit programme collapsed at the first whiff of contempt in the media. The Government showed itself to be entirely pusillanimous, back-pedalling and equivocating at its own subsequent press conferences.

After my experience as a consultant to and keynote speaker at the Summit, I was now interested to see what the commercial sector could do. I didn't expect the same kind of inertia and collapse from business when the first criticism came along. But I also hadn't quite understood how considerable are the resources the business community can call on when it is serious.

25   I'd known that a significant part of a product's cost was spent on marketing and advertising, but I hadn't appreciated how much time, labour and money could go into the development of a brand. As my work with Dove developed, I began to feel increasingly hopeful about how we might begin to challenge the negative aspects of what I'd come to call the visual musak—the ersatz femininity—around us and to include diverse, vibrant, pleasing and sexy images of women of all sizes, ages and physical types.

One of my key objectives was to get across the idea that recent times have seen a widening, a democratising, of the idea that everyone could be beautiful. Triggered by Twiggy and then fully realised by the Kate Moss generation (as much because of their class backgrounds as their skinniness), beauty had moved from being the interest of the few to the aspiration of all girls and women. This was pretty positive stuff in itself. But the terms and the expansion of beauty faltered on a paradox. The industry was simultaneously promoting an anti-democratic ideal of beauty that was narrow (literally) and excluding. Everyone had to be thin, thinner, thinnest.

If Dove was going to turn around the limited, destructive aspects of the beauty and dieting industries, then it was going to have to produce bold, startling, appealing images of women in all their sumptuous variety that would swagger in and dent the visual field. Dove would have to find a way to meet women where they had trained their eyes to be—on those images of skinny, untouchable and yet needy sexy women—and touch them deeply and humorously enough bring them to where I knew from my clinical practice they wanted to be: appreciated for their magnificent differences, their uniqueness, not their sameness.

Women have had enough of not finding themselves in the ads they look at. If Dove could get it right, other companies would be playing catch-up. And, of course, they did. Within months of the launch of the 'campaign for real beauty', Revlon hired Susan Sarandon as one of its faces. It was a vindication that not only had Dove and Ogilvy caught the zeitgeist, but others would follow and the aims of the campaign would be met not just by women flocking to their brand, but also by their competitors.

What impressed the most and continues to impress me is the commitment of the leadership team at Dove—Silvia Lagnado, Alessandro Manfredi, Erin Iles and Daryl Fielding and, of course, White. They're making the campaign work. Everyone doing Dove business now asks the questions I was brought in to help them confront in order to make the campaign effective. How does this marketing help women's and girls' self esteem? In what ways could it harm them? How does this product affect me? How do I want it to affect my daughter, my niece, my sister, my wife? How can I make a positive impact and turn the scourge of body hatred around? How can I be a global player in the beauty industry spreading good feelings about women's bodies rather than promoting insecurity?

30   How can I give girls and women a chance to enter into a new, contented relationship with their bodies?

These are deep, painful and complex issues. That's why they called in the shrink. But, as their performance so far shows, it is a really good start.

Reflect & Write

❏ In this article, Orbach chronicles the process she used to persuade Unilever, the makers of Dove beauty products, to embrace the new, radical campaign for new beauty. How did Orbach and the O&M team deploy strategies of pathos, ethos, and logos to accomplish their goals? Consider also the order in which they used these appeals. Why did they structure their patterns of persuasion in this way?

❏ In what ways is Orbach trying to make the same argument she makes to Unilever to the reader? In which paragraphs can you see places where she is making her case to both audiences?

❏ At one point in this article, Orbach claims that in order to be successful at this campaign, Dove was going to have to "produce bold, startling, appealing images of women in all their sumptuous variety that would swagger in and dent the visual field." Look at the images from the Dove campaign at their Website at http://www.campaignforrealbeauty.com. Has Dove accomplished this goal? What differences do you see between Dove's campaign and advertisements produced by other beauty product companies?

❏ **Write:** Some might argue that the Campaign for Real Beauty is simply an ethos appeal to the consumer. Write an essay in which you argue this point, considering whether or not the campaign has the potential to enhance or detract from the popularity of Dove's products—or whether it will have no distinguishable effect overall.

■ **John Riviello** *is a graphic designer specializing in Flash animations. This movie is part of Riviello's larger Website on body image issues and its relationship to the diet industry, fashion magazines, and the individual consumer's self-perception.*

What if Barbie Was an Actual Person?
A Flash Movie

John Riviello

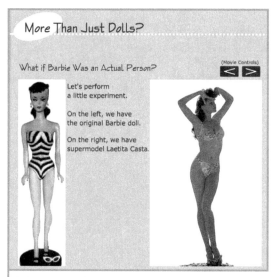

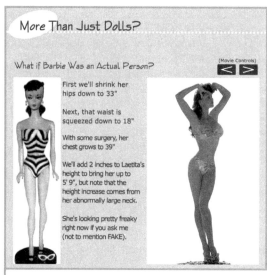

FIGURE 10.5 These screenshots from John Riviello's site juxtapose Barbie against a real model to demonstrate the differences between idealized versions of female beauty.

FIGURE 10.6

Reflect & Write

❑ In his visual argument (see http://www.johnriviello.com/bodyimage/barbie.html), Riviello pairs an image of a vintage Barbie with a photo of model Laetitia Casta. To argue his point, he both offers text of how he would transform Laetitia and then actually modifies her picture to reflect these alterations. What are the benefits of constructing his argument in this way? Why show both the Barbie and Laetitia? Why move from the silhouette to the color images? Is this an effective structure for the argument? Why?

❑ In the last frame (not shown), after Laetitia's eyes bulge cartoonishly in horror at her undersized feet, she disintegrates into a heap of dust, leaving us looking only at the vintage Barbie. Is this an effective conclusion? Why or why not?

❏   Visit the Flash animation itself at http://www.johnriviello.com/bodyimage/ barbie.html. How does watching the animation change the effect of the argument demonstrated by the static images alone? What does the new media component add to the argument?

❏   **Write:** Riviello could have written his argument as an academic essay, but he chose instead to use a Flash movie to argue his point. Write an essay in which you move through the same process of argumentation that he does, but use a more academic style. What adjustments did you have to make to convert his argument? Is one more effective than the other? Why or why not?

■   *Pop culture critic* **Mim Udovitch** *is a contributing editor for* Rolling Stone *and a regular contributor to* The New York Times, *where this essay was originally published in September 2002. "A Secret Society of the Starving" has also appeared online on the Website for About-Face, a nonprofit organization dedicated to combating distorted images of women in the media (http://www.about-face.org).*

A Secret Society of the Starving

Mim Udovitch

Claire is 18. She is a pretty teenager, with long strawberry-blond hair, and she is almost abnormally self-possessed for a girl from a small town who has suddenly been descended upon by a big-city reporter who is there to talk to her, in secret, about her secret life. She is sitting on the track that runs around the field of her high school's football stadium, wearing running shorts and a T-shirt and shivering a little because even though we are in Florida—in the kind of town where, according to Claire, during "season" when you see yet another car with New York plates, you just feel like running it down—there's an evening chill.

Claire's is also the kind of town where how the local high school does in sports matters.

Claire herself plays two sports. Practice and team fund-raisers are a regular part of her life, along with the typical small-town-Florida teenage occupations—going to "some hick party," hanging out with friends in the parking lot of the Taco Bell, bowling, going to the beach.

Another regular part of her life, also a common teenage occupation, is anorexia—refusal to eat enough to maintain a minimally healthy weight. So she is possibly shivering because she hasn't consumed enough calories for her body to keep itself warm. Claire first got into eating disorders when she was 14 or 15 and a bulimic friend introduced her to them. But she was already kind of on the lookout for something: "I was gonna do it

on my own, basically. Just because, like, exercise can only take you so far, you know? And I don't know, I just started to wonder if there was another way. Because they made it seem like, **write:** 'You do drugs, you die; be anorexic and you're gonna die in a year.' I knew that they kind of overplayed it and tried to frighten you away. So I always thought it can't be that bad for you."

Bulimia—binge eating followed by purging through vomiting or laxatives—didn't suit her, however, so after a little while she moved onto anorexia. But she is not, by her own lights, anorexic. And her name isn't Claire. She is, in her terms, "an ana" or "pro-ana" (shortened from pro-anorexia), and Claire is a variation of Clairegirl, the name she uses on the Web sites that are the fulcrum of the pro-ana community, which also includes people who are pro-mia (for bulimia) or simply pro-E.D., for eating disorder.

5   About one in 200 American women suffers from anorexia; two or three in 100 suffer from bulimia. Arguably, these disorders have the highest fatality rates of any mental illness, through suicide as well as the obvious health problems. But because they are not threatening to the passer-by, as psychotic disorders are, or likely to render people unemployable or criminal, as alcoholism and addiction are, and perhaps also because they are disorders that primarily afflict girls and women, they are not a proportionately imperative social priority.

They have been, however, topics of almost prurient media fascination for more than 20 years—regularly the subject of articles in magazines that have a sizable young female readership. In these forums, eating disorders are generally depicted as fundamentally body-image disorders, very extreme versions of the non-eating-disordered woman's desire to be thin, which just happen, rivetingly, to carry the risk of the ultimate consequence. "So many women who don't have the disorder say to me: 'Well, what's the big deal? It's like a diet gone bad,'" says Ellen Davis, the clinical director of the Renfrew Center of Philadelphia, an eating-disorder treatment facility. "And it is so different from that. Women

with the vulnerability, they really fall into an abyss, and they can't get out. And it's not about, 'O.K., I want to lose the 10 pounds and go on with my life.' It's, 'This has consumed my entire existence.'"

And now there's pro-ana, in many ways an almost too lucid clarification of what it really feels like to be eating disordered. "Pain of mind is worse than pain of body" reads the legend on one Web site's live-journal page, above a picture of the Web mistress's arm, so heavily scored with what look like razor cuts that there is more open wound than flesh. "I'm already disturbed," reads the home page of another. "Please don't come in." The wish to conform to a certain external ideal for the external ideal's sake is certainly a component of anorexia and bulimia. But as they are experienced by the people who suffer from them, it is just that: a component, a stepping-off point into the abyss.

As the girls (and in smaller numbers, boys) who frequent the pro-E.D. sites know, being an ana is a state of mind—part addiction, part obsession and part seesawing sense of self-worth, not necessarily correlating to what you actually weigh. "Body image is a major deal, but it's about not being good enough," says Jill M. Pollack, the executive director of the Center for the Study of Anorexia and Bulimia, "and they're trying to fix everything from the outside." Clairegirl, like many of the girls who include their stats—height,

weight and goal weight—when posting on such sites, would not receive a diagnosis of anorexia, because she is not 15 percent under normal weight for her height and age.

But she does have self-devised rules and restrictions regarding eating, which, if she does not meet them, make her feel that she has erred "I kind of believe it is a virtue, almost," she says of pro-ana. "Like if you do wrong and you eat, then you sin." If she does not meet her goals, it makes her dislike herself, makes her feel anxiety and a sense of danger. If she does meet them, she feels "clean." She has a goal weight, lower than the weight she is now. She plays sports for two hours a day after school and tries to exercise at least another hour after she gets home. She also has a touch of obsessive-compulsive disorder regarding non-food-related things—cleaning, laundry, the numeral three. ("Both anorexia and bulimia are highly O.C.D.," says Pollack. "Highly.")

10   And she does spend between one and three hours a day online, in the world of pro-ana. Asked what she likes best about the sites, Claire says: "Just really, like at the end of the day, it would be really nice if you could share with the whole world how you felt, you know? Because truthfully, you just don't feel comfortable, you can't tell the truth. Then, like, if I don't eat lunch or something, people will get on my case about it, and I can't just come out and

tell them I don't eat, or something like that. But at the end of the day, I can go online and talk to them there, and they know exactly what I'm going through and how I feel. And I don't have to worry about them judging me for how I feel."

Pro-ana, the basic premise of which is that an eating disorder is not a disorder but a lifestyle choice, is very much an ideology of the early 21st century, one that could not exist absent the anonymity and accessibility of the Internet, without which the only place large numbers of anorexics and bulimics would find themselves together would be at inpatient treatment. "Primarily, the sites reinforce the secretiveness and the 'specialness' of the disorder," Davis says. "When young women get into the grips of this disease, their thoughts become very distorted, and part of it is they believe they're unique and special. The sites are a way for them to connect with other girls and to basically talk about how special they are. And they become very isolated. Women with eating disorders really thrive in a lot of ways on being very disconnected. At the same time, of course, they have a yearning to be connected."

Perfectionism, attention to detail and a sense of superiority combine to make the pro-ana sites the most meticulous and clinically fluent self-representations of a mental disorder you could hope to find, almost checklists of diagnostic criteria expressed in poignantly human terms. Starving yourself, just on the basis of its sheer difficulty, is a high-dedication ailment—to choose to be an ana, if choice it is, is to choose a way of life, a hobby and a credo. And on the Web, which is both very public and completely faceless, the aspects of the disorder that are about attention-getting and secret-keeping are a resolved paradox. "I kind of want people to understand," Clairegirl says, "but I also like having this little hidden thing that only I know about, like—this little secret that's all yours."

Pro-ana has its roots in various newsgroups and lists deep inside various Internet service providers. Now there are numerous well-known-to-those-who-know sites, plus who knows how many dozens more that are just the lone teenager's Web page, with names that put them beyond the scope of search engines. And based on the two-week sign-up of 973 members to a recent message-board adjunct to one of the older and more established sites, the pro-ana community probably numbers in the thousands, with girls using names like Wannabeboney, Neverthinenuf, DiETpEpSi UhHuh! and Afraidtolookinthemirror posting things like: "I can't take it anymore! I'm fasting! I'm going out, getting all diet soda, sugar-free gum, sugar-free candy and having myself a 14-day fast. Then we'll see who is the skinny girl in the family!"

That ana and mia are child-like nicknames, names that might be the names of friends (one Web site that is now defunct was even called, with girlish fondness, "My Friend Ana"), is indicative. The pro-ana community is largely made up of girls or young women, most of whom are between the ages of 13 and 25. And it is a close community, close in the manner of close friendships of girls and young women. The members of a few sites send each other bracelets, like friendship bracelets, as symbols of solidarity and support. And like any ideology subscribed to by many individuals, pro-ana is not a monolithic system of belief.

15   At its most militant, the ideology is something along the lines of, as the opening page of one site puts it: "Volitional, proactive anorexia is not a disease or a disorder. . . . There are no victims here. It is a lifestyle that begins and ends with a particular faculty human beings seem in drastically short supply of today: the will. . . . Contrary to popular misconception, anorectics possess the most iron-cored, indomitable wills of all. Our way is not that of the weak. . . . If we ever completely tapped that potential in our midst . . . we could change the world. Completely. Maybe we could even rule it."

Mostly, though, the philosophical underpinnings of pro-ana thought are not quite so Nietzschean. The "Thin Commandments" on one site, which appear under a picture of Bugs Bunny smiling his toothy open-mouthed smile, leaning against a mailbox and holding a carrot with one bite taken out of it, include: "If thou aren't thin, thou aren't attractive"; "Being thin is more important than being healthy"; "Thou shall not eat without feeling guilty"; "Thou shall not eat fattening food without punishing thyself afterward"; and "Being thin and not eating are signs of true willpower and success."

The "Ana Creed" from the same site begins: "I believe in Control, the only force mighty enough to bring order into the chaos that is my world. I believe that I am the most vile, worthless and useless person ever to have existed on this planet."

In fact, to those truly "in the disorder"—a phrase one anonymous ana used to describe it, just as an anonymous alcoholic might describe being in A.A. as being "in the rooms"—pro-ana is something of a misnomer. It suggests the promotion of something, rather than its defense, for reasons either sad or militant. That it is generally understood otherwise and even exploited ("Anorexia: Not just for suicidal teenage white girls anymore" read the home page of Anorexic Nation, now a disabled site, the real purpose of which was to push diet drugs) is a source of both resentment and secret satisfaction to the true pro-ana community. Its adherents might be vile and worthless, but they are the elite.

The usual elements of most sites are pretty much the same, although the presenta-tion is variable enough to suggest Web mistresses ranging from young women with a fair amount of programming know-how and editorial judgment to angry little girls who want to assert their right to protect an unhealthy behavior in the face of parental opposition and who happen to know a little HTML. But there are usually "tips" and "techniques"—on the face of it, the scariest aspect of pro-ana, but in reality, pretty much the same things that both dieters and anorexics have been figuring out on their own for decades. There are "thinspirational" quotes—You can never be too rich or too thin"; "Hunger hurts but starving works"; "Nothing tastes as good as thin feels"; "The thinner, the winner!" There are "thinspirational" photo galleries, usually pretty much the same group of very thin models, actresses and singers—Jodie Kidd, Kate Moss, Calista Flockhart, Fiona Apple. And at pro-ana's saddest extreme, balancing the militance on the scales of the double-digit goal weight, there are warnings of such severity that they might as well be the beginning of the third canto of Dante's "Inferno": "I am the way into the city of woe. I am the way to a forsaken people. I am the way into eternal sorrow." The pro-ana version of which, from one site, is:

Please Note: anorexia is not a diet. Bulimia is not a weight-loss plan. These are dangerous, potentially life-threatening disorders that you cannot choose, catch or learn. If you do not already have an eating disorder, that's wonderful! If you're looking for a new diet, if you want to drop a few pounds to be slimmer or more popular or whatever, if you're generally content with yourself and just want to look a bit better in a bikini, go away. Find a Weight Watchers meeting. Better yet, eat moderate portions of healthy food and go for a walk.

However.

If you are half as emotionally scarred as I am, if you look in the mirror and truly loathe what you see, if your relationships with food and your body are already beyond "normal" parameters no matter what you weigh, then come inside. If you're already too far into this to quit, come in and have a look around. I won't tell you to give up what I need to keep hold of myself.

20   Most of the pro-ana sites also explicitly discourage people under 18 from entering, partly for moral and partly for self-interested reasons. Under pressure from the National Eating Disorders Association, a number of servers shut down the pro-ana sites they were hosting last fall. But obviously, pretty much anyone who wanted to find her way to these sites and into them could do so, irrespective of age. And could find there, as Clairegirl did, a kind of perverse support group, a place where a group of for the most part very unhappy and in some part very angry girls and women come together to support each other

in sickness rather than in health.

Then there's Chaos—also her Web name—who like her friend Futurebird (ditto) runs an established and well-respected pro-E.D. site. Chaos, whom I met in Manhattan although that's not where she lives, is a very smart, very winning, very attractive 23-year-old who has been either bulimic or anorexic since she was 10. Recently she's been bingeing and purging somewhere between 4 and 10 times a week. But when not bingeing, she also practices "restricting"—she doesn't eat in front of people, or in public, or food that isn't sealed, or food that she hasn't prepared herself, or food that isn't one of her "safe" foods, which since they are a certain kind of candy and a certain kind of sugar-free gum, is practically all food. ("You're catching on quickly," she says, laughing, when this is remarked on.) Also recently, she has been having trouble making herself throw up. "I think my body's just not wanting to do it right now," she says. "You have the toothbrush trick, and usually I can just hit my stomach in the right spot, or my fingernails will gag me in the right spot. It just depends on what I've eaten. And if that doesn't work, laxis always do."

Chaos, like Clairegirl, is obsessive-compulsive about a certain number (which it would freak her out to see printed), and when she takes laxatives she either has to take that number of them, which is no longer enough to work, or that number plus 10, or that number plus 20, and so forth. The most she has ever taken is that number plus 60, and the total number she takes depends on the total number of calories she has consumed.

While it hardly needs to be pointed out that starving yourself is not good for you, bulimia is in its own inexorable if less direct way also a deadly disorder. Because of the severity of Chaos's bulimia, its longstanding nature and the other things she does—taking ephedra or Xenadrine, two forms of, as she says, "legal speed," available at any health food or vitamin store; exercising in excess; fasting—she stands a very real chance of dying any time.

As it is, she has been to the emergency room more than half a dozen times with "heart things." It would freak her out to see the details of her heart things in print. But the kinds of heart things a severe bulimic might experience range from palpitations to cardiac arrest. And although Chaos hasn't had her kidney function tested in the recent past, it probably isn't great. Her spleen might also be near the point of rupturing.

Chaos is by no means a young woman with nothing going for her. She has a full-time job and is a full-time college student, a double major. She can play a musical instrument and take good photographs. She writes beautifully, well enough to have won competitions.

But despite her many positive attributes, Chaos punishes herself physically on a regular basis, not only through bulimia but also through cutting—hers is the live-journal page with the picture of the sliced-up arm. To be beheld is, to Chaos, so painful that after meeting me in person, she was still vomiting and crying with fear over the possible consequences of cooperating with this story a week later. "Some days," she says of her bulimia, "it's all I have."

One thing that she does not have is health insurance, so her treatment options are both limited and inadequate. So with everything she has going for her, with all her real-world dreams and aspirations, the palpitating heart of her emotional life is in the pro-E.D. community. As another girl I spoke with described herself as telling her doctors: "Show me a coping mechanism that works as well as this and I'll trade my eating disorder for it in a minute."

And while in some moods Chaos says she would do anything to be free of her eating disorders, in others she has more excuses not to be than the mere lack of health insurance: she has a job, she is in school, she doesn't deserve help. And what she has, on all days, is her Web site, a place where people who have only their eating disorders can congregate, along with the people who aspire to having eating disorders—who for unknowable reasons of neurochemistry and personal experience identify with the self-lacerating worlds of anorexia and bulimia.

Futurebird, whom I also met in Manhattan, says that she has noticed a trend, repeating itself in new member after new member, of people who don't think they're anorexic enough to get treatment. And it's true, very much a function of the Internet—its accessibility, its anonymity—that the pro-ana sites seem to have amplified an almost-diagnostic category: the subclinical eating disorder, for the girl who's anorexic on the inside, the girl who hates herself so much that she forms a virtual attachment to a highly traumatized body of women, in a place where through posts and the adoption of certain behaviors, she can make her internal state external.

30 Futurebird and Chaos are sitting in a little plaza just to the south of Washington Square Park, with the sun behind them. Futurebird is a small African-American woman. As she notes, and as she has experienced when being taken to the hospital, it is a big help being African-American if you don't want people to think you have anorexia, which is generally and inaccurately considered to be solely an affliction of the white middle class. Futurebird has had an eating disorder since she was in junior high school and is now, at 22, looking for a way to become what you might call a maintenance anorexic—eating a little bit more healthily, restricting to foods like fruits and whole-grain cereal and compensating for the extra calories with excessive exercising.

Like Chaos, she is opposed, in principle, to eating disorders in general and says that she hates anorexia with a blind and burning hatred. Although she also says she thinks she's fat, which she so emphatically is not that in the interest of not sounding illogical and irrational, she almost immediately amends this to: she's not as thin as she'd like to be.

Both she and Chaos would vigorously dispute the assertion that the sites can give anyone an eating disorder. You certainly can't give anyone without the vulnerability to it an eating disorder. But many adolescent girls teeter on the edge of vulnerability. And the sites certainly might give those girls the suggestion to . . . hey, what the hell, give it a try.

"What I'd like people to understand," Futurebird says, "is that it is very difficult for people who have an eating disorder to ask for help. What a lot of people are able to do is to say, well, I can't go to a recovery site and ask for help. I can't go to a doctor or a friend and ask for help. I can't tell anyone. But I can go to this site because it's going to quote-unquote make me worse. And instead what I hope they find is people who share their experience and that they're able to just simply talk. And I've actually tested this. I've posted the same thing that I've posted on my site on some recovery sites, and I've read the reactions, and in a lot of ways it's more helpful."

In what ways?

35 "The main difference is that if you post—if someone's feeling really bad, like, I'm so fat, et cetera, on a recovery site, they'll say, that's not recovery talk. You have to speak recovery-speak."

"Fat is not a feeling," Chaos says, in tones that indicate she is echoing a recovery truism.

"And they'll use this language of recovery," Futurebird continues. "Which does work at some point in the negative thinking patterns that you have. But one tiny thing that I wish they would do is validate that the feeling does exist. To say, yes, I understand that you might feel that way. And you get not as much of that. A lot of times people just need to know that they aren't reacting in a completely crazy way."

The problem is that by and large, the people posting on these sites are reacting in a completely crazy way. There are many, many more discussions answering questions like, "What do you guys do about starvation headaches?" than there are questions like, "I am feeling really down; can you help me?" And in no case, in answering the former question, does anyone say, "Um . . . stop starving yourself." A site like Futurebird's, or like the message board of Chaos's, are designed with the best intentions. But as everybody knows, that is what the way into the city of woe, the way to a forsaken people and the way into eternal sorrow are paved with.

What Clairegirl, sitting shivering on the running track, would say today is that when she reaches her current goal weight, she will stay there. But she can't ever really see herself giving ana up altogether. "I don't think I could ever stop, like, wanting to not eat. Like, I could keep myself from eating below 300 calories a day. But I could never see myself eating more than 1,000," she says, wrapping her arms around her knees. "I consider myself to be one of the extreme dieters. Like, I could never want to be—I mean, it would be so awesome to be able to say a double-digit number as your weight, but it would look sick, you know?" (Clairegirl is 5 feet 7 inches.)

40   And what about the people on the pro-ana sites who are not so happy, who describe the disorder as a living hell, who are in very bad shape? "Those girls have been going at it a lot longer than me. But you can't ever really say that ana isn't a form of self-hatred, even though I try to say that. If I was truthfully happy with myself, then I would allow myself to eat. But I don't. And it's kind of like a strive for perfection, and for making myself better. So I can't honestly say there's no. . . ."

She trails off, and gazes up, as if the answer were written in the night sky, waiting to be decoded. "Like, you can't say that every ana loves herself and that she doesn't think anything is wrong with her at all," she says. "Or else she wouldn't be ana in the first place."

Reflect & Write

❑ In writing this article, Mim Udovich structures her argument around interviews with three different young women with eating disorders. What is the effect of structuring the argument in this way?

❑ What rhetorical appeals is she relying primarily on in constructing this argument? How does the order of the interviews (i.e., which one is first, second, and third) impact the effectiveness of the argument?

❑ Twice when writing about her conversation with Chaos, Udovitch notes that there are things that would "freak" Chaos out if she saw them in print. How does this notation affect the reader's understanding of Chaos and change the way that we approach her as a primary source?

❑ **Write:** One of the elements that binds these girls together is their use of the Internet to participate in the pro-ana community. Write a blog entry in which you argue that pro-ana Websites and blogs should be shut down, using persuasive examples and evidence to support your point. Next, write a rebuttal to this position, in which you argue in defense of their existence. Finally, write a third position in which you try to find a middle ground between these two extremes.

■ *This poster is part of the* **National Eating Disorders Association**'s *broader campaign to promote new programs and academic curricula designed to educate the populace about the dangers of eating disorders. This campaign produces a variety of visual arguments, some of which address the problems associated with anorexia and bulimia, and others which promote girls' positive self image and a healthy relationship with food.*

2004 Get Real Campaign Ad
National Eating Disorders Association

FIGURE 10.7 This 2004 ad was featured as part of its "Get Real" campaign for National Eating Disorders Awareness Week.

Reflect & Write

❏ How does this advertisement create its argument through visual rhetoric?

❏ Do research online and locate statistics about anorexia in girls. Now create an alternative op-ad that relies more on a logos-driven argument to make its point. Be sure to incorporate rhetorically purposeful images to substantiate and reinforce your argument.

❏ Visit the parody ads Obsession and Reality at the Adbusters Website, linked through the *Envision* Website. Examine how they use different rhetorical strategies to make similar arguments. In each case, how are their purposes and audiences different?

❏ **Write:** What kinds of visual rhetoric might you design to address body issues for women of different races and colors? Do some research, and then draft a letter to the National Eating Disorders Association proposing a new campaign based on your findings.

COLLABORATIVE CHALLENGE

The posters created by the National Eating Disorders Association primarily focus on body image issues and eating disorders experienced by young girls. Working as a group, identify additional body image problems facing girls in your community. Now, as a team, sketch out a design for a parody poster to raise awareness about this issue. Next, working in your team, create a poster aimed at addressing body image in young boys. Be sure to decide upon your argument before drafting your poster: for instance, your poster could be designed either to promote positive body image or to call attention to male body image problems. Share your work with the rest of the class.

■ **Susan McClelland** *is an associate editor for* Maclean's, *a Canadian weekly newsmagazine, where this article appeared on August 14, 2000. She has also written an article on male body image, entitled, "The Lure of the Body Image: In Their Quest for the Beefcake Look, Some Men Try Extreme Measures."*

Distorted Images: Western Cultures are Exporting Their Dangerous Obsession with Thinness

Susan McClelland

When Zahra Dhanani was just seven years old, her four-foot frame already packed 100 lb.—so her mother, Shahbanu, put her on her first diet. "My mother, a fat woman, daughter of another fat woman, thought if I was skinny, different from her, I would be happy," says Dhanani. The diet, and many after, did not have the desired effect. By 13, Dhanani was sporadically swallowing appetite suppressants; at 17, she vomited and used laxatives to try to keep her weight under control. There were times when she wanted to die. "I had so much self-hate," recalls the 26-year-old Toronto immigration lawyer, "I couldn't look in the mirror without feeling revulsion."

The hate reflected more than just weight. "It was race," says Dhanani, who had moved with her family to Canada from East Africa when she was 4. "I was straightening my hair—doing anything to look white." Her recovery only began when, at age 19, she started to identify with women in other cultures. "I came to realize that there were people who revered large women of colour," says Dhanani, who now says she loves all of her 200 lb. She blames part of her earlier eating disorders on the images in western media: "When you have no role models to counteract the messages that fat is repulsive, it's hard to realize that you are a lovable human being."

Body image may be one of the western world's ugliest exports. Thanks to television, magazines, movies and the Internet, rail-thin girls and steroid-built beef-boys are being shoved in the faces of people all over the world. As a result, experts say, cultures that used to regard bulk as a sign of wealth and success are now succumbing to a narrow western standard of beauty. And that, in turn, is leading to incidences of eating disorders in regions where anorexia and bulimia had never been seen before. But body-image anxiety in ethnic cultures runs much deeper than weight. In South Africa, almost six years after the end of apartheid, black women still use harmful skin-bleaching creams in the belief that whiter is prettier. "We're seeing a homogenization and globalization of beauty ideals," says Niva Piran, a clinical psychologist at the University of Toronto. "It's white. It's thin. And the result is that people come to identify less with their own cultures and more with an image in the media."

In most cultures, bigger was considered better until the 19th century. "The larger a man's wife, the more he was seen as a good provider," says Joan Jacobs Brumberg, a professor of American women's history at Cornell University and author of *Fasting Girls: The History of Anorexia Nervosa*. That began to change during the Industrial Revolution, she says, as women in the United States and Great Britain began to see thinness as a way to differentiate themselves from the lower classes. By the 1920s, fat was seen as unhealthy. And in the burgeoning magazine, movie and fashion industries, the women depicted as being successful in love, career and finances were slim and almost always white.

5   Still, eating disorders are not a modern affliction. Records of women starving themselves (anorexia) date back to the medieval period (1200 to 1500). As Brumberg notes in *Fasting Girls*, during this time, a woman who did not eat was admired for having found some other form of sustenance than food, like prayer. Yet, until the last century, the number of women who fasted was low. But, particularly over the past 30 years, the number of anorexics and women who self-induce vomiting (bulimia) or use laxatives has

increased dramatically. "It's generally this obsession with the body, constant weight-watching, that introduces a person to these behaviours," says Merryl Bear of the Toronto-based National Eating Disorder Information Centre. It was commonly believed, however, that sufferers came predominantly from white, middle- and upper-class backgrounds. Experts thought ethnic minorities were immune because of their strong ties to communities that emphasize family and kinship over looks alone.

Studies done in the United States with Hispanic, black and Asian college students, however, show that women who are alienated from their minority cultures and integrated into mainstream society are prone to the same pressures of dieting as their white counterparts. In a recent study of South-Asian girls in Peel, Ont., 31 per cent responded that they were not comfortable with their body shape and size. Fifty-eight per cent compared their appearance with others, including fashion models—and 40 per cent wanted to look like them.

Some of the most compelling research comes from Harvard Medical School psychiatrist Anne Becker, who was in Fiji in 1995 when the government announced that TV, including western programs, would be introduced. "Fijians revere a body that is sturdy, tall and large—features that show that the body is strong, hard-working and healthy," says Becker. "Thinness and sudden weight loss was seen as some kind of social loss or neglect."

In 1998, Becker returned to Fiji and found that this had all changed. Her studies showed that 29 percent of the girls now had symptoms of eating disorders. Many said they vomited to lose weight. But what was most alarming were the girls' responses about the role of television in their lives. "More than 80 percent said that watching TV affected the way they felt about their bodies," Becker says. "They said things such as, 'I watched the women on TV, they have jobs. I want to be like them, so I am working on my weight now.' These teenagers are getting the sense that as Fiji moves into the global economy, they had better find some way to make wages and they are desperate to find role models. The West to them means success and they are altering their bodies to compete."

Cheryl McConney has felt the pressures to alter her body, too. The black 32-year-old native of Richmond Hill, Ont., co-hosts a daytime talk show on cable TV. And although it has not been difficult for her to get where she is in her career, she is concerned about how to navigate her next step. "Looking at Canadian television, I don't see many people who look like me on air," she says. At five-foot-five, and weighing about 145 lb., McConney has never been told she should lose weight. Still, in 1998, she went on a six-month, high-protein, low-carbohydrate diet, hoping to look better in front of the camera. She shed 20 lb. "I felt good. People in the studio thought I looked great, but it wasn't easy to maintain." Within a year, she had gained it all back.

10   For McConney, race has been more of an issue. An industry insider jokingly told her that she would do better if she dyed her hair blond. And just a few months ago, she was discouraged from applying for another on-air host position because of what the casting agents said they were looking for. "They wanted the 'girl next door' and 'peaches- and-cream' pretty, not chocolate and cream," says McConney, adding: "It was pretty clear some women were not invited to participate because of their skin colour." As to the girl next door part: "I said it just depends where you live."

While McConney says she is determined to make it on-air despite the barriers, Linda, who requested Maclean's not use her real name, may not be around to see her success. The 19-year-old—part South African and part East Indian—has anorexia. She says trying to fit into a Canadian suburban community played a big role in her illness. "I was never proud of my different religion, different skin colour," she says. "I would put white baby powder on my cheeks just to make me look white." What alarms her now, Linda says, is that with her skin pale from malnutrition and her weight fluctuating between 75 and 85 lb., other young women often come up to her and say, "You look so good, I wish I looked like you." But she adds: "What they don't know is that my body is decaying. People glamorize eating disorders. But what it is is a lifetime of hospitalization and therapy." As long as the western media promote thinness and whiteness as the pinnacle of beauty, stories like Linda's will remain all too familiar.

Reflect & Write

❑ In this article, Susan McClelland addresses not only the way body image relates to thinness but also its relationship to different racial features and skin color. Do you agree that the media tend to model its ideal of beauty around a Caucasian standard? What evidence can you cite from your own observations to support your opinion?

❑ What rhetorical appeals does McClelland utilize in this article? Pathos? Logos? Ethos? Which does she use most prominently and which is most powerful in solidifying her argument?

❑ **Write:** Look at international or culturally targeted beauty magazines at your local bookstore or news stand. Select a few images or ads, and draft your own argument concerning how that magazine defines beauty. Does it seem reliant on white, Western standards? Does it offer new or alternative visions?

■ *During the early twentieth century,* **Charles Atlas**, *inspired by a statue of Hercules, started body building and within a few years became known as "The World's Most Perfectly Developed Man." He and partner Charles P. Roman founded Charles Atlas, Ltd., a company dedicated to selling the secrets of masculine health and fitness. His advertisements, including "Hey Skinny," "97 lb. weakling", and "The insult that made a man out of 'Mac'" (right), appeared in the back of numerous comic books and newspapers and continue to circulate as examples of vintage American advertising.*

FIGURE 10.8 Blending cartoon and advertisement, this vintage Charles Atlas ad marketed a 32-page illustrated book designed to "make a man" out of the reader.

Reflect & Write

❏ How are pathos, logos, and ethos used in this advertisement to increase its persuasiveness?

❏ Visit the online Atlas archive at http://www.charlesatlas.com/classicads.html and examine other similar ads. How do these ads use similar strategies to the one shown here? Are there any that make more effective arguments? What elements make those arguments more persuasive?

❏ Consider the issue of male body image. Although the Atlas ads are dated, can you find examples of similar pressures in contemporary culture? Where would you be most likely to find stereotypes of male body image? How do pressures about male body image compare to pressures about female body image?

❏ **Write:** Considering the pressures that face men and boys today in terms of body image, storyboard your own advertisement for a fictitious contemporary product or service that will make a "man" out of a modern-day "Mac."

■ *This landmark article, which investigates the relationship between boys' body image and action toys, first appeared in the* International Journal of Eating Disorders *in 1999. The research later was featured in a key section of* The Adonis Complex *(2000), a book-length study of male body image.* **Harrison Pope** *and* **Amanda Gruber** *are professors of psychiatry at Harvard Medical School, and* **Robert Olivardia** *is a clinical instructor at the same institution.*

Evolving Ideals of Male Body Image as Seen Through Action Toys

Harrison G. Pope, Jr., Robert Olivardia, Amanda Gruber, and John Borowieki

Abstract: **Objective:** *We hypothesized that the physiques of male action toys—small plastic figures used by children in play—would provide some index of evolving American cultural ideals of male body image.* **Method:** *We obtained examples of the most popular American action toys manufactured over the last 30 years. We then measured the waist, chest, and bicep circumference of each figure and scaled these measurements using classical allometry to the height of an actual man (1.78 m).* **Results:** *We found that the figures have grown much more muscular over time, with many contemporary figures far exceeding the muscularity of even the largest human bodybuilders.* **Discussion:** *Our observations appear to represent a "male analog" of earlier studies examining female dolls, such as Barbie. Together, these studies of children's toys suggest that cultural expectations may contribute to body image disorders in both sexes.* © 1999 by John Wiley & Sons, Inc. Int J Eat Disord 26: 65–72, 1999.

Key words: male body image; male action toys; body image disorders

Introduction

A growing body of literature has described disorders of body image among men. For example, such disturbances are frequently documented in men with eating disorders. In one study, college men with eating disorders reported a degree of body dissatisfaction closely approaching that of women with eating disorders, and strikingly greater than comparison men (Olivardia, Pope, Mangweth, & Hudson, 1995). Other studies of men with eating disorders have produced similar findings (Andersen, 1990; Schneider & Agras, 1987). Even in studies of male students without eating disorders, the prevalence of body dissatisfaction is often striking (Mintz & Betz, 1986; Drewnowski & Yee, 1987; Dwyer, Feldman, Seltzer, & Mayer, 1969). Body image disturbances may be particularly prominent in American culture. In a recent cross-cultural comparison, groups of American college men reported significantly greater dissatisfaction with their bodies than comparable groups in Austria (Mangweth et al., 1997).

Another form of body image disturbance, also frequently affecting men, is body dysmorphic disorder (Phillips, 1991, 1997; Hollander, Cohen, & Simeon, 1993). Individuals with this disorder may develop obsessional preoccupations that their facial features are ugly, that their hairlines are receding, or that their penis size is too small—to name several of the more common presentations. Recently, we have described another form of body dysmorphic disorder found in both sexes, but probably more prevalent in men, which we have called "muscle dysmorphia" (Pope, Gruber, Choi, Olivardia, & Phillips, 1997). Individuals with muscle dysmorphia report an obsessional preoccupation with their muscularity, to the point where their social and occupational functioning may be severely impaired. For example, they may abandon important social and family relationships, or even relinquish professional careers, in order to spend more time at the gym (Pope et al., 1997). Many report that they refuse to be seen in public without their shirts on because they fear that they will look too small (Pope, Katz, & Hudson, 1993), Often they use anabolic steroids or other performance-enhancing drugs, continuing to take these agents even in the face of serious side effects because of persistent anxiety about their muscularity (Pope et al., 1993; Pope & Katz, 1994).

5   In many ways, muscle dysmorphia appears to be part of the "obsessive-compulsive spectrum" of disorders (Hollander, 1993; Phillips, McElroy, Hudson, & Pope, 1995). It is characterized by obsessional preoccupations and impulsive behaviors similar to those of classical obsessive-compulsive disorder. If this hypothesis is correct, it is natural to ask why modem American men with muscle dysmorphia would have developed this particular outlet for their obsessions, as opposed to a more traditional symptom pattern such as hand-washing or checking rituals.

One possible explanation for this phenomenon is that in our culture, the ideal male body is growing steadily more muscular. With the advent of anabolic steroids in the last 30 to 40 years, it has become possible for men to become much more muscular than is possible by natural means. Bodybuilders who won the Mr. America title in the presteroid era could not hope to compete against steroid-using bodybuilders today (Kouri, Pope, Katz, & Oliva,

1995). The public is exposed daily, in magazines, motion pictures, and other media, to increasingly—and often unnaturally—muscular male images. Some individuals, responding to these cultural messages, may become predisposed to develop muscle dysmorphia.

In an attempt to provide some quantitative data bearing on this hypothesis, we examined the physiques of American action toys over the last 30 years.

Methods

Action toys are small plastic figures, typically ranging from 3 3/4 in. to 12 in. in height, used by children in play, and frequently collected by adult hobbyists. Among the best known examples are the GI Joe figures, Star Wars and Star Trek characters, Superman, Spiderman, and Batman. Contemporary versions of these figures are readily available at toy stores and vintage figures may be purchased through a vast and well-organized collectors' market. Extensive reference works, such as the 480-page *Encyclopedia of GI Joe* (Santelmo, 1997), document the evolution of these figures over the years. We chose to study these toys because, unlike cartoon characters or movie stars, they can be readily physically measured, allowing accurate comparisons between figures of different eras.

We consulted with various action toy experts to ascertain toys which had been produced in various iterations by the same manufacturer over a period of 20 years or more. To obtain an objective index of the popularity of specific toys, we consulted the 1st through 15th annual sales surveys by *Playthings* magazine, published in the December issue of each year from 1983 to 1997 (*Playthings* magazine), to confirm that the toy had been among the 10 best-selling toy product lines in several years spanning the last two decades. We also required that the toy represent an actual male human being (such as a soldier or Luke Skywalker), rather than a nonhuman creature (such as Mr. Potato Head or the Teen-Age Mutant Ninja Turtles). Two toy product lines met all of these criteria: the GI Joe series manufactured by the Hasbro Toy Company since 1964 and the Star Wars figures manufactured by the Kenner Toy Company (a subsidiary of Hasbro) since 1978. We then purchased representative examples of these figures from different time periods. We also visited a branch of a large toy store chain and purchased additional examples of toys identified by store officials and by the most recent *Playthings* surveys as the most popular contemporary male action figures. Some of these latter figures, such as Batman and the Mighty Morphin Power Rangers, might not be considered completely "human," in that they possess powers beyond those of a real human being. Others, such as the X-Men, are mutants of human beings. However, they all possess essentially human bodies.

10   We then measured the waist, chest, and bicep circumference of all the figures and scaled these measurements using classical allometry (Norton, Olds, Olive, & Dank, 1996) to a common height of 1.78 m (70 in.).

Results

GI Joe

The action toy with the longest continuous history is GI Joe. The Hasbro Toy Company first introduced GI Joe as an 11 1/2-in. posable figure in 1964

Table 1.   Measurements of representative action toys extrapolated to a height of 70 in.

Toy. Date	Actual Measurements (in.)[a]				Extrapolated to Height of 70 in.[a]		
	Height	Waist	Chest	Biceps	Waist[b]	Chest[b]	Biceps[b]
GI Joe Land Adventurer, 1973 (with original body in use since 1964)	11.5	5.2	7.3	2.1	31.7	44.4	12.2
GI Joe Land Adventurer, 1975 (with new body introduced in 1974)	11.5	5.2	7.3	2.5	31.7	44.4	15.2
GI Joe Hall of Fame Soldier, 1994 (with body introduced in 1991)	11.5	4.8	7.1	2.7	29.2	43.2	16.4
GI Joe Extreme, 1998	5.8	3.0[c]	4.5[c]	2.2	36.5[c]	54.8[c]	26.8
The Gold Ranger, 1998	5.5	2.7	3.6	1.4[c]	34.4[c]	45.8[c]	17.8[c]
Ahmed Johnson, 1998	6.0	3.0	4.1	2.0	35.0	47.8	23.3
Iron Man, 1998	6.5	2.6	4.7	2.1	28.0	50.6	22.6
Batman, 1998	6.0	2.6	4.9	2.3	30.3	57.2	26.8
Wolverine, 1998	7.0	3.3	6.2	3.2	33.0	62.0	32.0

[a]Measurements estimated to the nearest 0.1 in.
[b]For comparison, the mean waist, chest, and biceps circumferences of 50 Australian soccer players, scaled to a slightly shorter height of 170.2 cm (67 in). were found to be 29.6 in., 36.3 in., and 11.8 in., respectively (19).
[c]These numbers are reduced by about 5% from actual measurments to compensate for the thickness of the figure's clothes and equipment.

(Santelmo, 1997). This figure continued without a change in body style as the GI Joe Adventurer in 1970 to 1973. It developed a new body style from 1973 to 1976 as the GI Joe Adventurer with kung-fu grip and lifelike body. In the late 1970s, production of the 11 1/2-in. figures was discontinued, being replaced by a series of 3 3/4-in. figures that was introduced in 1982. These smaller figures continued through 11 series over the next 10 years, eventually attaining a height of 4 1/2 in. and culminating in the GI Joe Extreme. This was a 5-in. figure (5.8 in. with knees and waist straightened) that was introduced in 1995 and is still available on the shelves of toy stores today. Meanwhile, the 11 1/2-in. figures were reintroduced in 1991 and continue to be manufactured to the present.

We purchased three representative 11 1/2-in. figures: a 1973 Adventurer with the original body in use since 1964, a 1975 Adventurer with the newer lifelike body, and a 1994 Hall of Fame figure. A photograph of these three figures appears in Figure 1 and their dimensions are shown in Table 1. Not only have the figures grown more muscular, but they have developed increasingly sharp muscular definition through the years. For example, the earliest figure has no visible abdominal muscles; his 1975 counterpart shows some abdominal definition; and the 1994 figure displays the sharply rippled abdominals of an advanced bodybuilder. The modern figure also displays distinct serratus muscles along his ribs—a feature

FIGURE 1. GI Joe Sergeant Savage, 1982 (left); GI Joe Cobra Soldier, 1982 (middle); and GI Joe Extreme Sergeant Savage. 1998 (right) (Hasbro).

FIGURE 2. Luke Skywalker and Hans Solo, 1978 (left); Luke Skywalker and Hans Solo, 1998 (right) (Kenner).

readily seen in bodybuilders but less often visible in ordinary men.

We also purchased several of the smaller figures for comparison—a 1982 Grunt, a 1982 Cobra soldier (GI Joe's arch-enemy), and a current GI Joe Extreme. As shown in Figure 2, the contemporary GI Joe Extreme dwarfs his earlier counter-parts with dramatically greater muscula-ture and has an expression of rage which contrasts sharply with the bland faces of his predecessors. Although the body dimensions of the earlier small action fig-ures cannot be accurately estimated be-cause of their layer of clothing, the GI Joe Extreme is more easily measured (see Table 1). If extrapolated to 70 in. in height, the GI Joe Extreme would sport larger bi-ceps than any bodybuilder in history.

Luke Skywalker and Hans Solo

A similar impression emerges upon examining the original (1978) versus the contemporary 3 3/4-in. figures of *Star Wars* characters Luke Skywalker and Hans Solo (manufactured by the Kenner Toy Company). As shown in Figure 3 [not shown here], Luke and Hans have both acquired the physiques of body-builders over the last 20 years, with particularly impressive gains in the shoul-der and chest areas. Again, the clothing on these small plastic figures precludes accurate body measurements, so that they are not included in Table 1.

Modern Figures

15   Figure 4 [not shown here] depicts five more examples from the most popular contemporary lines of male action figures. As mentioned earlier, it might be argued that most of these characters are not entirely human, in that they possess powers beyond those of real people. Nevertheless, they are given fundamentally human bodies, but with musculature that ranges from merely massive to well beyond that of the biggest bodybuilders (Table 1).

Discussion

We hypothesized that action toys would illustrate evolving ideals of male body image in the United States. Accordingly, we purchased and measured the most popular male human action figures which have been manufactured over the last 30 years. On both visual inspection and anthropomorphic mea-surement, it appears that action figures today are consistently much more muscular than their predecessors. Many modern figures display the physiques of advanced bodybuilders and some display levels of muscular-ity far exceeding the outer limits of actual human attainment.

These findings, however, must be interpreted cautiously for several rea-sons. First, we found only two lines of male human action toys which fully met our criterion of long-term documented popularity. Thus, it might be argued that these particular toy lines happened to favor our hypothesis by chance alone. However, on the basis of our discussions with action figure experts, we believe that the examples analyzed here are representative of the overall trend of body image in male action toys over the last several decades. The other leading contemporary toys, shown in Figure 4, support the impression that this trend toward a bodybuilder physique is consistent. The only notable exception to this trend is the Mattel Company's Ken, the boyfriend of Barbie. However, although the Barbie toy line overall has frequently ranked among the top 10 toy lines, Ken is but a small part of this market. Among boys in particular, Ken almost certainly ranks well below the popularity of the other male action figure discussed above (*Playthings* magazine).

Second, it is uncertain whether action toys accurately mirror trends in other media. It is our impression that comic strip characters, male models in magazines, and male motion picture actors have all shown a parallel trend toward increasing leanness and muscularity over the last several decades. However, more systematic studies will be required to confirm these observations.

Third, it is not clear to what extent these trends in toys, or parallel trends in other media, may be a cause or effect of an evolving cultural emphasis on male muscularity. Certainly, it would be premature to conclude that American men are prompted to develop disorders of body image purely as a result of boyhood exposure to muscular ideals of male physique. On the other hand, the impact of toys should not be underestimated. Male action toys as a whole accounted for $949 million in manufacturers' shipments in 1994 alone, with action figures accounting for $687 million of this total (*Playthings* magazine, 1995).

20 It should also be noted that similar theories have been advanced for many years regarding cultural ideals of thinness in women (Pope & Hudson, 1984; Cash & Pruzinsky, 1990). For example, one study found that both *Playboy* centerfold models and Miss America pageant contestants grew steadily thinner over the period of 1959 to 1978 (Garner, Garfinkel, Schwartz, & Thompson, 1980). A recent update suggests that this trend has continued at least through 1988 (Wiseman, Gray, Mosimann, & Ahrens, 1992). Similarly, in the area of toys, the literature has documented the inappropriate thinness of modern female dolls (Norton et al., 1996, Pederson & Markee, 1991; Rintala & Mustajoki, 1992; Brownell & Napolitano, 1995). Indeed, one report has found that Mattel Company's Barbie, if extrapolated to a height of 67 in., would have a waist circumference of 16 in. (Norton et al., 1996)—a figure approaching the impossibility of our male superheroes' biceps.

In any event, these striking findings suggest that further attempts should be made to assess the relationship between cultural messages and body image disorders in both men and women.

The authors thank Erik Flint of Cotswold Collectibles, Whitbey Island, WA; Vincent Santelmo of the Official Action Figure Warehouse, New York, NY; and Jeff Freeman of the Falcon's Hangar, Auburn, IN, for their assistance in the selection and purchase of action toys and in the preparation of this manuscript.

References

Action figures duke it out. (1995). Playthings magazine, 93, 26–28.

Andersen, A.E. (Ed). (1990) Males with eating disorders. New York: Brunner Mazel.

Brownell, K.D., & Napolitano, M.A. (1995). Distorting reality for children: Body size proportions of Barbie and Ken dolls. International Journal of Eating Disorders, 18, 295–298.

Cash, T.F., & Pruzinsky, T. (Eds), (1990). Body images: Developments, deviance, and change, New York: Guilford.

Drewnowski, A., & Yee, D.K. (1987). Men and body image: Are males satisfied with their body weight? Psychosomatic Medicine. 49, 626–634.

Dwyer, J.T., Feldman, J.J., Seltzer, C.C., & Mayer, J. (1969). Body image in adolescents: Attitudes toward weight and perception of appearance. American Journal of Clinical Nutrition, 20, 1045–1056.

Garner, D.M., Garfinkel, P.E., Schwartz, D., & Thompson, M. (1980). Cultural expectations of thinness in women. Psychological Reports, 47, 483–491.

Hollander, E. (1993). Introduction. In E. Hollander, (Ed.), Obsessive-compulsive related disorders. Washington, DC: American Psychiatric Press.

Hollander, E., Cohen, I. J., & Simeon, D. (1993). Body dysmorphic disorder. Psychiatric Annals, 23, 359–364.

Kouri, E., Pope. H.G., Katz. D.L., & Oliva, P. (1995). Fat-free mass index in users and non-users of anabolic-androgenic steroids. Clinical Journal of Sport Medicine, 5, 223–228.

Mangweth, B., Pope. H.G., Jr., Hudson. J.I., Olivardia, R., Kinzi. J., & Biebl, W. (1997). Eating disorders in Austrian men: An intra-cultural and cross-cultural comparison study. Psychotherapy and Psychosomatics 66, 214–221.

Mintz, L.B., & Betz., N.E., (1986). Sex differences in the nature, realism, and correlates of body image. Sex Roles, 15, 185–195.

Norton, K.E., Olds, T.S., Olive. S., & Dank, S. (1996). Ken and Barbie at life size Sex Roles, 84, 287–294.

Olivardia, R., Pope, H.G., Jr., Mangweth., B., & Hudson, J.I. (1995). Eating disorders in college men. American Journal of Psychiatry, 152. 1279–1285.

Petersen, E.L., & Markee, N.L. (1991). Fashion dolls; Representations of ideals of beauty. Perceptual and Motor Skills, 73, 93–94.

Phillips, K.A. (1991). Body dysmorphic disorder. The distress of imagined, ugliness. American Journal of Psychiatry, 148, 1138–1149.

Phillips, K.A. (1997). The broken mirror. New York: Oxford University Press.

Phillips, K.A., McElroy, S.L., Hudson, J.I., & Pope, H.G., Jr. (1995). Body dysmorphic disorder: An obsessive-compulsive spectrum disorder, a form of affective spectrum disorder, or both? Journal of Clinical Psychiatry, 56 (Suppl. 4), 41–51.

Playthings. (1983–1997). New York: Geyer-McAlister Publications, Inc.

Pope, H.G., Jr., Gruber. A.J., Choi, P.Y., Olivadia. R., & Phillips. K.S, (1997). Muscle dysmorphia: An under-recognized form of body dysmorphic disorder. Psychosomatics, 38, 348–557.

Pope, H.G., Jr., & Hudson, J.I. (1984). New hope for binge eaters. Advances in the understanding and treatment of bulimia. New York: Harper and Row.

Pope, H.G., Jr., & Katz, D.L. (1994). Psychiatric and medical effects of anabolic-androgenic steroids. A controlled study of 160 athletes. Archives of General Psychiatry, 51, 375–382.

Pope, H.G., Jr., Katz. D.L., & Hudson. J.I. (1993). Anorexia nervosa and "reverse anorexia" among 108 male bodybuilders. Comprehensive Psychiatry, 34, 406–109.

Rintala, M., & Mustajoki, P. (1992). Could mannequins menstruate? British Medical Journal, 305, 1575–1576.

Santelmo, V. (1997). The complete encyclopedia to GI Joe (2nd ed.). Jola, WI: Krause Publications.

Schneider, J.A., & Agras, W.S. (1987). Bulimia in males: A matched comparison with females. International Journal of Eating Disorders, 6, 235–242.

Wiseman, C.V., Gray, J.J., Mosimann, J.E., & Abrens A.H. (1992). Cultural expectations of thinness: An update, International Journal of Eating Disorders, 11, 85–90.

Copyright of *International Journal of Eating Disorders* is the property of John Wiley & Sons inc. and its content may not be copied or emailed to multiple sites or posted to a listserv without the copyright holder's express written permission. However, users may print, download, or email articles for individual use.

Reflect & Write

❏ Summarize the argument in your own words. How does the historical examination of action toys provide powerful evidence about social norms for male body image?

❏ How do the images work in conjunction with the written text to create a persuasive argument? What would be lost in terms of the argument's effectiveness without the images?

❏ What are the different pressures facing boys compared to those facing girls? How does the media shape body image standards along gender lines?

❏ Are the examples used in this article culturally specific? What kinds of toys or representatives of male bodies are common in different parts of the U.S., in cities versus the countryside, or in different parts of the world?

❏ **Write:** Pope's article is written for an academic audience. Draft a version of this article that could be published as a short opinion piece in a parenting magazine.

COLLABORATIVE CHALLENGE

Together with two or three classmates, go to a toy store or visit one online and do your own survey of recent toys for boys. Be sure to look at Transformers, Rescue Heroes, Bionicles, and comic book heroes like Spiderman, Batman, and the X-Men. Also look at the Star Wars line and G.I. Joe Sigma 6 toys. Write an essay in which you use your own observations on recent toys to either support, qualify, or refute Pope's assertions about body image as projected through toy culture for boys. You might take digital photos of toys you find at the store and use them in your essay. Convert your writing to a presentation and share your work with the rest of the class, making sure each team member takes a turn in presenting part of the argument.

■ **Kim Franke-Folstad** *is a columnist for the* Rocky Mountain News, *where this article was originally published on May 24, 1999 in reaction to Harrison Pope's 1999 study on action toys and male body images.*

G.I. Joe's Big Biceps are Not a Big Deal

Kim Franke-Folstad

Say it isn't so, Joe.

For years, I've been defending Barbie against accusations that she promotes an unrealistic body image for little girls.

And now it turns out good old G.I. Joe has been subjected to the same silly poking and probing, the same plastic-to-flesh measurement comparisons and similarly ugly allegations that he's encouraging young boys to seek an artificially enhanced physique.

Will this foolishness never stop?

5   The latest bit of bicep bashing comes from Harvard psychiatrist Harrison Pope, who's apparently spent years studying hard-bodied action figures and how they affect the way males feel their real-life bodies should look.

Big, bulging and buff.

According to Pope's research, the plastic playthings are getting ever more muscle-bound, and young men are, too—often by abusing anabolic steroids.

The doctor says he can't be sure which came first: bulked-up toys or bulked-up boys. But, either way, when a G.I. Joe's bicep measurement translates to an impossible 26 inches for a real he-man, it could mean a dangerous trend.

Here we go again.

10   Barbie's bust is too big, her waist is too small, her arches (both foot and eyebrow) are unreasonably high. G.I. Joe's arms are too thick, his chest is too chiseled and the muscles in his massive thighs are ridiculously rippled.

So what?

They are toys. We all know that. That's why we stop playing with them before we get out of grade school.

Well, most of us, anyway.

Besides, if anything, I'm more comfortable with the freakish physiques of today's action figures than I was with the more realistic and appropriately proportioned appearance of my brother's G.I. Joe back in the 1960s.

15   Now, instead of sending a dog-tagged doll that looks like your next door neighbor's older brother into battle, it's more like you've dispatched a cartoon superhero. Of course bullets bounce off his chest and he's never afraid—he's not a man, he's a mutant with a crew cut and really great accessories.

Let's face it: Boys have wanted to bulk up—and do it quickly—since Charles Atlas promised he could transform any 90-pound weakling into a muscle man proud to stroll the beach in his Speedo. These days, young men (and not so young men) may be influenced by Mark McGwire's 19-inch biceps and the knowledge that he takes an over-the-counter testosterone booster. They may have noted the equally hunky Bill Romanowski's propensity for modeling EAS apparel. Or they could be checking out the bulging necks—and wallets—of popular professional wrestlers Goldberg and "Stone Cold" Steve Austin.

But a plastic doll?

Please. To suggest that even little boys measure manliness by taking a ruler to their G.I. Joes is comical.

And from here it looks as though the "real American hero's" musculature isn't the only thing being blown out of proportion.

Reflect & Write

❑ What is Franke-Folstad's argument in this article? Is it an effective rebuttal to Pope's claims? Do you find her argument convincing?

❑ Consider the author's voice. Does it try to be academic? Informal? Objective? Is this an effective choice for her argument?

❑ **Write:** Franke-Folstad does not include images in her article. Select an image or set of images (you can find them through a Google image search or by visiting a toy store with your digital camera) and write captions for them so that they function in support of her argument. Also consider where in the article you would place your visual rhetoric.

■ *This audio essay originally aired on the March 15, 2005, installment of* **NPR's "All Things Considered."** *In it,* The Adonis Complex *author Dr. Harrison Pope extends his study of male body image to an international context.*

Cultural Differences Seen in Male Perceptions of Body Image

National Public Radio, "All Things Considered"

MICHELE NORRIS, HOST: From NPR News, this is All Things Considered. I'm Michele Norris.

ROBERT SIEGEL, HOST: And I'm Robert Siegel, with a story that points out another cultural difference between Asia and the West. This one has been pointed out by researchers at a psychiatric hospital in Massachusetts. A study from the Harvard-affiliated McLean Hospital says Taiwanese men are not as dissatisfied with their bodies as Western men. The findings are only preliminary, and researchers haven't yet explored why such a difference in body image might exist. But that didn't stop Sean Cole of member station WBUR in Boston from going out in search of some answers from the study's authors and beyond.

SEAN COLE REPORTING: One of the authors is a psychologist named Harrison Pope. For the last 20 years or so, he's been researching a disorder that he calls muscle dysmorphia, in which men are so fixated on building their bodies up that they've become pathological. Pope says the disorder is common enough that some guys have a nickname for it.

Dr. HARRISON POPE (Psychologist): Bigorexia, meaning sort of a reverse of anorexia nervosa, in which a guy looks in the mirror and thinks he looks too small when he's actually big.

5   COLE: Of course, it's a long way from wanting more muscles to having full-blown bigorexia, but Pope says a lot of men have a bit of the bigorexic in them. In the course of his research, he conducted a body image test with about 200

men in America and Europe. Each sat down in front of a computer screen depicting a little cartoon man that they could make fatter or thinner, brawnier or scrawnier. They were then asked to mold the cartoon into the image of their own body, the average male body, their ideal physique and the body women desire most.

Dr. POPE: In Austria, Paris and Boston, the men thought that women wanted a male body with about 20 or 25 pounds more muscle than an ordinary man. But when we then turned around and gave the computer to actual women in these cultures, the women chose a perfectly ordinary-looking male body without all of the added muscle packed on it.

COLE: Pope wondered if the same would hold true in Asian cultures, where attitudes surrounding masculinity are generally different than ours. So in June of 2002, he enlisted the help of Jeff Yang, a young Taiwanese-American Harvard student who happened to be going to Taiwan to visit family.

For the most part, Yang is a perfectly normal biochemistry major, a little on the slimmer side, maybe a little shy, and suddenly he finds himself administering this same computerized body image test to 55 Taiwanese college guys. As it turns out, they were a lot more accurate when it came to the body women desire most, overestimating by only five pounds of muscle. Yang says he also interviewed a bunch of doctors and trainers about body image while he was there, using the Mandarin word for muscle, which is. . .

Mr. JEFF YANG: Xixo(ph).

COLE: . . . the same as the Mandarin word for chicken meat. Yang says his interviewees became confused.

10 Mr. YANG: They thought I was asking if Taiwanese guys are afraid of chicken meat. The idea that somebody would be concerned about their muscularity is just so foreign in Taiwan that this word, uxixo,' they would associate it with chicken meat first.

COLE: Yang and Pope say muscle dysmorphia is almost unheard of in Asia. Their theories as to why this is range from differences in pop culture and media advertising to centuries-old ideas of what makes a man in both cultures. Yang told me that the Confucian ideal of masculinity is twofold. First, you have to have. . .

Mr. YANG: Wen.

COLE: That's W-E-N, which relates to a kind of cultural and academic prowess.

Mr. YANG: And also, wu.

15 COLE: Spelled W-U, which deals with physicality and martial or military skill.

Mr. YANG: The traditional notion of the ideal or essence of masculinity, it's put more emphasis on 'wen' over 'wu.'

COLE: But there's another factor in Asia that seems to blur the line between wen and wu a bit.

(Soundbite of person practicing kung fu)

COLE: We'll call it the Bruce Lee factor.

(Soundbite of person practicing kung fu)

Mr. YAO LI: I was brought up bringing for the wen, but I always liked wu.

20 COLE: This is Yao Li, a well-developed kung fu instructor in a martial arts school in Boston. We sat down in his studio together before his morning class. As a boy growing up in Taiwan, he says, he wanted to be like the heroes in the martial arts stories he was reading.

Mr. YAO: But I want to be more than just muscular. I want to learn the secrets, too. Like, the internal, like, Well, I'm going to use my chi to beat you up.'

COLE: 'Use my energy.'

Mr. YAO: Right, exactly. 'I'm going to use my chi to beat you up.'

COLE: The way Yao Li sees it, male physicality in America is actually trending away from brawn and more toward chi. Jeff Yang, on the other hand, says he's noticed that boy bands in Taiwan are starting to buff up a little bit, not that he listens to those bands. If that's true, the women of Taiwan might be a little bummed out about it.

(Soundbite of door slamming)

25 COLE: Since I didn't have time to actually go to Taiwan, I traveled from my office down one flight of stairs to an English-language school below.

(Soundbite of footsteps)

Unidentified Woman: OK. What's that word when you have three at one time?

Unidentified Student #1: Twins.

Unidentified Student #2: Twins.

Unidentified Student #3: Twins.

30 Unidentified Woman: Twins is two.

COLE: There were two Taiwanese women in the class I attended, and I'd heard something about one of them in particular that made me think she'd be a good spokesperson for the women of Taiwan. She usually goes by the name A-Mei.

A-MEI: In Taiwan, girls like men look fit. Fit.

COLE: Mm-hmm.

A-MEI: And if he has a big muscle and the girl will—How do you say?

Unidentified Woman: Run away.

35 A-MEI: Run away.

COLE: Run away?

A-MEI: Yes.

COLE: I'm sure that any guy that made A-Mei run away would be heartbroken. She's intensely beautiful. She is also one of the most famous pop stars in Asia, the Christina Aguilera of Taiwan. She just happens to be studying English in the

States for a few months. If you don't believe me, listen to how Jeff Yang reacted when I told him she was here. She's his aunt's favorite singer.

Mr. YANG: I really—I'm astonished.

40 COLE: Yeah. Yeah. I thought you would know who she was.

Mr. YANG: Oh, man. Wow.

COLE: I also told him what A-Mei said about muscle-bound men.

Mr. YANG: Anecdotally, I know, just talking with some friends in Taiwan, that for them, it's more important how a guy's facial features look rather than their muscularity. They might like Tom Cruise more than Vin Diesel or something.

COLE: Of course, if you're a single American male listening to this, none of what you've heard so far is going to be much help, unless you're planning to spend time in Taiwan. But rest assured, in another extremely scientific survey I conducted, of 12 American college girls, only one preferred really buff guys; good news for the average male, but not, as it turns out, for researcher Harrison Pope. That's right, Dr. Pope is jacked.
You know what's really ironic, Dr. Pope, is you are really buff. Like, you have huge arms. I'm looking at you, and you're like—I mean, how much can you bench press?

45 Dr. POPE: Well, I used to bench press 315, but now I have rotator cuff problems. So I can't do any bench presses at all, or else my shoulder starts to hurt.

COLE: Still, at least for now he probably won't be turning any heads in Taiwan. For NPR News, I'm Sean Cole in Boston.

Copyright ©2005 National Public Radio®. All rights reserved. No quotes from the materials contained herein may be used in any media without attribution to National Public Radio. This transcript may not be reproduced in whole or in part without prior written permission. For further information, please contact NPR's Permissions Coordinator at (202) 513-2030.Record Number: 200503152104

Reflect & Write

❏ Analyze the use of humor in this essay, from the construction of the term "Bigorexia" to the confusion about "xixo" as meaning "chicken meat." Why might the essay rely on international stereotypes in this way?

❏ How does the disclosure that Dr. Pope "is jacked" alter his credibility? Does it change the way you evaluate his claims about body image and masculinity?

❏ The essay makes a claim that boy bands in Taiwan are taking on American standards for physical appearance. How might this be true in other countries? Is there a reciprocal effect?

❏ **Write:** Conduct your own series of interviews about body image. Compose a script with your questions and then record your answers. You might show your subjects ads from magazines, clips of musical performers, or scenes from movies. How does the popular media influence constructions of body image across cultures?

PERSPECTIVES ON THE ISSUE

1. After analyzing billboards in your community, write an essay about the representations of female body image in contemporary advertisements. Draw upon at least two ads that you find on your own. Make a powerful argument about contemporary notions of ideal female beauty.

2. Visit the Love Your Body Day Website at http://loveyourbody.nowfoundation.org/oncampus.html. Analyze the visual banner that runs along the top of the site. How does this make an effective visual argument for "Love Your Body"? Now compare this banner to the Dove Real Beauty Campaign found at http://www.campaignforrealbeauty.ca/. What different strategies are used by each? Is one more successful than the other? If so, why?

3. Harrison Pope transformed his article, "Evolving Ideals of Male Body Image as Seen Through Action Toys" into a section of his book *The Adonis Complex* (NY: The Free Press, 2000). Locate this book in the library. Read pages 40–46 in *The Adonis Complex* and then write an essay in which you discuss the ways in which Pope developed the prose and content of his short piece into a longer research argument.

4. Having read the NPR transcript of "Cultural Differences Seen in Male Perceptions of Body Image," now listen to the audio essay itself on NPR.com through http://www.npr.org/templates/story/story.php?storyId=4536230. What do the audio elements add to the argument? Does the tone or mood of the piece change with the addition of sound? Are the two pieces equally persuasive? Why or why not?

FROM READING TO RESEARCH

1. Use a reference book such as Charles Goodrum and Helen Dalrymple's *Advertising in America* (NY: Harry N. Abrams Inc., 1990) or your own archival work with old magazines to get a sense of how magazines constructed ideals of beauty at a particular historical moment. Using specific examples from the advertisements and/or vintage magazine articles, write a persuasive essay that defines one of the foundations of beauty for that context.

2. Using both primary and secondary sources, write a research paper that compares contemporary concepts of male and female body image as represented in one of the following: advertising, television, or toys. You should focus on a specific historical period (the 1950s, the 1980s, current day) to narrow your argument.

FASHION STATEMENTS

Can we change the way people see us by purposefully altering our appearance through physical changes such as tattoos, piercings, or body art? Can we change how people look at us by deliberately putting on certain jewelry, clothes, or accessories? When we wear fashion, in many ways we seek to change the way we are seen by society. We use fashion to mark our bodies in a certain way and, in the process, we use visual markers to make a new argument about who we are. Sometime this change is subtle: a tattoo hidden under clothes or a small cross around our necks. Other times, these visual signs stand as announcements to the world, such as when we wear a mohawk or certain clothes. In this way, we use fashion to make a statement about what we like, what we believe, where we belong, and how we think of ourselves in the world. As we'll learn in the pages that follow, fashion has long been used to make a statement about identity, values, and meaning in society. That is, fashion statements have served as arguments for centuries.

From the earliest body etches on Easter Island to the most recent trend in Asian characters inked on American teenagers, tattoos have long conveyed great personal and cultural meaning. Specifically, tattoos represent a way of permanently marking the body—and therefore permanently making a public statement—about one's identity, one's loves, one's history, and one's community. As Margo DeMello explains in her essay in this chapter, tattooing in America was largely the practice of working-class men, and this history contributes to our stereotypical notion that only bikers, sailors, and convicts wear tattoos.

We are not surprised to find manly men wearing tattoos so that people will look at them a certain way. For example, the Detroit Pistons basketball player Rip Hamilton sports a tattoo that says "RIP," a nickname he shares with his father. According to *Sports Illustrated*, "the tombstone and the hand coming out of the grave means basketball for life." In this way, this athlete views his marked body as a sign of his professional commitment and his personal passion. Other celebrities with tattoos include Angelina Jolie, Tommy Lee, 50 Cent, the Rock, and Eminem, not to mention Dennis Rodman. We'll look at many such examples. But we'll also look at how everyday people choose tattoos as fashion statements with powerful messages. From firefighters in New York City using tattoos to communicate their grief, to women who are increasingly turning to tattooing as a form of writing, from full body art in Japanese motif to tribal bracelets worn by Britney Spears and tattoos on the Spice Girls, today, more and more people are turning to tattoos as a fashionable way to mark the body.

The model in Figure 10.9, walking down the runway at a fashion show while the crowd looks on, wears her tattoo as an accessory, the same way she would a bracelet or necklace. How might viewers be

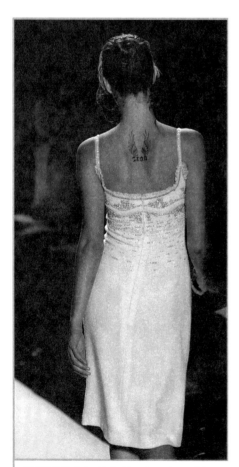

FIGURE 10.9 In this fashion show, the model shows off not only her outfit but the body art tattooed on her neck as well.

influenced by this fashion statement? What argument does the model make about her identity? How does tattooing work as writing on the body? How does this model's body suggest the way that writing in this medium has changed over the centuries since Captain Cooke first noticed men in Tahiti making markings on their bodies? How does the approval of the crowd in this photo support a shift in the cultural meaning of tattoos in society? As DeMello tells us, "Tattooing has moved from being a symbol of the outcast to that of the rock star, model, and postmodern youth, and with this shift in public perception has come a shift in meaning as well, as tattoo moves from stigma to status." We'll study the many ways that tattoos function as fashion statements, as arguments against society, and as ways of creating cross-cultural solidarity.

FIGURE 10.10 Fashion and personal identity are strongly interrelated in this photograph of a young girl shopping for clothes.

We'll also move from markings made on the body to clothing and accessories used to change the way the body looks. Specifically, we'll examine ways of using clothing fashion to make a statement about who we are, what we believe in, and how we want others to see us. Consider the woman in Figure 10.10. She wears a headscarf that matches her colorful outfit. She is shopping for jeans and showing a careful attention to style and the meaning of the clothes she wears. How does her choice of fashion shape the way we look at her? What if her headscarf and outfit were completely black? How would we look at her identity differently?

In the pages that follow, we'll study how clothing can function as a visible sign of our religious values—whether this be a cross, a yarmulke, or a headscarf. We'll ask whether, when we wear such items, are we freely expressing our private beliefs or are we making a powerful rhetorical statement to society at large? We'll also look at people who wear religion as a fashion trend and ask, is it a way of spreading the faith or a disrespectful tarnishing of sacred visual symbols? Has it become, as Paul Mitchell observes below, the "branding" or "commodification" of religion? These questions, and the recent debates over wearing religious jewelry or clothing in schools and countries across the globe, will be ones to explore.

Reflect & Write

- How do the two images shown here provide very different arguments about the values and cultures of the people?
- As we see in Figure 10.9, more and more women are choosing to mark their bodies through tattooing. Taking into account the rise of temporary tattoos, consider the way tattoos function as a fashion accessory and the statements they make in that context.
- Analyze the elements of Figure 10.10. What elements surprise you? What aspects can you relate to? Knowing that this image is one in a series from a photo essay entitled "Looking Beyond the Veil," what argument do you think this image is trying to make about fashion, religion, and youth culture?
- **Write:** When is a fashion statement a way of changing our understanding of religion? Write an essay in which you argue your stance on this subject; be sure to provide concrete examples on the subject and use images wherever possible.

■ **Margo DeMello** *published this article while in the Department of Anthropology at San Francisco State University. She is the author of* Bodies of Inscription: A Cultural History of the Modern Tattoo Community *(Duke University Press, 2000). She has also edited a collection entitled* Pierced Hearts and True Love: A Century of Drawings for Tattoos *(Hardy Marks, 1996). Currently, DeMello is the president and executive director of House Rabbit Society, the only nonprofit rabbit rescue organization, based in Richmond, California.*

"Not Just for Bikers Anymore": Popular Representations of American Tattooing

Margo DeMello

Consider the following scenes: On October 15, 1989, the Sacramento-based Living Art Association held their first "Living Art Exhibition" at the Hoggshead Saloon in Sacramento, California. The event was held in order to "elevate the status of tattooing to a legitimate art form" (Living Art Association pamphlet), and to correct what was seen as a negative perception of tattooing among the non-tattooed public. As such, local media representatives were invited to the show, and indeed, it made the 6:00 news. Another scene: From April 10th through the 14th, 1991, the National Tattoo Association held their twelfth annual show at the Garden Grove Hyatt Regency, in Southern California. Here, too, tattooed participants discussed tattooing with reporters in terms which were meant to legitimate tattoos. As one attendee put it, "It [tattooing] really is an art form. I mean, the sailor's tattoo is gone" (Nilsen E1). And finally, on December 5, 1992, at the American Anthropological Association's annual conference held at the San Francisco Hilton, there was a panel devoted to discussions of tattooing, piercing, cosmetic surgery and other forms of body modification. Liesl Gambold, from UCLA, discussed some of the motivations given by her informants for acquiring their fine art tattoos, which included self-control, empowerment, and a means of creating a sense of self.

The National convention, attended by over 4,000 tattooists, tattooees, and curiosity seekers from all over the world, was the most well-rounded, in terms of those attending, of the three events. Participants ranged from punks and members of the gay piercing subculture (many sporting facial piercings which at previous National shows had been disallowed) to bikers and professionals. The media focus on the convention was typical of most media treatments of tattooing today, in that it both perpetuated some common tattoo stereotypes, and at the same time attempted to dispel others. Nilsen, for example, in his article in *The Arizona Republic*, discusses the convention attendees, and notes a plethora of what he calls the "three B's: beards, breasts and beer bellies" (E1), yet he also maintains that the art itself has come a long way from "Popeye anchors, 'Death Before Dishonor' daggers, or 'Mothers'" (E1).

The Living Art Exhibit, on the other hand, was a strictly local event, attended by Sacramento area tattooists and their clients. Even though most of

Seeing Connections
Look at "Spotlight on your Argument" in Chapter 6 for a discussion of ways to develop your authorial stance in persuasive writing based on research.

the Sacramento tattooists at that time and a large number of their clientele were bikers, and the tattoos that they create are largely biker-style,[1] the organizers were eager to educate—via the journalists and their cameras—the public about the "fine art" aspects of tattooing, and to dispel any stereotypes of tattoos and their wearers being "low-class" ("low-class" and "biker" are terms that are usually equated in media portrayals of tattooing). Were they successful? To my mind, no. The event's participants did get to see themselves on the evening news (some of the women, and a few of the men, wore evening wear for this), but the coverage was limited to the spot at the end of the program (where they put the humorous or odd human interest stories).

And finally, the AAA conference panel included five papers on tattooing, three of which (by Liesl Gambold, Brenda Campbell and Elizabeth Miercke) focused on modern American tattoo culture. The tattooed individuals interviewed for these papers represented, like those at the Sacramento event, a small subgroup of the tattoo community. Unlike the bikers at the Hoggshead, however, the informants quoted in the AAA papers were all selected because of their non-traditional (read non-low class) status within the community. In other words, most were middle class, educated, and professional. These individuals, speaking through the anthropologists, discussed their relationship with their tattoos (all "fine art" tattoos) in such a way as to further distance themselves from bikers and other low status individuals. In response to why they chose to become tattooed, most informants employed the language of spirituality, self-help, or personal empowerment, a language which was also used by Fraser in her *SF Weekly* article (11) covering the panel.

5   What do all of these events, and the media coverage surrounding them, have in common? All were organized and attended by individuals eager to portray a new culture of tattooing, one that includes, not bikers and other "low lifes," but educated professionals, and which is based upon sophisticated, fine art designs by professional artists, which are again distinguished from the more "primitive" designs of old. The reporters covering the events also emphasized the distinction between biker, sailor, or convict tattoos and the modern forms being promoted at the events, yet they themselves could rarely distinguish between these forms. (This is no surprise because, as I mentioned regarding the Sacramento event, the individuals promoting fine tattooing are often themselves bikers who wear biker tattoos.) But do these portrayals of tattooing and tattooed people, both by the media as well as by members of the tattoo community itself, really give an accurate representation of the community? And if they do not, why would the tattoo community continue to portray itself in terms that are not representative of the whole subculture? Before I attempt to answer these questions, I wish to mention here one more event that I recently attended, but which was *not* covered in the mainstream press (although it has been covered in *Easyriders*, a national biker magazine): The Easyriders Motorcycle Rodeo, held at the Solano County Fairgrounds in Vallejo, California, over the weekend of October 11, 1992. While this was not a tattoo event per se, it did include seven tattooing booths, and a high proportion of the participants at the event were tattooed. There was no discussion at this show, among the organizers, the tattooists or the fans, of a "new" or "improved" tattoo mentality or culture. The tattoos available at the show were inexpensive, based on classic biker designs, and

made no pretensions to approximate fine art. In fact, in a recent issue of *Easyriders* (the biker magazine which sponsored the event), in an article entitled "Fantasies on Flesh," there is an explicit denial of any connection between tattoos and fine art. The author poses the question, "Are tattoos art? 'Fuck, no,' you say, 'tattoos are bitchin!' That's a good response. It shows you ain't a queer art critic" (Solan 39). The biker community represented by *Easyriders*, then, takes a very different stand in regard to the relationship between tattooing and art than we have seen at the other tattoo events.

What these different events, their participants, and the media accounts of them tell us is how modern American tattoo culture is represented by both individuals within and outside of the community. This paper looks at the different ways in which tattooing and tattooed people are defined, through an analysis of three different forums: Mainstream media reports on tattooing, and here I focus on what is said in these accounts, what is not said, and about whom it is said; academic treatments of tattooing, which tend to focus on specific trends within tattooing only *after* they have reached the popular media; and finally, what tattooed people say about themselves—to the press, in their own publications, and to each other. All three avenues contribute to what can be called the popular reading of tattooing in the United States today, a reading which, by focusing on certain privileged groups and meanings associated with tattooing, not only obscures other, equally valid readings, but which in effect silences many less privileged members of the community. Finally, this paper also looks at how such accounts not only represent American tattoo culture, but define and re-define it as well.

The Mainstream Media

I became interested in media representations of tattooing only by accident. For the last three years, friends and colleagues have been clipping articles on tattooing that they have encountered in magazines and newspapers, assuming that they would have something of value for my research on the American tattoo community. After reading a dozen or so of these, in journals as diverse as the *California Aggie*, the *Wall Street Journal,* or *The Los Angeles Times,* I came to the conclusion that they were of extremely limited value, because of the distorted picture of tattoos and tattooed people that they painted. It has only been recently that I've realized that these accounts are valuable precisely because of the distortions, half truths, and myths that they contain, and I began to take a closer look.

Most of the articles on tattooing that I've come across are similar enough in format and content to be placed into one of the following three categories: articles focusing on tattoo artists, articles which focus on tattooed people, and articles which center around events (like those cited in the introduction). Once we get past those basic distinctions, however, virtually all touch on the same themes. The first, and most important element, because it forms the article's prior text, deals with the question of who *used* to get tattoos, or what tattoos *used* to be. Some recent examples: "Tattooing, once only seen on bikers or drunken sailors . . ." (Bojorquez, "Scene" 1); "Americans associated tattoos with either a degenerate psychopath or a good-for-nothing biker" (McAuliffe 19); or "the stereotype of longshoremen or shanghaied sailors" (McCubrey, "Weekend" 8); all of which emphasize the "seedy" side of tattooing's history. This is a crucial element of most such articles because it serves as the foundation on which the author bases the next claim, which is that tattoo customers today are *different*: they are "middle-class, educated and professional, family people" (McCubrey "Weekend" 8), "who wouldn't know a Harley from a Kawasaki" (Bojorquez, "Scene" 1), and may include doctors, bankers, lawyers, and "PhD's." By contrasting these two groups of people (which one young woman, quoted in Werne, refers to as "the stereotypical and the new tattoo generation" (Werne 20), these accounts create a distinction between different types of tattoos and their wearers. Not only do they make a number of claims about bikers, convicts, and other "low lifes" and their tattoos, they place them in the realm of the historical—they *used to* get tattoos, but not any more. This approach is significant as it makes the "new tattoo generation" the only group who now wears tattoos (or at least the only group of significance), thus rendering all others invisible—indeed, it denies them the right to exist, at least in the public eye. But it is also important because these articles give this "new" group of tattooists and their clients a voice with which to represent themselves, as these articles are generally based on interviews with selected tattooed people. Bikers and their ilk are not interviewed for these pieces, and are effectively silenced through this maneuver.

If certain (middle-class, educated) tattooed people are allowed to speak about tattooing in these mainstream publications, what do they say, and about whom do they say it? Those who were interviewed for the articles which I've seen tend to discuss their tattoos in terms of the following general ideas: personal aesthetics, individuality, and spirituality or personal growth. Many of those interviewed maintained primarily aesthetic reasons for getting tattooed, such as the women who commented, "I think it's sexy and sensuous" (McCubrey, "Weekend" 8), or "It's got beauty, it's got spirit, and it speaks to people" (McAuliffe 19). On the other hand, a common sentiment was expressed by one man: [The tattoos express his desire to] "go against what people want you to do. All your life you're computerized to do what people want you to do" (19), and by another who said "It's a way of defining yourself. . . . It's a way of saying, I'm unique, I'm one of a kind" (19), and a third, "The power of the tattoo is in its ability to express individuality and in its permanence" (Werne 20). These men choose to focus on the uniqueness of their tattoos, and how the tattoo in rum makes them unique. But by far the most popular tattoo discourse today centers around notions of personal growth and borrows its language from the New Age and self-help movements of the 1970s and 1980s. Explanations which draw on these arenas can be simple, "My name means moon in Sanskrit [to explain a moon tattoo]" (Bojorquez, "Scene" 1) or complicated, "For me they are rites of passage. . . . My tattoos usually come at important times in my life" (McAuliffe 19) or "Tattoos are something you can relate to in a visceral way, they are archetypal" (Nilsen El). For many individuals interviewed, the following quote could summarize their experiences as well:

[The respondent's] attitude toward tattoos is one of great mysticism. Every tattoo on his well covered body means something to him. He researches his ideas in books and magazines. Sometimes he even has visions in his dreams of what to get next. "For me, it's very spiritual . . . I wear them for balance in life and in the universe." (Orvino 29)

All three discourses—aesthetics, individuality, and personal growth and spirituality—are extremely common in most popular readings of American tattooing today, and can be contrasted with the unspoken, but nevertheless understood, reasons for why people *used to* get tattooed, i.e., they were drunk, it's a macho thing, to fit in with the crowd, or even worse, for no real reason at all. Like the young man quoted above, the middle-class tattoo wearers interviewed for these articles emphasized the amount of time and effort spent preparing for a tattoo, planning what to get, where to have it placed, etc. Tattoos for this group are not a spur-of-the-moment decision, but are a "commitment to the highest degree" (Werne 20). All of the factors which are highlighted in such articles—the educational and professional status of the individual, the aesthetic appeal of the tattoo, the tattoo's ability to create a sense of a self separate from others, and the spiritual potential of the tattoo—can be appreciated and understood even by the non-tattoo wearing, middle-class public. Thus, by first focusing their articles around a select group of middle-class individuals, most of whom have relatively small, inoffensive tattoos; by second, denying all of those who do not fit this category the right to be represented, except as the absent unit of comparison; and third, by centering the discussion around ideas which are very popular outside of the tattoo community, the journalists are able to make the world of tattooing a safe and understandable place for the reader. While many middle-class readers may still view tattooing with a great deal of unease, these articles nevertheless construct a set of meanings for these "new" tattoos that serves to reduce this discomfort, and create a shared understanding.

The Academic Approach

10 Academic treatments of tattooing in the last five years have not deviated very much from the model presented by the mainstream journalists. Most draw the same distinctions between middle-class and low-class tattoo use, without recognizing the role that the media plays in the creation of this boundary.[2] Rubin (233–62), for example, discusses the "primitive" style of traditional American tattoos but quickly dismisses these tattoos in order to focus on the modern, art-influenced styles favored by well known tattoo artists. Nowhere is there an attempt to distinguish between the different forms of traditional tattoo (i.e., biker, sailor, convict, gang, etc.), nor is it noted that these forms are still very much in existence in this country. Such accounts uncritically accept the media portrayals of tattooing, replicating their one-sided view of the community, and once again, they silence those who do not fit the model. Both Rubin (233–62) and Blanchard (11–21) write accounts which attempt to present a summary of the culture, although they are not based on interviews with tattooed individuals, but which focus exclusively on the modern manifestations of tattooing.

In their conference presentations, Gambold, Campbell and Juana Smith all based their research on interviews with members of the tattoo community, but following the popular model, all limited their informant base to include only middle-class individuals with Fine art tattoos. Furthermore, these informants, as well as the researchers who interviewed them, all discussed their tattoos using the same language that we saw used in the popular articles, and in fact, were often better able to articulate some of the more complex and spiritual notions. (Some of those interviewed even used the language of anthropologists—one of Smith's subjects not only described her tattoos as being rites of passage, but cited Victor Turner as well—in their discussions.) Whether because the subjects in these treatments were speaking about their tattoos to anthropologists (who have a well known interest in ritual), or because these people were chosen because they shared a similar philosophy about tattoos with the researchers, these individuals claim that their tattoos provide "a way of making sense of [their] urban lives, which are otherwise nearly devoid of personal rites" (qtd. in Fraser 11), "a sense of personal empowerment" (Smith) and can be used to "assert control over their physical beings to attain more control over their emotional lives" (qtd. in Fraser 11). As in the mainstream publications, these people invest a great deal of meaning in their tattoos, making the analysts' jobs quite easy. The informants seem to have spent so much time thinking through their various motivations for becoming tattooed, and the ways in which the tattoos provide them with a sense of fulfillment, identity, and control, that the anthropologists were left with little analysis of their own to do. Perhaps this is why these articles never do more than accept their subjects' explanations for their tattoos, perhaps restating them in more academic and less pop-psychology terms.

Tattooed People: What They Say About Themselves and Each Other

As we've seen from the media and academic accounts of tattooing, only certain members of the tattoo community are represented in such accounts. Again, I ask the question, do these people speak for the entire community? Through an examination of those publications which are produced within the tattoo community, we can see a greater variety of tattoos, tattooed people, and meanings associated with tattoos than we do in the mainstream and academic treatments, although some elements of the community (such as convicts) continue to remain, for the most part, invisible.

Tattoo Advocate was a glossy magazine produced for two years by Shotsie Gorman, a New Jersey tattoo artist. This magazine promoted fine art tattoos and actively disparaged other, less sophisticated forms of tattoo, as well as the magazines (*Easyriders, Outlaw Biker*, etc.) which display them. The language used in *Tattoo Advocate* reflected the New Age tone that we've seen in popular accounts of tattooing, and indeed, the magazine almost reads as a bible for those seeking spiritual aid through tattoos. The articles focus on Buddhism, the Occult, and tattoos from exotic (i.e., more "spiritual" than our own) cultures and make a number of claims about the "healing potential" of tattoos.[3] This magazine differs from other tattoo publications in that the editor's progressive political and social beliefs are also promoted in its pages, which are definitely not shared by many (most?) members of the tattoo community. *Tattoo Advocate*, while filled with beautiful photographs of fine art tattoos, did not have the support of the community and folded in 1990.

TattooTime, published since 1985, also represents a "highbrow" perspective, and aims at an educated audience (Ed Hardy, the magazine's publisher and editor, maintains that *TattooTime is not* a "fan magazine"). It also deals with issues like spirituality and magic, but it does not come across as "preachy," like *Tattoo Advocate*. The language used here is less New Age, and more academic (indeed, Hardy makes a point of inviting scholars with an interest in tattooing such as Clinton Sanders, Alan Govenar, and Tricia Allen to contribute), and the magazine includes no interviews with tattooed people (unless they are artists). Instead, the emphasis is on the art, history, and cross cultural perspectives of tattooing, and thus spends little time on individuals' personal motivations for getting tattooed. However, *TattooTime* does contribute to the current elitism surrounding tattooing by including in their pages only fine art tattoos, professionally educated and trained tattooists, and middle-class clients. Furthermore, the magazine's cost ($20 per issue) prohibits many lower income people from buying it, thus restricting its readers to those of a certain socio-economic status.

15   *TattooTime* also helped create a popular tattoo discourse through its first issue, called "The New Tribalism." This issue was devoted to the documentation of tattooing in "tribal" cultures such as Borneo, Samoa, New Zealand, Hawaii, and Native America, and included photographs of the tattoos that are being worn among middle-class clients in the West in imitation of this style, called "new tribalism." This magazine was extremely influential in not only creating and promoting a new tattoo style, but also in discussing—for the first time—the international tattoo culture in terms of a "tribe." The concepts of "tribe" and "tribal" have since become, within certain circles, a metaphor for the entire tattoo culture, incorporating as it does notions of both community as well as the currently popular ideology of "primitivism" (or "modern primitivism" per Vale and Juno). Many members of the tattoo community who are also involved in piercing, scarification, branding or other forms of body modification, see themselves as enacting, through body manipulation, ancient rituals which impart deep meaning into their lives. As one heavily tattooed and pierced member of this subculture explained, "Culturally speaking, all primitive societies have done things like this [tattooing, piercing, branding] since the dawn of time. It's a basic, intuitive practice. I share with primitive peoples a certain ideal in my life. I am practicing ritual. It's a religious practice" (Marchand 23). While *TattooTime* does not actively promote this type of lifestyle, their first issue did spark much of the interest in these "primitive" modifications, as well as provide the anthropological and historical background for the new ideology.

     Tattoo has been published since August 1989, and claims to be a magazine produced by and for the mainstream tattoo community, yet it is published by *Easyriders*, a prominent biker magazine, and, like *Easyriders*, it can only be purchased by adults (due to the female nudity). *Tattoo* is a curious magazine, as it aims, like the other publications discussed, to promote the art of tattooing, yet includes in its pages examples of fine art tattoos alongside biker tattoos—tattoos which would be considered low-class by the other publications mentioned. While the editors of *Tattoo* seem unaware of this contradiction, the issue is often taken up by the magazine's readers in the letters to the editor. For instance, in the "Tattoo Mailbox" in the June 1992 issue, Staci L. writes in to express her distaste at "biker-type" tattoos which she feels are "ugly and unattractive" and project an image which "turns off many people".

For the next three months, other readers responded to Staci's letter, most angrily. Iden Rogers, for example, writes:

Staci L., you ask that there be fewer biker-type tattoos in *Tattoo* magazine. You state that they are "ugly and unattractive." I am a long-time Harley rider so, sweet thing, you just pulled on my chain. My Harley, the Harley scene, and "biker-type" tattoos are all very meaningful to me—very much a part of my life. I appreciate jail-house tattooing as well. Biker tattoos, though admittedly often of a grim theme, are not ugly and unattractive to me. (14)

Eric Eberhardt also responds:

Staci L., if you don't like "biker-type" tattoos, then get yourself a fucking fingernail growers handbook to read. . . [She had also requested that fingernail art be included in the magazine.] And the next time you want to see ugly, outlaw biker tattoos, send me your address and I'll make a trip to your place and give you a demonstration of something real. (16)

These letters express the contradiction inherent in a magazine which is both dedicated to promoting mainstream tattoo art, but which also has a committed readership (and staff) of bikers.

Another debate often expressed in the pages of *Tattoo* involves the way in which tattooed women are represented. *Tattoo* features between ten and fifteen different artists and "collectors" in its pages each month, both men and women. The men who are chosen tend to have a large part of their body covered with tattoos; generally a full back piece, both sleeves (arms), and perhaps some leg work or other body work. Women featured in the magazine, on the other hand, often have as few as two or three small-to-medium size tattoos, and are very often shown nude, or at least topless (even when the tattoos are easily visible while clothed). Recently, women have begun writing in to *Tattoo* to complain about the abundance of female nudity in the magazine and have received the following responses:

Your July 1992 issue Mailbox contained a lot of whining about female nudity and untoward sexuality in your magazine from people who claimed to love tattoos but not naked women. These individuals have the option of buying the latest feminist publications and reading them. Let them write to their spirit guides in Now's (sic) publications and ask them to cover tattooing for them Now-stylc. (Kirkham 18)

. . . In her letter she states how distasteful she found female models who, in your magazine, "let everything they own hang out." First, stick to speaking for yourself. If the rest of us would like you to speak for us we will let you know. Second, what those ladies choose to bare is their decision. (Kerns 14)

These letters express not only the writers' feelings about the question of female nudity in the magazine, but also their indignation at what they consider to be *their* magazine being taken over by "yuppies," "queers," and "feminists." As one of the only forums in which bikers, and others considered to be low-class (including convicts, whose letters, and occasionally, art work, can often be found in the magazine), can express themselves and their tattoos. *Tattoo* provides an important arena for tattoos, collectors, and lifestyles excluded from most every other discussion.

The New Hegemony

While tattoos themselves may be counter-hegemonic in the ways in which they challenge dominant notions about the body and how the body is to be used, I would argue that the current discourse found in popular readings of tattooing is not. Through a careful combining of popular discourses of personal growth, self help, and individualism, those promoting tattoos as a middle-class fashion statement/statement of identity have succeeded in making tattoos increasingly safe and sane. Appealing to the post-sixties generation, the modern tattoo culture provides both the symbols, as well as the ideologies, of spiritual, aesthetic and emotional fulfillment. Given that tattoos previously had one reading, derived from their exclusive association with members of the lower classes, how has this reading come to be supplanted, and what are the implications?

American tattooing is a tradition which, since the mid-nineteenth century, has belonged primarily to working-class men, and as we have seen, it has more recently become in addition, a middle class, and often feminine, tradition. Andrew Ross, in his discussion of the appropriation of 1940s Hollywood glamour in gay camp, writes that camp is the "recreation of surplus value from forgotten forms of labor . . . by liberating the objects and discourses of the past from disdain and neglect" (151). In a sense, this is what the modern users of tattooing have done: tattoos have become "liberated" from the province of low lifes, and can now be properly positioned as aspects of fine art. But these (working-class) forms of labor, unlike those used by camp, are not forgotten or deceased, but are still very much in use by other people. As Judith Williamson has pointed out (116), like other fashions that are borrowed from lower-class or Third World peoples (i.e., dressing in "rags," being suntanned, etc.), such looks are only fashionable when the individuals who wear them are not themselves poor or dark-skinned. Black people don't try to tan themselves (and in fact, often try to appear as light-skinned as possible) and poor people, when they can, try to dress up to separate themselves from their working-class lifestyles. This type of middle-class appropriation on the part of the middle-class purveyors of tattooing, while it may appear liberatory, "shows how characteristics of social difference are appropriated within our culture to provide the trappings of individual difference" (116).

20   Eric Hobsbawm, in his introduction to *The Invention of Tradition*, looks at how traditions are often invented, and notes that such traditions are rarely grounded in an existing system of beliefs and actions. Aram Yengoyan, in his paper on the development of traditions in Southeast Asia, maintains that such traditions are not created in a vacuum, but must be based on a prior text that "provides the intellectual and emotional grounding from which the new symbols and institutions are understood and recast to maintain continuity" (10). While I agree with Yengoyan that the notion of prior text is crucial in order for a new cultural symbol to become tradition, there are complicating factors operating when such a symbol is borrowed, rather than wholly invented *in situ.* In the case of American tattooing, the symbol was appropriated from the working class into the middle class in the 1970s, while continuing to remain, as well, within the working class community. As the new middle-class tattooists and their customers did not, and still do not, possess the lower- or working-class prior text (economic and social marginalization, as well as a

more practical, less "sacred" conception of the body) necessary to make tattoos a meaningful part of their lives, the previous text is ignored and a new text created.

This new text was created through three different operations, the first of which involved the creation of two separate tattoos, one lower-class and one middle-class, each with separate levels of artistry, and separate levels of meaning. Through a recasting of American tattoos into two opposed groups, traditional/low-class vs. fine art, and by associating certain individuals with each group, differences in tattoo forms are linked to patterns of social stratification. Thus the borders between the groups are maintained, not for aesthetic purposes, but for social and political ones. By publicly denouncing the lower-class forms, and even (as we have seen in recent media publications) denying that they even exist, the promoters of this new form are able to separate themselves from a tradition that is seen as negative, yet they are able to retain the symbol itself. As Yengoyan states, "The wholesale borrowing of foreign and distant ideologies into contexts not possessing the prior texts does not invoke the intellectual and emotional sustenance required of action and political mobilization unless these foreign ideologies are culturally mediated" (10). This cultural mediation occurs in the pages of popular (and academic) journals across the country which redefine tattooing, and thus restratify the tattoo community, on the basis of middle-class standards of taste—standards which ultimately form the basis for the new prior text. This prior text, which includes notions of fine art, spirituality, personal growth, and personal empowerment, has much of its origins in the New Age movement which began in the 1970s, and thus the language which would later serve to define modem tattoos was born at the same time that tattooing began to spread into the middle-class.

Finally, as the history of tattooing in the United States has been denied, a new history must be created, this one based not on an American history of sailors, prostitutes, criminals and bikers, but on a mythical, primitive past. This fictionalized past thus gives legitimacy to a cultural tradition which is seen as low-class, and furthermore, naturalizes it. It is my contention that this final stage in the redefining of American tattooing occurred around 1985 with the publication of the first issue of *TattooTime,* called "The New Tribalism." Since that magazine came out, many in the tattoo community have come to envision all tattooed people as belonging to a tribe, and sharing a culture based on a natural, or instinctive, impulse. This "primitivist" philosophy, articulated most clearly in the Re/Search volume, *Modern Primitives,* represents a desire on the part of its adherents to return to a primitive past, which was supposedly honest, egalitarian, full of ritual, etc.[4] That people have practiced tattooing and other forms of body modification in most "primitive" societies around the world at one time or another gives extra support to the claim that tattooing is a "natural" act. Not only is tattooing a means to symbolically undo the conquest of the primitive world, but it is itself conceived of as a natural symbol (which partly explains the popularity of symbolic anthropologists Victor Turner and Mary Douglas in many people's accounts).

In summary, tattooing has moved from being a symbol of the outcast to that of the rock star, model, and postmodern youth, and with this shift in public perception has come a shift in meaning as well, as tattoo moves from stigma to status. A final question: does the fact that tattoos have become absorbed into certain segments of the middle class as symbols of identity and fashion mean that their subversive meaning has been entirely neutralized? Does appropriation necessarily mean recuperation? According to Kaja Silverman, in her article "Notes on a Fashionable Discourse," it does not. Rather, she writes that because "deviant dress" is often absorbed by the fashion industry, it means that it has:

won not only a style war, but a pitched cultural battle. It is no small thing to effect a change in mainstream fashion. . . . Clothing not only draws the body so that it can be seen, but also maps out the shape of the ego . . . then every transformation within a society's vestimentary code implies some kind of shift within its ways of articulating subjectivity. (149)

Whether this is the case with tattooing remains to be seen. If a shift of this magnitude can occur within a period of less than ten years, through a simple process of denying the past (and to some extent, the present) and then recreating it to appeal to a different population, this says something about the ability of individuals to invent not only tradition, but meaning as well. That this transformation occurred largely within the pages of mainstream and non-mainstream media publications about tattooing in turn tells us something about the power of the media to affect, if not real social change, but at least symbolic transformations.

Notes

[1] I define biker tattoos according to style and imagery. Stylistically, biker tattoos are generally all-black, although many have some additional color, and are created with a one-needle machine which gives the tattoo a "fine-line" (rather than bold) appearance. The images favored in biker tattoos include Harley-Davidson motorcyles and HD engines, skulls, and other death images, anti-social slogans ("Fuck the World," "Live Fast, Die Young"), nude women, and fantasy imagery such as dragons, wizards, and castles. Technically, these tattoos can range from extremely well executed to extremely primitive, depending on the skills of the artist.

[2] For exceptions to this, see Govenar ("Variable Context"), who gives a close reading of tattooing among Chicanos and convicts; and Sanders, who conducts his interviews at a number of tattoo studios and does not limit his informants to educated members of the middle class.

[3] See Govenar for a discussion of how tattoos became, in the 1970s, not only chic, but during this time they also "appealed to what Christopher Lasch has called the 'therapeutic sensibility'" (*Issues* 93). Some tattoo artists during this time assumed a therapeutic role, and likened themselves to psychologists or psychiatrists in their ability to help customers/patients overcome emotional difficulties.

[4] In the introduction to *Modern Primitives*, Vale and Juno allow that this notion of the primitive is "dubiously idealized and only partially understood" (4), and thus state "What is implied by the revival of 'modern primitive' activities is the desire for, and the dream of, a more ideal society" (4). Here then is the attempt not only to mimic an idealized past, but to (per Yengoyan) *outdo* it.

Works Cited

Blanchard, Marc. "Post-Bourgeois Tattoo: Reflections on Skin Writing in Late Capitalist Societies." *Visual Anthropology Review* 7. 2 (1991): 11–21.

Bojorquez, Jennifer. "Body Images." *The Sacramento Bee* 10 July 1992: Scene 1–3.

Campbell, Brenda. "Mirrors and Windows: The Movement of Meaning in Tattoo." American Anthropological Association conference, San Francisco, Dec. 1992.

Eberhardt, Eric. Letter. *Tattoo* June 1992: 16.

Fraser, Laura. "Tattoo You: The Psychology of Body Manipulations." *SF Weekly* 9 Dec. 1992: II.

Gambold, Liesl. "Personal Symbols and Public Displays of Affliction: Tattoo Culture in Urban America." American Anthropological Association conference, San Francisco, Dec. 1992.

Govenar, Alan. *Issues in the Documentation of Tattooing in the Western World.* Ph.D. diss., University of Texas, Dallas, 1984.

Govenar, Alan. "The Variable Context of Chicano Tattooing." *Marks of Civilization.* Ed. Arnold Rubin. Los Angeles: Museum of Cultural History, UCLA, 1984: 209–17.

Hobsbawm, Eric. Introduction. *The Invention of Tradition.* Eds. Eric Hobsbawm and Terence Ranger. Cambridge: Cambridge UP, 1983: 1–14.

Kerns, Michael. Letter. Tattoo. Oct. 1992: 14.

Kirkham, Ray. Letter. Tattoo. Sept. 1992: 18–19.

Kodl, Kim. "Tattoos: Campus Skin Sketches." *The California Aggie 7* Nov. 1990: Praxis 1–2.

Libman, Gary. "Illustrated Man Is No Skinflint." *Los Angeles Times* 20 Apr. 1990: E1.

Marchand, Shoshana. "Hooked: Mind and Body Games among the Modern Primitives." *Bay Guardian* 27 May 1992: 23–25.

McAuliffe, Mike. "Body by Hardy." *Argus* 19 Feb. 1990: 19-20.

McCubrey, Joanne. "Walking Art." *Mountain Democrat* 9 Feb. 1990: Weekend 8–9.

Miercke, Elizabeth. "American Ethnography and Body Tattoos." American Anthropological Association conference, San Francisco, Dec. 1992.

Nilsen, Richard. "Fine Art in the Flesh." *Arizona Republic* 14 Apr. 1991: E1.

Orvino, Rachel. "Pins and Needles: Tattoo Art Struts Its Stuff." *Sacramento News and Review* 18 June 1992: 28–29.

Rogers, Iden. Letter. *Tattoo* Sept. 1992: 14–16.

Ross, Andrew. *No Respect: Intellectuals and Popular Culture.* New York: Routledge, 1989.

Rubin, Arnold. 'Tattoo Renaissance." *Marks of Civilization.* Ed.. Arnold Rubin. Los Angeles: Museum of Cultural History, UCLA, 1988: 233–62.

Sanders, Clinton. *Customizing the Body: The Art and Culture of Tattooing.* Philadelphia: Temple UP. 1989.

Silverman, Kaja. "Notes on a Fashionable Discourse." *Studies in Entertainment: Critical Approaches to Mass Culture.* Ed. Tania Modleski. Bloomington: Indiana UP, 1986: 139–52.

Smith, Juana. "Women and Tattoos." American Anthropological Association conference, Chicago, Nov. 1989.

Solan, J.J. "Fantasies on Flesh." *Easyriders* Oct. 1992: 39–43.

Vale, V., and Andrea Juno. *Modern Primitives.* San Francisco: Re/Search, 1989.

Werne, Lisa. "Joining the Realm of the Marked. *Orion* 25 Sep. 1991: 20.

Williamson, Judith. "Woman Is an Island." *Studies in Entertainment: Critical Approaches to Mass Culture.* Ed. Tania Modleski. Bloomington; Indiana UP, 1986: 99–118.

Yengoyan, Aram. "Culture and Ideology in Contemporary Southeast Asian Societies: The Development of Traditions." Unpublished ms., 1989.

Reflect & Write

❏ This article opens with an examination of some of the persuasive messages reflected by bodies marked with tattoos: "self control, empowerment, and a means of creating a sense of self." Do such messages, sported by the new professional class of tattoo bearers who prefer "fine art" over "primitive" designs, actually pose a challenge to "biker, sailor, or convict" tattoos? Or can you see a connection between such seemingly distinct groups of people?

❏ Margo DeMello wrote this article as a contribution to the field of cultural anthropology. How does she establish her own authorial stance in the first four pages? How does she insert her "I" into this argument and is this an effective tool of persuasion for her piece?

Seeing Connections
Look at "Spotlight on your Argument" in Chapter 6 for a discussion of ways to develop your authorial stance in persuasive writing based on research.

❏ How does DeMello make her concluding question—whether tattooing has shifted from stigma to status symbol or from subversive message to sign of conformity—part of a larger argument about the role of the media in shaping our opinions about the visual world?

❏ **Write:** Locate a variety of tattoos both in magazines and on the Internet. Following DeMello's example, conduct a rhetorical analysis and compare three of them to compose your own argument about class and meaning.

■ *As tattoos have become more accepted in popular culture, they have become increasingly featured as modes of self-expression. From PETA's anti-fur "Think Ink, Not Mink" campaign (which has featured celebrities as varied as rock star Tommy Lee, NBA player Dennis Rodman, and actress Franka Potente) to photographic tributes, such as Scott Veldhoen's striking photographs of tattoo culture, reproduced in Michael Atkinson's* Tattooed: The Sociogenesis of a Body Art *(2003), the image of the tattooed body increasingly functions as a means of making a cultural argument.*

Visual Reading

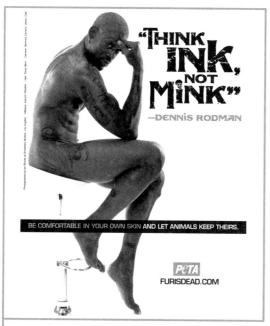

FIGURE 10.11 Dennis Rodman showcases his tattooes in this poster for the "Think Ink, Not Mink" PETA campaign.

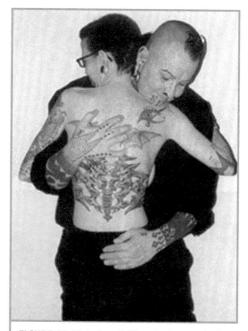

FIGURE 10.12 In Scott Veldhoen's photograph of a close embrace, the couple's body art contributes to their dramatic self-expression.

Reflect & Write

❏ What arguments do these two images pose about the changing meaning of tattoos in our culture—from outlaw to fashion follower, from rebel to conformist? Analyze the message of each image.

❏ What message is Dennis Rodman sending through posing for a PETA poster? If you learn that this poster is part of the campaign against wearing fur, how does this change your interpretation of his body as a text? What difference does it make if a person tattoos for individual reasons or if a person poses as a tattooed person for a particular cause?

❏ How might the second image of the couple be used as part of a poster campaign? What would be the message? Draft a proposal for the production of this poster.

❏ **Write:** Search out additional tattoos and write a short review of the patterns in marked bodies you discover. What arguments are being made by the wearers of these fashion statements?

■ **George Bodarky**, *assistant news and public affairs director for WFUV, has covered New York City issues ranging from humorous examination of local hipsters to serious stories on homelessness or historic architecture. In 2002, Bodarky's Saturday morning program,* Cityscape, *won a gold medal for Best Public Affairs Program for a show delving into the September 11th terrorist attacks. The following is a transcript of an interview conducted by George Bodarky as a follow-up to the September 11th attacks. The transcript integrates Bodarky's report with notations on the environmental sound effects (NATSOTs) used to punctuate his narrative.*

Interview: Tattooing Their Grief

George Bodarky

The arms, chests, and backs of scores of New York City firefighters and police officers are now lifetime memorials to their lost colleagues. Many are choosing to get tattoos to remember the September 11th attacks—giving them a way to silently wear their grief. George Bodarky reports. . .

((NATSOT)) tattoo drilling

Since September 11th, Island Tattoo on Staten Island has inked memorial pieces onto more than 250 New York City firefighters and police officers.

The parlor's owner, who goes by the name of Dozer, is a heavy-set man with long, frizzy hair in a pony tail. He's wearing blue scrubs and gold chains around his neck. His arms are covered in tattoos. Ironically one of them features the Manhattan skyline and includes the now crumbled Twin Towers. Dozer says he's donating 50 dollars from every 100 dollar tattoo to charities for the families of uniformed personnel killed in the September 11th attacks. He says since the disaster, there have been days when all his staff works on is memorial pieces for firefighters and police officers—who often share their stories about their lost colleagues or what happened at Ground Zero . . .

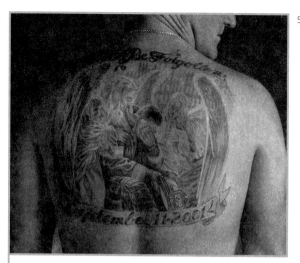

FIGURE 10.13 Tattooing functions as a form of memorial for many firefighters who lost co-workers on September 11, 2001.

5   "The tattoo means so much to these firemen. Some of them say it's a closure act. That they finally feel that they've done something that helps them heal."

Dozer says most firefighters are choosing to get a tattoo designed by the son of a Staten Island firefighter and four other firemen. The tattoo is in the shape of the firefighter's badge with the twin towers on the inside. In the very back—an American Flag—flapping in the wind. The top has the letters FDNY. On the bottom are four "fives"—the fire departments' code for fallen firefighters. Dozer recalls one firefighter who wanted the initials of all of the members of his department who were killed on September 11th to be included in his tattoo. The fireman was from Rescue Five on Staten Island. The station lost a total of eleven firefighters. . .

"The way that he was when I started writing down, tattooing the initials on him. I honestly didn't think he was going to sit for the whole entire thing. Every time I got to one set of initials. This man watched every set that I put on his leg and every time I put one set down, he felt the pain of that person lost. And it took a lot for me not to lose it myself."

((NATSOT)) police scanner, street sound

So far, four firefighters from Staten Island's Rescue Five have decided to turn their bodies into permanent memorials to their lost colleagues. Firefighter Peter Greibesland says he lost a lot of friends on September 11th and wanted a way to show his appreciation for what they did for New York. He's wearing blue FDNY shorts—which makes it hard to miss the tattoo on his outer, right calf—an FDNY badge with angel wings. . .

10   "It symbolizes that a—we'll never forget what happened. And we a—we hope nobody else ever forgets

What happened either. All the men that laid down their lives for others."

The tattoo on Greibesland's right leg is his first and only.

((NATSOT)) tattoo drilling

Dozer—with Staten Island Tattoos—says that's not uncommon. . .

"About 80 percent of these firefighters don't have any tattoos. They come in here and this is the only one they have. The only one they want. That shows you how much and how close they mean to each other."

15   Dozer says his parlor has inked many more tattoos on New York firefighters than police officers—but he says there's no question that members of the NYPD are also turning to body art as a way to remember. And he says that's allowed him to make a very interesting observation. Dozer says the tattoos help to show

that September 11th has drawn The FDNY and the NYPD—which have not always seen eye to eye—closer together. . .

"The majority of tattoos that we did on the NYPD had both a fireman's badge and a policeman's badge right next to each other. That's what they were getting tattooed on them—with the towers behind them. Or a silhouette of a fireman next to a police officer with the towers behind them."

Dozer says aside from New York's finest and bravest, his parlor hasn't seen too much demand for September 11th-related tattoos. . .

"The only general public that gets any type of memorial-type of tattoo with what happened. We are finding out are the relatives of the unfortunate—didn't make it. The son of a firefighter. We got quite a bit of those."

((NATSOT)) tattoo drilling

20   Inside a small room at Staten Island Tattoos, a young Italian man wearing a blue FDNY shirt and red shorts—has his right sneaker off and his leg is resting on a stool. Anthony D'Amico is getting a tattoo on his right, outer calf. Something he designed himself—a firefighters' patch—with a skull in the middle—and a cross around it. Anthony is the son of a firefighter. His father was not on duty at the time of the attacks and is still with us, but seven other members of Ladder Company 132 in Crown Heights, Brooklyn—who Anthony says he knew well—died on September 11th. Anthony says for him getting a tattoo is the right thing to do. . .

"I think it's for pride. I have a lot of pride in these guys. I would have probably done the same thing if I was on the job."

A tattoo artist by the name of Chachi—who's wearing blue scrubs, a sports cap on backwards and has a shot glass through his left ear piercing—is working on Anthony's tattoo. The way Chachi sees it—for those with very close ties to the terrorist attacks—going to a tattoo parlor—is like going to a counseling session. . .

"You hear so many stories from all different guys. Cause I mean these are the guys that were there the whole time for almost the whole thing and they're coming in, getting tattoos and telling you stories about what was happening down there and I don't know. It kind of—I guess it helps them and you know. I guess it's like a therapy."

While some may think a tattoo is the best way for them to honor the victims of 9/11, Doctor Annie Kalayjian, a visiting psychology professor at Fordham University, says it's not something they should rush into. . .

25   "They may be sorry about their actions a couple of months down the line and it may be very difficult to undo those marks and you know tattoos. So I would really caution them before really doing it and talk with someone before doing it."

((Nat Sound)) tattoo parlor sounds

At Staten Island Tattoo—getting memorial pieces inked on their bodies—isn't the only thing that is helping firefighters and others deal with their grief.

The parlor's owner—Dozer—says the so-called "Wall of Honor" he's set up—has also had therapeutic effects. Every time a firefighter gets a memorial tattoo—a Polaroid is taken and posted on the front wall—along with their names and fire companies. . .

"When other firemen come in—or families of the firefighters come in—they go over to the wall and the wall seems to help them. I've had people come here and look at wall. And they swore that one or two of these guys didn't make it and to them that photograph just made their day. They're just so much happier that he wasn't one of the ones. He did get through."

((Nat Sound)) fire engine sound

30   Back at Rescue Five—firefighter Scott Wonica—may be the next to find himself on Dozer's "Wall of Honor..."

"I like drawing. I'm artistic and uhm, I'm planning on designing something with the buildings, the skyline, an angel just looking over Manhattan."

I'm George Bodarky.

Reflect & Write

❏ Describe Bodarky's introduction strategy. How does he replicate writing techniques through his use of sound? How does the transcript reveal this?

❏ Bodarky interviews members of the Staten Island Rescue 5 as well as the tattoo artist who helps survivors use tattoos as visual rhetoric markers. How do such visible signs, etched permanently into the body, help with grief, healing, comfort? What surprising outcome occurred in the use of tattoos as a marker of solidarity between the firefighters and police officers?

❏ Analyze the elements of the 9/11 tattoo carefully. What contribution does each visual element make in constructing the argument about the grief and loss experienced that day? How does choice of image, color, tone, and arrangement persuade the wearer and the viewer to "never forget"?

❏ **Write:** Draft your own radio essay on the power of tattoos to bring together a community in grief. Conduct interviews, record sounds, and compose your transcript.

COLLABORATIVE CHALLENGE

Working in a group of three or four, write your own how-to guide for getting the best tattoo. Base your team's recommendations on research about what can go wrong. You might choose one of the issues presented in this case study—such as how to choose tattoos for self-empowerment, redesigning visual elements for tattoos as memorial, picking a tattoo that has historical meaning, keeping tattooing legal, defying class and gender stereotypes about tattoos—or you might make up your own issue, such as tattoos and hygiene, telling your parents you have a tattoo, or what to do when you no longer love the person whose name is permanently inked on your skin. Include images in your report. When you are done, present your team project to the rest of the class.

■ *In the photo, a woman is wearing a "chador" (a type of open cloak that covers the head), that marks her as belonging to the Islamic religion. What other elements do you notice in the photo? How does it raise questions about identity, purpose, and audience? What might be the photographer's comment on her country of Iran?*

Women of Allah: Rebellious Silence
Shirin Neshat

Reflect & Write

❏ Despite not knowing the background of this Iranian woman, or what the writing on her face even says, what would you say is the argument of this strategically posed photograph?

❏ How does the presence of the gun in the photo change the argument? How does the woman's facial expression contribute to your interpretation?

❏ According to one photography critic, "the chador has an ambiguous character: on the one hand, it is a symbol of the masculine oppression and the violence, but, by another one, it is an identity sign, a resistance sample before the loss of traditions." How might you make multiple, perhaps conflicting, interpretations of this photo as a visual argument about gender, culture, and identity?

❏ **Write:** What does it mean to mark the body with tattoos in this way? Compose three captions for this image that reveal your argument. Write a short explanation of your reasons for composing the captions you did. What have you learned about fashion statements made of tattoo writing, clothing, and props such as guns?

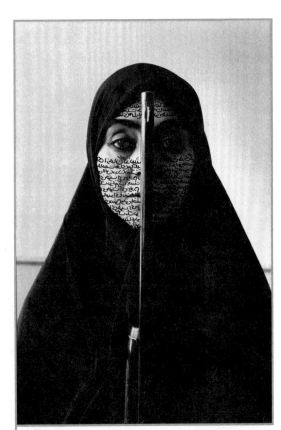

FIGURE 10.14 "Rebellious Silence" is a photograph from Shirin Neshat's series, Women of Allah (1993–1997).

Source: "Rebellious Silence" by Shirin Neshat, 1994. B&W RC print and ink, 11x14 inches (photo taken by Cynthia Preston). Edition of 10+1AP. Copyright Shirin Neshat 1994. Courtesy Gladstone Gallery, New York (SN008).

Persepolis, *a graphic novel by* **Marjan Satrapi***, shares the story of a young girl's experiences growing up in Iran in the middle of the 1979 revolution, as an increasingly fundamentalist regime changed the way she experienced childhood. The part of the novel shown here demonstrates a change in the way girls had to dress for school. The author explains that she uses books to help people understand other cultures: "If people are given the chance to experience life in more than one country, they will hate a little less…That is why I wanted people in other countries to read* Persepolis, *to see that I grew up just like other children." Satrapi has completed a sequel to* Persepolis, *(Random House, 2003); she now lives and writes in France.*

"The Veil," *Persepolis: The Story of A Childhood*

Marjan Satrapi

FIGURE 10.15 This page from Marjane Satrapi's graphic novel *Persepolis*, provides a child's perspective on headscarves in Iranian culture.

Source: "The Veil," translated by Mattias Ripa & Blake Ferris, from PERSEPOLIS: THE STORY OF CHILD-HOOD by Marjane Satrapi, translated by Mattias Ripa & Blake Ferris, copyright (c) 2003 by L'Association, Paris, France. Used by permission of Pantheon Books, a division of Random House, Inc.

Reflect & Write

❏ What is the rhetorical stance of the main character with regard to wearing the veil?

❏ The author states that she wrote *Persepolis* because she was a pacifist; she wanted people "to see that I grew up just like other children." Analyze this scene for the commonalities depicted between the main character and children you know. How does Satrapi construct childhood in Iran as both similar to and different from growing up in America? What message do you think she is trying to convey in this part of the book?

❏ Satrapi asserts that "images are a way of writing." How is that true in this passage from her graphic novel? Make your case by citing concrete evidence from the text.

❏ **Write:** Emulate Satrapi's strategy of writing by story-boarding your argument through cartoons. Then compose a brief description of your project for a future audience.

■ **Ruth La Ferla** *writes articles on fashion for* The New York Times, *where this article originally appeared on March 29, 2005.*

Wearing Their Beliefs on Their Chests

Ruth La Ferla

from top left, a cabala charm over a "coexist" T-shirt; a Derek Lam wrap; cher; a Dsquared sweater; a necklace from Intuition in Los Angeles; Larry favorite T-shirt; a Jesus bag; Trapper Blu at Christopher's in New York.

Source: The New York Times.

Late last week, Trapper Blu, a ski and snowboarding instructor from Wanship, Utah, dropped in with his family at Christopher's, a T-shirt shop in Greenwich Village, and tried on a shirt emblazoned with an image of Jesus and the slogan "Put Down the Drugs and Come Get a Hug." "I would wear this, you bet," Mr. Blu, 23, said, scrutinizing his reflection in the mirror. "The shirt is funny," he added, as he tweaked the brim of his cowboy hat, "but it doesn't make fun of Jesus or anything."

A few blocks south at Urban Outfitters, part of a youth-oriented chain that sells T-shirts along with shag rugs, coffee mugs and multitiered hippie skirts, Jurek Grapentin, visiting from Germany, looked on as a young friend of his examined a shirt printed with a rosary entwined with the words "Everybody Loves a Catholic Girl."

"It's a nice message," Mr. Grapentin, 22, said. "Catholic people most of the time can be so traditional in their thinking. To me this looks more new, more in."

Mr. Blu and Mr. Grapentin are among the legions of the faithful, or the merely fashionable, who are increasingly drawn to the religious themes and imagery—portraits of saints, fragments of scripture—that have migrated in recent months from billboards and bumper stickers to baseball caps, T-shirts, flip-flops and even designer clothing. Such messages are being embraced by a growing number of mostly young people, who are wearing them as a testament of faith or, ironically, as a badge of hipness.

5 "There is no question, religion is becoming the new brand," said Jane Buckingham, the president of Youth Intelligence, a trend-forecasting company. "To a generation of young people eager to have something to belong to, wearing a 'Jesus Saves' T-shirt, a skullcap or a cabala bracelet is a way of feeling both unique, a member of a specific culture or clan, and at the same time part of something much bigger."

There was a time when such symbols were worn discreetly and were purchased mostly at gift shops or Bible stores. Now, emboldened perhaps by celebrities like Ashton Kutcher and Paris Hilton, who are photographed brandishing spiritual messages on shirts and caps, aspiring hipsters and fashion groupies as well as the devout are flaunting similar items, which are widely available at mass-market chains and online.

A casual survey of the Internet last week, including mainstream marketers like Amazon.com, turned up T-shirts, bowling bags, belt buckles and dog tags by the hundreds bearing messages like "Inspired by Christ," "Give All the Glory to God," "I <heart> Hashem" (a Hebrew term for God), "Moses Is My Homeboy" and "Buddha Rocks."

Plastic tote bags and tank tops bearing images of Jesus and the saints stock the shelves of drugstore and cosmetics chains like Walgreens. Some items have worked their way up the fashion chain to stores like Atrium, a New York sportswear outlet popular with college students, which offers polo shirts with images from the Sistine Chapel; and Intuition, a Los Angeles boutique that sells rosaries, cabala bracelets and St. Christopher medals as fashion jewelry.

Come fall, members of the fashion flock, at least those with pockets deep enough, will find chunky sweaters that read "Jesus Loves Even Me" from Dsquared, a label that only a season earlier traded in fashions stamped with obscene images and slogans; a Derek Lam blanket wrap embroidered on the back with a torso-length cross; and Yves Saint Laurent coats and evening dresses seeded with ecclesiastical references.

10 Fashions with spiritual messages are just the latest expression of religion as a pop phenomenon, one that has steadily gained ground with consumers since the best-selling "Left Behind" series of novels, based on a fundamentalist Christian interpretation of apocalyptic prophecy, turned up on bookshelves, and "The Passion of the Christ" became a box-office hit. Their popularity arrives at a time when faith-based issues, including school prayer and the debate over the definition of life, are dividing Americans, a rift reflected to some degree among those who wear the new fashions.

Tanya Brockmeier, 19, another German visitor browsing last week at Urban Outfitters, wears a cross and sees nothing amiss in wearing a religious-theme T-shirt, "so long as it looks modern," she said. "These things are a way of showing my faith." But Larry Bullock, 41, treasures a T-shirt with an image of Jesus as a D. J. Mr. Bullock, the general manager of the Civilian, a gay club on Fire Island, N.Y., was brought up as a Roman Catholic. "But for me," he said, "wearing this shirt is a way of mocking the rhetoric that goes on over religion, which I think is just ridiculous."

The commodification of religious faith "is born of a consciousness that any religious movement, to stay viable, has to speak the idiom of the culture," said Randall Balmer, a professor of American religion at Barnard College in New York. Dr. Balmer also observed that airing one's religious views in public, which would have been regarded as unseemly or even presumptuous 20 years ago, has become acceptable. "We live in a multicultural, pluralistic environment," he said, "and acknowledge implicitly that individuals have a right to differentiate themselves. In fact, there is cachet in that."

Whatever is driving the popularity of message-driven merchandise, it is generating robust sales. Last year sales of apparel and accessories at Christian bookstores and gift shops reached about $84 million, according to the Christian Booksellers Association, a trade association of retailers. Teenage Millionaire, the Los Angeles-based makers of the "Jesus Is My Homeboy" T-shirt, a million of which have been sold, reported $10 million in sales last year, up from $2 million three years ago.

The Solid Light Group of Columbus, Ohio, which sells T-shirts with legends like "Jesus Rocks," does not disclose sales figures but is projecting a 40 percent increase from a year ago. "Ours has become a mainstream business," said Debbie Clements, a sales manager of the company. "It won't be too much longer before you see more designers in the secular marketplace doing religious fashions."

15   Chris Rainey, the director of marketing for Kerusso, a company in Berryville, Ark., that sells wristbands that say "Live for Him" and T-shirts with messages like "Dead to Sin, Alive to Christ," maintains that his wares make faith seem relevant. "We're just doing what a lot of churches have started to do, using marketing to reach a new generation," he said.

Still, the concept of religion as a wearable commodity rankles some consumers. "I would not wear clothing with a religious message," said Megan Schnaid, 27, a New York University graduate student from Los Angeles. "I'm not used to putting my faith on such loud display."

Many retailers, too, balk at selling fashions with an aggressively religious bent. Aurelio Barreto, who runs a Southern California chain of five stores called C28 (a reference to the biblical verse Colossians 2:8), recalled that when he first tried to sell his Not of this World line of tank tops and hoodies to secular stores at California malls, he was shown the door. "I was told, 'There is no way we will buy this,'" "Mr. Barreto said." 'We're not going to have God in here.'"

Michael Macko, the men's fashion director of Saks Fifth Avenue, who viewed the Dsquared collection in Milan last winter, said he was somewhat taken aback. "Hmm, I thought, 'Religion as a fashion theme. That's a little different from corduroy or camel. How do we handle this?'" "Undeterred, Saks bought the Dsquared line for its stores across the country. "We bought it as a fashion item, not as a moral statement," said Ronald Frasch, the chief merchant of Saks. "We sell crosses, and it's not a big step from crosses to sweaters."

Not surprisingly, some secular retailers stock religious-based paraphernalia because they are loath to miss an opportunity. "We don't just want all the punks and rockers to walk into the store," said Priti Lavingia, the owner of the T-Shirt Stop in Marino Valley, Calif., which carries the Not of This World line. "Maybe 20 percent of the people in this area are very religious," Ms. Lavingia said. "I want their business also."

Reflect & Write

❑   Why do you think some merchants view religious rhetoric on clothing so differently, as either an imposing moral statement or as a meaningless fashion trend? How does LaFerla's organization of quotes in this article—her choice to alternate diverse perspectives throughout the piece—offer a nuanced view on this issue? What additional perspectives might you want to add to this article?

❑   Compare this argument with Ruth La Ferla's August 19, 2001, article in *The New York Times* entitled "Noticed; Religious, Rebellious or Chic, Crosses Are Forever." How has the trend of wearing religious symbols as jewelry or clothing changed in subsequent years? What rhetorical strategies does she use in this article to make her argument (for instance, quoting her interview sources, using concrete detail, ending with an implicit thesis)? Which piece is more persuasive?

❑   **Write:** Compose a narrative about the religious visual rhetoric you encounter in one week on campus or in your hometown.

COLLABORATIVE CHALLENGE

Find two partners for this activity. Together, locate the article "Thousands protest head scarf ban: French parliament's lower house voted Tuesday to approve law." CNN.com (Saturday, February 14, 2004) http://edition.cnn.com/2004/WORLD/europe/02/14/france.headscarves.ap/. According to the CNN article, the protestors marched against a new French law banning all kinds of religious apparel in school, including Jewish skullcaps and large Christian crosses from public schools. The law received global criticism for infringing on religious freedom, and protesters in Paris carried banners marked "The veil, my voice," "Secularism: Shame," and "School is my right. The veil is my choice. France is my shelter." As a team, develop your own slogans for a rally to protest governmental regulations on wearing religion in school. Now, compose a speech from the school president defending the law's rationale. Use all three rhetorical appeals in both the slogans and the presidential speech. Share your work with the rest of the class and discuss what you learned from this exercise.

Mary is My Homegirl T-shirt

FIGURE 10.16 Religion meets teen culture in this "Mary is My Homegirl" t-shirt.

Reflect & Write

❏ Analyze the photo in Figure 10.16. What is the fashion statement? What elements catch your eye? How do the model's stance, expression, and body language contribute to the argument of the image?

❏ Compare the T-shirt in Figure 10.16 to the the Derek Lam blanket wrap with an embroidered cross that appeared on a fashion runway in New York, shown in Ruth La Ferla's article. Does featuring a cross in a fashion show or as T-shirt art signify a disrespectful use of the visual rhetoric of Christianity? Or is it a sign of importance of religious culture in the United States?

❏ If freedom of expression is considered a natural right for all Americans, then can freedom of expression through fashion also be considered a right? Discuss this question with regard to the religious T-shirt shown here.

❏ **Write:** Compose your own T-shirt by sketching out the words and design on a sheet of paper. Then, draft a proposal to a manufacturing company. Explain the argument of your fashion article and how you are trying to change the way people look at you through this article of clothing.

■ *An Australian author and poet,* **Paul Mitchell** *has published a collection entitled* Minorphysics *(2003). This article originally appeared in the June 1, 2005, issue of* BreakPoint, *an online journal that offers a Christian perspective on current fashion trends and news items.*

Faith and Fashion: The Power of T-shirt Evangelism

Paul Mitchell

Nineteen ninety-two marked the birth of the grunge look. Mudhoney and Dinosaur Junior t-shirts graced the backs of 20-somethings who, along with fuzzed up power chords, also discovered body piercing. The famous Nirvana t-shirts (featuring a baby swimming underwater in pursuit of a one-dollar bill on a hook) were *de riguer* for the rock set.

I was a young Christian at the time and eager to attend the Australian rockfest known as "The Big Day Out." Hundreds of bands would be playing for 12 hours under hot Melbourne skies that cooled off only slightly at night. But the big question for me was not which bands I would catch, it was what t-shirt I would wear. The crowd would be wearing t-shirts featuring rock, metal, and dance acts from around the world. How could I best demonstrate my devotion to Christ?

I had been reading a lot of authors from the Apophatic tradition (St. John of the Cross, etc.), so I considered wearing a plain white t-shirt. I figured that my absence of "idols" would demonstrate the foolishness of theirs'. But that idea, in a strongly visual culture, didn't have me reaching for my t-shirt drawer.

Next, I toyed with the idea of wearing a U2 t-shirt. Even though they wouldn't be playing at The Big Day Out, wearing their t-shirt was an obvious way to make a Christian statement. Besides, lots of people would be wearing t-shirts of bands that wouldn't be playing, I reasoned. But I left my U2 shirt folded up in the drawer—basically because they were too mainstream to wear to such an *alternative* rock fest. Also, a part of me wanted to make a stronger statement.

5   In the end, I settled on a Christian t-shirt. But even then, I didn't pick just any Christian shirt. You see, there were lots of Christian shirts in the early '90s. Some showed burnt toast popping out of toasters—an attempt to symbolize Hell. Others portrayed a single peaceful fish swimming in one direction while a school of piranhas swam in the other. Maybe it was because of my intellectual pride, but I decided against those types of shirts. Instead, I wore a white t-shirt which had a full color copy of a perhaps 17th century painting of the Crucifix-ion." (My "intellectual pride" didn't extend far enough to bother finding out who was the artist or in what century the work was produced.)

To my surprise, none of my non-Christian friends at The Big Day Out com-mented on my shirt. Neither did anyone in the crowd, even though I didn't see anyone else wearing a t-shirt like mine. I expected someone to say something, anything. But no one did.

What I was doing that day was what Christians have tried to do for centuries—make some kind of outward sign of their inner conversion, to show the world that yes, I'm *different*. Something has happened to me and I want you to see it. And I want you to see it because I want you to experience what I have experienced.

The ancient Jewish people had the sign of circumcision to show that they belonged to God. But early Christians were not so, well, in a period of history without anesthesia, "lucky" isn't quite the right word. Yet the desire to *show* our Christian faith to the world on our person hasn't abated. While nuns, priests, monks, and members of the ruling class in Anglicanism and Catholicism have always worn clothes that showed their Christian status, the rank and file in early Christendom had to make do with wearing crosses.

Then, in the late 20th century, along came the mobile billboard called the t-shirt. And almost since its inception, Christians have seen it as a way to both show and propagate their faith. Through text and the psychedelic styles of the 60s and 70s, the Jesus People movement continues to disseminate the evangelical message about the end of the world and the coming of Christ's reign.

10   The early 21st century, however, has seen the mainstream culture make a mockery of such t-shirts. For example, I've seen shirts with pictures of a '70s-looking Jesus or Mary figure accompanied by the words "Jesus is my Homeboy" or "Mary is my Homegirl"—a spoof from the film *Saved*. (Sadly, I even know Christians who wear them.) Some shirts parody Christian concepts. One such shirt reads, "In case of rapture, please cheer." (This is supposed to be an antidote to the many t-shirts and bumper stickers that show the results of Christians being raptured, i.e., driverless cars crashing.)

We could say that the previous examples are typical of a culture that ignores God. Or we could view them as simply being an assault on sloganeering in general. After all, they're not unlike the shirts with a Nike swoosh and the words: "Sweatshops: Just Don't Do It." Such shirts clearly attack the ubiquitous advertising slogans propagated by multinational companies.

Spoof Christian t-shirts give the same message to Christendom that spoof advertising t-shirts give to big companies: we see through your propaganda, and your slogans have become meaningless and even offensive to us.

It's obvious that Christians will continue making t-shirts with 'turn or burn' Christian messages and non-Christians (maybe even Christians?) will continue making shirts that spoof them. One company, however, has a different approach to Christian fashion messages. Luke's T-shirts creates garments that integrate high fashion and color design with a picture of a lion and the words, Tribe of Judah. There's a refreshing subtlety to this kind of work, which neither spoofs nor overtly proselytizes. Instead, these t-shirts more closely mirror the parables Jesus so often used.

Christian sloganeering—which is, of course, not restricted to the fashion world—has become too similar to the world's omnipresent advertising slogans.

Consequently, it has diminished its ability to grab people's attention. Advertisers are all too aware of this phenomenon. That's why they try numerous approaches to garner the attention of consumers who are deadened by the sheer number of slogans that confront them every day. The reality of t-shirts that spoof Christian slogans spells the end of this kind of approach to communicating the faith.

15   In the end, Christianity is not a brand—it's a relationship whose depth can't be reduced to slogans. Any attempt to do so will only make our faith appear thin and open to parody. To outwardly communicate our Christianity, we must use the oldest and best method—our love.

Reflect & Write

❏ Consider Paul Mitchell's strategy: he begins his article first with Kairos, or establishing the context, and then with ethos, or introducing his experience as an appeal to authority. How does this strategy construct the tone for the piece and invite readers to consider his position? As he strategically integrates references to theology as well as contemporary culture, his article becomes a well researched argument. What is the effect of this added material?

❏ Mitchell describes the T-shirt as offering "some kind of outward sign of . . . inner conversion" and yet, he warns, the T-shit runs the risk of parody. Which way do you read the visual rhetoric of the T-shirt? How might others see it?

❏ **Write:** Compose a rebuttal to Mitchell in which you use his quotations and references but come to a different conclusion.

Seeing Connections
For a further discussion on Kairos, see Chapter 2.

PERSPECTIVES ON THE ISSUE

1. Margo DeMello mentions the stereotype of the "aging biker" as the most popularly perceived tattooed body. According to her article, what has contributed to the change in which bodies now bear tattoos? How has the tattoo as a visual mark itself transformed as the body bearing it has changed with time? How does the gender of the tattooed body carry great importance—for firefighters, for biker culture, for the Iranian woman with a gun, and for the examples of tattooed bodies throughout history?

2. Now add to the above question considerations about the legal battles over tattoos. What do age limits on tattoos signify about a culture's values and beliefs? Should there be different laws for different kinds of tattoos, or for body piercing, tattooing, and head spikes?

3. Explore the subcultures of extreme body modification: nail art, body piercing, and branding, to name a few. How are responses to such visual rhetoric on the body shaped by cultural values and shared beliefs?

4. Compare the recent controversies over Christian T-shirts in America, in which Christians themselves find them potentially offensive as disrespectful visual rhetoric, against the debates over headscarves in France, where government officials are telling religious students not to make themselves visible as such in schools. What are the similarities between these issues? Where do the parallels end? Can there be a blanket policy for wearing religion in public? Does it depend on context, audience, and

the argument of the rhetoric itself? How does the visual rhetoric of attire that merges religious and nationalist rhetoric make a persuasive argument?

5. Visit and study the following log of news events concerning religious clothing and jewelry in schools at http://www.religioustolerance.org/sch_clot2.htm and http://www.religioustolerance.org/sch_clot5.htm. How does this list provide evidence for the way students choose to wear clothing that suggest their arguments on an issue? Pick one or two examples from the list and discuss them in relation to the articles by LaFerla and Mitchell. Then write a short report naming instances of people at your school using fashion to convey a strong political or religious message. If you want, you can convert your report into a blog. Add hyperlinks to indicate your research and photographs wherever you can.

6. In an article entitled "Wearing your Religion," published in *The News-Star* (June 3, 2005), a newspaper in Northeast Louisiana, writer Magin McKenna seems to offer an objective report on a new trend in wearing religious icons on T-shirts. Yet what do her research findings reveal about the differences between American and European markets, or about the predominance of certain religions? Compare these T-shirts with the racial T-shirts printed (and then recalled) by Abercrombie & Fitch; see http://modelminority.com/modules.php?name=Newsfile=articlesid=21 and http://www.geocities.com/tarorg/shirts.html

FROM READING TO RESEARCH

1. Historical inquiry into global cultures will bring you new perspectives on tattoos as an important cultural ritual. Go to your library and locate two issues of *National Geographic* to find their images and create a photo essay in which you match these examples of tattooed bodies to examples in your own community: Alexandra Boulat, "Bold strokes of saffron mark a woman in Zaouia Ahansal," *National Geographic* (January 2005); "A Yemini woman displays the handiwork of a local artist who uses dye made from henna plants and a paint called khidab," *National Geographic* (February 2005). Now apply the argument from one of the scholarly pieces in this case study to the issue of henna. Analyze the issue from a historical perspective using your research and looking at temporary henna tattoos used in wedding ceremonies and parties, on boardwalks and in traditional cultures. How does henna have a similarly rich and complex history in terms of what it means to mark the body in this way? Conduct a research paper on this issue and compose your own contribution to scholarship.

2. According to the Anti-Defamation League, "Religious messages on T-shirts and the like may not be singled out for suppression. Students may wear religious attire, such as yarmulkes and head scarves, and they may not be forced to wear gym clothes that they regard, on religious grounds, as immodest." See "Religion in the Public Schools," Anti-Defamation League http://www.adl.org/religion_ps_2004/dress_codes.asp. Consider the fact that some students see wearing an athletic uniform as an imposition on their religious or cultural values. How might you make an argument to defend students who seek to avoid such visual rhetoric on their bodies? Conduct a survey of your peers in college or in your community. Then, using the survey results along with your reading in this chapter, develop a research paper on this issue. Craft a thesis and make your argument with ample references to your sources.

CHAPTER 11

Sports and Media

When we see sports on television or covered in our favorite magazine, are we just viewers enjoying the show of athletics or does the media shape our experience of sports in some way? Why are certain sports favored by certain cultures? What role does the media have in shaping these choices? Who gets to be represented in sports coverage?

We'll tackle some of these questions in the pages that follow. We come to agree with scholar Paul Mark Pederson, who has suggested, "Sport and mass media are inextricably linked together in a symbiotic relationship. These two institutions rely on each other—the mass media sell sport and sport sells the mass media."

We can see this relationship represented in Figure 11.1, the *Time Magazine* cover with which we have chosen to open this chapter. The Olympics as a modern spectacle speaks to the power of spectatorship, the sporting arena, and the way the media brings international events back to the fans across the world. The picture itself presents a convergence of many of the themes that we explore in this chapter: the glorifying of both Michael Johnson's performance and his physique as an athlete, as he stands proud atop his pedestal; the international context of the Olympics offset by the patriotism of this staged photo; and the way that sports help shape our collectively held notions about race and masculinity. We'll examine these issues and many more, exploring questions about sports, identity, culture, gender, race, and how the media shapes our very experience of watching the games we love to see.

FIGURE 11.1 Track star Michael Johnson poses on part of the American flag for a cover of the *Time* special issue on the Olympics.

ENGINEERING A BETTER ATHLETE

Brawny arms, chiseled abs, bulky forearms, hardened cheek muscles, increased weight, and tight skin: are these our ideals of physical perfection? Are they the visible results of the successfully trained athlete? Or are these signs of illicit steroid use meant to bolster the body's natural abilities? Perhaps they are the result of a strict diet of vitamins and nutritional cocktails—not quite illegal—or even innovative and completely legal training regimens such as sleeping at high altitudes or in oxygen-rich tents. What do sports actually test? How can we be sure that all athletes are performing on a level playing field? These questions have wracked a sports industry now battered by drug abuse scandals that have led to severe consequences on many levels. Once-revered sports like baseball have been defamed, and even at the Olympics, officials spend more time and money testing athletes for illegal and potentially dangerous performance-enhancing chemicals than they do judging events. In the most extreme cases, the quest for physical perfection and maximum performance has lead to the death of star athletes, like baseball prospect Steve Bechler who died after using chemicals he believed would help improve his game.

To complicate matters, the quest for top athletic performance—and the achievement of perfection it suggests—is often a passion embraced by more than the players on the field or the runners on the track. Trainers, team owners, coaches, parents, pharmaceutical companies, and even national leaders all have a stake in the accomplishment of sports figures. As Mike Sokolove writes in his article for this chapter, "A whole subculture of athletes—and the coaches and chemists who are in the business of improving their performances—is eager for the latest medical advances." The newest methods of changing athletic looks and acts are found not only in bottles of Xenadrine or chemicals such as the human growth hormone erythropoietin (EPO); they are also located within such technological advances as the "Speedo Fastskin Suit," high-oxygen sleep chambers, genetically engineered food, and nonstick spike sport shoes.

In the articles that follow, you'll learn about the effects steroid abuse has on the body, as showcased in the op-ad in Figure 11.2. Just as each part of the visual depicts a consequence of taking performance-enhancing drugs, so will each article explore why we have so much invested in winning that we turn to such drastic methods. We'll consider, with Steven Shapin, whether "steroid use is the natural con-

FIGURE 11.2 The "Steroids: Body of Evidence" poster itemizes steroids' effects on the different parts of the body.

sequence of the hyper-competitiveness and performance anxiety of our entire culture" and we'll wonder with Thomas Murray "if sport continues to be overwhelmed by the performance at all costs principle, it could become something like a high-level circus exhibition, like professional wrestling or an activity of that sort." We'll study how standards of masculinity shape decisions for some athletes, such as Dominican Republican baseball hopefuls, to take veterinary steroids, and how witnessing their sports heroes succumbing to steroid abuse affects the younger generation of athletes.

Reflect & Write

❏ What is the target audience of this poster? How is it designed specifically to appeal to that audience?
❏ What rhetorical appeals (pathos, logos, ethos) are at work in this poster? Is one prioritized over the others? Which one, and how can you tell?
❏ **Write:** Write a memo to the company that produced this poster about how they should revise it to more directly target high school athletes. Be sure to include references to specific revisions as well as a rationale for your suggestions.

In recent years, the All-American image of baseball has been tarnished by repeated accusations of steroid use and doping among its players. This visual reading compiles a range of responses by cartoonists to the debate about the role of doping in professional baseball.

Political Cartoons: Steroids & Baseball

FIGURE 11.3 This cartoon by Bill Day relies exclusively on images to make its argument about steroid use in professional baseball.
Source: Bill Day: (c) Commercial Appeal/Dist. by United Features Syndicate, Inc.

FIGURE 11.4 James Casciari's cartoon uses a then-and-now comparison in its argument about the recent change in "equipment" used by baseball players.
Source: James Casciari/Scripps Howard News Service.

FIGURE 11.5 Gary Varvel re-works a classic Peanuts scenario in this 2005 cartoon about baseball and steroids.

Source: By permission of Gary Varvel and Creators Syndicate, Inc.

Seeing Connections
Review the PreWriting Checklist at the end of Chapter 1 for ideas about how to use elements such as character, setting, composition, captions, layout and imagery to convey your argument in your cartoon.

Reflect & Write

❏ How does each cartoonist's rhetorical style provide an argument about the visible effects of steroids and performance-enhancing drugs? Notice the alterations to the body presented in each cartoon.

❏ Why does Bill Day show the player's arms in the light but his face in the shadow? How does he use symbolism to make his point?

❏ How does James Casciari use both visual and verbal strategies of argument to suggest the way "the game" has changed? What does he mean through this play on words and images?

❏ What argument is made about influence in the Charlie Brown cartoon by placing in Snoopy's hands a book about Jose Canseco (a famous baseball player from Cuba whose best-selling book, *Juiced: Wild Times, Rampant 'Roids, Smash Hits, and How Baseball Got Big* claimed that 85% of major league players took steroids)? How does the book, together with Snoopy's steroid-inflated body, offer a perspective on cause and effect? Is Charlie Brown's comment strong enough in response? How might you rewrite the bubble?

❏ **Write:** Draft a short position paper about your perspective on the recent steroid abuse scandals in sports. Having done so, convey the same argument—but this time by sketching a cartoon. Now exchange essays and cartoons with a classmate and discuss the ways the different media affected the composition and the reception of your argument.

■ *"Clean Up Hitters" originally appeared in the April 18ᵗʰ, 2005, issue of the* New Yorker. *Although it begins as a book review of Jose Canseco's eye-opening expose* Juiced: Wild Times, Rampant 'Roids, Smash Hits, and How Baseball Got Big, *social historian* **Steve Shapin** *expands his argument to provide a historical context for the controversy and to demonstrate the complexities behind the medical and ethical implication of steroid use. Shapin is the Franklin L. Ford Professor of the History of Science at Harvard University.*

Clean Up Hitters: The Steroid Wars and the Nature of What's Natural

Steven Shapin

One young man leads another to a toilet stall, cautiously looking around to make sure they're not being observed. Then he has him lower his trousers so that he can get at his buttocks. What follows is a matter of enormous public interest.

Years later, President George W. Bush makes a speech condemning it. Congressional hearings are held to investigate it and to frame public policy.

It is the summer of 1988; the toilets are in the home locker room of the Oakland Athletics;

and Jose Canseco is injecting Mark McGwire with anabolic steroids. Or so Canseco recounts in "Juiced: Wild Times, Rampant 'Roids, Smash Hits, and How Baseball Got Big" . . . . "It was really no big deal," Canseco writes. "We would just slip away, get our syringes and vials, and head into the bathroom area of the clubhouse to inject each other." By the late nineteen-nineties, according to Canseco, teammates were pairing off together in bathroom stalls with such regularity that it became an object of clubhouse drollery: "What are you guys, fags?"

Anabolic steroids are synthetic variants of such naturally occurring hormones as testosterone. They're called anabolic because they work in "constructive metabolism," during which simple materials provided to the gut or the bloodstream are built up into complex living tissue. Among the main effects that athletes want is a boost of skeletal muscle mass, and anabolic steroids help you get big fast. Canseco says he started doing anabolic steroids and growth hormone in 1985—the first baseball player to use steroids "in a serious way," he claims—and he put on twenty-five pounds of solid muscle in just a few months. More followed. McGwire grew massive, too, and he and Canseco became known as "the Bash Brothers."

Canseco explains that oil-based anabolic steroids require a large-gauge needle, so you have to be careful where you inject yourself. If you're a baseball player, you don't want to use your quad or calf muscles, because it may hamper your running, or your shoulder muscles, because you're doing a lot of throwing and catching. That leaves the buttocks. It takes a lot of practice to be able to do it yourself; when you start out, you need a little help from your friends. Once you become more accomplished, you can inject yourself, and then you'll want to become "an ambidextrous injector," he says, "because you definitely are going to want to hit both sides of your glute." (If you keep hitting the same spot, he warns, "it can get nasty.") Steroid use, as Canseco tells it, is itself a form of athleticism. Different steroids do different things: if you want just to build muscle mass, one sort will do; if you want to run fast, there are steroids to increase your fast-twitch muscle fibres. The congeries of bodybuilding substances

Canseco claims to have used includes Deca-Durabolin, Winstrol, Equipoise, and Anavar, as well as human growth hormone. He delightedly recalls that early in his steroid-fuelled career he was dubbed "the Natural."

5   Canseco writes that steroid use is no big deal, but he's wrong. President Bush made the remarkable decision to use his 2004 State of the Union address to denounce its dangers ("The use of performance-enhancing drugs like steroids in baseball, football, and other sports is dangerous, and it sends the wrong message—that there are shortcuts to accomplishment, and that performance is more important than character"). The U.S. Anti-Doping Agency sees it as a threat to sportsmanship ("Deterring the use of drugs in sport is necessary to preserve the integrity of sport in the United States"). The National Institute on Drug Abuse is alarmed at a range of irreversible side effects associated with steroid use by bodybuilding adolescents. There are fans who now wonder, say, whether there should be an asterisk by Barry Bonds's home-run record. And, of course, it's a criminal offense to possess anabolic steroids without a valid prescription.

Among the justifications for banning these substances are their side effects. For males, these may include breast development, atrophied testicles, and reduced sperm count, as well as baldness, severe acne, jaundice, tremors, an enlarged prostate, problems in liver and kidney function (with the possibility of tumor formation), hypertension, elevated risk of stroke and heart attack, and mood swings—the enhancement of masculine aggressiveness popularly known as "'roid rage." When administered to adolescent bodies still in the course of development, steroids may cause permanently stunted growth; their use has been implicated in some teen-age suicides. Sentiment against steroid use also flows from a widespread sense of fair play and equity. The ideal of the level playing field translates broadly into the belief that all competitors should come to play with normal bodies, functioning normally.

So it may come as a surprise that "Juiced" celebrates steroid use as part of a new era of "clean living" in baseball, driving out alcohol, cocaine, marijuana, and even amphetamines—the "greenies" that Jim Bouton wrote about in "Ball

Four," back in 1970. With the "trend toward better fitness that came with steroid use," Canseco maintains, "you saw bigger, stronger, faster, and *healthier* athletes, instead of those raggedy, run-down, pot-bellied ball players of previous eras." Steroid use among athletes has clearly aroused national passions, but passionate arousal isn't the ideal frame of mind for reasoned debate. Are the medical and moral evils of steroids in competitive sport really so unambiguous?

Nothing in "Juiced" suggests that Canseco was using steroids under a physician's care, or even on a doctor's advice. He seems to have had himself periodically checked out by doctors, but that's all. He was, instead, part of the great civic tradition condensed in the old motto "Every man is his own physician." Canseco learned the techniques of steroid use by noticing how his own body reacted to the chemicals, and adjusting dosages and combinations accordingly. Yet steroid use also belongs to the history of mainstream modern medicine, and John Hoberman's excellent "Testosterone Dreams: Rejuvenation, Aphrodisia, Doping" . . . tells much of the story of how and why steroids came to the pharmacy shelves.

In the late eighteen-eighties, a septuagenarian French physiologist named Charles-Edouard Brown—Sequard announced that he had been rejuvenated-and had the arc of his urine lengthened—by injecting himself with extracts from the sex glands of a dog and a guinea pig. Brown-Sequard's "organotherapy" created a considerable market for these crude extracts, and by the nineteen-tens the transplant of animal testicles and testicular extract was heralded as a treatment for homosexuals, who could thereby achieve an "energetic and manly aspect." But the real breakthrough came with the artificial production of androgenic and estrogenic hormones in the nineteen-thirties, especially the synthesis of testosterone in 1935. In testosterone, the medical profession saw hopes for restored virility and vigor, the extension of life, the cure for a range of disease, the management or elimination of sexual deviance, and enhanced performance in a variety of life functions. That year, *Newsweek* declared that the hormone could prevent "premature sterility and feminine characteristics in men."

10 In a familiar pattern, the transformation of previously "natural" features of human life into diseases marched in step with the trade in hormones: one medical historian calls them "drugs looking for diseases." Testosterone has, in recent years, been prescribed for "the andropause"—the decline in testosterone levels supposedly suffered by many men over sixty-five—and for women who consult doctors for low libido. Elder sex is completing the transition from deviance to embarrassment to a chemically assisted new normal. It's the pharmaceutical version of "If you build it, they will come," and you can find a parable to this effect in "Juiced." Canseco says that when he joined the Texas Rangers he introduced Rafael Palmeiro to steroids, and Palmeiro's newfound prowess on the field led to a lucrative deal to endorse Viagra.

So there has always been the thinnest of lines between medical augmentation and medical restoration. Is the task of the physician to maintain and restore normal function? If so, what is to count as normal? Or is it to enhance and release the full range of human potential? Hoberman plausibly predicts that "the future of testosterone drugs will evolve within the contest between a wide-open medical ethos—one that approves medical interventions to enhance a range of life functions"—and our traditional sense that a well-lived life follows a natural trajectory from birth to death and that aging is a fate, not a disease."

Hormonal therapies lie right at the heart of these tensions, along with the chemical dosing of rambunctious kids, gastric-bypass surgery, and the more exotic forms of infertility medicine. Hoberman worries that "physicians who cater to patients' demands that are motivated by vanity or social fashion diminish the stature of practitioners by making them as much beauticians as healers." But who is to judge what pain is suffered by the obese or the wrinkled, not to mention the parents of aggressive and inattentive children? And who has the right to say which conditions you must live with and which you may mobilize the resources of chemical or surgical art to avoid?

The notion of what is normal—and, therefore, of what physicians may seek to restore and what they should leave untouched—isn't arbitrary, but neither is it unambiguous. A recent celebration of the biotechnological future, Ramez Naam's "More than Human: Embracing the Promise of Biological Enhancement" . . . points out that athletes' use of injectable erythropoietin (epo) to boost their red-blood-cell count, and thus their endurance, may come to be replaced by some sort of gene therapy—a once-and-for-all introduction of the genes allowing individuals to produce a higher level of red blood cells as long as they live. Is it an unnatural result when it's produced by your own un-drugged body?

When anti-doping organizations condemn steroids as a threat to the "integrity" of sport, they take a view about what should count as artificial enhancement and what as legitimate treatment. So it's worth noting that anabolic steroids not only helped Canseco turn into a home-run-hitting monster but also, he says, allowed him to recuperate from a series of back surgeries which could otherwise have ended his career. "I was on steroids and growth hormone," he recounts of his third surgery, "so I guess they accelerated the natural healing process."

15   There's overwhelming evidence that professional cycling, and particularly the Tour de France, is a chem lab on wheels, but even here the line between the augmentative and the recuperative use of drugs is deeply unclear. Scaling the Alpe d'Huez is painful, and rebounding from *hors categorie* climbs to ride the next day calls for extraordinary recuperative powers. Is it unethical for a doctor to assist cyclists in managing that pain and restoring that extraordinary version of "normal" function which allows them to do their job? Physicians who make their living doing so can plausibly see themselves as healers. Spectators following the Tour de France seem to understand that. Even at the height of the doping revelations of 1998, the public continued to show their support for the cyclists. And one reason they did so was, as Hoberman says, "their appreciation of the physical ordeal the riders had to endure. Many ordinary people who depended on cigarettes, caffeine, or alcohol to make it through their days had no trouble sympathizing with men whose suffering could be read on their drawn and haggard faces."

In one way or another, we've always been juiced. When coffee and tea were new in the Western world, they were seen as powerful (and often dangerous) mind- and body-altering substances. The historical anthropologist Alan Macfarlane has recently argued for a causal link between the rise of British tea-drinking and the burst of physical energy that accompanied the Industrial Revolution. Opiated artists and coke-stoked musicians inspire both a tragic sense of damaged lives and a widespread appreciation of their chemically modified imagination and chemically managed psychic pain. And what do we say about the socially transformative effects of the steroidal birth-control pill? Do we put an asterisk next to the sexual revolution?

So the notion of the natural doesn't resolve the baseball issue; nor does the notion of harm or the notion of proper medical practice. The right question to ask is whether steroid use among competitive athletes is *fair*. To be sure, the definition of what's fair (as opposed to what's cheating) isn't any less contestable than the notion of what's normal. Nothing but shifting cultural preference lies behind our view that Lance Armstrong is not cheating if he sleeps in a pressure chamber to boost his red-blood-cell count but would be cheating if he used epo; or our view that it's all right to use methylxanthines (the stimulants in coffee) but not ephedra. These are ethical matters, and although ethical judgments are historically changing and culturally variable, the conventions express who we are and what we value. We can't live without them. It's possible to imagine a future in which the medically supervised and regulated juicing of athletes will become the norm. (Even then, "natural" athletics would undoubtedly continue as a specialty taste, comparable to the organic-foods section in the supermarket.) But it's impossible to imagine any competitive sport or social practice in which some forms of advantage-seeking aren't defined as cheating and sanctioned accordingly. To complain that the rules are contingent and somewhat arbitrary is beside the point: games are the celebration of such rules. That's what makes them games.

It's a matter of debate what damage "proper" steroid use might cause to baseball players and other athletes, as is the precise extent of current use. Hoberman maintains that steroid use is the natural consequence of the hyper-competitiveness and performance anxiety of our entire culture, and, if he's right, steroids are the price we pay for the spectator goods we demand. I suspect the matter is more complicated than that. The public is perfectly aware that the demand for performance creates the conditions for cheating in sport, as it does for fraud in science or in bookkeeping. But at the same time much of the public holds cheaters accountable for succumbing to competitive pressure. We've now decided that steroid use crosses the line. Yes, we're the ones who drew that line, and we could have drawn it somewhere else. But what of it? To understand all is still not quite the same as to forgive all.

❏ "Steroid use, as Canseco tells it, is itself a form of athleticism," and writes Shapin. Analyze this claim. Do you agree? What evidence does Shapin use to support it?

❏ The voice of Shapin as author emerges clearly in paragraph 5; what do you make of this tone shift? How does he support his rhetorical stance through appeals to ethos, logos, and pathos consecutively?

❏ **Write:** Compose a response to Shapin's argument that supports, advances, or contests his claims. Use direct quotes from the article to support your position; be sure to use proper MLA parenthetical form in doing so.

Reflect & Write

❏ How effective is the opening scene as an introduction to the article's main argument? What kind of issues does the scene between two men in a bathroom raise? What are the logical fallacies in connecting sexuality, masculinity, and legality for an article on steroid use?

Seeing Connections
Review Chapters 6 and 9 for suggestions about integrating and citing quotations effectively.

Claudia Dreifus, *a science interviewer for* The New York Times *and freelance writer for periodicals such as* The Atlantic, Mother Jones, *and* The New York Times, *has interviewed many notable figures from Toni Morrison to the Dalai Lama. Her book,* Interview *(1999), a consideration of the art of interviewing, is used broadly across academia. In this piece, from an August 2004 issue of* The New York Times, *she interviews Thomas Murray, president of the Hastings Center, a bioethics research organization.*

Olympian Talent, and a Little Artificial Help: A Conversation with Thomas H. Murray

Claudia Dreifus

THOMAS H. MURRAY, president of the Hastings Center, a bioethics research group in Garrison, N.Y., spends a large part of his day considering the culture, philosophy and ethics of the sporting world.

As the author of several papers on the use of science in sports, Dr. Murray, a social psychologist, has served on the United States Olympic Committee's anti-doping panel, an experience he describes as "the most frustrating work I've done."

He also recently became chairman of the World Anti-Doping Agency's ethical issues review panel, which, he said in a recent interview, "is really serious about dealing with abuses."

Dr. Murray, 58, is an avid bicyclist. But he has no plans to go to Athens next week. "I've never been to a single Olympics," he said, with a smile. "There are jobs within the Olympic movement that come with lots of perks. The job I had wasn't one of them."

5 INTERVIEWER: *Recently, a major ethical or medical issue has dominated the headlines of each Olympics. The Atlanta Games were dubbed the "EPO Games," after erythropoietin, the human growth hormone. What do you think the Athens Games will be called?*

SPEAKER: Perhaps the "Gene Games?" The hot new topic is genetic manipulation or gene transfer, and people are getting very excited and worried that athletes might try to genetically enhance themselves.

But of course, the technology is not here yet. Lee Sweeney at University of Pennsylvania is working on a technique that could be therapeutic for people with muscular dystrophy, but that might also be used by athletes to enhance muscle size. Thus far, his work has only been with mice. Indeed, the whole technology of gene therapy is very much in its infancy. So while there will be a lot of talk about it, I don't expect there will be any genetically enhanced athletes in Athens, although there might be some who think they have been.

How can a person "think" they've been genetically enhanced?

Because there are scads of scoundrels promoting all kinds of things to athletes. Some athletes are gullible. They hang out with these people, listen to them.

In the sports world, there's something called "five-ring fever," which is a desire to be associated with the Olympic movement. If you're not an athlete yourself, you get closer by currying favor. There are athletes who will pay for all kinds of services they think will enhance their strength and endurance. In many cases, they're getting nothing. In others, they are ingesting some very dangerous substances.

Is the problem here the technologies or, rather, how some people use them?

In almost every case, the technology that is being used for enhancement wasn't developed for that, but for some therapeutic use. EPO, which you mentioned earlier—it's for people who have chronic anemia. It helps them make red cells. Athletes pretty quickly figured out, "If this substance can get my blood up to normal, why can't I get it a little above normal and then maybe I can run or cycle a little faster."

Would you say that there's a subculture of self-experimentation among athletes?

It's been around for decades, though it's gotten more elaborate, more formalized and in some cases, state-sponsored. There was an enormous sports doping industry in East Germany. It involved over a hundred scientists and doctors and thousands of athletes. It was a horrendous activity that damaged a lot of people.

Aside from the damage that some of the enhancements do to individual athletes, what is the harm in using them?

The first thing: It changes the whole idea of a level playing field.

What most athletes hate is losing to a cheater. If you could give athletes a way to compete without performance enhancements and have a fair shot at winning, most would prefer that.

The other thing is that enhancements bring into question the very meaning of athletic endeavors. In the past, sports have been a combination of natural talents and old-fashioned virtues like tenacity, endurance, willingness to suffer pain—and in the case of team sports, playing unselfishly. If all of that is reduced to a drug or an injectable, the meaning of sport may be altered irrevocably. If sport continues to be overwhelmed by the performance at all costs principle, it could become something like a high-level circus exhibition, like professional wrestling or an activity of that sort.

10 *Will we be seeing Olympics in the future where the sports physicians and scientists are the real contenders?*

"Best body sculptor?" I'm afraid you're frighteningly realistic.

There are branches of the sport of power lifting that give us a glimpse into that sort of future. Because within power lifting there is widespread use of performance-enhancing drugs and steroids, the sport has split into a myriad of governing bodies, including a "drug free" power lifting association and another "anything goes" association. The latter is very clear: "We don't monitor, we don't test for drugs. Whatever allows you to lift the greatest weight is what we permit."

So what will happen to the meaning of competition if all sports go that way in the future? Will victory go to the person with the best drugs and gene therapists?

What does the current investigation into the Bay Area Laboratory Co-Operative teach us?

That there are cadres of reasonably skilled scientists willing to work surreptitiously to dope athletes, including the creation of entirely new drugs, such as THG tetrahydrogestrinone, a synthetic steroid, which was thought to be undetectable.

The track star Marion Jones, whose name has been linked to the Bay Area laboratory inquiry, feels she's been given a raw deal because she hasn't failed any physical testing. Does she have a point?

Testing isn't the only way to check against doping. For a fairly long time it's been possible to find an athlete guilty of doping from evidence other than a laboratory test, if the evidence is sufficiently clear and independent.

For example, it's possible to find evidence of the "old-fashioned" blood doping where you got a blood transfusion, but you get it far enough ahead of the competition so that you've urinated away the excess fluid volume, but you still have the extra red cells. In such cases, if you found items like IV bags, or testimony by people who've administered the blood, that could be evidence. It was the only way to be fair to other athletes against whom this person was competing.

For more than a decade, you served on a United States Olympic Committee panel charged with monitoring sports doping. Did you find it a waste of time?

No, because I met some wonderful people among the athletes who also served. But what happened was that we would get partial information, provide the advice we were asked to give and then we'd never find out whether the advice was followed.

I felt frustrated. The U.S.O.C. had to have some form of drug control program; that's what I felt we were doing there. But there was the feeling that the leadership of the U.S.O.C. as well as the various sports governing bodies, with rare exceptions, was not really committed to this.

Now with the U.S.A.D.A.—the United States Anti-Doping Agency—things have changed. U.S.A.D.A. seems to be very serious about trying to give us a different path.

Dr. Gary Wadler, a well-known sports physician, claims that sports doping is a public health issue. Do you agree with him?

Absolutely. Anabolic steroids are the example. They are used by a frightening number of high school and college-age students. They take them because they think it will make them stronger, and if they are male because they think it will make them look more masculine.

These young people hear of their sports heroes using them, and if their role models are using steroids to pursue performance at any price, they think, "Why not?"

Another thing I worry about—for the young and the old—is this feeling out there that our bodies are mere objects to be manipulated and optimized by whatever means available. If 14-year-olds are taking steroids, this is bad news for all of us.

Reflect & Write

❑ Why do Claudia Dreifus and Thomas Murray rename the Olympics the "EPO Games" and the "Gene Games"? What is the effect of these changes? What do such titles reveal about their stance on this situation?

❑ Murray contends that the problem with doping is "it changes the whole idea of a level playing field." Why is this a problem? Discuss with regard to comparisons Murray makes to other sports in which the visual spectacle necessarily includes big, bulky bodies: circus performance, professional wrestling, and power lifting.

Student Writing

See Nicholas Glacomini's article, "FDA Should Be Given Control Over the Marketing of Dietary Supplements" as part of his cutting edge online magazine, "Revolutionizing Healthcare"

www.ablongman.com/envision/236

❏ Murray talks about visible and hidden signs of doping. Do the different signs relate to character, emotions, or logic in some way? How do visible versus hidden signs affect sports fans differently?

❏ **Write:** Compose a list of questions for a possible interview with your coach about these issues. Construct questions designed to uncover the reasons why a particular physical look or body matters to athletes. You might seek to interview a coach who supports performance enhancement in order to develop a strong counter-argument.

COLLABORATIVE CHALLENGE

Together with three or four classmates, design a brief survey or interview questionnaire to conduct on your campus or in your community concerning doping in professional sports. You might decide to interview coaches, players, parents, and community or school leaders. Based on your reading in this chapter so far, what key questions might you ask? How do each of these groups perceive the situation of performance-enhancing drugs? Analyze rhetorically the answers you receive to determine your community's stance. Write a report based on the interviews and quote from people you interview. Present your findings to the class.

■ *This chart is part of CBS News's online interactive article, "Dope & Glory." Other features of this story include information on the most popular steroids and those athletes who have most recently been found to have used steroids during competition.*

Chart: Olympic Drug Testing

CBS News Interactive

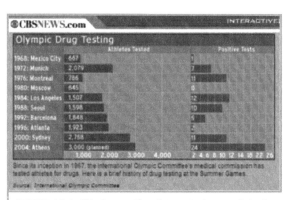

FIGURE 11.6 This chart on Olympic Drug Testing provided evidence to support CBS news' feature on "Dope & Glory."

Reflect & Write

❏   Is this an effective information graphic for discussing steroid use in the Olympics? Why or why not? What argument is it making?

❏   How could the information in this graphic be presented differently? How would the changes you suggest alter its argument?

❏   **Write:** Draft a paragraph that makes an argument about the state of steroid use in Olympics over the last 40 years, using this chart as evidence and drawing on specific information from the chart to make your argument.

Michael Sokolove *is a contributing writer for the* New York Times Magazine *and the author of* The Ticket Out: Darryl Strawberry and the Boys of Crenshaw *(2004). A longer version of this article was originally published in the Sunday, January 18, 2004 edition of the* New York Times Magazine. *Two days later, during his State of the Union address, President Bush called for stronger measures to curtail the use of performance enhancers in baseball.*

Drug in Sport: The Shape to Come

Mike Sokolove

On a brisk day last December, I was led through a warren of red-brick buildings on the campus of the University of Pennsylvania in West Philadelphia and then up to a fifth-floor molecular physiology laboratory. I had come to visit some mice—and to take a peek at the future of sport.

I had heard about these mice, heard them called 'mighty mice', but I was still shocked at the sight of them. There they were in several small cages, grouped with normal mice, all of them nibbling on mouse chow pellets. The mighty mice looked like a different animal. They were built like cattle, with thick necks and big haunches. They belonged in some kind of mouse rodeo.

The Penn researchers have used gene therapy on these mice to produce increased levels of IGF-1, or insulinlike growth factor-1, a protein that promotes muscle growth and repair. They have done this with mice before birth and with mice at four weeks old. A result has been a sort of rodent fountain of youth. The mice show greater than normal muscle size and strength

and do not lose it as they age. Rats altered in the same fashion and then put into physical training— they climb little ladders with weights strapped to their backs—have experienced a 35 per cent strength gain in the targeted muscles and have not lost any of it 'detraining', as a human being will when he quits going to the gym.

To H. Lee Sweeney, chairman of Penn's department of physiology, and Elisabeth Barton, an assistant professor, the bizarre musculature of their lab specimens is exciting. This research could eventually be of immense benefit to the elderly and those with various muscle-wasting diseases.

'Our impetus, going back to 1988, was to develop a therapy to stop people from getting weak when they get old,' Sweeney explained. 'They fall and injure themselves. We wanted to do something about that.'

Barton has the broad shoulders and athletic build of the competitive cyclist and triathlete she once was. 'You see children with muscular dystrophy and their parents are just so broken up because it's so sad,' she said. 'You see grandparents who can't get out of bed. These are the people this is for.'

But the Penn team has become acutely aware of a population impatient to see its research put into practice—the already strong, seeking to get stronger still. Sweeney gets their emails. One came from a high-school football coach in Pennsylvania not long after Sweeney first presented his findings at a meeting of the American Society for Cell Biology. 'This coach wanted me to treat his whole team,' he said. 'I told him it was not available for humans, and it may not be safe, and if I helped him we would all go to jail. I can only assume he didn't understand how investigational this is. Or maybe he wasn't winning, and his job was on the line.'

Other calls and emails have come from weightlifters and bodybuilders. This kind of thing happens often after researchers publish in even the most arcane medical and scientific journals. A whole subculture of athletes—and the coaches and chemists who are in the business of improving their performances—is eager for the latest medical advances.

Sweeney knows that what he is doing works. The remaining question, the one that will require years of further research to answer, is how safe his methods are. But many athletes don't care about that. They want an edge now. They want money and acclaim. They want a pay-off for their years of sweat and sacrifice, at whatever the cost.

10 'This was serious science, not sports science,' Dr. Gary Wadler, a United States representative to the World Anti-Doping Agency, said when I spoke to him about the Penn experiments. 'As soon as it gets into any legitimate publication, bingo, these people get hold of it and want to know how they can abuse it.'

Sweeney's research will probably be appropriated before it is ever put to its intended medical purpose. Someone will use it to build a better sprinter or shot-putter.

There is a murky quality to sport at the moment. We are in a time of flux. The rules are ambiguous. Everything is a little suspect.

Two positive tests last summer brought the drugs issue into sharp focus. Samples taken from British sprinter Dwain Chambers on 1

August revealed traces of the new 'designer steroid', tetrahydrogestrinone (THG), produced by the San Francisco-based Bay Area Laboratory Co-Operative, known as Balco. Three weeks later, a veteran American sprinter named Kelli White ran the track meet of her dreams at the world championships in Paris. She took gold in the 100 and 200 metres, the first American woman ever to win those sprints in tandem at an outdoor world championships. In both events, the 5 ft 4 in, 135 lb White, a tightly coiled ball of power and speed, exploded to career-best times.

On a celebratory shopping trip on the Champs-Elysees, White, 26, glimpsed her name in a newspaper headline and asked a Parisian to translate. She learnt that she had failed a post-race drug test and that her medals and $ 120,000 in prize money were in jeopardy. Later, she acknowledged that she had taken the stimulant modafinil, claiming that she needed it to treat narcolepsy, but had failed to list it on a disclosure form. What she added after that was revealing, perhaps more so than she intended. 'After a competition,' she told reporters, 'it's kind of hard to remember everything that you take during the day.'

15 The THG scandal and the attention focused on Balco, which has advised dozens of top athletes (including White) on the use of dietary supplements, has opened the curtain on the fascinating cat-and-mouse game played between chemists and the laboratory sleuths who try to police them.

But White's statement exposed another, deeper truth: elite athletes in many different sports consume cocktails of vitamins, extracts and supplements, dozens of pills a day—the only people who routinely ingest more pills are Aids patients—in the hope that their mixes of accepted drugs will replicate the effects of the banned substances taken by the cheaters. The cheaters and the non-cheaters alike are science projects. They are the sum total of their innate athletic abilities and their dedication—and all the compounds and powders they ingest and inject.

A narrow tunnel leads to success at the very top levels of sport. This is especially so in

Olympic non-team events. An athlete who has devoted his life to sprinting, for example, must qualify for one of a handful of slots on his Olympic team. And to become widely known and make real money, he or she probably has to win one of the gold medals that is available every four years.

The temptation to cheat is human. In the realm of elite international sport, it can be irresistible.

After White failed her drug test, the United States Olympic Committee revealed that five other American athletes had tested positive this summer for modafinil. Did they all suffer from narcolepsy? That would be hard to believe. More likely, word of modafinil and its supposed performance-enhancing qualities (perhaps along with the erroneous information that it was not detectable) went out on the circuit. It became the substance du jour.

20   For athletes, performance-enhancing drugs and techniques raise issues of health, fair play and, in some cases, legality. For the fans, the issues are largely philosophical and aesthetic. On the most basic level, what are we watching, and why? If we equate achievement with determination and character, and that, after all, has always been part of our attachment to sport—to celebrate the physical expression of the human spirit—how do we recalibrate our thinking about sport when laboratories are partners in athletic success?

Major League Baseball seems to have decided that the power generated by bulked-up players is good for the game in the entertainment marketplace. The record-breaking sluggers Mark McGwire and Sammy Sosa have been virtual folk heroes and huge draws at the gate. Their runs at the record books became the dominant narratives of individual seasons. But the sport is much changed. 'Muscle baseball' is the near opposite of what I and many other fans over 30 were raised on, a game that involved strategy, bunting, stolen bases, the hit-and-run play—what is called 'little ball'.

Professional basketball is not generally suspected of being drenched in steroids and other performance enhancers. But anyone who has seen even a few minutes of old games, from, say, 20 years ago, is immediately struck by the evolution of players' physiques. Regardless of how it happened, today's NBA players are heavier and markedly more muscled and the game is tailored to their strengths. It is played according to a steroid aesthetic. What was once a sport of grace and geometry-athletes moving to open spaces on the floor, thinking in terms of passing angles-is now one primarily of power and aggression: players gravitate to the same space and try to go over or through one another.

But it is sports that have fixed standards and cherished records that present fans with the greatest conundrum. If what's exciting is to see someone pole vault to a new, unimaginable height—or become the 'world's fastest human'—how do we respond when our historical frame of reference is knocked askew by the suspicion, or known fact, that an athlete is powered by a banned substance?

But in elite sport, the substances themselves are murky. Because America's $18 billion-a-year (£10bn) dietary-supplement industry is (at best) loosely regulated, some items on sale at ordinary health food shops could well be tainted by steroids or growth hormones. The United States Food and Drug Administration only banned ephedra last month, long after the herbal stimulant was blamed for numerous serious health problems, along with the sudden death last year of Steve Bechler, a Baltimore Orioles pitcher.

25   The whole situation cries out for a dose of clarity, but the closer you look, the fuzzier the picture. Start with the line between what's legal and illegal when it comes to enhancing performance. The line, already blurry, is likely over time to disappear entirely. I visited a US swimmer last September as technicians sealed up his bedroom, after which they installed equipment that reduced the amount of oxygen in his room and turned it into a high-altitude chamber. This is a common and legal training method that Ed Moses, America's best male breaststroker, said he hoped would increase his count of oxygen-carrying red blood cells. A whole team of long-distance runners sponsored by Nike lives in a much more elaborate simulated high-altitude dwelling in Portland, Oregon. The desired effect of the so-called 'live high, train low' method—sleep at altitude, train at sea level—is the same

as you would get from taking erythropoietin, or EPO, which increases red-blood-cell production and is banned in sports.

Two other US swimmers, in the lead-up to the Olympic Games in Sydney, were on a regimen of 25 pills a day, including minerals, proteins, amino acids and the nutritional supplement creatine, an effective but not necessarily safe builder of muscle mass. Much of the mix may well have been useless, but athletes tend to take what's put in front of them for fear of passing up the one magic pill.

'I like to think we're on the cutting edge of what can be done nutritionally and with supplements,' the swimmers' coach, Richard Quick, said then as his athletes prepared for the 2000 Games. 'If you work hard consistently, with a high level of commitment, you can do steroid-like performances.' One of his swimmers, Dara Torres, who increased her bench press from 105 pounds to 205 pounds and swam career-best times at the age of 33, said at the time that her goal was to 'keep up with the people who are cheating without cheating'.

And who are the cheaters? Everyone else. One primary motivation to cheat is the conviction that everyone else is at it. To draw the often arbitrary lines between performance enhancing and performance neutral, between health endangering and dicey but take it at your own risk—to ensure that sport remains 'pure'—a vast worldwide bureaucracy has been enlisted.

At the lowest level are those who knock on the doors of athletes in their homes and apartments in the United States and Europe and in the mountain villages of Kenya and at the training sites in China and demand 'out of competition' urine samples. Higher up on the pyramid are the laboratories around the world chosen to scan the urine (and blood) of elite athletes for the molecular signatures of any of hundreds of banned substances. At the top of the drug-fighting pyramid are the titans of international sport—the same people who often cannot see to it that a figure-skating competition is fairly judged.

30   Nearly every drug that is used by athletes to boost performance started out as a therapeutic miracle. Steroids are still prescribed for men with serious testosterone deficiencies. Aids patients and others with muscle-wasting conditions are dosed with steroids.

Until the mid-Eighties, people suffering from severe anaemia, as a result of chronic renal failure or other causes, had to have frequent blood transfusions. The development of recombinant human erythropoietin was a godsend. Instead of transfusions, anaemics could get injections to boost their red-blood-cell count. But what would the effect of EPO be on a person with a normal or better than normal red-blood-cell count? What could it do for an already genetically gifted, highly trained endurance athlete? Just what you would expect: make a super-endurance athlete.

EPO swept the European professional cycling circuit, nearly destroying the sport. There were police raids, huge stockpiles of EPO confiscated from cyclists' hotel rooms, arrests, trials, wholesale suspensions of competitors. 'Each racer had his little suitcase with dopes and syringes,' a former doctor said about one incident. 'They did their own injections.'

EPO migrated to other endurance sports, including cross-country skiing, marathoning and orienteering. Inevitably, it showed its fatal flip side.

'In simplest terms, EPO turns on the bone marrow to make more red blood cells,' says Dr Gary Wadler, the American delegate to the World Anti-Doping Agency. 'But there's a very delicate balance. You can have too much EPO. The body is a finely tuned instrument. It has feedback mechanisms to keep it in balance. What these athletes are often trying to do is get around the feedback, to trick their own bodies.'

35   Between 1989 and 1992, seven Swedish competitors in orienteering—that mix of running and hiking that is sometimes called 'cross country with brains'—died, apparently from heart attacks. Nearly all were in their twenties. As many as 18 Dutch and Belgian cyclists died under similarly mysterious circumstances between 1987 and 1990. 'At first they said it was some kind of virus, a respiratory virus,' Wadler says. 'But what kind of virus only knocks off the most fit individuals in their country? The autopsies were private. All the deaths were not definitively linked.' That it must have been EPO, he added, was obvious.

For weightlifters and competitors in the throwing sports of shot-put, javelin, discus and hammer, the performance enhancer of choice has long been steroids. Anabolic steroids (anabolic means tissue building) increase muscle mass and enhance the explosiveness needed for a wide range of other athletic endeavours: sprinting, jumping, swimming, serving a tennis ball, swinging a baseball bat, delivering a hit on the American football or rugby field. Their use is starkly high risk, high reward. Other side effects include liver tumours, impotence, breast enlargement and shrunken testicles in men and male sexual characteristics in women. (Some of the side effects for women include enlargement of the clitoris, deepening of the voice, facial hair and male-pattern baldness.)

If you want a peek at the future of performance-enhanced sport—at what drug-laced athletes can accomplish—look back to the mid-Eighties, the apex of East Germany's shameful and ruthlessly effective doping programme. The East Germans were not the only practitioners of extreme pharmacological sport, only the most flagrant and well organised. (East Germany is the only nation known to have systematically doped athletes, often minors, without their knowledge.)

Steroid usage works particularly well for women athletes, because they naturally make only a fraction of the testosterone that men produce. John Hoberman says: 'In the 1980s, what we saw was this new breed of monster athletes, particularly on the female side.'

Certain records from this heyday of unpoliced steroid abuse—particularly in sports in which raw strength is a primary requirement—suggest that performances were achieved then that are unlikely to be matched by a clean competitor. The top 14 men's hammer throws in history occurred between 1984 and 1988. In the women's shot-put, you must go all the way down to the 35th farthest throw in history to find one that occurred after 1988.

40 Until last April, the top 10 men's shot-put throws in history occurred between 1975 and 1990. Then, at a competition in Kansas, the American shot-putter Kevin Toth finally broke into that elite group. His distance, 22.67 meters,

was the farthest that anyone had put the shot in 13 years. Six months later, Toth's name was among the first to surface in the Balco scandal. Published reports said he had tested positive for THG, the new designer steroid.

In women's sprinting in the 1980s, the star—and still the world-record holder in the 100m and 200m—was Florence Griffith-Joyner, Flo-Jo. Americans loved her style, her body-hugging track suits, her long and fabulously decorated nails, her ebullience. Elsewhere in the world, and even in the United States among those with a knowledge of track and field, Flo-Jo's exploits were viewed with more scepticism.

After Joyner died in 1998, at 38 (the cause was related to a seizure), a strange hybrid of a column appeared in the *New York Times* sports section. Written by Pat Connolly, who had coached Evelyn Ashford, the woman whose 100m record Joyner smashed, it was partly a tribute and partly a posthumous indictment. 'Then, almost overnight, Florence's face changed—hardened along with her muscles that now bulged as if she had been born with a barbell in her crib,' Connolly wrote. 'It was difficult not to wonder if she had found herself an East German coach and was taking some kind of performance-enhancing drugs.'

Flo-Jo had been a very good, but never a champion, world-class sprinter. Her 1988 performance in Seoul was—in the damning parlance of international sport—anomalous.

Baseball is rarely thought of in the context of hammer throwing, shot-putting or women's sprinting. But in terms of anomalous performance, baseball is potentially East Germany in the 1980s: a new frontier. Just as in the steroid-drenched days of Olympic sport, a deep suspicion has attached itself to baseball and its lenient testing programme, not least because of the grotesque, bloated appearance of some of the players.

45 The question of how many home runs it is possible to hit in one season is more open-ended than, say, the fastest possible time a person can achieve in the 100m. Factors such as the size of the ballpark, liveliness of the ball and skill of opposing pitchers affect the outcome. Nevertheless, a century's worth of experience amounted

to a pretty persuasive case that around 60 home runs, for whatever combination of reasons, was about the limit.

In 1927, Babe Ruth slugged 60, which remained the record until 1961, when Roger Maris (in a slightly longer season) hit 61. But in 1998 McGwire of the St Louis Cardinals obliterated Maris's record by hitting 70 home runs.

Late in that season, a reporter snooping around McGwire's locker spotted a bottle of androstenedione, or andro, a substance usually described as a steroid 'precursor' that provides a steroid-like effect (and that is still unregulated in the major leagues). McGwire was forced to acknowledge that his strength was neither entirely 'God given' nor acquired solely in the weight room. But McGwire entered baseball already big and as a prodigious home-run hitter: he hit 49 in his first big-league season, a record for rookies. Contrast that with the career arcs of Barry Bonds and Sammy Sosa, which are unlike any in the game's long history. Bonds had never hit more than 46 home runs until the 2000 season and in most years his total was in the 30s. But at age 35, when players normally are on the downside of their production, he hit 49 home runs. The following season he turned into superman, breaking McGwire's record by hitting 73.

Bonds's totals in the next two seasons, 46 and 45, were artificially low because pitchers walked him a staggering 346 times. His new capabilities had thrown the balance between pitcher and hitter completely out of whack: the new Barry Bonds was too good for the game. He needed a league all of his own.

Sosa's progression was even more unusual. In his first eight major-league seasons he averaged 22 home runs, although his totals did steadily increase and he hit 40 in 1996, then a career high. He was selected an All-Star exactly once. Unlike Bonds, he was not considered among baseball's elite players.

50   Then in 1998, McGwire's record-breaking year, Sammy Sosa hit 66 home runs—six more than the great Babe Ruth had hit in his best season. Sosa wasn't done. The following year he hit 63, followed by seasons of 50, 64 and 49—the best five-year total in baseball history.

There is no evidence that Bonds and Sosa have used steroids, but that there is steroid use in baseball, at all levels, is undeniable. Ken Caminiti, voted the National League's most valuable player in 1996, admitted his own use in a *Sports Illustrated* sarticle in 2002 and estimated that at least half the players in the big leagues built strength with steroids. The former slugger Jose Canseco has acknowledged steroid use. In a 2002 *USA Today* survey of 556 big-league players, 44 percent said they felt pressure to take steroids.

Last year, the *Washington Post* published a sad series of stories revealing that teenage prospects in the baseball-rich Dominican Republic, the source of nearly a quarter of all players signed to US professional contracts, are taking veterinary steroids to try to get strong enough to attract the interest of scouts.

Nobody has presented evidence that Sosa or Bonds has built home-run power chemically. And both vehemently deny it. Sosa's name has not surfaced in the Balco case and he has not testified before the grand jury. Bonds did testify in December but he has not been accused of any wrongdoing.

Bonds has acknowledged patronising Balco, which under Victor Conte, its founder, has specialised in testing athletes' blood to determine the levels of elements such as copper, chromium and magnesium and then recommending supplements. Experts I talked to say they consider Conte's theories medical mumbo jumbo, but he consulted dozens of top athletes, including Marion Jones, Amy van Dyken (an Olympic champion swimmer) and Bill Romanowski, a linebacker in the NFL with the Oakland Raiders. Jason Giambi of the New York Yankees was also a client and also testified before the grand jury.

55   The World Anti-Doping Agency—imperfect as it may be—is generally considered an improvement over the patchwork approach to drug enforcement that preceded it. Created in 1999 at the World Conference on Doping in Sport in Lausanne, Switzerland, the agency was intended to bring coherence to anti-doping regulations and harmonisation among all the different nations and sports bodies expected to enforce them. In theory, it is the ultimate authority on matters of drugs and sport—looming over

national Olympic committees and the national and international federations of all the individual sports and making it more difficult for those parochial interests to protect athletes caught doping.

Wada's medical committee devoted several years to compiling an impressively voluminous list of banned substances. But the role of Wada and its president, Dick Pound, is mainly bureaucratic and political. Wada can't slow science down—or influence a culture that hungrily pursues human enhancements of all kinds.

'All of these issues are going to be moot in 20 or 30 years,' says Paul Root Wolpe, a professor of psychiatry at Penn and the chief of bioethics at Nasa. 'We already are seeing a blurring of the line between foods and drugs, so-called nutraceuticals. In the future, it will be more common, accepted. We'll eat certain engineered foods to be sharp for a business meeting, to increase confidence, to enhance endurance before a race or competition.'

What I learnt during my visit to Lee Sweeney's lab at the University of Pennsylvania is that lifting his research for purposes of athletic enhancement is not from some sci-fi future. It's possible—now. Sweeney and his team know for sure they can build muscle mass and strength. Their next step as they try to determine if their methods are safe for humans will be to experiment on larger animals, most likely dogs with muscular dystrophy.

I asked Elisabeth Barton what would happen if some rogue nation or outlaw conglomerate of athletes asked her to disregard scientific prudence and create a human version of the mighty mice. Could she do it?

60   'Could I?' she answered. 'Oh, yeah, it's easy. It's do-able. It's a routine method that's published. Anyone who can clone a gene and work with cells could do it. It's not a mystery.'

Behind her, Sweeney nodded his head in agreement. 'It's not like growing a third arm or something,' he said. 'You could get there if you worked at it.'

There is a parallel from the past for the entire issue of performance-enhancing drugs, one tied to what was once another unwelcome substance in sports: money. Some casual followers of the Olympic movement may still not fully realise that nearly all of the participants are now paid professionals.

There never was any big announcement that the cherished concept of amateurism—athletes competing for the pure love of sport—had been discarded. But over time, the changed reality has been accepted. Top athletes profiting from under-the-table payments? The public didn't care, and the ideal of amateurism expired, outdated and unenforceable.

One of the last things Pound said to me indicated that he knows, too, that Wada's mission has an expiry date pending. Maybe genetic enhancements really won't work for athletes, he speculated. 'If you strengthen the muscle to three times its normal strength, what happens when you break out of the starting blocks? Do you rip the muscle right off the bone?'

65   Pound seemed to like the thought of this gruesome image. He paused, then extended the thought. 'That would be nice if that happened,' he said. 'It would be self-regulating.'

Reflect & Write

❏ Why does the article open and close with the image of "mighty mice"? Considering that "Mighty Mouse" was a popular cartoon character twenty years ago, how might the image reflect cultural attitudes toward doping athletes today?

❏ Sokolove claims that once a drug's benefits appear in "a legitimate publication," then people clamor for it. How might appearing in print validate a drug? Is this an effect of ethos or logos? What does the look of scholarly research contribute to the economic value and social cache for a drug product?

❏ Why does Sokolove consistently compare athletes taking drug, vitamin, and nutrition supplements to AIDS patients? How does this writing strategy affect his overall argument?

❏ **Write:** How have sports taken on a new set of visual stereotypes? Locate Sokolove's use of descriptions such as "heavier" "marked," "gruesome," "monster," "bulged," "grotesque," and "bloated," and write a rhetorical analysis as to why his choice of language contributes to his argument.

■ **Andrew Tilin** *currently serves as the editor for the "What's Cool" section for* Business 2.0, *a magazine focused on business, technology, and innovation published by Time Warner. Tilin has contributed articles to numerous publications, including* The New York Times Magazine, Rolling Stone, *and* GQ, *and served as a contributing editor to* Wired. *This article originally appeared in the September 2000 issue of* Wired.

Ready, Set, Mutate!

Andrew Tilin

Italian physicist Ciro Fusco thinks he knows exactly what could stop a muscled-up sprinter from winning gold at this month's Summer Games in Sydney, Australia—the spikes on his or her shoes, which have a tiny-but-measurable "glue effect" when they stab a track's surface. Fusco has spent the last four years studying such minutiae while developing adidas gear for the 2000 Olympics. He and a team of engineers used computer modeling to rethink the existing shape of track spikes; what emerged was a shallow Z-shaped cleat, made from a ceramic-aluminum alloy, that doesn't poke into the runway. Instead the shoe grabs the running surface and then easily lets go.

It all sounds a little obsessive, but at a time when jocks are maxing out the body's capabilities, micro-innovations can add up. "Athletes have reached certain physical limitations," says Fusco. "And now technology is optimizing their performance."

Of course, the five-ring brass gets nervous when it hears talk of enhancements beyond extra effort, pep talks, and Gatorade; they're forever scrambling to control technology's growing influence on sports. Witness the absence (due to tubing size restrictions) from Sydney's velodromes of the aerodynamic, carbon-fiber bikes that were rolled out four years ago in Atlanta, and the mandate given to Speedo, in the name of fair play, to dole out its sleek new swimsuits to any competitor who wants one. As for drugs, notorious test-tube elixirs like human growth hormone and erythropoietin are coming under more scrutiny than ever. Nevertheless, International Olympic Committee officials have all but conceded that their ability to test for banned substances isn't reliable enough to catch everybody.

Which raises a point: It may be time to reexamine this whole athletic purity thing and say to hell with it. Within at least five years, elite athletes will be able to obtain genetic upgrades, injecting mutated nucleotide chains that stimulate the production of oxygen-toting red blood cells or increased musculature. Olympic officials might not be able to stop that either, so wouldn't it be better to make sure everybody, including those teensy badminton players from South Korea, gets a safe, reliable gene boost? (And while we're at it, could we put Flubber tips on the shuttlecocks to liven up the action?)

5   In celebration of this escalating pursuit of faster-higher-stronger, we've compiled a cutting-edge athlete's duffel of techno-enhanced clothing, equipment, and drugs that will help the world's athletes mine gold starting September 15 and running through the October Paralympics. After that comes some innovations for the future. Although these optimizers may take a while to debut, an Olympic year is the perfect time to recognize the spirit they represent: Screw purity—what we want is possibility.

Arrow Dynamic

To battle Sydney's 20-knot springtime gusts and enhance the accuracy of the venerable X10 arrow long used in archery competition, Easton Technical Products sought out technology from a Defense Department contractor that builds tank-killing shells. The new addition to the barrel-shaped, aluminum/carbon-fiber shaft is a tungsten tip that's 2.2 times denser than conventional steel. With more of the arrow's weight concentrated at the front, the upgraded X10 travels straighter in a crosswind.

Fuel Injection

Sports drugs now come in more blends than you'll find at Starbucks. With the threat of a new Olympic dope test that could detect EPO (the popular hormone that stimulates the formation of red blood cells and thereby increases aerobic capacity by up to 15 percent), endurance athletes have found a new way to boost the transport of oxygen to redlining muscles. The illicit concoction is a blood expander—an undetectable and experimental synthetic plasma that carries additional oxygen and was originally designed for people in need of transfusions. Problem is, the shelf life of these red-cell substitutes can be short, and they may have been responsible for trauma-patient deaths in clinical trials. "The artificial blood could cause an allergic reaction, get stuck in your kidneys, and cause them to fail," warns Don Catlin, an opponent of such tactics who directs UCLA's Olympic Analytical Lab.

Skin Trade

The most impressive of the new uniforms debuting Down Under is Speedo's intricately textured Fastskin. Following four years of development, the full-body stretch-nylon swimsuit is covered with tiny scales and sharklike, V-shaped ridges. Water literally breaks off the Fastskin, lowering hydrodynamic drag by 6 percent over conventional spandex. Meanwhile, adidas' One-Armed Throwing Suit for javelin and discus competitors, as well as shot-putters, has a Power Lycra sleeve that compresses the athlete's arm to heighten proprioception, or the awareness of where one's limbs are in space. And Nike's Swift Suit has golf ball-style dimples on the arms and legs to cut down runner-generated turbulence.

Thrust and Parry

Fencers' feet perform distinctly different tasks, so adidas designers concluded that fencing footwear should follow suit. The lead shoe (far right) is always pointing at the opponent and moving back and forth, so the rubber tread runs side to side for maximum traction. A generous helping of foam cushioning provides for softer landings during Zorro-style attacks. The rear shoe, positioned perpendicular to the lead shoe, is canted toward the arch, easily rolling inward when an athlete lunges forward.

Live High, Train Low

10 One big conundrum for endurance athletes is finding a way to sleep at high elevations (where thin air prompts the body to produce more red blood cells) and train at sea level (where oxygen-rich air permits exercise at the greatest intensities). Solution: the Hypoxico Tent System. The collapsible tent can accommodate a queen-sized bed and is attached to a hypoxicator, or air-separation generator, that withholds enough oxygen molecules to simulate conditions up to 9,000 feet. Olympic race-walkers and cyclists have been snoozing between the nylon walls since late last year.

Internal Combustion

The night-before group spaghetti-feed has been delivered a death blow: Performance diets are now tailored to the requirements of individuals and their sports. It begins with a prick of the finger in the lab, where white blood cells are isolated and analyzed down to the DNA level. After testing the effectiveness of various nutrients on the cells, a nutritionist determines specific responsiveness to such things as carbs and protein, and builds a custom diet that can result in fewer injuries and better performance. "Athletes in the same event can have very different dietary needs," says Jeffrey Bland, a nutritional bio-chemist and president of Washington's Institute for Functional Medicine, which is attracting the doctors of Olympic cyclists and runners.

Spring Action

Some Paralympic runners will strap on Flex-Foot's latest Sprint-Flex III prosthetic, a carbon-fiber, bowed spring of a lower limb, to speed them down the track. Drawing on feed-back from athletes, designers at the Aliso Viejo, California, company built the Sprint-Flex III's toe about 2 inches longer than earlier models for increased ground contact and better stability when launching out of the blocks. Look for the 2.5-pound artificial shin to propel a 100-meter competitor under the previously unassailable 11-second barrier.

Coming Soon!

High Style

What athletes wear to future games will be considerably more than just a fashion statement. Record-breaking bodyware will carry chemicals that convert sweat into energy or trigger timed, in-body adrenaline releases. "Nanofactories will synthesize chemicals directly on the fabric," says Stephen Michielsen, a professor of textile and fiber engineering at the Georgia Institute of Technology in Atlanta. Another closet possibility: duds knitted with optical fibers to transmit an athlete's voice and physiological data (heart rate, for instance) to a coach pacing the sidelines.

Manmade Muscles

Researchers at MIT are growing tissue in their petri dishes that could make prosthetics more human and less contraption, adding developed calf muscle, for example, to an already powerful, energy-rebounding limb like the Sprint-Flex III. Genetic- and nerve-related hurdles, as well as circulation-system issues, are currently keeping manmade muscles from being as good as the real thing. But the big brains believe their cultured muscles can grow stronger with use, and run less on battery power than sugar water. "The idea is that machines will be somewhat like us," says Hugh Herr, the MIT project director and a double-below-knee amputee. "In my lifetime, I would love to feed my prosthetic ankles."

Contact Lenses

15 Talk about synchronized swimming: Goggles with heads-up displays will make sure athletes swim their race by the numbers. Inside the goggles' lenses, stroke rate, elapsed time, and other key data will be projected the way vital information is flashed onto a fighter pilot's windshield. In addition, a poolside computer would be fed physiological statistics via telemetry so coaches could analyze the numbers and send radio-communicated advice to swimmers wearing remote headsets attached to goggle straps. By the time athletes make a splash in Athens four years from now, they'll be able to get and give feedback with nary a pause between strokes.

Redefining Runway

Nike engineers are betting that a high heel, not a sneaker, will produce the fastest times. Observing that full-tilt runners never come down off the balls of their feet during the first 10 meters of a race, researchers hypothesize that if an athlete could continue for the next 90 meters using the same stride, records would be broken. "The foot needs to act as a lever so the power coming from the rest of your body doesn't vanish," says Tom Carleo, head of shoe development for Nike's Olympic runners. "We're trying to improve on natural locomotion." Swooshed pumps, with heels kept high by springs, could be prototyped within two years.

Turbo Tablets

Who says performance-enhancing pills have to mess with your chemistry? Already being used by astronauts and soldiers to avert overheating and dehydration, one disposable sensor capsule from Palmetto, Florida's HTI Technologies could be repurposed by solo endurance athletes and team players to measure everything from body temperature to heart rate. Readings from the ingestible devices are sent to a Polar receiver and displayed on a handheld telemeter. While still only theory, another concentrated tablet envisioned by physiologist Bob Murray, director of the Gatorade Sports Science Institute, could release carbohydrates over time, ensuring optimal performance.

Reflect & Write

❑ How does the author use tone, diction, and even humor in this piece? How does this tone differ from that of other pieces about performance-enhancement you've read in this chapter?

- All the points in this piece are based on research; how is research deployed and represented here?
- What image of future Olympians does this article conjure up for you?
- **Write:** Choose one of the innovations mentioned above and develop a marketing campaign for that product. Identify a target audience and a means of distribution (radio ads? commercials? print ads? Web ads?) for your marketing. You might choose to roll out your marketing campaign at the 2012 Olympics in London. Draft one sample advertisement for this marketing campaign and share it with the class. Carefully consider how to use rhetorical appeals and your understanding of kairos and the rhetorical situation to make a persuasive advertisement. Write a reflection to accompany your ad in which you identify your target audience, your means of distribution (radio? television? newspapers? magazines? billboards? Websites?) and your rationale for choosing this means. Finally, explain which rhetorical strategies you used in your ad and why.

■ *In 2000, Speedo began development on a technological innovation to help swimmers. Through studying shark skin, Speedo developed Fastskin, a full body suit composed of different fabrics and textures designed to optimize the swimmer's stroke potential. As mentioned in "Ready, Set! Mutate!," Fastskin premiered at the 2000 Sydney Olympics.*

Fastskin Advertisement

Speedo

FIGURE 11.7 Designed to evoke science fiction film, this Speedo ad features a group of young people wearing "Fastskin" swimwear.

Reflect & Write

- Analyze the imagery of this poster. What is the theme that is used to market Fastskin? How is that theme realized in the design and arrangement of this poster? Why do you think that the artists chose to use this theme?
- Does this poster rely most heavily on logos, pathos, or ethos in producing its argument? Explain your response.
- How are "Ready, Set, Mutate" and this poster making similar arguments about performance enhancement? What is that argument?
- **Write:** Visit the Speedo website http://www.speedo.com and read about Fastskin. Now draft an alternative poster based on a different rhetorical appeal than the one used in the poster Figure 11.7. Share your poster and your rhetorical strategies with your class.

COLLABORATIVE CHALLENGE

The USADA (United States Anti-Doping Agency) houses several videos on its Website designed to educate kids about the use of steroids and performance-enhancing drugs. Either in class or in small groups in a computer lab, watch the videos that link from the Envision Website. What rhetorical choices are evident in the composition of these films? How are words and images used in combination? How is the USADA represented in the films? If you were to revise one of the videos, how would you do so? Together with your peers, storyboard two or three scenes that you would add into the film to make it more effective for its target audience. Present your group storyboard and rationale to the class.

www.ablongman.com/envision/237

REFLECTING ON THE ISSUE

1. Look back to the cartoon by Nick Anderson at the beginning of Chapter 1 and compare it to the cartoons in this chapter. What argument does Nick Anderson make concerning the effects of steroid use on children? Consider at least three different possibilities; support your answer with specific visual details from the cartoon. Now write a comparative essay contrasting Anderson's cartoon to one of the ones you have analyzed in this chapter. You might also want to bring in additional cartoons from Daryl Cagle's expansive "Steroids 'n Baseball" collection (http://cagle.slate.msn.com/news/BaseballSteroidsRoundup/main.asp). Write an analysis essay in which you compare the different arguments and strategies found in these cartoons.

2. One the major issues presented by these articles is articulated by Steven Shapin: "What is to count as normal?" Write your own response to this question, responding explicitly to quotations you take from the second half of Shapin's article as well as to points made in the interview with Thomas Murray and the article by Mike Sokolove.

3. When Michael Sokolove revised his *New York Times Magazine* article for publication in the *Observer Sports Magazine,* he cut the article by almost half. Find and read the original article by locating it in the library. Then compare the two versions. What did he excise during revision? Did the revision change the content of his argument? Did it change the delivery of his argument? Is one version more persuasive than the other? Why?

4. Compare Andrew Tilin's piece against Michael Sokolove's piece for their different strategies of relying on research. Which article makes its iceberg of research most visible? Which one seems more academic and which more popular? Can you identify each author's rhetorical stance? Compare their use of descriptive language as well. Which article seems to you more persuasive about the issue of "performance and perfection"?

5. What lies ahead for the future of sports? Will we ever return to an age of "purity"? How do we draw the line between synthetic chemicals, technological innovations in shoes and clothing, innovative training regimes, oxygen sleep chambers, and medical advancements? Craft an argument in which you take a stand on this issue. Use quotations from the articles in this chapter if you wish to respond to their arguments. Follow the Guidelines in Chapter 6 in order to craft your own perspective on this issue.

FROM READING TO RESEARCH

1. Visit the Speedoaqualab through its Website at http://www.speedoaqualab.com/. How does this part of the Website function as a marketing tool? Consider this Website in conjunction with the Fastskin poster reproduced earlier in this case study. Now draft an analysis and evaluation of Speedo's marketing strategies for Fastskin—use the research sources available on Envision online for Chapter 2 in "Surveying the Field" to help you compose your research argument about the Website. Then transform your analysis into a persuasive argument. That is, write as if you were the advertising agency proposing it to Speedo for the first time and be sure to use a solid rationale for explaining why you feel this marketing approach would be successful. When you are finished, compare the two writing genres. Which one is more compelling to you? To your instructor? To the business community? How do the different forms of writing rely on similar sources?

2. Relying not only on the knowledge you've gained in reading the articles for this Chapter, but also on additional research you conduct in the library, write a research paper about the veterinary steroids taken by young Dominican Republican baseball hopefuls. Then, transform your paper into an op-ad. Compare your op-ad to the image in Figure 11.2. What governs the rhetorical choices you make in terms of design, image, color, and verbal accompaniment? Use your op-ad as a cover for your research paper on the situation in the Dominican Republic concerning recruitment and training conditions. Ask your librarian for help locating additional sources you might use in this written document.

GLOBAL SPORTS AND NATIONAL IDENTITY

Today, sports athletes are superstars with global fame. Consider the most popular names we hear on television, the radio, in advertisements, on the Web, and even in film. Tiger Woods, Ichiro Suzuki, Yao Ming, and Sammy Sosa?these are a few recent stars who have globalized sports. These individuals stand for more than a single player in a single sport. Tiger Woods, whom some call "a global citizen," has changed the identity of the American athlete by transforming the popular representation of golf. Ichiro Suzuki symbolizes new global exchanges between not only Japan and America, but potentially between other countries such as the Dominican Republican as well, where baseball is Americanizing culture and where local athletes are hoping to help make America more international. Many look to Yao Ming as a "bridge" figure between China and America, but also between Chinese and Asian Americans as well as among various minority

FIGURE 11.8 This poster for Beijing Olympics, 2008, features the slogan "New Beijing—Great Olympics," and shows many nationalities coming together.

communities in America.

However, it is not just the individual athlete who fosters a connection between different contexts and cultures. Sporting events themselves have also come to serve a pivotal role in the globalization of sports. From the Olympics to the World Cup, international competition serve the dual role of both reinforcing the idea of global unity while simultaneously re-positioning each team firmly within its national identity. The athletes might come together on one playing field, but in some ways they are never more identified with nationhood as during these global events.

In this chapter, we'll examine such trends as we look at "Global Sports and National Identity." How do athletes stand for more than individual achievement? What is it that enables them to stand as visual signs of nations, cross-cultural identity, communities in transition, or the force of globalization? Moreover, we'll examine how the representation and media coverage of sports works in our visual world. If, as Emma Wensing argues in this chapter, "Sporting events are one of the few public spheres where nations compete against each other without causing harm," then how do games such as the Olympics provide an important social function for our world?

Reflect & Write

❑ How does the design of the poster convey the idea of global unity or partnership? To what extent do these design choices successfully convey these ideas?
❑ Considering the context of the photograph (taken on the streets of Beijing), what argument does the photograph itself make? Think about issues like perspective, composition, and arrangement.
❑ **Write:** Building from the discussion of persona in Chapter 3, write a brief op-ed from the perspective of the person in the photograph discussing to what extent the Olympics represents a moment of global unity and cooperation.

A PhD candidate at the University of Toronto, **Emma Wensing** *is a specialist in Physical Education and Health. The argument of this article, published in* Yale Global *in August 2004, is drawn both from from her Masters thesis and her further research on media and culture.*

Olympics in an Age of Global Broadcasting

Emma Wensing

When the XXVIII Olympiad opens in Athens, get ready for the bursts of national pride. Since the 1964 Tokyo Games, when the Olympics were telecast live for the first time, they have become the most global sporting event in the world. Gathering together athletes and sport officials from over 200 countries as well as global corporations, the Olympic broadcast now attracts an audience of billions. Yet despite these globalizing features, the Olympics, with its televised flag-raising and national anthems for the winners, actually serves to reinforce the political and cultural distinctiveness of individual nation-states.

It is at international sport competitions, like the Olympics, that sentiments of national identification and belonging come to the fore in media coverage. Sporting events are one of the few public spheres where nations compete against each other without causing harm. International sport, in this context, can be seen as a substitute for war, as physical prowess becomes a measure of a nation's standing on an international stage. The country that wins, or receives the most number of medals, is simply superior.

However, this one-dimensional perspective means that only one country can therefore 'win' the overall medal tally. Yet countries from around the world still manage to celebrate their Olympic athletes as national heroes. While taking images from the host Olympic broadcaster, many countries also send their own television crews to the Games to provide nationally focused commentary and discussion. Western-centered research on the Olympics and other large international sporting events (like soccer's World Cup and the Commonwealth Games) has shown that sports media coverage typically emphasizes national athletes and symbols, plays up desired national characteristics, and emphasizes locally-relevant rivalries in order to make the event meaningful for the viewers back home.

Each nation's Olympic coverage focuses on its own athletes, because the media believe that is what people 'back home' want to see. Commentators often refer to national teams as 'our team' or 'our athletes', which reinforces for audiences that they too should be identifying with 'their' national representatives. As well, giving athletes or teams nicknames—such as equestrian 'Captain Canada' Ian Millar or the American basketball 'Dream Team'—further helps audiences form a connection with specific national athletes. On-screen graphics, like national flags in the corner of the screen, are also used to make Olympic coverage nationally distinct.

5   Every country values different qualities and characteristics in its citizens, and these transfer to national representatives. A country's general sense of its place on the world stage, in combi-nation with desired traits, will shape the Olympic broadcast in that nation. For example, New Zealand, as a small country, is highly unlikely to win more medals than China, Germany, or the United States. So the New Zealand media tend to downplay success as the sole factor in evaluating their athletes' performances. Instead, their coverage emphasizes how hard the athletes have trained, their 'good sports' ethic, and the value of simply participating and sharing in such a wonderful event. These characteristics reflect the qualities desired in 'typical' New Zealanders who give their all. By highlighting the intrinsic elements of athletic performance, the New Zealand media reduce the risk of embarrassment if the athletes fail to perform. If the athletes do win, their success can be celebrated as a bonus.

In contrast, Australia's Olympic coverage emphasizes winning. Although Australians are unlikely to top the overall medal tally, winning more medals than specific rivals is of paramount concern. Beating the United Kingdom plays an essential role in confirming Australia's national identity by proving it has overcome relatively humble beginnings as a British penal settlement and colonial outpost. Surpassing the performance of colonial neighbor New Zealand is taken as a given although rivalry in certain sports, such as equestrian and rowing, is still strong. Today, the main rivalry for Australians is the United States, especially in swimming. Success in the pool marks Australia as unique in the face of an increasingly American-dominated national and popular culture.

Countries that are geographically close, have co-dependent economies and/or political allegiances also use sporting competitions as a means of ensuring cultural distinctiveness. However, it is typically in countries under 'threat' from these globalizing forces that events like the Olympics take on greater national significance. The cultural value and importance of Olympic sports that embody the determined nature of Canadians is indicated by the extensive public demonstrations of national pride following victories over their neighbor, the United States. After Canadian victories in the ice hockey competitions at the 2002 Winter Olympics, flag waving, wearing 'Canada' t-shirts, street parties and parades were common. In contrast, the United States, as an already established cultural, political and economic leader, has relatively less to gain from successful Olympic performance in terms of building national identity and pride. Indeed, the United States appears so secure in its place as a world leader, that participating in localized and internally-focused sports like Major League Baseball, NBA Basketball, and NFL Football is enough to reinforce key national values such as success, athletic mastery, and upwards economic mobility.

While media coverage of the Olympics emphasizes difference between nations, it can also narrow the definition of what it means to belong to a particular nation and further undermine the Olympic rhetoric of uniting people. By presenting only one version of the nation's Olympic story, media coverage can reinforce ideological power relations within individual nations. An example is broadcasts that focus on the athletic achievements of male athletes, and the domestic roles (wife/mother/daughter) of female athletes. Different reporting styles for male and female athletes can reinforce cultural ideas about gender difference rather than focusing on the shared physical and mental abilities needed to become the best in the world. In addition to gender, sports media coverage can also emphasize preferred cultural values of class, race, sexuality and dis/ability.

When sports performances are deemed to have extraordinary political, cultural or economic significance, internal national divisions may be overridden in coverage of high profile, successful, individual athletes. At the Sydney 2000 Olympics, the performance of Indigenous Australian 400-metre runner Cathy Freeman was tied to the contentious political issue of progress on Aboriginal reconciliation. Freeman was presented by the media as a person who could unite Australia through athletic success, and this unity could then be transferred to political pressure on the Australian government to apologize for past injustices to Indigenous peoples. In this instance, Freeman's status as a symbol for national unity and reconciliation appeared to negate her ideologically subordinate positions of being female and Indigenous.

10   It is clear that the Olympic sports media context is important for maintaining and constructing the collective identity of individual nations. Sports media coverage helps nations define themselves as unique, whether through success or the valuing of particular characteristics. In addition, commercial pressures to provide large audiences for Olympic and broadcast sponsors means that local broadcasts will be tailored further to increase the meaningfulness of the event for particular national audiences. In this way, Olympic broadcasting is simultaneously tied to both the local and the global contexts. As the Olympics are staged over the next two weeks, watch cautiously and think critically about the way the broadcast is shaped for your particular national audience. Remember that what you are watching is not just athletes competing, but a carefully planned and managed television product designed to keep you interested by reinforcing where your allegiances should lie.

Reflect & Write

❑ Wensing identifies the flag as an example of the visual rhetoric of nationalism. What other examples make the Olympic coverage nationally distinct by country? How are victories celebrated through visual rhetoric? What about the visual appearance of winners themselves? Discuss four examples from the article and the meaning of each.

❑ How does coverage of the Olympics in diverse countries reflect those countries' national values? How are such arguments created based on a premise of shared values?

❑ Does the thesis of this rhetorical analysis essay stand true today? Consider the context of world powers, recent political events, sports wins, and the location of the next Olympics.

❑ **Write:** The conclusion to this article takes a rather strong turn and reveals the writer's stance about the influence of the media concerning national identity. Can you rewrite the conclusion to offer a more open-ended perspective?

■ *To commemorate the summer 2006 World Cup,* National Geographic *published excerpts from* The Thinking Fan's Guide to the World Cup *in its June 2006 issue. The excerpts, collected under the title "The Beautiful Game: Why Soccer Rules the World," detailed its influence on nations as varied as Spain and Angola. The following articles, on Argentina and Croatia, are taken from this* National Geographic *feature story. Thomas Jones, author of "Ode to Maradona," serves as an editor and contributor to the* London Review of Books. *Courtney Angela Brkic, the author of the selection on Croatia, is an American of Croatian descent, known primarily for her award-winning collection of stories,* Stillness, *and for her work with victims of Srebrenica, Bosnia, which she described in* Stone Fields: An Epitaph for the Living.

The Beautiful Game: Why Soccer Rules the World

National Geographic

Ode to Maradona: Falklands' Revenge

Thomas Jones

The highest compliment anyone could pay any-one else when I was growing up in England in the 1980s was "skill" (as in "man, your new skateboard is so skill"), and nobody was more skill than Diego Armando Maradona. His name was invoked as the highest form of praise, on the soccer field and elsewhere ("man, your new skateboard is so Maradona"). It took me a while to realize that the word referred to a human be-ing, let alone a soccer player. Then I saw him score against Italy in the 1986 World Cup, leap-ing several feet into the air outside the left edge of the six-yard box to tap the ball deftly over the outstretched right leg of the Italian captain, past the outstretched arms of the keeper, and into the bottom right-hand corner of the goal. It was evi-dent, even to me, that Maradona was not merely skillful, but skill embodied.

The next time Maradona scored was June 22, the day Argentina played against England. The two nations had last clashed four years ear-lier, not on a soccer field but in the Falklands War, which Argentine writer Jorge Luis Borges later compared to "a fight between two bald men over a comb." By the time Britain had re-taken the islands from Argentina, more than 900 men (most of them Argentines) had lost their lives. The victory saw Margaret Thatcher's pop-ularity soar in Britain; the defeat contributed to the downfall of the right-wing military junta that had ruled Argentina since 1976.

Group Therapy: A Nation is Born

Courtney Angela Brkic

Not so long ago, when Croatia was part of Yugoslavia, soccer was an expression of ethnic-ity, of political orientation, of self. Many feel that a 1990 match between Zagreb's Dinamo and Belgrade's Red Star marked the beginning of Croatia's war for independence. At the begin-ning of the match, fans from both sides clashed in the stands and on the field. The Serb-dominated police beat Croatian fans while allowing Serb fans to run amok, and the events caused the al-ready bubbling frustrations with Yugoslavia to boil over. Even the players were not immune. Upon witnessing a policeman beating a fallen Dinamo fan, midfielder Zvonimir Boban karate-kicked him, becoming a hero of the growing independence movement.

The war that followed was long and brutal. More than ten thousand people were killed, and one thousand are still missing today. Not surpris-ingly, tourists stopped visiting the Croatian coast, and the region became associated with suffering. For a country so rich in potential, so enthusiastic about what it could achieve now that it was on its own, being classified simply as a war zone or a former Yugoslav republic was a blow.

Croatia's independence was recognized in 1992, but the 1998 World Cup brought another form of recognition. Elation had already begun to sweep the country when Croatia beat powerhouse Germany in the quarterfinals. "Is it really possi-ble?" people seemed to be asking one another,

All that was ancient history four years later—or so both teams insisted before the game. Maradona scored both of Argentina's goals in a 2-1 victory over England. The second of them, 11 dazzling seconds of superhuman skill, was voted Goal of the Century in 2002. When Maradona executed an exquisite arabesque, stretching his right leg elegantly behind him, I wouldn't have been surprised if he'd taken off into the air and started flying. He appeared to be moving through a different time frame from the England players, who came to tackle him only once he was already past them.

To my surprise, nobody I knew wanted to talk about that second, extraordinary goal. All anyone wanted to talk about was the one he'd scored four minutes earlier, with his fist. Maradona's one-time fans were seething with fury, as if he'd betrayed them personally. Overnight his name had become an insult, a by-word for cheating. I was baffled. What became known as the Hand of God incident just didn't seem so bad to me; it still doesn't. For one thing, I find it impressive that Maradona, five feet five inches (164 centimeters) tall, should have beaten the goalie, who was nearly a foot taller, to the ball. And weren't the referee and linesman most at fault, for not spotting the foul and for allowing the goal? I've always suspected that high-minded censure of the Hand of God is a way of dressing up disappointment and frustration that England lost; that the behavior for which England fans will never be able to forgive Maradona is not his cheating, but his running around five England players like so many wooden posts to score the greatest goal that's ever been scored and knock England out of the World Cup.

unable to contain their optimism. In Zagreb, large-screen televisions were set up on the city squares so people could watch the Croatia-Netherlands third-place match in raucous groups. It was a Saturday, and I watched in my apartment with friends, drifting out to the balcony to listen to the excited conversations and shouts coming from the cafés below. The sound of cheers filled the air when Croatia scored. It was like the city was one gigantic living room, everyone's eyes on a single television set. Traffic all but stopped, and the street below was empty. When the game finished with Croatia the winner, people flooded the streets. They filled the main square, and that night, all night, we heard happy, drunken voices singing.

Coming nearly three years after the war ended, it was an emotional moment in a young country's history. On television, reporters interviewed grown men who could not stop weeping. The country had not seen such unified celebration since its declaration of independence. Now no one could deny Croatia its place on the map.

Reflect & Write

❏ Jones begins by introducing the term "skill" as a popular expression. How does this set the stage for his brief article? What do we come to expect as readers based on this opening?

❏ Analyze the title for Jones's piece. How is the article both an "ode" and a reflection on history? Why does the title work? What nations are at play in the meat of his argument?

❏ Brkic describes the Croatia victory as an emotional moment not just for individual spectators but for the whole country. How does she lead up to this point? What essential information did she provide earlier in her article to prepare the reader for this argument?

❏ How did Croatia transform from an isolated and war-ravaged country to one where grown men are weeping? Point to specific lines and passages that show the author's account of this change. How, in this sense, can we understand soccer as "The Beautiful Game"?

❏ **Write:** Draft a brief column for a sport that offers, in your perspective, a "Beautiful Game" in the ways explored here—as healing for a community, as revenge for a historical wrong, or as a way to bring people together.

COLLABORATIVE CHALLENGE

For many contributors to the June 2006 special issue of *National Geographic,* soccer is, to borrow Brkic's words, "an expression of ethnicity, of political orientation, of self." In groups of three or four, explore several other of the brief articles written by fans for this magazine issue. You can either look up the magazine issue in your library or visit the magazine feature story online at the Envision Website. Then, as a group, compose an American contribution to this collection. Include a photo and a rationale for why you selected that image to accompany your argument. How might soccer be (or not be) an expression of American identity, political orientation, or self?

www.ablongman.com/envision/238

■ *The first of these two photographs, published on the* National Geographic *Website, shows a group of young Zambian boys playing soccer with a ball they had created by knotting together strips from discarded plastic bags. The photographer, Gideon Mendel, took the photo in 1993 following the death of 18 national soccer team payers in a plane crash. The tragedy crushed Zambia's prospects for the 1994 World Cup and, Mendel notes, "children everywhere [. . .] imitated the hops and skips of the national team's training dance." The second photo, taken by Themba Hadebe, provides a window into the international popularity of soccer as enjoyed by adults and children both.*

Heads-up Move

Photographs by Gideon Mendel, and Themba Hadebe

FIGURE 11.9 This photo's center focus on children in Zambia, who look up to their handmade soccer ball created from plastic bags, makes a powerful argument about the role of the game in Zambian culture.

FIGURE 11.10 The dynamic action of adults jumping up on a dusty field in this color photo, provides insight into the importance of soccer to people in Zambia.

Reflect & Write

❏ Analyze the first photo for its rhetorically strategic elements. What is the effect of looking straight at the boy launching the ball in the air? What do you make of the condition of the ball? Now, knowing the history behind this photo—namely, that it was taken shortly after a plane crash killed nearly every member of the soccer team—what argument do you think the photographer is trying to make through this composition?

❏ How does the condition of the ball in the top photo shape your response as a viewer or persuade you to interpret the photo in a particular way? How does the impression that the ball seems homemade serve to make a comment on social conditions and poverty in Zambia?

❏ Compare the two photos. How does the second one (Figure 11.10) complicate the argument made by the first photo alone? Notice that until you see the ball in the left of the frame, you think you're just looking at a portrait of poverty; does seeing the soccer ball change the way the viewer sees the picture? Does the type of ball change the argument?

❏ **Write:** Compose captions for both photos, offering your interpretation made by the argument of the image. Then draft a short article about soccer in Zambia that might use these images as part of its persuasion.

David Leonard is an assistant professor of comparative ethnic studies at Washington State University, specializing in videogame culture, African-American film, and sports and race relations. He has written numerous articles for both academic and popular journals, including Journal of Sport and Social Issues, Simile, and Popmatters. He originally published this article in a 2003 issue of Colorlines: Race | Culture | Action, a nationally distributed magazine focused on issues related to race and American culture.

Yo, Yao! What Does the "Ming Dynasty" Tell Us About Race and Transnational Diplomacy in the NBA?

David Leonard

Fans and commentators alike have heralded Yao Ming's arrival and acceptance in the NBA as an indicator of the increasing social standing of Asians in the U.S., and the breaking down of boundaries with China. But in actuality, the Rockets' center's popularity reflects the maintenance of dominant stereotypes (sports commentator Brent Musburger blamed the "hordes" of Chinese voting for him as the reason Yao got to start in the All-Star Game). He embodies both ideological usefulness as a model minority in the world of basketball (among the "gangstas"

of the league) and economic importance in a global sports market—at the same time being a symbol of pan-Asian pride through his successful presence as an Asian man in the hypermasculine world of professional basketball.

Yao as Commodity

The star power of Yao Ming is not the result of his extraordinary stats for the Houston Rockets. He averages a respectable 13 points and 8.2 rebounds per game. The flurry of magazine covers, billboards, and television commercials featuring Yao reflect the desires of American and Chinese companies to cash in on Yao's popularity. Beyond the efforts to sell basketball to more than 2 billion Chinese nationals, the NBA hopes to capitalize on the sudden explosion in ticket sales to the Asian American market.

Asian Americans buying group packages for Rockets games represent 11 percent of the buying public, 10 percent more than last year. In cities across America, Yao attracts fans to the Rockets' away games to such an extent that a number of stadiums, in places like Detroit, Boston, and Oakland, have offered special "Asian American nights." When the Rockets played the Golden State Warriors this spring, the Oakland arena announced parts of the game in Mandarin. Rockets' coach Rudy Tomjanovich frequently boasts of Yao's importance in bridging cultural and political gaps. In other words, Yao is presumably schooling America about Chinese culture and history.

It's dubious that Yao's dunking and product promotions will provide Americans a meaningful introduction to China, especially because Yao's popularity and public persona is rooted in old-school stereotypes about Chinese culture and identity. For example, in honor of Yao's debut appearance in Miami, the American Airlines Arena passed out fortune cookies to all 8,000 fans in attendance. In other cities, teams have celebrated Yao with dragon dances and other "traditional" ceremonies. While understandably a source of cultural delight, the attempts to attract Asian fans through stereotypes and decontextualized cultural festivals reflect the NBAs economic and cultural hopes for the "Ming Dynasty." Asian identity and cultural values now have a place at the NBA table and within the global marketplace, but the visibility of Asianness comes through a homogenized and flat presentation of cultural identity, not unlike the representation of black NBA stars.

5   Yao's popularity has little to do with his inside game or America's total acceptance of Asians. The constructed Yao serves a particular purpose within the NBA. As noted by Ric Bucher, a columnist for *ESPN: The Magazine,* he is "humble" and has a "team-first attitude that blows through the NBA like a blast of fresh air into a collapsed mine shaft." In a world of supposedly greedy black ball players, Yao isn't hustling for a bigger slice of the pie. He's a nonthreatening foreigner who provides an example of desirable change to the white folks at the head office.

A Freak and a Foreigner

At seven foot five, 298 pounds, Yao defies commonsense ideas about Asian men. Take Apple's most recent commercial, a kind of circus freak show juxtaposing Yao with MiniMe (Vern Troyer). Yao, able to take his laptop from the overhead compartment of an airplane without standing, is huge in comparison to his tiny computer. Further racializing their difference, Troyer watches "Crouching Tiger, Hidden Dragon" on his massive computer. Yao's popularity is also tied to this fascination with his freakish height and size.

The discourse surrounding Yao Ming frequently centers on his foreign status. Announcers and sports writers continually focus on his difficulties behind the wheel of a car, his strange eating habits, and the difficulties he has with the English language. Undoubtedly, many international players have had problems adjusting to English and "American" culture, but Yao's difficulties are placed in the foreground. His frequently-aired Visa commercial, which debuted during the Super Bowl, reinforces the dominant assumptions made about certain foreigners. Yao, wanting to buy a miniature version of the Statue of Liberty (he is already a patriotic American), attempts to write a check. Despite his excellent English, Yao is unable to discern the giant sign prohibiting purchases by personal check. What follows is a back-and-forth repartee between Yao and the Puerto Rican female clerk, in which she says "Yo!" and he corrects her with "Yao," lightheartedly illustrating for us their basic inability to communicate like civilized citizens of the United States.

"Black-Asian Conflict"

While the traditional stereotype of Asians is that they are timid and passive, Yao's future success, according to teammates, is dependent upon his ability to transcend his "Asianness," and perform with a more authentic masculinity, exemplified by the NBAs black players. Steve Francis, a Rockets teammate, has commented on the need to teach Yao how to be more aggressive and cutthroat, since Chinese culture leads Yao to want to share the ball with others and not attack his competitors when they are "down." Francis implies that Asian masculinity is feminine, weak, and passive, vis-a-vis a black masculinity that aggressively attacks without consideration for ramifications, bringing to the surface the question of race within American sports culture.

In a now famous incident, Shaquille O'Neal was asked on a nationally syndicated sports talk show what he thought of Yao Ming. He replied: "Tell Yao Ming, ching-chong-yang-wah-so." While nobody responded to this racial blast, its re-airing in December elicited a significant amount of controversy. Writer Irwin Tang, in Asian Week, called Shaq a racist. Moreover, Tang concluded that the public silence surrounding Shaq's comments, compared with the hammering of Trent Lott for his Dixiecrat remark, revealed the acceptability of anti-Asian racism and the double standards employed within American racial discourses.

10   Leaders in the Asian American community demanded a public apology, fearing that without a response, the media was condoning anti-Asian prejudice. Diane Chin, executive director of Chinese for Affirmative Action, said Shaq's un-retracted comments sent a problematic message: "It gives license, a green light, to others that says that kind of action is acceptable."

While the comment was reprehensible, the way activists like Chin often frame the problem reflects a simplistic approach to consciousness-raising and anti-racist organizing within the world of sports. It was the rare commentator who took the time to contextualize Shaq's remark within the historic pattern of stereotyping Asian Americans in popular culture.

Globalizing Basketball

Shaq's comments reflect not simply individual prejudice, they bring up a larger issue facing the NBA: the friction between African American players (who make up the majority of the league) and the growing number of international players who have signed on in the last few years. In 1999–2000, international players, mostly from Europe, made up 11 percent of the NBA roster. The preparedness of overseas imports to immediately contribute, the affordability of signing these players, and usefulness of international players in lightening the color of the league all contribute to this trend of siphoning off the world's best talent—"B-1 visa" style.

An influx of international stars are systematically displacing the up-and-coming "diamonds in the rough"—the proverbial tenth man on the bench—from the pool of national draft choices. "Europeans have now squeezed [blacks] out of the draft, unless they are a 'can't miss' talent," reports Andy Katz of ESPN.com. The 2001–2002 NBA draft saw 17 players drafted from overseas. Tony Ronzone, an international scout for the Detroit Pistons, predicted, in *ESPN: The Magazine,* that within the next five years, 40 percent of NBA players will be "foreign."

The media marketability and sheer skill of foreign players is also a factor in displacing black players. For the 2001–2002 season, the NBA named Pau Gasol, a Spanish player for the Memphis Grizzlies, rookie of the year. Yao Ming, who was the first pick in last year's NBA draft, is likely to corner the title for 2002-2003, further eroding the dominance of black ball players. Unlike their American counterparts, foreign-born players are able to turn professional at an early age, so that by the time they enter the U.S., their skills—especially their offensive skills—are much more developed. O'Neal's mockery of Yao Ming reflects this growing tension among players for control over the NBA—which often plays itself out racially.

15   The fact that international players, including Yao, are continuously praised as model players—fundamentally sound, hardworking, coachable, good immigrants—while black players are riddled with a barrage of critiques, complicates the Shaq incident. The February issue of *Sports Illustrated* reported that more than 70 percent of fans approved of the "foreign invasion." Like Asians in society as a whole, Yao (and other international players) is set up as a model minority, whereas the shorts-sagging, trash-talking, tattooed black "gangstas" in the NBA get blamed

for the league's demise. Refusal to acknowledge this reality and the league's very public attempts to market international players oversimplifies the Shaq remarks. If we really face the phenomenon head-on, it becomes apparent that the popularity of Yao Ming, as a racialized body conveying sportsmanship and a work ethic, does not reveal America's acceptance of "Chinese culture" but rather conveys a racialized distaste for the majority of other players—who are black.

An Alternative Masculinity

But Yao Ming also represents a complicated racial phenomenon. He is not simply a stooge of globalized capitalism, nor a perfect foil to Shaq's racism. He is indeed a reflection of globalization in the NBA, in terms of the border crossing of athletes and the efforts to sell basketball (and America) around the globe. Moreover, he surely is a model minority in the NBA, a commodity, and a useful image in a larger project of cultural imperialism. These realities help explain the phenomenon known as the Ming Dynasty, but so does his place as a symbol of Asian American pride, especially for males. He challenges the dominant conception of Asian American masculinity. Yao's dominance in a world defined by masculinity and body reflects his transgressive presence in Asian America. Connected to a world of hyper-masculinity, defined by the presence of the most "authentic" black male bodies, Yao offers Asian American males an alternative conception of self—a masculinity of power, strength, and machismo seldom available publicly. Given this confluence of complex factors, it shouldn't be surprising if the Ming Dynasty has a long reign in the United States.

A Bastion of Multiracial Appreciation?

Although the TV networks and sports merchandisers would have us believe otherwise, the world of professional sports is not a bastion of multiracial appreciation or integration, or by an even longer shot, of anti-racism. Like other star athletes of color, such as the Williams sisters or Tiger Woods, Yao Ming is often cited as an example of how the world of sports is destroying its own internal racist barriers.

But the simplistic formula of access and opportunity equaling racial progress denies the complexity of racism and its globalized effects on sports and society as a whole. Despite the gradual integration in professional sports, racialized ideas and white supremacy dominate the way athletes are represented and merchandised to the starsearching American public.

Reflect & Write

❑ Do you agree that Yao Ming has been marketed as the epitome of stereotypes? What does this mean in terms of global sports? What cultural stereotypes are perpetrated by this article?

❑ Notice the way the subheads function as writing devices in this article. How do they anticipate or extenuate the argument of each subsection? Are they stronger or more moderate in tone than the the rest of the writing? Why might the writer have chosen this technique?

❑ Why, according to Leonard, is the global expansion of the NBA happening right now? What explanations are offered for Yao Ming's appeal, and what has Yao Ming done for the NBA and international sports in general that other sports figures have not? Use evidence in the article to support your response.

❑ How does the writer broaden out to larger ideas at the end of the article? Do you agree with his conclusion?

❑ **Write:** Compose a counterargument to Leonard's piece, proposing that Yao Ming does in fact offer Americans a meaningful introduction to China and Chinese culture. How might you rebut Leonard's argument point by point?

Movie Poster: *The Year of the Yao*

Fine Line, 2005

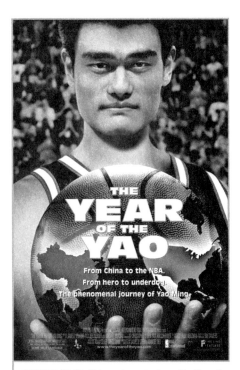

FIGURE 11.11 This movie poster from *The Year of the Yao* (2005) makes a visual argument for Yao as a "bridge figure" between cultures.

Reflect & Write

❑ The original title for this movie was "The Yao Ming Movie." Analyze the difference between the two titles and the argument they make about Yao Ming and the content of the movie. Which one is more appealing to the audience? Why?

❑ Look carefully at the visual details of the poster. What are the implications behind Yao holding "the world in his hands"? How is color used purposefully in this image? How does the blurring of the audience in the background enhance the image's argument, if at all?

❑ **Write:** Create a draft for an alternative movie poster for "The Year of the Yao" either by hand or using Photoshop. Now write a brief reflection on your rhetorical choices— what argument were you trying to make and how did you employ visual rhetoric to do so?

■ **Jane Juffer** *is a professor at Pennsylvania State University with interests in Latino/a culture. She has published on immigration policy, Central American refugees, and pornography. This article originally appeared in the November 2002 issue of* The Journal of Sport & Social Issues, *an academic journal featuring sociological studies of sports culture. "Who's the Man" focuses on the media coverage of Sammy Sosa during his 1998 homerun competition with Mark McGwire.*

Who's the Man? Sammy Sosa, Latinos, and Televisual Redefinitions of the "American" Pastime

Jane Juffer

Latino and Latin American baseball players have expanded the boundaries of the "American pastime," asserting their ethnic and national identities even while being accepted as representatives of the sport most closely aligned with a white United States identity. This redefinition is achieved in part via cable and satellite technologies that carry images of Latinos to homes throughout the United States at a time when the Latino population is growing and becoming more dispersed, raising the possibility that baseball will lessen racism and xenophobia. However, media coverage is at times nostalgic for a more bounded sense of home and nation and often emphasizes players' individual mobility, erasing the economic and political conditions that have brought Latin American players to the United States. The author shows how these tensions play out in Chicago superstation WGN's coverage of Cubs star Sammy Sosa, who has emerged as a national hero in both the U.S. and the Dominican Republic.

There is the moment before every Major League Baseball (MLB) game when the fans rise perfunctorily to mutter the words to the national anthem, turning in the direction of a flag that most of them cannot see or do not bother to seek out. Children eat hot dogs, already bored; men doff their caps and balance beer cups in one hand, already drunk; people who have brought homemade signs wave them, already convinced they will not get on television. Yet after the events of September 11, the routine was no longer routine. It was denaturalized, and all the taken-for-granted elements of the national pastime—that baseball is the epitome of competition, good sportsmanship, nationalism, and masculinity and hence an arena for defining what it means to be American— were suddenly called out for rearticulation.

That was no clearer than at Wrigley Field, home of the Chicago Cubs, where on September 27, the Cubs played their rival in the division title chase, the Houston Astros, in the first game at Wrigley since the attacks. As did nearly all MLB teams, the Cubs organized a pregame ceremony in honor of the victims and heroes of September 11. No one could miss the flags draped across the apartment buildings that surround Wrigley Field. Eyes became teary when the Chicago Police Department's bagpipes and drums of the Emerald Society played "Amazing Grace," and Cubs' catcher Joe Girardi, who had played 4 years for the New York Yankees, gave a speech that ended with his voice breaking. After the game, he told a reporter, "Sometimes you just can't hold back tears. Men are supposed to portray an image of toughness but [the tragedy] just hit too close to home" (Reader, 2001). But the clincher came when the Cubs' star, right fielder and homerun slugger, Sammy Sosa, a native of the Dominican Republic, stepped to the plate in the first inning and lofted a homer into right-center field. As he rounded first base, coach Billy Williams handed him a flag, and Sosa carried it around the bases to thunderous applause, waving it again after emerging from the dug-out for a curtain call. One fan held up a sign that read "In Uncle Sammy we trust." Commentators praised Sosa's timing and his conduct (as appropriately humble); even the opposing pitcher, Shane Reynolds, conceded that "it was patriotic" (a concession facilitated by the Astros' 6-5 win). The next morning, Sosa was for a moment baseball's ambassador of patriotism, as the image of him holding a flag, head slightly bowed as he rounded the bases, was replayed constantly by television news and sports shows around

Journal of Sport & Social Issues, Volume 26, No. 4, November 2002, pp. 337–359
DOI: 10.1177/0193732502238253
© 2002 Sage Publications

the country. Sosa's act became the opportunity for celebrating baseball's diversity, an indicator of a great and tolerant United States (as opposed to the intolerant enemy). One MLB columnist wrote that Sosa was a very appropriate player to carry the flag, for "coming from less materially blessed circumstances in the Dominican Republic, the man may have a more genuine appreciation for some aspects of the American dream than many Americans" (Bauman, 2001).

Sosa is one of many Latinos—now roughly 25% of major league players—who have redefined the "national" in "national pastime," no small feat given the strength of that association. In 1976, for example, Michael Novak, author of *The Joy of Sports,* wrote (quoted in Sobchack, 1997) that

> baseball is as close a liturgical element of the White Anglo-Saxon Protestant myth as the nation has. It is a cerebral game, designed as geometrically as the city of Washington itself, born out of the Enlightenment and the philosophies beloved of Jefferson, Madison, and Hamilton. It is to games what the Federalist papers are to books, (p. 180)

The articulation of Sosa, a Black Dominican for whom English is a second language, to patriotism following September 11 illustrates that not only is Novak's characterization no longer true but also that no one wants it to be true. Baseball still tells a powerful story about the greatness of America, but America is now inclusive, indeed more representative of all of the Americas. The role that Latinos have played in this redefinition of the national pastime can be gauged partially by the rise of Sosa to national/international hero, a status gained during the 1998 season when he and the St. Louis Cardinals' Mark McGwire competed to break Roger Maris's nearly 30-year record for homeruns in a single season. Although McGwire, a burly, red-haired, White man who easily falls into the line of home run heroes still most often mythologized in the image of Babe Ruth, eventually won the race with 70 homers, it was the charismatic Sosa who won the hearts of American viewers. By the end of the 1998 season, Sosa had remarkably (and I suppose arguably) emerged as "The Man," both in the United States and in the Dominican Republic, and elsewhere as well. This status was most clearly indicated in Sosa's off-the-field appearances, at sites imbued with national sentiment: He was invited by the Clintons to help light the White House Christmas tree in 1998; not long thereafter, he sat next to Hillary Clinton during the president's State of the Union address, receiving a special acknowledgment from the president for his hitting prowess and his philanthropy.

5   Interestingly, the rearticulation of U.S. national identity has not required Latino baseball stars to forsake their own national identities; in fact, the emergence of highly visible Latino and Latin American stars including Pedro Martinez, Mariano Rivera, and Alex Rodriguez has relied on a complex mix of the local, national, and global. In part, the redefinition of the national pastime works because players such as Sosa do not purport to be fully American. Sosa has always stressed his Dominican identity: for example, throughout the homerun race, when reporters asked him, "Who's the man?" Sosa would answer, "He [McGwire] is the man

here, and I'm the man in the Dominican Republic." Occasionally, Sosa would add, "Excuse me, Mark, but I'm the man in Chicago." Even as he posits a Dominican national pride, Sosa skillfully—it would seem—negotiates his insider/outsider status, often thanking the "great country of America" for the opportunity to play baseball here—suggesting, as often goes the rhetoric around Latin American players—that he is not truly making claims on citizenship—he's only here to play ball. This humility acts to contain the fear of invasion implicit in the rhetoric of announcers who now regularly comment on the fact that so many players come from Latin America—lumping together U.S.-born Latinos with Latin Americans under the rubric of "Other."

A similar rhetoric is at play in coverage of the 2000 census figures, which revealed that the number of people identifying themselves as of "Hispanic origin" grew 58% since 1990 to about 13% of the population. Also, Latino populations are becoming more widely dispersed as more Latinos move from traditional areas of settlement, such as the Southwest, North-east, and major urban areas into the more rural South and Midwest. Latinos are the largest minority in 18 states, including Iowa, New Hampshire, and Nevada. Hence, a critical question to ask of baseball as a global sport:[1] What are the effects of Latino ballplayers' increasing acceptance as part of the national pastime, their televisual presence in living rooms from Chicago to Iowa to the Dominican Republic? Does baseball contribute to a greater understanding of how globalization has widened the gap between rich and poor, forcing people into migratory routes, leaving homes that are decimated by the effects of transnational corporations? Or does baseball only serve to create the illusion of upward mobility—in focusing on individual stars, does baseball elide the material conditions of inequality in the home countries in part by holding stars responsible for philanthropic efforts (as Sammy Sosa with hurricane relief in the Dominican Republic)? The answers to these questions hinge in no small part on where and how baseball is disseminated via media technologies—newspaper, radio, broadcast, cable, and satellite coverage and, to some degree, on new media technologies linked to the Internet and sports computer games. In this article, I focus on television, which is still the primary media-ating technology of private and public for most U.S. households, presenting, in different ways, the same dilemma it has since the 1950s: Docs television sanitize images for armchair tourists? And/or does it present new places and identities in a nonthreatening yet potentially expansive manner (see Morley, 2000; Spigel, 1997)?[2]

These questions have been reframed by globalization and new media technologies: as such, this article is also a contribution to the developing conversation about globalized, mediated sport, situated in what Wenner (1998) described as the "corporate landscape that has come to define the upper echelon of what can only be called MediaSport" (p. 4). ABC's ESPN International now reaches more than 127 million households in 150 countries; Rupert Murdoch's News Corp., which among its many holdings includes Fox, Fox Sports, and the Los Angeles Dodgers, reaches two thirds of the world's television households (Bellamy, 1998, p. 77). In the global economy, however, other sites do not drop out; as Randy Martin and Toby Miller (1999) argued,

In sport, the national, global, local, and personal coexist through the same practice, although all of these spatial configurations may spin in different directions
rather than support each other. The geography of sport is not calibrated on any
single map, and the affiliations and attentions that point to powers not subsumed
by the national take place on grounds that are at once local, national, and global.
(p. 12)

We must attend to these different sites, to their complex interrelationships, so
as to understand power, access, and mobility—who is moving where, under
what conditions, with what effects. This article begins to answer those questions in relation to Latinos, baseball, and television by examining, in the Fou-
cauldian sense, how the material dissemination and televisual representation
of Latino baseball players make possible the statement of certain truths about
race, ethnicity, and gender.

The redefinition of the national pastime has occurred simultaneously with
the expansion of baseball on cable and satellite into most middle- and upper-
class homes in the United States as well as throughout parts of the world. These
material changes have reshaped baseball's self-representation; for example,
ESPN now offers a block of programming in Spanish on Sunday evenings,
ESPN Deportes TV. Also, even during games announced in English, ESPN
sometimes deploys its Spanish-speaking baseball reporter, Alvaro Martín. At
one game, for example, when the Cubs' rookie pitcher Rubén Quevedo's parents
were in the stands, Martín interviewed the Venezuelan couple in Spanish,
providing his own immediate translations.[3] Other baseball announcers now even
try to pronounce Spanish names correctly. In stark contrast to his grandfather,
the famously crude Cubs' announcer Harry Caray, who mispronounced Latino
names with great relish, his grandson and new Cubs' announcer, Chip Caray, is
taking Spanish lessons, pronouncing some Latino surnames with an impressive
accent, and even sprinkling his commentary with Spanish phrases.[4]

Yet there is an underside to this valorization of Latino identity: the era-
sure of the many material inequalities that produce Major League Baseball's profits. Latin American ballplayers are signed by U.S. scouts for
small sums and often languish for years in the minors, sometimes ending
up as undocumented workers in U.S. cities. The viability of Latin American
leagues has been hurt as the best players try to make it in the United States;
Major League Baseball functions as any multinational corporation, weakening local economies by encouraging dependence on an external power.
Furthermore, media coverage and broadcasters' banter often reveals an undercurrent of the fear of invasion from the South combined with versions
of nostalgia for the time when the game was truly a game—a purely American game.[5] This nostalgia for a time when borders seemed more impervious
and the location of home and nation more clearly defined is reflected in the
recent valorization of local and regional sports by Fox Sports Net. One series of their commercials, for example, depicts various "barbaric" sports acts
in unnamed "third world" countries and ends with the tag line: "Fox Regional Sports. Sports news from the only region you care about. Yours."

10   This nostalgia reveals the ongoing power of national identity—precisely
because of globalization; television, as David Morley (2000) said, functions
powerfully to shape the national sense of who belongs and who does not
(p. 118). Baseball on U.S. television becomes particularly interesting in light

of citizenship construction because there are so few Latinas/os else-where on television; baseball and some other professional sports, such as boxing, is one of the few genres in which Latino representation matches or surpasses their demographic representation (in fact, one of the few series for adults that focuses on a Latina/o family—Showtime's *Resurrection Boulevard*—features a family of boxers). Of course, national borders are constantly traversed; television helps to create imagined communities between Latinas/os throughout the United States and Latin Americans in their home countries. As Arjun Appadurai (1996) said, television produces a "mutual contextualising of motion and mediation" as "moving images meet deterritorialised viewers. Important new diasporic public spheres are created and sustained that quite transcend the orbit of the nation state" (p. 4). However, the degree to which a "diasporic public sphere is created" will depend on who has access to participation in that sphere—hence on the broader social, political, and economic conditions for Latinos and Latin American immigrants in the United States. I argue here that for the influx of Latinos in baseball to have a beneficial impact on race and ethnic relations in the United States, the dissemination and representation of baseball must foreground the connections and power relations that shape people's movement between places; for example, between Chicago, the Dominican Republic, and small towns throughout the rural United States, where Latino immigrants move in search of employment in meat-packing and chicken processing plants. In the terms of geographer Massey (1994),

> Instead, then, of thinking of places as areas with boundaries around, they can be imagined as articulated moments in networks of social relations and understandings, but where a large proportion of those relations, experiences, and understandings are constructed on a far larger scale than what we happen to define for that moment as the place itself, whether that be a street, or a region, or even a continent. And this in turn allows a sense of place which is extroverted, which includes a consciousness of its links with the wider world, which integrates in a positive way the global and the local. (p. 155)

Baseball has played an important role in making these connections, possibly reshaping ideas about Latino and U.S. identity for some baseball fans. However, this progressive potential is also limited because the various places that are linked remained bounded rather than overlapping; the discourse on Latin ballplayers has definitely redefined the American in American pastime, yet not often in a manner that shows the imbrications of the national, the global and the local, and the power imbalances wrought by globalization and lived at the level of the local.

Notes

1. As several sports scholars have noted, the scholarship on sports, media, and race is lacking—especially in regards to Latinos. More attention has been given to African Americans (Kimkema & Harris, 1998).
2. Spigel (1997) described how, historically, "broadcasting, like the telephone and telegraph before it, was seen as an instrument of social sanitation . . . Numerous commentators extolled the virtues of television's antiseptic spaces, showing how the medium would allow people to travel from their homes while remaining untouched by the actual social contexts to which they imaginatively ventured" (p. 215). Similarly, Morley (2000) argued that "via television's transmission into the home, the covalence of alterity is more strongly

established than ever before, as that which is far away is made to feel both very much 'here'—right in our sitting rooms—and precisely 'now'" (p. 182).

3. The game aired August 13, 2000.

4. Roberto Clemente, the great Pittsburgh Pirate star from Puerto Rico, struggled throughout the 1950s and 1960s to be called "Roberto" instead of "Bob" by the media and other sports personnel. My son has a baseball card of Clemente that calls him "Bob Clemente," The star was killed in an airplane crash on New Year's Eve of 1970 when he was on his way to deliver earthquake relief to people in Nicaragua.

5. Representations of baseball on film have been subject to various stages of nostalgia, as Sobchack (1997) noted. In particular, she comments on Ken Bums' 1994 PBS documentary *Baseball,* which she calls a "highly nostalgic and elegiac" exercise, less about "historical analysis" than about "constituting a collective memory"(p. 193).

Acknowledgments

Thanks to Holly Flynt for her research assistance on this article and to Ralph Rodriguez for his astute reading. Thanks to my parents, Ron and Peg Juffer, for insights on what it means to be Cubs fans living in Iowa, and most of all to one of Sosa's biggest fans, Alex Juffer, for sharing his 118 Sammy baseball cards.

References

Armour, T. (1998, September 12). On deck; Pitchman Sammy, achievements, personality mean endorsements for Sosa. *The Chicago Tribune, p.* 3: 3.

Appadurai, A. (1996). *Modernity at large,* Minneapolis: University of Minnesota Press.

Barmann, T. (2000, July 16). Telecom Act delivers a scrambled price picture to consumers. *Knight Ridder/Tribune Business News.*

Bauman, M. (2001, September 28). *A Wrigley night to remember.* Retrieved September 29, 2001 from www.MLB.com

Bayless,S. (1998a, August13). Is Sosa really having more fun than we are? *The Chicago Tribune,* pp. 4:1, 3.

Bayless, S. (1998b, September 8). McGwire's tag team trumps Sosa. *The Chicago Tri bune.* *pp.* 4:1, 3.

Bellamy, R. (1998), The evolving television sports marketplace. In L. Wenner (Ed,), *MediaSport* (pp. 73–87). New York: Routledge.

Bjarkman, P. (1994), *Baseball with a Latin beat.* Jefferson, NC: McFarland.

Breton, M. (2000, Spring), Fields of broken dreams: Latinos and baseball. *ColorLines,* pp. 13–17.

Hersh, P. (1998, September 9), Dominican reaction: In Sosa's town, night is still. *The Chicago Tribune,* p. 4:4.

Kinkema, K. M., & Harris, J. C. (1998). MediaSport studies: Key research and emerging issues, In L. Wenner (Ed.), *MediaSport* (pp. 27–54), New York; Routledge.

Klein, A. (1991). *Sugarball; The American game, the* Dominican *dream.* New Haven, CT. Yale University Press.

Martin, R., & Miller, T, (1999). Fielding sport: A preface to polities? In R. Martin & T. Miller (Eds.) *SportCult* (pp. 1–13). Minneapolis: University of Minnesota Press.

Massey, D. (1994). *Space, place, and gender.* Minneapolis: University of Minnesota Press.

McAvoy, K. (2000, March 27). Batting clean up. *Broadcasting & Cable,* pp. 32, 36–37,

McClellan, S. (1993, March 15). Fear of falling fees, ratings haunt MLB. *Broadcasting & Cable,* pp. 42–43.

McClellan S. (2000, April 20). The rights of spring. *Broadcasting & Cable,* pp. 26–27, 30.

Morley, D. (2000). *Home territories: Media, mobility, and identity.* New York; Routledge.

Reader, H. (2001, September 28). *Emotional Girardi salutes victims.* Retrieved September 29, 2001, from www.Cubs.com

Regalado, S. (1998). *Vina baseball! Latin major leaguers and their special hunger.* Chicago: University of Illinois Press.

Rogers, P. (1998a, August 24). Friendly fire: Lima's HR pitches to Sosa raise questions. *The Chicago Tribune, p.* 3:3.

Schlosser, J.(1999, July 12). Fox's sporting chance. *Broadcasting & Cable,* pp. 23–24.

Sherman, E. (1998, September 25). Networks hope fans will tune in after Sosa, McGwire are tuned out. *The Chicago Tribune,* p. 4:5.

Sobchaek, V. (1997). Baseball in the post-American cinema, or life in the minor leagues. In A. Baker & T. Boyd (Eds.), Out *of bounds: Sports, media, and the politics of identity* (pp. 175–197). Bloomington; University of Indiana Press.

Spigel, L. (1997). The suburban home companion: Television and the neighbourhood ideal in post-war America. In C. Brundson, J. D'Acci, *&.* L. Spigel (Eds.), *Feminist television criticism: A reader* (pp. 211–235). Oxford, UK; Clarendon.

Sullivan, P. (1998a, August 1). Obscurity no bother to Sosa: Says playoff chase outweighs record. *The Chicago Tribune,* p, 3:3.

Sullivan, P. (1998b, August 9). Inside the Cubs: McGwire's biggest cheerleader? Sosa. *The Chicago Tribune,* p. 4:3.

Sullivan, P. (1998c, August 27). Super Sammy goes flying again. *The Chicago Tribune,* p. 4:1, 3.

Sullivan, P. (1998d, September 1). 1 blast, 2 bows for Sosa: Takes curtain call after 55tb, stands in after Wood Homers. *The Chicago Tribune,* p. 4:1, 2.

Sullivan, P. (1998e, September 6). Sosa banks 58th, keeps 2-race pace. *The Chicago Tribune,* pp. 3:1, 2.

Tribune's Tower in TV. (1993, March 22). Interview with Jim Dawdle. *Broadcasting & Cable,* pp. 15–17.

"Vande Berg, L. R. (1998). The sports hero meets mediated celebrityhood. In L. Wanner (Ed.), *MediaSport* (pp. 135-153). New York: Routledge.

Wasko, J. (1994). *Hollywood in the information age: Beyond the silver screen,* Austin: University of Texas Press.

Wenner.L. (1998). Playing the MediaSport game. In L. Wenner (Ed.), *MediaSport* (pp. 3–13). New York; Routledge.

Zimbalist, A. (1992). *Baseball and billions: A probing look inside the big business of our national pastime.* New York: Basic Books.

Reflect & Write

❏ According to Juffer, how has Sammy Sosa been elevated to "hero status"? Do you agree or disagree with this label? Why or why not?

❏ How well does Juffer answer her own questions about the effects of the media on sports' globalization? What is her argument?

❏ Juffer talks about the "valorization of Latino identity" in her article; how does this valorization affect peoples' view of Major League Baseball? What does Juffer argue needs to happen for the influx of Latinos in baseball to positively impact race and ethnic relations in the U.S.?

❏ According to Juffer, how has global dispersion of sport—in particular baseball— affected American national identity? Do you agree or disagree? Explain your response.

❏ **Write:** Compare Sammy Sosa's place in baseball to Yao Ming's place in basketball; do both figures demonstrate Americans' openness to a "global sports community"? Explain your answer in a brief essay.

■   *The* Sports Illustrated *cover below features Sammy Sosa, Ken Griffey Jr., and Mark McGwire (March 6, 2000) during their homerun spree. The DVD image of the 2002 Major League Baseball Productions film* Rising Sons *provides an overview of the rapid rise and influence of Japanese baseball players into U.S. Major League Baseball. The coverage begins with Masanori Murakami, recruited to the San Francisco Giants in 1964, and ends more than 30 years later with Ichiro Suzuki's successes with the Seattle Mariners.*

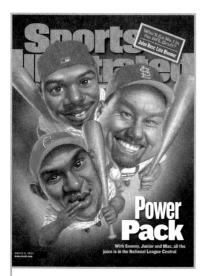

FIGURE 11.12 A March 2000 *Sports Illustrated* cover clearly captures the multicultural transformation of American baseball.

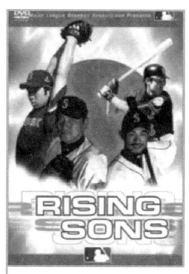

FIGURE 11.13 The *Rising Sons* DVD cover marks in both words and images its focus on Japanese players in American baseball leagues.

Reflect & Write

❑   Compare the two images—the *Sports Illustrated* cover and the Major League Baseball Productions DVD cover. What different strategies and techniques are being used to make an argument about the power of each player?

❑   How does the kairos of the home run race factor into the visual arguments being made?

❑   Do either of these images seem to support or refute the argument present in Jane Juffer's article, "Who's the Man?" How so? Notice the position of each player, where your eye moves first, the embodied rhetoric and rhetoric of gesture, and the facial expressions.

❑   **Write:** Compose a letter to the editor of *Sports Illustrated* or the production manager for the DVD *Rising Sons,* commenting on the visual rhetoric strategies of one or both images. Base your letter on your responses to the questions above.

COLLABORATIVE CHALLENGE

Together with a team of four people, create the proposal for a new marketing company in which you offer in-depth analysis of international trends in Asian athletes coming to America, American athletes representing multicultural values, and minority athletes challenging the white male American dream. Start with Tiger Woods, Ichiro Suzuki, Yao Ming, and Sammy Sosa and compose a rhetorical analysis of current market practices used to popularize and acclimatize these athletes. Next, identify four new areas in global sports and make a persuasive case for how your group can serve international companies or American sports franchises. Storyboard your marketing campaign, draft a written proposal, and present your pitch to the class.

PERSPECTIVES ON THE ISSUE

1. As we've seen, the branding process, from Olympic winners to soccer champions, from baseball recruits to basketball stars, revolves around carefully chosen slogans and visual symbols. Pick two figures from this chapter and explore more recent ads featuring these athletes. Analyze the meaning of the visual and verbal choices made by advertisers in constructing a "brand image." What are the consequences for our understanding of global sports and national identity?

2. How do the articles in the *National Geographic* special issue on soccer present the sport as a truly global and international passion? How would you characterize America's attitude toward soccer and toward the recent World Cup? What other sports fall into this category of more international than American?

3. Many of these articles have focused on individual sports figures. How do athletes like Ichiro Suzuki, Yao Ming, and Sammy Sosa stand for more than individual achievement? What is it, according to the articles you've read here, that enables them to stand as visual signs of nations, or cross-cultural identity, or communities in transition, or the force of globalization? Compose your response in a short argument; include appropriate quotations from each of the articles here.

4. Look at the series of Fox sports commercials that Jane Juffer describes in her article as "blatantly racial." Write an essay in which you explain why she made this determination and whether or not you agree with it.

FROM READING TO RESEARCH

1. Explore additional videos on the official Olympic Website to consider how the Olympic Committee promotes unity amid competition. How are the Winter Games marketed differently from the Summer Games? How is China responding to allegations of crimes against Human Rights in its marketing campaign for the 2008 Beijing Olympics? Write a research-based analysis in which you present your argument about the marketing strategies used by the Olympics. Now translate that writing into a script for your own commercial video. Be sure to consider not only the actual words, but also some of the images that you intend to use. Who would you use to narrate? What would be the argument?

2. Take your answer to question 2, above, further by consulting several research sources: *Offside: Soccer and American Exceptionalism,* by Andrei S. Markovits and Steven L. Hellerman (Princeton University Press, 2001); *Football Culture: Local Contests, Global Visions,* edited by Gerry Finn and Richard Giulianotti (London: Frank Cass, 2000), *Games, Sports and Cultures,* edited by Noel Dyck (Oxford, 2000); *Sports Matters: Race, Recreation; and Culture,* edited by John Bloom and Michael Nevin Willard (New York University Press, 2002). Drawing from these reference books, or your own field research work, develop your understanding of the perceptions about soccer across the globe. Using specific case studies, write a persuasive research essay that argues for the function of soccer as a definer of culture. Alternatively, you might also choose to focus on a different sport, such as swimming (see Carly Geehr's paper in Chapter 5) or women's rugby.

PLAYING AGAINST STEREOTYPES

Sports figures play many different roles in contemporary culture. These roles range from figures of physical perfection to embodiments of national pride; they span from representations of local identity to symbols of global community. For many viewers and readers, these figures become much larger than life.

How is the media complicit in this process? We'll see in the following pages that the media constantly projects images of athletes to the consumer public: this might include images of athletes grimacing with concentration as they hit a speeding ball (see Figure 11.14), images of athletes soaring through the air as they make that impossible basket, and images of athletes gliding effortlessly through the water, lap after lap, exalting in victory and bowing their heads with defeat. In this way, athletes become symbols of determination, excellence, and performance.

You can see this in the covers shown in Figure 11.14–11.16. Analyze these images of three athletes for what arguments the covers make—not only about the individual players, but also about the sport, about the team, about the nation as a whole, and about the race and gender of the athlete.

As you analyze these images, you might come to the conclusion that too often images such as these are flat and two-dimensional, even if projected in surround sound, on a high-definition TV. That is, we tend to see not complex, fully-developed individuals, but instead figures that feed into and perpetuate certain cultural stereotypes. So a key question emerges: how do sports—and in particular the media coverage of sports—both reinforce and dismantle stereotypes?

In the readings that follow, we'll uncover how sports figures become subject to gender and race stereotyping by reading articles that examine sports coverage, advertising, and photojournalism in depth. You'll learn to turn a critical eye on all future media

FIGURE 11.14 This cover of *Sports Illustrated* from May 26, 2003 features a powerful photo of tennis great Serena Williams.

FIGURE 11.15 *Sports Illustrated* chooses a different approach in its cover photo of Anna Kournikova from the June 5, 2000 issue.

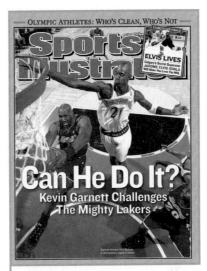

FIGURE 11.16 The May 31, 2004 *Sports Illustrated* cover features NBA all-star Kevin Garnett.

coverage of the sports you may love—and those that may be quite new to you. In the process, you'll have a chance to contribute your own responses to this ongoing debate about "Sports and Media."

Reflect & Write

❏ What stereotypes do you think dictate our impressions of athletes? Which of these covers most clearly depicts these stereotypes? Is there a stereotype that is not represented here?

❏ Compare the way Anna Kournikova and Serena Williams are posed in each of their *Sports Illustrated* cover shots; observe both their facial expressions and their postures. How, if at all, do these images perpetuate the potential stereotypes of female athletes?

❏ How does the portrayal of the two female tennis players compare and contrast to that of the male basketball players? How does each reinforce or dismantle stereotypes, if at all?

❏ **Write:** Compose a letter to the editor of *Sports Illustrated* and present your perspective on the covers.

■ **Thad Mumford** *has been involved in the television industry for over 30 years; as a writer and producer, his credits include work on* M.A.S.H., A Different World, *and* Coach. *In this article, first published in May 2004 in* The New York Times, *he invokes the concept of minstrelsy, a form of American entertainment from the nineteenth and early twentieth century characterized by actors painting their faces black with charcoal in order to perform comic skits in "blackface." A form of burlesque, minstrelsy or black vaudeville often relied on stereotypical racist portrayals of African Americans to depict them as lazy, naïve, superstitious, or clownish.*

The New Minstrel Show: Black Vaudeville with Statistics

Thad Mumford

There has never been a better time to be a black athlete. Moneywise, it is now a sum-of-zeros game. (If only my parents had seen the long-term value of studying Rod Carew's books on hitting instead of math and chemistry.) African-Americans have turned white football and basketball players into tokens. And while our representation in baseball continues its decline, the percentage of blacks who dominate the game continues to surge. The reign of Tiger Woods and the Williams sisters could lead to a time when country club athletic equipment will be on back order in Harlem's sporting goods stores.

Advertisers now line up to have black sports figures push their products, especially to the audience they covet, with near-liturgical zeal, 18-to-25-year-old white suburban males, many of whom are mesmerized by the idiomatic hip-hop jargon, the cock-of-the-walk swagger, the smooth-as-the-law-allows attire of their black heroes.

But there is a downside to all this. The unsayable but unassailable truth is that the clowning, dancing, preening smack-talker is becoming the Rorschach image of the African-American male athlete. It casts a huge shadow over all other images. This persona has the power to sell what no one should buy: the notion that black folks are still cuttin' up for the white man.

Any ethnic group that ever found itself on the periphery of equality and acceptance has had to create coping mechanisms. Some who were victimized by bigotry secretly mimicked the prejudicial perceptions of their oppressor with exaggerated, self-deprecating depictions of their behavior, their very private burlesque that gave them brief respites from their marginalization.

5 For African-Americans, burlesque as healing balm became the essential comedic ingredient of black vaudeville. Comics would strut and cakewalk through now classic routines that savagely lampooned minstrel shows, popular staples of mainstream vaudeville in which white performers in blackface and coily-haired wigs further dehumanized their own creation, the darkie prototype.

Black vaudeville would become a casualty of expanding educational opportunities that created an evolving black middle class with deep concerns that minstrel-like characterizations were degrading and would only perpetuate the accepted attitude that the Negro was the slap-happy court jester for whites.

But a variety of factors, in particular the canonizing of youth culture, the de-emphasizing of wisdom and the glorification of the boorishness inherent in America's look-at-me culture, has played a major role in putting black vaudeville back on the boards. The featured attraction? A number of black athletes.

When we see a wide receiver strut and cakewalk to the end zone, then join teammates in the catalog of celebratory rituals, which now feature props, or hear a cackling, bug-eyed commentator speaking Slanglish ("Give up the props, dog, they be flossin' now!"), we are seeing our private burlesque, out of context, without its knowing wink and satiric spine. Minus these elements, what remains is minstrel template made ubiquitous by Stepin Fetchit and the handful of black actors who worked in the early motion pictures.

But unlike the Stepin Fetchits, left with no alternative but to mortgage their dignity for a paycheck, who often suffered tremendously under the weight of tremendous guilt and shame, some of today's black athletes have unwittingly packaged and sold this nouveau minstrel to Madison Avenue's highest bidders, selling it as our "culturally authentic" behavior, "keepin' it real," as they say.

10   Nothing could be less real or more inauthentic. Or condescending. How can 38 million people possibly have a single view of reality or authenticity? But the athletes who have exhumed the minstrel's grave keep alive these shopworn condescensions.

"The danger of the domination of these one-dimensional images is that they deny the humanity and the intellectuality of an entire people, eliminating the possibility of them being taken seriously," said Dr. Harry Edwards, a professor of sociology at San Jose State who is a consultant to the National Football League.

White adults, whose knowledge of black life is generally limited to what they see in pop culture, take burlesque at face value. This reinforces what was considered culturally authentic, that black people are funny as all get-out.

But the athletes aren't the main culprits. That, of course, would be television, which has brought its two major contributions to American culture, sex and excess, to every sport. TV has erased the line that separated sports from entertainment and created a product that encourages the marketing of black burlesque. Call it athle-tainment.

"We now allow people to take the pride and dignity from our athletes by celebrating them when they play for the camera," said Al Downing, a veteran of 15 major league seasons, now doing public relations for the Los Angeles Dodgers.

15   It can be a dizzying ride. Today's African-American athletes have been handled like porcelain eggs from the moment it became clear that preparing for the next game was of greater significance than preparing for the SAT. Then once they become seven- and eight-figure Hessians, they are walled off from the real world, and all accountability, by management, agents and corporate sponsors, who are all blessed with fertile amounts of unctuousness ("You rule, bro!"). The word no has become a museum piece. As the football Hall of Famer Deacon Jones once said, "There's no school that teaches you how to be a millionaire."

But does this mean that athletes who feel the need to pay homage to every tackle with a dance step, who triumphantly crow in the face of opponents after monster dunks, should be excused for not knowing the line between exuberance and bad sportsmanship?

"I'm more impressed by someone like a Barry Sanders, athletes who do their jobs without having to show up the opposition," said Bill White, whose major league career spanned 13 years.

Issues of cultural identity are complicated, contradictory and complex. One person's ethnic burlesque is another's sense of cultural autonomy. Questions beget more questions. If we keep our burlesque private, are we capitulating to people who feel we should be ashamed of this behavior? Aren't there more appropriate times and places to have fun with our own stereotypes? But does regulating this behavior inadvertently marginalize those African-Americans trapped in burlesquelike worlds? Is there a possible connection between the actions of the white fan who cheers rabidly after sack dances on Sunday, then may be reluctant to grant bank loans for black businesses on Monday?

Those most vulnerable to this confusion are the children, far too many growing up with mangled notions of race, manhood and sports. Black athletes who take our burlesque public could tell them, in the lingua-slanga they share, that there is a difference between having style and actin' the fool. Or that reading and speaking proper English isn't a punk white-boy thing. Or that their chances of playing professional sports are extremely remote. So, if these children do have athletic ability, they should think of using it for one purpose, to get a free education.

They'd get their props. Because that's keepin' it real.

Reflect & Write

❑ What does Mumford mean when he writes that "the clowning, dancing, preening smack-talker is becoming the Rorschach image of the African-American male athlete"? Do you agree? Why or why not?

❑ Who, in Mumford's opinion, should bear partial responsibility for perpetuating the stereotypical image of the African-American athlete? How convincing is his argument? Explain your response.

❑ Toward the end of the article, Mumford questions, "If we keep our burlesque private, are we capitulating to people who feel we should be ashamed of this behavior? " What is your response to this question?

❑ **Write:** Draft out your argument using vivid language from your community. Include quotations from the article here as part of your argument.

A nationally recognized commentator on American popular culture, **Dr. Todd Boyd** *is a professor of Critical Studies at the USC School of Cinema-Television. He has published widely on race, sports, hip hop culture and the media, contributing articles to newspapers as varied as* The New York Times, the Chicago Tribune, *the* Boston Globe, *and the* Charlotte Observer. *Boyd also has published several books on his area of specialty, including* The New H.N.I.C.: The Death of Civil Rights and the Reign of Hip Hop *(2002);* Am I Black Enough for You?: Popular Culture from the 'Hood and Beyond *(1997); and* Young Black Rich and Famous: The Rise of the NBA, the Hip Hop Invasion, and the Transformation of American Culture *(2003), from which this excerpt is taken. Boyd also has appeared as an expert on popular culture on many news programs as well as served as a commentator on ESPN and NPR's* News and Notes *with Ed Gordon.*

"Doin' Me": *from* Young, Black, Rich, and Famous
Todd Boyd

As the players in question get to be younger and younger, it is certain that the influence of hip hop will continue to reign supreme. Hip hop at this point is more than just the music that the players listen to on their ubiquitous headphones, in the same way that basketball is more than just another game. Hip hop is a way of life that best defines the worldview from which these contemporary players emerge.

Hip hop has always been about having an upward trajectory. An abiding sense of social mobility abounds. Basketball has become the way that many who are talented enough and fortunate enough get to experience that mobility. This is their opportunity to showcase their skills and become rich in the process. What angers and alarms so many is the fact that a lot of these players have no interest whatsoever in imitating the ways of mainstream White society. This is evident in the style choices favored by so many contemporary players. Cornrows have replaced the bald head. Long baggy shorts are de rigueur. Tattoos are the order of the day.

The exception to this is a player like Tim Duncan, he of West Indian descent. West Indians have often been considered as better able to assimilate into mainstream America than their African American counterparts; think Sidney Poitier and Colin Powell, for example. Duncan then seems to be a throwback, a player from a previous time whose fundamental style of play and extremely unassuming disposition make him stand out among a league of players deeply ensconced in the hip hop milieu. No matter how much attention is lavished on Duncan by approving league and media starmakers, he is the exception, not the rule. Hip hop–minded players dominate the game and the conversations around it.

Though Duncan may be a throwback, it is a player like Rasheed Wallace who to me epitomizes the idea of retro. Wallace alternates between cornrows and a nappy old-school 'fro, also in the signature shoe of the hip hop generation, the now vintage Nike Air force One. Wallace has also been a source of controversy throughout his tenure in the league. He was one of the first players that the league fined for wearing his shorts too long, for instance.

5   Obviously the length of someone's shorts has nothing to do with how he plays basketball. A player wearing long shorts does not in any way gain a competitive advantage over a player in shorter pants. As the length of all basketball shorts has gotten longer over time, the extremely long shorts are about style, and especially hip hop style. This is where the problem comes in. The NBA wants to control the players' image and suppress expression of this hip hop style on the court. The result is the enforcement of nonsensical rules about ultimately insignificant issues like the length of shorts.

John Stockton, the older White superstar of the Utah Jazz, continues to wear his shorts at the same length they were worn back in the old days. His especially "short shorts" are worn to make a statement that he is not like the younger Black players in the league. Stockton's shorts are like basketball's version of the Confederate flag; an attempt to hold on to an antiquated and outdated sense of the NBA in spite of the obvious changes that abound.

Many of the younger Black players in the league, like Rasheed Wallace, wear their shorts long to make an equally provocative statement: "This is our league, and we will do things in accordance with our culture." Early in the 2001–2002 season, several Black players, including Kobe Bryant and Shaquille O'Neal, were fined and told to make the length of their shorts conform to league standards.

Hip hop–minded players like Rasheed Wallace are constantly being criticized for other things as well. The media has tended to focus on Wallace's excessive number of technical fouls, of which admittedly there are many. Wallace's emotion on the court is a demonstration of his desire to play the game at a high level. No one knows what to do with a Black man who exhibits emotion though. Unlike others, Black men are not allowed to exhibit anything remotely approximating passion. It is too often misperceived as a violent threat. In this regard they seem to be caught in a frustrating catch-22. If someone is angry, they are too emotional. And if they are laid back, they are not angry enough.

This double standard was most clearly at work when Rasheed Wallace was called for a technical foul in a playoff game against the Lakers back in 2000. Wallace was charged with a technical for an "intimidating stare" pointed in the direction of referee Ron Garretson. Though Wallace's reputation of being given to outbursts preceded him, this call was ridiculous. The call was the equivalent of accusing Wallace of "reckless eyeballing," a Jim Crow charge often leveled against Black men when it was perceived that they had been looking at a White woman or looking in a way thought disrespectful to a White person.

10   Though players like Wallace have come to represent the majority of players in the league, they are often still being discussed and manipulated by people of another generation and from another disposition altogether. Gone are the days when Jackie Robinson broke the color line in baseball and Black athletes were simply content to be included. Things have now changed quite drastically. One cannot honestly discuss sports in American society without including the contributions of Black people as a primary part of that conversation. After several generations of prominent Black athletes, their significance in sports is very much like their significance in the music industry: unquestionable. These are two areas of the culture where Black people have not only excelled, but where they are the standard by which all others are measured.

This being the case, contemporary Black athletes feel no need to simply be content because they are being Included. Unfortunately, their inclusion on the athletic side of things often mirrors a relative exclusion in other realms of the sporting world. Many members of the main stream media are White and of a different generation. They often want to impose the dictates of the past on the Black athletes of the present. They tend to have the same expectations of an Allen Iverson as they did of a Joe Louis. Allen Iverson did not grow up in the same world that Joe Louis did, and he has not had the same experiences either. So why should he be expected to think and act in the same way? Contemporary Black basketball players have a great deal of money at their disposal along with a great deal of visibility and power. Yet the people who tend to control the aspects of the game off the court—the media, the league— reflect these old ideas and expectations.

I have often found that the incongruity of these circumstances is best reflected in the term "role model." To me, this is a modern-day version of saying that someone is a "credit to their race," as they said about Joe Louis and others in the past. Role model is another way of saying to the young. Black, rich and famous, "Stay in your place, speak when spoken to, and do as you are told. . . be thankful for what you've got." In response, the young, Black, rich and famous raise an extended middle finger. This seems to have resulted in an impasse. The proverbial unstoppable force meets the immovable object.

What emboldens the young, Black, rich and famous is that they know they are the reason people are paying attention in the first place. They are the reason for being. This reflects a shift in power relations. This is not to say that Black basketball players run things, but they do have a say-so. They are the attraction and they are the straws that stir the drink. Like stars in Hollywood who draw people to their movies, these basketball players command the box office. When the media, the establishment, and those fans with their heads in the sand wake up, they will realize all of this too. You cannot force a Black square peg into a round White hole. You cannot draw White blood from a Black turnip. You can however turn the game of basketball into a global entertainment commodity, with Black players at the center of a new definition of what now constitutes America.

Reflect & Write

- ❏ In this section of his book, Boyd claims that Hip Hop is a way of life that defines the culture of basketball players; it is a style choice. How does he support this assertion? Point to specific evidence. Is he convincing?
- ❏ How does Boyd strategically use diction to convey his argument about Black basketball players? Which terms are most familiar to you?
- ❏ Why does Boyd provide a historical and contemporary perspective on the notion of the "role model"? What is his point? Do you agree with it?
- ❏ **Write:** What is Boyd's point about the length of shorts being a sign of race and cultural identity? Pick another item of clothing and compose a blog entry explaining how this clothing serves as visual rhetoric for a cultural group in your community.

■ *Produced by the Media Education Foundation, a nonprofit organization specializing in providing educational resources designed to encourage media literacy,* Playing Unfair *(2003) is a short film designed to provide analysis of the role of gender in sports 30 years after Title IX legislation mandated equal privileges for female athletes. The film integrates short clips from media footage with commentary by three prominent media scholars: Mary Jo Kane from the University of Minnesota, Pat Griffin from the University of Massachusetts, and Michael Messner from the University of Southern California.*

Transcript: **Playing Unfair**

The Media Education Foundation

Introduction—The Best of Times and The Worst of Times

[News voice-over] Is the American public ready to embrace professional women's teams and the image of a tough, physical, female athlete?

MARY JO KANE: As we enter a new century, we are in what I call the Best of Times and the Worst of Times with respect to media representations of female athletes. There has been both widespread acceptance and movement of women in sport that was unheard of thirty years ago, and at the same time there's been an increasing backlash about their success and their presence.

MICHAEL MESSNER: I think not too long ago, it was very easy to equate athleticism, strength, physical power, with men, and by contrast to think about women as weak, as supportive for men, purely as sexual objects. Now that landscape has changed somewhat with the tremendous growth of girls, and women's sports.

[Sports commentator] *There's Rebecca Lobo with a jumper!*

MICHAEL MESSNER: Everybody has the opportunity to see strong, powerful, physically competent, competitive women and I think that really challenges that simple gender dichotomy that we used to take so much for granted.

PAT GRIFFIN: Sport is not just a trivial activity for fun. It has real, deep cultural meaning in this society. And I think that to challenge that meaning in terms of what it means to be a man in this culture, by inviting women in and acknowledging that women are also athletic and muscular and strong, is a real challenge to that cultural norm that we live in.

5 MARY JO KANE: There is a cultural assumption that I think persists even to this day, that because of the definition of masculinity and sport, part of the birthright of being male in this culture is owning sport. You own sport. As women move into this once exclusive domain of male power and privilege and identity, there's been a tremendous backlash, and a desire to push back, and either to push women out of sport altogether or certainly to contain their power within in and keep them on the margins.

Out of Uniform—The Media Backlash Against Female Athletes

MICHAEL MESSNER: If you just watch the sports news, and you just watched ESPN, and if you just picked up *Sports Illustrated Magazine* for your main print source of information about what's going on in the sports world, it would be easy to continue to conclude that there is no women's sports happening.

MARY JO KANE: Women are significantly underrepresented with respect to amount of coverage, even though women represent 40% of participants nationwide in terms of sport and physical activity. What all the studies indicate is they represent about 3-5% of all the coverage. So we give viewers a very false impression if you just rely on the media, that women simply aren't participating in sports in the numbers that they are.

MICHAEL MESSNER: Over the course of a decade that we were doing research on the coverage of women's and men's sports, our dominant finding was how much the coverage of women's sports had not changed. About 5% of the airtime was given to women's sports. In our most recent study, ten years later that had gone up to about 8%, which is still miniscule. I mean it's really a tiny increase in over a ten year period in coverage of women.

[NBC News] *They are very excited. The NBA playoffs have arrived and while the Knicks are dominating. . .*

MICHAEL MESSNER: You set the tone and make a statement about what's most important and what the key happenings of the day were with your lead story.

[NBC News] *a big night coming up in sports as the Islanders. . .*

10 MICHAEL MESSNER: What we found is almost always the lead stories were about men's sports. They put a lot more production value into the men's coverage. There's tape, there's graphics, there's interviews and so forth.

[ESPN promo] *June heats up on ESPN.*

MICHAEL MESSNER: When women do kind of peak into the frame, though, it's usually in ways that are mostly dismissive or disrespectful.

[ABC News Channel 7] *Finally, a hearty erin go braugh to my countrymen and-women out there, and in your honor we have a little Erin Go Bra-less.*

MICHAEL MESSNER: In our study, one of the longest stories that was done on the sports news for instance was on a female nude bungee jumper on St. Patrick's Day who had painted her body green and jumped off of a bridge and they did a very long story on this—on the sports—meanwhile ignoring all the sports women had been playing that day: a major golf tournament and so forth.

[ABC News Channel 7]
— That's wonderful; do we have to slow that down?
— That was amazing, I'll remember it forever.
— . . . And so will we.

MICHAEL MESSNER: Well we all know that news isn't totally objective, but it's supposed to be a picture of what happened today in the world.

MARY JO KANE: What we know in terms of the data is that women athletes are significantly more likely than male athletes to be portrayed off the court, out of uniform, and in these hyper feminized roles. The thing that we infrequently see is images of women athletes as athletes. I think we need to talk about why that is and who benefits from *not* seeing women athletes as athletes.

15 PAT GRIFFIN: Who's controlling the images that we see in the media, and I think particularly if you look at sports media, by and large, the decisions about what images are portrayed, what images are used, who gets coverage, are still made by men. They're part of a culture that sees women in a particular way. And so I think they prefer to see women athletes portrayed in a more feminine way, it's more comfortable.

MICHAEL MESSNER: When television does cover women's sports, they're most likely going to cover women's tennis, and during certain seasons and certainly during the Olympics, women's figure skating. There's a traditional equation of femininity with tennis and figure skating that makes some sports commentators more comfortable with covering them—they fit more in their own ideological frame about what women are supposed to look like and how they're supposed to act. There's still a tendency, we found, in the play-by-play coverage of tennis to call women athletes more often by their first names, as though there's some sort of familiarity that the commentator has with them.

[Tennis commentator] . . . *to counter Jennifer's return.*
[Tennis commentator] . . . *you just never know which Amelie's going to show up.*
[Tennis commentator] . . . *Monica, trying to hang on, but Serena's serve. . .*

MICHAEL MESSNER: And to call men athletes by their last name or by their last and first name.

[Tennis commentator] . . . *Cand Ruzesky takes the game. . .*
[Tennis commentator] . . . *Agassi, through to the semis, and coming off his French Open win.*

MICHAEL MESSNER: People who work in an office, the boss will call the secretary by her—or his, if it's a male secretary—first name, and the referent the other way is always "Mr." or "Mrs." or some title.

PAT GRIFFIN: I think what's going on is we still have a lot of cultural anxiety about strong women and what that means about them as women. And until we can sort of move much further, as a culture in opening up the boundaries for what we consider to be OK for girls and women in sport, we're always going to have that ambivalence there.

20 MARY JO KANE: As we went into the women's World Cup soccer, nobody knew who Brandi Chastain was. We knew who Mia Hamm was, but we didn't know who Brandi Chastain was. We know who she is now.

[Newscaster] World Cup hero Brandi Chastain, throws the first pitch—tank top, no sports bra.
[ABC News Channel 7] And uh, Brandi did keep her shirt on, but did take a sweater off, during warm-ups.
[ABC News Channel 7] It was announced Nike will exploit Brandi Chastain's strip tease by attaching her to a line of sports bras.

MARY JO KANE: It immediately got turned into "Brandi Chastain took her shirt off," rather than "what fabulous athletes these women are!"

MICHAEL MESSNER: How many times did we see images of Jenny Thompson actually swimming in *Sports Illustrated*? But when she posed for *Sports Illustrated* in that way, we saw her and now we know who she is.

MARY JO KANE: What got taken up in the press and the public discourse wasn't who Jenny Thompson was and what she'd accomplished as a great swimmer, an Olympic swimmer, but what did it mean to have Jenny Thompson take her shirt off?

[Montage of images of female athletes and non-athlete models]

MARY JO KANE: And the images that you see of women being physically powerful and strong and contrast that to the images of women athletes as little sex kittens, it's an enormous difference. And it is such a powerful contrast that I would argue that is exactly why those images are suppressed. Because sport is all about physical, emotional, and mental empowerment. And so what do you do with all these women who are becoming great athletes and learning the lessons of empowerment and self respect and pride that you get from participating in sport? How are you going to keep that force at bay? And one way that you do that is to do a very time honored and tested mechanism of keeping women's power at bay and that is to sexualize them, trivialize them, and marginalize them.

There are more and more images of women athletes that bear alarming resemblances to soft pornography. What you see is an emphasis, not on their athleticism and their athletic achievements, or their mental courage and tough-ness, but on their sexuality, their femininity, and their heterosexuality. So what better way to reinforce all of the social stereotypes about femininity and mas-culinity than to pick up *Sports Illustrated* or *Rolling Stone* or *Maxim* or *Gear* and see an image of a female athlete, not as strong and powerful but as somebody that you can sexualize and feel power over. I don't think that there's a more overt example of that these days than in the world of professional tennis in the image of Anna Kournikova. She has the most corporate sponsorship of any professional female athlete and it is not because of her athletic competence because she is as of this date, still has never won any singles tournament, let along a Major.

25 PAT GRIFFIN: What it says to me is that an athlete's sexual appeal quotient is much more important than her athletic ability quotient and her athletic accom-plishment quotient. And it's very difficult to imagine the same kind of thing happening in men's tennis—a player who has never won a major tournament getting the kind of attention—media attention and endorsement in terms of money that Anna Kournikova gets. And I think that as long as that's possible, it really gives us a pretty good gauge of what are the important things in women's sports.

MICHAEL MESSNER: One of the new things over the last several years is there definitely is more media sexualization of men and men athletes in particular. Men are being viewed as sexy, mostly because of what they do. Of course they have to look good, but they're viewed as sexy primarily for what they're doing on the court or on the field, how good an athlete they are, how powerful they are, how they move when they play. Women are being viewed as sexy not for what they're doing on the court or for what they're doing on the field, but for how they look and what they wear off the field and how they pose off the field, and that's the key difference.

[ESPN: World's Sexiest Athlete] The world's sexiest athlete? Anna Kournikova, hands down. Have you seen the billboard of it? That explains enough.

Kournikova: All athletes are entertainers. As long as people like what they're seeing, they're going to keep coming back, so I think that's good.

Playing Along—Empowerment or Exploitation?

MARY JO KANE: It's not just how the media portray women athletes. It's how they are promoted and how they portray themselves. They simply feed into and keep the engine going of the way in which the media portray women athletes.

[Entertainment Tonight!: Brandi Chastain interview] It was something that I'm glad I did and if it got attention for soccer, then good.

MICHAEL MESSNER: Those are paradoxical images that both suggest empowerment for women and suggest that this media is still trying to frame women in conventionally sexualized ways. And I think that plays into very easily the idea that I, as an individual, need to feel empowered or do feel empowered by taking off my clothes and posing and getting myself into a major national magazine and maybe getting some endorsements.

PAT GRIFFIN: There are other women that I've talked to—young women—who see this in a real different way. They don't really see that as compromising or an expression of concern about how people see them. They just see that as— "that's just my individual way of expressing myself." And I think that certainly could be true for a certain number of them. But what I always want to say to them is it's important to look at the larger picture of pressures, that it's not just about individual choice. That if you look at how women athletes portray themselves, and how they're portrayed in the media, it's a part of a much larger cultural expectation. Is this the kind of image that we want young girls who are interested in sport to aspire to? Do we want them to think that in order to be respected as an athlete, they have to strip?

30 MARY JO KANE: And a very common retort is "what's wrong with being portrayed as feminine?" and "we want to be portrayed as well-rounded" and "there's nothing wrong with showing off our bodies. We're *proud* of our bodies." And on the surface, I think that all of those are very legitimate arguments. The problem that I have is that for women to show that they have strong and powerful bodies, it does not require them to take their clothes off. The way that those images get taken off is basically in terms of locker room titillation. It has absolutely nothing to do with men sitting around, saying, "Boy, I really respect them as fabulous athletes." It's about consuming their bodies for men's sexual pleasure. So that in no way empowers them or is done as an empowering image.

MICHAEL MESSNER: I don't think you'd have near the amount of controversy or debate if a woman occasionally decides to pose half-clothed in front of a camera for *Sports Illustrated* or something. But it's the dearth of coverage of women and the dearth of respectful coverage of women's athletics in those major media that makes those images stand out so much and be so controversial.

The Glass Closet—Homophobia in Sport and Sports Media

MARY JO KANE: Homophobia is in the bone marrow of women's athletics, you simply cannot get around it.

[ABC News] Billie Jean King, the undisputed Queen of Tennis. Last Friday, facing what is certainly the most serious crisis of her career, thirty-seven year old Billie Jean admitted she had had a homosexual affair with her former Marilyn Barnett.

[NBC News] Billie Jean King's contract to make television ads for ER Squibb Company is not being renewed. The New York Daily News quotes a company official as saying she was too strong a personality, that she was overpowering the product. He denied that the company's decision had anything to do with Mrs. King's disclosure of a lesbian relationship. The News says Avon Products is reviewing its connection with Mrs. King cautiously.

35 MARY JO KANE: I think its pretty clear that if you're a female athlete and you want corporate sponsorship, you'd better project a wholesome image. And part of that wholesomeness is the assumption that you are not lesbian, that you are heterosexual. So you'll have a disproportionate number of images of women athletes with children, with boyfriends, with husbands, to clearly mark themselves as heterosexual.

PAT GRIFFIN: Sometimes I refer to that as sort of the protective camouflage of feminine drag that women athletes and coaches feel sort of compelled to monitor in themselves and in others. Certainly it's this need to reassure people— I'm an athlete, I may be a great athlete, but don't worry, I'm still a normal woman.

MARY JO KANE: The acronym for the professional golf tour is the LPGA, as in the Ladies Professional Golf Association and I think it has been widely known or feared for many years that the "L" stands for "lesbian." The LPGA and the women who've played in the Tour have taken great pains to distance themselves from that lesbian image and to again, very overtly and explicitly identify themselves as heterosexual.

[TV ad] Hey Laura Baugh, UltraBrite toothpaste would like to proposition you.

***Laura**: Right here? On national television?*

MARY JO KANE: Jan Stephenson who was a well-known professional golfer was part of an LPGA calendar—"we're professional golfers by day but we're really sexy gals by night." A disproportionate amount of the coverage given to Nancy Lopez who's one of the greatest golfers ever on the Tour was about her marriage to Ray Knight who's a professional baseball player with the Mets, and her role as a mother. There were lots of pictures of Laura Baugh when she was pregnant and playing on the Tour. The LPGA rarely gets any media coverage and yet there was a lot of media coverage around "is she going to be able to get through the round and the tournament and not go into labor?" The media or the corporate sponsors or the women athletes themselves specifically identify themselves with the role of wife and mother, which clearly marks them as heterosexual.

[ABC News] For Chris Evert this will be her nineteenth and last US Open.

MARY JO KANE: In the late 1980s, one of the greatest professional tennis players this country has ever produced, Chris Evert, announced her retirement. *Sports Illustrated* chose to put her on the cover: "Now I'm going to be a full time wife." They chose to portray her as somebody who was giving up her career to become a full-time wife. On the inside, with the profile, they had a pictorial chronology of Evert's "career" in sport. This isn't in "Bride Magazine" or in "Heterosexual Magazine"—its in *Sports Illustrated,* talking about her retirement as being a professional tennis player, and yet the focus, certainly in terms of the visual images you were given, was of Chris Evert as a heterosexual wife and mother.

PAT GRIFFIN: The more we focus on women athletes as heterosexual and sexy and feminine, the more lesbians in sport become invisible. It's difficult enough in many cases to be a lesbian in sport, but to be held up against that standard that is not about me—that sense of being made to feel as if I must be invisible for the sake of women's sports, for the sake of not creating controversy—it's a huge pressure, and it keeps us from really dealing with some of the key issues in women's sports which have to do with heterosexism and homophobia.

[ABC News] It has added to the torment she has long suffered, from the public acknowledgement of her homosexuality.

Martina: It's much easier being heterosexual, believe me. It's much easier pretending.

PAT GRIFFIN: There are heterosexual women in sport who are very much threatened by the idea that someone might think that they're a lesbian, or would call them a lesbian. And lesbians in sport are very much concerned—and rightly so—about being discriminated against, if they're identified in sport. And you put that together and it really drives a wedge between women in sport. And that wedge serves a larger social function of keeping women from forming alliances to really further women's sport as a whole.

[Tennis commentator] . . .I mean she came out and openly declared her sexuality and in team sports of course that would be suicidal—I don't mean that literally, but I mean it would be a very, very hard thing

40 PAT GRIFFIN: I think it's amazing to me that in the WBNA, there is not one publicly out basketball player. And yet we know that there are many lesbians in basketball as there are in any sport. But none of them have felt personally safe enough, or I think another factor is feeling like the league itself, the women's

basketball professional league, is safe enough to withstand the potential media scrutiny of acknowledging that there are lesbian players. You know, the weird thing is everyone knows there are lesbian players. So we have this strange sort of paradox of lesbians feeling that they need to hide, yet everyone knows that they're there—I often call it the "glass closet."

MARY JO KANE: The WNBA is very much aware that a large part of their fan base is lesbian. They're a new league, they are struggling to survive. So they certainly don't want to alienate any section of their fan base, especially one that's so prominent and loyal. On the other hand, they take great pains to market themselves as a family-friendly entertainment venue. And so because of homophobia and cultural stereotypes, we see that there's this contradiction on the one hand wanting to market yourself as family values entertainment, and on the other hand, what do you do with the fact that you have these lesbians in the stands?

MICHAEL MESSNER: There are stars that were put forward to promote the league, were positioned as the "girl next door," like Rebecca Lobo, a mother—Cheryl Swoops, or a fashion model—Lisa Leslie. And in doing that what they did was they pushed certain women forward as representing the league, who could exemplify what they saw as pretty conventional, heterosexual roles for women.

MARY JO KANE: I think the struggle is, how do you show athletic competence, athletic strength, athletic power—beating up and beating down your opponent—in ways that don't trigger cultural stereotypes about women athletes being too butch, being too manly, being too aggressive?

[Basketball Coach Pat Summit] *Get tough! Get tough!*

MARY JO KANE: In order for women athletes to be taken seriously as athletes, they have to be portrayed as competent, which in sports like basketball, by definition means being big, strong, tough, fast, powerful. You can't have one without the other, and yet to equate them means to challenge every stereotype and construction of femininity and masculinity we have in the culture.

Fair Play—Women Athletes in Action

45 PAT GRIFFIN: Masculinity and femininity are not natural things. You know, boys don't pop out of the womb with a football in their arm, and girls don't pop out with a doll. We have to be *taught* very carefully how we're supposed to act to conform to those artificial expectations of masculinity and femininity. And to the extent that sport is very gendered in this culture—its one of the ways that masculinity and femininity are taught.

MICHAEL MESSNER: One of the things that people haven't really talked about that much though is that having more images of powerful women, respectful coverage of women's sports, is also potentially very good for boys. Boys are growing up in a world where they're going to have women co-workers, women bosses—the foundations for their views of women are being laid during their childhood. If what they're seeing is a sea of imagery that still suggests to them that athleticism is to be equated entirely with men and masculinity and that women are there simply as support objects or as objects of ridicule or as sexual objects, that is helping to shape the images that boys have of women. I don't believe that there's a conspiracy in the media to say "let's not cover women's sports" or "lets make fun of women athletes," but I think that especially sports desks and sports news people have not caught on to the fact yet that the culture has changed.

PAT GRIFFIN: Well, I don't think any social change happens in a nice, smooth sort of step-by-step path, onward and upward. If you look at any social change movement, whether we're talking about the black civil rights movement, the women's movement in general, the gay, lesbian, bisexual, transgender movement—when there are changes, there's always a pushback. And so change sort of happens in that way, and I think that's what we're seeing here.

MARY JO KANE: All I'm asking is, turn the camera on, and let us see what it looks like when women participate in sports. And what we'll see is that they are terrific athletes who are enormously gifted and enormously committed to something that many people in this country love, and that's sport.

Reflect & Write

❏ Paraphrase the assumptions that society makes about the meaning of sports, as well as about women and men in sports. How have these continued today even with the passage of Title IX?

❏ What issues concerning sexuality and the female body are raised by this film transcript?

❏ How do the speakers raise concrete points of evidence concerning the media's unfair depiction of women in sports? Discuss the use of names, the framing, the tapes, the particular sports shown, the focus on clothes and on sexual preference. Which of these media infractions do you think has the greatest consequences? Why?

❏ Do you agree with the contention that the media representation of several female athletes verges on "soft porn"? Argue for both sides of this debate.

❏ **Write:** Draft a letter to *Sports Illustrated* from the perspective of Chris Evert, Rebecca Lobo, and Anna Kournikova. How would each woman respond to the arguments made by this film? Quote from passages in the transcript in your letter.

COLLABORATIVE CHALLENGE

Get into groups of three for this activity. Using at least three different examples of a single type of sports coverage (for instance, three news reports, three newspaper articles, or three articles in a sports-oriented magazine), explore how the amount and tone of coverage of women athletes reveal the relationship between gender stereotype and sports media. Pick two recent and concrete examples to prove your assertions. Compose a Multiple Sides feature article (following the guidelines in Chapter 3) and present your findings to the class.

PERSPECTIVES ON THE ISSUE

1. Consider the portrayal of African-American athletes in sport, as featured in this Chapter: Kevin Garnett, Michael Jordan, Serena Williams. What does each portrayal have in common? How does each portrayal support or dismantle racial stereotypes? Gender stereotypes?

2. Compose a script in which you put into dialogue the arguments made by Boyd and Mumford. See the directions in Chapter 5 on the dialogue of sources. What would each writer have to say in response to the argument of the other? What new synthesis of perspective on race and stereotypes in sports might you come to through a conversation with these authors?

3. Compare the portrayal of tennis stars Anna Kournikova and Serena Williams on the *Sports Illustrated* covers and the way women athletes are featured in the *Playing Unfair* transcript. Write an essay in which you use these diverse representations as evidence for discussing the stereotypes and challenges facing women and girls in sports coverage today.

4. Visit *Sports Illustrated*'s cover archive through its Website and look at the covers from a few years. Look at different ways that male athletes have been represented. Write an essay in which you analyze the stereotypes of femininity, masculinity, heterosexuality, ethnic identity, and race at work in these covers. Center your argument around how far the media has—or hasn't—come in its representations of athletes.

FROM READING TO RESEARCH

1. Choose an advertisement that features an African-American athlete. Use it as evidence to support, modify, or refute the arguments offered by Mumford or Boyd. First perform a rhetorical analysis of the image. Then assess the image in context by using quotations from the articles in this chapter as secondary source support for your claims. You may also draw on additional primary and secondary source materials by consulting your library. See Chapter 5 for various kinds of research you might consult and Chapter 6 for strategies on incorporating sources in your writing.

2. Explore the importance of Title IX in the history of women's participation in sports and the consequent representations of gendered athletes. Conduct research on the topic and formulate your perspective into a research argument. You might want to interview coaches as well as athletic women from diverse generations to get a range of viewpoints on this issue. Construct a list of questions based on the issues raised by the film *Playing Unfair*. For added challenge, transform your research report into a script for a film, with your interviewees as the key players in your movie.

CHAPTER 12

Copyright and Creativity

What exactly is "copyright" and how does it shape our culture? Can we think of "copyright" as similar to the notion of property—or how people can own certain things such as land and houses? How can we connect this notion to books, or music, or movies? Does this mean that in our own creative work (if we write poems, songs, movies, or other texts), we have to be careful about how we "borrow" ideas and about how our ideas might in turn be taken from us?

These questions get at the heart of issues of copyright. As we'll explore in this chapter, there is a paradox at the heart of modern copyright issues: although now copyright often is seen as designed to limit creative freedom, it originally was intended to *encourage* artists to produce new cultural texts by providing them with the incentive of profiting from their work. But today, we are confounded by the ambiguity that lies between the creation of cultural texts and those laws designed to protect an artist's rights.

Take, for instance, the artistic image of Heidi Cody's "American Alphabet" in Figure 12.1. Looking at this text, you are looking at our culture through the lens of legal battles. What at first seems a creative approach to drawing letters is actually a sign of monetary and court battles over who owns the right to represent ideas in certain ways—and this has significant implications for creativity.

FIGURE 12.1 Heidi Cody re-mixes letters from recognizable brand labels to construct her "American Alphabet."

So, what do you see in the image? At first glance, you might simply see a rather creative rendering of the standard English alphabet. A more careful scrutiny, however, might bring terms to mind not usually associated with the ABCs: Campbell's Soup, M&Ms, Oreos, Reese's Peanut Butter Cups, York Peppermint Patties. Each of the letters, you probably realize, is taken from the logos of common grocery products, producing a collage that comments on much more than the alphabet: it also argues for the way in which copyrighted materials—from brands, to songs, to ads—provide the fundamental building blocks for contemporary American culture.

"Can she do that?" you might ask as you think about the implications of Cody using such recognizable symbols in her collage. These symbols are trademarked by the different companies, which implies ownership over their use. Thus the image forces us to ask, "Is she breaking the law?" Clearly Cody intended to prompt such questions; in fact, her collage is featured in the Illegal Art exhibit, a collection of artistic creations that push the boundaries of copyright and trademark infringement. The goal of the exhibit was to make people think about who owns culture and how culture itself is produced.

But it is not only artists like Cody who prompt us to think about the regulations surrounding media and copyrights. Let's take two serious legal cases as examples. In 1996, artist Lebbeus Woods successfully sued Universal Studios, claiming that the studio used one of his sketches as the inspiration for an interrogation room set in the Bruce Willis film *Twelve Monkeys* (1995). That same year, Warner Brothers faced a similar suit for *Batman Forever* (1995); in that case, sculptor Andrew Leicester alleged that his sculpture had been featured at least eight times as a backdrop in the film without his permission. The courts, however, did not find in his favor. Around the same time, filmmaker Jon Else was forced to digitally remaster a segment of his documentary on the San Francisco Opera when Fox Studios placed their copyright fee at $10,000 for him to include a four-and-a-half-second clip of *The Simpsons* that was playing on the television in the background of a scene he shot showing the opera stage hands relaxing backstage. More recently, Paramount Pictures sought an injunction against a New York filmmaker to prevent him from distributing his independent, ten-minute film that they alleged was based on a bootleg copy of Oliver Stone's script for *World Trade Center* (2006). The filmmaker has argued that his movie was created as part of his master's thesis for Yale University and was never intended for commercial distribution. Thus was it an infringement of property rights or not? What are the consequences for creativity and the work of artists everywhere?

The complicated relationship between regulation, creativity, and culture is the focus of this chapter. In the first part of the chapter, "Copyright Matters," we'll move away from approaching copyright as a black and white issue—one of restriction and infringement—and explore instead how copyright has been tested, redefined, and, at times, modified by organizations like Creative Commons to keep pace with our increasingly digital culture. In "Who Owns Popular Culture?" we'll spend some time investigating one of the most common types of copyright infringement: the downloading and sharing of digital files, whether they be from music, TV, or film. Finally, in "Remixing Culture," we'll return to the question of how American culture is created. We'll look specifically at the new artistic texts being generated out of a fusion of existent ones—musical mashups, engaging photo collages, and even remixed and remastered films. After completing these readings, you should have a greater understanding of the complexities of this issue and its implication for your own use and production of cultural texts.

COPYRIGHT MATTERS

FIGURE 12.2 This image from the Creative Commons website visually captures the "Spectrum of Rights" that consumers face in their use of other people's original work.

Have you ever downloaded music from a P2P site? Copied an image from an online search to use it in a paper? Installed a friend's software into your computer? If so, you already have ventured into what one cultural critic calls the "Copyright Jungle"—that dense wilderness filled with tangled legal jargon, ethical ambiguities, and general confusion. Since oral culture gave way to print culture, copyright—or the *right* to *copy*—has always been a pressing legal issue. However, with the advent of digital technologies, the problem has been exacerbated; with the prevalence of photo scanners, digital copy and paste tools, seemingly omniscient online search engines, and the ever-expanding reach of the Internet, the possibilities for copying, sharing, and distributing materials are in more people's reach than ever before. As a result, questions of authorship and ownership have become more abundant, more adamant, and more public as they move into newspaper headlines, classroom discussions, and even into the courtroom.

Perhaps you feel like the figure in our opening image—juggling a host of media and usage limitations, from traditional copyright to the public domain. Yet issues of copyright are perplexing and the right choices are not always clear. Many questions surround copyright regulation: Who owns a creation? Who can use it? Who can profit by it? In this chapter, we'll read a series of texts concerned with these questions, including selections from a comic book produced by the Duke law school, designed to educate readers about fair use; an article from the *Atlantic Monthly* that investigates the implications of overseas piracy of American products; and a speech by Stanford Law Professor Lawrence Lessig that provides an evocative argument for alternative models of regulation. Together, these texts will provide you with a range of perspectives on the different ways contemporary intellectuals negotiate between the ideas of individual ownership and community property for all types of cultural productions.

Reflect & Write

- ❑ How does the graphic from the Creative Commons website use a simple line drawing to create a visual argument about the complexity of copyright issues?
- ❑ **Write:** Visit the Creative Commons Website through **www.ablongman.com/ envision/239** and write a brief analysis that explains the overall purpose and argument of the site.

This excerpt is taken from Bound by Law? Trapped in a Struggle She Didn't Understand, *a comic book produced by the Duke Law School's Center for the Study of the Public Domain. This 53-page visual argument was developed by* **Keith Aoki,** *the Philip H. Knight Professor of Law at the University of Oregon School of Law, a specialist in intellectual property law and author of* Seed Wars: Cases and Materials on Intellectual Property and Plant Genetic Resources; **James Boyle,** *one of the founders of the Center for the Study of the Public Domain, a board member of Creative Commons, the William Neal Reynolds Professor of Law at the Duke Law School, and author of* Shamans, Software and Spleens: Law and the Construction of the Information Society; *and* **Jennifer Jenkins,** *Director of the Center for the Study of the Public Domain and a specialist in intellectual property and copyright infringement.* Bound by Law? *follows a documentary filmmaker through the process of understanding the implications of copyright restrictions for her intended film on New York City.*

Excerpt:
Bound By Law?

**Keith Aoki,
James Boyle, and
Jennifer Jenkins**

FIGURE 12.3–12.8
These pages from *Bound By Law?* use comic book form to explore issues of intellectual property and copyright.

FIGURE 12.4

FIGURE 12.5

FIGURE 12.6

FIGURE 12.7

FIGURE 12.8

Reflect & Write

❏ Why do you think that these law professors chose to write their explanation of fair use in comic book form? Do you think this was a successful choice? Why or why not?

❏ Which panel or sequence of panels struck you as most effectively accomplishing the comic book's purpose? What elements of these panels make them particularly effective?

❏ How are point of view, persona, and stance reflected in this set of panels? What is the significance of the choice of characters? What roles do they serve in relation to the audience and the overall purpose of the text?

❏ **Write:** Choose one panel from those contained above and perform a rhetorical analysis in which you examine how rhetorical strategies of arrangement, style, and invention are used to produce an argument. Write up your analysis, being sure to include reference to specific detail.

Seeing Connections
Review the "Prewriting Checklist" at the end of Chapter 1 for tips on analyzing a cartoon.

■ **Charles C. Mann** *has written prolifically on issues related to technology, science, and commerce for numerous publications, including* The New York Times, Smithsonian, Business 2.0, *and the* Washington Post. *In addition, he has published several books, the most recent of which,* 1491 (2005), *describes life in the Americas prior to Columbus's arrival. He has received writing awards from the American Bar Association, the Alfred P. Sloan Foundation, the American Institute of Physics, and the Margaret Sanger Foundation, and has been a National Magazine Award finalist three times. He also is a contributing editor for the* Atlantic Monthly, *where this article appeared in September 1998.*

Who Will Own Your Next Great Idea?

Charles C. Mann

About twelve years ago I walked past a magazine kiosk in Europe and noticed the words *"temple des rats"* the cover of a French magazine. Rat temple! I was amazed. A few months before, a friend of mine had traveled to northwestern India to write about the world's only shrine to humankind's least favorite rodent. The temple was in a village in the Marusthali Desert. That two Western journalists should have visited within a few months of each other stunned me. Naturally, I bought the magazine.

The article began with a Gallic tirade against the genus *Rattus. Le spectre du rat, le cauchemar d'humanité! Quel horreur!*—that sort of thing. Then came the meat: an interview, in Q&A form, with a "noted American journalist" who had just gone to the rat temple. The journalist, who was named, was my friend. No such interview had

occurred: the article was a straight translation, with fake Interruptions by the "interviewer" such as *"Vraiment?"* and *"Mon Dieu!"*

I was outraged. To my way of thinking, these French people had ripped off my friend. I telephoned him immediately; he had the same reaction. Expletives crackled wildly across the Atlantic. Reprinting his copyrighted article without permission or payment was the same, we decided, as kicking down his door and stealing his CD player.

We were wrong. Although the magazine had done my friend wrong, what was stolen was not at all like a CD player. CD players are physical property. Magazine articles are *intellectual* property, a different matter entirely. When thieves steal CD players, the owners no longer have them, and are obviously worse off.

5   But when my friend's writing was appropriated, he still had the original manuscript. What, then, was stolen? Because the article had been translated, not one sentence in the French version appeared in the original. How could it be considered a copy? Anomalies like this are why intellectual property has its own set of laws.

Intellectual property is knowledge or expression that is owned by someone. It has three customary domains: copyright, patent, and trademark. Copyrighted songs, patented drugs, and trademarked soft drinks have long been familiar denizens of the American landscape, but the growth of digital technology has pushed intellectual property into new territory. Nowadays one might best define intellectual property as anything that can be sold in the form of zeroes and ones. It is the primary product of the Information Age.

All three forms of intellectual property are growing in importance, but copyright holds pride of place. In legal terms, copyright governs the right to make copies of a given work. It awards limited monopolies to creators on their creations: for a given number of years no one but Walt Disney can sell Mickey Mouse cartoons without permission. Such monopolies, always valuable, are increasingly lucrative. For the past twenty years the copyright industry has grown almost three times as fast as the economy as a whole, according to the International Intellectual Property Alliance, a trade group representing film studios, book publishers, and the like. Last year, the alliance says, copyrighted material contributed more than $400 billion to the national economy and was the country's single most important export.

These figures may actually understate the value of copyright.

The digital world has created new problems for copyright owners. If the cost of manufacturing and distributing a product falls, economic forces will drive down its price, too. The Net embodies this principle to an extreme degree. Manufacturing and distribution costs collapse almost to nothing online: zeroes and ones can be shot around the world with a few clicks of a mouse. Hence producers of digital texts, music, and films will have trouble charging anything at all for copies of their works—competitors can always offer substitutes for less, pushing the price toward the vanishing point.

10   In addition, creators must deal with piracy, which is vastly easier and more effective in the digital environment. People have long been able to photocopy texts, tape-record music, and videotape television shows. Such leakage, as copyright lawyers call it, has existed since the first day a reader lent a (copyrighted) book to a friend. With the rise of digital media, the leakage threatens to turn into a gush. To make and distribute a dozen copies of a videotaped film requires at least two videocassette recorders, a dozen tapes, padded envelopes and postage, and considerable patience. And because the copies are tapes of tapes, the quality suffers. But if the film has been digitized into a computer file, it can be E-mailed to millions of people in minutes; because strings of zeroes and ones can be reproduced with absolute fidelity, the copies are perfect. And online pirates have no development costs—they don't even have to pay for paper or blank cassettes—so they don't really have a bottom line. In other words, even as digital technology drives the potential value of copyright to ever greater heights, that same technology threatens to make it next to worthless.

This paradox has engendered two reactions. One is to advocate eliminating copyright altogether. "Information wants to be free" is the apothegm of choice here. In this view, copyright restricts what people can do with the intellectual property coming through the wires. Futilely but dangerously, it tries to fence the electronic frontier. It unjustly creates monopolies in information. It is a relic of the past and should be expunged.

The other, opposing reaction is to strengthen the hand of copyright owners. Realizing the growing economic import of copyright, Congress is rapidly trying to overhaul the nation's intellectual-property regime. The changes would give copyright owners more control for longer times; some would make it a crime to work around copyright-protection schemes. A different tack is being taken by state governments, which may bypass copyright altogether by amending the laws governing sales contracts. If they succeed, copyright owners will be able to ask individual customers to agree to contracts regulating the zeroes and ones flowing into their homes.

Before we send this vintage episode of Seinfeld *to your computer, please read the following conditions and terms, paying careful attention to the clauses that forbid taping or replaying the program even once. After you click "OK," the transmission will start.*

Because I make much of my living from copyright. I find the to-and-fro fascinating, and have a vested interest in the results. But issues bigger than the financial status of writers are involved. Copyright is the regulatory authority for the marketplace of ideas. It lays out the economic ground rules to create the hubbub of debate that the Founders believed necessary for democracy—one reason that they included copyright in the Constitution (Article I, Section 8, instructs Congress to "secur[e] for limited Times to Authors and Inventors the exclusive Right to their Respective Writings and Discoveries"). Copyright law allows Michael Jackson to make a fortune from the Beatles catalogue, and Bill Gates to add to his untold wealth by licensing electronic reproductions of the photographs of Ansel Adams. But its real purpose is to foster ever more ideas and ever more innovation from ever more diverse sources. When, in 1790, George Washington asked Congress to enact copyright legislation, he argued that it would increase the national stock of knowledge. And knowledge, he said, is "the surest basis of public happiness."

Today the marketplace of ideas is being shaken up by the competing demands of technology, finance, and law. Large sums of money are at stake. Change seems inevitable. One way or another, we will lay a new institutional foundation for literary culture in the United States. How we do it will play a big role in determining our future well-being. It would be comforting to believe that decisions will be made thoughtfully and well. But little evidence suggests this is true. Indeed, we may be heading into a muddle that it will take us a long lime to escape.

In December the MPAA estimated that piracy, chiefly in the form of illegal videocassettes, costs the U.S. motion-picture industry more than $2.5 billion a year.

15   Movies are not the only losers. Publishers complain that pirates knock off expensively produced textbooks in fields ranging from business management and computer science to medicine and English. Music companies hire a firm called GrayZone to hunt down bootleg-CD makers and Web-site pirates around the globe. In some countries—Russia and China, for example—more than 90 percent of all new business software is pirated, according to the Business Software Alliance and the Software Publishers Association, the two major trade associations in the field. The International Intellectual Property Alliance claims that foreign copyright infringement alone costs U.S. firms as much as $20 billion a year.

Critics charge that these huge figures are absurd, and not only because of the obvious difficulty of measuring illicit activity. While researching this article I obtained a CD-ROM called "CAD Xpress" for about $30 ("CAD" is the acronym for "computer-assisted design"). It contained a copy of the current version of AutoCAD, the leading brand of architectural-drafting software, which has a list price of $3,750. According to the Software Publishers Association, my copy of CAD Xpress represents a $3,750 loss to Autodesk, the manufacturer of AutoCAD. This assumes, of course, that I, and every other buyer of CAD Xpress, would otherwise pony up thousands of dollars for AutoCAD.

More important, in the view of Stanley Besen, an economist at Charles River Associates, a consulting firm in Washington, D.C., the huge estimates of piracy losses don't take into account the copyright owners' responses to copying.

"Suppose I know that people are going to copy Lotus 1-2-3," he said to me. "So I sell it for $500, knowing that four people will make copies of each program, whereas I might sell it for only $100 if all five users purchased programs for themselves." The price takes copying into account, and no loss occurs.

Such accommodations might insulate software firms from some of the effects of copying. But Besen does not think that they can insulate the companies from all of them, especially when a single bootleg can spawn so many other illicit copies that the original company can't raise the price enough to compensate for the losses incurred. I bought CAD Xpress at the Golden Shopping Centre, in Hong Kong. The Golden Shopping Centre was a kind of shopping mall for copyright infringement: three stories of pirated video games, CDs, videotapes, and software. Situated next to the Sham Shui Po subway station, in Kowloon, the mall was not hard to find—the address was in my *Fodor's Citypack* guidebook to Hong Kong.

20   The mall consisted of an unlovely concrete block jammed with small, kiosklike stores. Stores on the first floor sold mainly bootleg video games and devices that permit players illicitly to use games built for one company's machines on machines made by another. The second floor was full of pirated music and film. I wasn't interested in the music, but I was intrigued by the stacks of digital video disks. DVDs are compact disks that contain entire movies (they are sometimes called video compact disks, or VCDs). Expatriate cinéastes complain that most theaters in Hong Kong are devoted to the local product: action pictures starring the fleet-footed likes of Jackie Chan and Chow-yun Fat. But the stacks of illegal DVDs included such esoteric fare as the works of the late Polish director Krzysztof Kieslowskl. *Grand Illusion* for $6,001 *The Crying Game* for $8.00! Fellini's *Satyricon* for next to nothing! I began to see what low-cost distribution was all about.

    The third floor was devoted to computer programs. Here I bought CAD Xpress. In a gesture to the law, it was sold under the counter. Actually, what was under the counter was looseleaf binders that catalogued the store's illicit wares. Confused by the descriptions, which were written in garbled English, I asked a woman at one store if she sold AutoCAD, and she spoke to a young person who ran off and ten minutes later reappeared with the CD-ROM. "How much is it?" I asked. She wrote "240" on a slip of paper—240 Hong Kong dollars, then about $30 U.S. Because I make my living from copyright. I felt funny about buying pirated software. To satisfy my curiosity without arousing my conscience, I had decided to buy software that my family already owned. This idea collapsed when I saw CAD Xpress and its ilk. Competition among pirates ensures that their CD-ROMs are crammed with software; buying a single program wasn't easy. According to my local Autodesk dealer, my $30 copy of CAD Xpress contains more than $20,000 worth of computer-assisted-design software.

For me, the software was less than ideal. Most of the instructions were in Chinese, and some of the programs didn't work (or at least I couldn't make them work). But overall the disk was still a good buy. For another $30 I bought a CD-ROM called Power Dragon Software. One of its forty-eight programs was Quicken, the popular accounting software. Given the relatively small size of Quicken, I presumably paid less than a dollar for it—indeed, less than a quarter. In another store I bought the same version of Quicken on two floppy disks. This cost $25—about a hundred times as much, and almost as much as the whole CD-ROM, which included forty-seven other programs. The difference was that the floppy disks came with a photocopy of the manual, which is more informative than the program's help screens.

Many stores in the Golden Shopping Centre sold compilations of computer games, fifty or so per CD-ROM. It occurred to me as I flipped through them that I was inspecting a kind of precursor to the electronic book. I had recently written a book. Completely formatted, the manuscript was about 600,000 bytes in size. A CD-ROM holds more than 600 million bytes, enough for scores of books.

Complaining too loudly about illicit software exposes Americans to a charge of hypocrisy. During the nineteenth century U.S. copyright law did not extend to foreigners' works. New York City became the piracy center of the world. Charles Dickens's *A Christmas Carol* sold for the equivalent of $2.50 in England. On this side of the Atlantic bootleg editions cost six cents. U.S. publishers were unmoved by the plight of their writers who were pirated in England: they could make more money by stealing *Little Dorrit* here than by selling *Little Women* there. Only in 1891 did Congress pass international-copyright legislation.

25   I asked the man who sold me Power Dragon if the threat of prosecution worried him. He asked a friend to translate. The friend said, "He is not worried. Soon, very soon, his boss will sell on the Internet. They will send the programs through another country." Iraq, India, Bulgaria, somewhere in Africa, the friend said. In a world made up of hundreds of nations, someone would always be willing to assist his operations.

Reflect & Write

❏ What strategies, such as those discussed in Chapter 2, does Mann use to develop his argument? Were these effective rhetorical choices for his piece?

❏ What is Mann's attitude toward foreign markets for pirated goods? Identify particular passages, sentences, or allusions where that becomes clear.

❏ In the article, Mann describes his own different reactions to copyright infringement—from outrage to ambivalence to, arguably, complicity. How does representing this spectrum of reactions produce a different argument than had he portrayed himself in just one way? What does this do to the reader's experience of the copyright issue?

❏ Mann's article is clearly dated at some points—such as the moment where he defines the term DVD for the reader. Does this datedness undermine the argument? Why or why not?

❏ Consider the conclusion of the piece. Why do you think that Mann ends his discussion in this way?

❏ **Write:** Draft a brief letter to Mann that comments on his argument in relation to the changes in dissemination of media since he wrote it— TiVo; pay-based downloads of music, TV shows, and movies from the Web; computers being equipped with DVDRWs. How have current changes in technology and information management either fulfilled or undercut his vision?

■ **Lawrence Lessig** *is a professor of law at Stanford University and the chair of Creative Commons, an organization devoted to developing alternative licensing to encourage more productive sharing of authored works. He is one of the leading figures in copyright and intellectual property debates. Lessig originally delivered this presentation as the keynote for the July 2002 Open Source Convention. He is the author of several books on intellectual property and creativity, including* The Future of Ideas *(2001) and* Free Culture *(2004).*

Free Culture
Lawrence Lessig

I have been doing this for about two years—more than 100 of these gigs. This is about the last one. One more and it's over for me. So I figured I wanted to write a song to end it. But then I realized I don't sing and I can't write music. But I came up with the refrain, at least, right? This captures the point. If you understand this refrain, you're gonna' understand everything I want to say to you today. It has four parts:

• Creativity and innovation always builds on the past.
• The past always tries to control the creativity that builds upon it.
• Free societies enable the future by limiting this power of the past.
• Ours is less and less a free society.

In 1774, free culture was born. In a case called Donaldson v. Beckett in the House of Lords in England, free culture was made because copyright was stopped. In 1710, the statute had said that copyright should be for a limited term of just 14 years. But in the 1740s, when Scottish publishers started reprinting classics (you gotta' love the Scots), the London publishers said "Stop!" They said, "Copyright is forever!" Sonny Bono said "Copyright should be forever minus a day," but the London publishers said "Copyright is forever."

These publishers, people whom Milton referred to as old patentees and monopolizers in the trade of book selling, men who do not labor in an honest profession (except Tim here), to [them] learning is indebted. These publishers demanded a common-law copyright that would be forever. In 1769, in a case called Miller v. Taylor, they won their claim, but just five years later, in Donaldson, Miller was reversed, and for the first time in history, the works of Shakespeare were freed, freed from the control of a monopoly of publishers. Freed culture was the result of that case.

Remember the refrain. I would sing it, but you wouldn't want me to. OK. Well, by the end we'll see.

5   That free culture was carried to America; that was our birth—1790. We established a regime that left creativity unregulated. Now it was unregulated because copyright law only covered "printing." Copyright law did not control derivative work. And copyright law granted this protection for the limited time of 14 years.

That was our birth, and more fundamentally, in 1790, because of the technology of the time, all things protected were free code. You could take the works of Shakespeare and read the source—the source was the book. You could take the work of any creativity protected by the law and understand what made it tick [by] studying it. This was the design and the regime, and even in the context of patents, there were transparent technologies. You didn't take, you didn't need to take the cotton gin [for example] and read the patent to understand how it worked, right? You could just take it apart.

These were legal protections in a context where understanding and learning were still free. Control in this culture was tiny. That was cute, right? Control, tiny . . . OK. And not just then, right? Forget the 18th century, the 19th century, even at the birth of the 20th century. Here's my favorite example, here: 1928, my hero, Walt Disney, created this extraordinary work, the birth of Mickey Mouse in the form of Steamboat Willie. But what you probably don't recognize about Steamboat Willie and his emergence into Mickey Mouse is that in 1928, Walt Disney, to use the language of the Disney Corporation today, "stole" Willie from Buster Keaton's "Steamboat Bill."

It was a parody, a take-off; it was built upon Steamboat Bill. Steamboat Bill was produced in 1928, no [waiting] 14 years—just take it, rip, mix, and burn, as he did [laughter] to produce the Disney empire. This was his character. Walt always parroted feature-length mainstream films to produce the Disney empire, and we see the product of this. This is the Disney Corporation: taking works in the public domain, and not even in the public domain, and turning them into vastly greater, new creativity. They took the works of this guy, these guys, the Brothers Grimm, who you think are probably great authors on their own. They produce these horrible stories, these fairy tales, which anybody should keep their children far from because they're utterly bloody and moralistic stories, and are not the sort of thing that children should see, but they were retold for us by the Disney Corporation. Now the Disney Corporation could do this because that culture lived in a commons, an intellectual commons, a cultural commons, where people could freely take and build. It was a lawyer-free zone.

(Audience applauds.)

It was culture, which you didn't need the permission of someone else to take and build upon. That was the character of creativity at the birth of the last century. It was built upon a constitutional requirement that protection be for limited times, and it was originally limited. Fourteen years, if the author lived, then 28, then in 1831 it went to 42, then in 1909 it went to 56, and then magically, starting in 1962, look—no hands, the term expands.

10   Eleven times in the last 40 years it has been extended for existing works—not just for new works that are going to be created, but existing works. The most recent is the Sonny Bono copyright term extension act. Those of us who love it know it as the Mickey Mouse protection act, which of course [means] every time Mickey is about to pass through the public domain, copyright terms are extended. The meaning of this pattern is absolutely clear to those who pay to produce it. The meaning is: No one can do to the Disney Corporation what Walt Disney did to the Brothers Grimm. That though we had a culture where people could take and build upon what went before, that's over. There is no such thing as the public domain in the minds of those who have produced these 11 extensions these last 40 years because now culture is owned.

Remember the refrain: We always build on the past; the past always tries to stop us. Freedom is about stopping the past, but we have lost that ideal.

Things are different now, [different] from even when Walt produced the Walt Disney Corporation. In this year now, we have a massive system to regulate creativity. A massive system of lawyers regulating creativity as copyright law has expanded in unrecognizable forms, going from a regulation of publishing to a regulation of copying. You know the things that computers do when you boot them up? Going from copies to, not just copies of the original work, but even derivative works on top of it. Going from 14 years for new works produced by a real author—there are fewer and fewer of those people out there—to life plus 70 years. That's the expansion of law, but also there's been an expansion of control through technology.

OK, so first of all, this reality of opaque creativity, you know that as proprietary code. Creativity where you don't get to see how the thing works, and the law protects the thing you can't see. It's not Shakespeare that you can study and understand because the code is, by nature, open. Nature has been reformed in our modern, technological era, so nature can be hidden and the law still protects it—and not just through the protection, but through increasing control of uses of creative work.

Here's my Adobe eBook Reader, right. Some of you have seen this before, I'm sure. Here's *Middlemarch;* this is a work in the public domain. Here are the "permissions" (a lawyer had something to do with this) that you can do with this work in the public domain: You are allowed to copy ten selections into the clipboard every ten days—like, who got these numbers, I don't know—but you can print ten pages of this 4 million page book every ten days, and you are allowed to feel free to use the read-aloud button to listen to this book, right?

15   Now, Aristotle's *Politics,* another book in the public domain [that was] never really protected by copyright, but with this book, you can't copy any text into the selection, you can't print any pages, but feel free to listen to this book aloud. And

to my great embarrassment, here's my latest book, right? No copying, no printing, and don't you dare use the technology to read my book aloud. [Laughter] I'll have a sing button in the next version of Adobe. Read a book; read a book.

The point is that control is built into the technology. Book sellers in 1760 had no conception of the power that you coders would give them some day in the future, and that control adds to this expansion of law. Law and technology produce, together, a kind of regulation of creativity we've not seen before. Right? Because here, here's a simple copyright lesson: Law regulates copies. What's that mean? Well, before the Internet, think of this as a world of all possible uses of a copyrighted work. Most of them are unregulated. Talking about fair use, this is not fair use; this is unregulated use. To read is not a fair use; it's an unregulated use. To give it to someone is not a fair use; it's unregulated. To sell it, to sleep on top of it, to do any of these things with this text is unregulated. Now, in the center of this unregulated use, there is a small bit of stuff regulated by the copyright law; for example, publishing the book—that's regulated. And then within this small range of things regulated by copyright law, there's this tiny band before the Internet of stuff we call fair use: Uses that otherwise would be regulated but that the law says you can engage in without the permission of anybody else. For example, quoting a text in another text—that's a copy, but it's a still fair use. That means the world was divided into three camps, not two: Unregulated uses, regulated uses that were fair use, and the quintessential copyright world. Three categories.

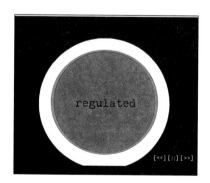

Enter the Internet. Every act is a copy, which means all of these unregulated uses disappear. Presumptively, everything you do on your machine on the network is a regulated use. And now it forces us into this tiny little category of arguing about, "What about the fair uses? What about the fair uses?" I will say the word: To hell with the fair uses. What about the unregulated uses we had of culture before this massive expansion of control? Now, unregulated uses disappear, we argue about fair use, and they find a way to remove fair use, right? Here's a familiar creature to many of you, right? The wonderful Sony Aibo Pet, which you can teach to do all sorts of things. Somebody set up a wonderful aibopet.com site to teach people how to hack their dogs. Now remember, their dogs, right? And this site actually wanted to help you hack your dog to teach your dog to dance jazz. Remember (Europeans are sometimes confused about this), it's not a crime to dance jazz in the United States.

This is a completely permissible activity—even for a dog to dance jazz. In Georgia, there are a couple jurisdictions I'm not sure about [laughter], but mainly, dancing jazz is an OK activity. So Aibopet.com said, "Here, here's how to hack your dog to make it dance jazz." If anything, it would be a fair use of this piece of plastic that costs over $1,500. You would think, "This is a fair use," right?

Letter to the site: Your site contains information providing the means to circumvent Aibo, where copy protection protocol constitutes a violation of the anticircumvention provisions of the DMCA. Even though the use is fair use, the use is not permitted under the law. Fair use, erased by this combination of technological control and laws that say "don't touch it," leaving one thing left in this field that had three, controls copyright, [thereby] controlling creativity.

20   Now, here's the thing you've got to remember. You've got to see this. This is the point. (And Jack Valenti misses this.) Here's the point: Never has it been more controlled ever. Take the addition, the changes, the copyrights turn, take the changes to copyrights scope, put it against the background of an extraordinarily concentrated structure of media, and you produce the fact that never in our history have fewer people controlled more of the evolution of our culture. Never.

Not even before the birth of free culture, not in 1773 when copyrights were perpetual, because again, they only controlled printing. How many people had printers? You could do what you wanted with these works. Ordinary uses were completely unregulated. But today, your life is perpetually regulated in the world that you live in. It is controlled by the law. Here is the refrain: Creativity depends on stopping that control. They will always try to impose it; we are free to the extent that we resist it, but we are increasingly not free.

You or the GNU, you can pick, build a world of transparent creativity— that's your job, this weird exception in the 21st century of an industry devoted to transparent creativity, the free sharing of knowledge. It was not a choice in 1790; it was nature in 1790. You are rebuilding nature. This is what you do. You build a common base that other people can build upon. You make money, not, well, not enough, but some of you make money off of this. This is your enterprise. Create like it's 1790. That's your way of being. And you remind the rest of the world of what it was like when creativity and innovation were a process where people added to common knowledge. In this battle between a proprietary structure and a free structure, you show the value of the free, and as announcements such as the RealNetworks announcement demonstrate, the free still captures the imagination of the most creative in this industry. But just for now. Just for now. Just for now, because free code threatens and the threats turn against free code.

Let's talk about software patents. There's a guy, Mr. Gates, who's brilliant, right? He's brilliant. A brilliant business man; he has some insights, he is even a brilliant policy maker. Here's what he wrote about software patents: "If people had understood how patents would be granted when most of today's ideas were invented and had taken out patents, the industry would be at a complete standstill today." Here's the first thing I'm sure you've read of Bill Gates that you all 100 percent agree with. Gates is right. He is absolutely right. Then we shift into the genius business man: "The solution is patenting as much as we can. A future startup with no patents of its own will be forced to pay whatever price the giants choose to impose. That price might be high. Established companies have an interest in excluding future competitors." Excluding future competitors.

Now, it's been four years since this battle came onto your radar screens in a way that people were upset about. Four years. And there have been tiny changes in the space. There have been a bunch of "Tim" changes, right? Tim went out there and he set up something to attack bad patents. That was fine. There were a bunch of Q. Todd Dickinson changes. He was a former head of the patent commission—never saw a patent he didn't like. But he made some minor changes in how this process should work. But the field has been dominated by apologists for the status quo. Apologists who say, We've always patented everything, therefore we should continue to patent this. People like Greg Aharonian, who goes around and says every single patent out there is idiotic. But it turns out that the patent system's wonderful and we should never reform it at all. Right?

25   This is the world we live in now, which produces this continued growth of software patents. And here's the question: What have we done about it? What have you done about it? Excluding future competitors—that's the slogan, right? And that company that gave birth to the slogan that I just cited has only ever used patents in a defensive way. But as Dan Gillmor has quoted, "They've also said, look, the Open Source Movement out there has got to realize that there are a lot of patents at stake, and don't imagine we won't use them when we must."

Now, the thing about patents is, they're not nuclear weapons. It's not physics that makes them powerful, it's lawyers and lawmakers and Congress. And the thing is, you can fight all you want against the physics that make a nuclear weapon destroy all of mankind, but you can not succeed at all. Yet you could do something about this. You could fuel a revolution that fights these legal threats to you. But what have you done about it? What have you done about it?

(Audience applauds.)

Second, the copyright wars: In a certain sense, these are the Homeric tragedies. I mean this in a very modern sense. Here's a story: There was a documentary filmmaker who was making a documentary film about education in America. And he's shooting across this classroom with lots of people, kids, who are completely distracted at the television in the back of the classroom. When they get back to the editing room, they realize that on the television, you can barely make out the show for two seconds; it's "The Simpsons," Homer Simpson on the screen. So they call up Matt Groenig, who was a friend of the documentary filmmaker, and say, you know, Is this going to be a problem? It's only a couple seconds. Matt says, No, no, no, it's not going to be a problem, call so and so. So they called so and so, and so and so said call so and so.

Eventually, the so and so turns out to be the lawyers, so when they got to the lawyers, they said, Is this going to be a problem? It's a documentary film. It's about education. It's a couple seconds. The so and so said 25,000 bucks. 25,000 bucks?! It's a couple seconds! What do you mean 25,000 bucks? The so and so said, I don't give a goddamn what it is for. $25,000 bucks or change your movie. Now you look at this and you say this is insane. It's insane. And if it is only Hollywood that has to deal with this, OK, that's fine. Let them be insane. The problem is their insane rules are now being applied to the whole world. This insanity of control is expanding as everything you do touches copyrights.

So, the broadcast flag, which says, "Before a technology is allowed to touch DTV, it must be architected to control DTV through watching for the broadcast flag." Rebuild the network to make sure this bit of content is perfectly protected, or amend it for . . . chips that will be imposed on machines through the law, which Intel referred to as the police state in every computer, quite accurately. And they would build these computers, but are opposed to this police state system.

30   And then, most recently, this outrageous proposal that Congress ratify the rights of the copyright owners to launch attacks on P2P machines—malicious code that goes out there and tries to bring down P2P machines. Digital vigilantism. And not only are you allowed to sue if they do it and they shouldn't have done it, but you have to go to the attorney general and get permission from the attorney general before you are allowed to sue about code that goes out there and destroys your machine . . . when it shouldn't be allowed to destroy your machine. This is what they talk about in Washington. This is what they are doing. This is, as Jack Valenti says, a terrorist war they are fighting against you and your children, the terrorists. Now you step back and you say, For what? Why? What's the problem? And they say, It's to stop the harm which you are doing.

So, what is that harm? What is the harm that is being done by these terrible P2P networks out there? Take their own numbers. They said last year [that] five times the number of CDs sold were traded on the Net for free. Five times. Then take their numbers about the harm caused by five times the number sold being traded for free: A drop in sales of five percent. Five percent. Now, there was a recession last year, and they raised their prices and they changed the way they counted. All of those might actually account for the five percent, but even if they didn't, the total harm caused by five times being traded for free was five percent. Now, I'm all for war in the right context, but is this the ground one stands on to call for a "terrorist war" against technology? This harm? Even if five percent gives them the right to destroy this industry, I mean, does anybody think about the decline in this industry, which is many times as large as theirs, caused by this terrorist war being launched against anybody who touches new content? Ask a venture capitalist how much money he is willing to invest in new technology that would touch content in a way that Hilary Rosen or Jack Valenti don't sign off on. The answer is a simple one: Zero. Zero.

They've shut down an industry and innovation in the name of this terrorist war, and this is the cause. This is the harm. Five percent.

And what have you done about it? It's insane. It's extreme. It's controlled by political interests. It has no justification in the traditional values that justify legal regulation. And we've done nothing about it. We're bigger than they are. We've got rights on our side. And we've done nothing about it. We let them control this debate. Here's the refrain that leads to this: They win because we've done nothing to stop it.

There's a congressmen: J.C. Watts. J.C. Watts is the only black member of the Republican Party in leadership. He's going to resign from Congress. He's been there seven and a half years. He's had enough. Nobody can believe it. Nobody in Washington can believe it. Boy, not spend 700 years in Washington? He says, you know, I like you guys, but seven years is enough, eight years is too much. I'm out of here. Just about the time J.C. Watts came to Washington, this war on free code and free culture began. Just about that time.

35   In an interview two days ago, Watts said, Here's the problem with Washington: "If you are explaining, you are losing." If you are explaining, you're losing. It's a bumper sticker culture. People have to get it like that, and if they don't, if it takes three seconds to make them understand, you're off their radar screen. Three seconds to understand, or you lose. This is our problem. Six years after this battle began, we're still explaining. We're still explaining and we are losing. They frame this as a massive battle to stop theft, to protect property. They don't get why rearchitecting the network destroys innovation and creativity. They extend copyrights perpetually. They don't get how that in itself is a form of theft. A theft of our common culture. We have failed in getting them to see what the issues here are and that's why we live in this place where a tradition speaks of freedom and their controls take it away.

Now, I've spent two years talking to you. To us. About this. And we've not done anything yet. A lot of energy building sites and blogs and Slashdot stories. [But] nothing yet to change that vision in Washington. Because we hate Washington, right? Who would waste his time in Washington?

But if you don't do something now, this freedom that you built, that you spend your life coding, this freedom will be taken away. Either by those who see you as a threat, who then invoke the system of law we call patents, or by those who take advantage of the extraordinary expansion of control that the law of copyright now gives them over innovation. Either of these two changes through law will produce a world where your freedom has been taken away. And, If You Can't Fight For Your Freedom . . . You Don't Deserve It.

But you've done nothing.

(Audience applauds.)

There's a handful, we can name them, of people you could be supporting, you could be taking. Let's put this in perspective: How many people have given to EFF? OK. How many people have given to EFF more money than they have given to their local telecom to give them [poor] DSL service? See? Four. How many people have given more money to EFF than they give each year to support the monopoly—to support the other side? How many people have given anything to these people, Boucher, Canon... . This is not a left and right issue. This is the important thing to recognize: This is not about conservatives versus liberals.

40   In our case, in Eldred [Eldred v. Ashcroft], we have this brief filed by 17 economists, including Milton Friedman, James Buchanan, Ronald Kost, Ken Arrow, you know, lunatics, right? Left-wing liberals, right? Friedman said he'd only join if the word "no-brainer" existed in the brief somewhere, like this

was a complete no-brainer for him. This is not about left and right. This is about right and wrong. That's what this battle is. These people are from the left and right. Hank Perritt, I think the grandfather of cyberspace—the law of cyberspace running in Illinois—is struggling to get support, to take this message to Washington. These are the sources, the places to go.

Then there is this organization. Now some of you say, I'm on the board of this organization. I fight many battles on that board. Some of you say we are too extreme; you say that in the wrong way, right? You send e-mails that say, "You are too extreme. You ought to be more mainstream." You know and I am with you. I think EFF is great. It's been the symbol. It's fought the battles. But you know, it's fought the battles in ways that sometimes need to be reformed. Help us. Don't help us by whining. Help us by writing on the check you send in, "Please be more mainstream." The check, right? This is the mentality you need to begin to adopt to change this battle. Because if you don't do something now, then in another two years, somebody else will say, OK, two years is enough; I got to go back to my life. They'll say again to you, Nothing's changed. Except, your freedom, which has increasingly been taken away by those who recognize that the future is against them and they have the power in D.C. to protect themselves against that future. Free society be damned.

Thank you very much.

Reflect & Write

❏ How and why does Lessig use his "refrain" in this lecture? What is the effect on the argument to have a refrain? Compare the ways that Lessig uses the refrain to the way in which it is used in Justin Cone's piece at the opening of Chapter 9.

❏ Think about the relationship between Lessig's tone and his subject. Why do you think he adopted this particular tone? How did he tailor his tone to his subject and to his expectations about his audience?

❏ Lessig begins the discussion by talking about historical context. Why do you think he begins his talk in this way? What are the benefits of doing so?

❏ Look carefully at the Steamboat Willie example. How does this example function in relation to the rest of the argument? Consider how Lessig's choice of example and his treatment of it influence his audience's response to his argument as a whole.

❏ Does the purpose of Lessig's lecture change at the end? Or does his entire speech actually build to this point? Analyze the conclusion and its relationship to the argument as a whole.

❏ **Write:** Included in this selection are two PowerPoint slides from Lessig's talk. Using your own design, create at least three other rhetorically effective slides for this talk. Then, in small groups, deliver sections of his talk to your partners, using your slides as visual aides.

COLLABORATIVE CHALLENGE

In small groups, watch the Flash version of Lessig's talk online through the link on the *Envision* Website. Pay special attention to the relationship between his script and his PowerPoint slides. Together construct a list of observations about the rhetorical strategies that govern his use of PowerPoint in this lecture. How does he use them to further his argument? How does this differ from other PowerPoint presentations that you have seen? Now together redesign these observations into an oral multimedia presentation in which you use the same strategies as Lessig did to present your argument to the class (you may use transparencies or posters for slides if you do not have access to PowerPoint). Deliver your presentation to your class and afterward talk about your own reactions to using visual and oral rhetoric in this way.

www.ablongman.com/envision/240

Chaired by Lawrence Lessig, Creative Commons is an organization that has developed a new system for sharing authored texts online while still adhering to the traditional copyright system. On its Website, it provides several overviews of its system, including "Licenses Explained," from which this sequence of panels is taken.

Licenses Explained

from the Creative Commons Website

FIGURE 12.9–12.11 Images from *A Spectrum of Rights* explain how Creative Commons licenses work.

FIGURE 12.10

FIGURE 12.11

Reflect & Write

❏ What is the benefit of providing this information in this format? Why do you think that Creative Commons opted for a cartoon strip approach rather than one that was more heavily word-based?

❏ Look carefully at the overall design of the individual frames. How would you characterize it? Think about the way the characters are drawn, the placement of images, the use of words, and the design of the background. What is the effect of these rhetorical choices?

❏ Compare the first and second panels. How does the difference between the arrangement and design of these images reflect Creative Commons's argument about how copyright affects the relationship between the consumer, the artist, and the text itself?

❏ Which panel do you think makes the most powerful visual argument? Why?

❏ **Write:** Draft a prose summary of each cartoon panel. Synthesize all the panels into one culminating report and present it to the panel class.

PERSPECTIVES ON THE ISSUE

1. Compare the section on Fair Use in *"What Is Copyright?"* (http://www.copyright.com/ccc/viewPage.do?pageCode=cr100-n) to the excerpt from *Bound by Law?* How does each one make its argument using the possibilities of the medium that it's working in? What audience does each seem to be intended for? Is one more successful than the other? Why?

2. Consider Lawrence Lessig's keynote address. How do you think that Lessig constructed this piece specifically to be delivered orally? What elements (strategies of develop, rhetorical appeals) does he seem to be employing in direct awareness of the differences between written and oral argumentation? As a reader, how were you affected by the inclusion of parenthetical asides such as "audience applauds"? Finally, in the end, Lessig transforms his argument into a call to action. Was this structure evident from the beginning of the text? How did his appeal for financial donations at the end affect your overall appraisal of the argument?

3. Visit the full text of "Licenses Explained" (http://creativecommons.org/about/licenses/comics1/) and look carefully at the full visual argument. Write an analysis of these images in which you discuss the ways in which visual elements are used to produce a definitive introduction, evidence, and conclusion for this argument. How are elements arranged, altered, and echoed to create a structure and sense of development for this argument? You might also consider the difference in design between this visual argument and the one found in *Bound by Law?* How do these differences resonate with differences in audience, purpose, or argument?

FROM READING TO RESEARCH

1. Locate from the library and read Lessig's published piece "Innovating Copyright," which can be found in *Cardozo Arts & Entertainment Law Journal* 20.3 (2002) 611–623. Write a paper in which you explore how his written and oral arguments differ in their awareness of audience, their strategies of development, and their overall goals. Use direct quotations from the texts to support your points.

2. In June 2004, *Wired* magazine produced an issue about intellectual property, copyright restrictions, and remixed culture. Find that issue in your local library or browse it online. Look at the section entitled "Free and Unfree." How do the different information graphics work in conjunction with the written introduction to the section to produce an argument? Now translate the "Free and Unfree" section from a predominantly visual argument to a more traditional essay. Be sure to reproduce the argument and stance of the original in your translation. Use direct quotes or information from the graphics and introduction in your writing as appropriate.

WHO OWNS POPULAR CULTURE?

While lawyers and academics debate issues of intellectual property, consumers are confronting issues of copyright head on. First limited to the file-sharing of music, the debate has now broadened to include questions of downloading digital media. As the op-ad from the Electronic Frontier Foundation demonstrates (see Figure 12.12), ordinary citizens—from homemakers, to businessmen, to college students—increasingly are finding themselves under intense scrutiny for their role in peer-to-peer (P2P) sharing of copyrighted materials. This chapter explores different perspectives on the sharing of digital media—both audio and visual—and how the question of ownership has impacted questions of consumer rights and use.

FIGURE 12.12 This poster from the Electronic Frontier Foundation undercuts the typical cultural association between illegal file sharing and teenagers.

Reflect & Write

❏ How does the visual image of the Electronic Frontier Foundation poster make a visual argument? Why do you think EFF chose this group of people and pose them in this way?

❏ Based on the image and caption for the poster, what kind of organization do you expect the Electronic Frontier Foundation to be? How would you describe its purpose or mission?

❏ **Write:** Compose a brief analysis of the EFF poster that explains the argument it is trying to make. How does EFF want viewers to respond to this poster?

■ *This article is the first of a pair of articles published on September 12, 2003, by* Salon, *examining both sides of the music file-sharing issue. Each article takes the Electronic Frontier Foundation op-ad campaign, featured in Figure 12.12, as a starting point.*

The author of this first article, **Scott Matthews***, has participated in discussions about file-sharing not only on the pages of* Salon, *but also with Lawrence Lessig and on the* David Letterman Show. *As a software developer, he is responsible for creating Andromedia (a program that streams music on the Web), the Bitty Browser (an embedded browser for Webpages), and Baudio (a program that converts computer files into audio files).*

Copying Isn't Cool

Scott Matthews

As the record industry prepares hundreds of lawsuits targeting people suspected of illegally copying music over the Internet, a broad coalition of leading academics and civil libertarians is standing up for "file sharing" with the intention of ushering in a new copyright system.

Case in point: The Electronic Frontier Foundation, longtime defender of free speech and privacy online, is sponsoring an advertising campaign with the slogan "File Sharing: It's Music to Our Ears." Seeking to recruit new members who are "tired of being treated like a criminal for sharing music online," the ad's message is clear: It's cool to copy music, regardless of the copyright status.

The EFF's goal, like that of many legal scholars, software coders and media pundits, is a new system of compensation for copyright holders that would legitimize file sharing, generally through some new tax on Internet use that would be redistributed to content creators.

But the tacit endorsement of copyright violation seems intended to force the change rather than open it to debate: The more people engage in file sharing, the stronger the case that it can't be stopped, and that our current system of copyright must therefore be scrapped.

5   This is a bad idea propagated in bad faith. Rather than cheering on file sharing, the EFF should be presenting us with the details of its alternative so that we can measure it against our current copyright system, and collectively decide which system we prefer.

The major record companies—mostly in the guise of their lobbying group, the Recording Industry Association of America, or RIAA—have been widely criticized as being heavy-handed in their response to file sharing. But the tactics and goals of those leading the charge against them have generally avoided scrutiny. It's time to take a closer look.

Music industry critics would have us believe that their objective is to rein in an evil cartel, but there's much more to it than that. Their intention is to dictate new terms to all digital authors, regardless of whether they are working for an oligopoly or toiling away in a garage.

As an independent software developer, I don't much appreciate the effort to recast copying others' work as a cool and revolutionary act. What's worse, civil liberties advocates are promoting alternative systems that compromise free speech and privacy, bedrock principles that we have traditionally relied on them to defend.

The first thing to note is that this debate isn't just about music, it is about copyright in general. All leading file-sharing applications are designed to copy any kind of file. If the goal is to legitimize the activity over these peer-to-peer (P2P) networks through a new tax, then we should expect such a system to apply to all digital works—not just music, but also movies, software, photographs, ebooks and so on.

10   So how is free speech compromised?

Under these alternative systems, compensation for cultural expression is shifted to governmental control—the government collects the tax, divides it up, and pays the artists. But this is also the same government that has a long record of denying public funding for "offensive" art.

As a simple example, consider that pornography makes up as much as 40 percent of file-sharing traffic. Are we to believe that those copyright holders would receive their proportionate share of the P2P tax? It seems far more likely that the government will instead decide to exclude "adult" works, drawing a line between art and offense.

This isn't just about porn. The FCC regularly censors the infamous "seven dirty words" from public airwaves, and it's a safe bet that the trend will continue with P2P payouts—certain works will be deemed not worthy of compensation by public funds.

There is no reason to believe that the First Amendment would apply here—after all, nothing would be stopping such works from being exchanged over file-sharing networks. It's just that the government isn't going to pay the author when they are. And since it is not possible to remove the corresponding works from file-sharing networks, such a system further marginalizes the economic opportunity of fringe artists.

15   This is a genuine free-speech concern, and music industry critics should address it with something better than their reflexive mantra: "Well, the RIAA sucks."

Free speech isn't the only traditional value that civil liberties advocates compromise with the alternative copyright systems that they propose—privacy takes a beating too.

One of the leading goals of these alternative systems is to better compensate underrepresented works, and that sounds great. But in order to account for every song—not to mention every movie, photograph, software program and so on—the government would have to create a vast technical oversight system to track Internet use.

A privacy debacle inevitably follows.

Some argue for a limited statistical sample, but think about the math: To statistically "notice" those less-popular, nonmainstream works you would have to sample the habits of a huge population, if not the entire population. This cannot be a relatively simple, Nielsen-type analysis of 100 TV channels, nor would it be at all analogous to the current system that now tracks what plays on the radio; it's an ongoing record of how we use the Internet.

20   Next, remember that this isn't just about music and ask yourself: Do you want the government to have access to a running record of what you listen to, what you look at, what you have, what you know? If, alternatively, the intention is to somehow make these records truly anonymous, there would be no way to detect efforts that artificially boost the popularity—and corresponding compensation—of a particular work.

Given the current focus on terror, it is hard to imagine the government building a system that ensures anonymous communication. However, it isn't hard to imagine the government taking an interest in new tools that better track Internet use.

This is exactly the sort of privacy threat that civil libertarians should be concerned about. Oddly, the traditional watchdogs of privacy are now embracing the very attitude that they typically warn us about: "Trust us." Gee, no thanks.

To avoid the specter of government control, the EFF and others sometimes call for a "voluntary" solution. Such rhetoric sounds nice, but clearly the record companies would have to be forced into voluntarily licensing their works for P2P, and file sharers would have to be forced into voluntarily paying for it. And music fans can already get music from licensed sources, including Rhapsody, EMusic, Apple's iTunes Music Store, CD Baby and others.

There may indeed be a better way to compensate digital authors, but we deserve a chance to debate the details and choose between alternatives, including our current system of copyright. The tiresome "RIAA vs. freedom" spin oversimplifies the situation and distracts us from making an informed and important decision.

25   And the more you ask questions, and try to get answers, the more you might realize that you actually prefer the copyright system that we have now, and the less you'll appreciate the efforts to destabilize it.

Record industry critics will undoubtedly heckle as the RIAA sues people for illegally copying music, but the same copyright laws also protect lots of people like me—independent musicians, filmmakers, programmers, authors and so on. Our lives are mixed up in this too.

The EFF and aligned academics blunder when they trade privacy and free speech for piracy and free music.

Reflect & Write

❏   In his article, Scott Matthews defines the ad's message as: "It's cool to copy music, regardless of the copyright status." Looking at this ad (Figure 12.12), do you agree? How would you interpret the message? How does your interpretation of the EFF ad influence your understanding of Matthews's broader argument? Considering that, while the ad was linked to the original article, it was not reproduced within the article itself, how does Matthews's interpretation guide the audience's understanding of the EFF's position in relation to downloading?

❏   Look at the way in which Matthews introduces the issue of free speech. How is this designed to influence the reader's approach to the issue of downloading?

❏   Consider how Matthews uses ethos in this article—both in terms of his own ethos and in constructing a sense of the EFF's and downloader's ethos—to enhance his argument.

❏   **Write:** Look at the final line of this article. Does Matthews make a solid case for the oppositions that he defines here? Do you agree with these oppositions? Write a response to Matthews in which you either support or challenge the oppositions he defines in his conclusion.

■ *The author of this article,* **Jason Schultz,** *specializes in intellectual property issues and is a staff attorney for the Electronic Frontier Foundation, a nonprofit civil liberties organization that focuses on the regulation of information and individual liberties on the internet. This article was written as a direct response to Matthews's discussion of "Copying Isn't Cool".*

File Sharing Must Be Made Legal

Jason Schultz

The Recording Industry Association of America (RIAA) has finally launched its campaign of lawsuits against the 60 million Americans who file-share. And already, we've seen the first casualties—a 12-year-old girl and her mother in New York must pay $2,000 they don't have in a hastened settlement; a 71-year-old grandfather in Texas has to hire a lawyer to defend himself and his grandkids; a single mother in Colorado searches for legal advice she can't afford. These are the horror stories of the current copyright wars.

It doesn't have to be this way. There are alternatives. That's why EFF launched the Let the Music Play Campaign, to create a showcase for reasonable solutions that don't involve endless lawsuits. None of them is perfect; all of them have flaws and drawbacks. But all of them are preferable to thousands of lawsuits against individual American families. A good solution will get artists paid, while protecting the privacy and free-speech rights of fans.

Some critics worry that changes made in the copyright law for music may be detrimental to changes in the copyright law for software, books and other copyrighted works. This is a perfectly legitimate concern and has been addressed in several of the plans on our site. For example, the "voluntary collective licensing" plan is specific to the music industry and does not apply to software or other copyrighted works. Just as ASCAP and BMI collect blanket licensing fees from radio stations today, so could similar organizations collect fees from P2P users for file-sharing music. No other copyright owners would be affected by such a plan.

Another solution might be compulsory licensing—Congress could step in and force the record labels to accept file sharing in exchange for reasonable compensation from file sharers. This is what happened with webcasting. It is also how cable companies and satellite companies pay for TV programming. These historical solutions have only affected specific industries; there is no reason that we cannot limit the P2P solution as well.

5   Copyright law has always been a patchwork quilt, treating different works in different ways. For example, there is a specific compulsory license for making a cover song. If you want to record your own version of Bob Dylan's "Like a Rolling Stone," you don't have to get Bob's permission. A specific section of the copyright law allows you to simply go ahead and record and sell your version—as long

as, in return, you pay Bob eight cents for every copy you sell. This special exception doesn't affect any other copyright holders, just songwriters. Of course, if other industries such as the book, movie or software industry like this idea, they could adopt it as well. That's the beauty of having reasonable alternatives. Everything is on the table; consumers and content owners can negotiate via the marketplace and Congress to ensure the best plan is worked out.

Privacy and free speech are certainly considerations that we must take into account with any proposed solution. But consider the ways in which the current copyright system is already costing us privacy. Under the Digital Millennium Copyright Act (DMCA), any copyright owner can issue a "secret" subpoena to your ISP and force them to reveal your name, address, e-mail, and personally identifying information simply on the basis of a "good-faith belief" that you are infringing one of their copyrights; they don't even have to file a lawsuit or go before a judge for approval. It is true that on the Internet we are all copyright owners. Every e-mail, every Web page, every comment post is copyrighted. While government surveillance today is as scary as ever, we must also protect ourselves and our privacy against reckless copyright owners who wish to snoop on our activities as well. A system that legalizes file sharing also immunizes file sharers against DMCA subpoenas, since copyright owners would no longer have any basis to obtain file-sharer names. Given that the RIAA has issued more than 1,500 such subpoenas in the last two months alone, this would create a tangible and concrete protection of privacy.

Critics also worry about government involvement in the P2P solution. While a P2P compulsory licensing solution may require congressional involvement to change the copyright law, there is no reason to assume that the government needs to be involved in collecting or distributing any funds collected from file sharers. Much like ASCAP and BMI, private organizations can manage the job of distributing money to artists. Private companies like those that assemble the Nielsen ratings can take care of sampling who is listening to what music. And while aggregate sampling may require some access to what we listen to, there is no reason that it cannot be done anonymously and voluntarily.

Again, these are all principles that we can forcefully advocate during congressional hearings or discussions with artists. The big picture, however, is that right now, today, hundreds and potentially thousands of individual music lovers face lawsuits that may bankrupt their families and invade our privacy, technology companies face legal actions that chill innovation, and there is no clear end in sight. We cannot bury our collective head in the sand and hope that everything works out. We must consider reasonable alternatives that make file sharing legal and pay artists. To ignore these options leaves the future of music and the future of digital media technology almost entirely in the hands of organizations like the RIAA and out of the hands of consumers and innovators. Meanwhile, all of us, whether we file-share or not, are paying a price, perhaps not in terms of dollars and cents, but certainly in terms of privacy and innovation.

Reflect & Write

❏ Compare the way in which Schultz opens his article with how Matthews opens his piece. How do these different introductions reflect a difference in focus and argument?

❏ If Matthews evokes ethos frequently in his argument, Schultz often deploys pathos. How do you see this operating in his text? Is pathos used effectively? Why or why not?

❏ In what ways is Schultz's argument constructed as a direct response to Matthews? Find places in the text where he implicitly replies to "Copying Isn't Cool." Why do you think he didn't write the article as a more direct rebuttal?

❏ What is at stake in this debate, according to Schultz? Are these stakes different from those identified by Matthews? How do these similarities or differences impact the persuasiveness of their arguments when read together?

❏ **Write:** Draft a comparative analysis of the two pieces in which you argue which you find more persuasive, referring to specific elements of the essays to support your points.

COLLABORATIVE CHALLENGE

Working with a group, rework the Schultz and Matthews pieces as a dialogue of sources, using the model provided in Chapter 5. To facilitate the dialogue, create a moderator figure designed to facilitate the discussion. Be sure to accurately represent Schultz and Matthews, even if you don't use direct quotes, and feel free to include alternate examples drawn from your own experience or research to develop the discussion. When you are done, compare your dialogue with that generated from another group and discuss the way in which you developed stance and argument through style in this challenge.

The three editorial cartoons on this page all comment using both visual and verbal rhetoric on the debate surrounding file downloading. **Gary Brookins** *is an editorial cartoonist for the Richmond (Virginia)* Times-Dispatch. **Daryl Cagle** *is editorial cartoonist for MSNBC.com and one of the most widely read cartoonists in the world.* **John Pritchett** *is an editorial cartoonist for the* Honolulu Weekly *and he also publishes illustrations on environmental issues for* Environment Hawaii.

Political Cartoons: File-sharing and the Music Industry

FIGURE 12.13 Gary Brookins's cartoon pits the Music Industry against a spectrum of illegal file-sharers.

Source: Gary Brookins, © 2005 Richmond Times-Dispatch.

FIGURE 12.14 Daryl Cagle provides an alternate perspective on the relationship between the RIAA and the consumer.

Source: © 2003 by Daryl Cagle and CagleCartoons.com. All rights reserved.

FIGURE 12.15 John Pritchett's editorial cartoon trades on religious analogy to make its argument about music downloading.

Source: Cartoon by John S. Pritchett.

Reflect & Write

❏ Compare the "They All Did It" cartoon to the EFF poster in Figure 12.12. Look at the similarities in theme and setting; how do they suggest a common argument? Now look at the differences—in perspective, in composition, the use of captions, and characters. How do these differences indicate subtle differences in the force, focus, or stance of the argument?

❏ Look carefully at the Figure 12.4 cartoon. How is the RIAA (Recording Industry Association of America) represented? How is the downloader represented? Which is the cartoon more sympathetic to? What visual details lead you to this conclusion?

❏ What is the effect in the final cartoon of overlaying religion on the issue of music downloading? What does this conceit imply about organizations like the RIAA? About the relationship of the average consumer to this organization? Is there added significance in making the mandate not to download music into a commandment?

❏ **Write:** Draft a paper that persuasively argues which cartoon makes the most powerful statement about file sharing or music downloading. Use careful rhetorical analysis of the cartoons to support your position.

■ **Lev Grossman** *is a notable book critic and interviewer, who has interviewed figures as varied as Tom Clancy, Bill Gates, and Salman Rushdie. His writing has appeared in numerous prominent publications, including* Time Magazine, The New York Times, Lingua Franca, *the* Village Voice *and* Salon. *This article was first published in the May 5, 2003, issue of* Time.

It's All Free! Music! Movies! TV Shows! Millions of People Download Them Every Day. Is Digital Piracy Killing the Entertainment Industry?

Lev Grossman

James Phung saw *Phone Booth* before you did. What's more, he saw it for free, in the comfort of his private home-screening room. Phung isn't a movie star or a Hollywood insider; he's a junior at the University of Texas who makes $8 an hour at the campus computer lab. But many big-budget Hollywood movies have their North American premieres in his humble off-campus apartment. Like millions of other people, Phung downloads movies for free from the Internet, often before they hit theaters. *Phone Booth* will fit nicely on his 120-GB hard drive alongside *Anger Management, Tears of the Sun* and about 125 other films, not to mention more than 2,000 songs. "Basically," he says, "the world is at my fingertips."

Phung is the entertainment industry's worst nightmare, but he's very real, and there are a lot more like him. Quietly, with no sirens and no breaking glass, your friends and neighbors and colleagues and children are on a 24-hour virtual smash-and-grab looting spree, aided and abetted by the anonymity of the Internet. Every month they—or is it we?—download some 2.6 billion files illegally, and that's just music. That number doesn't include the movies, TV shows, software and video games that circulate online. First-run films turn up online well before they hit the theaters. Albums debut on the Net before they have a chance to hit the charts. Somewhere along the line, Americans—indeed, computer users everywhere—have made a collective decision that since no one can make us pay for entertainment, we're not going to.

As crimes go, downloading has a distinctly victimless feel to it—can anything this fun be wrong?—but there are real consequences. Click by click, file by file, we are tearing the entertainment industry apart. CD shipments last year were down 9%, on top of a 6% decline in 2001. A report by Internet services company Divine estimates pirates swap between 400,000 and 600,000 movies online every day. It's information-superhighway robbery.

If you ask the pirates, they'll say they're just fighting for their right to party. If you ask the suits, they'll say they're fighting for their lives. "If we let this stand, you're going to see the undoing of this society," says Jack Valenti, head of the Motion Picture Association of America (M.P.A.A.). "I didn't preside over this movie industry to see it disintegrate like the music industry." Them's fightin' words, and the battle lines are being drawn. Two landmark legal decisions last week, one in favor of the entertainment industry and one against it, will shape the way we deal with digital movies and music for years to come. The only thing left to decide is which side of those battle lines you're on.

5   It's easy to see why the pirates do what they do. Right now you can find thousands of free movies online if you know where to look—a glance at one popular website yields links to copies of *Holes, Malibu's Most Wanted* and even the Rowan Atkinson comedy *Johnny English,* which won't hit U.S. theaters until July. Just about every song ever released—as well as quite a few that haven't been—is available online for nothing more than the effort it takes to point and click. Record-industry types have a cute nickname for this phenomenon: "the celestial jukebox."

Most online piracy happens through what is called file-sharing software, such as Kazaa, Gnutella and Direct Connect, that links millions of computers to one another over the Internet. File-sharing software takes advantage of the fact that music and movies are stored as digital data—they're not vinyl and celluloid anymore, but collections of disembodied, computerized bits and bytes that can be stored or played on a computer and transmitted over the Internet as easily as e-mail. Using file-sharing software, people can literally browse through one another's digital music and movie collections, picking and choosing and swapping whatever

they want. If you've never tried it, it's hard to describe how seductive it is. Start up a program like Kazaa, type in the name of your favorite rock band, and a list of song titles will instantly appear on your screen. See something you like, click on it, and it's yours. An average song might take two minutes to download to your computer if you have a broadband connection. Log on any night of the week and you'll find millions of users sharing hundreds of millions of songs, movies and more.

Ask your average high school kids if they use Kazaa, and the answer is a resounding "duh." Stewart Laperouse and Jennifer Rieger, a couple at Cy-Fair High School in Houston, log on as part of their regular after-school routine—it's the new milk and cookies. Often they do their downloading a deux, after he gets out of lacrosse practice. His collection is relatively small: 150 songs and about 50 music videos. She's the real repeat offender, with 400 pilfered tracks on her hard drive. "Who wouldn't want to do this?" Rieger says. "It's totally free and it's easy." Look for pangs of guilt and you'll get only shrugs.

This isn't how it was supposed to be. A little more than three years ago the Recording Industry Association of America (R.I.A.A.), which represents most U.S. record labels, filed suit against Napster, the granddaddy of file-sharing services, for "contributory and vicarious copyright infringement." The R.I.A.A. won; Napster lost. A judge ordered its servers shut down. End of story?

Hardly. The file-sharing services didn't go away. They evolved, getting smarter and more decentralized and harder to shut down. Napster's network relied on a central server, an Achilles' heel that made it easier to unplug and shut down. But Kazaa, now the most popular file-sharing software, is built around a floating, distributed network of individual PCs that has no center. There's no single plug to pull. Kazaa has savvily chosen a decentralized business strategy too: it's a mirage of complicated partnerships with the official owner, Sharman Networks, tucked away on the South Pacific island of Vanuatu. So far, its diffuse structure has kept its management off U.S. soil and out of U.S. courtrooms.

10   It isn't just the file-sharing companies that are evolving; the Internet is too. Broadband Internet access has become cheaper and more widespread—analysts expect the number of households with broadband to jump 41% this year—and that means we can move bigger, fatter files in less and less time. Personal computers have also evolved. In 1992 the average hard drive was 120 megabytes. Now it's 40 gigabytes, 300 times as big—perfect for stashing whole libraries of audio and video. CD and DVD burners used to be expensive peripherals; now they come standard. Every new PC is a self-contained entertainment studio, right out of the box. What we have here is not a failure to communicate; it's a raging, runaway success.

The consequence of the high-tech evolution is a new generation of technologically empowered consumers for whom free entertainment isn't a windfall, it's a basic right. Just ask Sean Farrell, a senior at Yale. A sophisticated listener, he dabbles in jazz and classical along with the usual hip-hop. But he hasn't bought a CD in four years. Instead, he has 5,000 songs on his computer's 430-GB hard drive, and more in the 20-GB MP3 player—an Apple iPod—that is permanently attached to his hip. When he and his roommates have parties, they don't bother with CDs, they just run cables from the computer in Farrell's bedroom to the stereo in the common room and blast the free tunes straight off his PC. "I don't feel really guilty," he says. "The music industry has to realize that this is here to stay; it's not going away." See the pattern yet?

For years people wondered whether all this downloading would actually affect the entertainment industry's bottom line. Now that last year's numbers are in, we have the answer. According to Nielsen SoundScan, CD album sales slid from 712 million units in 2001 to 680 million in 2002. CD sales in the first quarter of 2003 were down 15 million units from last year. Or look at it this way: in 2000 the top 10 albums in America sold 60 million copies; in 2001, 40 million; in 2002, 33 million. Nobody knows for sure exactly how much of the decline is caused by piracy, but it's safe to say the answer is somewhere between "some of it" and "most of it." Sure, the economy had a down year, but people found enough spare change in their couches to boost sales of MP3 players 56% over 2001. And while consumers bought about 680 million albums last year, they purchased 1.7 billion blank CDs—up 40% from the year before. The clear implication: users are downloading free music and burning it onto blank CDs. Industry analysts are reduced to fairy-tale metaphors to describe the change. The genie is out of the bottle. Pandora's box is open. The dikes have burst, and the Dutch boy has gone surfing.

Which isn't to say music executives are sitting around wringing their hands. It takes time for any corporation to recognize that its universe has changed, and major labels don't exactly turn on a dime. For Martin Bandier, chairman and CEO of EMI Music Publishing, the dime dropped three years ago when his 11-year-old son Max gave him a present: his 100 favorite Motown songs. "I said, 'But we have hundreds of copies!'" Bandier recalls. "He said, 'This is in a different place—on my hard drive.' It was scary." Bandier immediately convened a war council to figure out how to protect EMI's precious song catalog, which ranges from Judy Garland to Norah Jones. "People did not think it was real in the beginning," he says. "It's as real as can be."

Reality bit, and deep. In 2001 EMI brought in new top management, including chairman of EMI Recorded Music Alain Levy, to help navigate the brave new digital world. The administration promptly laid off 1,800 employees (20% of EMI's staff), which helped absorb the impact when sales fell 10% in 2002—and created an executive position, global head of antipiracy. It also brought in executive vice president John Rose, an e-commerce ace from consulting firm McKinsey. "The fundamental premise of hiring someone like me," says Rose, "is that this industry needs to be re-engineered." Since last summer, EMI has been holding weekly three-hour lunch meetings with artists, managers, agents and lawyers, a dozen at a time, to explain to them, as Rose puts it, "how the world needs to evolve."

15   First order of business: evolve some claws. Some labels (they're reluctant to identify themselves) hire professional counterhackers, companies like Overpeer, based in Manhattan, that specialize in electronic countermeasures

such as "spoofing"—releasing dummy versions of popular songs onto file-sharing networks. To your average Kazaa user they look like the real thing, but when you download them, they turn out to be unplayable. Movie studios, meanwhile, staff screenings with ushers wearing night-vision goggles to suss out would-be pirates with camcorders. When Epic Records distributed review copies of the new Pearl Jam album last fall, it sent them inside CD players that had been glued shut. The White Stripes went further: review copies of their new album Elephant were sent on good old-fashioned vinyl, which is trickier to copy. In the copy-protection wars, low tech is the new high tech.

For EMI, the plan is not to prohibit copying, just to keep us from doing it quite so much. In theory, the CD of the future will be smart enough to let its owner make one copy of a song for the computer, one for the iPod, and maybe burn an extra for the car, but that's it. But even that might annoy consumers who are used to making as many copies as they want. Even if the smart CD of the future becomes a reality, to work at all it will have to work absolutely perfectly. If just one copy leaks onto Kazaa, anywhere in the world, millions of people can have all the copies they want.

Of course, there's an even older-fashioned way to keep people from stealing your stuff. It's called the law. "What we're dealing with is thievery, plain and simple," says the M.P.A.A.'s Valenti. "People try to use a lot of sophistry to get away from that fact." The legal landscape on which the war against piracy will be fought is being defined right now. In January a federal judge ruled that Verizon, a telephone company that is also an Internet service provider (ISP), must honor the R.I.A.A. subpoena to reveal the identity of one of its customers, a Kazaa user whom they suspect of downloading more than 600 songs. Verizon asked for a stay of the decison, and a flurry of briefs from the M.P.A.A. (backing the record companies) and numerous privacy and consumer organizations (on behalf of Verizon) ensued. On Thursday, the judge denied Verizon's request. Unless it can get a reprieve from an appeals court, the company has 14 days (and counting) to come up with the name.

The message is clear: If you're going to download music, don't expect to hide behind the anonymity of the Internet. On the other hand, if you're in the business of making file-sharing software, you have a lot less to worry about. On Friday a federal judge ruled that two companies—Grokster and StreamCast Networks, which makes a program called Morpheus—were not liable if users of their file-sharing software infringed on someone else's copyright. In his decision Judge Stephen Wilson cited the legal fuss that sprang up in the 1980s over Sony's Betamax technology. Like file sharing, it was a tool that could be used for both legal and illegal copying. Then, as now, the former was deemed to outweigh the latter.

The ruling is a stinging blow for the R.I.A.A. and the M.P.A.A., which brought the suit (and will appeal it), and it tells us a lot about how the war against piracy will be fought. If file-sharing services won't sit still and be sued, individual users will make easier targets. Case in point: lawsuits filed last month against students at Princeton, Michigan Technological University and Rensselaer Polytechnic Institute that seek billions of dollars in damages—$150,000 for each pirated song. Nobody thinks piracy can be stopped by suing one user at a time, but if companies focus on major uploaders—people who make huge numbers of files available for others to download—a few high-profile busts may scare off some of the rest. "In the Verizon case, we got the judgment that we really needed," says Andrew Lack, chairman and CEO of Sony Music Entertainment, "which is that on an individual basis you are being ripped off, and you have a right to stop that."

20   The pace is picking up as Big Media head to court with everybody they can think of. The M.P.A.A. is wrangling with a company called 321 Studios over the legality of one of 321's products, software that enables consumers to make free copies of movies from DVDs. The FBI busted a Los Angeles man last week for camcording movies off the big screen and selling copies—a legal first. Universal Music Group and EMI have even filed suit against venture-capital firm Hummer Winblad just because it invested in Napster back in 2000.

But the legal fight is far from a sure thing. Copyright laws are slippery and subjective—the judge in the Grokster case made a special plea in his ruling asking Congress to fix gaps in the laws that cover file sharing. Enforcing those laws is also tricky. Colleges, where a lot of the downloading goes on, like to think of themselves as bastions of privacy and free speech, not copyright police. The international reach of the Internet makes enforcement even dodgier. Case in point: in 1999 Jon Johansen, a Norwegian teenager, figured out how to break the copy protection on commercial DVDs, making possible the cheap, high-quality, a la carte copying of movies. This information became, shall we say, fairly popular on the Internet, earning Johansen, who was 15 at the time, the nickname "DVD Jon." In 2000 Norwegian prosecutors, egged on by the M.P.A.A., charged him with violating digital-security laws. In January the verdict came in: Johansen got off. An appeals hearing is scheduled for December.

There's another problem with suing people: it doesn't make you popular with your customers—and Big Media are already fighting a major p.r. battle. Everybody who has ever watched VH1's Behind the Music has heard musicians bad-mouth their record labels, and no one is going to feel bad for ripping off the suits who ripped off their favorite rock star. File sharing has become cool, a way to fight the power, to stick it to the Man. Re-engineering the public image of studio executives probably isn't in the cards—these are, after all, the same companies that coughed up $143 million last October to settle a class action accusing them of price fixing—but in the past few months, more and more artists have begun speaking out, and they stand a better chance of winning sympathy. For years musicians and other artists were reluctant to address file sharing, in part because they saw how uncool Metallica's James Hetfield looked when he tried. But in September the likes of Nelly, the Dixie Chicks, Brian Wilson and the incontrovertibly cool Missy Elliott delivered televised antipiracy scoldings. In April, Ben Affleck appeared in an antipiracy spot on behalf of the movie industry. Still, you don't have to be Alanis Morissette to spot the irony in a zillionaire celebrity pleading for sympathy. After a spoofed version of Madonna's new album, *American Life,* started circulating on the Net, featuring a recording of the Material Girl saying "What the f___ do you think you're doing?", a hacker took over the singer's website,

Madonna.com, and posted real, downloadable MP3s of every song on the album.

The entertainment industry's grand plan for surviving piracy isn't just about the stick; there's a carrot too, a big one. The Internet offers a whole new way of selling music, and when music and movie executives are not expressing their outrage over downloading, they are salivating over a potentially massive revenue opportunity. There are already a couple of dozen legal, pay-to-play downloading services, including Pressplay, Listen.com's Rhapsody and Music Net. Apple Computer has a new service, which was slated for rollout this Monday, that's meant to integrate seamlessly with its iPod MP3 player and its iTunes music software. Movie and TV downloading websites are sprouting up as well. Movielink, which is backed by five major Hollywood studios, made its debut in November and features a library of more than 300 films. SoapCity.com offers online episodes of daytime serials.

But these services face competition you wouldn't wish on Bill Gates. Unlike, say, Kazaa, they have to clear each song or movie or show for digital distribution with each individual artist and studio. They have made significant progress—Pressplay, for example, has upwards of 300,000 tracks available for download, with membership starting at $9.95 a month—but it's slow work. The for-pay services also mire users in a mesh of restrictions that limit what they can do with the music they download. That $9.95 plan at Pressplay buys you unlimited downloads, but you can't move the songs to your portable MP3 player or burn copies of them onto a CD, and you can listen to them only so long as you're a Pressplay subscriber. Miss a payment, and the files lock up. For $8 more a month, Pressplay gives you 10 "portable" downloads that are free of those constraints. But compare that with the roughly infinite number of unrestricted, unconstrained, infinitely copyable downloads that Kazaa offers for roughly nothing, and you can see that Pressplay has an uphill battle on its hands.

25   Pressplay and the other "legitimate" music services are more reliable than Kazaa and its ilk. For one thing, there's no porn and no spoofing, and Apple's new offering is expected to

give the whole process a more streamlined, user-friendly feel. These services also give customers the peace of mind that comes with not breaking the law. It will be interesting to see how much that's worth. But for now listeners are staying away in droves; industry analysts estimate that the legitimate downloading services have fewer than 300,000 users in all. Still, if the retail-music business is going to survive, this may be what it has to look like, and for the business side, that's the real significance of the digital revolution. "It's not piracy per se but a transition to a digital world that will transform what a record company is and how it works," says EMI's Rose. "While downloading is an important issue, it's just symbolic of a much more fundamental shift in how music will be moved and acquired by consumers and be used."

Can the for-pay services compete? Maybe. Can antipiracy laws be enforced? Perhaps. Can copy protection stand up to a hacker army of teenage Jon Johansens? It's possible. But all this raises an interesting question: What if the pirates win? If you play the thought experiment out to its logical extreme, the body count is high. After all, you can't have an information economy in which all information is free. The major music labels would disappear; ditto the record stores that sell their CDs. The age of millionaire rock stars would be over; they would become as much a historical curiosity as the landed aristocracy is today. Instead, musicians would scratch out a living on the touring circuit, since in an age of free music the only commodity they would control is live performance, along with any merchandise they could hawk in the parking lot after the show. Hollywood would also take a hit. People might still pay to watch movies in the theater—viewing on the big screen beats watching movies on your computer—but Hollywood would have to do without revenue from video stores. Who's going to rent what they can download for free? TV studios would likewise have to do without their cushy syndication deals, since the Net would become the land of infinite reruns. Hope you like product placement—you'll be seeing a lot of it. Already this July the WB network and Pepsi plan to launch an American

Bandstand—style TV show called Pepsi Smash, featuring performances by big-ticket music acts. Alternative revenue streams never tasted so good.

In a sense, the future is already here. You can see it in action in Asia. Piracy is a growing phenomenon in the U.S., but in some developing countries, it is a fact of life. There's a marketplace in Karachi, Pakistan, where you can buy a DVD of *How to Lose a Guy in 10 Days* for 100 rupees (about $1.75) even while it's playing in first-run theaters in the U.S. Karachi boasts five optical-disc factories, just one of which churns out 40 million pirated discs a year. If you think American teenagers are guiltless, file-swapping punks, try talking to a Karachi shopkeeper. "We make copy of everything!" says Mohammed Haris. "Even George Bush cannot dare to come over here. We will keep the original and send his copy back home."

This kind of commercial piracy has devastated the Asian entertainment industry. In China, where piracy rates for movies, music and software are all more than 90%, record companies trying to develop local talent have bled money for years. Every time they try to build up a star, the pirates siphon off the profits. "There's no point in spending money to drive demand," says Samuel Chou, Warner Music's CEO for China and Taiwan, "because what you drive all goes to piracy."

30   It's a scary cautionary tale—but at this point, hypothetical horror stories are almost beside the point. The people have spoken, and they say they want a revolution. File sharing isn't going to save us from corporate entertainment the way the Beatles saved Pepperland from the Blue Meanies, but if it allows more people to listen to more music in more ways than they ever have before, can it be all bad? And does good or bad even matter? Technology has a way of sweeping aside questions of what is right or wrong and replacing them with the reality of what is possible. Recorded entertainment has gone from an analog object to a disembodied digital spirit roaming the planet's information infrastructure at will, and all the litigation and legislation in the world won't change it back. The genie is out of the bottle, and we're fresh out of wishes.

Reflect & Write

- Look carefully at Grossman's rhetorical choices in his first paragraph. How does he situate the reader in relation to Phung? What stylistic tools does he use to accomplish this? Now look at the second paragraph. What is the effect of qualifying the statement "Every month they download . . ." with the phrase "or is it we?"? Does this change the audience's stance? Look elsewhere in the article to see how he uses personal pronouns ("we" and "you") to subtly influence his argument.
- How does Grossman represent both sides of the argument? Find two places in the article where he gives both the pro-downloading and the anti-downloading positions on this issue. Does he seem to favor one more than the other? How can we tell?
- How does Grossman use logos—facts and statistics—to build his argument? How does he use specific example?
- **Write:** Look carefully at the structure of this article. Write a reverse outline for this piece (that is, try to reconstruct the outline that Grossman might have used in drafting. Why does Grossman choose to develop his argument in this way? Was this an effective structure for his argument? Why or why not? How does his structure reflect his understanding of the rhetorical situation in which he was writing? Compose a reflection based on your answers to these questions.

■ The **Motion Picture Association of America** *is the major trade association of the American film industry; it serves as the voice and advocate for the industry as a whole.*

You Can Click, But You Can't Hide

from the Motion Picture Association of America

Reflect & Write

- Focus for a moment on the header for this ad. It provides a revised version of the adage, "You can run, but you can't hide." What relationship does this header establish between the audience and the MPAA? Why do you think that the designers chose this approach?
- What visual elements relate form and content in this ad? How is the position of the hand and the composition of the photo (what is contained in the image, and what was left out) significant?
- Think about the rhetorical appeals used in this ad. What elements reflect the pathos appeal? ethos? logos? Now consider how these appeals factor into the arrangement or layout of the ad itself. What is the effect?
- **Write:** Define the target audience for an MPAA ad that argues against illegally downloading movies online. Create a mock-up of an advertisement designed to target that audience. Present your draft to the class and talk about the significance of your rhetorical decisions.

FIGURE 12.16 This 2004 ad is now featured on the RespectCopyright.org Website, a site set up by the Motion Picture Association of America (MPAA) to educate visitors on copyright law and illegal downloading.

COLLABORATIVE CHALLENGE

Working with a group, pretend that you are a liaison from either the MPAA or the RIAA visiting a local high school to convince teenagers not to illegally download or share materials online. How would you convince them? Script a five-minute argument using some form of multimedia (audio, film clips, PowerPoint) to aid your presentation.

■ **Michael Eisner,** *then-CEO of the Walt Disney Company, delivered this address to Congress on June 7, 2000, as part of the Internet Caucus Speaker Series. This program, sponsored by the Internet Education Foundation, was designed to allow leading members in the Internet and business community to share with Capitol Hill their ideas about the "Opportunities Facing the Internet."*

Address Before Members of the United States Congress

Michael Eisner

Thank you, Senator Hatch, for that kind introduction. You have been a leader in public-policy with regard to the Internet in particular and entertainment industries in general. We are grateful for your leadership.

I also want to thank Senators Leahy and Burns, and Congressmen Hyde, Conyers, Goodlatte and Boucher for hosting today's lunch. And, a thank you to Jerry Berman of the Internet Education Foundation for his assistance.

What's more, I want to thank all of you for being here today. You comprise the busiest audience on earth. I realize that each of you has tremendous demands on your time as you go about the business of running our country.

Because you are all such busy men and women, I am not here simply with my mouse ears on to sing the praises of our company. Rather, I'd like to talk about a much wider issue beyond Disney. . .one that directly affects the future of all of the entertainment companies, the future of all consumers and even the future of our nation's balance of international trade.

5   I realize that there are great risks when one attempts to speak so much about the future. I am reminded of a story you may have heard about a notice posted on a college bulletin board. It read: "This evening's meeting of the Clairvoyance Society has been canceled due to unforeseen circumstances."

However, I am willing to accept the risks of talking about the future because the implications of my subject today, I believe, will be undeniably enormous in the century that stretches before us.

And, that subject is: the protection of intellectual property in the digital age.

But, talk alone isn't adequate to cover this issue. After all, intellectual property encompasses more than just words—it's about art, music and imagery as well. So, I figured I would be doing a disservice by just delivering the usual 20-minute speech. What's more, if it is true that a picture is worth a thousand words, how many words are *ten thousand* pictures worth? Actually, not just pictures, but dramatically original computer-generated images.

Enough words. Let me show you.

[VIDEO - Opening of *Dinosaur,* freeze-framing abruptly as the pterodactyl is flying over herds of dinos]

10   O.K., let's stop right there. As you have probably figured out, you've just seen the first few minutes of our new film, *Dinosaur* which has already grossed more than $100 million in the U.S. But, I did not show it to you out of a shameless urge to promote our product—though I'm sure you and your families would enjoy going to see it this weekend, playing at a theater near you.

The debate over intellectual property often gets buried in jargon. The term "intellectual property" itself is obtuse legalese that sounds like a euphemism for the jar holding Albert Einstein's brain.

So, I thought I'd try and move away from the jargon and simply show you what the debate is all about—a piece of authentic intellectual property.

Of course, intellectual property is a rather wide-ranging category that covers everything from piano songsheets to computer software. But ultimately, it is about the work of the human imagination, such as what you see here on the screen.

What is now urgently needed is the implementation of a legislative, economic and technological environment that will foster creativity and encourage the legitimate use of all those silicon chips to create more flights of fancy like this. Otherwise, the same technology that enabled our artists to create these incredible images could also make them go away.

[Screen goes to black]

15   This is the perilous irony of the digital age.

Thanks to computer technology, filmmakers have been able to take us to incredible places in the last few years. They have hurled us into the heart of a tornado, they have invited us on board the Titanic, they have rocketed us to a galaxy far, far away. And today, they enable us to walk among the dinosaurs.

But, unfortunately, just as computers make it possible to create startlingly pristine images, they also make it possible to create startlingly pristine copies.

To fully appreciate the extent of this dilemma, I believe it's instructive to take a brief dino tour of the history of American cinema.

[VIDEO - *The Lost World*]

This was one of the first Hollywood blockbusters—*The Lost World,* made in 1924. It may look crude today, but back then it was magic to audiences who had little idea how the filmmakers were able to seemingly bring dinosaurs back to life.

[VIDEO - "*King Kong*"]

20   In 1933 came *King Kong,* which made a giant leap in special effects—and, of course, it added sound, which allowed audiences to hear the incessant screaming of Fay Wray.

[VIDEO - Fay Wray in King Kong's paw screaming]

[VIDEO - *Godzilla*]

The next landmark film on this dino tour was *Godzilla* in 1954. *Godzilla* may have spawned any number of cheesy sequels, but the first one set a new standard in the depiction of scaly monsters, and entranced and terrified audiences from Tokyo to Tacoma.

[VIDEO - *Jurassic Park*]

In 1993, as I'm sure you all remember, *Jurassic Park* came along. This film raised the dino bar even higher by utilizing the creative power of the computer to seamlessly integrate completely authentic-looking dinosaurs in a live-action film. I might add that we have received legal clearances to show you all this terrific copyrighted intellectual property of our competitors.

These dinosaur movies offer just one slice of the progression of our industry. I could just as easily have tracked the evolution of any number of other genres—gangster movies, from Cagney to Coppola . . . comedies, from Chaplin to Carrey . . . adventures, from Fairbanks to Ford . . . romances, from Hepburn & Tracy to Ryan & Hanks.

As you may have noticed, none of the films I've referred to came from The Walt Disney Studios. This is completely intentional. Our studio has a proud history, but we have hardly cornered the market on creating great intellectual property. For a variety of reasons, an incredible array of talent came to Southern California and built what were rightly called "dream factories," thereby inventing an industry. Throughout the century, this industry acquired ever-increasing importance to the entire American economy, since the products it produced were embraced by people across the nation and around the world.

25   To appreciate just how important, consider the significance of America's copyright-related industries, which include motion pictures, television, home video, music, publishing and computer software. In 1977, these industries added $160 billion to the U.S. economy, or roughly 3.6% of GDP. In 1997, this figure had grown to nearly $530 billion, representing 6.3% of GDP.

This growth is all the more significant when you consider that a tremendous amount of these revenues are generated overseas. In just six years—from 1991 to 1997—the foreign sales and exports of copyright-related industries nearly doubled from $36 billion to $66 billion. As a result, foreign sales from copyright industries are now greater than almost every other industry category, including such major exporters as the automotive industry and the agriculture industry. Earlier this year, the U.S. experienced its greatest foreign trade imbalance ever. Imagine how much worse the situation would have been without the positive impact of our content-based industries.

We now need to ensure that the necessary steps are taken to make sure that the success story of American intellectual property during the 20th century is not undermined during the 21st. At a time of burgeoning trade deficits, we must act to assure the security of one of America's few positive trade assets.

To give you an idea of what's really at stake, allow me to return to prehistoric times. We left off the *Dinosaur* clip with this shot.

[VIDEO - Freeze frame of pterodactyl flying over dinos]

Even being held in freeze frame for you to scrutinize, this looks like an impeccable aerial shot following a pterodactyl as it flies over a herd of dinosaurs. Unfortunately, we weren't able to find any real dinosaurs to star in the film—and if we had, I understand they're terribly hard to train. So, we had to digitally birth them ourselves, bit by bit.

30   It took more than four years, and it required the invention of proprietary technologies.

First, we had to shoot the live-action backgrounds. To do this, we designed something we called a "dino cam."

[VIDEO - Dino cam at work]

As you can see here, it is a camera suspended by cables that are attached to two 70-foot towers. This allowed us to make extremely fluid tracking and crane shots that could quickly go from the height of a 50-foot brachiosaur down to the eye level of a lemur. Our camera team spent 18 months taking the dino cam to a range of locations that included Australia, Jordan, Venezuela, Hawaii, Western Samoa—and even so far as the Los Angeles County Arboretum in exotic Arcadia.

Of course, there was no point to the "dino cam" if there were no dinos. So, we built our own digital animation studio back in Burbank and filled it with an extraordinary team of computer animators.

[VIDEO - Dinosaur production montage to illustrate the following]

These animators first created digital skeletons to better understand how dinosaurs were engineered.

35   Then they layered on musculature so their creations could move realistically.

Then there was the skin. Not only did it have to look completely real, but it had to have a sense of mass and weight that would convincingly relate the tremendous size of these animals.

Then our animators took on another challenge that was completely unknown in the Cretaceous Era. Our dinosaurs would talk. So, each dinosaur needed to be designed in such a way that it could convincingly mouth words.

All of this resulted in a tremendous amount of data that had to be processed. So, we built what we called a "render farm." This "farm" was a room full of computers running 24 hours a day to crunch all those billions of zeros and ones.

To give you some sense of the detail that went into the film, let's look again at one brief shot.

[VIDEO - Dinosaur running through the water amidst giant dinosaur legs, then freeze frame]

40   Let me build that scene for you step by step.

[VIDEO - "Build" to illustrate the points]

First the dino cam filmed a tracking shot across a pond.

Then we added the brachiosaurs in the background.

Next, we created rough animation of the youthful dinosaur.

Then we introduced the final animation of the dinosaur along with a flock of birds flying and the giant legs of some more brachiosaurs.

45   Next, we inverted all of these images in order to show their reflections in the water.

In order to make it look like the dinosaur is really interacting with the water, we added splash and ripple effects.

Finally, we composited all of these elements to produce the finished scene.

[VIDEO - Run the finished sequence]

This is one magic trick where even once you know how it was done, it still dazzles.

I'll resist the temptation to go on and on about the countless ingenious tricks that our animators and technicians devised to make this film, because my point isn't to promote the film. My point is that we have created a movie that took four years to make, during which 45 million megabytes were crunched—or enough data to fill 70,000 CDRoms—all to generate the necessary data for an 80-minute film—which, were it to get in the wrong hands, could be compressed onto a single DVD disk in a matter of minutes and instantaneously put on the Internet while the film is still in the theaters.

50   In other words, this film represents the flesh and bones—or, in this case, scales and bones—of that highfalutin legalistic term, "intellectual property." And, it is all put in jeopardy by an old-fashioned everyday term—"piracy."

But, in this context, I'm not talking about the comical characters sailing the high seas at the Pirates of the Caribbean. Rather, I'm talking about an underground of secretive and sequestered Pirates of Encryption—the hackers who shamelessly assert that anything they can get their hands on is legally theirs.

You may be familiar with the recent controversy over a company called *iCrave.com,* which claimed the right to pluck television signals off the air and stream them on the Internet for all the world to see. You may also be aware of software programs like Napster, Wraptster, Freenet and Gnutella, which allow college kids to build vast music collections on the hard drives of their lap top computers without ever buying a single CD.

These Internet programs enable the piracy of intellectual property. Their use is rapidly escalating, with a potential impact on our culture and our economy that is comparable to other Internet-related issues that many of you have expressed concerns about—such as cyber-security, credit card security and the safety of your children's web surfing.

There is no question that the Internet is an exciting and dynamic new force in commerce and entertainment. But so were, in their time, radio and television. And they had to play by the same boring old rules involving copyright infringement.

55   Today's Internet pirates try to hide behind some contrived New Age arguments of cyberspace, but all they are really doing is trying to make a case for Age Old thievery. When they hack a DVD and then distribute it on the web, it is

no different than if someone puts a quarter in a newspaper machine and then takes out all the papers, which, of course, would be illegal and morally wrong.

The pirates will argue that this analogy is unfair, maintaining that all they're doing is cracking a digital code. But, by that standard, it would be justifiable to crack a bank code and transfer the funds from someone else's account into your own. There's just no way around it—theft is theft, whether it is enabled by a handgun or a computer keyboard.

The piracy of intellectual property takes all forms. I don't know if any of you have ever seen one of the videotapes for sale on the sidewalks of many major cities. Here's what they can look and sound like.

[VIDEO - Pirated scene from *Tarzan* in which the visuals are blurry and shaky, the sound is muffled and echoy]

As you can see, these tapes are barely watchable. But, they crop up with alarming speed—videos of *Dinosaur* have already been seen on the streets of Malaysia. Now look at the same scene from *Tarzan* as it could be downloaded directly off the Internet.

[VIDEO - Excellent quality scene from *Tarzan*]

Instead of one bad quality videotape for sale on the street, we could soon be talking about unlimited numbers of high quality copies available on the Internet. And, new technology is making it faster and easier for users to download this kind of material.

60   The Internet pirates who produce these contraband copies have found some odd bedfellows in the intellectual community and in industry.

Social critics, like Esther Dyson, have spoken out against traditional copyright protection on the web. Ms. Dyson once listed the "new rules" of the Internet and went on to say, and I quote, that "Chief among the new rules is that 'content is free'." I must say that I find this assertion interesting, since at the bottom of Ms. Dyson's newsletter, one can clearly read that it is copyrighted—and, as her subscribers can attest, her newsletter is most certainly not free.

Regrettably, Ms. Dyson is not alone in this self-serving hypocrisy. The same scholars and companies who advocate a "content is free" philosophy scrupulously protect their own intellectual property with copyrights, trademarks and patents. Just yesterday, it was reported that Napster is taking legal action against a punk rock group that has been selling t-shirts, hats and bumper stickers featuring the Napster logo. Apparently, they don't find copyright infringement so virtuous when they're the ones being infringed upon.

I find it especially remarkable when Internet hardware companies refuse to protest piracy—because I believe they are acting against their own long-term interests. This is because the Internet needs content—and it needs more of it every day.

The fact is that nobody signs up for the Internet because of the elegance of its routers. Nobody logs on because of the micro-chip inside. No, they use the Internet in ever-growing numbers because of the content. Right now, that content is largely information. But, increasingly, it will also be entertainment. The growth of bandwidth will increasingly make possible full video experiences.

But, this expansion of Internet entertainment will stall if the creators of the content cannot enjoy the full rights of ownership of that content.

65   It does not take a CPA to figure out that a movie like *Dinosaur* does not come cheap. However, it is an investment worth making if there can be substantial reward in success. But, if this reward is allowed to be pirated away, then the creative risktakers will put their energies elsewhere, and the Internet will become a wonderful delivery system with nothing wonderful to deliver.

One of the fallacies of the intellectual property debate is that it's really just a conflict between the pro-technology members of the "New Media" against the anti-technology members of the "Old Media." As I hope I made clear with the discussion of *Dinosaur,* this characterization couldn't be more wrong. At Disney we embrace technology. And we always have.

Throughout his career, Walt Disney recognized new technology as the friend of the storyteller. He kept pushing the envelope with the first sound cartoon, the first color cartoon, the first use of the multi-plane camera, the first use of stereophonic sound, and the development of robotics for his theme parks. Walt was also almost alone among movie studio chiefs in the 1950s when he recognized television as a new opportunity and not a threat.

At Disney today, we are not only seizing the tremendous possibilities offered by technology in movies, as with *Dinosaur*—we are also active participants in the expansion of the Internet with our GO.com family of sites, such as Disney.com, ESPN.com, ABCNews.com, ABC.com and Family.com. And, we believe we are helping to pioneer the convergence of the Internet with television through the development of Enhanced TV, which allows viewers to become active participants in the programming, accessing stats during a football game, playing against the contestants on "Millionaire" and guessing the winners on the Oscars.

We intend to continue to pour resources into the Internet—but not if this requires surrendering the rights to things we own.

70   Just as our society is beginning to address other security threats posed by the Internet, we must address the security of copyrights. With this in mind, our company is undertaking a wide-ranging strategy to make the Internet truly secure for intellectual property. This strategy consists of five main elements.

First of all, we are turning to our representatives in Washington with both defensive and offensive requests. And, we do so clear in the understanding that this issue has fundamental roots in our nation's Constitution. Intellectual property rights are really no different from ordinary property rights. If you own something, you expect the government to respect your right to keep it from being stolen.

On defense, we ask the Congress to refrain from mandating a compulsory license for redistribution of creative works over the Internet. There are numerous factors that make compulsory licensing ill suited to a global medium like the Internet.

On offense, we ask you to begin to explore with us legislation that would assure the efficacy of technology solutions to copyright security. As we seek to develop measures such as watermarking, we need the assurance that the people who manufacture computers and the people who operate ISP's will cooperate by incorporating the technology to look for and respond to the watermarks. This same mandate could be part of the solution to a host of other Internet security issues as well.

The second element of our strategy to protect intellectual property is to work with governments around the world to respect our rights. We are actively involved in the Global Business Dialogue on E-Commerce, and our company is serving as chair of the Intellectual Property Work Group. The Internet is international. The issues involving it cannot be viewed with a myopic American eye. Instead, we must think and act globally.

75   The third element is education. Most people are honest and want to do the right thing. But they can't do the right thing if they don't know that they're doing a wrong thing. I am always amazed when I walk the streets of New York and stroll past an open fruit stand. Thousands of people go by each day respecting the fact that if they want an apple they need to pay for it, even though it would be incredibly easy to just take it. When it comes to the Internet, most people simply aren't aware that the same issues apply. According to a recent *Newsweek* cover story, college kids are simply oblivious to the legal and moral implications of downloading copyrighted material off the Internet. Working with Jack Valenti and the MPAA, we are advocating a more aggressive campaign to make people aware of intellectual property rights on the Internet, in much the same way as the FBI warning at the front of videotapes.

Fourth, we believe that the entertainment industry as a whole—and I mean all the companies with a stake in the e-future—should take meaningful technological measures. To an extent, piracy is a technical problem and must be addressed with technical solutions. The studios, broadcasters and record companies—working in cooperation with the technology companies—need to develop innovative and flexible watermarking or encryption systems that can stay one step ahead of the hackers.

The fifth and final of our initiatives is economic. History has shown that one of the best deterrents to pirated product is providing legitimate product at appropriate prices. In the music industry, we have already seen that most people will gladly pay fair prices for legally-produced product even when it can be easily reproduced and unlawful copies can be easily acquired. I am certain that the same person who pays a reasonable price for an apple at his local fruit stand will pay a reasonable price for a video on his local hard drive.

To be sure, none of these measures represents a silver bullet that will stop piracy in its tracks. But, that's o.k. Markets are messy, and, over time, these initiatives will be refined and new ones will emerge. But, there first needs to be a recognition and a commitment—in government, in industry and among the general populace—that theft will not be tolerated in any form—whether it's someone shoplifting in a store or downloading on the Net.

All we need is for this basic rule of society to be acknowledged and enforced in the cyber world as it is in the real world. If this can be achieved, then the possibilities of the Internet—for communication, for education, for entertainment and for commerce—will be as limitless as the lightspeed at which it has brought the world together.

80   Indeed, as long as intellectual property rights are adequately protected, then I firmly expect that the pirates will be defeated and the entertainment industry will not go the way of the dinosaur.

[VIDEO - Pick up the *Dinosaur* clip where we left off]

Rather, like our digital pterodactyl, we will continue to take wing and fly on toward new creative horizons, to the benefit of our industry, our audience and our nation.

Thank you very much.

Reflect & Write

❑   How does ethos figure into Eisner's argument?

❑   Consider the way in which Eisner uses examples to increase the persuasiveness of his argument. What do you think about his choice of multimedia examples? How does this reflect an awareness of his audience and of the *kairos* of his argument? Was his use of these examples a successful or less successful choice? Why?

❑   After his series of video clips, he points out, "As you may have noticed, none of the films I've referred to came from The Walt Disney Studios." Why is this an important point to make for his argument? Would his argument have been strengthened or weakened if he had limited himself to examples from his own studio? Why or why not?

❑   Eisner spends a lot of time detailing the process of making one scene from the Disney movie *Dinosaur*. Why do you think he decided to spend time doing this? How does this support his argument?

❑   How does Eisner's tone shift as he moves past his example to discuss Internet "pirates"? Does this tone shift undermine or reinforce his argument?

❑   Look at the structure of Eisner's argument. How does his introduction work in conjunction with his conclusion?

❑   **Write:** Draft a response to Eisner's argument in the persona of a person who advocates the exchange of free content—including movie downloads—on the Internet.

PERSPECTIVES ON THE ISSUE

1. Compare the image in Figure 12.12 ("Tired of being treated like a criminal . . .") to the image at the beginning of Chapter 4 ("When you pirate MP3s . . ."). How does each use different rhetorical strategies to make a similar argument?

2. Having read the RIAA's antipiracy statement, visit its Website at http://www.riaa.com/issues/piracy/default.asp. Now visit its "Quotes from the Artists" page at http://www.riaa.com/about/artists/quotes.asp. How do the quotes affect your view on music downloading? What were the intended effects of these quotes? Do the quotes accomplish these goals?

3. Visit the RespectCopyrights.org Website and look at the online equivalent of the Figure 12.16 ad. How does the dynamic nature of the online version change the persuasiveness of the ad? Is the print ad or the animated ad more effective? Why or why not? Now browse the rest of the site, especially the links to "What is Copyright?," "What is Piracy?" and "So What's It to Me?" Who is the audience for this site? Does this site seemed successfully designed to persuade that audience? Why or why not? Be sure to consider the properties of online rhetoric in your analysis.

4. Read Lev Grossman's article carefully. What is Grossman's stand on the issue of downloading? How does the article use word choice, examples, structure, and rhetorical appeals to suggest its argument to the reader?

5. Read Michael Eisner's address to Congress. Is it a successful argument? Why or why not? What rhetorical appeals does he use to make his argument? Pay careful attention to his structure: how does he craft his introduction, his conclusion, his metaphor, and his example to make a persuasive oral argument? How does he use visual rhetoric? Do you think this was an effective choice? Why or who not? Discuss with a partner how he might have rescripted this argument if he discovered that he would have no multimedia capabilities during his presentation.

6. The two pieces from *Salon* offer differing perspectives on music sharing. Draft two op-ed pieces, one pro and one con, about the issue of downloading TV and film online.

FROM READING TO RESEARCH

1. Using your favorite search engine, search the terms "Disney" and "copyright." Read at least two of the articles that you uncover. How do these articles either complement or provide a contrast to Eisner's perspective as he presented it to Congress? Write a paper that uses direct sources from all three texts (Eisner's address as well as the two articles you found) to support your own argument about Disney's relationship to copyright issues.

2. Do some primary research on the illegal downloading of media from the Internet (such as music, film, television shows, software) by conducting a series of interviews and surveying your classmates and professors on the issue. You may choose to narrow your focus to one type of media or focus more broadly on the ethics of the issue as a whole. Be sure to refer to Chapter 5 for advice on surveys and interviews. Once you have compiled your data, create a multimedia presentation, complete with information graphics, in which you share your findings and your argument about this issue to your class.

REMIXING CULTURE

FIGURE 12.17 This student-created ad for the campus TV station in the Media Center at the University of Örebro, Sweden, relies on a remix of visual culture images.

Underlying the debate over copyright lies the concern that what is being regulated by legislation is not just individual content, but culture itself. In fact, as we've seen, Lawrence Lessig and others argue that culture itself is formed precisely by a "remixing" of established texts—that is, old images, songs, and films are revisited, and incorporated to create new culture. We can see this process at work in the student-created poster in Figure 12.17, which revises the famous World War I propaganda poster depicting America's Uncle Sam (see Figure 4.4) to address a new audience: Swedish youth at the University of Örebro. This remix of culture is international, cross-cultural, contemporary, and effective—it draws students to work for the television station in the media center.

The practice of remixing culture pervades further than just student-created ads: Disney remixes Japanese *sentai* TV shows into the kid hit, *Power Rangers,* for a U.S. audience; DirecTV remixes scenes from *Dukes of Hazzard* and *Back to the Future* to advertise its High Definition offerings; Gwen Stefani adapts the lyrics and melody from the classic *Fiddler on the Roof* song, "If I Were a Rich Man," to suit her own point of view. Culture literally is revised and remade every day.

But the practice of remixing culture is still hotly contested, especially when that process involves deliberate sampling, ripping, burning, and fusing existing cultural texts. With advances in digital technologies and the rise of sharing sites such as Flickr, we've recently seen an explosion in such new and unexpected texts: lyrics and musical accompaniments are remixed to produce original songs; new dialogue is superimposed upon film to create a new viewing experience; photographs are collaged, cropped, and modified to make original political statements. These remixed texts are exciting, fresh, and innovative—and they implicitly challenge traditional notions of consumption and production, purchase and profit.

If, as Creative Commons would argue, "creativity always builds on the past," then how does restricting the use of existent texts inhibit the development of a rich culture? Conversely, what are the ramifications of making all texts public domain, always available for reassembling and remixing at the user's whim?

Reflect & Write

❏ Why do you think students in Sweden would use the familiar image of Uncle Sam for their poster? How might Uncle Sam resonate differently with Swedish students than with U.S. students?

❏ **Write:** Find three examples of "remix" culture and write a brief essay that explains how old images (and other texts) can be used to create new culture. In what ways do your examples support or refute Lessig's claim that culture always builds on the past?

■ **Sasha Frere-Jones** *is a regular contributor to* The New Yorker, *where this article was origi-nally published in its January 10, 2005, issue. He also publishes articles on music and culture in* Slate, The New York Times, *and the* Village Voice.

The New Math of Mashups

Sasha Frere-Jones

In July of 2003, Jeremy Brown, a.k.a. DJ Reset, took apart a song. Using digital software, Brown isolated instrumental elements of "Debra," a song by Beck from his 1999 album "Midnite Vultures." Brown, who is thirty-three and has studied with Max Roach, adjusted the tempo of "Debra" and added live drums and human beat-box noises that he recorded at his small but tidy house in Long Island City. Then he sifted through countless a-cappella vocals archived on several hard drives. Some a-cappellas are on commercially released singles, specifically in-tended for d.j. use, while others appear on the Internet, having been leaked by people working in the studio where the song was recorded, or sometimes even by the artist.

After auditioning almost a thousand vocals, Brown found that an a-cappella of "Frontin'," a collaboration between the rapper Jay-Z and the producer Pharrell Williams, was approximately in the same key as "Debra." The two songs are not close in style—"Debra" is a tongue-in-cheek take on seventies soul music, while "Frontin' " is hard and shimmering computer music—but the vocalists are doing something similar. Brown exploited this commonality, and used his soft-ware to put the two singers exactly in tune.

Both Beck and Williams are singing in an impaired but enthusiastic shower-stall falsetto. Williams's goofy come-on—"Don't wanna sound full of myself or rude, but you ain't look-ing at no other dudes, because you love me"—is both musically and conceptually in sync with Beck's own daft chorus: "Girl, I wanna get with you, and your sister. I think her name is Debra." Brown's collage sounds not like two songs stitched together but one single theme song for inept Romeos everywhere. After several months of work, he completed the track, called it "Fron-tin' on Debra," and posted it on his Web site. With an enthusiastic push from Beck, "Frontin' on Debra" was made commercially available in October on iTunes.

"Frontin' on Debra" is an example of a "mashup," in which, generally, the vocal from one song is laid over the music from another. The best-known mashup in the United States is an unauthorized album-length project called "The Grey Album," assembled by Brian Burton, known professionally as Danger Mouse. The vo-cals are from Jay-Z's "The Black Album," and the musical bed is a highly processed and reor-ganized version of the Beatles' "White Album." Occasionally compelling, "The Grey Album" is not a great example of a mashup, because the musical bed is processed so radically that its source is sometimes not clear. One of the thrills of the mashup is identifying two well-known artists unwittingly complementing each other's strengths and limitations: bacchanalian rapper Missy Elliott combined with morose English rock band Joy Division, ecstatic Madonna work-ing with furious Sex Pistols. The most celebrated mashups are melodically tuned, positing a har-monic relationship between, say, Madonna's voice and the Sex Pistols' guitars.

5   Mashups find new uses for current digital technology, a new iteration of the cause-and-effect relationship behind almost every change in pop-music aesthetics: the gear changes, and then the music does. If there is an electric guitar of mashup, it is a software package called Acid Pro, which enables one to put loops of different songs both in time and in tune with each other. Mark Vidler, known professionally as Go Home Productions, explained some other benefits of

digital technology to me in London not long ago: "You don't need a distributor, because your distribution is the Internet. You don't need a record label, because it's your bedroom, and you don't need a recording studio, because that's your computer. You do it all yourself."

A legally cleared album of mashups called "Collision Course" is currently in the *Billboard* Top Ten. It is a sort of "Black Album" footnote, a combination of Jay-Z's work on "The Black Album" and other albums, and the music of Linkin Park, the multiplatinum rock band. "Collision Course" is not a particularly good mashup—Linkin Park's adequate rhyming and bleating vocals only detract from Jay-Z's authority and swing—but it's a good example of why major record labels have taken so long to embrace the form.

As Jennifer Justice, of Carroll, Guido & Groffman, Jay-Z's law firm, explained, "Jay's song '99 Problems' uses two huge samples and has four different credited publishers. That's before you've added anyone else's music to it, which would be yet another publisher or two. Making a mashup with that song means the label issuing the mashup has to convince all the publishers involved to take a reduction in royalty—otherwise, it won't be profitable for the label. The publishers are not going to agree to this if we're not talking about two huge artists. With Jay-Z and Linkin, it's like found money, but less well known artists might not be sexy enough or big enough." This may be true, but lawyers and considerations of profit have little to do with how mashups happen, or why they keep happening.

In April of 2000, an English bass player and MTV v.j. named Eddy Temple-Morris inaugurated a radio show called "The Remix" on London's XFM network. A remix, traditionally, was simply a song taken apart and enhanced by the addition of new elements but not actually combined with another song. Temple-Morris played remixes, many of them rock songs reworked by dance-world producers, and mashups made by friends of his like the producer Garret (Jacknife) Lee. By the end of the year, Temple-Morris was receiving unsolicited CD-Rs from people using aliases like McSleazy and Osymyso.

In October of 2001, a d.j. named Roy Kerr, calling himself the Freelance Hellraiser, sent Temple-Morris a mashup called "A Stroke of Genius," laying Christina Aguilera's vocal from "Genie in a Bottle," a lubricious pop song, over the music from the Strokes' "Hard to Explain," a brittle, honking guitar song. "Stroke" is a perfect pop song, better than either of its sources. What was harmonically sweet in the original songs becomes huge and complex in the combination. Aguilera's vocal is an unabashedly expressive ode to her sexuality, and her control over it. (She will unleash the genie from her bottle only if rubbed the right way.) The Strokes' track is compressed and jittery, as if made by hipster robots, but the chord changes are lovely. The original vocal, by Julian Casablancas, is a good rock snarl, but it is a delivery more of attitude than information. Each song targets a demographic that wants nothing to do with the other—teen-agers texting their friends while cruising the mall, and twenty-somethings drinking cheap beer in expensive New York bars—but Hellraiser brokers an amazing musical détente between the two styles. Stripped of "Genie in a Bottle"'s electronic beats, Aguilera's sex-kitten pose dissipates, and she becomes vulnerable, even desperate. The opening lines now sound less like strip-club small talk and more like a damsel pining from a tower: "I feel like I've been locked up tight for a century of lonely nights, waiting for someone to release me." After another line, she shifts into a wordless "oh, oh" that lays over the Strokes' chord changes so deliciously you can't imagine why the song didn't always do that. After hearing it twice, you can't remember when it didn't.

10 In fact, "A Stroke of Genius" is so good that it eventually led Freelance Hellraiser to do official remixes for Aguilera and others, and he has just completed, at Paul McCartney's invitation, an entire album of McCartney remixes. "Stroke" also inspired a fourteen-year-old named Daniel Sheldon to start a Web site called boomselection.info. "The Remix" remains England's main hub for mashups, but the rest of the world is being served through Sheldon's site and getyourbootlegon.com, a message board started by Grant McSleazy, who recently graduated to doing legitimate remixes of Britney Spears.

I visited Temple-Morris at the XFM studios in Central London in October. He is a tall, rangy man who gestures quickly and smiles almost constantly. His basic mode is deep enthusiasm and his favorite word is "love," which he uses without irony. "We get our wrists slapped by the record companies and publishing companies and whatever," he said. "But these days there's much more love, there's much less paranoia."

Temple-Morris was broadcasting "The Remix" as we talked. He moved briskly behind the console, speaking continuously to the seven or eight people in the room. In mid-conversation, he smiled, nodded, and leaned toward the microphone. The "on air" light went on without warning, and the track playing in the studio cut off abruptly.

"Love it. Want to take it out to dinner. Wanna marry it. There are some tunes, I don't know what it is, it's the rolling beat, it's that incredible bass line, it's just, there's something really, really sexy about this record. And so I thought, I've got to play you a new really sexy record that I found."

Temple-Morris proceeded to play a record that, under normal circumstances, would have seemed fairly sexy, but, following his salesmanship, sounded like the National Anthem of Sex. This is Temple-Morris's gift: he was born to the job of loving music and persuading others to love it as much as he does.

15   Also in the room was Mark Vidler, a.k.a. Go Home Productions, one of the more reliable mashup-makers. Once a graphic designer working for a company that made travel pillows, and long before that a guitarist in a rock band called Chicane, Vidler, too, was converted in October of 2001. "I heard 'A Stroke of Genius' on the radio and I thought, That's clever. I could do that," he said. By April of 2002, Vidler was making his own mashups. His first was called "Slim McShady," a combination of Eminem and Wings. "I created it on a Saturday, posted it on the Tuesday, and got played on the radio that Friday, on 'The Remix.'"

Vidler is responsible for several mashups that have the same uncanny brilliance as "Stroke of Genius." "Girl Wants (to Say Goodbye to) Rock and Roll" brings Christina Aguilera back to sing over the Velvet Underground's "Rock and Roll." "Ray of Gob" combines Madonna's "Ray of Light" and the Sex Pistols' "God Save the Queen," and both Madonna and the Pistols admired it.

Mashup artists like Vidler, Kerr, and Brown have found a way of bringing pop music to a formal richness that it only rarely reaches. See mashups as piracy if you insist, but it is more useful, viewing them through the lens of the market, to see them as an expression of consumer dissatisfaction. Armed with free time and the right software, people are rifling through the lesser songs of pop music and, in frustration, choosing to make some of them as good as the great ones.

Reflect & Write

❏ In his introduction, Frere-Jones moves from a specific example to a definition. Why do you think he adopted this strategy? Was this an effective choice?

❏ How does Sasha Frere-Jones use descriptive language to make his writing more vivid? Find at least three examples where he uses descriptors effectively.

❏ Early in his article, Frere-Jones contends that "*The Grey Album* is not a great example of a mashup, because the musical bed is processed so radically that its source is sometimes not clear." What argument is he making here about the qualities of a "great" mashup? How does the relationship between the sources and the new musical creation speak to issues of intellectual property?

❏ Look carefully at a paragraph in which Frere-Jones describes the audible qualities of a song, such as the paragraph that begins "In October of 2001." What strategies does he use to convey his impressions of the music to the reader?

❏ **Write:** In his conclusion, Frere-Jones for the first time brings up the term *piracy*. How would his argument have changed if he had included *piracy* in his opening paragraph? If there is any "blame" in the creation of mashups, where does his conclusion place it? Write out your responses in a position paper and then draft a cover letter to send your paper to *The New Yorker.*

■ *In February 2004, DJ Danger Mouse sent out 3,000 promo copies of* The Grey Album, *his remix of the Beatles'* White Album *and Jay-Z's* The Black Album. *Shortly afterward, he received a cease-and-desist notice from EMI, an organization that owned the rights to the Beatles' album. Although Danger Mouse stopped distributing* The Grey Album, *fans of his work continued to make it available on the Internet. After extended litigation, the case was dropped, and* The Grey Album *remains available for Internet download.*

Cover: The Grey Album

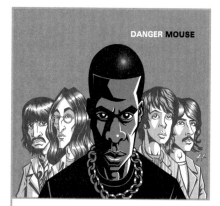

FIGURE 12.18 The cover of DJ Danger Mouse's *Grey Album* visually represents the album's musical remix.

Reflect & Write

❏ How does the cover of *The Grey Album* reflect the fact that it is a mashup? Consider how contrast, arrangement, style, and color impact the argument.

❏ Choose a musical mash-up that you like. Now design a cover for it that reflects the way that it combines different artists and musical styles. Share you cover art with the class.

❏ **Write:** Draft a letter to EMI in which you support or contest the cease-and-desist notice.

■ **Jon Healey,** *a staff writer for the* Los Angeles Times, *has published stories on copyright infringement lawsuits, online music, and the convergence of media and technology.* **Richard Cromelin,** *also a staff writer for the* L.A. Times, *brings his specialty in pop music criticism to the collaboration; he has written previously for* Creem *and the* Phonograph Record. *This article first appeared in the March 21, 2004 edition of the* Los Angeles Times *and focuses principally around the controversy over DJ Danger Mouses's remix,* The Grey Album.

When Copyright Law Meets the 'Mash-up'

Jon Healey and Richard Cromelin

Record producer Brian Burton knew he'd done something technically illegal when he electronically blended tracks from the Beatles' "White Album" and vocals from Jay-Z's "The Black Album" into a CD called "The Grey Album."

But he was so excited by the mix of Fab Four riffs and Jay-Z raps that he badly wanted people to hear it. "When I was finished, it was the biggest sense of accomplishment I've had over anything," he said. So in January, the Los Angeles-based Burton, who records as DJ Danger Mouse, made a couple of thousand copies of the disc and started mailing them out.

His wish to be heard has come true many times over, although not in the way he expected. On Feb. 10 the Beatles' record company, EMI Music, stopped Burton from distributing "The Grey Album." That action triggered an online revolt that led tens of thousands of people to download digital copies of the CD, generating enough buzz to draw reviews from such mainstream outlets as CNN.

EMI's move against Danger Mouse was a spectacular backfire in the war over what's fair when the muse runs afoul of copyright law in the Digital Age. Technology is making it easier than ever to sample and rework recordings, and to the chagrin of entertainment companies and some artists who hold copyrights, the public is showing little sympathy for their efforts to control original works.

5   Fred E. Goldring, a Beverly Hills-based music-industry lawyer, likened EMI's response to "The Grey Album" to the major labels' earlier mishandling of the Napster file-sharing service. "By creating a controversy and trying to shut it down, they actually attracted more interest in it," Goldring says. "They created their own hell." He adds, "It became probably the most widely downloaded, underground indie record, without radio or TV coverage, ever. I think it's a watershed event."

That's the dilemma faced by entertainment companies and other copyright holders in a sampling, file-sharing world. The law may be black and white, but among artists and audiences, the creative landscape has been remixed in shades of gray.

A Landmark Skirmish

The main force behind the online release of Burton's album was a loosely organized confederation of websites and online activists who believe copyright holders in general, and the major record labels in particular, have gone too far in trying to enforce their rights.

To them, "The Grey Album" epitomized how new digital tools allow artists to build on earlier works in unexpected ways, enriching society by turning old creations into new ones—this time by using the originals as raw material, not just inspiration.

It's not in the public interest to hold back that kind of creativity, argued the free-"The Grey Album" forces. So despite threats from EMI's lawyers, they recruited more than 150 websites to offer downloadable versions of the work on Feb. 24 as part of a protest called Grey Tuesday.

10   It was a landmark skirmish in a battle that dates to the mid-'80s, when digital recorders, or "samplers," found their way into studios. Soon hip-hop artists were routinely borrowing snippets of sounds from LPs without seeking permission from the artists who recorded them or from their labels.

Those freewheeling days didn't last long. Objections from R&B giant James Brown, among others, forced some samplers to pay for the material they used. Then, in 1991, a federal judge in New York staggered the sampling world by granting British songwriter Raymond "Gilbert" O'Sullivan's request for an injunction against rapper Biz Markie, who had built a song around samples from O'Sullivan's biggest U.S. hit, "Alone Again (Naturally)."

Not only did U.S. District Judge Kevin Thomas Duffy order the rapper's label to reclaim and destroy every unsold copy of the offending record, but he also referred the case to the U.S. attorney's office for possible prosecution. Biz Markie wasn't hauled back into court, but Duffy had sent a clear—and chilling—message to everyone in the field.

Today, most copyright experts say that the rule on sampling is pretty clear. With limited exceptions, artists can't use a recognizable sample from someone else's recording unless the copyright holder grants permission. The copyright holder is in the driver's seat, able to set the price for a sample (ranging from a few hundred dollars to a share of the revenue from the song) or to withhold permission entirely.

The Beatles, for one, have never given their approval to any sampling requests. Jay-Z, on the other hand, doesn't seem to mind. He released a vocals-only version of "The Black Album," which was widely viewed as an open invitation to people like Burton to use his work. (The Beatles did not respond to requests for comment on "The Grey Album." Jay-Z was not available but said through a representative,

"I applaud creativity in any form.")

As Grey Tuesday organizers see it, the law gives copyright owners too much control, in part because getting permission to sample an existing work is rarely as simple as one artist calling another and asking. They tend to peg the artists' record labels as the bad guys and unsung musicians as the victims.

"Sampling is something that's been sort of made illegal by the major labels over the last decade and a half," says Nicholas Reville, co-founder of Downhill Battle, an independent-music advocacy group based in Worcester, Mass., that spearheaded efforts to distribute Burton's work.

"It sounds hyperbolic, but they really have banned an art form from the mainstream. This wasn't about getting whatever album for free just to defy the major labels, it was about making sure that they weren't able to censor this work of art and about [demonstrating] why there needs to be a reasonable and practical sampling right."

"Reasonable" and "practical," though, are somewhat in the eye of the beholder. Ask Dexter Holland, the lead singer of the Offspring, how he'd feel if someone mixed his band's hit album "Smash" with, say, Dylan's "Blonde on Blonde," and he says: "Honestly, I'd be flattered. I would think that would be a good thing. That's a tough line, like exactly how can you control your music in all ways and all respects?"

Of course, if someone sold that remix, "that would be a different story," the Huntington Beach-based musician says. "But in terms of just having it, putting it up for people to listen to, I think that's totally fine."

Then there's L.A.-based Chris Carter, whose band Dramarama has heard its song "Anything, Anything" mashed up with Pink's "Get the Party Started."

"I think it's extremely clever," he says of "The Grey Album." His concern is over potential commercial release of such works. "It's the Beatles' musicianship, songwriting and performing that you're benefiting from. It's the actual recording. That's what they own. They own the masters. You can't take something someone else owns."

Carter, who also hosts the "Breakfast With the Beatles" radio show Sunday mornings on KLSX-FM (97.1), doesn't buy the argument that intellectual property falls into a different, less protected category from "real" property such as a car or a house.

"It's real property. A master tape, I could hit you over the head with it. It would hurt."

But inhibiting creators like Burton would hurt the public more, argues Creative Commons, which is supplying some of the intellectual firepower behind the pro-sampling forces. The group of copyright and technology experts says its mission is "to build a layer of reasonable, flexible copyright" in what it sees as an increasingly restrictive environment.

Board member Lawrence Lessig, a Stanford law professor, says the group is trying to develop a "sampling license" that recording artists could use to tell other musicians that their works could be sampled. The inspiration, he says, came from noted Brazilian singer and songwriter Gilberto Gil, who wanted other artists to be able to sample his songs for free.

Sampling licenses, though, would require the labels to play along. And so far, Lessig says, they've resisted allowing their artists to give permission for sampling. The labels often say they're trying to protect their artists when they sue file-sharing networks and their users for infringement, so, Lessig says, "If their artists say, 'OK, fine, I'm happy to have other people remixing my work,' they ought to respect that too."

Bowie Chimes In

One reason artists may want to keep White Albums from being mashed into Grey ones is concern about the integrity of their works.

"Taking it to extremes," says the Offspring's Holland, "what if someone took one of your records and put Adolf Hitler over it—something you don't believe in and despise? If you really think about it, if you're OK with it one way, you've got to be OK with it always. I think that's part of what free speech is in America. It'd be a bummer, though."

David Bowie, whose records are popular material

30   "I would always give the artist the chance to present to me what he wishes to do," says the veteran rock star by e-mail. "I would not give permission if I felt the work to be morally or politically repugnant. I would expect to be compensated for the work used. Outside of that, I'm fairly easygoing, as long as there's some kind of communication between the artist and myself. I think that is the important part."

To some copyright experts, "The Grey Album's" online release was a direct attack on artists and their moral rights as creators. The "moral rights" concept, which is strongest in Europe, holds that artists should have the power to stop their work from being altered or reused in ways that affect their reputations. Under this view, even if the Beatles sell their copyrights to EMI, they still have a moral right to protect the integrity of their recordings.

Russell G. Weiss, a copyright-law expert at Morrison & Foerster in Los Angeles, says the concept of moral rights is rarely applied in the U.S. to music. Still, he says, the idea of uncontrolled sampling doesn't gibe with the original purpose of American copyright law, which was "to encourage people to take the time and energy to make creative works" by enabling them to benefit from their work's commercial success. Forcing copyright holders to allow others to sam-

among Internet music-mashers and mixers, says he reserves the right of refusal because of just such a possibility.

ple and transform their work reduces the incentive to create, he argues.

Samplers are "kind of trading on someone else's property," Weiss says. "You shouldn't be forced to allow someone to transform your work. . . . You might not want to give other people that leg up, because you worked so long and hard."

The pro-sampling forces retort that artists have been building on their predecessors' efforts for centuries. In a sense, "creativity is about standing on the shoulders of giants in ways that we haven't before," said John Palfrey, executive director of the Harvard Law School Berkman Center for Internet & Society.

35   "I don't see why that's so different than the Beatles listening to a Chuck Berry song or trying to cop a certain vibe of someone else's sound and put it through their filter to create their new sound," says record producer Rick Rubin, whose original, sample-based backing track on Jay-Z's "99 Problems" was replaced by a "Helter Skelter" sample on "The Grey Album." (Rubin says he loves the result.)

Given how technology is changing the way the public interacts with art and enabling more people to be creators, Palfrey said, sampling-fueled works "shouldn't be stopped by a set of legal doctrines that no longer make sense."

Should Bowie and Holland be able to stop a sampler from using their recordings in a way they find repugnant? Sure, Palfrey says—but not by

using copyright law. Instead, he said, they can rely on other legal doctrines to protect their reputations and their brands.

Goldring disagrees, but he's pragmatic about sampling.

"Artists should have the absolute right to control their work," he says. "The problem is, how do you control that in the new world? The argument is, all of the fundamentals of copyright law are sound, and all of the fundamentals of copyright law should be enforced to protect artists' rights. Absolutely. [But] what does that mean in a world where everything can be digitized and transmitted around the world at the push of a button?"

'Mash-ups' in the Mainstream

40   Fueled by the digital power of the Internet, "mash-ups" like Burton's are making their way into the mainstream, and so are protests against the record companies trying to prevent them.

An unauthorized mash-up of Nelly's "Work It" and AC/DC's "Back in Black" that circulated online is in the regular rotation at KIIS-FM, the most listened-to station in Los Angeles. And two other Southern California outlets, KDLD-FM in Santa Monica and KDLE-FM in Newport Beach, have aired mash-ups by Go Home Productions that blend the Sex Pistols with Madonna.

"It's all heating up," says Mark Vidler of Watford, England, the man behind Go Home Productions. The field is becoming so popular, he says, a growing number of record companies have come calling with authorized mash-up projects.

45   Downhill Battle's Reville estimates that more than 100,000 copies of "The Grey Album" were downloaded on Feb. 24 alone. That's a remarkable number if it's accurate, but there's no way to know because of limited record-keeping by the Grey Tuesday participants. Eric Garland, chief executive of Big Champagne, a firm that monitors file-sharing networks, says that on Feb. 24 "The Grey Album" "was on a short list of the most popular records, period."

Five years ago, widespread acts of civil disobedience against EMI and the Recording Industry Assn. of America because of the way they enforced copyrights would have been inconceivable, says Lessig of Creative Commons. "This is how far the RIAA has pushed the world by its own extreme behavior."

Downhill Battle is still considering its next move, Reville says. A spokeswoman for EMI, meanwhile, would say only that the company intends "to protect our artistic content related to this matter to the fullest extent of the law." And EMI is no longer alone in the fight. Sony/ATV Music Publishing, which controls the Beatles' songwriting copyrights, has asked at least one Internet service provider to disconnect a website offering "The Grey Album." The site—illegal-art.org—switched Internet providers, got a lawyer and went back online.

Weiss of Morrison & Foerster said EMI doesn't have much choice. "The alternative to not pursuing your legal remedies is no one's going to be afraid to infringe," he says. If EMI sues and wins, he adds, "the message that you'll see is, A, you don't do this, and B, if a cease-and-desist is sent, you better [stop] right away."

In the meantime, the pro-sampling forces continue to press their case at the grass-roots.

A group aligned with Downhill Battle has compiled "The Jay-Z Construction Set," offering musicians a primer on how to make mash-ups on their home computers. The set, which includes "The Grey Album" and other remixes of Jay-Z's work, is circulating through file-sharing networks.

"What these technologies are making possible is a new form of expression that is not going to be able to be contained by something as simple as the law and enforcement of the law," says Palfrey of Harvard.

50   He favors allowing works to be sampled while ensuring that the original creator gets paid. The law won't change, though, unless people believe they have a stake in what might otherwise seem to be an arcane legal fight.

"The only way this is going to work is if people get a sense for why it matters," Palfrey says. "Real art is being created here."

If so, it's art being created in uncharted territory.

"A one-off, isolated thing like 'The Grey Album,' yeah, it's interesting," Carter says. "But I think we're going to be getting a lot of it. You're going to get 'The Dark Side of the Moon' album put together with this, 'Sandinista' with Bob Marley. It's gonna be crazy. I think it's gonna get out of control."

Bowie has observed parallel conflicts played out and resolved, to some degree, in the world of visual art, where appropriation of one artist's pictorial image by another has led to litigation involving such major names as Robert Rauschenberg and Helmut Newton. He's more philosophical.

55   "It will all slowly sort itself out into some kind of workable mess," he says, "but will continue to be a gray area for years to come. But that is life, isn't it?"

Reflect & Write

❏ What structural similarities are there in the way in which Frere-Jones and Healey and Cromelin start their articles? What are the significant differences for their overall arguments?

❏ Healey and Cromelin spend some time developing the historical context of *The Grey Album* case. How does this context enrich or detract from their argument? Why?

❏ Do the authors do an effective job of presenting both sides of the argument? Point to places in the text where each side is represented. Do they offer any insight into additional perspectives on this issue? If you had to develop a third response to the question of mashups, what would it be?

❏ In many arguments against mashups, critics point to the financial implications of creating "new" music this way. In this article, the authors spend some time developing the concept of "moral rights." Do they make a persuasive case about the validity or lack of validity of this position? What rhetorical strategies do they use to accomplish this?

❏ **Write:** Modeling your response on the multiple sides project in Chapter 3, assume personas and write an argument from each of their perspectives on this issue.

■ *Canadian-based artist* **Tom Forsythe** *staged and photographed "Food Chain Barbie" in 1999 as a means of commenting on his view of the materialism and gender bias endemic to contemporary society. Shortly after he posted the images on his Website, he was sued by Mattel, the makers of Barbie, for copyright and trademark infringement. The courts eventually ruled in Forsythe's favor. "Food Chain Barbie" has since appeared as part of "Illegal Art," a live and Web-based exhibit of images that challenge the limitations of copyright law.*

Photograph from "Food Chain Barbie"

Tom Forsythe

Reflect & Write

❏ What visual argument is "Food Chain Barbie" making about Barbie, about society, and about art?

❏ Setting the court decision aside, does it seem to you that the image is disturbing enough to prompt Mattel's response? Why or why not? Do you think Mattel should be able to restrict the use of Barbie's image in works of this nature? Explain your answer.

❏ Compare this image with the Body Shop ad (Figure 7.8) found in Chapter 7. Which makes the most powerful argument? Why?

❏ **Write:** Draft the plans for your own remix (photograph, cartoon, or sculpture) featuring Barbie that would make an argument about some aspect of society or cultural values. Share your design with your classmates.

FIGURE 12.19 Tom Forsythe's controversial "Food Chain Barbie" photographic series prompted legal action by the Mattel corporation.

Source: Fuji Supergloss Print, 11" x 14", Edition of 20 by Tom Forsythe, 1999. Courtesy of the artist.

■ **Bill Werde** *writes for* The New York Times, *where this article was first published on June 7, 2004, a few days after the release of* Harry Potter and the Prisoner of Azkaban, *the third installment in the Harry Potter film series.*

Hijacking Harry Potter, Quidditch Broom and All

Bill Werde

On Friday night *Harry Potter and the Prisoner of Azkaban* sold out theaters all over the globe. But in a makeshift screening room in a Brooklyn warehouse, more than 75 film-goers paid $7 each to watch the first film in the series, *Harry Potter and the Sorcerer's Stone.* Sort of.

On the screen *The Sorcerer's Stone* played as it was released by Warner Brothers. But the original soundtrack, dialogue and all, was turned down and replaced by an alternate version created by a 27-year-old comic book artist from Austin, Tex., named Brad Neely. He calls his soundtrack "Wizard People, Dear Reader," and it is one more breach of 5 the media industry's control of its products.

With Mr. Neely's gravelly narration, the movie's tone shifts into darkly comic, pop-culture-savvy territory. Hagrid, Harry Potter's giant, hairy friend, becomes Hagar, the Horrible, and Harry's fat cousin becomes Roast Beefy. As imagined by Mr. Neely, the three main characters are child alcoholics with a penchant for cognac, the magical ballgame Quidditch takes on homoerotic overtones, and Harry is prone

to delivering hyper-dramatic monologues. "I am a destroyer of worlds," bellows Mr. Neely at one point, sending laughter reverberating through the warehouse Friday night. "I am Harry" expletive "Potter!"

Mr. Neely, a fan of the series, created his alternate soundtrack last summer after joking about the notion with friends in an Austin nightspot. "Usually those kinds of jokes just die in the bar," he said. This time Mr. Neely burned his creation to CD, sent copies to friends and gave some to local video rental stores; several bundled his soundtrack with rentals of *The Sorcerer's Stone.*

The alternate soundtrack did not receive much attention until March, when it was shown at the New York Underground Film Festival. The festival's director, Kendra 10 Gaeta, received a gift from her boyfriend weeks before the festival: a painting by Mr. Neely, who threw in a CD of his Potter narration. "It was just so funny," she said.

Among those attending that festival was Carrie McLaren, whose Web site, Illegal-art.org, functions as an online museum for copyright-infringing art.

Ms. McLaren has since offered the huge digital file of "Wizard People" for download and raved about the sound-track on her site.

"We think Neely has crafted an as of yet unnamed new art form," she wrote, "one everyone should experience for themselves."

There is a brief history, at least, to alternative sound-tracks. Woody Allen's 1966 movie *What's Up, Tiger Lily?* substituted Mr. Allen's comic dialogue and descriptions for the soundtrack of a bad Japanese spy movie. But while Mr. Allen bought the rights to the original film and distributed his new version in theaters, subsequent ventures in the digital era, like Mr. Neely's, have taken liberties without permission and let the Web take care of distribution.

In 2001, for example, an anonymous *Star Wars* fan was so displeased with the helium-voiced character Jar Jar Binks in *Star Wars, Episode I: The Phantom Menace* that he recut the film, removing the character, a stunt that became known as "the Phantom edit."

George Lucas, the creator of *Star Wars,* initially was intrigued by the alternative version of the film. But when bootleg copies began selling at comic book conventions, and other edited versions began to trade online, his firm, Lucasfilm, sent letters to the news media indicating that it viewed such projects as copyright infringement.

A spokewoman at Warner Brothers said that the studio was unaware of "Wizard People, Dear Reader" and declined to comment further.

It is not clear that Mr. Neely's soundtrack violates the studio's copyright. Jonathan Zittrain, co-director of the Berkman Center for Internet and Society at Harvard Law School, said that while the copyright holder retains the rights to derivative works, it was possible "Wizard People" was protected under the rules that allow "fair use" of copyrighted works for purposes like criticism, comment and news reporting.

"The long-term strategic threat to the entertainment industry is that people will get in the habit of creating and making as much as watching and listening, and all of a sudden the label applied to people at leisure, 50 years in the making—consumer—could wither away," he said. "But it would be a shame if Hollywood just said no. It could very possibly be in the interest of publishers to see a market in providing raw material along with finished product."

Mr. Neely has not let the lack of legal clarity stop him from making plans to perform the "Wizard People" soundtrack live at an Austin theater July 23 through 25, as well as one night each in Seattle, Portland and Olympia, Wash., in August.

He is also working on his next project, a similar concept with a different style. The films need to have a lot of action, he said. "I'm thinking maybe *Jurassic Park*."

Reflect & Write

❏ At one point in the article, Bill Werde describes "Wizard People, Dear Reader" as "one more breach of the media industry's control of its products." Does Werde overall seem critical of the consumer remixing of popular movies? Why or why not?

❏ How does the Woody Allen example function in the article? Does it support the contention that consumers like Brad Neely should be able to remix film or undermine it? How?

❏ Look at the sources that Werde uses in his article. What additional sources or quotations might Werde have included to make his argument more persuasive? What would these sources contribute to the article?

❏ **Write:** Listen to part of "Wizard People, Dear Reader" (http://www.illegal-art.org/ video/wizard.html) online and then write a film review of this movie version of Harry Potter that makes clear your position on the issue of cultural remixing.

COLLABORATIVE CHALLENGE

In "Hijacking Harry Potter," Bill Werde describes the way in which one person "customized" Harry Potter to produce his own multimedia experience. Working with a small group, choose a short video clip—a commercial, a segment of a televised speech, a portion of a TV show—that you can replay either using a VCR, DVD player, or the Internet. Watch it with the sound off and then script your own remix narration for it. Share your remix with your class, either reading your narration live or playing a recorded version to accompany the clip.

■ *Revelations is a non-profit Star Wars fan film produced and released on a very small budget by Panic Struck Productions. All of the artists who worked on the film were volunteers.*

Movie Poster: Revelations

Panic Struck Productions

FIGURE 12.20 This movie poster advertises the Star Wars fan-produced film, *Revelations*.

Reflect & Write

❏ Nowhere on the *Revelations* poster is the phrase "Star Wars" prominently displayed. Looking at the poster quickly, did you associate it with the *Star Wars* franchise? Why of why not?

❏ What aspects of the posters have been specially chosen to try to "brand" it as a *Star Wars* film?

❏ Compare this poster with an official poster for one of the recent *Star Wars* films. Are there any differences that announce this poster as a "remix"?

❏ **Write:** Draft your plan for a remixed poster of a popular film. Include political figures and a strong argument about contemporary culture in your sketch.

■ *This article originally appeared in* Shift, *a magazine devoted to issues related to digital culture.* **Bret Dawson** *has written several articles on digital culture, including articles on digital money and one on data mining and invasion of privacy.*

The Privatization of Our Culture

Bret Dawson

A few days after airplanes crashed into the World Trade Center, the nephew of a friend of a friend had his fourth birthday party. In classic fourth-birthday-party style, there was cake and ice cream, pin-the-tail-on-the-donkey and a loot bag for each guest when it was time to go home. There was a piñata, too, a big one shaped like Bart Simpson.

Most of the grownups there chose not to play pin-the-tail-on-the-donkey or tag or hide-and-seek, and instead stayed in the kitchen, far from the piñata, sipping coffee and chatting nervously about What This World Is Coming To. These were the days, remember, when CNN was still showing the 767-hits-tower footage on a five minute rotation, the days when you couldn't turn on the TV without seeing fireballs erupting and skyscrapers collapsing and panicked office workers jumping to their deaths. You remember the fear, the horror, the sick panic of the teens of September. You do, don't you?

As the mood grew darker in the kitchen, one of the party guests wandered in, bored of hide-and-seek and curious what everybody was talking about.

"Oh," the little interloper guessed, "all those people in New York who got sick."

5   Around the kitchen, the grownups nodded wistfully.

"I've been wondering about something about that," the four-year-old continued. "When the bad men stole those airplanes, where was Batman?"

The little kids in your own life, be they your siblings or your children or the nephews and nieces of your friends' friends, were all talking a lot about Batman last autumn, wondering where he and Spider-Man and the Flash were when the terrorists struck, wondering why the men in tights have forsaken us. Maybe you've wondered the same thing.

I think I have the answer. Batman was unavailable to the panicked citizens of NY on 9/11, was MIA in that hour of great need, because he is private property. Because he is private property and his owners are keeping him on a Los Angeles soundstage, where he is filming TV commercials for the OnStar concierge service, available on selected General Motors cars and other fine automobiles.

This essay is not about terrorism. It is not about little kids who say the darndest things. Neither is it terribly concerned with why a man in a cape and a rubber mask with pointy ears failed to save the day on September 11. So what is the point? Here is a convenient thesis statement for you: The discoveries, eureka-moments, fables, characters, songs and jokes that form the only common ground we share as citizens—the set of ideas collectively known as "The West"—are now the property of a few multinational corporations. Our entire culture has fallen into private hands, taking with it our right to tell our stories, our right to keep our personal lives personal, even our right to heal our sick. THIS SUCKS. THIS IS VERY BAD.

10   It need not be the end, however. Not if we as citizens, as Westerners, as participants in our own culture, can find the will and the resolve to reclaim what is ours.

Ours is a culture steeped in the art of make-believe. From the moment kids are old enough to watch the Teletubbies, they spend their waking hours soaking in a hot bath of wonder and whimsy, of magical stories full of amazing things that never happen in real life. We teach children to believe in Santa Claus and the Easter Bunny and Jack Frost and Monsieur Lactose (who causes tooth decay), and they do believe, and their excited musings and speculations about what really goes on at the North

Pole delight us endlessly. A few years later, with a little more experience and a little more wisdom, the kiddies toss out make-believe about Santa and the Tooth Fairy and M. Lactose as "babyish."

But here is what these older, wiser kiddies do not toss out: Batman, Pokémon, Barbie, *Rugrats, Crash Bandicoot, The Lion King,* "It's Not Easy Being Green," "C is for Cookie," *The Powerpuff Girls, Sailor Moon,* Mario, Hello Kitty, *Metal Gear Solid, Enterprise, Buffy, Dawson, Felicity, Smallville,* "D'oh," Zoom Zoom, "Oh, for God's sake, Niles!" Master of Puppets Master Of The House Master Of My Domain, Etc.

This is not a bad thing all by itself, this life-long attachment to the Neighbourhood of Make-Believe, and it is not a bad thing because it is making somebody rich. It is a bad thing because it means most of the thoughts passing through your head at any given moment are private property, subject to the whims and desires and litigious controls of the companies that own them.

During the big Harry Potter media pigout late last year, you probably heard a lot about the battle over internet domain names between Harry's pubescent fans and the meanies at Warner Bros. In case you didn't, here's how it went:

1. Fans of the books start Potter fan sites.
2. WB buys Potter film/merchandise rights.
3. WB begins aggressive lawyerly campaign to take possession of domain names with connections to Potter—most notably fifteen-year-old Claire Field's harrypotterguide.co.uk.
4. Field and her father raise media stink.
5. Sensing potential P.R. nightmare à la McLibel, WB backs off, saying it will leave noncommercial fan sites alone—for now.

15 Ah, a victory for little people the world over, right? Sure, provided you only cared about preserving your ability to praise somebody else's intellectual property on your website, and also provided you never, ever hoped to earn a living on the strength of those efforts.

No matter what you make of boys who fly on broomsticks, Harry Potter is a big big part of early twenty-first-century culture, a part too large for any but the most dogged of us to avoid. What Claire Field and all the other Pottersite proprietors were doing was merely what kids and grownups have been doing for as long as people have been telling stories: They were taking a tale that spoke to them, holding it close and making it their own.

A little historical context here: The Brothers Grimm did just that with Rapunzel and Snow White and Rumpelstiltskin and earned a hearty living at it. King James I did that when he decreed that the current crop of English bibles was a little lacking and it was time for a new edition. Ditto for the children who kept "Ring Around the Rosie" alive since the Plague. Robin Hood, Punch and Judy, Jesus Christ of Nazareth—they and many thousands of others have all had their stories edited and retold and re-tooled as their host culture evolved and changed over the years. That was the prerogative of the people who lived surrounded by those ideas, who went to sleep singing those songs. Well, we still live surrounded by ideas and we still go to sleep singing songs, but all those ideas and songs belong to companies with Big Expensive Lawyers.

The Potter flap ended because some of those Big Expensive Lawyers threw some kids a bone, not because anybody recognized the kids' right to play in their own sandbox. The distinction is important.

When napster finally went dark last summer, hardly anybody in the music industry did a victory dance. Oh, the famous internet song-trading service had finally been brought to heel, and the Ricky Martin MP3s were no longer flowing the way they once had, but the music still wanted to be free. On the Gnutella network, through spiffy new applications like BearShare and LimeWire, on a new service from Holland called KaZaA, on Morpheus and URLBlaze and OpenNap, people were shaking their bon bons like never before.

20 A lot of smartypants media types thought this was hilarious, that the public was showing Lars Ulrich and the RIAA who was boss, and that from now on we'd all make as many copies of "Enter Sandman" as we frickin' pleased, thank you very much. The war for free tunes was not over, however, and it is still not over today. As experiments with copy-protected CDs blossom and wilt, the legal resolve of the record companies and the music publishers hardens with every report of falling sales and every retail bankruptcy.

That legal resolve is now downright steely, as in gigantic, coconut-sized steel balls. Witness the Recording Industry Association of America's recent contribution to the War On Terrorism—a proposed amendment to the USA Act that would allow copyright holders to hack into private computers and delete illicit tunes and videos and pictures. The version that got the President's signature was blissfully free of that particular dingleberry, but the RIAA is unbowed, vowing to seek similar authority as legislative opportunities present themselves.

What are we really talking about here? We are talking about an industry, or a collection of industries, that produces and sells something called content. Here are some examples of content:

1. *Seinfeld*
2. Windows XP
3. *Men Are From Mars, Women Are From Venus*
4. *Star Wars Episode II: Attack of the Clones*
5. *"Sweet Caroline,"* by Neil Diamond

In other words, songs, movies, TV shows, software and all that. These are products that by their very nature are well suited to digital production and distribution. They may be sold in physical form (on CDs or DVDs or what have you), but at heart they are merely patterns of information, easily copied from one medium to another and one hard drive to another.

Napster, and by extension the Internet itself, so frightened the people who owned all this content because it threatened to leave them without a way to make their customers actually, you know, pay for the products they watched and listened to. Everybody, even those with MP3 collections numbering in the six-digit range, can understand that fear. There are billions and billions of dollars at stake, and all the aforementioned smartypants media blather notwithstanding, copyright owners are not going to say, "OK downloaders, you win; the new Slipknot record's on us."

25   Here is what they're going to say instead: "You. Downloader. We see you have made yourself a copy of the new Slipknot record. Give us money now or we will erase it." They will say this because they will have the ability to say it, because they will find a way to protect their valuable assets from freeloaders.

If song-swapping cannot be stopped at the server level or the network level, it will be stopped by snooping. (What's that you got there on your hard drive, fella? You paid for that?) It will be stopped by shoot-first-ask-questions-later litigation. It will be stopped by the creeping development of new pay-for-play media. It will be stopped by networked hardware that never plays a song or a movie without first getting clearance from a permission server. It will be stopped because money talks, because nobody with pockets that deep facing threats that great ever says "Uncle." It will be stopped because intellectual property is the real estate of the twenty-first century.

What does this mean for you? Consider how much of your life, your worktime and your playtime involves interacting with IP products, with software and media and information and entertainment. Now consider what it would mean to have your every move through that digital swamp tracked and recorded, all in the name of enforcing copyright. It would mean the Viacoms and the Disneys and the News Corporations of the very near future would own great volumes of information about your comings and goings, enormous databases full of your private life.

This is not a life anyone in the Western world can opt out of, remember. Choosing to avoid computers, music, television or movies brands you a crank, an eccentric. Avoiding all of them and still participating in society at large is completely out of the question.

On october 16, 2001, the canadian government placed an order for $1.5 million of fluoroquinolone antibiotic with Apotex, a drug manufacturer specializing in generic equivalents of brand-name medications. Exactly what happened in the days before and after that order was placed is still the subject of dispute, but here is an approximation:

1. Anthrax infects several people in the U.S. Panic ensues.
2. Canadian government officials approach Bayer AG (Cipro patent-holder) for assurances that there will be enough fluoroquinolone-class antibiotic to go around.
3. Bayer allegedly cannot supply the number of tablets requested.

4. Canadian government officials approach Apotex, placing an order for a generic Cipro-equivalent, in knowing violation of the Bayer patent.
5. Bayer cries foul.
6. Public dustup ensues, with much disagreement over who offered how many pills when. Opposition makes hay with Health Canada's decision to break law of the land.
7. Deal reached. Bayer agrees to make its own pills available with forty-eight hours notice, and everyone agrees that if Bayer cannot deliver, the Apotex ones will stop the gap. Agreed-upon cost: about $1.30 per tablet, a discount over the regular price.
8. The media finds something else to pay attention to. Nobody mentions that generic Cipro is available in Colombia and Guatemala for about five cents a pill.

30 Cipro, which is generically known as ciprofloxacin, is protected by U.S. patent #4,670,444. What this means is that for the next couple of years (protection expires in 2003 in the U.S., 2004 in Canada), Bayer—along with any licensees it chooses to designate—has a monopoly on this now-famous antibiotic. Nobody else is allowed to run the string of chemical reactions described in the patent document, nobody else is allowed to manufacture products incorporating that chemistry, and certainly nobody else is allowed to sell any of it. Bayer owns the idea itself, the information, the A-leads-to-B-leads-to-C instruction set.

And even when panic is at an all-time high, even when innocent letter carriers are dying of hemorrhagic lung failure and nobody knows how big the whole deal could get, the company can still insist in public discourse that its patent will not be frickin' violated, thank you very much, and no one on the board of directors will lose a moment's sleep worrying about armed revolution.

Last October, a private entity's right to own ideas went head-to-head with a nation's right to use an idea to save its citizens from death by melting lung tissue. Guess which one prevailed?

In her neo-prog classic *no logo*, naomi klein wrote that "when we try to communicate with each other by using the language of brands and logos, we run the very real risk of getting sued." True enough. But the ugly truth, the one we really need to talk about, is that everyone who lives in the West does that all day every day. We can't communicate any other way.

Here, in keeping with the spirit of this essay, is an unauthorized dance remix of a few paragraphs from pages 177–8 of the hardcover version of *No Logo*:

Many alleged violators of copyright are not trying to sell a comparable good or pass themselves off as the real thing. When I write a hot, dirty, porn story featuring Captain Kirk . . . with Mr. Spock . . . and post it on my website, I am not pretending to be Paramount Pictures, UPN, the estate of Gene Roddenberry or anybody but myself.

As branding becomes more expansionist, however, a competitor is anyone doing anything remotely related, because anything remotely related has the potential to be a spin-off at some point in the synergistic future. It also has the potential to seep into the public domain, where ordinary citizens will swap it and reshape it and republish and retell it. Lord knows, if enough people find themselves hollering and writing "Hello, Newman!" and "D'oh!" and "Motion to suppress!" at each other without legal interference, we're going to get the idea that it's generally OK for us plebes to talk to each other in our own mother tongue, the language of the media culture into which we were born.

And then just imagine what might happen: Mom 'n' Pop costume stores could stitch Batman Halloween capes without seeking or receiving the blessing of DC comics. Teachers could ask their students to write stories about Ash Ketchum and Team Rocket and Pikachu, could offer Pokémon Trainer badges for achievement prizes, could legitimately engage children in the lively, subtle, endlessly nuanced culture they live in. Competing publishers could produce mildly or wildly different editions of the same books, could bring familiar characters to unfamiliar situations and vice versa.

Artists will always make art by reconfiguring our shared cultural languages and references, but as those shared experiences shift from firsthand to mediated, a new set of issues raises serious questions about out-of-date definitions of freedom of expression in a branded culture. But artists are just the tip of it.

Yes, the underlying message of copyright bullying is that culture is something that happens to you, something you buy at the Virgin Megastore or rent at Blockbuster. But culture is more than that, all the efforts of armies of brand managers notwithstanding. Culture may begin as something you buy at the Virgin Megastore or rent at Blockbuster, but it only flowers into its true form when people turn those movies and tunes into conversations and ideas and personal, life-changing moments.

35 OK, enough already. This is not just about fancypants loft-dwellers making art about how media-soaked our society is. This is about our right to communicate with each other as citizens in the language we know best. It is about being able to say a ditzy pal is "being totally Phoebe," and know the choice of words is legitimate. It is about being able to call Bill Clinton "the teflon President" without a capital "T," about being able to say "velcro" without adding "brand fastener." It is about the important weight of trivial turns of phrase, about stories and jokes and ideas. It is about exactly the same things that unite people and ignite struggles the world over.

All our archetypes are private property. We should make them public again.

Here, then, is a manifestic closing for you.

A powerful movement is building even now, of people uniting to oppose the bullying thuggery of multinational corporations and their brands. This is generally a pretty good idea, as sweatshops are bad and so is environmental degradation and collusion with evil anti-democratic governments. Ugly corporate behaviour should be exposed and the people responsible should be shamed and fined and jailed.

But consider the real source of corporate power, the insidious force that allows and empowers all that ugly behaviour. It is copyright and trademark and patent. It is intellectual property. It is the exclusive right to emblazon a swoosh on a shoe, the exclusive right to call a sandwich a "Big Mac," the exclusive right to tell stories about the characters we care about, the exclusive right to produce certain kinds of fluoroquinolone-class antibiotics.

40 If anyone could open a restaurant and put up a big sign with golden arches on it and serve two-all-beef-patties-special-sauce-lettuce-cheese-pickles-onions-on-a-sesame-seed-bun, how much longer do you suppose there would still be a McDonald's Corporation to get up to no good around the globe?

If anyone with a sewing machine could put the Tommy Hilfiger blue-red-white icon on a shirt, how much longer do you suppose the original Hilfiger would be around to outsource his production to Southeast Asia?

If anyone could turn Batman into a hero or a rogue or a terrorist, if anyone could rewrite the story of his secret origin, if anyone could don the cape and the cowl, how much longer would our culture remain in private hands?

Let's not be any more naïve than we have been already. Copyright will not go away in our lifetime. Neither will trademarks and neither will patents. But consider this: As new technologies undermine the business models of the big intellectual property owners, those big intellectual property owners are seeking new ways to defend and enlarge their turf, and *this is not a done deal.* New and odious bits of IP statute and regulation are showing up in our legislatures and our Parliaments all the time, but they can be stopped, the same way anything else ugly and stupid can be stopped.

45 They can be stopped by vigorous and sensible public debate, by people who know their culture is under seige and who are committed to helping their fellow citizens understand. This is not pretty or simple, but making law and influencing public policy have never been pretty or simple. Our culture is private because the law has allowed it to become so, and the law can begin to swing the pendulum back, but making it so will require a delicate and persistent effort in the backrooms, in the courts, and in the streets.

They can be stopped by large and small acts of civil disobedience, by the willful and deliberate and unauthorized use of those precious trademarks in media large and small—on your school notebook, on your website, on your TV show. Eventually, they'll lose their power, becoming as generic and empty and valueless as "Kleenex" and "Aspirin" and "Thermos" have become.

They can be stopped by encouraging and supporting those public officials who understand something is wrong. On that score, the Cipro affair showed much promise, inasmuch as it was about a government department screwing up the nerve, just for a moment, to say to hell with your precious property rights.

They can be stopped if we dare to stop them, if we dare to take our archetypes and our icons and our superheroes and make them our own once more.

Batman *can* save the day, really he can, if only we have the courage to write that story.

So go ahead.

50 Just do it.

Because you're worth it.

Zoom zoom.

Reflect & Write

❏ Why does Dawson start his article with a birthday party, 9/11, and Batman? Was this an effective choice? Why or why not? How did his decision to start the essay this way affect the way in which he presented his argument? Did this make his argument stronger or weaker? Why?

❏ How would you characterize Dawson's voice in this article? Find at least three specific moments in the article where he establishes this voice through word choice, structure, or tone. How does the type of ethos he establishes as an author affect the way in which you receive his argument?

❏ Consider the examples that Dawson uses in this article: Harry Potter, Napster, Apotex. Why do you think that he selected these examples? How did he anticipate they would render his argument more convincing? Was he correct?

❏ What was your reaction to reading Dawson's "unauthorized dance remix" of the paragraphs from Naomi Klein's *No Logo*? Did the fact that it was a remix detract from its persuasiveness as a piece of evidence? Did Dawson's experimentation with the form he was discussing increase his overall persuasiveness? Explore the implications of this particular "quotation."

❏ Look at the three "If anyone" examples toward the end of the article. Why are these important questions to ask at this point in the essay?

❏ Examine the final sentences of the article. How do they work in conjunction with the rest of the argument? Do they provide an effective capstone to the discussion? Why or why not?

❏ **Write:** Draft an analysis of Dawson's writing style.

PERSPECTIVES ON THE ISSUE

1. Some critics have likened the remixing of cultural texts to a return to something more like oral or folktale tradition, where stories were continually shared, adopted, and transformed by multiple tellers. Do you agree with this assessment? If so, why do you think this return to a more oral-based tradition is so threatening to so many people? Write a blog entry in which you work through this assertion and its ramifications for contemporary culture.

2. Search the Web for a fansite or visit a bookstore to find a fan magazine devoted to a particular film or TV show (for instance, *LOST, Battlestar Gallactica, Star Trek, Buffy the Vampire Slayer,* or *Star Wars*). Examine one piece of fan fiction that generates its narrative from the characters and/or setting of the original. Now write a piece of analysis in which you argue for the role of fan-produced texts in the spread—or the crippling—of American popular culture.

FROM WRITING TO RESEARCH

1. Look up the original paragraphs from Naomi Klein that Bret Dawson remixed in "The Privatization of Our Culture" and compare the two. Now write an analysis about the extent of the remixing, its impact on Klein's argument, and your evaluation on how such "remixes" should be used in articles and formal arguments.

2. Research other contemporary remixes of the Uncle Sam poster (Figure 4.4). How has this image been used over the years to reflect changes in culture? What do you learn about Kairos from studying these examples? Now research the poster in your library. When was it first published and reprinted? How do contemporary remixes complicate this cultural heritage? Has Uncle Sam become an international figure? How so or how not? Compose your argument based on research. Use the guidelines in Chapters 5–6 to help you.

CHAPTER 13

Gaming Culture

A ten-year-old boy battles imperial storm troopers in *Lego Star Wars II*. A second-grade girl gives Barbie a French manicure in *Barbie Fashion Designer*. A summer intern plays a quick game of sudoku on his laptop during his lunchbreak. A group of high school friends banter while playing Capture the Flag in *Halo 2*. A college student logs in to join fellow guild members across the country to complete a quest in *World of Warcraft*. Each is participating in modern gaming culture; each demonstrates the way that video games have expanded their audience to reach beyond the arcade, into elementary schools, onto university campuses and beyond.

But with the protean reach of video games—from Gameboy to PlayStation 3 to computer screen—comes questions about their social implications. Is the gaming world, as games like the *Sims 2* suggest (see Figure 13.1), just a simulation, a practice run for reality? What is the relationship between gameplay and lived experience? How do computer games alternately undermine and reinforce gender stereotypes, both on screen and off? What relationship do video games centered on aggression have to real-life acts of violence? And, more broadly, to what degree do video games provide platforms for education, amusement, and social interaction and to what extent do they promote social isolation and political apathy?

FIGURE 13.1 One user's screen capture shows the diversity of characters she created playing *The Sims 2* game.

In this chapter, we will explore some of these issues in relation to gaming culture. In "Gender Games," we will investigate the role of gender politics in the design and play of computer games, looking at both the female avatars, like the Sims women in Figure 13.1, who often seem to be pixilated visions of male fantasy, as well as the female players and designers struggling to find their niche in an industry still dominated by men. In "Violence and Video Games," we'll turn our attention to games like *Doom 3, Grand Theft Auto,* and *Full Spectrum Warrior*—games that come under frequent attack for their violent content.

We'll engage a range of views, from critics that argue that violent gaming provides a needed outlet for human aggression, to those who contend that simulated violence leads to real violence, to those who argue for the purposeful use of such gaming to prepare young adults for military service. Finally, in "Games with an Agenda," we'll focus on one of the most recent and innovative genres of computer games: games designed deliberately to produce an argument. We'll look at advergames (games advertising a product), campaign games (games designed to argue a political candidate's position), and even online activism, investigating the extent to which gameplay can operate as an innovative and effective mode of persuasion.

GENDER GAMES

FIGURE 13.2 The highly gendered persona of Lara Croft from *Tomb Raider: Legend* combines "ideal beauty" and sexuality with aggressive gun wielding.

From the curvaceous daring of Lara Croft in Figure 13.2 to the perfect pixilation of the contestants in the Miss Digital World pageant, the female presence on the computer screen is hard to miss. With advances in graphics technology and screen resolution, the female avatar appears as a figure of ideal beauty, and ironically, as less real than ever before. Her presence raises a crucial question: How are women represented as characters in video games?

Meanwhile, on the other side of the screen, we find the female player and producer of contemporary computer games, and a new set of questions arise about gender and video games: How do the women on the screen compare with the women who play the games? What role can women have in changing the way games are designed, produced, marketed, and played? Is there a market for games tailored specifically toward women? What qualities should those games contain? Or should gender be factored out of the equation in game design? These are questions debated constantly among cultural critics, gamers, and feminists alike.

The texts that follow offer a variety of viewpoints on this difficult issue: from Sheri Graner Ray, who takes the computer industry to task for not considering the female gamer market, to Richard Cobbett, who satirically questions the very way we analyze and write about the subject of girls and video games. In keeping with this rich body of perspectives, this chapter is designed not to argue for one position on this issue, but instead to open multiple windows into the complicated dialogues taking place alongside these gendered games.

Reflect & Write

❏ Analyze the rhetorical qualities of Figure 13.2. What aspects denote gender identity? What appeals are at work?

❏ What audience do you think is targeted by the image in Figure 13.2? Support your argument with evidence from your analysis of the image.

❏ **Write:** What ideas do you have about gender games now, before reading the essays in this chapter? Write up your assumptions about gamers and game design, about representations of women onscreen and the significance of those representations. Share your essay with the class.

■ **Suneel Ratan** *has contributed articles to* Fortune *and* Time *magazines and currently writes about video games for* Wired News. *He also has been involved in the online operations at Channel One and Electronic Arts. This article first appeared in* Wired News *on July 15, 2003.*

Game Makers Aren't Chasing Women

Suneel Ratan

A visit this past Saturday afternoon to a busy video-game store in San Francisco was a snapshot of a gaming industry that continues to be run by post-adolescent males for post-adolescent males.

Of the 25 or so people in *Electronics Boutique,* six were women. Three of them looked bored—they were accompanying their gamer boyfriends. Two Korean-American girls were in the store on their own, but they were buying a copy of *Warcraft III: The Frozen Throne* for a male relative. And the last woman? She was working one of the cash registers.

The IDS numbers don't offer a breakdown between console and PC, and don't account for online games. The group's figures do show that women are primarily playing card, board and puzzle games. Female console game players—who are still regarded as a small piece of the overall console market—do seem to be trying their hands at driving, role-playing and action games.

What both studies reinforce is that women generally are not flocking to the games that are the gaming industry's current bread and butter. Those range from sports games like those from industry-leading Electronic Arts to violent first-person shooters such as Microsoft's *Halo,* id

Software's *Doom* and *Quake* series, and *Half-Life* from developer Valve Software.

Card, board and puzzle games are typically played for free over the Internet or often represent low-priced console and PC titles.

Analysts cited a few key reasons why the industry doesn't seem to be exactly rushing to make bigger, better games that have more appeal to women.

One is that the industry has become risk-averse as game development budgets climb. It increasingly relies on tried-and-true formulas and movie licenses.

Another is that designers simply haven't figured out how to design more games with crossover appeal. Perhaps that's because not enough designers are women—they are only slowly penetrating production and development teams in the industry.

"Who writes the checks?" asked Kelly Verchere, a former assistant producer with EA in Vancouver, British Columbia. "It's a guy who says, 'These sports games are doing really well, so let's make more of those.' You don't have women writing the checks or making the games. I really don't think you're going to see amazing games for women for another 10 years."

10   IDSA President Douglas Lowenstein said the fact that women are playing card, board and puzzle games shouldn't be discounted, as they are an important part of the gaming universe.

Still, he acknowledged, "This industry is nowhere near fully exploiting its potential to deliver content that appeals to girls and women. We're doing more of that than in the past, but we're still scratching the surface."

Certainly, the topic of women and gaming isn't new—even if there seems to be a renewed frankness about the need to adjust designs to reach both genders and to open up the industry to women producers, developers and executives.

Laurel's Purple Moon, which was founded and folded in the late 1990s, was part of a movement toward "pink games"—titles and activities aimed specifically at young girls and women. Now the thinking seems to be geared toward getting the industry to make more games like the King's *Quest* series and *The Sims* that both genders like to play.

"I'm not a big fan of pink games," said T.L. Taylor, an assistant communications professor at North Carolina State University who has done extensive research on women and gaming. "Making games in which you get women to do 'women things' isn't a very successful strategy. Women enjoy combat in ways that go beyond the stereotypical notion that women are social and men like to fight."

15   Some of Taylor's most recent research involves examining women in the context of massively multiplayer online role-playing games such as Sony's *EverQuest* and EA's *Ultima Online*. She notes that women make up an estimated 20 to 30 percent of the players of such games, "despite the fact that (they have) not been designed with them in mind, and in fact may at times actively disenfranchise some of them."

One of the key ways such games can exclude women is in the "hyper-sexualized" avatar choices they are offered, with distended Lara Croft-like physiques, Taylor said. The proportion of women playing such games would likely increase if they were given more freedom to choose the way in which they're electronically represented.

"If you talk to women who are EverQuest players, they hate their avatar choices," Taylor said. "It's like they have to wear chain-mail bikinis."

Other analysts said that key steps for reaching women include having more female characters, taking a keen look at interfaces to ensure accessibility, and marketing games that appeal to women in places they might see them. That might mean selling games in bookstores instead of just CompUSA or the game section of Wal-Mart.

What blocks those simple changes from being incorporated into industry practice is the game industry's macho culture, which makes it difficult for women to break into the production and development side of the business, let alone survive and thrive in it.

20   EA's Verchere, for instance, noted that she was one of two or three women at any given time on a development team of 25.

"Many people were fine about it—'great, fine, you're a woman,'" Verchere said. "But there were others who tried to trip you up and would say, 'How much do you know about games?' I'm not a tomboy gamer, and I wasn't going to defend the number of hours I spent playing Quake."

A contrasting view came from Caroline Trujillo, a producer and designer at Vivendi Universal Games who is currently working on the *Spyro* franchise. The game industry may be dominated by men, she said—but she doesn't believe things would be much different if there were an equal number of men and women in production and development.

"The reality is that boys do play games more than girls do and, at some point, boys are buying more games than girls are," Trujillo said. "It's not that we're failing to tap into that audience because there aren't enough women on our end. It's just the nature of the industry and the product we're developing. It's like saying men would buy more makeup if more men were working in that industry."

Trujillo's comments notwithstanding, slow change may be in the works. Many of those interviewed for this story noted that more women attended this year's Game Developers Conference than ever before. Indeed, the International Game Developers Association has started a Women in Game Development committee that is examining questions such as hiring and employment.

25   Still, Laurel isn't particularly optimistic—and said the industry largely remains caught in a loop in which male gamers are making games for people like themselves, despite evidence that companies could reap huge rewards by expanding their audience. That goes beyond women to include men who don't fit the gamer archetype or tastes.

"The game business persists in serving a niche market, and the products being produced are only appealing to a niche market," Laurel said. "It's a self-fulfilling loop."

Reflect & Write

❏ According to this author, why aren't game-makers chasing women? What factors are contributing to this situation?

❏ Why does Ratan begin his article with the scene in the store? How does this hook the reader into his argument?

❏ Suneel Ratan interviewed several different people for this piece. List the different people interviewed and evaluate why he chose them and what they contribute to his article. If you had to choose one additional person or type of person to interview for this article, who would it be?

❏ **Write:** Ratan mentions several reasons that contribute to the scarcity of women gamers. Choose the one that seems most persuasive or controversial to you and write a blog entry in which you explore your opinion on that subject.

■ **Sheri Graner Ray** *is an award-winning game designer who began her career working on the* Ultima *game series. In 2004, she was listed by the* Hollywood Reporter *as one of the Top 100 Most Influential Women in the Computer Game Industry. This selection is the final chapter of her 2003 book,* Gender Inclusive Game Design: Expanding the Market, *an important contribution to the ongoing discussion about women's role in the gaming industry.*

But What If the Player Is Female?

Sheri Graner Ray

When Barbie Fashion Designer (Mattel) showed up on the retail computer game shelves in 1996, it blew away the largest misconception in the game development industry—that girls don't play computer games. The financial success of Barbie® titles soon had publishers scrambling to develop something that would capture a piece of this exciting, new, and lucrative market.

Unfortunately, this did not result in better-designed games or an honest evaluation of what females wanted in computer entertainment. With the exception of a few intrepid developers, it resulted in an industry that simply tried to recreate the Barbie title numbers by cloning these games again and again. Thus, the girls' market came to be defined not so much as a market, but as a genre of shopping, make-up, and fashion games for girls ages 6–10—a market which was then quickly saturated.

When these titles didn't succeed like their progenitor, the industry decided the market was not as lucrative as they thought. So they went back to developing titles for the traditional market of males, ages 13–25.

What the industry overlooks is that this short-sightedness has left a huge hole in the market. Girls that play Barbie games do grow up. With no titles for them to graduate to, they simply spend their money elsewhere. It doesn't have to be this way.

5 By looking at the differences in male and female entertainment criteria, and applying this information to the titles the industry is developing, it is possible to remove the barriers that prevent the female market from accessing those titles. And it is possible to do this without putting Doom into a pink box or making games about fuzzy kittens.

It can be done by looking at some of the basic foundations of game design and recognizing that males and females may deal with game basics in very different ways. From the first contact with a title, their differences in approach can be seen.

The avatar is the first thing a player comes in contact with, usually on the package cover. How the players experience the game through their avatars can be greatly enhanced with an understanding of the importance of avatar presentation and representation. When the female avatar is hypersexualized, it is highly likely the female player won't even consider the title. This 'eye candy' may be pleasing for male players, but they are a barrier for female players.

Also, providing avatars that are gender stereotyped in their roles in the game, or are limited in their scope, serves to push away the female audience. Likewise, if designers know that sexually-oriented humor that contains 'put-downs' of females will cause female players to walk away, they can avoid inadvertently adding content that will drive away a sizeable portion of their sales audience.

Differences in learning styles can affect whether or not a player actually plays the game when they first come in contact with the tutorial and, if it is a demo, whether the player actually buys it. Females want a modeling style of learning, whereas males prefer a more explorative method. If designers keep this in mind, they can work to develop tutorial styles that will best benefit both genders and make game tutorials seamless and natural for all players; the player is encouraged to enter the game, and their level of enjoyment is increased (Gottfried 86).

10 Even the basic concept of the game can be a barrier for some players. The concept of conflict usually serves as the basic premise for any game title. If it is apparent from the game description that the resolution of the conflict is only going to be handled in the traditionally male manner—that is, a confrontational resolution—then this will dissuade those players that would normally choose other resolution styles, such as negotiation or compromise. With the knowledge of how each gender handles conflict, designers can build resolutions into their games that complement both styles and appeal to both audiences.

The stimuli designers use to capture their audience and keep their attention can have an effect on which markets find the title engrossing as well.

Males are physically stimulated by visual input. Females may enjoy visual stimulus, however, they do not have a physical response to it. Their response comes from emotional or tactile input. So games that rely on fast movement and visual special effects may not capture the female market as well as they do the male market. By understanding this difference, designers can balance the stimuli they are using for their game and attract and keep a greater percentage of their players.

When the players have actually entered the game, how they are rewarded for their successes can either reinforce a positive game experience or it can demotivate the players. While males prefer punishment for error in a game, females prefer forgiveness. Punishment for errors is the classic method by which games are resolved. The player is given a limited number of 'lives' and has only so many 'chances' to succeed. If they do not succeed, then they are usually returned to the beginning of the level, and all progress on that level is lost.

Forgiveness for error means the loss is not permanent. Instead, it is a temporary loss, or progress toward the final goal is slowed; but it can be regained quickly, normal gameplay resumed, progress can be continued. There is no 'dying' and starting over.

Often for females, the reward of 'winning' or achieving a high level is simply not enough reason to play a game. They want to find a solution that is mutually beneficial and socially significant. They want to accomplish something, rather than 'win.' By understanding this, designers can adapt their reward system and their victory conditions to better accommodate different player expectations.

15   Even how males and females use computers is basically very different. Males wish to conquer the machine. They want to use it as an expression of physical power. Females want to work with the machine. They want to use it to expand their communications powers. However, because of the limited amount of cross-gender entertainment software, females have come to view computers not so much as an entertainment medium, but as a communications and productivity tool instead (Turkle 98).

Why is it important for females to play games? There are two reasons. One reason is ideological, and the other is economic.

Ideologically, it is vitally important that girls play and enjoy computer games because it increases their comfort level with technology, and this is essential for them to maintain economic parity with males in today's society. If girls are not allowed to have fun with technology today, we cannot expect them to excel with technology tomorrow.

However, the more economic reason is that the game industry must expand to other markets if it wishes to sustain growth. There are only so many males age 13–25 in the world at any given time. If no other audiences are farmed, then the game industry will outgrow its market, resulting in loss of revenue and ultimately a contraction of the industry. Add to that the fact that females control an ever-growing percentage of the disposable income, then it makes sense to appeal to them if this industry wants 'a piece of the action.' However, to do this, designers must be willing to look at play patterns and models that are not necessarily their own. It is going to take producers/publishers who are willing to diversify their workforces by making a concerted effort to seek out qualified female candidates. It also means that those women who are already in the industry must be willing to serve as role models and mentors for the women who want to break into the industry. And overall, it's going to take an industry that is willing to step back, take a look at their titles, and ask themselves, "But what if the player is female?"

References

Gottfried, Allen W. and Catherine Caldwell Brown, *Play Interactions, The Contribution of Play Materials and Parental Involvement to Children's Development,* Lexington Books, Mississippi, 1986.

Turkle, Sherry, "Computational Reticence; Why Women Fear the Intimate Machine," In C. Kramare (ed), *Technology and Women's Voices,* New York: Routledge & Kegan Paul.

Reflect & Write

❏ Does Ray make a persuasive argument? Why or why not?

❏ Some critics have suggested that she relies too heavily on generalization and stereotypes. Do you find this a valid criticism?

❏ Select some places in the argument where she might have added in more specific examples to be even more persuasive. What examples would you use?

❏ Ray is writing for a very specific audience here: game designers. How do you see this concern over audience reflected in the structure, tone, and execution of her argument? How does she make her argument matter to this audience?

❏ **Write:** Sheri Graner Ray provides some very specific advice for game developers about how to create games that appeal to girls. Building from her advice, work with a group to draft a proposal for a new game that would fulfill the need for games aimed at an adult female audience. In your proposal, include an overview of the gameplay and story, a description of the main characters, and mock up either an advertisement or a cover for your game. Present your proposal and other materials to the class.

■ *The* My Scene *characters are a spin-off of the Barbie line updated for today's modern girls. MyScene.com offers its users several gaming opportunities, including "Beauty Studio," where players give the* My Scene *girl of their choice a makeover; "Room Makeover," where players decorate their own ideal room; "Shopping Spree," where players take two My Scene friends shopping for clothes; and "Fashion Designer," where players chose fabrics and styles for a new wardrobe for one of the* My Scene *characters.*

Screenshots: *My Scene* Online Game

FIGURE 13.3 This screen capture from myscene.com features the Beauty Studio where users can give their characters a full makeover.

FIGURE 13.4 Two myscene.com characters try on clothes during a Shopping Spree.

Reflect & Write

❏ Look at the design of the *My Scene* Website as shown in these screen shots. How is it designed to appeal to girls? Think carefully about layout, imagery, color, style, arrangement, and tone. Do you think this is targeted more to young girls (under 10) or older girls (in their teens)? What elements lead you to this conclusion?

❏ Some people might suggest that it is important to analyze games aimed at younger audiences very carefully because they teach important lessons about life. Based on your observations of these screen shots, what lessons are these games teaching?

❏ **Write:** Visit the game section of the *My Scene* Website (http://myscene.everythinggirl.com/games) and play the games. Then write a short review for a parenting magazine in which you evaluate the site's appeal and appropriateness for young girls. As an alternative, write a review instead for a feminist magazine.

Bonnie Ruberg *is a creative writer who has published fiction in* Hobart Pulp, Word Riot, *and* Juked, *and who serves as editor-in-chief for the literary magazine* Verse Noire. *Ruberg is also an avid gamer and staff reporter for* Nintendo World Report, *a gaming news Website. This editorial appeared on Planet GameCube (now* Nintendo World Report) *on February 20, 2005.*

Games for Girls

Bonnie Ruberg

You've seen them in the stores. You've walked the aisles of your favorite gaming retailer and sighed, wondering, Why are these here? You've skimmed the wall of GBA boxes, searching for a new release, and noticed their brightly-colored presence among the normal, better titles. You've started to ignore them. You don't even consider them real games anymore. After all, they're just for kids. Or even worse, for girls.

Girl games. Where did they go wrong?

There's a plethora of bad girl games floating around right now. As far as Nintendo products are concerned, most of them are for the GBA. Take, for example, the Mary-Kate and Ashley line from Acclaim. *Girls Night Out* seems to have worked its way into the realm of acceptable mediocrity, but *Sweet 16*, which received a 45% review average on *IGN* says *Sweet 16* "arrives as a clear *Mario Party* clone with the Olsen twins license slapped on for good measure." Disney's *That's SO Raven* offers only more of the same: girly (sometimes insulting) objectives, awkward controls, and shallow gameplay. Top that all off with the fact that the game itself isn't even fun.

A few recent girl games have begun the upstream battle toward quality. A2M's *Lizzie McGuire 2: Lizzie Diaries,* the sequel to a stereotypically poor original, shows serious signs of improvement, including clear graphics and actually enjoyable mini-games. Stifled by extremely short play time, and the almost total lack of replay value, *Lizzie McGuire 2* still manages to have a leg up on the other titles in its genre. *Kim Possible 2,* another sequel from A2M, seems to even have legitimate, non-girl-game promise. IGN has named it their sleeper hit of the year. With more complicated gameplay and a strong plot, it hasn't just moved to the top of the girl game class, it's proved itself worthy of entering a different category all together.

5 Which brings up an important point about girl games: a really good girl game isn't a girl game anymore. It's just a game.

"Funny thing is" says IGN, "this deserving sleeper might actually find a second fanbase. You've got a platformer with polished design, tight control, plenty of replayability, and a hot gal in the lead role as the butt-kicking, high-flying, belly-shirt-sporting hero chick. Think Castlevania set in So-Cal, or Catwoman with some class. It's certainly a game that you gamer boys shouldn't be ashamed of picking up . . . if you think you can keep up with her."

But what exactly defines a girl game in the first place? Female characters? Girly missions? Slapdash designs? In my mind, a girl game is one that has been specifically created for and marketed to girls. The primary concern of those in charge of its production is not quality gaming, but picking up on sales from a profitable niche market. Not that every game publisher doesn't have money on the mind, but in the case of girl games, that desire for profit is rarely followed up by the healthy market competition that forces production teams to put out a worthwhile product in order to stay afloat. It's a widely accepted element of the industry: girl games suck.

Or, if it's unfair to say they outright "suck," it's obvious that they receive considerably less development care than other, non-girl titles. An overwhelming number of them, instead of deriving from original concepts, are based off of movies and television shows. Girls, the industry seems to be saying, don't need originality. They don't need nuanced gameplay, well-rendered graphics, or interesting sound. Girls don't want innovation; they want mini-games and flashy puzzles. Why waste time in development that will go unappreciated? Girls want what's girly. They want what sucks.

Who, exactly, are these girls? College students? Stay-at-home moms? Grandmothers in rockers cradling their GBAs? No, in the case of girl games, when the industry says "girls", the word is synonymous with "children" (an issue ridiculous enough to warrant an entirely different editorial). So maybe these games are justified in their over-simplicity because they are made for kids.

10   Maybe. But if little girls get crummy girls games, why don't little boys get crummy boy games? Sure there are other poor, but less "girly," TV and movie-based titles. But we don't call these boy games. We just call them bad.

What do young girls really want? Could it be the industry actually has female kids pegged with these (usually) at best luke-warm games? If it seems that way, it's only because girls aren't exposed to other types of gaming. They try out the things the media tells them they'll like. They watch other girls, ones just like themselves, enjoying these games in the ads on TV. They can't see themselves in *Halo 2* advertisements. Why would they? From all that they've been told, from what they've seen, girls don't play those sorts of games.

What about older girls, women—should they get their own games too? How many sales is the industry missing out on by not putting out equally shoddy titles for female adults? The only reason they haven't taken advantage of the opportunity like they have with girl games is that they think women wouldn't buy. Even designing crummy games would be waste of money. Women don't game. For now, and for the sake of holding back a swarm of bad "women's games," let's not tell them the truth.

And how much of a difference would it make if these games were good? If girl games got just as much time and attention in development as normal games, would they be morally ok? There's no answer to that question, because such an approach could never actually happen. Girl games are designed for "peripheral" gamers. They are, as such, peripheral games. If they were not, if they were good, as mentioned before, they would cease to be girl games. They might continue to be "girly," but they would not be girl games.

In the end, the idea of creating gender-specific games, whether for girls or for boys, is just demeaning. By putting out these titles, game makers are implying that girls can't, and don't want to, handle real games. Sometimes that might seem right, but only because it's an accepted (by both sexes) preconception, and not because it's innately true.

15   Many people, game publishers and female gamers alike, stand up for girls games, claiming they serve as a necessary entry-point for many girls into the world of gaming—a gateway to more legitimate games. But do the girls who play girl games really ever move on to better, more complicated titles? Is this gateway really a gateway, or is it more like a cul-de-sac?

In my opinion, playing girl games has none of the desired effects. That is, girls who play them do not continue to game. For plenty of consumers, girl games and their primary platform (the GBA) are separate from the rest of the gaming market. As noted on *Game Spot,* according to a recent Club Nintendo survey, 22 percent of Japanese DS owners are female. It's become acceptable, in fact somewhat normal, for girls to own handheld systems, but not consoles. The girls I know who are into gaming (and I mean actual, dedicated gamers) certainly did not come in through girl's games. In fact, the majority of girls I've met who used to or still do play girl games foster the expected dislike for normal gaming that already-established gamers find so frustrating.

What the industry needs to do, both to help out with issues of gender-equality and to make things more money, is to change the face of general, quality, non-gender-specific gaming. If little boys can like real games, so can little girls; it's just a question of perspective, marketing, and (please!) a little more equal representation in the games themselves. If reluctant, potential girl gamers need gateway games, then Nintendo should be pushing titles like *Animal Crossing* and *Pikmin,* quality games with some girl-attractive aspects. Don't start newbies out by showing them what's bad and sexist in gaming; show them the cool stuff. Then they'll be no more need for girl games, just good ones.

Reflect & Write

❏ Both Bonnie Ruberg and Sheri Graner Ray recognize the same problem: the lack of games that adult women want to play. However, the way they approach this problem is different. What is Ruberg's solution to this issue? Consider also Ruberg's audience. How does this audience influence the solution that she proposes?

❏ Compare the styles of Ruberg's and Ray's articles. How do they execute their argument differently? Is one more compelling than the other? Why?

❏ At one point in this editorial, Ruberg uses a series of rhetorical questions to advance her argument. Is this an effective strategy? What does it bring to the argument that more conventional expository discourse wouldn't?

❏ **Write:** Adopting the persona of Bonnie Ruberg, write a rebuttal to Sheri Graner Ray's article that uses direct quotes from Ray in its argument.

■ *These images, taken from two recent video games, offer an intriguing glimpse into the way women are portrayed in the growing genre of interactive media.*

Screen Shots: Female Avatars

FIGURE 13.6 Kurenai, an Asian female avatar, drops down from a rooftop in *Red Ninja: End of Honor.*

Source: Image courtesy of Vivendi Games, Inc. and is under license.

FIGURE 13.5 The half-vampire protagonist of the *Blood Rayne* combines sexuality with aggression and physical prowess.

Reflect & Write

❏ Look at the screen shots of these popular female avatars. Both of these characters, as well as Lara Croft (in Figure 13.2), are the main protagonists of their games. What similarities do you see between them?

❏ Consider how sexuality and power work in conjunction with one another in each image. How is stereotype reinforced and also subverted?

❏ In these games, the avatar's appearance has been crafted by the game designer. However, in some games, such as *The Sims,* the player has much more control in selecting the appearance of the characters. How does this issue of control inform the discussion about the appearance of these characters? Is one model of character selection preferable?

❏ The October 2004 issue of *Playboy* magazine featured several female avatars (including BloodRayne and Kurenai) in provocative poses. How does their inclusion in this magazine contribute to your understanding of the relationship between the design of these characters and real-life appraisals of female beauty?

❏ **Write:** Draft a letter from Lara Croft to *Playboy* magazine declining the offer to appear in their October 2004 spread featuring female avatars. Create an argument that engages some of the issues of gender, gaming, and identity that have been explored by the authors of the articles you have read in this chapter.

COLLABORATIVE CHALLENGE

In a small group, make a list of female game characters that you are familiar with. Put them into categories according to audience: Are they designed for men or for women? For adults or for children? How does their design reflect this attention to audience? For each one, determine what argument that character is making through her design or characterization. Make a poster that categorizes and synthesizes your analysis (using both words and images) and share that poster with the class.

■ **Zoe Flower's** *Girlspy column appears biweekly on Gamespy.com, a news site for the gaming community; she has a popular column on the* Official Playstation Magazine *(OPM); she co-produces with her friend Stephanie Drinnan an action series about female extreme sports athletes called "Hardcore Candy"; and she toured America in 2002 as "GamerGirl," in which role she did TV and radio spots to discuss issues related to the gaming community. This article, published January 1, 2005, in* OPM, *focuses on her area of specialty: girls and gaming.*

Getting the Girl: The Myths, Misconceptions, and Misdemeanors of Females in Games

Zoe Flower

It was 1996 when a little development house out of the U.K. finished work on a lush new adventure game featuring a brunette archeologist named Lara Croft. It was a defining moment for me as I watched her strut seductively across my screen and into the sex symbol status that would turn the gaming world on its head. Fast-forward eight years through the evolution of next-gen hardware, multimillion-dollar budgets, and massive acceptance of games in pop culture. Still, Lara Croft continues to personify an ongoing culture clash over gender, sexuality, empowerment, and objectification. It was while standing in my first-ever ladies' room line at E3 2004 as I pondered the Playboy bunnies, the return of Leisure Suit Larry, and the slew of buxom virtual ladies headlining each booth that I questioned whether the industry had evolved at all.

It might seem like a simple puzzle to solve: trying to understand why female representation in videogames—whether it's as characters, developers, or gamers—is important. But it seemed the more questions I asked, the more elusive the

answers became. And it wasn't long before my own stereotypes were called into question.

When I requested an interview to discuss Cyberlore's *Playboy: The Mansion,* I never even considered that the senior designer on the Sims-style project might be a woman—one pregnant with twins, in fact. As I expected, Brenda Brathwaite has a lot to say about females in today's games. But I can guarantee it's not what you might expect.

"If you're going to animate breasts, animate them properly," admonishes Brathwaite. "The breasts in the original *Dark Alliance* drove me nuts. If my breasts moved like that, I'd go to the doctor . . . or call an exorcist."

5   While this industry veteran shows a sense of humor and perspective concerning her work, there are many who won't find the idea of creating a *Playboy* magazine simulator funny. "I suspect that those who feel it's a gender controversy have probably not seen an issue of *Playboy* magazine. They have it stereotyped," suggests Brathwaite. "I find that *Playboy* is a celebration of women and goes out of its way to be respectful. On *Playboy: The*

Mansion, we were committed to making a good, tasteful game."

I got a similar response regarding Majesco's *BloodRayne;* Rayne, coincidentally, just appeared in *Playboy*'s "Sexiest Game Characters" spread. And here too, the product manager for the goth queen was herself female.

"If you don't have the gameplay to back up the character appeal, T&A will only get you so far," effuses Liz Buckley. "*BloodRayne* resonates very well with our target audience of males ages 17 to 34, but Rayne has a huge female following as well. I think that's attributable to her strength and attitude—it's definitely empowering to play as her."

So if it's all about personality, why bother with the heaving bosom and leather chaps? It turns out Rayne was an ugly duckling before her transformation to voluptuous vixen. "Initially, Rayne had a militant, dark gothic look. She was a brunette with tight buns in her hair and a very severe body line," explains Buckley. And I even found myself admitting I'd rather play the "extreme makeover" version of the vamp.

Maybe it's not a crime to sex up the leading ladies, particularly if they retain some character development. But what about Vivendi's upcoming *Red Ninja,* which claims to incorporate sexuality as a gameplay mechanic, allowing main character Kurenai to seduce unsuspecting guards?

10 "It's a challenging concept to attempt when body language and atmosphere are confined by things like polygon limits," admits Associate Producer Melissa Miller. "Early on, we conducted a focus test specifically with female gamers. They liked the concept of Kurenai but felt she was showing too much skin with the short kimono. Once we justified the need for some sexiness with the seduction mechanic, they bought into Kurenai completely and were really excited about playing her."

Producer Yozo Sakagami of Namco's *Death by Degrees,* featuring Tekken's Nina, expressed a similar design challenge when trying to achieve what his team calls "functional beauty in combat." It turns out that Nina's bikini and catsuit are more than just eye candy. "The outfit designs were based on ease of movement and variation in appearance," states Sakagami.

"Depending on whether an attack connects with bare or clothed skin, the resulting damage differs."

Right. And are female gamers buying into it? "We've received favorable reactions from women toward Nina in this game. We were surprised because these women saw in Nina the character image we had hoped to create but feared we hadn't attained. Intangible elements such as these can easily be obscured while developing a game."

With such a positive response to stereotypical female protagonists, I began to question whether it was possible to design a strong female character without the requisite augmented body and sexual references.

"These types of character designs are not necessary; it is an easy way out," argues Ubisoft's Tyrone Miller. "*Beyond Good & Evil* shows us that you can convey the same strength and likability in a female character without having to use blatant sex appeal."

15 Interestingly enough, *BG&E*'s protagonist Jade is the brainchild of game designer Michel Ancel (*Rayman, King Kong*). "Rumor has it that Ancel's wife actually served as the main inspiration and muse for Jade's look and personality," informs Miller. "Ancel wanted to create a realistic lead character with a persona that players could connect to and identify with. As you play the game, you really develop an attachment to her."

So with men designing approachable leading ladies of realistic proportions and women enthusing over the feminine aspects of *Playboy* and goth queens, I realized that the issue might have less to do with gender and more to do with how sexuality is perceived in today's games.

"It's wrong to single out female characters when their male counterparts are usually just as superficial," argues Amy Hennig, game director for Naughty Dog. "We seem to be at that 'naughty' stage, where some developers are testing the limits to see what they can get away with. Games aren't considered just toys anymore, but we haven't matured beyond juvenile titillation."

Karin Yamagiwa, 2D-texture lead for Sucker Punch (*Sly Cooper*) points out, "Sexuality can be powerful, but it depends on how it's used. Games like *Rumble Roses*...some of my female friends find them a bit offensive, while others find them hilarious. Is it for boys to ogle? Of course! But I also know plenty of men who are embarrassed by it."

Anna Kipnis, a programmer for Double Fine Studios, adds, "Games can have story elements and amazing gameplay that can appeal to people regardless of gender. I believe that is what game developers should strive for, and perhaps not enough do."

20   Aletheia Simonson of Sony CEA's product evaluation group agrees. "Games for women are there; the hurdle is getting a woman who has never played a videogame to try one. It will probably be some time before the game equivalent of the romantic comedy is a blockbuster hit," she explains.

Well, one developer seems to have combined gender equality with mass appeal. EA Maxis' *The Sims* franchise has laid claim to a whopping 50 percent female audience. And it's not as if this series is without its gender stereotypes and sex appeal. One look at *The Urbz: Sims in the City* reveals a prevalence of thong panties and revealing clothing. So just whom is this game meant for?

"Were we planning to entice the male? Well, it does make them look twice in the office!" jokes Virginia McArthur, lead producer on *The Urbz* Handheld. "But you will find when women play, they tend to choose the hip low-riders, as it really fits in with the culture of the location."

As for the secret of *The Sims'* success, McArthur answers confidently: "When we brought *The Urbz* to consoles, we realized that what keeps females interested in our products is the customization and real-life interactions and scenarios they can play out as an Urb. Female players on consoles wanted to spend more time socializing and unlocking items and outfits; they wanted to spend less time on motives and watching animations."

But isn't it generalizations like those above that have been packaged into the dreaded concept of the "girl game"? "It's silly and patronizing to think there's some magic 'girl game' formula, that if the box is pink and there's shopping in the game, girls will buy it in droves," warns Naughty Dog's Hennig, who believes this stereotyping disenfranchises girls all the more. "In general, I think women prefer games that include exploration, problem-solving, customization, and non-linear play. When we incorporate these elements into our games—whether it's *GTA* or *The Sims*—we're going to attract a wider demographic."

25   However, despite the recent growth spurt of women making and playing games, there remains a great divide between male and female gamers. Many women report feeling intimidated, whether it's because of an overwhelming amount of product on store shelves or the often aggressive behavior of other gamers. It's no secret that it can be tough to become part of the hardcore online community, even for the most talented players.

In an attempt to bridge the gender gap, Ubisoft has created and funded a fully female gaming team known as the Frag Dolls, a group of hardcore twitch gamers with panache who play *Splinter Cell* and *Rainbow Six*. At first impression, this could be taken as a marketing gimmick by Ubisoft to attract more males to their products. Not true, claims the publisher.

"We're creating role models for a whole legion of girls out there who may have been too intimidated to play games online—or even play at all," explains Ubisoft's online community manager, Nate Mordo. "For those who have bemoaned the fact that in-game heroines have tended to adhere to a certain template, I think that more women playing games means that we'll see more games that cater to this newly diverse audience."

The Frag Dolls are looking to debunk the myths associated with girl gamers and help support other women looking to play. But it's still naive to think that all gamers are treated equally: One visit to the girl team's forums (www.fragdolls.com) demonstrates the uphill battle to convince male gamers that girls are worthy adversaries and teammates.

So it appears, in fact, that publishers are finally accepting the existence of the once mythical female market. However, whether the industry can mature and evolve to capture their interests still remains to be seen. What I can guarantee is a sentiment echoed by every woman I spoke with: The more women that get involved, the more power they have to evoke change from within. It may take time and effort, but I don't know anyone who ever said getting the girl was easy.

Reflect & Write

- ❏ Zoe Flower conducted a long interview with Brenda Brathwaite—think about the quotation she chose to introduce Brathwaite with. Why this particular quotation? How does it affect the way that the reader is introduced to Brathwaite? How does it affect the way the reader understands the development of Flower's argument?

- ❏ While discussing the character Rayne, Flower admits that she herself would rather play the "extreme makeover" version of this character. How does this personal revelation about her own feelings about female characters affect the persuasiveness of her overall argument?

- ❏ Midway through the article, Flower writes, "I realized that the issue might have less to do with gender and more to do with how sexuality is perceived in today's games." What is the difference between gender and sexuality as Flower constructs it in this article? Do you agree with her statement or not?

- ❏ Analyze Flower's conclusion. What are its strengths? What would you have added or done differently if you were writing this article?

- ❏ **Write:** Flower did not include any images with this article. Using a Google image search, choose three images and place them at strategic places in the article to contribute to the argument. Write a brief reflection on why you chose the images you did and how you intended them to work in conjunction with Flower's existing argument.

■ *The Frag Dolls, a touring team of professional women gamers, are sponsored by game publisher Ubisoft to promote gaming for women.*

Screen Shot: Frag Dolls About Us Webpage

FIGURE 13.7 The Frag Doll "About Us" page aims to deliberately debunk stereotypes about women and gaming.

frag /frag/ *n. & v. · n.* 1 number of kills. 2 a fragmentation grenade. · *v.* 1 to eliminate other players in multiplayer shooters (fragging).

rag·doll physics /ragdol fiziks/ *n.* 1 a program allowing videogame characters to react with realistic body and skeletal physics.

frag·doll /fragdol/ *n.* 1 a female gamer with the skills to dominate in multiplayer shooters. 2 a lady with the sass to use the laws of physics to her incontestable advantage.

The Frag Dolls are a team of gamers recruited by Ubisoft to represent their video games and promote the presence of women in the gaming industry. Started in 2004 by an open call for female gamers, the Frag Dolls immediately rocketed to the spotlight after winning the Rainbow Six 3: Black Arrow tournament in a shut-out at their debut appearance. Soon after, the team began appearing in major gaming publications like *Electronic Gaming Monthly,* and filmed episodes for three different G4 television shows. They followed their early success by taking open challenges in *Splinter Cell: Chaos Theory* for 32 undefeated hours during the four-week Electronic Gaming Championship.

The Frag Dolls celebrated their one-year anniversary at the 2005 Penny Arcade Expo and repeated their shut-out performance in a new tournament, *Ghost Recon 2: Summit Strike*. Soon after they appeared on the pilot episode of the popular new *Gamehead* television show on Spike TV. The team then toured with the Major League Gaming circuit for the 2005 season, taking open challenges in a variety of Ubisoft titles. They moved to the World Series of Video Games circuit in 2006 where they compete in *Ghost Recon: Advanced Warfighter* with other professional-level teams.

The Frag Dolls are known not only for being skilled gamers in multiple titles, but for their advocacy of female gamers. The Frag Dolls have spoken on panels at the Women's Game Conference and two of the Women in Games International conferences. They have stated a desire for more female gamers in multiple interviews and have developed a gaming community friendly to other women interested in trying out video games.

5   The Frag Dolls can be found online or offline playing a variety of videogames in every genre, from RPGs and point-and-click PC adventures to FPS on the Xbox 360. Each week they write blogs about events, news in the industry, and their experience as gamers. You can find them online during regularly scheduled times, or talk with them in their community forums.

Reflect & Write

❑ How do the different visual elements of this Webpage work in conjunction to create an identity for the Frag Dolls? Do they produce a unified identity? How do the different images compete with one another? How does the page represent both women's identity on-screen (as characters) and off-screen (as gamers)? What differences do you notice about these different identities?

❑ Look at the Frag Dolls' graphics in comparison to the earlier *My Scene* screen shots. What similarities do you see? What differences?

❑ The site uses the strategy of definition quite literally to introduce the Frag girls to the readers. What is the effect of heading the written text with a definition in this way? Analyze the different definition entries as well as the way that they work together to help develop a specific argument about this group's identity.

❑ Compare the visual representation of the Frag Dolls with the written definition. Do they seem to be defining these girls in the same way? Why or why not?

❑ In a previous version of the About Us Website, the Frag Dolls included the following for their written description of themselves:

Okay, boys. The days of cooties have gone the way of *Centipede*. Girls are into games now, and we're just as hooked as you are. In fact, girl gamers make up 43% of all gamers, according to the ESA. So, where *are* all the ladies in the house?

Enter the Frag Dolls, a group of girl gamers out to have a little fun. We're here to represent the ladies in gaming with the taste and talent for beating you at your own games. So, for all you guys who think the only gals in gaming are the leather-clad, pixilated beauties on your screens, think again. We're real, and we've got the skills to teach you a few tricks of our own. So hang around and check out our blogs, or come challenge us online. You just might learn something.

Compare the style and voice of this description to the one reproduced above. What differences do you notice? How do you think this is tied to *kairos* and the rhetorical situation of the different versions of the Wepages? How is ethos utilized in each example?

❏ **Write:** Draft a proposal for an alternative Website design for the Frag Dolls. Be sure to provide a rationale for your redesign.

■ **Amanda Fazzone** *specializes in writing about the arts and media and has served as the assistant managing editor of the* New Republic, *as well as contributing articles to* Salon, Spin, *and* Slate. *This article appeared in the July 2, 2001, issue of the* New Republic.

Game Over

Amanda Fazzone

I have more than a few things in common with Lara Croft, the gun-toting, Bigfoot-slaying, back-flipping, treasure-hunting, aristocratic English heroine who stars in the video game *Tomb Raider*, recently spun off into the number-one movie in the United States, *Lara Croft: Tomb Raider*. We both have dark hair and dark eyes. We both enjoy music and the arts. We both like corgis. We both write for a living. And we both have breasts. But while Lara's 34Ds unwaveringly float mid-bicep, I, like most women, rely on an armada of brassieres to ballast what nature never intended skin to buoy. The 5-foot-9-inch, 130-pound Lara—even with the enviable measurements of 34D-24-35—seems not to have any breastcontrol issues at all. Whether she's fighting giant lizards or rappelling in the Himalayas, they invariably stay put.

Her secret? Lara Croft isn't real. She doesn't actually weigh in at 130 pounds (and her breasts don't weigh anything at all), the "stats" in her lengthy promotional "bio" notwithstanding. She's a synthespian: a computer-generated virtual woman with the pixels and the moxie to engender crushes in the hearts of the millions of gamers who made *Tomb Raider* one of the most successful video game series of all time. The

game's tag line: "Sometimes a killer body just isn't enough."

But not being human hasn't kept Lara from taking heat for her unnaturally perfect body. Feminists say that, with the advent of computer-generated cybermodels and synthespians, the bar for real women has been raised even higher. Asks Germaine Greer: "How many women do you know with broad chests and narrow waists like [Lara Croft]? Men should wake up to the fact that women have big bums. Whatever these characters are, they're not real women." Princeton University Professor Elaine Showalter claims that "Croft and the cybermodels epitomise the era of power grooming. No longer can women depend on a dab of powder and lipstick before they face the public." Today's woman, Showalter writes, employs "[l]iposuction, exfoliation, laser-blasting, Botox and collagen [to] take the skin to pix[e]lated smoothness and tautness." Life imitating art.

The outrage isn't surprising. Feminists have long decried the alchemy employed to create women of Barbie doll proportions, charging that such images cause men to objectify women, and contribute to the lack of female self-esteem that leads to depression, eating disorders, and the operating table. And with Lara and her virtual compatriots, that alchemy—and presumably the suffering it spawns—has taken a giant technological leap forward. Still, there may be an upside to all this pixelation. After all, feminists aren't the only ones infuriated by the emergence of cybermodels—the "real" modeling industry has good reason to be upset as well. Cybermodels may do more than put human models out of work; their explicit fakeness might just force people to admit that the whole modeling enterprise has been fake from the start.

5   From *Toy Story* to *Titanic* to *Shrek,* we're growing increasingly accustomed to recognizing synthespians for the man-made products they are. On the Internet, cybernewscasters Vandrea (modeled on British newscaster Andrea Catherwood) and Ananova have become celebs. And Webbie Tookay (that's "2-K"), the first virtual model, was dubbed "the most valuable model in the world" with an estimated market value last year of $15 million, thanks, in part, to contracts with Nokia and Sony. (By contrast, Gisele Bundchen, the world's highest-paid human model, earns a mere $5 million per year.) But cybermodel celebrity is a consciously cynical phenomenon. Their creators aren't trying to trick us into believing these images are real. They're just simulating reality.

What's more, even as girls' magazine marykateandashley dubs Lara "an Indiana Jonesesque girl" and as Angelina Jolie, the 26-year-old Academy Award-winning actress, doubles for Lara on film, it's almost impossible not to notice that Croft and her cyberpeers aren't real. It's true, as Naomi Wolf wrote in her 1991 book *The Beauty Myth,* that " 'Computer imaging'—the controversial new technology that tampers with photographic reality—has been used for years in women's magazines' beauty advertising." But the whole point of computer imaging was that magazine readers didn't know—or at least didn't think much about the fact—that the woman on the cover didn't look that way in real life. And so young girls could aspire to look the way Gisele looks on this month's cover of *Vogue.* But they can't ignore Lara's inauthenticity, because her inauthenticity is central to her fame. "When I first played the game, I thought [Lara's breast

size] was ridiculous," said one 15-year-old girl I interviewed after the film. "How could she run and jump dressed like that?" And you can see it on the video screen. Lara barely speaks, is controlled by the player, and is primarily seen from behind. A clear case of art trying—and failing—to imitate life.

Of course it's possible that, as technology improves, it will become increasingly difficult to distinguish real women from their computer-generated counterparts. And if that's the case, beauty-industry handlers will have even more reason to prefer synthetic women. "She is the perfect model," cheers Webbie Tookay's agent, John Casablancas—the founder of Elite Model Management who left his post last year to found the first-ever cybermodel agency, Illusion 2K. "Webbie can eat nothing and keep her curves. . . . [S]he will never get a pimple or ask for a raise." With a Screen Actors Guild strike looming, speculates a recent *Entertainment Weekly* article, the demand for synthespians may grow even higher. And, unlike most reed-thin models and actresses, cybermodels have no need for breast augmentation, airbrushing, padded bras, or industrial-strength double-stick tape.

Still, would it be so bad if technology grew sophisticated enough to trump reality, if synthespians replaced women in all those forms of entertainment feminists have historically derided—modeling, beauty pageants, pornography? Who would protest if we no longer expected women to look like models, just as we never expected anyone to climb walls like Spider-Man or have supersonic hearing like the Bionic Woman?

Perhaps cybermodels and synthespians will help us admit that what men have been getting off on all these years—and what women have been emulating at unrecoupable cost—are, like Lara Croft, little more than cartoon characters. And with that admission might come a more natural definition of what's sexy, by which the genuine confluence of health and DNA is deemed preferable to the handiwork of a Photoshop virtuoso. Were that truly to come to pass, of course, it wouldn't only be the human supermodels whose careers would suffer: Presumably, Lara's would as well. But she'd manage. After all, she'll always have her writing.

Reflect & Write

- What argument is Fazzone making about female avatars and body image?
- Fazzone opens her essay by identifying her similarities to Lara Croft. Why start her argument in this way? How does it enhance her larger goals?
- List the different sources that Fazzone draws on in her article. How does her selection of sources reflect her awareness of audience and the purposes of her argument? Look for moments in her article when she makes the reader aware of the research that underlies her argument.
- Fazzone uses a lot of specific language and imagery in her writing. Find two different sentences in which you think she uses this vivid style effectively and share them with your class.
- Fazzone's second to last paragraph is composed of two rhetorical questions. Why do you think she chose to use this technique at this point in the article? Is it an effective choice?
- **Write:** Many writers use a deliberate framing technique in opening and closing their arguments. In this case, Fazzone opens using a comparison to herself, but closes with only an implicit reference to that opening strategy. Write an alternative conclusion for this article that uses a more deliberate frame, closing with a more direct comparison between the author and Lara Craft in the same manner used in the introduction.

Helen W. Kennedy *teaches interactive media theory at the University of East London. She is co-editor of* Cyborg Lives? Women's Technobiographies *(2001), an anthology of first-person narratives about the relationship between technology, gender, and power, and has written many articles on the same subject. This article appeared in the December 2002 issue of* Game Studies, *an online, cross-disciplinary journal dedicated to computer game research.*

Lara Croft: Feminist Icon or Cyberbimbo?

Helen W. Kennedy

As the title suggests, the feminist reception of Lara Croft as a game character has been ambivalent to say the least. The question itself presupposes an either/or answer, thereby neatly expressing the polarities around which most popular media and academic discussions of Lara Croft tend to revolve. It is a question that is often reduced to trying to decide whether she is a positive role model for young girls or just that perfect combination of eye and thumb candy for the boys. It is also increasingly difficult to distinguish between Lara Croft the character in *Tomb Raider* and Lara Croft the ubiquitous virtual commodity used to sell products as diverse as the hardware to play the game itself, Lucozade or Seat cars. What follows then is an analysis of the efficacy and limitations of existing feminist frameworks through which an understanding of the kinds of gendered pleasures offered by Lara Croft as games character and cultural icon can be reached. I will begin by analyzing Lara primarily as an object of representation—a visual spectacle—and then move on, considering the ways in which the act of playing *Tomb Raider* as Lara disrupts the relationship between spectator and "spectacle."

There is no doubt that *Tomb Raider* marked a significant departure from the typical role of women within popular computer games. Although a number of fighting games offer the option of a female character, the hero is traditionally male with females largely cast in a supporting role. In this respect alone Lara was a welcome novelty for experienced female game players. "There was something refreshing about looking at the screen and seeing myself as a woman. Even if I was performing tasks that were a bit unrealistic. . . I still felt like, Hey, this is a representation of me, as myself, as a woman. In a game. How long have we waited for that?" (Nikki Douglas in Cassell and Jenkins 1999).

When *Tomb Raider* hit the games market, it did so with a good degree of corporate muscle behind it: indeed the game was launched as a significant part of the Sony Playstation offensive. It was a game which deployed the latest in technical advances in games design. Featuring a navigable three-dimensional game space, a simple but atmospheric soundtrack and a level of cinematic realism previously unattainable.[1] The game also made use of a familiar and popular adventure-based narrative format. A great deal has been said already about the extent to which *Tomb Raider* pillages the *Indiana Jones* movies for its narrative structure and setting. The success of the game is arguably attributable to this synchronicity between new techniques, a highly immersive and involving game space and game narrative and the controversial (and opportunistic) use of a female lead. Lara is provided with a narrative past appropriate to her status as an *adventurer* and an aristocratic English accent—a greater degree of characterization than the norm. Certainly, fans and critics suggest that none of these factors alone can explain the world beating success of the first game and its many sequels. "Lara's phenomenal success wasn't just about a cracking adventure, other games had that too. Lara had something that hooked the gamers like nothing has before. At the center of *Tomb Raider* was a fantasy female figure. Each of her provocative curves was as much part of the game as the tombs she raided. She had a secret weapon in the world of gaming, well . . . actually two of them" (Lethal & Loaded, 8.7.01). For this fan, judging from the tone, it seems that Lara herself is *at least* as significant as the story or gameplay. This comment also signals Lara's status as an object of sexual desire, a factor which the marketing/advertising of *Tomb Raider* was keen to reinforce.

It is clear that the producers of Lara wanted to market her as a character *potentially* appealing to women; her arrival on the game scene dovetailed nicely with the 90's "girlpower" zeitgeist

and could potentially have hit a positive chord with the emergent "laddette" culture which very much centred around playing "lads" at their own game(s). In *Killing Monsters* Gerard Jones locates Lara amongst a number of feisty and highly sexualized female characters that rose to prominence in the 90s—including *Buffy the Vampire Slayer* (2002). These characters have a strong "bimodal" appeal in that they manage to engage a large following of both young men and women. The console games market has traditionally been very explicit in their exclusive address to a male audience. In the late 80s and early 90s both Nintendo and Sega made it very clear that to attempt to market games for girls would threaten their real market—boys and young men. Sony's Playstation, by addressing youth culture in general, broke with this tradition[2]. The featuring of Lara Croft as girl power icon and cover girl for *The Face* magazine (1997)—where she is compared to both Yoda and Pamela Anderson—demonstrated the success of the marketing campaigns and signaled her penetration within a wider cultural landscape: people who had never played *Tomb Raider* could not help but have some awareness of Lara the character/icon.

Lara Croft as Action Heroine

5   The obvious connection between *Tomb Raider* and film narrative conventions and the way in which the game deploys themes and tropes from other popular cultural forms means that a feminist critique at the level of the politics of representation is somewhat inevitable. One such possible feminist approach might be to welcome the appearance of active female heroines within traditionally male or masculine genres. Lara Croft is by no means the first gun-toting action heroine and the iconography of her representation conforms to conventions deployed from *Annie Get Your Gun* onwards, but also has forerunners in comic book heroines such as *Tank Girl*. If, for example, we were to compare her to the representations within the female buddy-movie *Thelma and Louise* we can find many key commonalities. *Tomb Raider* also reworks a male-dominated genre and features a female central character: Lara totes a gun as she navigates a hostile landscape fraught with danger. Consider

also the ending of *Thelma and Louise*—they die within the story yet the white screen and the snapshots of them during the credits offer other possible, more positive, endings; with Lara this process becomes even more elaborated as she is resolutely immortal—with each death there is the possibility to replay the level over and over until it comes out right. The popular media and feminist response to *Thelma & Louise* was also similarly polarized around the issue of their representation—did the fact that they wielded guns guarantee or undermine the films status as feminist?[3] The juxtaposition of physical prowess and sexuality continues to produce a great deal of ambivalence amongst feminist and non-feminist commentators.

Thelma and Louise, and other action heroines such as Trinity in *The Matrix,* can also be considered as what Mary Russo describes as "stunting bodies" (1994): Female figures which, through their performance of extraordinary feats, undermine conventional understandings of the female body. Thelma and Louise, Trinity and Lara explosively take up space within a particularly masculinized landscape—the desert, dark urban landscapes, caves and tombs—and in doing so offer a powerful image of the absolute otherness of femininity within this space. The action genre is typically masculine so this type of characterization is often celebrated as at least offering some compensation for the ubiquity of oppressive representations of women and the preponderance of masculine hard bodies. The general absence of such characters is part of the reasons why fans become so invested in these characters and helps to explain why the popular, critical and academic response is often so polarized. The transgressive stunting body of the action heroine is replicated in the figure of Lara. Her occupation of a traditionally masculine world, her rejection of particular patriarchal values and the norms of femininity and the physical spaces that she traverses are all in direct contradiction of the typical location of femininity within the private or domestic space. If women do appear within these masculine spaces their role is usually that of love interest (often in need of rescuing) or victim. Lara's presence within, and familiarity with, a particularly masculine

space is in and of itself transgressive. By being there she disturbs the natural symbolism of masculine culture.

The absence of any romantic or sexual intrigue within the game narrative potentially leaves her sexuality open to conjectural appropriation on the part of the players. The fact that little evidence can be found of lesbian readings of Lara does not in itself prove that this does not or cannot happen. The ubiquity of the heterosexual readings and re-encodings of Lara leaves little space or legitimacy for this form of identification and desire. Within the masculine culture that pervades gaming practice/discussion and dissemination it is unlikely that female gamers will feel adequately empowered to make such a position explicit. However, the fact that a number of the female fan drawings/images of Lara are ones which portray her in sexually coded poses at least hints at this possibility. (For examples of this artwork see http://www.ctimes.net, http://www.eidos.co.uk; http://network.ctimes.net/volcl). So within this particular feminist framework there is some cause for celebration of Lara's presence as marking a significant breakthrough in the representation of women within the game space itself.

Lara as Fatal *Femme*

There is another feminist film studies approach that is much less inclined to celebrate the presence of masculinized female bodies. Psychoanalytically informed approaches which have developed from the insights offered by Laura Mulvey's landmark essay (1975) on the function of women within film narrative have a very different take on the tropes of this type of image. Two key insights which appear relevant to Lara are Mulvey's argument that the female body operates as an eroticized object of the male gaze and the fetishistic and scopophilic pleasures which this provides for the male viewer. The second argument was that "active" or "strong" female characters signify a potential threat to the masculine order. This is a more complex argument, dependent as it is on a pyschoanalytic reading of unconscious processes. Within this narrative the female body is a castrated body and as such it represents the threat of castration itself.

This threat, it is argued, is disavowed or rendered safe by the phallicization of the female body. It could be argued that Lara's femininity, and thus her castratedness, are disavowed through the heavy layering of fetishistic signifiers such as her glasses, her guns, the holster/garter belts, her long swinging hair.

What is certainly apparent is the voyeuristic appeal of Lara. This is clearly expressed in the critical analysis of Lara by Mike Ward. In a discussion of the relationship between the male player and Lara, he describes his initial discomfort when faced with a photograph of the latest model posing as Lara for marketing purposes (Lara Weller). What disturbs Ward about this image is that Lara is looking directly out at the viewer of the photograph, a look he interprets as signaling her awareness of herself as the object of the gaze. This is something which never happens in the game—voyeuristic pleasure depends upon being empowered to look without being seen. For Ward this appears to betray the contract between the player and Lara. In his view "If Lara never returns the ever-present look, she demonstrates her awareness of the player in other ways: her only spoken word is a terse, slightly impatient, 'no' if you try to make her perform a move that isn't possible. To the novice player at an impasse, there seems to be a frustrated potentiality in the way she stands and breathes, the user's ineptitude holding all her agility and *lethality* at bay"(Ward 2000, my emphasis).

10   By looking back, Lara disrupts the "circle" of desire which he describes: "And even if she incorporates my banality, my ordinariness, still, she's beautiful. The player's gaze is a strange closed circle of the desiring look and the beautiful, powerful exhibition. In fact, the look and the exhibition are one and the same, bound into a single, narcissistic contract safer and more symmetrical than anything Leopold von Sacher-Masoch was ever able to dream up" (Ward 2000). What is curious about this article by Ward is both his apparent awareness of the complex range of scopophilic pleasures which Lara affords and his utter acceptance of, if not abandonment to, these pleasures. In his reference to Sacher-Masoch he also signals an awareness of their potentially sadistic nature. It has been argued that the internal spaces of game worlds stand in for the mysterious and unknowable interior of the female body; deploying Lara's *lethality* to navigate and master this space could be argued to enhance these pleasures. Ward does acknowledge that Lara is not real, yet his investment in her and the pleasure he derives from looking at her appear to be very real. Lara is the perfect "object" of desire in what he describes as the equivalence between his look and her performance: she is unwittingly consumed and incorporated through this look. This pleasure is only disrupted when she is made flesh in the form of Lara Weller who *can* look back, and through this can express a subjectivity outside of this phantasmic circle. The discussion of Lara as a male fantasy object can, however, foreclose any discussion of how she might equally be available for female fantasy. The encapsulation of both butch (her guns/athletic prowess) and femme (exaggerated breast size, tiny waist, large eyes, large mouth) modes of representation makes Lara open to potentially queer identification and desire.

There are also limits to the applicability of this theory to a games character who is simultaneously the hero (active) and the heroine (to be looked at). Lara is closer to Mulvey's later work on the Pandora myth which she explores in *Fetishism and Curiosity* (1996). Lara too has "a beautiful surface that is appealing and charming to man [which] masks either an 'interior' that is mechanical or an 'outside' that is deceitful" (1996). Mulvey argues that "Pandora prefigures mechanical, erotic female androids, all of whom personify the combination of female beauty with mechanical artifice." (1996) Whilst relating Pandora to the femme fatale Mulvey finds this productive of a more interesting reading when discussing an active female protagonist. "Pandora's gesture of looking into the forbidden space, the literal figuration of curiosity as looking in, becomes a figure for the desire to know rather than the desire to see, an epistemophilia" (1996). Mulvey's conceptualization allows us to move from considering "activity" as masculine within the dynamics of the spectacle. Within this framework Lara's active negotiation of these hostile landscapes can be conceptualized as a feminine coded "desire to know"—a curiosity which enables us to sidestep the "rather too neat binary opposition between the spectator's gaze, constructed as active and voyeuristic, implicitly coded as masculine, and the female image on the screen passive and exhibitionist." (1996) Whilst this is a useful framework which allows for a more positive reading of Lara it cannot account for how the processes of identification and desire may be enhanced or subverted through playing the game. By focusing on Lara as an agent and a spectacle there is little here that would differ from a reading of the film version of *Tomb Raider* (2001), and this does not account for the specificity of the *experience* of playing as Lara.

But Playing as Lara. . . What Then?

What difference does it make to the argument if we focus on Lara as a character within a game and not a film? One response is to suggest that there may be something of interest in the fact that it is typically a male player who, at least for the duration of the game, is interacting with the game space as a female body. In the game it is the player who determines the actions, so the involvement is potentially that much greater than with other media forms—the computer "functions as a projection of certain parts of the mind . . . producing the uncanny effect of the computer as a second self" (Sofia 1999). Thus, interaction with, and immersion in the game "affords users the narcissistic satisfaction of relating to a technological second self," in this case a *female* second self (Sofia 1999). The relationship between male player and Lara when playing the game could be seen as analogous to the relationship between Case and Molly in Gibson's *Neuromancer* (1984). Case is a "console cowboy" who is able to "jack-in" to Molly's sensorium and experience her actions and sensations—she becomes an extension of his nervous system. "Between self and other, subject and object, [the interface] permits quasi-tactile manipulation of computational objects that exist on the boundary between the physical and the abstract" (Sofia 1999). This collapse offers a promise of a utopian subjectivity which is free from the constraints of fixed gender boundaries.

Thus, in this complex relationship between *subject* and *object* it could be argued that through having to play *Tomb Raider* as Lara, a male player is transgendered: the distinctions between the player and the game character are blurred. One potential way of exploring this transgendering is to consider the fusion of player and game character as a kind of queer embodiment, the merger of the flesh of the (male) player with Lara's elaborated feminine body of pure information. This new queer identity potentially subverts stable distinctions between identification and desire and also by extension the secure and heavily defended polarities of masculine and feminine subjectivity. Through this transgendering process, the Lara/player interface is open to two possible queer readings. One is that she is a female body in male drag—a performance of masculinity that undermines its reliance upon a real male body and highlights the instability of masculinity as an identity. Or conversely, Lara could be considered a female drag performer in that the bodily signifiers of femininity are grossly exaggerated to the extent where they threaten to collapse. "What drag exposes. . . is the 'normal' constitution of gender presentation in which the gender performed is in many ways constituted by a set of disavowed attachments or identifications" (Butler 1993). However, this transgendering process can only be argued through if we agree that Lara is in fact a feminine subject in any real sense. Lara's feminity is only secured through these key exaggerated signifiers (or perhaps just the two). This femininity is immediately and irrefutably countered by other phallic signifiers.

Furthermore, the potential transgendering function of playing as Lara does not appear to have any real consequences in the gaming culture sustained by the male players. If anything, any kind of identification with Lara is disavowed through the production of stories and art that tends to want to securely fix Lara as an object of sexual desire and fantasy. The fact that Lara has no sexual or romantic encounters within the game also suggests that the male players and, of course, the designers might feel uncomfortable with identifying her as the object of male desire. It also means that Lara has no sexual identity or subjectivity. To date there are no male-authored fan sites which deal with the question of "how it feels to play as a woman" and it is hard to imagine that there ever could be. Instead, you have a proliferation of sexualized imagery dominating the official and unofficial websites. Alongside these images, there exist rumours and discussions about game patches which enable the player to play with a nude Lara—the legendary "Nude Raider" game patch, or to get her to perform a strip tease. These appear to be more grounded in fantasy than reality, although there are nude images of Lara available on the web. There are also a number of web pages which offer "fragging" opportunities for female gamers to "set fire to" these nude images (see for example http://www.grrlgamer.com/fraggednude.htm). It is the presence of both the official and unofficial highly sexualized images of Lara which is often the focus of critical discussion.

15   It seems much more likely that the pleasures of playing as Lara are more concerned with mastery and control of a body coded as female within a safe and unthreatening context. The language and imagery remains resolutely sexist and adolescent. However, Jones (2002) argues that "indirectly, these boys are accommodating shifting gender roles, building confidence that they can find even strong, challenging women attractive and that they won't be overwhelmed by their own fears as they deal with real girls." Jones sees these sexy and powerful female characters as providing complex resources for both fantasy and identification as stable gender roles are eroded. Playing as Lara, enables engagement with an active female fantasy figure, providing opportunities for exploration of alternative versions of themselves. He argues that although "these kids may approach their bad girls as objects at first, as the game or movie or the tv show begins to unfold, they are clearly identifying with them" (2002). Even the apparent use of sexist imagery within the fan culture does not necessarily foreclose a feminist reading of playing as Lara. Jones goes on to argue that young men often choose to play games as a female character (when provided the choice or given the opportunity to design their own) as it enables them to experience a greater range of emotional complexity. For Jones, the popularity of these games and the female characters is a positive sign of greater gender flexibility and a general license to experiment with alternative identities. (2002).

But we are still some way from a full analysis of the game/player interaction. It may be that the relationship between player and game character advances in phases as the player becomes increasingly proficient at working the controls. As this proficiency or expertise develops the game character may become an extension of the player herself and Lara's separateness as a female body is eventually obliterated. "Engagement is what happens when we are able to give ourselves over to a representational action, comfortably and unambiguously. It involves a kind of complicity, we agree to think and feel in terms of both the content and conventions of a mimetic context. In return, we gain a plethora of new possibilities and a kind of emotional guarantee" (Laurel 1993). Thus the technology (including Lara) becomes a mask which signals our participation in an artificial and immersive reality and simultaneously "signals that we are role-playing rather than acting as ourselves" (Murray 1997). As a liminal space the game world allows a transgression of social and cultural norms—as an act of play we recognize the time spent playing as separate to other forms of interaction and unbound by conventional rules of behaviour. When what Murray describes as "the symbolic drama" reaches a level of intensity we become compelled to complete the game, often neglecting other activities in order to do so. The sense of presence we experience within the game world means that it can be hard to "jack out" of the game sensorium and attend to mundane matters. Thus, potentially, the fact that the polygons within the game are arranged in such a way as to denote a female body adds an extra dimension in developing an understanding of the game playing experience.

For the female game player, these complex and visceral experiences may provide further opportunities for the gratification of fantasies of omnipotence and may allow for empathic experience of the pleasures of exploration and adventure which are absent in the real world.

This may even be enhanced by the possibilities of identification with the game character— "empathy is subject to the same emotional safety net as engagement—we experience the characters' emotions as if they were our own, but not quite; the elements of 'real' fear and pain are absent" (Laurel 1993)[4]. From this we might also speculate that some of the desperate re-encoding of Lara as "sex object"—on the part of male players—may arise from an anxiety over the fact that these experiences *are* mediated by a female character and thus signify an attempt to deny any empathy/identification with Lara.

Virtual Lara: Cyborg Embodiment

Don't look at the Idoru's face. She is not flesh; she is information. She is the tip of an iceberg, no an Antartica, of information. . . she was some unthinkable volume of information. She induced the nodal vision in some unprecedented way; she induced it as narrative. (Gibson 1996)

In 1996, Kyoko Date—another virtual character—released a single in Japan. She was created by the Visual Science Lab in Japan and was promoted through a successful talent agency Hori Pro. Kyoko's personality and performance were scripted and controlled in exactly the same way as Stock, Aitken and Waterman managed and controlled the identity and image of Kylie Minogue or Jason Donovan. As virtual commodities invested with a specifically human backstory and personality it could be argued that Date & Lara destabilize the reality of more human idols. It could be argued that Madonna is no more real or approachable than Lara or Date. In a sense, Lara the game character is no more virtual than the images of real movie or pop stars: they too are representations which are carefully managed. Gibson's *Idoru*, published in 1996 at the same time as the launch of *Tomb Raider* and Date, pivots around the romance between a real rock star and Idoru herself, a virtual performer/artist.

The Idoru appears omniscient within this story. She is able to reflect and respond to whoever she communicates with—each encounter with her is particular to the interlocutor and

Idoru herself demonstrates no central subjective coherence—she is as depthless as a mirror. The same is true of Lara, who will perform differently (and reflect differently) depending on the skill and proficiency of the player. These virtual "babes" are ludic postmodern signifiers par excellence (Morton 1999), endlessly available for resignification, and providing multiple possibilities for narcissistic pleasure. When the game is mastered the player experiences Lara's mobility, agility and athleticism as his or her own. The creation and maintenance of a fairly complex backstory for Lara is an attempt to secure control of her virtual identity—she is a commercial product after all. Providing Lara with a (fairly) plausible history gives her some ontological coherence and helps to enhance the immersion of the player in the *Tomb Raider* world, and abets the identification with Lara. What Idoru, Lara and Date all highlight is the willingness on the part of real humans to invest erotically in fictional characters. It could potentially be argued that this is in no way a new insight—people have always invested emotionally in literary, film and television characters. This could also be seen to underline the fact that male sexual desire and fantasy are always bound up in an image of femininity which is virtual (in the sense that it is not *real*). Femininity is thus finally exposed as an empty signifier, a sign without a referent.

20   These occasions for both virtual embodiment and "erotic interfacing" (Springer 1999) need to be more fully understood as complex experiences in their own right.

"The phantasmic mobility of virtual bodies not only satisfies our infantile desires for omnipotence and omnipresence, but can provide hallucinatory satisfaction to those whose real body's mobility is impaired in some way" (Sofia 1999). This celebration of virtuality is also premised on an understanding that "computers are machines for producing postmodern forms of subjectivity" (Sofia 1999) and that these may help to bring about the collapse of other more oppressive subjectivities. As with the examples above, these more celebratory readings remain somewhat utopian in the face of the extent of the proliferation of virtual female bodies which are mere "objects." "Lara Croft is the monstrous off-spring of science, an idealized eternally young female automaton, a malleable, well-trained technopuppet created by and for the male gaze" (Schleiner 2000). Technology becomes a means of extending or transcending the body as the final site of the monstrous feminine other, as well as providing opportunities for the playing out of fantasies of conquest and control of this "other." These hypersexualized versions of virtual femininity are strategies of containment which need to be understood as such. The trenchant encoding of the technological imaginary as a masculine preserve and the positioning of femininity as an aesthetic rather than agentic (i.e. the player is the agent) presence within this landscape serves to maintain the exclusion of girls and women from the pleasures of the interface, erotic or otherwise.

These virtual "babes" are *not* welcomed by some feminists. Elaine Showalter argues that "since the computerized cover girls are patched together from the best features of real models and stars no real woman can ever hope to equal them; but their popularity . . . nonetheless is part of the millennial taste, for elaborate feminine artifice, especially an artifice shrewdly designed to look natural" (*Sunday Times*, 10 June 2001:6). Like the earlier discussion around transgendering, this *elaborate artifice* could serve to underline the very constructedness of conventional ideals of femininity. However, Showalter and others fear that we will have a generation of young girls who grow up even more dissatisfied with their own bodies and who are willing to make more and more drastic interventions in order to recraft their bodies in line with these impossible images, there is a sad irony in the idea that real women are more and more likely to use technology in order to become more like virtual women who fundamentally *are* just technology. "More generally, Croft and the cybermodels epitomize the era of power grooming. No longer can women depend on a dab of powder and lipstick before they face the public" (Showalter 2001).

In the end it is impossible to securely locate Lara within existing feminist frameworks, nor is it entirely possible to just dismiss her signifi-cance entirely. These readings demonstrate the range of potential subversive readings, but there exists no real "extra-textual" evidence to back this up—hence the focus on the text itself, which is on its own inadequate to explore the range of pleasures available from playing as Lara—we can only conjecture. The girl gaming community which communicates via the internet has its own highly critical discourse about the imagery and content within computer games. They not only complain about the degree of sexist portrayals of women but also bemoan the stupidity of many female games characters and lack of strong female leaders in role playing games.[5] This critique must be acknowledged and addressed by designers and producers of games if they intend to attract and retain this audience.

Where are the game companies that say its okay to be girl who doesn't think like one? ... I refuse to be charted like a map, and confined to several "common" characteristics. I am uncommon. Make games for me. (Douglas 1998)

If we are going to encourage more girls into the gaming culture then we need to encourage the production of a broader range of representations of femininity than those currently being offered. We also need to offer a critique of the entire discourse around gaming which serves to create the illusion that it is a masculine preserve. Feminist film criticism has had an impact (albeit only to a limited extent) on the representation of women in cinema. This critique has inspired many writers and directors, both within and outside the Hollywood system, to increase the range of possible subject positions offered to women. It is similarly vital that in the construction of a critical discourse about games we encourage and stimulate innovative and alternative images of men and women that do not simply reinstate doggedly rigid gender stereotypes.

25   In this article, I have tried to be attentive to what might be different about the relationship between representations within the game world and the experience of playing the game. It is clear that games *are* an increasingly sophisticated representational and experiential medium and that we need analytical tools which are precise enough to

capture both the similarities *and* the differences to other forms of leisure consumption. Simultaneously, it is becoming more and more evident that the interactive and immersive modes of engagement so central to gameplay are the model driving other forms of computer mediated consumption. This means that feminist theory cannot afford to ignore the games paradigm. By the same token, the politics of representation—and here I would extend this to racist and homophobic as well as sexist modes—is a vital issue which the games industry should not ignore.

References

Balsamo, Anne (1995) "Forms of Technological Embodiment: Reading the Body in Contemporary Culture," *Body & Society* 1 (3-4):215–237.

Bell, David (2001) *An Introduction to Cybercultures,* London: Routledge.

Butler, Judith (1993) *Bodies That Matter: On the Discursive Limits of "Sex,"* London: Routledge.

Cassell, J. and Jenkins, H. (1999) *From Barbie to Mortal Kombat: Gender and Computer Games.* MIT Press.

Demaria, Cristina & Mascio Antonella, *Little Women Grow Up: A Typology of Lara Croft's Sisters* http://www.women.it/4thfemconf/workshops/laracroft5/demariamascio.htm. Accessed 21.06.2001.

Douglas, Nikki (1998) "Uncommon Me" *Grrl Gamer* http://www.grrlgamer.com/gamergrrl04.htm. Accessed 05.02.2002.

Gamman, L. and Marshment, M. (Eds) (1988) *The Female Gaze: Women as Viewers of Popular Culture,* London: The Women's Press Ltd.

Gibson, William (1997) *Idoru,* Penguin Books.

Gibson, William (1984) *Neuromancer,* Penguin Books.

Hayles, N. Katherine (1999) *How We Became Posthuman: Virtual Bodies in Cybernetics, Literature, and Informatics,* University of Chicago Press.

Herz, J.C. (1997) *Joystick Nation: How Videogames Gobbled Our Money, Won Our Hearts and Rewired our Minds,* Abacus Books.

Jones, Gerard (2002) *Killing Monsters: Why Children Need Fantasy, Super Heroes and Make Believe Violence.* NY: Basic Books.

Laurel, Brenda (1993) *Computers as Theatre,* Addison Wesley Longman Ltd.

Lethal & Loaded, Documentary Channel 5, 8th July, 2001.

Mitchell, Juliet (1987) *Psychoanalysis and Feminism: A Radical Reassessment of Freudian Psychoanalysis,* Penguin Books.

Morton, Donald (1999) "Birth of the Cyberqueer," pp. 295–313 in J. Wolmark (ed) *Cybersexualities:*

A Reader on Feminist Theory, Cyborgs and Cyborgs. Edinburgh University Press.

Mulvey, Laura (1975) "Visual Pleasure and Narrative Cinema," *Screen* 16 (3):6–18.

Mulvey, Laura (1996) *Fetishism & Curiosity,* London: BFI.

Murray, Janet (1997) *Hamlet on the Holodeck: The Future of Narrative in Cyberspace,* Mass: MIT Press.

Oliver, Kelly (1997) *The Portable Kristeva,* Columbia University Press.

Poole, Steven (2000) *Trigger Happy: The Inner Life of Videogames,* Fourth Estate Ltd.

Read, Jacinda (1999), "Popular Film/Popular Feminism: The Critical Reception of the Rape-Revenge Film" 29.11.99. in *Scope Online Journal* www.nottingham.ac.uk/film/journal/articles/popular_feminism.htm

Russo, Mary (1994) *Female Grotesque: Risk, Excess and Modernity,* NY: Routledge.

Sawicki, Jana (1991) *Disciplining Foucault: Feminism, Power and the Body,* Routledge.

Sawyer, Miranda (1997) "Lara Croft: The Ultimate Byte Girl," *The Face.*

Schleiner, Anne Marie (2000) "Does Lara Croft Ware Fake Polygons: Gender Analysis of the '1st person shooter/adventure game with female heroine' and Gender Role Subversion and Production in the Game Patch" available Switch: Electronic Gender: Art at the Interstice at http://switch.sjsu.edu/web/v4n1/annmarie.html. Accessed 19/06/01.

Showalter, Elaine (10th June, 2001) *The Sunday Times.*

Shulusky, Edward *In Love with Lara: Reflections on an Interactive It-Girl,* http://www.tombraiders.com/lara_croft/Essays/Edward_Shulusky/default.htm accessed 19/06/01.

Sobchack, Vivian (1987) *Screening Space: The American Science Fiction Film,* NY: Ungar.

Sofia, Zoe (1999) "Virtual Corporeality: A Feminist View," pp.55–68 in J. Wolmark (ed) *Cybersexualities: A Reader on Feminist Theory, Cyborgs and Cyberspace,* Edinburgh University Press.

Springer, Claudia (1999) "The Pleasure of the Interface," pp. 34–54 in J. Wolmark (ed) *Cybersexualities: A Reader on Feminist Theory, Cyborgs and Cyberspace,* Edinburgh University Press.

The Matrix (1999) The Wachowski Brothers.

Thelma & Louise (1991) Ridley Scott.

Turkle, Sherry (1984) *The Second Self: Computers and the Human Spirit,* NY: Simon & Schuster.

Ward Gailey, Christine (1994) "Mediate Messages: Gender, Class, and Cosmos in Home Video Games," *Journal of Popular Culture* 27 (4): 81–97.

Ward, Mike, 14 January 2000, "Being Lara Croft, or, We are All Sci Fi," *Pop Matters.* Available at http://popmatters.com/features/000114-ward.html. Accessed 19/06/01.

Woolley, Benjamin (1993) *Virtual Worlds: A Journey in Hype and Hyperreality*, Penguin Books.

Endnotes

1. Sony are alleged to have invested $500 million in the hardware behind the Playstation and a further $500 million in the software. These figures are quoted in *The Face* (1997) but also in Poole (2001).
2. See Poole (2001), Herz (1997) but ample evidence for this address to a male audience is provided in early marketing campaigns and was certainly a factor in the *Tomb Raider* adverts. This is most particularly evident in the "Where the Boys Are" advertising campaign for *Tomb Raider II*.
3. For an overview of the complex debates around *Thelma & Louise* see Read, Jacinda (1999), "Popular Film/Popular Feminism: The Critical Reception of the Rape-Revenge Film" 29.11.99. in *Scope Online Journal* www.nottingham.ac.uk/film/journal/articles/popular_feminism.htm
4. The degree to which fear and pain are *not* experienced by the player is debatable. I know that my heart rate rockets, my palms sweat, I leap out of my chair and develop calluses on my thumbs. The experience of playing *Tomb Raider* has often left me shaken and exhausted.
5. For some fairly typical examples of this discourse see www.grrlgamer.com & www.chiq.net.

Reflect & Write

❏ Late in the article, Kennedy suggests that men playing *Tomb Raider* have a "transgendered" experience. Do you agree or disagree with this claim? Consider the fact that in first person shooter games, the player sees through the character's eye—and that in *Tomb Raider* the player watches the character of Croft actually perform the actions. How does this difference between *Tomb Raider* and the first person shooter genre support or undermine Kennedy's points?

❏ Both Fazzone and Kennedy in their articles suggest connections between computer gaming and popular culture: Whereas Fazzone discusses Lara Croft and other female figures in relation to the magazine and modeling industry, Kennedy refers to film. How does their use of these comparisons differ?

❏ Like Fazzone, Kennedy refers to Elaine Showalter in her article. How do the two authors use this source differently?

❏ The "about" page of *Game Studies* requests that articles submitted should be free of jargon. Do you feel that Kennedy accomplishes this goal? If not, identify a place in the article where you feel Kennedy could have eliminated jargon and draft a revision.

❏ **Write:** Identify Kennedy's main argument and then rewrite this article as an editorial for your school newspaper. Share your editorial with your class and discuss the modifications you made to content, tone, and structure to accommodate the different audience and publication.

■ **Richard Cobbett** *is the features editor for* PC Plus *magazine. This popular satirical article originally appeared on his online journal in June 2005.*

Writing a "Girls in Gaming" Article
Richard Cobbett

Your ten-step guide to writing a truly . . . unique article about the bizarre creature that is woman.

I am the Alpha and the Omega; leftie *and* rightie . . .

At some point in your writing career, it's almost guaranteed that you'll think it's a good idea to write one of these articles. If you're a guy, that is. By and large, female writers have better things to do with their time than obsess over their gender while playing a game, and tend to be into gaming because they like—how can I put this? Oh, yes, playing games, rather than out of a burning need to practice amateur sociology.

But never mind that. Here's your ten-step path to success.

1. Be a Warrior for Righteousness

5   Yes, you, sir—damn near all these things are written by sirs, any that aren't can be discounted as a statistical glitch—are a champion of chivalry! Once knights rescued damsels on horseback, in shiny silver armour (actually, no, but never mind)—now you can get the same effect by complaining about Lara Croft's chest. Which brings us to...

2. Evidence A: Lara's Chest

This is your introduction; your jumping off point. How you tackle this thorny issue will affect the whole tone of your cutting article. Refer to "Lara's chest," and you sound debonaire and suave, aware of the connotations, yet subtly removed from them. A sly reference to "Lara's boobs" and you're with the everyman; casual, yet aware. "Lara's assets" show you as a dispassionate observer of life's rich tapestry. And "Lara's back! And her front too!" translates literally as "I am a man with no sense of humour."

Discussion of character should be avoided at all costs; fighting the objectification of female game figures by ignoring irrelevant details like personality, background, stance, objectives, voice work, dialogue, relationships, and all that other junk, in favour of obsessing over breasts. You know. The important things.

3. Break Down Gender Gaps

It's important to set the tone for your feature, and make it welcoming for any girls who happen to pick up a copy. Don't worry that the tone is inevitably aimed at guys, and full of words like 'we should' and 'female gamers are.' You can compensate by putting your words on a lurid pink background, and covering it with hearts and lipstick kisses. Puppies are optional. Pictures of attractive game groups like the Fragdolls are not. Find the photos with the tightest T-Shirts, preferably on a very cold day, and express your shock and outrage via the magic that is 'the sardonic caption.' This should not stop this being the largest image on the page, preferably re-used throughout. Similarly, rather than using words like 'gamers,' make sure to say 'girl gamers,' or better yet, simply 'females.' Nothing says enlightened cosmopolitanism like talking like a Ferengi.

If you absolutely have to put a picture of a regular female gamer, a thumbnail or something is perfectly acceptable. In no circumstances may you begin with anything other than a physical description, moving onto the actual 'gaming' part only as time permits—in much the same way that no write-up of Jonathan "Fatallty" Wendell ever goes without a discussion of his latest hairstyle, or the pertness of his ass.

10   Oh, and always express at least some level of surprise—if only by feeling the need to point it out—at female gamers being able to play as well as the menfolk. You don't need to hide it. As we all know, the railgun is powered by testosterone, but the memo about moving a mouse being entirely unrelated to one's collection of reproductive organs has yet to circulate properly. Speed it on its way with some vague talk about multitasking. And something about asking for directions, because jokes aren't sexist if applied to men.

4. Women Are Interchangeable

Seriously, all the same. If you've got a quote from one, you've got one from all of them. "Women don't like violent games." "Women like constructive experiences." It's just like all us guys loving football, muesli, Leonard Cohen and fartjokes. Any evidence to the contrary, such as this example from *Pro-G,* is clearly the result of freakish brain-parasites at work; most probably cooties.

"Women are more interested in good games," says McShaffry. "And women are less interested in crap."

"I binge read *Heat* when I go to my friend's house," says Krotoski.

Needless to say, this means that because games aren't appealing to women, girl gamers are mistaken about enjoying the games they play right now. They just don't realise it yet. Your article may just be what they need to stop kicking your arse with *Christie.* Remember: only ever deal in absolutes. Absolutes are always 100% accurate.

15   IMPORTANT NOTE: Should you actually be of the female persuasion while writing your article, this rule counts double. Feel free to bring down the hammer on incredibly specific examples of What Women Don't Like, safe in the knowledge that nobody will ever dare argue or have a contrary opinion. Just like when Mary Whitehouse was alive.

5. It's Not Enough to Just Dislike Something

No, you might think it is, but really it's not. You're not allowed to find, say, *Elexis Sinclaire* tacky and embarassing without adding "and demeaning" or "and exploitative" or "and sexist" or "and insulting," or something else which takes great offense on someone else's behalf instead of your own.

And under no circumstances wuss out by trying to be rational, like *WomenGamers*. . .

It is not our wish to impose one view of what a female character should look like, sound like, etc. We hope you will share YOUR IDEAS about female characters, and what you would like to see in future games. Hopefully, part of what WomenGamers.com is helping to create is a greater range of choices in female characters. We are not looking to eradicate all female characters with huge boobs, as we realize some gamers enjoy them.... but it would be nice if not ALL female characters had them! Get the point?

Honestly, they'll be talking about *gameplay* next . . .

6. Cherry Pick Your Examples

20 Games like *Leisure Suit Larry* are perfect fodder for righteous scorn. True, some critics might point out that there's nothing in there you wouldn't see in a *Carry On* film . . . and the *Carry On* films are pretty popular with everyone. And that the series had a pretty strong female following throughout, due to being a harmless comedy designed to get laughs rather than get players off. And that the jokes come from Larry being a loser, not a lover. Oh, and that his real objective in most of the games isn't getting a cheap shag—something which the game almost invariably presents as an empty experience, if it ever actually happens, and usually never actually does—but rather finding *actual love* and happiness; right down to getting married three times to at least two women who ultimately come to reject him despite his hopes, and constantly bumbling through embarassment after humiliation in the hope of acceptance, with almost all of his 'conquests' based on trying to be helpful and solve peoples' problems in the hope of acceptance and later nocturnal reciprocation rather than directly pursuing perversion—unless a single guy who likes being around pretty ladies is automatically a pervert these days. And all that other 'actually played the game' yadda yadda.

It may help your argument's credibility if you add a three-step walkthrough on reproducing asexually. Make sure to include screengrabs.

Alternatively, if you feel like playing devil's advocate for a paragraph or too, *The Sims* should be held up as a counter-example, because it's like a doll's house, and girls like playing with dolls. And while obviously *everyone* grows out of *The Hardy Boys* or *Just William* or Winnie the Pooh, Nancy Drew is timeless. This is because girls never age, and have no interest in anything but childrens' toys and high culture. At some point they magically move from Barbie to Dostoyevsky and all else is immature silliness. But since the closest we're likely to get to the latter in computer games is *The Brothers Kalashnikov,* it doesn't really matter.

The fact that the overwhelming majority of games, from adventures to RPG to platformers to strategy to beat-em-ups to quiz games to puzzle games couldn't give the faintest stuff what gender you are should never be mentioned. There must be more Girl Games! Equality through segregation! It's not patronising at all! No, it's why all books, movies, magazines and even foodstuffs come specially wrapped in blue and pink paper, just so everyone knows what they should be paying attention to. Or, y'know, not. Don't waste too much time checking or anything.

(For bonus points, say you've been playing *Super Princess Peach* and liked it; quickly adding that you had to take insulin shots to get past Level 5.)

7. The World Is Made of Doom and Gloom

25 You've only got four pages to correct millions of years worth of gender coding, evolutionary development, and entrenched perceptions, and still need to shoe-horn in your manifesto, your clever idea for an all-encompassing game that will make the girls of the word go 'Squeee!' in unison, the boxout about accidentally testing the state of the world by playing a female MMORPG character on *All The Cliches Turn Up At Once Day,* and the follow-up anecdote, where you annoyed a lady-Quaker by delivering a lengthy lecture on sexism to the guy she put on Ignore several sentences back, resulting in the bomb going off and your team losing the round but winning the war . . . on sexism!

With this in mind, everyone will understand that you didn't have time to mention, say, Jeanette/Therese in *Bloodlines,* Annah/Fall-From Grace and Ravel in *Planescape,* SHODAN in *System Shock,* Zoe Castillo and April Ryan from the *Longest Journey* games, Nico from *Broken Sword,* Farah in *Prince of Persia,* Grace from *Gabriel Knight,* Rinoa, Cate Archer, Meche in *Grim Fandango,* D'Arcy Stern from *Urban Chaos, Starcraft*'s Kerrigan, *Monkey Island*'s Elaine Marley/Threepwood, Angel and Spirit and Flint and Rachael from *Wing Commander*, *Realms of the Haunting*'s Rebecca Trevisard, Jade from *Beyond Good and Evil, Syberia*'s Kate Walker, Laura Bow, the unnamed heroine of *Plundered Hearts,* or the princesses of *Tribes: Vengeance,* or *Quest for Glory*'s Katrina, or *Thief*'s Viktoria. . . certainly, you won't have the space for names like Sierra designers Jane Jensen, Lori Cole, Christy Marx and Lorelei Shannon, or to point out that *Everquest*'s oft-criticised art design was done by Rosie Cosgrove, or that *Playboy: The Mansion* was designed by Brenda Braithwaite, who also chairs the IGDA's 'Sex in Games' sections and has a book coming out on the subject, or Emily Short's legendary status in the interactive fiction community, or Dan/Dani Bunten Berry, the designer Warren Spector didn't want to meet for fear of *sounding like a dribbling fanboy*. . .

After all, none of that stuff matters. It's more important to highlight the glaring gaps in the industry than give practical examples of just how a wider perspective has actually helped—tiresome, irrelevant junk like how damn near every game that's had the nerve to cover sexual topics on an adult level has had a female designer at the helm.

Don't worry though: there's always enough space to namecheck *Custer's Revenge.* Some things are just too important to slip into obscurity, and if that doesn't include a rape-based action game for the Atari 2600, I don't know what does.

8. Everyone Really Loves Games

The only people who don't are the ones who haven't been fixed yet. Remember, getting a non-gaming girlfriend into *Quake* isn't like you being cajoled to get into *Mills and Boon*—it's like handing over the whole entire world of reading in one beautiful go! And nothing's more fun than having someone read over your shoulder, especially when they keep complaining you're reading the wrong way, or reading too slowly, or not appreciating the finer details of the articles you *totally* buy the magazine for. Which leads us neatly to:

9. The Industry's Bottom Line Is Your Problem

30 Never make the thrust of your argument 'girls should play games because they might find them fun,' or 'sharing the fun with a loved one,' or anything gay like that. Serve up as much data as you can find on the financial side, of how many more copies of games the companies could sell, and what percentage of the market is going untapped. It's not about the experience, or enjoyment, but the rampant commercialism. That XX% of the market isn't merely a shame because many people who don't play games, male and female alike, would have a great time with the hobby we love; it's a worldwide travesty not seen since the dinosaurs disappeared.

This may seem an odd thing to focus on, but look at it this way: the bigger the industry is, the more features you can write about it being too commercial! Everyone wins!

10. Ignore Everything in this Post Except this One Line and the Bit About the "Lara's Back" Joke, Because Seriously People, Stop It Already

I have four feet, my bottom is bright green, and I live in an igloo on Saturn.

Reflect & Write

❏ What is Cobbett's implicit argument in this piece? Why do you think he chose this format to convey it? What effect did these choices have on you, as a reader, and the way that you were persuaded by his argument?

❏ At which points in the article do you find similar points or themes that you encountered in other readings in this chapter? Did you find them to be more or less persuasive here?

❏ This piece was originally written as an article on Cobbett's online journal—that is, on his Weblog. How do you see the choice of genre affecting the way in which he composed this piece in terms of invention, arrangement, and style?

❏ Look at the last point. Why do you think he ends this way? How does this affect the overall persuasiveness of his argument?

❏ How did Cobbett's formulaic approach to writing about women and gaming culture influence the way you think about your own ideas or writing about the subject? Are there other types of essays that have a similar static form?

❏ **Write:** Rewrite this list as a more formal editorial; keep the voice strong, but use more conventional essay structure with a developed introduction that moves through a main body with supporting points and then into a conclusion that underscores its argument. Read your version against Cobbett's; what did the more traditional form bring to the argument? What was lost in the translation?

In a group, identify another issue related to gaming that is similarly formulaic in its argument. For example, you might choose to write about violence and video games or about the digital divide (the technology gap between rich and poor). Now together draft your own top ten list about writing an article on this subject. Having done so, quickly mock up an article that follows your own rules. Share your rules and your article with your class.

1. Each of these articles takes a slightly different stance on the issue of women and gaming. Choose the essay that you *least* agree with and draft a response paper, using direct quotes and evidence from that article as well as examples from your own experience.

2. Visit your local toy or electronics store or an online store such as Amazon.com and browse the computer games targeted toward young children. How many games seemed to be targeted toward a specific gender? Are there any "pink" games? Which games seemed to be targeted toward a general audience? Select one game in particular and write a blog entry or opinion piece in which you analyze the visual rhetoric of the packaging in relation to the issue of gendered games.

3. Visit some online games directed at girls, such as those found at Everything Girl (http://www.everythinggirl.com), American Girl (http://www.americangirl.com/fun.html), and The Adventures of Josie True (http://www.maryflanagan.com/josie/). Spend some time playing the games and studying the multimedia representations of girls on those sites. Now compose one of the following three texts: an article for a newspaper about the state of gaming for girls; an op-ad for a parenting magazine; or an article for a girls' magazine. Showcase your work for the class and discuss your rhetorical choices and how they would have been different had you chosen one of the other two options.

4. At one point in her article, Amanda Fazzone argues that the very inauthenticity of video game female characters makes them less of a threat to real women's sense of beauty. Compare this argument to the one made in Kim Franke-Folstad's argument about G. I. Jose in the Imagining the Ideal Body section of Chapter 10. Does one author make a more persuasive argument than the other? Why?

FROM READING TO RESEARCH

1. Write out a series of questions and interview female gamers in your class or dorm to discover the way women play and the reasons they do so. Present your findings to the class.

2. Building from your fieldwork for the previous question, brainstorm a game that would appeal to a woman gamer. Storyboard some of the initial action of the game, write an abstract description, and design an ad or box design for the game. Next, create a PowerPoint presentation and marketing pitch aimed at the executives of a successful but relatively conservative gaming company, making a case for why this game would be successful with its target audience. Deliver your presentation to the rest of the class.

VIOLENCE AND VIDEO GAMES

When officials discovered in the wake of the 1999 Columbine High School shootings that the two student gunmen were avid players of the computer games *Doom* and *Quake,* the stage was set for a widespread reevaluation of the relationship between virtual and real life violence. Artist Jon Haddock offers his own opinion on the matter in his 2001 piece "Cafeteria"; by redesigning the scene from the Columbine cafeteria to resemble a screenshot from the popular *Sims* computer game, Haddock suggests an interrelationship between gameplay and real-life actions. The extent of this interrelationship, however, remains a matter of contention, especially as computer animation, game design, and game sales continue to advance. Players and critics alike debate: Does playing at virtual violence predispose gamers to real-life violent acts? Or do violent games simply provide an

FIGURE 13.8 Artist Jon Haddock recreated the Columbine Massacre in his "Cafeteria" scene of the Sims game.

outlet or form of harmless entertainment to help people relieve tensions online rather than in real life? Adding greater complexity to the discussion is the recent surge in video games modeled on real-life military situations. How does our appraisal of video game violence change in a time of war?

In this section, we'll read a variety of perspectives on this issue, from that of Gerard Jones, who argues that "Violent Media is Good for Kids" in an essay of that title, to the argument made by Eugene F. Provenzo, Jr., who turned his research about the effects of interactive violence on children into testimony presented before a Senate committee. We'll also ask you to consider this issue from your own perspective, looking at screenshots from military games and drawing on your own knowledge about the implications of funnelling aggression and violence into interactive games.

Reflect & Write

❏ By reformatting the Columbine tragedy as a scene from *The Sims,* Haddock suggests a relationship between virtual worlds and real-world perspectives. However, *The Sims* is a nonviolent game. How does this knowledge change your interpretation of his argument in this image?

❏ How might Haddock have modified his design to make a stronger argument about the relationship between school shootings and video game violence?

❏ **Write:** Draft a blog response to the *Sims* creation above in which you present your current opinion about video game violence. Revisit this blog after you work through the readings and questions in the rest of the chapter.

San Francisco-based media critic **Gerard Jones** *has written on sitcoms and the American dream and on the history of comic books. He has also written text for several comic books, including titles featuring Batman, Superman, and the X-Men. His 2000 book* Killing Monsters *argued for the benefits of allowing children to indulge in fantasy violence. This article, published originally in the June 28, 2000, issue of* Mother Jones, *condenses this argument, focusing primarily on comic book violence, but makes important points relevant to video games.*

Violent Media Is Good for Kids

Gerard Jones

At 13 I was alone and afraid. Taught by my well-meaning, progressive, English-teacher parents that violence was wrong, that rage was something to be overcome and cooperation was always better than conflict, I suffocated my deepest fears and desires under a nice-boy persona. Placed in a small, experimental school that was wrong for me, afraid to join my peers in their bumptious rush into adolescent boyhood, I withdrew into passivity and loneliness. My parents, not trusting the violent world of the late 1960s, built a wall between me and the crudest elements of American pop culture.

Then the Incredible Hulk smashed through it.

One of my mother's students convinced her that Marvel Comics, despite their apparent juvenility and violence, were in fact devoted to lofty messages of pacifism and tolerance. My mother borrowed some, thinking they'd be good for me. And so they were. But not because they preached lofty messages of benevolence. They were good for me because they were juvenile. And violent.

The character who caught me, and freed me, was the Hulk: overgendered and undersocialized, half-naked and half-witted, raging against a frightened world that misunderstood and persecuted him. Suddenly I had a fantasy self to carry my stifled rage and buried desire for power. I had a fantasy self who was a self: unafraid of his desires and the world's disapproval, unhesitating and effective in action. "Puny boy follow Hulk!" roared my fantasy self, and I followed.

5   I followed him to new friends—other sensitive geeks chasing their own inner brutes—and I followed him to the arrogant, self-exposing, self-assertive, superheroic decision to become a writer. Eventually, I left him behind, followed more sophisticated heroes, and finally my own lead along a twisting path to a career and an identity. In my 30s, I found myself writing action movies and comic books. I wrote some Hulk stories, and met the geek-geniuses who created him. I saw my own creations turned into action figures, cartoons, and computer games. I talked to the kids who read my stories. Across generations, genders, and ethnicities I kept seeing the same story: people pulling themselves out of emotional traps by immersing themselves in violent stories. People integrating the scariest, most fervently denied fragments of their psyches into fuller senses of selfhood through fantasies of superhuman combat and destruction.

I have watched my son living the same story—transforming himself into a bloodthirsty dinosaur to embolden himself for the plunge into preschool, a Power Ranger to muscle through a social competition in kindergarten. In the first grade, his friends started climbing a tree at school. But he was afraid: of falling, of the centipedes crawling on the trunk, of sharp branches, of his friends' derision. I took my cue from his own fantasies and read him old Tarzan comics, rich in combat and bright with flashing knives. For two weeks he lived in them. Then he put them aside. And he climbed the tree.

But all the while, especially in the wake of the recent burst of school shootings, I heard pop psychologists insisting that violent stories are harmful to kids, heard teachers begging parents to keep their kids away from "junk culture," heard a guilt-stricken friend with a son who loved Pokémon lament, "I've turned into the bad mom who lets her kid eat sugary cereal and watch cartoons!"

That's when I started the research.

"Fear, greed, power-hunger, rage: these are aspects of our selves that we try not to experience in our lives but often want, even need, to experience vicariously through stories of others," writes Melanie Moore, Ph.D., a psychologist who works with urban teens. "Children need violent entertainment in order to explore the inescapable feelings that they've been taught to deny, and to reintegrate those feelings into a more whole, more complex, more resilient selfhood."

10   Moore consults to public schools and local governments, and is also raising a daughter. For the past three years she and I have been studying the ways in which children use violent stories to meet their emotional and developmental needs—and the ways in which adults can help them use those stories healthily. With her help I developed Power Play, a program for helping young people improve their self-knowledge and sense of potency through heroic, combative storytelling.

We've found that every aspect of even the trashiest pop-culture story can have its own developmental function. Pretending to have superhuman powers helps children conquer the feelings of powerlessness that inevitably come with being so young and small. The dual-identity concept at the heart of many superhero stories helps kids negotiate the conflicts between the inner self and the public self as they work through the early stages of socialization. Identification with a rebellious, even destructive, hero helps children learn to push back against a modern culture that cultivates fear and teaches dependency.

At its most fundamental level, what we call "creative violence"—head-bonking cartoons, bloody videogames, playground karate, toy guns—gives children a tool to master their rage. Children will feel rage. Even the sweetest and most civilized of them, even those whose parents read the better class of literary magazines, will feel rage. The world is uncontrollable and incomprehensible; mastering it is a terrifying, enraging task. Rage can be an energizing emotion, a shot of courage to push us to resist greater threats, take more control, than we ever thought we could. But rage is also the emotion our culture distrusts the most. Most of us are taught early on to fear our own. Through immersion in imaginary combat and identification with a violent protagonist, children engage the rage they've stifled, come to fear it less, and become more capable of utilizing it against life's challenges.

I knew one little girl who went around exploding with fantasies so violent that other moms would draw her mother aside to whisper, "I think you should know something about Emily. . . ." Her parents were separating, and she was small, an only child, a tomboy at an age when her classmates were dividing sharply along gender lines. On the playground she acted out "*Sailor Moon*" fights, and in the classroom she wrote stories about people being stabbed with knives. The more adults tried to control her stories, the more she acted out the roles of her angry heroes: breaking rules, testing limits, roaring threats.

Then her mother and I started helping her tell her stories. She wrote them, performed them, drew them like comics: sometimes bloody, sometimes tender, always blending the images of pop culture with her own most private fantasies. She came out of it just as fiery and strong, but more self-controlled and socially competent: a leader among her peers, the one student in her class who could truly pull boys and girls together.

I worked with an older girl, a middle-class "nice girl," who held herself together through a chaotic family situation and a tumultuous adolescence with gangsta rap. In the mythologized street violence of Ice T, the rage and strutting of his music and lyrics, she found a theater of the mind in which she could be powerful, ruthless, invulnerable. She avoided the heavy drug use that sank many of her peers, and flowered in college as a writer and political activist.

I'm not going to argue that violent entertainment is harmless. I think it has helped inspire some people to real-life violence. I am going to argue that it's helped hundreds of people for every one it's hurt, and that it can help far more if we learn to use it well. I am going to argue that our fear of "youth violence" isn't well-founded on reality, and that the fear can do more harm than the reality. We act as though our highest priority is to prevent our children from growing up into murderous thugs—but modern kids are far more likely to grow up too passive, too distrustful of themselves, too easily manipulated.

We send the message to our children in a hundred ways that their craving for imaginary gun battles and symbolic killings is wrong, or at least dangerous. Even when we don't call for censorship or forbid "*Mortal Kombat*," we moan to other parents within our kids' earshot about the "awful violence" in the entertainment they love. We tell our kids that it isn't nice to play-fight, or we steer them from some monstrous action figure to a *pro-social doll*. Even in the most progressive households, where we make such a point of letting children feel what they feel, we rush to substitute an enlightened discussion for the raw material of rageful fantasy. In the process, we risk confusing them about their

natural aggression in the same way the Victorians confused their children about their sexuality. When we try to protect our children from their own feelings and fantasies, we shelter them not against violence but against power and selfhood.

Reflect & Write

❏ Do you find Jones's article persuasive? How does your own childhood experience or your observation of other children's experience with fantasy violence support or undermine his claims?
❏ Consider Jones's allusion to the Victorians and their attitudes on sexuality in the last paragraph. Why do you think he chose to include this comparison?
❏ **Write:** While Jones makes a powerful argument for the benefits of fantasy violence for children, only at the end does he explicitly mention video games. Write a short editorial in which you expand on his argument, focusing specifically on current video games.

Brian Farrington *is an editorial cartoonist for the* Arizona Republic.

Political Cartoon
Brian Farrington

Reflect & Write

❏ How is the relationship between violence and media represented in the cartoon? What remedy could you surmise that Brian Farrington might suggest for this situation?
❏ The focus of the cartoon could easily have been just the boy playing the video game. What is the effect of including the father? Consider his position in relation to the child as well as his written comment.
❏ Look carefully at the detail included in the area where the boy is sitting. How do details like the video game cover and the gaming accessories contribute to the argument?
❏ **Write:** Draft a rhetorical analysis of the cartoon. Refer to Chapter 1 for guidelines.

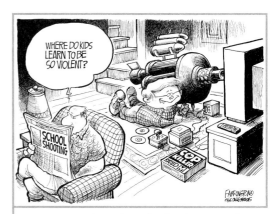

FIGURE 13.9 Brian Farrington's political cartoon works through the irony of the parent's question, "Where do kids learn to be so violent?"

Source: Courtesy of Brian Farrington/Cagle Cartoons.

COLLABORATIVE CHALLENGE

With your group, visit the link below to view a series of cartoons, that draw a relationship between shootings and the media. How do they provide different perspectives on the issue? Or, alternately, how do they represent the same perspective in different ways? How do the different rhetorical choices impact the image's argument? Which cartoon seems to offer the bleakest message? Why? Synthesize your findings and present them to the class, offering close analysis of the images during your presentation.

   www.ablongman.com/envision/241

■ **Eugene F. Provenzo Jr.** *is a professor at the School of Education at the University of Miami, who focuses his research on the impact of computer culture on children and education. His research has been featured in articles in* The New York Times, Mother Jones, *and* The Guardian, *as well as on National Public Radio. His expertise in this area led him to be asked to testify twice before government subcommittees about violence in video games. The following testimony represents his remarks made on March 21, 2000, before the Senate Committee on "The Impact of Interactive Violence on Children," chaired by Senator Sam Brownback.*

Testimony Before the Senate Commerce Committee Hearing on "The Impact of Interactive Violence on Children"

Eugene F. Provenzo Jr.

My comments this morning must be brief. Much of what I will discuss is found in a new book I am working on entitled *Children and Hyperreality: The Loss of the Real in Contemporary Childhood and Adolescence.* It continues a line of inquiry I began in 1991 with *Video Kids: Making Sense of Nintendo,*[1] as well as in a number of articles and book chapters.[2] In this work, I am arguing that children and teenagers are spending much of their time in simulations, rather than in the natural or "real" world. It is an argument, which if true, has serious implications for not only our children, but also for the future of our society. Essentially, I believe that the unreal, the simulation, the *simulacra* has been substituted for the real in the lives of our children. This occurs at many different levels: in the video games that are so much a part of the experience of contemporary childhood; in the shopping malls and "commercial civic spaces" where our children spend so much of their time; in television programs, advertisements and movies; in the theme parks where we vacation; in the online chat rooms and discussion programs through which we communicate and exchange information; and finally, in the images of beauty and sexuality that run as a powerful undercurrent through much of our culture and the lives of our children.

As suggested above, the hyperrealities that increasingly shape and define the experience of childhood and adolescence come in many different shapes and forms. Some are clearly more detrimental than others.

Since this hearing focuses on "The Impact of Interactive Violence on Children," I will concentrate on what I consider to be the most disturbing aspect of my research—the increasing "romanticization" of violence—and more specifically, the frightening power and potential of the new video game technologies.

Let me begin by reflecting a bit on the information included on the recently released videotapes made by Eric Harris and Dylan Klebold shortly before the Columbine High School shootings last year.

5   It is very clear that Harris and Klebold wanted to tell the world a story whose script they seem to have learned through the entertainment media—particularly from ultra-violent films and video games. Harris tells his story in front of a video camera with a bottle of Jack Daniels and a sawed-off shotgun cradled in his lap. He calls the gun Arlene, after a favorite character in the *Doom* video game. Harris and Klebold saw themselves as important media figures, whose story would be worthy of a filmmaker like Steven Spielberg or Quentin Tarintino. The fact that Harris and Klebold created these videotapes reminds me of the Mickey and Mallory characters in Oliver Stone's film *Natural Born Killers* who became media stars as a result of a murderous rampage across the country. It is no accident that the film was a favorite of Harris and Klebold. I would like to argue that films and video games not only teach children about violence, but also how to be violent.

When violence is stylized, romanticized and choreographed, it can be stunningly beautiful and seductive. At the same time, it encourages children and adolescents to assume a rhetorical stance that equates violence with style and personal empowerment.

It does matter that we romanticize and stylize violence in films and video games.

It does matter that children and adolescents can put themselves into the virtual body of a killer in first-person shooter games. It matters because a computer or video game is a teaching machine. Here is the logic: highly skilled players learn the lesson of game through practice. As a result, they learn the lesson of the machine and its software—and thus achieve a higher score. They are behaviorally reinforced as they play the game and thus they are being taught. Have you ever considered what it is they are being taught?

Consider first-person shooter games such as *Quake, Blood, Doom* or the recently released *Daikatana*. These are games that provide the player with a real view perspective of the game. This is very different from the earlier tradition of video games like *Street Fighter II* or *Mortal Kombat,* in which the user viewed small, cartoon figures on the screen and then controlled their actions by manipulating them through a game controller. In contrast, a first-person shooter actually puts you inside the action of the game. The barrels of weapons like pistols and shotguns are placed at the bottom center edge of the computer screen. You can look right or left, up or down, by manipulating the computer mouse or game controller. The effect is one of literally stepping into the action of the game as a participant holding the weapon. Lieutenant Colonel David Grossman, a former Professor of Psychology at West Point, argues that first person shooter video games "are murder simulators which over time, teach a person how to look another person in the eye and snuff their life out."[3]

Games like *Doom* are, in fact, used by military and police organization to train people. The Marine Corps, for example, has adapted *Doom* to train soldiers in the Corps. Some critics claim that there is little difference between what goes on in a first-person shooter and playing a game of Paintball, where players divide up on teams and hunt each other in a wood or elaborately constructed game room. To begin with, Paintball is acting that takes place in the real world. You run around a little, get tired and winded, bumped and scrapped. There are serious consequences for getting out of control as you play—in other words—the fact that the game is physical and tangible means that it has limits. These limits not only include your own endurance, but the rules and procedures followed by your fellow players.

In a first-person shooter like *Quake* there are no boundaries or limits. The more "extreme" you are (a terminology often used in describing the action of the games), the more likely you are to win. Paul Keegan explains that in John Romero's recently released first-person shooter game *Daikatana*:

Physical reality suggests that you are sitting in a chair operating a mouse and a keyboard. But with the computer screen replacing your field of vision, you believe you're actually creeping around a corner, causing your breath to shorten. Afraid an enemy is lying in wait, you feel your pulse quicken. When the monster jumps out, real adrenaline roars through your body. And few things in life are more exhilarating than spinning around and blowing the damn things to kingdom come, the flying gibs so lifelike you can almost feel wet blood.[4]

What is going on here is clearly different than just a game of Paintball or "Cowboys and Indians." However, the creators of first-person shooters just don't understand that there is a problem. John Carmack, the main creator of *Quake,* for example, considers the game nothing more than "playing Cowboys and Indians, except with visual effects."[5] In a recent interview, Carmack was reminded that in the past kids playing Cowboys and Indians weren't able to blow their brothers' heads off. His response was to laugh and say: "But you wished you could."[6]

10   Keep in mind this important face: in first-person shooter games, players are not responsible for what they do. There are no consequences for other children, for families, or for society. As Mark Slouka explains in reference to the CD-ROM video game *Night Trap,* the game allows its players: "To inflict pain. Without responsibility. Without consequences. The punctured flesh will heal at the touch of a button, the scream disappear into cyberspace."[7]

Games that employ a first-person shooter model represent a significant step beyond the tiny cartoon figures that were included in *Mortal Kombat* in the mid-1990s. In fact, there has been a continuous evolution of the realism of these games as computing power has increased and become cheaper. Much of this has to do with the enormous increase in computing power. A moderately fast desktop computer with a Pentium II chip that could be purchased for under $1,000 today has the speed of a $20 million Cray supercomputer from the mid-1980s.[8]

Even more interesting is the availability of inexpensive game consoles. Sony's dominance of this market has recently been challenged by Sega's amazing 200 Mhz Dreamcast game machine—available for nearly a year now in North America. It will soon be superseded by Microsoft's X-Box, which is designed specifically for interactive gaming, and which is set for release in the fall of 2001. The X-Box will be driven by a 600 Mhz Intel Pentium III chip. It will cost less than $500 and will allow players to go online to play games. The machine and the programs that will drive it represent what is potentially an extraordinary virtual reality simulator.

Larry Smarr, director of the National Center for Supercomputer Applications in Champaign-Urbana, Illinois, believes that systems like these represent "the transition from people playing video games to a world where we will create our own fantasies in cyberspace."[9]

In many respects, the content of violent video games represents a giant social and educational experiment. Will these ultra violent games actually teach children to behave and view the world in markedly different ways? To repeat an earlier argument, video and computer games are, in fact, highly effective teaching machines. You learn the rules, play the game, get better at it, accumulate a higher score, and eventually win. As Mark Slouka argues, the implications of new technologies like video games "are social: the questions they pose, broadly ethical; the risks they entail, unprecedented. They are the cultural equivalent of genetic engineering, except that in this experiment, even more than the other one, we will be the potential new hybrids, the two-pound mice."[10]

15   It is very possible, that the people killed in the last few years as the result of "school shootings" may in fact be the first victims/results of this experiment. If this is indeed the case, it is an experiment *we* need to stop at once. Some things are too dangerous to experiment with.

Notes

1. Eugene F. Provenzo, Jr., *Video Kids: Making Sense of Nintendo* (Cambridge: Harvard University Press, 1991).
2. See: Eugene F. Provenzo, Jr., "'Brave New Video': Video Games and the Emergence of Interactive Television for Children," *Taboo: The Journal of Culture and Education* Vol. 1, #1, Spring 1995, pp. 151–162; and Eugene F. Provenzo, Jr., "Video Games and the Emergence of Interactive Media for Children," in Shirley R. Steinberg and Joe L. Kincheloe *Kinderculture: The Corporate Construction of Childhood* (Denver, CO: Westview Press, 1997), pp. 103–113.
3. Deborah Claymon, "Video-game industry seeks to deflect blame for violence," *Miami Herald,* July 2, 1999, 3E.
4. Paul Keegan, "A Game Boy In the Cross Hairs," *The New York Times Magazine,* May 23, 1999, p. 38.
5. Ibid, p. 39.
6. Ibid.

7. Mark Slouka, *The War of the Worlds: Cyberspace and the High-Tech Assault on Reality* (New York: Basic Books, 1995), p. 13.
8. David E. Sanger, "High-Tech Exports Hit Antiquated Speed Bumps, *The New York Times,* June 13, 1999, WK 5.
9. John Markoff, "Silicon Valley's Awesome Look at New Sony Toy," *The New York Times,* March 19, 1999, p. C1.
10. Ibid.

Reflect & Write

❏ Provenzo designed this argument to be presented to a Senate Committee. How does it differ in tone and style from Jones's piece that was written for the popular magazine *Mother Jones*? What choices did Provenzo make to create an argument that would be effective for his specific audience?

❏ Although many would argue that the typical video game does not "argue" a particular position, Provenzo suggests that "it encourages children and adolescents to assume a rhetorical stance that equates violence with style and personal empowerment." Do you agree with this claim? Why or why not? How does your assessment of this claim influence how you think about the persuasive power of video games?

❏ **Write:** At one point in these comments, delivered in 2000, Provenzo looks forward with apprehension to the X-Box gaming system and the expanding ability for gamers to go online. Write a letter to Provenzo articulating your appraisal of X-Box and/or online gaming technology and its relationship to either remedying, modifying, or worsening the effect Provenzo argues that violent gaming is having on society.

■ *This article appears on the Velvet-Strike Website and is authored by the organization's founder,* **Anne-Marie Schleiner,** *an Assistant Professor of Fine Art at the University of Colorado, Boulder. Schleiner is well known in the digital world for her role as a techno-culture critic and her work in gaming art and design. Velvet-Strike, a site that promotes online activism against the violence in the multiplayer game* Counter-strike, *is part of her larger website, Opensorcery.net, that focuses on open source digital art forms and online activism.*

Velvet-Strike: War Times and Reality Games (War Times from a Gamer Perspective)

Anne-Marie Schleiner

When I first heard about the attacks on September 11, just a fraction before I felt a wave of sadness, a nauseating thought passed through my mind. What terrible timing—with this president in office, perhaps even more so than previous ones, he could use this event as justification for dangerous actions on a global scale and at home. A few weeks later, I left for Spain to give a workshop on modifying computer games. When I arrived the next morning at the workshop I learned that the U.S. had declared war on Afghanistan. The workshop organizers had installed a new demo of *Return to Castle Wolfenstein,* a remake of an old Nazi castle shooter game, on all the PC's. The sounds of the weapon-fire echoed off the concrete walls of the workshop warehouse space—what I once approached with playful macho geek irony was transformed into uncanny echoes of real life violence. At that moment, that room was the last place I wanted to be. Joan Leandre, (one of the artists presenting at the workshop), and I discussed creating some kind of anti-war game modification.

Not long after the Sept 11 attacks, American gamers created a number of game modifications for games like *Quake, Unreal* and *The Sims* in which they inserted Osama Bin Laden skins and characters to shoot at and annihilate. Since *The Sims* is not a violent game, one Osama skins distributor suggested feeding the Sims Osama poison potato chips. If you can't shoot him, then force him to overeat American junk food, to binge, death by over-consumption, death by capitalism. (*The Sims* is essentially a game whose rule sets are based on capitalist algorithms, although according to *The Sims* designers these rules are balanced by other factors.)

The most disturbing Osama mod I saw was on display in October 2001 at a commercial game industry exhibit in Barcelona called Arte Futura. To give the exhibition organizers the benefit of the doubt, they were probably unfamiliar with urban American ethnic cartography. In this mod, Osama is represented as an Arab corner grocery story owner, as is common in many tough inner city neighborhoods in North America. The goal of the mod is to enter the corner liquor grocery store and kill the Arab owner. (At the time I saw this I had just gotten an email from my sister in Seattle describing how she and other college students were taking turns guarding mosques from vandalists.)

Harmless release of tension or co-conspirator in the industrial war complex? Playful competition or dangerous ethnic and gender politics of the other? The first computer game, created at MIT by Slug Russell and other "hackers", was called *Spacewar,* an outer space shooter influenced by cold war science fiction. Since *Spacewar,* computer games evolved and bifurcated into multiple genres, some related to war and fighting simulation, (and using technology occasionally directly funded by the US military), and others less so. (RPG, Real Time Strategy, Shooter, God Game, Action/Adventure, etc). In the 1990's, within the shooter genre, characters evolved from white guy American soldiers into oversize funny male monsters of all shapes and stripes and pumped female fighting machines. It seemed to be about a kind of monster fantasy workshop, humorous macho role-play, taking things to their frag queen extremes. Within online *Quake* and game hacker culture, gender restrictions and other boundaries opened up.

5   Then beginning with *Half-life* and continuing with shooter games whose alleged appeal is "realism," a kind of regression took place. In terms of game play games like *Half-life* are universally seen as advancements. Yet in *Half-life* you are only given one white guy everyman American geek guy to identify with. And all of the NPC researchers and scientists in the game are male. *Half-life*

remaps the original computer game target market back onto itself, excluding all others and reifying gamer culture as a male domain. (Not that I didn't play *Half-life* but I would have enjoyed it more if I could have played a female character.)

The trend towards what male gamers call "realism" solidified in 2000 with the *Half-life* mod *Counter-Strike*. *Counter-Strike* is a multi-player game where you choose to play on either the side of a band of terrorists or on the side of counter-terrorist commandos, (all male). The tactics of the terrorists and the counter-terrorists are essentially indistinguishable from each other. (Perhaps this similarity between terrorist and counter-terrorist is telling about the current situation in Israel and other places where the "war on terrorism" has been forged for a while or is only just beginning.)

People who love *Counter-Strike* have told me that the appeal is the "realism"—its not about "silly" muscly monsters bouncing around space ports like in the Quake Series—in *Counter-Strike* you play realistically proportioned soldiers and commandos killing each other in stark bombed out bunkers. When you are killed in *Counter-Strike* your character really "dies" instead of immediately regenerating. (Although you get to play again in a few minutes as soon as the next round begins.) So "realism" is not about faster game engines, graphics processing and "photorealism." It is about reproducing characters and gameplay environments that are considered closer to "reality" and farther from fantasy.

But now, in the wake of Sept 11, are these games too "real"? Or is the real converging with the simulation? Who defines what is real? According to an email rumor, President Bush recently approved of a deal between an American television network and the US military to create a series of wartime docudramas of US soldiers fighting the "war on terrorism" abroad. The news section of the TV network was apparently miffed at the arrangement because they had been unable to gain access to reporting on the war in Afghanistan. (Recall in Orwell's *1984* the merging of state controlled war time news and docu-fiction.) The trend in brutal reality TV, beginning with popular shows like *Cops,* and continuing with a slue of reality game shows like *Survivor* is another field of *convergence.*

You are for or against us, you are with us, "the one", or you are with the enemy is the underlying logic of the West, as I understood a talk by Marina Grzinic at an international cyberfeminist conference in Germany in December 2001. (Pre-axis of evil.) Although computer games replicate this binary competitive logic maybe there is something ultimately subversive in the knowledge that it is only a game, that at any moment you may switch sides with the "other," you may play the terrorist side in *Counter-Strike.* But reality games pretend to erase this awareness. And if you are going to converge network shooter games and contemporary middle eastern politics into a game, (*Counter-Strike*), then you leave out a number of complexities such as economics, religions, families, food, children, women, refugee camps, flesh bodies and blood, smell etc.

10   Maybe the problem is that convergence with "reality" is happening with the wrong game genre. Instead of replicating the binary logic of the shooter genre, of Cowboys and Indians, of the football game, if the US government

borrowed tactics from real time strategy gamers or RPGers, we might be looking at a different global response. (But then again given who our leadership is now, its unlikely he is capable of the intellectual planning required of a strategy gamer.) "Winning" or advancement in massively multi-player Role Playing Games like *Everquest* is enhanced by strategically building social bonds amongst players. And strategy games like *Warcraft* and *Command and Conquer,* while directly enacting tactics of imperialist colonialist expansionism, at least take into account other factors in addition to military might.

After playing *Counter-Strike* for a couple weeks I must confess it incorporates social maneuvers beyond shoot and kill, (and I must also confess to enjoying many aspects of the game—I have actually always enjoyed shooters). Team play and communication between members on your side are complex, including live voice radio, and a number of coded chat "smileys" and automated radio commands that take some time to learn. Formulating strategies is also necessary for survival, as in other network shooters. As a *Counter-Strike* newbie I was sometimes even able to solicit help from my enemies, indicating a clear awareness of the game as fictional play space. Some of the combat environments are quite beautiful. But I still am critical that this domain, the network of thousands of international *Counter-Strike* servers spanning Taiwan to Germany, has been reified as an exclusively male "realistic" combat zone. (You can hear live audio voices of male players on many servers.) I am also disturbed that the binary logic of the shooter is being implemented on a global military scale.

Personally I would like to see computer games move towards fantasy, away from military fantasy which pretends to "realistic." I like fantastic environments where there is more room for imaginative habitats and characters. Japanese games for children and adults are engaged in this undertaking, filled with curious animal Pokemon creatures, Robo-cats, transformers, Anime people, monsters, demons and fairies, of all genders. I identify more with these characters than with counter-terrorist or terrorist soldiers and they are what I want to be my reality. Reality is up for grabs. The real needs to be remade by us.

Reflect & Write

❏ How does the post-September 11th climate, in Schleiner's view, change the stakes for issues of violence in video games? Compare her argument to Provenzo's.
❏ Schleiner worries about the fact that many current players have the capability to modify the content and look of games. How does this concern play out for Schleiner? Find passages to quote in support of your answer.
❏ Does Schleiner's bias undermine her argument?
❏ **Write:** At the end of her piece, Schleiner remarks that she would like games to move back toward fantasy, away from simulated reality. Write a response to her article in which you argue about the difference (or lack of difference) between violent content in fantasy-based vs. reality-based games in relation to her fears about the social effects.

■ *These in-game screen shots represent the progression in visual realism in recent war games.*

Screen Shots: War Games

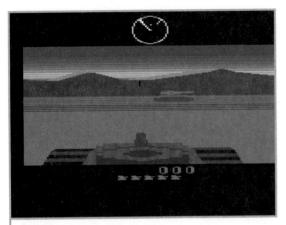

FIGURE 13.10 This screenshot from the 1980s Atari game *Battlezone* puts the player in the shooter's seat of a tank in the middle of battle.

Source: Battlezone (r) image courtesy of Atari Interactive, Inc. (c) 2007 Atari Interactive, Inc. All rights reserved. Used with permission.

FIGURE 13.11 The recently released online game Kuma/War features realistic graphics that insert the player into the middle of real-life military encounters.

Reflect & Write

❑ The images shown here mark the shift from original war games, with their heavily pixilated and object-oriented graphics, to the newer, more realistic interfaces. How does the experience of playing these games change with the move from firing a tank to holding a gun or pursuing an objective based on real-life events?

❑ Analyze the different perspectives represented in these screen shots. Considering Provenzo's discussion about how violent games force the gamer to assume a certain rhetorical stance, identify the stances that are suggested by these images.

❑ **Write:** Go online and watch a trailer for either Counter-strike or Kuma/War. Write a blog entry in which you investigate the relationship between violence and visual rhetoric in the trailer that you watched.

A 2003 Knight science-journalism fellow at MIT, **Clive Thompson** *specializes in writing about technology and society. He contributes articles regularly to* The New York Times Magazine, Wired, Details, *and the* Boston Globe, *and serves as the video-game columnist for* Slate. *Thompson also posts his insights on collisiondetection.net, his blog about technology and culture. This article was published in the August 22, 2004, issue of* The New York Times.

The Making of an X Box Warrior

Clive Thompson

It was only a virtual Baghdad, baking under a virtual sun. As in real life, though, troops were dodging gunfire. I was at the Institute for Creative Technologies in Marina Del Rey, Calif., playing a new X box video game called Full Spectrum Warrior. Leading eight men in an Army squad on a patrol of the war-torn city, I got a taste, however approximate, of why Iraq is such a hard place to be a soldier these days. My job, as squad leader, was to order my soldiers where to go and what to do. First, I sent half of my men into an alleyway, where they immediately came under fire from insurgents hiding nearby. Scrambling for safety, I ordered us to duck into a building, pausing to marvel at the detail of the architecture. I then led us back out onto the street, directing my team to crouch behind a car while we tried to locate the snipers. This was a bad idea. Despite what you see in action movies and other video games, cars do not provide good cover from bullets. The snipers cut loose, and my troops crumpled to the ground. It was surprisingly distressing. In barely three minutes, I had

led every single one of my soldiers to his death.

I play video games regularly and, modesty aside, usually do quite well. Though this was my first attempt at *Full Spectrum Warrior,* the reason that I played poorly was not that I was inexperienced but that the game was not designed solely for entertainment. *Full Spectrum Warrior* was created by the Institute for Creative Technologies, with help from the Army, to teach soldiers realistic strategies for surviving what the armed forces call "military operations in urban terrain." As a result, the game is unforgivingly precise. The soldiers you command are programmed to respond the way a real soldier would. There are no magic weapons to bail you out. All you have going for you is the real world. "This is what you'll really see when you're out there," said Maj. Brent Cummings, a soldier then stationed at Fort Benning, Ga., who worked as a consultant on the game and walked me through it.

For the past three years, the military has been entertaining the surprising idea that

video games, even those that you play on a commerical system like Microsoft's Xbox, can be an effective way to train soldiers. In fact, the Army is now one of the industry's most innovative creators, hiring high-end programmers and designers from Silicon Valley and Hollywood to devise and refine its games. Some of these games are action-packed, like *Full Spectrum Warrior.* Others, like one that the military's Special Operations Command is currently designing to help recruits practice their Arabic, are less so. All the games, however, speak to the military's urgent need to train recruits for the new challenges of peacekeeping efforts in places like Iraq.

Teaching someone to be an accurate shot is not particularly hard to do. Military trainers have learned that if you put someone through a week of intensive work with a point-and-shoot simulator (not unlike today's commercially available shoot-'em-up video games), he will be reasonably good with a rifle. Teaching judgment, however, is much harder than teaching hand-eye coordination. Today's military is in the market for games that train soldiers, in effect, how not to shoot—how to avoid conflict whenever possible, to recognize danger and find a route around it. As a squad leader in *Full Spectrum Warrior,* you do not even carry a gun that fires, which makes it the first military-action video game in which the player never discharges a weapon.

5   Some skeptics worry that if the military's games are not realistic enough, they will encourage bad habits and incorrect strategy—tactics that work on the screen but get soldiers killed on the battlefield. It is certainly true that many video games for sale in stores would be disastrous for training and would trivialize a task that is literally a matter of life and death. James Korris, the creative director of the Institute for Creative Technologies, said that he once analyzed the behavior of the computerized enemy forces in the commercial game *Command & Conquer Generals.* At first glance, the enemy appeared to be marching in intelligent formations, but on closer examination, he said, they were revealed to be "sort of running laps."

But for now the skeptics will have to hold their breath. The Army is already preparing plans to ship out copies of *Full Spectrum Warrior* to soldiers, and its creators envision the game being played by troops in Iraq, where Xboxes are popular among Americans looking to unwind. Many of the military's young soldiers, members of the PlayStation generation,

spend much of their downtime each week playing games. As the military sees it, they might as well be playing games that hone their skills. "When a soldier is off-duty," Cummings said, "he's going to go back to his barracks, and he's going to play Tony Hawk's *Pro Skater.* What if I give him a simulation instead?"

Modern military simulations have existed since the Second World War, when projected films of planes were used to train gunners to identify aircraft and mocked-up cockpits were physically rocked side to side to replicate the feeling of a dogfight. The military began to create highly sophisticated simulators in the 80's, taking the electronic instrument panels of helicopters, ships and tanks and wiring them to computers that could display virtual targets. With these installations, still regarded as the most accurate training technology available for learning complex battle maneuvers, hundreds of soldiers could fight together as if on one battlefield, practicing moves that they had previously been able to discuss only theoretically.

In the early 90's, however, the military lost some of its dominance in the field of computer simulations as the video-game industry began to take off. Groundbreaking games like *Quake* and *Counterstrike*—so-called first-person shooters, because the players view the action from a first-person perspective—were pioneers of a style of graphics that depicted

combat from an individual's perspective. Computer-game designers in the 80's looked enviously at the state-of-the-art graphics available to the military. Now military experts could walk into a Wal-Mart and buy games off the shelf that had crisper visuals and smarter artificial intelligence than some of their own tools. Michael Zyda, director of the Navy Modeling, Virtual Environments and Simulation Institute, remembers the moment when that shift occurred. "We'd show our stuff to generals," he said, "and they'd say, 'Well, my son is playing something that looks better than that, and it only cost $50.'"

The military's simulators, of course, were still elite tools. But they were prohibitively expensive (a single military flight simulator can cost up to $30 million), and they were products of the cold-war era, designed for combat in which large armies face one another head-on. In the eyes of someone like Neale Cosby, director of the simulation center of the Institute for Defense Analyses, a private group that advises the Pentagon, the old technology was outdated. "We do not have good simulations for combatants who walk to work," he said. "Tanks, Bradley vehicles, that's all cold-war stuff." For the needs of today's lighter, more flexible Army and its urban campaigns, in which soldiers walk door to door, video games that made you stroll through dungeons looking to slay shrieking monsters suddenly seemed relevant.

10   Before long, military experts began to approach private-sector game designers, looking for opportunities to collaborate. Video games have even been used as a form of outreach, the military's public face to American youth. More than 10 million people have downloaded a first-person shooter game called *America's Army* that the Army gives away as a recruiting tool. It now ranks as one of the most popular games ever. (In a recent poll by 1 to 1 Research, 30 percent of a group of young people with a favorable view of the military said they had developed that view from playing *America's Army*.)

Not only did the military seek out game designers, but after Sept. 11 there were instances of game designers reaching out to the military to offer their services. "It was the reversal of the cultural flow," Zyda said. He remembers fielding phone calls from people saying, "Well, I've been doing entertainment for years, but now I want to do something for the country." One of the designers who got involved was Robert Gehorsam, the C.E.O. of the games company Forterra Systems, who as a Sony executive oversaw the development of the wildly popular online video game *EverQuest*.

Gehorsam lives three blocks away from ground zero, and even before Forterra released a commercial game called *There* last year, he wondered whether the military might find it useful. The game *There* is what is known as a "massively multiplayer online world": for a yearly membership of $50, you can log onto the game any time from any computer connected to the Internet. You select a character, or "avatar," and then wander around a vast 3-D world, engaging with other players who have logged on from their computers in any number of ways. Some people choose to race dune buggies; others take potshots at one another with goofy weapons or just hang out and talk. (There is even a book club of *There* players who meet and talk online in the game's universe.)

Unlike other online games of this genre, many of which are modeled on fantasy worlds like that of The Lord of the Rings, There is scrupulously realistic. All the avatars look human and even appear to breath and blink in convincing ways. Gehorsam suspected that with certain modifications, There might allow soldiers around the world to train with one another. Battle-hardened officers in Baghdad, he speculated, could participate in urban-warfare scenarios, in real time, with fresh-faced recruits in the Midwest. Friendly Iraqis could log on and take part in a virtual mob scene, complete with abuse hurled in Arabic.

In 2002, Gehorsam showed *There* to some people in the field of military simulations, and they agreed that he was onto something. In early 2003, he landed a $3.5 million, four-year contract from the Army Research, Development and Engineering Command to build a simulator geared to model warfare against insurgents in urban settings. Forterra's game designers immediately set to work creating a new, parallel version of their online world—a separate, cordoned-off virtual earth for the Army's exclusive use. In this souped-up version, the world in which your avatar lives and moves is based on a remarkably accurate, roughly one-to-one counterpart to the real earth, derived from satellite data. "If your avatar was standing in New York, and you wanted to go to San Francisco," Gehorsam explained, "you'd have to walk the exact same distance as in real life—step by step." Forterra's designers also started erecting a Middle Eastern city reminiscent of Baghdad and before long had produced one square mile of tightly nested buildings, which Army soldiers all over the world could roam simultaneously.

15   After Gehorsam demonstrated a prototype this spring on the high-tech cable channel TechTV, he received a call from Jim Kondrat, a captain in the Illinois National Guard. Kondrat wanted his troops to try it out.

In June, I traveled to Moline, Ill., to watch Kondrat and a team of soldiers give *There* its first military test drive. Though the system was still, at that point, a prototype, Gehorsam wanted feedback from real soldiers who might be deployed in the near future. In light of the military's recent stop-loss orders, all the soldiers in the room had been alerted to the possibility of deployment to

Iraq. (And, indeed, one captain was scheduled to depart a few weeks later.)

Gehorsam's *There* team set up the game in the convention room of a Holiday Inn, while Kondrat lounged at the back of the room in his Army fatigues. A tall, round-faced man, Kondrat radiated a sort of wry calm, which seemed fitting since, as he explained, he is a Buddhist. When I remarked that it was appropriate that a Buddhist would experiment with a virtual-reality world, he chuckled and said he was willing to try anything to help prepare his soliders for potential combat. He explained that equipment for on-the-ground training is hard to come by. "We don't even have ammunition to do training," he said. "They need it all in Iraq."

Kondrat's unit, a battalion, particularly needed to practice convoy maneuvers—piloting a large number of vehicles down a road while keeping them safe. Kondrat said that he would like to take the battalion more often to one of the Army's desert outposts in California, where installations are set up like Iraqi villages, but that those resources, too, are now in high demand.

Instead, Kondrat's soldiers hoped to use *There* to create a virtual village that a battalion might drive through. "We can go out, try it, screw it up, reset, do it 20 times again—before we go out there burning diesel in the real world," explained Capt. William Ehrhardt, a burly man who combs what is left of his short-cropped hair straight down over his forehead.

One of Gehorsam's team members sat in front of a computer to demonstrate how to create a virtual city. At the keyboard, he pecked at a few keys and called up a blank expanse of land. He selected an avatar and walked him out onto an empty plain. With a few mouse clicks, he picked the shape and size of a building, and with one more click, it zoomed into place. A few more clicks generated rugged hills and scrub grass to cover them. In a final flourish, he reached up and turned off the sun. Presto: one Iraqi building at dusk.

The soldiers were visibly impressed. "Cool," one said, exhaling. "It's like *The Matrix*."

Each soldier then logged onto one of the dozen computers in the room and started experimenting with the game. Mostly in their late 20's and early 30's, many were longtime video-game players, and they quickly mastered the basics of moving about, drawing their rifles and driving a vehicle. At first, they mostly horsed around, intoxicated by a world that was void of real repercussions. Two soldiers piled into a car and began hunting for another vehicle to slam into. "Let's play chicken!" one said. Another soldier practiced aiming his machine gun: when he pointed it at his comrade's head, his friend just laughed.

As they became more expert at the keyboard controls, though, the soldiers became more serious and hunkered down. When they were given a military exercise to run, they became engrossed. At one point, the soliders set up a roadblock and practiced preventing unauthorized drivers from going past. Cars trundled up full of virtual Iraqis (operated by real-life soldiers, some of whom had logged onto the game from California). Each player was equipped with a headset microphone, so when he spoke, you could hear their voices in the game.

"I need to get through to my wife!" one of the Iraqis shouted. "I need to get through to the marketplace!"

"Back up, sir," the squad leader said. "This way is closed. You'll have to find another route."

The Iraqi was furious. "You Americans! You come in here, and you just make stuff up!"

Soon, several other cars had pulled up, and nobody was retreating. The atmosphere turned palpably tense. "You've got 10 seconds," the leader warned, training his gun on the cars.

Then chaos broke out. An Iraqi hopped in his car and made a break for it, driving straight through the blockade. The soldiers opened fire, but the driver got through safely and escaped down the street.

"Another one coming!" shouted one of the soldiers, as a second Iraqi ran up with a machine gun and stormed past the sandbags. This time, the guardsmen wheeled in unison and fired. The terrorist flopped to the ground.

"Well," said one soldier, "that'll make the evening news."

Not everyone in the military is convinced that receiving training in a game is possible or even useful. Army culture is deeply physical: training is about sweating hard and keeping your boots in the mud. Video games, in that context, can seem like a frivolous or even dangerous detour from real-world experience.

One of the biggest concerns that skeptics voice is the danger of so-called negative training. If a game is programmed with unrealistic physics and behavior, it can teach soldiers incorrect techniques—potentially deadly when they eventually enter combat. In a game like *Full Spectrum Warrior,* where the enemy is made up of computerized opponents with artificial intelligence, the obvious concern is that the preparation will not give a human-enough sense of how devious, or inept, a real enemy can be.

The soldiers in Illinois generally found *There* impressive, but they offered several criticisms of its realism. One soldier pointed out that you should not be able to jump inside a vehicle and drive it unless you are licensed for it. "I don't even know how to drive a Bradley," he said, "but I just got in one and drove it downtown."

A lieutenant wondered whether the game was too exciting for its own good. Boredom is a key part of training, he said, since part of the challenge of gun battles is that they often come out of nowhere after hours of tedium. All agreed that *There* could better simu-

35 late exhaustion: a virtual soldier who stands around in Iraqi heat ought to become fatigued, they argued, unless he is drinking lots of virtual water.

Even the enthusiasts agreed that the games can be oversold. Cummings, the consultant on *Full Spectrum Warrior,* worried aloud about the possible perception that a simulation would be taken as something more than just that—a rough approximation. "I think people will see it, and they'll say, 'Oh, jeez, I can't believe you're training your army this way,'" he said. He even shies away from using the word "game" to describe the simulations. "Global war on terrorism is not a game," he said. When he was posted in Afghanistan, he recalled, it was so hot that his sweat erased notes he was making on a map. In a video game, he said, "you can't replicate that."

On the other hand, what if the games are accurate, but they fall into the wrong hands? The Army made *Full Spectrum Warrior* in two versions: one for the military and a slightly modified form for the public. The commercial version instantly became a best seller. Today, you can walk into a game store, buy it and get a taste of what it is like to manage troops under Arab fire. (The decision to release the game to the public was driven by an interesting business consideration. Microsoft, which created the Xbox, reserves the right to approve any game that another company creates to

run on it, and it charges a fee for each copy of the game that sells. Microsoft will typically only green-light a game with a sufficiently large market—in the case of *Full Spectrum Warrior,* one that included not just soldiers but the general public.)

If a game like *Full Spectrum Warrior* is an accurate representation of Army training, you might wonder about the wisdom of selling it to the public. Real-life terrorists might well use it to learn about the urban-warfare tactics of American soldiers. Granted, the version of *Full Spectrum Warrior* available to the public is not as precise about military doctrine (ambulances carry ammo, for example), and it has bigger, Hollywood-style explosions. But it turns out that the military-grade version of the game also resides on the disk of the public version. Anyone who can figure out the "unlock" code can buy the public game, unlock it and play the military one.

James Korris of the Institute for Creative Technologies said that *Full Spectrum Warrior* includes only classic battle drills, with which Al Qaeda, and most foreign countries, are already familiar. "If there were classified content," he said, "there's no way it would end up on a commercial product with a static access code." Still, even nonclassified information can be useful. To prepare for the 9/11 attacks, terrorists used commercially available flight simulators, not secret Pentagon ones.

Some military experts argue that while it is possible for the games to provide useful training for terrorists, the benefit of some of these games to the Army far outweighs any potential security hazard its theft might pose. "This is going to give us a bigger edge than it gives to somebody else," said William Davis, who heads the lab that created the virtual weapons for the recruitment game *America's Army.*

40   In June, when I met with Brent Cummings at the Institute for Creative Technologies, he was slightly abashed about being dressed down in jeans and a golf shirt. When he first came to the West Coast from his spit-and-polish military base in Georgia, it was a bit of a culture shock. "I wasn't a hard-core gamer," he said. "I'm thinking: O.K., these Hollywood flakes, what am I going to get out of it? They all probably smoke dope."

But he said he was quickly impressed by the commitment of the programmers at the Institute for Creative Technologies to make an accurate game. Cummings's job was to ensure that *Full Spectrum Warrior* conformed to military doctrine. He brought military manuals so that he could show the programmers the myriad details of how soldiers are really trained to act, down to the way they go into a room when they are entering and clearing a building. Particularly crucial, he said, was developing the "nudge"—the player's ability to physically grab a fellow soldier and point him in the desired direction. "A squad leader is very physical," he said. "He goes up, and he grabs people literally on the shoulder and says: 'Hey, knucklehead. Over here.' He drags people around."

The game was booted up for me, and on a huge screen in an auditorium, an institute staff member guided the squad around the city. He was much better at the game than I was: when he encountered insurgents taking potshots from behind a barrier, he sent a team of his men to neatly flank them.

But can you learn strategy from the game? Cummings said he believes so. Out in Illinois, Jim Kondrat, the captain in the Illinois National Guard, said that he had seen firsthand the results of training with *Full Spectrum Warrior.* He bought a copy of the game when it was publicly released and watched his young recruits gather around an Xbox to play it. "When you have wounds and action going on around you," he said, "it starts to stress the leader. We had one guy with both his teams pinned down by fire, and I was saying: 'What are you going to do? What are you going to do?' And he was freaking out." Then one soldier hit upon a plan to fire a smoke grenade. It worked: the enemy was confused, and the soldiers successfully flanked them.

In fact, the virtual world offers some unequalled ways of visualizing a battlefield. Consider how the game facilitates "after-action review," a key part of training. After soldiers practice a technique, they talk about it to analyze what went wrong. Typically, soldiers will argue about precisely what happened on the field. With video games, however, they can literally replay the scene to find out.

45   Cummings showed me a game called *Full Spectrum Command,* currently in use at Fort Benning, Ga., in which you control a company of up to 150 people. For my benefit, he had a staff member run a mission infiltrating a building where terrorists were holed up. The soldiers advanced, blowing a hole in the gate, and terrorists began firing back. All of a sudden, Cummings froze the scene, as in a "bullet time" moment in *The Matrix.* Red lines onscreen showed the flight paths of enemy bullets. The camera zoomed along one of the lines, showing us what the bullets "saw" as they raced toward the soldiers. With another keystroke, Cummings made the walls on the buildings vanish so we could see where the enemy had been crouching.

He pointed to a red line that showed where one of the soldiers was hit. "See that?" he said. "That was our vulnerability."

Cummings conceded that the games have limits. "You can't play *Full Spectrum Warrior* and become a squad leader," he said. "It doesn't work that way. But you can experience a few things. You can make a few mistakes. You can learn from those mistakes."

For all the critiques of the video games, the fact is that real-life physical exercises are not perfect themselves. When I spoke with Neale Cosby of the Institute for Defense Analyses, he described some of the Vietnam-era training exercises as being no better than playing cowboys and Indians. "You walked through the forest," he said. "You shot at each other, and you yelled: 'Bang! Bang!'" In the 80's, the military devised a system of laser tag called the Multiple Integrated Laser Engagement System, which, it turned out, could not fire through bushes.

It is the grim paradox of all training for war: unless you are actually risking your life in battle, it is not real. As Stephen Goldberg, a psychologist who works for the Army, told me, any type of play-acting—whether in the field or on the computer—is liable to teach you something wrong. "Whatever you're doing other than fighting the enemy has compromises that make it artificial," he said. "Our motto is 'All but War Is a Simulation.'"

Reflect & Write

❏ How does Thompson use the first paragraph to hook the reader into his essay? What strategies does he use?
❏ How does Thompson establish his ethos in this piece?
❏ Schleiner presented a concerned look at the interface between war and gaming. Does Thompson share her concern? How does he see the relationship between the military and video games evolving?
❏ **Write:** Choose part of Thompson's argument and transform it into a five-minute presentation. Script and deliver that presentation to your class, then write an analysis of how you had to transform his written material for oral delivery.

COLLABORATIVE CHALLENGE

Many of the authors included in this chapter argue diametrically opposed positions on the issue of media violence. In order to think through their different stances on the topic, work with a group and draft the transcript of an imaginary radio roundtable discussion where each of the writers gets a turn to have his or her say on the subject. Ask each member of the group to assume the persona of one of the authors—you can refer to the articles or even quote from them directly if you like. Once you have drafted the discussion, role play it for your class, then discuss whose position was the most persuasive.

PERSPECTIVES ON THE ISSUE

1. Brian Farrington in his political cartoon and Eugene Provenzo in his address to the Senate committee both make arguments about the detrimental effects of violent video games. Where do each of these authors place blame for this? Analyze the different rhetorical strategies that each uses to accomplish this end. How does the medium in which they were arguing (political cartoon vs. testimony in a government hearing) influence their choice of strategies?

2. Some critics have argued that games like *Kuma/War,* which are based on real-life military encounters, serve as a form of interactive journalism. Watch one or two of the War mission videos from the Kuma site (http://www.kumawar.com/downloads.php) then consider the validity of that assertion. To what extent is *Kuma/War* a type of interactive journalism? To what extent does it function as a type of wartime propaganda? Do games like *Kuma/War* promote greater awareness of the lived experience of wartime in the Middle East? How does interactivity change the journalistic function of these missions? Be sure to consider the alternation between simulation, real-life footage, and the newscast format used in these mission downloads.

3. Visit the *Kuma/War* (http://www.kumawar.com/main.php), *America's Army* (http://www.americasarmy.com/), and *Full Spectrum Warrior* (http://www.fullspectrumwarrior.com/index.php) Websites. Analyze the argument of each site and how they use visual rhetoric to create this argument. What distinguishes the recreational game sites (such as Kuma) from the military-funded sites (such as America's Army)—both in terms of the visual and textual elements?

FROM READING TO RESEARCH

1. Do some research into the console war games from the 1980s such as Atari's *Battlezone* and write a research paper comparing military games then and now.

2. Identify your own stance on the relationship between gaming violence and real-life violence. Collect a series of images through a Google image search and through capturing screen shots that seem relevant to your argument. Combine these images into a photo essay—you could do a photo essay without words, one that utilizes just captions, one that includes both images and text, or one that takes advantage of multimedia possibilities and includes audio and animation to make your point.

GAMES WITH AN AGENDA

In this chapter, we have pushed video games beyond the idea of entertainment to look at the persuasive power beneath the surface. Whether it be the gender stereotypes of *Tomb Raider,* the adrenaline-charged violence of *GTA,* or the interactive journalism of *Kuma/War,* we have investigated the way these games implicitly or explicitly construct and reinforce a certain world view. Video game theorist Ian Bogost clearly articulates the relationship between gaming and real world perspectives: "Videogames are cultural artifacts," he states in one article. "They are steeped in ideology. In this very broad sense, all games are political."

Some games, however, are more deliberately political than others. As the poster from the 2004 "Videogames with an Agenda" exhibit demonstrates (see Figure 13.12), there are a growing number of games that resonate with social and political activism. While many designers prioritize marketability and entertainment, a growing number of video game developers have begun to capitalize on the persuasive potential of games as a form of visual rhetoric. You probably have already come across some of these games: maybe you've battled with straws in *Pepsi Lime and the Straw Fight* or fed the hungry in Burger

King's *Sneak King*, or maybe you even indulged in a game of *John Kerry: Tax Invaders* during the 2004 presidential election. In each case, you were being asked not just to play—to have fun—but to allow yourself to be persuaded to try a new drink, to consider buying a fast car, or to take action against a specific political platform.

What defines a "game with an agenda," therefore, is less its content than its purpose: it is designed to argue a particular position. As we shall examine in the articles and images that follow, these persuasive games take on many different causes: marketing, environmental issues, public policy, quitting smoking and even political protest. Persuasive gaming has proven itself useful in many different arenas; however, some questions remain: Can an online game really change someone's mind about an issue? Where do we draw the line between persuasion and propaganda? Finally, is persuasive gaming simply a passing fad?

FIGURE 13.12 The poster for a 2004 exhibition on video games uses visual echoes of previous protest movements (the Black Panthers) to make its argument.

Reflect & Write

❏ Analyze the poster in Figure 13.12 rhetorically. What strategies of persuasion are at work?

❏ Like many of the posters discussed in Chapter 4, this poster echoes propagandistic images from the mid-twentieth century as part of its modes of persuasion. Analyze the poster, considering not only its arrangement and style, but also the way in which this resonance with twentieth-century propaganda is used.

❏ **Write:** Sketch an alternative poster for this exhibit and then write a one-page reflection discussing your rhetorical decisions.

■ *In this article from the June 11, 2005,* Economist, *the authors discuss a relatively recent innovation in marketing: the advergame—online games used to market products or ideas. Organizations as varied as Pepsi, Peugeot, the Truth Campaign, and the United Nations World Food Programme feature advergames on their Websites.*

And Now, a Game from Our Sponsor

Cross the popularity of a new medium with the demands of advertisers, and the result can be a whole new genre of entertainment. In the 1930s, the sponsorship of radio serials by makers of household-cleaning products led to the soap opera. Listeners were enthralled by episodic, melodramatic storylines, and advertisers were guaranteed a big audience. Today, the same thing is happening with another new medium. Video games have been crossed with advertising to produce a new genre: the advergame.

Advergames appeal to both advertisers and gamers alike. Advertisers face the problem that many young people are watching less television in favour of gaming and internet surfing. A report published last year by Nielsen, a market-research firm, found that time spent watching television was declining among American men aged 18–34, and was decreasing even faster among gamers of the same age. Given that internet users are finding ways to avoid pop-ups, flashing banners and spam, putting advertisements into games is an obvious way to reach them. Perhaps surprisingly, gamers seem to feel positive towards in-game advertising. Football, driving and other sports games look more realistic with real advertisement hoardings rather than generic ads for made-up products. And the popularity of many advergames suggests that gamers are evidently quite happy to put up with advertising in return for free entertainment—just as soap-opera fans were in the radio age.

In-game advertising is not new, but until recently it was limited to static product-placement, inserted rather awkwardly into console games, says Denise Garcia of Gartner, a consultancy. She estimates that less than 10% of console games carry such "embedded" ads, and they account for a mere 0.25% of revenues at Electronic Arts, the world's biggest games publisher. In the long term, ads will be piped directly into games over the internet, allowing games publishers to update in-game advertisements as often as they want and to collect information about how in-game advertising is viewed. This may even lead to new, advertising-supported pricing models.

Today, however, few games consoles are connected to the internet. So while there is vast potential for in-game advertising on consoles, the near-term opportunity lies in advergames, which are specifically designed around advertising—the product is often the protagonist—and are either downloaded on to PCs or played inside web browsers. American firms spent around $90m last year on advergames, compared with $20m on in-game adverts and product placements, says the Yankee Group, a consultancy.

5   A successful early example of the genre was *America's Army*, an advergame first released as a recruitment tool in 2002 which is based on *Unreal*, a shoot-'em-up. This strikingly realistic war game, which covers basic training, tactical

planning and a variety of missions, now has over 5m registered players. About 100,000 people download the game free every month. But advergames can promote peace as well as war, as a more recent example, *Food Force*, demonstrates. This advergame, launched in April by the United Nations World Food Programme, is intended to raise awareness of global hunger. Players are cast as emergency aid workers who must pilot helicopters, negotiate with rebels and help to rebuild communities.

Kris Oser, a video-game specialist at *Advertising Age,* an industry magazine, says old-style television, print and radio advertising "just throws brands at people." Compare that with Dodge's advergame, *Race the Pros*, in which the company's cars can be driven to victory in a hyper-realistic simulation. Every Friday, real NASCAR race times are uploaded into the computer-controlled cars, and the track is dotted with the virtual billboards of dealerships close to the player (who must enter a zip code to take part). Such driving advergames also neatly sidestep rules that prohibit boasting about a car's top speed in TV adverts.

Richard Schlasberg, a Coca-Cola marketing manager based in Hellerup, Denmark, says the beverage-maker, long a fervent believer in television advertising, is now siphoning funds from its TV budget to maintain a regularly updated suite of games. A 30-second prime-time slot on American television can cost half a million dollars, whereas an advergame rarely costs more than $50,000 to develop and can be posted on the Internet for months or years. Mr. Schlasberg notes that, with television, potential drinkers just stare, briefly, at Coca-Cola. With advergames, consumers are "actually playing you," he says, and they then associate the brand with fun.

The simple, browser-based games offered by Coca-Cola and other firms may not be as sophisticated as *America's Army*, but they have merits of their own. They are easy to access and do not require players to download an enormous installer file, so they are well suited to casual play in lunch hours or coffee breaks.

Such games also have a broader appeal than traditional games. They can be found on mainstream websites, and nearly half of players are women.

Kimberly-Clark, a maker of feminine sanitary products, launched an advergame called *KT's Impossi-Bubble Adventures*. The game avoids mentioning tampons altogether—girls have to keep a brutish brother from reading their diaries. But after the game, they are ushered to a page that does discuss tampons. The advergame, put on line in mid-February, was played 500,000 times in its first six weeks. Given that it cost $25,000 to develop, that works out at a cost-per-play of just $0.05. Andy Stawski, a brand manager at Kimberly-Clark, says the game is having a significant effect on sales.

10 Advergames have been used in some unlikely ways. America's National Christmas Tree Association launched an advergame last year to promote real trees over plastic ones. In Britain, the Food Standards Agency launched a game called *Sid the Slug* to encourage people to eat less salt. (This rankled the Salt Manufacturers' Association, which has been lobbying—so far in vain—to kill the game.) And excitement over the potential of advergames has led some would-be pioneers astray. Ian Bogost of Persuasive Games, based in Atlanta, dreams of building games that go "outside the sphere of entertainment" into "rhetorical tools". One of his efforts is *Activism, the Public*

Policy Game, which was paid for by the Democratic Congressional Campaign Committee. Alas, the slow-paced action of tax reform is neither motivating, fun, nor terribly educational.

Reflect & Write

❏ In the article, the author refers to Kris Oser's contention that traditional advertising simply "throws brands at people." How is this type of advertising different? Do you think that it would be more or less effective? With what audience?

❏ Consider the analogy that opens this article. Why do you think that the author of an article on a new media technology started by referring to the 1930s? Was this an effective strategy? Why or why not?

❏ What effect does it have on the article's treatment of the topic to end with those advergames that have gone "astray"? How does this impact the readers' understanding of advergames as a viable advertising medium? What would be an alternative way to end this piece? How would that change the argument?

❏ **Write:** Visit the advergame archive at the Adverblog Website to access one or more advergames (http://www.adverblog.com/archives/cat_advergames.htm). Write an analysis of the game that you play, arguing about its persuasiveness as a new form of advertising for a product.

Jim Downing *is a reporter for the* Seattle Times, *where this article first appeared in the December 7, 2004, issue.*

Army to Potential Recruits: Wanna Play?

Jim Downing

Shaun Henry huddled in the snow behind a thin pillar. Nothing moved in the early-morning mist. Five enemy soldiers had taken the towers halfway across the bridge, and it was Henry's job to eliminate them.

He hoisted his M-16 and stepped into the clear.

A rifle report split the air. He fell back behind the pillar.

"We didn't have good cover," Henry later recounted. "I kept getting shot in the foot."

5   Back in the real world, a drizzly recent Saturday in Woodinville, Henry's toes were intact. He was in the final round of a video-game tournament sponsored by the U.S. Army.

In 10 minutes, Henry, 18, was "dead," his position overrun by five "soldiers" from Bellevue.

This is *America's Army,* a computer "first-person shooter" game, in which players advance through the stages of soldierhood—drilling in basic training, taking target practice with an M-16, studying basic emergency medicine and, finally, going into combat.

It's been such a hit that the Army has recently gone one step further with the game, organizing video-game parties around the country like this one in Woodinville, offering free game play, free "chow" and plenty of exposure to the Army's recruitment tactics. Woodinville and Bellevue recruiters plan to repeat the events every three months.

The Army makes no bones about the fact that it designed the game to attract a new generation of potential soldiers reared on ever-more-realistic video games. Information on joining the Army is a mouse-click away through an Internet link.

10   Since the Army released the game in July 2002, it has proved to be a low-cost advertising jackpot. The game has been downloaded more than 16 million times, and the Army estimates that nearly a third of all young people of prime recruitment age have been exposed to it.

But the game has drawn criticism from parents and anti-recruiting activists. The national group Veterans for Peace, for example, this year adopted a resolution condemning the Army's use of video games and the recruitment of anyone under 18 in general.

The critics say the new round of *America's Army* tournaments is just one more way for recruiters to get into the heads of impressionable high schoolers, a notion the Army rejects.

"I think [the game is] particularly questionable and exploitative of young people because it develops attitudes and propensities among younger children [more] than most of the other recruiting tools do, and at a more subliminal level," said Todd Boyle, of Kirkland, a Vietnam-era Navy veteran and founder of Washington Truth in Recruiting, a group that provides parents with information about the military that counters recruiters' messages.

"The Army games are particularly objectionable because they also include an indoctrination component, deepening the ideology of war," Boyle said. The games are "preying on [teenagers'] natural interest in affiliation—all Madison Avenue stuff."

15   Last month, Sgt. 1st Class Alvin Martin, one of two recruiters at the Army's Woodinville office, rented a computer-gaming business called LanWerX for the tournament. The same day, recruiters hosted a parallel event at another LanWerX branch 12 miles away in Bellevue.

Martin put up fliers and made phone calls to offer free food and a day of free *America's*

Army gaming to any interested boy, girl, man or woman over age 13—no commitments required. A khaki Humvee was parked outside.

Thirty-five players showed up in Woodinville to compete. The six winners then took on the winning team from the Bellevue tournament, via a high-speed Internet connection.

But the Bellevue squad was good.

"It's like they were all Special Forces," Henry said.

Martin, a 17-year Army career man, wore his camouflage field uniform and combat boots for the event. The Army looks for "that outgoing personality" in its recruiters, he said.

Martin disagrees with critics who see the game as a sinister way for the Army to get into the heads of ever-younger children.

"This isn't some kind of psychological thing to brainwash anybody," he said. "It's getting the U.S. Army name out there in a positive light.

"It's like Coca-Cola. You see the shape of the bottle and you know what it is. It's branding."

Martin signed up one new recruit from the Woodinville tournament. From the Bellevue event, recruiters said last week they have signed up one new soldier and are finishing testing and background checks to sign up two others.

In the recruiting game, that's a pretty good rate of return. At a recent series of three tournaments in New York City,

recruiters generated 320 new leads but only two enlistments. Each new soldier counts. Together, Martin and his recruiting partner in Woodinville, Sgt. 1st Class Harold Hunt, have a 46-enlistee annual quota.

Across all the armed services, recruiting costs about $4 billion annually, according to a 2003 government study. Between 1998 and 2002, the military's annual advertising expenditures alone more than doubled, from $299 million to $607 million.

That's why the *America's Army* video game has proved such a bargain. The first version cost $7 million; costs of updating the game and operating the *America's Army* Web site are about $5 million per year.

A survey by the Army this year showed that 29 percent of all young American adults ages 16 to 24 had had some contact with the game in the previous six months.

As part of the recruitment effort, Martin brought in active-duty soldiers with battle experience to join in the tournament.

Staff Sgt. Jonathan Selves, an infantryman in Haiti in 1993, said the video game portrayed the Army's weapons, equipment and approach to small-squad warfare quite well.

"You learn a lot of the tactics that we use on the battlefield," he said. "The whole purpose is to minimize casualties."

What the game lacks, of course, are real bullets.

"It's a game," Selves said. "It's not your life."

At the Woodinville tournament, Henry was joined by several young men who had already enlisted; they declined to be interviewed. Others said they were there only for the game, which drew mixed reviews.

"This game actually kinda sucks," said 19-year-old Matt Rayfield, of Monroe. He said he prefers a game called *Counter-Strike*. And he said he doesn't plan to enlist.

"Getting shot isn't as much fun as it looks," he said.

Henry said he likes the action in the *America's Army* game. But what he is really excited about are the job opportunities in the Army. And recruiters, he said, have been offering to bring order to his life.

Henry has attention-deficit disorder and struggled to graduate from Bothell High School last spring. He said he had been spending most of his time since then "lounging at home."

Henry was interested in the Army before he played the game, but the tournament, he said, is one of the things making him feel better about signing up. The Army says he has to lose 30 pounds first, though.

"The Army is talking to me about how quick I'd rise in the ranks, how they'd pamper me if I did a good job in basic [training]," he said. "They'll have me take a survey, and they'll put it in a computer and it'll spit out what I'm good at."

Reflect & Write

❏ How does the introduction of this article hook the reader? What strategy does Downing use to get the reader engaged?

❏ Consider the final comments about Henry at the end. Did they change the way you interpreted the argument of this article? Why or why not? Does Downing seem supportive of the Army's advergame techniques or critical of them?

❏ **Write:** Visit the *America's Army* site and then visit the *Counter-strike* site. Do the two differ? Write a blog entry in which you explore the differences and similarities between the advergame and the mainstream video game.

COLLABORATIVE CHALLENGE

Take on the persona of an Army recruiter and write a response to this article as a letter to the editor. Be sure to use pathos, logos and ethos in your letter, but feature one appeal more prominently than the others. When you share your letter with your class, explain your rhetorical choices.

Daniel Terdiman *specializes in writing about technology and Internet culture, and has contributed articles to* The New York Times, Salon.com, Time Magazine, *and* Wired, *where this article originally appeared on April 22, 2004.*

Playing Games with a Conscience

Daniel Terdiman

At first, the game looks like so many other first-person shooters: cross hairs aiming missiles at a raft of enemy targets.

But *September 12th* isn't like other games. Because when a missile shot at Arab terrorists kills an innocent bystander in the game's fictional Afghani village—and it's nearly impossible not to—other villagers run over, cry at their loss and then, in a rage, morph into terrorists themselves.

"The mechanics of the game are about this horrible decision, whether to do things, to take actions that will inevitably kill civilians," says Noah Wardrip-Fruin, co-editor of *First Person,* a collection of essays about the relationship between stories and games.

Indeed, *September 12th* has a point to make: that our actions have consequences, and that we should try to understand why other people take to arms. As Wardrip-Fruin puts it, the goal of the game is to develop in the player "empathy for the people who will become terrorists out of that experience, of having seen innocent people killed."

5   Earlier this week, the Simon Wiesenthal Center issued its annual report looking at websites and online games that promote hate, racism and anti-Semitism.

The report seeks to raise awareness about how hate groups are exploiting technology to spread their message, says Mark Weitzman, director of the center's Task Force Against Hate.

Such use of technology "teaches us that there always have been people in our society that will use whatever means is available to send out a message of hate," Weitzman says. "Our concern is how to deal with it."

He points to games like *Concentration Camp Manager, Ethnic Cleansing, Ghettoopoly* and others as examples of games put out by extremist groups.

"There's suicide-bombing games, (and) the full range taken from today's headlines," says Weitzman. But "you won't find them advertised, especially because some of them are rip-offs of legitimate games. I don't think the people at Monopoly would be very happy about *Ghettoopoly.*"

10　　But rather than focus on games that disseminate messages of hate, Wardrip-Fruin, *September 12th* designer Gonzalo Frasca and Persuasive Games founder Ian Bogost would prefer that people instead consider games that foster understanding and tolerance of other cultures.

"I think that what is essential is allowing players to freely experiment within a virtual environment and encourage them to discuss what they play with their peers," says Frasca. "*September 12th* carries its own humanistic message, but I think that eventually, it would be even better if players would be able to use games as small laboratories for exploring—and contesting—their own beliefs."

Bogost says there are a growing number of games that promote positive messages and mutual understanding. For example, he thinks that *Real Lives 2004* does a good job of helping players see what it would be like to experience life as a member of another culture.

"You're taking on the role of another person who is not you," says Bogost. "Maybe (it's) a person from rural India. You're implicating yourself in all the trials or tribulations or difficulties that you might not think of."

Another game Bogost likes is *Civilization III*, because of the way it makes players work together, regardless of race or religion.

15　　To Wardrip-Fruin, it's just as important to look at how a game is built as it is to look at a game's message.

"It's important to think about the structure ᵒ game," he says, "not just from these hate sites, but from mainstream publishers, if we're going to understand these issues."

He thinks that hate groups are doing no more than exploiting a style of game—for example, first-person shooters—for their own purposes.

"If you think about what these people are doing on these hate sites, they're taking a set of well-understood game mechanics that are about hating someone—about hating the Germans during World War II—and finding them and killing them," Wardrip-Fruin explains. "So it's very easy to just slap (on) the image of the group you hate. I would argue the message is the same: Find the group you hate and go and kill them."

Frasca agrees.

20　　"Keep in mind that a lot of commercial games—following the Hollywood tradition—use token enemies like Arabs (and) Vietnamese," he says, "which are shot in these games without the players thinking twice about the ideological message that these games carry. Lots of people start thinking about this when, say, Hezbollah launches an anti-Israel game, but there are plenty of anti-Arab games that are available at Wal-Mart at $39.95."

Still, that's not to say that all violence discourages mutual understanding.

"I do not think that killing virtual people is wrong, though—it is a lot of fun, indeed," Frasca says. "But virtual killing is totally different from real killing. As long as we can make that difference within a critical attitude, the situation does not need to be problematic."

But Frasca also says there are countless games that promote neither hate nor violence.

Wardrip-Fruin concurs, and says open-ended simulation games like *The Sims* do a very good job of encouraging constructive thought in game players.

25　　"It's very hard to imagine one that is about hating some ethnic or religious other," he says. "I'd say that the fundamental thing about a computer game is the structure of what you do as a participant, and the structure of something like *SimCity* or *The Sims* is about understanding a system, and trying to make it grow in the way you want it to grow."

Frasca goes so far as to say that some massively multiplayer games, even ones involving violence, help players understand each other better.

"Online games such as *EverQuest* foster cooperation between players from all over the world," he explains. "Even if there can be language barriers that can interfere with the communication, *EverQuest* allows players to work together based on their skills, without focusing on their gender, age, nationality (or) religion."

According to Bogost, there is a bright future for games that promote mutual tolerance and understanding.

But right now, says Frasca, games with such agendas are few and far between.

30   "Games for tolerance are (in) their infancy," he says. "But I think they have a great potential because games always allow you to be in somebody else's shoes and viewing the world through their eyes. And that is the essential requirement for tolerance: Understanding that other people

have different realities that may not be the same (as) ours."

Reflect & Write

❏   What is the argument made by this article? How does Terdiman's selection of which games to mention and which descriptions to develop factor into the construction of this argument?

❏   At one point in the article, Terdiman mentions that Gonzalo Frasca suggests that even violent multiplayer games have their positive side. Do you agree with this assertion? Why or why not?

❏   **Write:** Draft a response to the Terdiman piece that argues for the benefits of venting "hate" online through gaming. You might choose to develop the position offered by Chris Kaye in the October 2004 issue of *Esquire*. In his article, "Joystick Jihad," he wrote, "Casting our enemy as the villain [in video games] can be as lucrative as a Halliburton contract in an oil-rich war zone (and a hell of a lot more fun)" (p. 114).

■   **Gonzalo Frasca,** *a game designer, specializes in video game development and rhetoric. He edits Ludology.org, a resource for scholars interested in computer games; he co-edits—with Professor Ian Bogost of Georgia Tech—a blog about persuasive gaming called WaterCoolerGames.com; and he also co-curated a recent exhibit, "Videogames with an Agenda" with Bogost. He is also a founding member of Newsgaming.com, an organization dedicated to producing games with a political purpose. In this piece, Frasca describes the process through which he and his colleague Bogost conceived and designed the controversial persuasive game September 12, a game that offered commentary on the U.S. reaction to the September 11, 2001, terrorist attacks. This article was first published in the November 2003 "Ivory Tower" column through the Digital Games Research Association, a nonprofit, international organization of video game scholars.*

Ideological Videogames: Press Left Button to Dissent

Gonzalo Frasca

"Videogames do not necessarily need to be entertaining." Such a statement is still likely to trigger passionate debates (albeit less likely than a few years ago). Who would play a game that is not fun? The answer, of course, relies on how you define fun and entertainment.

The question is trivial in other media, such as books or films. Certainly, thousands of movies and novels are made every year with the sole goal of entertaining their audience, while a similar amount supposedly aim at more serious goals such as generating debate, making a point, explaining something or sharing knowledge. The latter are not fun under the broader definition of the term, even if they do provide certain pleasures.

The question should be trivial in games, too. Actually, videogames were born for non-entertaining uses, as military simulators designed for training. There is also an extensive history of educational videogames with an explicit pedagogical agenda. These examples, which exist since the very beginning of the genre, should suffice to make the point that videogames can certainly have non-entertaining purposes. However, in my experience, most players react negatively to the idea of games that do not just aspire at being fun.

If videogames are indeed persuasive tools, then they can be used for conveying passionate ideas. If you want to know if a medium is ready to deliver an ideological message, simply ask if somebody would be willing to endanger her life for it. There are multiple cases of this in literature (i.e. Salman Rushdie) and it certainly happens in films, even though on a minor degree (Martin Scorsese's *Last Temptation of Christ* was violently boycotted).

5 Would somebody be willing to die for a videogame? I guess the answer is still no. Currently, it is more likely that games can simply trigger passionate arguments and some foul language. As a matter of fact, the moment I knew that my game *September 12th* had succeeded at conveying its ideas was when the first piece of hate mail arrived to my inbox.

Ideological videogames are games that you can agree or disagree with. Certainly, nobody disagrees with *Tetris*. However, as games started dealing with more realistic simulations of human life, the situation changed. A clear example is *The Sims,* which has been criticized for its supposed consumerist ideology (and defended by its author as anti-consumerist). Still, I think *The Sims* was clearly designed primarily as entertainment. Of course, there is nothing wrong with that, but personally I would also love to see more games with a clear agenda.

Before professionally working as a game designer, I worked in advertising and journalism. The connection between videogames and ads was clear for me since I saw a Budweiser banner displayed in *Tapper,* the classic bartender game. It was while working at CNN that I started daydreaming about creating games that would complement news with editorial statements, like political cartoons do. A few years later, I was finally able to launch Newsgaming.com with the help of a group of collaborators.

Newsgames, or games based on news events, are certainly not new. There are countless examples of games based on political and social events, as well as many created after the events of 9-11. It is on this tradition that I created *September 12th,* a game (even if its instructions provocatively claim that it is not a game) that tries to make a point about the war on terror.

Basically, the game models a Middle Eastern town showcasing mostly civilians and some terrorists. The player controls a crosshair with which it is possible to launch missiles. It is almost impossible to kill the terrorists without generating "collateral damage." Every time that a civilian dies, others will mourn him or her and, suddenly, become terrorists. After a few minutes of play, the number of terrorists is out of control.

10 If you are looking for a more detailed description of my experience with crafting *September 12th,* please see "Playing with reality," at Game-Research.com. I am not going to refer here to some common objections, such as the game being one-sided and its failure to showcase terrorists in action. Nevertheless, I would like to summarize in this article just a few aspects.

September 12th was conceived with two goals in mind. One was conveying a simple idea through a simple model: violence will create more violence. It was my hope that this idea would contribute to generate debate around the issue of the civilian casualties of the war on terror. The other goal was exploring the problems of creating actual ideological videogames instead of just writing about them from my nice and tall ivory tower.

The game certainly generated debate. A few weeks after its launch, more than 100 thousand people from all over the world have played *September 12th.* More importantly, half of the links pointing to it came from online forums and weblog comments, where both the game and its topic were discussed.

The game also generated criticism and was very often dismissed as too simplistic (which, of course, it obviously is). In part, this rejection may be due to what Sherry Turkle identifies in her book *Life on the Screen* as "simulation denial": some people believe that simulations cannot help us in understanding reality because they always offer a limited model of it. However, I think that a big part of this critique is due to the fact that political videogaming is not yet a well-established genre. Nobody would ever criticize a printed political cartoon on the basis of being too simplistic: caricatures are simplifications by definition. In spite of this, cartoons make a point and this is why they remain a useful journalistic tool.

We need more games that make statements. Surely, games and simulations will always be limited. Games will always be biased. Games will always be interpreted (and manipulated) in ways that its authors never foresaw. However, I agree with Sherry Turkle that games could also provide great insight:

"Understanding the assumptions that underlie simulation is a key element of political power. People who understand the distortions imposed by simulations are in a position to call for more direct economic and political feedback, new kinds of representation, more channels of information." (*ibid*)

15   In order to accomplish this, us academics must join forces with developers and provide them with practical game theory or, even better, start making our own games. Personally, I see *September 12th* as a small experiment on game rhetoric. But the potential of videogames for critical thinking and debate is, I believe, much larger. It lies, I think, in providing players with tools to contest the game's ideological assumptions by designing their own games. Eventually, games will allow us to model our ideas and let others play with them and vice versa.

One of my most vivid childhood memories was witnessing my mother and aunt crying together as they burned most of their books in our backyard. This was during my home country's military dictatorship, when owning certain books was enough reason for being imprisoned and/or tortured. I wonder if some day somebody would hold a match in front of a pile of videogames and seriously consider burning them down in order to maintain their freedom. If that ever happens, it would mean that our civilization would have been able to turn a supposedly trivial medium into something that really matters. Thanks to Ray Bradbury, we know that books flame at 451 degrees Fahrenheit. Who knows how much heat is needed to burn videogames?

Reflect & Write

❑   In this piece, Frasca starts by establishing a connection between video games and books and films. How does this strategy contribute to the persuasiveness of his argument?

❑   In the paragraph that begins "The game also generated criticism . . .", Frasca addresses some of the critiques of *September 12*. Do you find his response to the critics convincing? Why or why not?

❑   The concluding paragraph of this piece, with its narrative about book burning, is very striking. Why do you think that Frasca chose to end with this story and analogy? Does this final image and rhetorical question alter the argument of the article as a whole?

❑   **Write:** Frasca distinguishes between nonideological video games (such as *Tetris*) and ideological video games ("games that you can agree or disagree with" — i.e. that are, however subtly, suggesting a particular worldview or opinion). As a group, brainstorm a list of ten video game titles. Each member of the group should then individually rank the titles as Ideological, Nonideological, or Undecided. Convene as a group and discuss your rankings. Then choose one of the games that you marked as "ideological" and develop a brief PowerPoint presentation in which you explain to the class how its serves this function.

■ *Velvet-Strike, a Website maintained by Anne-Marie Schleiner, is a repository for a series of strategies to combat violence and video games. Schleiner, promoting online activism against violence in Counter-Strike, an online multiplayer game modeled on military combat, includes a link to these "Recipes," which have been submitted by visitors to her site, for nonviolent protests online.*

Velvet-Strike Intervention Recipes

The following are instructions for how to intervene in *Counter-Strike* and some other online shooters with the intent to disrupt gameplay as usual with performative art actions. Please send us your own intervention recipes.

Recipe for Salvation by Graphical User Intervention(GUI):

1. Enter a Counter-Strike Server with a hostage scenario as a member of the Terrorist Team.
2. Rescue the Hostages you are supposed to be guarding.

Recipe for Crashing by Brody(aka sylo):

1. Join a vehicle heavy Tribes2 server.
2. Create and pilot a transport ship.
3. Gather friendly warriors in the transport pretending that you will soon fly to the enemy base.
4. When everyone is in, fly away from the enemy base, into the endless beautiful landscape.
5. Convince your passengers that this is a shortcut, or you are taking them on a nice tour, to calm them down.
6. Fly as far as possible.
7. Upon landing (or crashing), your passengers will be so far from the battle they must commit a mass suicide (ctrl-k) to return to the fighting.

Recipe for Martyrdom by John Brennan(aka BigJB):

1. You and several friends join a busy Counter-Strike server.
2. During the battle, tell everyone you are martyrs for peace, then jump off the tallest structure in the level, killing yourselves.

Recipe for Friendship by A.M.S.

1. Find a Counter-Strike server with 0 or 1 other player on line.(If you go to an empty one most likely someone will show up to see who you are.)
2. Shoot a few times at your enemy.
3. Tell them you are newbie and ask them to show you how to plant the bomb.
4. Ask them which country they are from.
5. Ask them all about themselves.
6. Arrange to meet another time.

Recipe for Heart Stand-in by A.M.S.

1. Ask the members of your Counter-Strike team, (must be at least 14), Counter-Terrorist or Terrorist, to stand in a large, low, flat open area in the game that can be viewed from above.
2. Arrange everyone to stand in the shape of a heart. Do not move or return fire.
3. On all player chat send out the message repeatedly: "Love and Peace"
4. Retain position stoicly.

Reflect & Write

❏ Do you think that virtual performance art of this type is effective? Why or why not?
❏ How do the visual and the textual combine in the last recipe?
❏ Notice how each recipe contains a reference to the person who authored it. Why do you think author attribution is included? What is the effect on the reader? On the gaming community? How would it be different if the Website listed full names, rather than just initials?
❏ **Write:** Draft your own recipe for nonviolent protest in a multiplayer game to add to this list.

■ *Another feature of the Velvet-Strike site is that it hosts a series of "sprays" that can be downloaded for use in* Counter-Strike *gameplay. When active, these sprays replace the* Counter-Strike *bullets with spraypaint so that instead of showering players with bullets, Velvet-Strike operatives paint an antiviolence mural on the wall for all players to see. Velvet-Strike also invites* Counter-Strike *players to submit their own sprays, which they make available for downloading on their site.*

Velvet-Strike Sprays

FIGURE 13.13–14 These examples of *Velvet-Strike Sprays* show how gunfire is converted into anti-violence graffiti during gameplay.

Reflect & Write

❏ Compare these images to those found in the Counter-Strike clips found at http://www.steamgames.com/v/index.php?area=media&cc=US. Do you feel that this is an effective means of subverting violent gameplay? Why or why not?

❏ Look back at the recipes for intervention. Which do you think would make a more effective statement—the recipes or the sprays? Why?

❏ Which of the two sprays seems most effective? Why?

❏ **Write:** Visit the Velvet-Strike site and look at the sprays available for download. Then sketch out your own spray and write a letter to Schleiner to accompany it, explaining the rhetorical choices behind your design.

PERSPECTIVES ON THE ISSUE

1. Many of the articles above discuss the ways in which video games have been used as persuasive political tools. However, each writer approaches this topic in a very different way. Look carefully at the style, tone, structure, and evidence in the articles. How do they differ? Is one article more persuasive than the others? Why?

2. Visit some of the political games mentioned above and play them. Do these seem to be effective modes of persuasion? What audience are they targeted at? Do you think they will become powerful tools in upcoming elections? Why or why not?

3. Play *September 12* at http://www.newsgaming.com/newsgames.htm. Having played the game, how does your understanding of Terdiman's and Frasca's article change? Would their articles have benefited from including screen shots as visual evidence? Which image would you chose, and where in their article would you place it?

4. Choose a campus issue (workers rights, alcohol on campus, student fees) and with a group, brainstorm the design for a game that would help people learn about these issues. Share your ideas with the class.

FROM READING TO RESEARCH

1. Ian Bogost writes about one of the Truth's advergame's in a July 27, 2004, blog entry on Watercoolergames.com (http://www.watercoolergames.org/archives/000202.shtml). Read Bogost's comments, then visit the Truth Website and try to find the game that he describes. After looking at it, browse the different "issues" of Truth to find a different advergame. Now write your own blogpost analyzing its rhetorical effectiveness, using Bogost's post as a research starting point for a model.

2. Working in groups, research an important local or national issue and develop a stance on the subject. Conduct field research about this issue by interviewing members of the community. Draft a storyboard for an online game designed to persuade viewers to your point of view. Prepare a pitch for a fictional candidate or governing board in which you argue for the effectiveness of your game in their campaign. Be sure in your pitch to touch on the following: who the game will reach; how players will access the game; what the rhetorical features of the game are in terms of design and content; and why this form of interactive media would be an effective campaign tool.

CHAPTER 14

Representing Reality

How do images represent reality? Can they capture the "truth" of an event or does a photograph actually work as a tool of persuasion? This chapter will explore a range of instances in which photography and ethics collide. We'll look at both domestic photographs—snapshots of American communities—and international perspectives—images snapped at moments of crisis across the globe. In all these examples, we will encounter challenging questions about the ethics of photography: Who can take a photo? Who is captured by print? What does it mean to freeze identity in time and place? Can photos ever tell the truth? How are arguments made—about people, places, events, and history—through the snapping of a photo?

Consider, for instance, the photograph in Figure 14.1, taken days after the levees broke outside New Orleans. What is the argument of this photograph? Notice the image of a man and woman walking down the street. In another context, this would seem to be an image of the ordinary. But what effect do the other photographic elements have? How do the high water and the military vehicle in the background transform this into an image of crisis? What is the line between these two categories? Now consider the written caption used by the newspaper:

FIGURE 14.1 This photograph from the *Dallas Morning News* juxtaposes the figures of people wading through the flooded streets of New Orleans with the image of a tank, sent to aid the victims of hurricane Katrina.

> New Orleans, LA—Tossed together by crisis, 81-year-old Louis Jones (left) and 62-year-old Catherine McZeal join forces to navigate Poydras Street in their trek to the Superdome and a chance at evacuation. *(September 1, 2005. Photo by Michael Ainsworth.)* © 2005 The Dallas Morning News.

How do the words in turn shape our interpretation of the meaning of the image? How do words and pictures combine to create a compelling argument about what happened in New Orleans?

In capturing this moment, the photographer makes an argument—about our lives and our realities. How we interpret such images will be the focus of this chapter. In looking at images, captions, and arguments about these representations of reality, we'll come to a deeper understanding of how the media shapes our understanding of reality, our lives, and our world.

Our first perspective on this issue will take a close look at seemingly simple photos: those moments when we see normal people living their lives. But we'll ask how the moment in time actually turns into an argument when we consider these images as visual rhetoric. Take, for instance, a family in America at the dinner table. If we saw a photograph of this family holding hands and saying grace, we might come to some conclusions about the religious practices of this racial group, class status, geographic location, or era in time. But what if we took a photo of the family at a moment of debate, or what Susan Sontag calls a "pessimistic perspective" such as when the father places his fist on the table or the child seems about to break into tears. Perhaps this could be a passing moment, but it would send a message to viewers about the lives of this family and their values, experiences, and identity. We'll ask questions about how images of the ordinary shape what we might know about the reality of the subject. As we'll learn from writer Patrick Cox, images do this by capturing identity, freezing it in time, and making an argument for the viewer. We'll end this section with a consideration of how video blogs and new technologies such as Flickr and YouTube enable people to share personal images with a wide public.

In the second part, we'll look at how images of crisis—moments of conflict, tragedy, horror, or devastation—seem to capture national or international moments in time in ways that convey fixed arguments about what is happening. In doing so, as Daniel Okrent tells us, they thereby persuade viewers to interpret a situation in a given light. This section of the chapter will not only examine images of natural disasters but also images from wartime, perhaps one of the most fraught situations in which photography and ethics collide. Your reading of Chapter 3 introduced you to war photography, and early images such as those by Alexander Gardner in which he purposefully moved the bodies of war dead to create more of a pathos-laden scene for his viewers. Since the Civil War, war photography and photojournalism have evolved with changing technologies to include color images and film footage, political positions on how much the public can see, and ethical concerns over the morale, confidentiality, and consequence of war coverage. We'll look at the most recent form of photojournalism in war, what the military and the media call embedded journalism—the practice of assigning photographers to a military unit. We'll ask, with Dirck Halstead and Jim Lehrer, how the position of the photographer shapes the reality he or she represents for a viewing audience.

Seeing Connections
Explore the history of war photography—and the way photos work as visual arguments—in Chapter 3.

SNAPSHOTS OF THE ORDINARY

FIGURE 14.2 This photograph from *America 24/7* captures one perspective on everyday suburban existence in America.

Photography takes an instant out of time, altering life by holding it still.

—*Dorothea Lange*

Look at the photo of the mom in Figure 14.2. Without a caption, we are faced with the challenge of interpreting the photograph as a text—as an image of the ordinary life in America. And yet, there is something special about the image: this mom seems rather extraordinary, with her ability to multitask by literally balancing babies and house chores. Clearly, our interpretation about her history, her current situation, her husband, her class status, her lack of a babysitter, her beliefs and values, and her future is based on our reading of the photo as a text. In this way, the photo makes an argument about this woman's life—and in the process, we learn a bit about her reality through this representation. In fact, the original title for the photo exhibit read *America 24/7: Extraordinary Images of One American Week*. The writer found the photo "extraordinary" as well. Words and images combine to make an argument that this American mom is pretty special, and so too perhaps by extension is suburban America.

But does this photographed image accurately reflect the reality of this woman's life outside this one moment? Maybe she posed for the camera. Maybe she has never mowed the lawn before. Or maybe she does this every weekend. In a sense, we must take this image as evidence—it is all we have. As Patrick Cox asserts in his review of the *America 24/7* exhibit, "Photographs play an essential role in defining our character."

This chapter will look at images of the everyday and the ordinary. We'll start with photographs that people—such as yourself—take of their own families, and then we'll study ways in which photography has been used to define American culture. As part of this analysis, we'll look at what Susan Sontag named the "pessimistic turn" in American visual culture, a movement away from Kodak moments to less filtered views of contemporary life. Finally, we'll come back full circle to a moment of optimism for the power of the photographic image, exploring how the new technologies of Flickr and YouTube allow people to share once again photos of the ordinary and post them on the Web as representations of their everyday reality.

Reflect & Write

❏ What do you think is the context and circumstance for the photo?
❏ What argument is the image making about women's roles in America today?
❏ **Write:** Draft our own caption for this photo. What argument are you trying to make by appending those words to this image? Now, visit the exhibit online and read the original caption at http://dirckhalstead.org/issue0311/247_04.html to compare your interpretation of the image to the actual caption and story provided by the photographer.

Lenore Skenazy, *a columnist for the* New York Daily News, *has written widely on American popular culture, politics, and family life. As a writer, she is known for her humorous, often ironic style. Her articles have been reprinted in numerous publications, including the* Miami Herald, *the* Montreal Gazette *and the* Detroit Free Press. *This article originally appeared in the* Daily News *on January 5, 2003, and was read on NPR in March 2003.*

Don't Smile for the Camera

Lenore Skenazy

A 2-year-old was visiting our home the other day—clinging, crying, demanding juice then milk, no, JUICE!—and frankly, we found him fascinating. We simply could not remember any time that our own kids, ages 4 and 6, had ever been that horrid.

Er, young.

The 2-year-old's parents looked a tad peeved at our amnesia, until my husband, Joe, figured out the source of our self-satisfaction: "We took our videos at all the wrong times."

Bingo. If you look at the video record of our kids (bring some No-Doz), you will find a twosome so sweet, they could actually rot teeth. But you won't find real life.

5   Here they are pretending to toboggan through our living room, after a double timeout (not shown).

Here they are dancing to a Beatles song—after a half-hour, untaped, of Joe trying to get the CD player working.

And ah, just look at them there, stirring the brownie batter—with the camera expertly snapped off the second one started screaming, "You're licking too much!"

No, our family looks pretty perfect on film, as must yours, because if there's one thing we have all learned, it is what constitutes a Kodak moment: It is the moment our life most conforms, however briefly, to the way we'd like it to be. And it is about as reliable a record as a souvenir postcard.

"All families want to be seen as happy, friendly and successful," says Dan Gill, a freelance photographer. "However, these Kodak moment pictures are a far cry from our daily lives."

10   Not only do we instinctively reach for the camera only when our kids are acting like the ones on "The Cosby Show," often we wait until far-flung relatives have assembled and the house is clean and the dog isn't sniffing anywhere embarrassing. In this way, we create our own mythology of a perfect family.

Mythology? Yes, that's what you'll find between the covers of most family photo albums, says Arthur Dobrin, professor of humanities at Hofstra University.

A little history, here: In the days before photography and the industrial revolution,

cultures passed down their myths orally: We are the people of the trees! Our chief is the son of thunder, etc. Everyone learned the same story about their collective ancestors.

But with the advent of photography, families were suddenly able to record their own individual history: This is our very own grandfather. We descended from *him*.

"Very few cultures present themselves negatively," says Dobrin. "And neither do very many photo albums. They can't! The family's identity depends on it.

15   So in our pictures, "Children are always laughing and smiling. We also photograph ourselves loving and hugging," says Dobrin—including those of us who don't hug much. And of course, we photograph our great successes: graduation, marriage, the 30-inch striped bass.

When something goes wrong—say, a breakup—many are the miffed who will snip the discarded spouse out of the picture. There—that never happened.

Likewise, you won't find many portraits of loved ones sick in the hospital, or even sitting on the couch, watching reruns. That's not the stuff of myth. That's the stuff of real life.

The stuff that slips away.

Kodak moments may make us feel proud of who we are and where we come from, but they do a disservice to memory. When we don't have pictures of the toy-strewn house, mom in her bathrobe, grandpa drinking his soup, the life we really lived disappears. By the time we want to remember it, we can't.

20   We have gained a Kodak moment and lost the story of our lives.

Seeing Connections
For guidelines on writing an essay about the argument of a photograph, see Chapter 3.

Reflect & Write

- ❏ How does Skenazy's distinctive voice and style contribute to the persuasiveness of her column? How appropriate is it to the argument she is conveying? How would her argument have changed if she had used a more formal voice?
- ❏ How does the introductory example set up the argument that follows?
- ❏ Skenazy uses the phrase "Kodak moment" a few times in her article. What does she mean by this phrase? What does this phrase mean to you?
- ❏ **Write:** Look in a family photo album or select a photograph (one that you have or one that you remember) that is representative of your own family photos. Do your photos support Skenazy's assertion about the Kodak moment? Write an essay responding to her argument and using your own personal photographs as evidence.

■ *In this article,* **Patrick Cox** *introduces the photography exhibition,* America 24/7. *Dr. Cox specializes in twentieth-century American political, media, and social history with an emphasis on Texas and the Southwest. He is the assistant director of the Center for American History at the University of Texas, Austin, and has authored a biography on the late U.S. Senator Ralph W. Yarborough. This article originally appeared in the November 2003 issue of the* Digital Journalist, *a monthly online magazine focused on visual journalism.*

America 24/7: A Family Photograph Album, November 2003

Patrick Cox, PhD.

Americans have maintained a long love affair with their lives and images.

In *America 24/7*, Rick Smolan and David Elliott Cohen captured a remarkable series of images of the lives of everyday Americans during one week in May 2003. Instead of attempting to capture America's epic moment on film, the authors chose to select the digital photographs of professional and amateurs from around the nation. Americans at work and play, pictures of celebration and meditation, urban and rural landscapes the pages contain photos that portray the ideas and lives that represent the very fabric of our nation.

Photographs play an essential role in defining our character. In the modern era, films and television provide a popular format for news and entertainment. Most people will state that they obtain information and visual images from television and the movies. Yet every family in America maintains their own highly prized collection of photos of their family and their history. These are the most coveted of all family treasures. Early in my life, working as a young reporter at a newspaper, I interviewed the local volunteer fire department chief about residential fires. I don't remember much of the story, but one statement always stayed with me. When a person's home catches on fire, people always want to save their loved ones, their pets and their family photographs.

Photos of everyday life are treasures. I have hundreds of family photos and pictures in my personal albums—my exuberant daughter with her first car, my wife and I on a secluded beach in Mexico, my dogs in the back of the pickup truck, a scenic waterfall on a back trail at Yellowstone, childhood photos when we were all slim and trim, family shots with everyone squeezed in front of the Christmas tree (and trying to have everyone smile and keep their eyes open).

5 One of my favorite photos is an 8 × 10 black and white picture of two great gentlemen who befriended me as a young newspaper editor. Standing on the left is Chester Franklin, white hair with a cowboy hat, and on the right is Beven Varnon, balding with a white beard. They are standing next to Indian Rock on the Blanco River in Wimberley, a small town about 40 miles southwest of Austin. Both men are smiling as they have just finished some great tale. In my early career, these two men were the wise old sages and the guiding forces who helped steer me through treacherous waters of my formative adult years. Both are now deceased, but their image and influence is firmly embedded in my mind. But they are the people who represent the best in American ideas and values.

These are the images and ideas that are captured in *America 24/7*. As the authors state in the book, the product is a visual patchwork. This is not a glitzy version of a Hollywood personality venue that is often promoted as the image desired by Americans. And this is not a public relations production intended to show only the desirable, edited photos for marketing a corporate brand. The photos capture the true essence of American character and communities. Just like the family photo album, this includes pictures from everyday life and records a week of American history for posterity.

Reflect & Write

❏ Patrick Cox begins his article with a premise that "Americans have maintained a long love affair" with images. How does this trope serve as a unifying thesis for his short piece? How does Cox connect this thesis to the idea of photos as treasures?

❏ Analyze the use of anecdotes and narration as an argumentative strategy—one discussed in Chapter 2—and consider the effectiveness of this writing technique for a review essay. How does the use of story reflect the decision of the exhibition editors to tell a story with pictures?

❏ The editors of the exhibit, Rick Smolan and David Elliot Cohen, address directly the question of ethical and equal representation. Analyze their argument for selection; do you find this argument persuasive? Why or why not? Here is the argument: "*America 24/7* is not intended to be fair. Not every state, race, religion—or photographer—is represented; nor is every point of view included. This is not a book for tourists or one created by a public-relations firm to explain America to the world. It's a visual patchwork, woven by Americans from every walk of life."

❏ **Write:** Imagine that you are Lenore Skenazy and write a column from her point of view that reviews the *America 24/7* exhibit.

■ *Described as the largest collaborative photography exhibit in history,* America 24/7 *collected photos from over 25,000 amateur and professional photographers to create a visual chronicle of everyday life in America.*

Visual Reading: Images from *America 24/7*

FIGURE 14.3 A snapshot into domestic life in Pinehurst, Georgia, shows Howard "Curly" Borders reading his evening paper. What argument does this visual representation make about life in the American South?

FIGURE 14.4 Alphanso "Chippy" Edwards looks out from the kitchen window in Hartford, Connecticut.

FIGURE 14.5 Boys dive into the 80-mile-long All-American Canal on a hot day on the California/Mexico border.

Reflect & Write

❏ How does each visual text—as a photographic reading—serve to produce a sense of America's identity in a particular way? What specific rhetorical elements shape the composition of the text? Use the checklist at the end of Chapter 3 to help you answer this question.

❏ Taken together, how do these images constitute parts of the American "family album"? What do they say about this "family"? What images do you think should be included here as well?

❏ How are race, gender, and social class constructed by these images? Compare Figures 14.3 and 14.4 in particular, which show two men, two windows, but very different arguments about "America."

❏ The captions reproduced for these photographs are part of the original exhibit. How do the captions work in conjunction with the images? The captions read as follows:

Figure 14.3: "Pinehurst, Georgia: Howard "Curly" Borders loves old houses and old cars. He's restored both his prized '29 Buick and the 100-year-old Victorian house he shares with wife Elaine." Figure 14.4: "Hartford, Connecticut: When Alphanso "Chippy" Edwards, 60, started his restaurant, Chippy's, 20 years ago he was one of only a handful of African-America business owners in Hartford. Today his domain also includes the Laundromat next door." Figure 14.5: "Calexico, California: The 80-mile All-American Canal not only irrigates California's Imperial Valley, it's also a perfect swim spot along the Mexican border. Although climbing through the westernmost edge of the border fence from Mexico into America is technically illegal, on particularly hot days the Border Patrol tends to look the other way."

❑ Consider the information contained in each caption and the order in which that information is presented. How is style, word choice, and voice used to create a certain impression? Why do you think each caption begins with the geographic location? How do the captions contribute to pulling together the individual photographs into a unified exhibit and argument about *America 24/7*?

❑ **Write:** Review other photographs in the *America 24/7* exhibit by visiting http://www.digitaljournalist.org/issue0311/247_01.html. Choose three photographs and write your own review of their rhetorical elements, meaning, and significance.

COLLABORATIVE CHALLENGE

As a group, conduct your own *America 24/7* project. Use a digital camera and take photographs of everyday people during the course of one week. Building on your knowledge of photo essays from Chapter 8, arrange your photos into a sequence that tells a story and add captions. Finally, compose a cover article as both an introduction and review essay, explaining your rhetorical choices as well as the argument of your final project. Present your group work to the class. For added challenge, use a film recorder to complete the same project described above. This time, capture scenes from everyday life and then, during your editing process, include a "director's cut" with a voice-over providing the rationale for your images and the arguments they make about your life and culture.

Seeing Connections
Consult the guidelines for composing a photo essay in Chapter 8.

■ **Susan Sontag** *was a famous essay writer as well as an experimental novelist, short story writer, film writer, director, and photographer. Her work has been published in* The New Yorker, The New York Review of Books, The Times Literary Supplement, Art in America, Antaeus, Parnassus, The Threepenny Review, The Nation, *and* Granta. *Her final book,* Regarding the Pain of Others, *looked at both art and photography from a moral and social point of view. The excerpts of this essay are taken from* On Photography *(1977), a best-selling book on visual culture. The essay was originally published as "Freak Show," in* The New York Review of Books *on November 15, 1973.*

America, Seen Through Photographs, Darkly

Susan Sontag

Walt Whitman tried to see beyond the difference between beauty and ugliness, importance and triviality. It seemed to him servile or snobbish to make any discriminations of value, except the most generous ones. Great claims were made for candor by our boldest, most delirious prophet of cultural revolution. Nobody would fret about beauty and ugliness, he implied, who accepted a sufficiently large embrace of the real, of the inclusiveness and vitality of actual American experience. All facts, even mean ones, are incandescent in Whitman's America—that ideal space, made real by history, where "as they emit themselves facts are showered with light."

The Great American Cultural Revolution heralded in the preface to the first edition of

Leaves of Grass (1855) didn't break out, which has disappointed many but surprised none. One great poet alone cannot change the moral weather; even when the poet has millions of Red Guards at his disposal, it is not easy. Like every seer of cultural revolution, Whitman thought he discerned art already being overtaken, and demystified, by reality. "The United States themselves are essentially the greatest poem." But when no cultural revolution took place, and the greatest of poems seemed less great in days of Empire than it had under the Republic, only other artists took seriously Whitman's program of populist transcendence, of the democratic transvaluation of beauty and ugliness, importance and triviality. Far from having been themselves demystified by reality, the American arts—notably photography—now aspired to do the demystifying.

In photography's early decades, photographs were expected to be idealized images. This is still the aim of most amateur photographers, for whom a beautiful photograph is a photograph of something beautiful, like a woman, a sunset. In 1915 Edward Steichen photographed a milk bottle on a tenement fire escape, an early example of a quite different idea of the beautiful photograph. And since the 1920s ambitious professionals, those whose work gets into museums, have steadily drifted away from lyrical subjects, conscientiously exploring plain, tawdry, or even ugly material. In recent decades, photography has succeeded in somewhat revising, for everybody, the definitions of what is beautiful and ugly—along the lines that Whitman had proposed. If (in Whitman's words) "each precise object or condition or combination or process exhibits a beauty," it becomes superficial to single out some things as beautiful and others as not. If "all that a person does or thinks is of consequence," it becomes arbitrary to treat some moments in life as important and most as trivial.

To photograph is to confer importance. While there are subjects that cannot be beautified, there is no way to suppress the tendency inherent in all photographs to accord value to their subjects. But the meaning of value itself can be changed—as it has been in the contemporary culture of the photographic image which is a parody of Whitman's evangel. In the mansions of pre-democratic culture, someone who gets photographed is a celebrity. In the open fields of American experience, as catalogued with passion by Whitman and as sized up with a shrug by Warhol, everybody is a celebrity. No moment is more important than any other moment; no person is more interesting than any other person.

The epigraph for the superb book of Walker Evans's photographs is a passage from Whitman that sounds the theme of American photography's most prestigious quest:

> I do not doubt but the majesty & beauty of the world are latent in any iota of the world.... I do not doubt there is far more in trivialities, insects, vulgar persons, slaves, dwarfs, weeds, rejected refuse, than I have supposed. . . .

Whitman thought he was not abolishing beauty but generalizing it. So, for generations, did the most gifted American photographers, in their democratizing pursuit of the trivial and the vulgar. But among American photographers who have matured since World War II, the Whitmanesque mandate to record in its entirety the extravagant candors of actual American experience has gone sour. In photographing dwarfs you don't get majesty & beauty. You get dwarfs.

Starting from the attic gallery-workroom Alfred Stieglitz ran for thirteen years (1905–1917) at 291 Fifth Avenue (first called the Photo-Secession Gallery, later simply "291"), the most ambitious forum of Whitmanesque judgments, American photography has moved from affirmation to erosion to, finally, a parody of Whitman's program. In this history the most edifying figure is Walker Evans, who, if not the greatest American photographer, was surely the greatest photographer of America.[1] Evans is the last great photographer to work seriously and assuredly in a mood deriving from Whitman's euphoric humanism, summing up what had gone before, anticipating much of the cooler, ruder, bleaker photography that has been done since. (For example, the prescient series of "secret" photographs of anonymous New York subway riders that Evans did between 1938 and 1941.) But Evans broke with the heroic mode. He found Stieglitz's work arty.

Like Whitman, Stieglitz saw no contradiction between making art an instrument of identification with the community and aggrandizing the artist as a heroic, romantic, self-expressing ego. Paul Rosenfeld praised him in his florid, brilliant book of essays, *Port of New York* (1924): "Alfred Stieglitz is of the company of the great affirmers of life. There is no matter in all the world so homely, trite, and humble that through it this man of the black box and chemical bath cannot express himself entire." Photographing, and therefore redeeming, the homely, trite, and humble is also an ingenious means of individual self-expression.

"The photographer," Rosenfeld writes of Stieglitz, "has cast the artist's net wider into the material world than any man before him or alongside him." Photography is a kind of overstatement, a heroic copulation with the material world. Evans sought a more impersonal kind of affirmation, a heroic reticence, a lucid understatement. Neither in the impersonal architectural still lifes of American facades and inventories of rooms that Evans loved to make nor in the moving portraits of Southern sharecroppers he took in the late 1930s (which became the book with James Agee, *Let Us Now Praise Famous Men*) was Evans trying to express himself.

Even without the heroic inflection, Evans's project still descends from Whitman's: the leveling of discriminations between the beautiful and the ugly, the important and the trivial. Each thing or person photographed becomes—a photograph; and becomes, therefore, morally equivalent to any other photograph. Evans's camera brought out the same formal beauty in the exteriors of Victorian houses in Boston in the early 1930s as in the store buildings on main streets in Alabama towns in 1936. But this was a leveling up, not down. Evans wanted his photographs to be "literate, authoritative, transcendent." The moral universe of the 1930s being no longer ours, these adjectives are barely credible today.

10   Whitman preached empathy, concord in discord, oneness in diversity. Psychic intercourse with everything, everybody—plus sensual union (when he could get it)—is the giddy trip that is proposed explicitly, over and over and over, in the prefaces and the poems. This longing to proposition the whole world also dictated his poetry's form and tone. Whitman's poems are a psychic technology to chant the reader into a new state of being (a microcosm of the "new order" envisaged for the polity); they are functional as mantras, ways of transmitting charges of energy. The repetition, the bombastic cadence, the run-on lines, and the pushy diction are a rush of secular afflatus, meant to get readers psychically airborne, to boost them up to that height where they can identify with the past and with the community of American desire. But this message of identification with other Americans is foreign to our temperament now.

The last sigh of the Whitmanesque erotic embrace of the nation, but universalized and stripped of all demands, was heard in the "Family of Man" exhibit organized in 1955 by Edward Steichen, Stieglitz's contemporary, and cofounder of Photo-Secession. Five hundred and three photographs by two hundred and seventy-three photographers from sixty-eight countries were supposed to converge—to prove that humanity is "one" and that human beings, for all their flaws, are attractive creatures. The people in the photographs were of all races, ages, classes, physical types. Many of them had exceptionally beautiful bodies; some had beautiful faces. As Whitman urged the readers of his poems to identify with him and with America, Steichen set up the show to make it possible for each viewer to identify with a great many people depicted and potentially with the subject of every photograph: citizens of World Photography all.

It was not until seventeen years later that photography again attracted such crowds at the Museum of Modern Art: for the retrospective of Diane Arbus's work that was shown between November, 1972, and February, 1973. In the Arbus show, a hundred and twelve photographs all taken by one person and all similar—that is, everyone in them looks (in some sense) the same—impose a feeling exactly contrary to the reassuring warmth of Steichen's material. Instead of people whose appearance pleases, representative folk doing their human thing, the Arbus show lines up assorted monsters and border-line cases—most of them ugly; wearing grotesque or unflattering clothes; in dismal or barren surroundings—who have paused to pose and, often, to gaze frankly, confidentially at the viewer. Arbus's work does not invite viewers to identify with the pariahs and miserable-looking people she photographed. Humanity is not "one."

The Arbus photographs convey the antihumanist message which people of good will in the 1970s are eager to be troubled by, just as they wished, in the 1950s, to be consoled and distracted by a sentimental humanism. There's not as much difference between these messages as one might suppose. The Steichen show was an up and the Arbus show was a down, but either experience serves equally well to rule out a historical understanding of reality.

Steichen's choice of photographs assumes a "human condition" or a "human nature" shared by everybody. By purporting to show that human beings are born, work, laugh, and die everywhere in the same way, the "Family of Man" systematically denies the determining weight of history—of genuine and historically embedded differences, injustices, and conflicts. Arbus's photographs suggest a world in which everybody is an alien—hopelessly isolated, immobilized in mechanical, crippled identities and relationships. But both the pious uplift of Steichen's photograph anthology and the cool horror of the Arbus retrospective render history and politics irrelevant. One does so by universalizing the human condition, into joy; the other by atomizing it, into horror.

15   Diane Arbus's photographs are a good place to examine more closely this recent and widespread turn of the American sensibility downward—into a pessimism that, at the turn of the century, would have been routinely labeled as decadent, but which now is hailed as simply tough-minded. Professional and successful as a fashion photographer since her late teens, Arbus began doing serious photography only around 1958 when she was thirty-seven, and died in 1971; about a decade of work is represented in the Museum show and the book. Only three of the 112 photographs in the retrospective are landscapes: either dead, or, literally, fake. The rest are portraits, most of them of a single person or some kind of couple; and all the people are grotesques.

The ambiguity of Arbus's work is that she seems to have enrolled in one of art photography's most visible enterprises—concentrating on victims, the unfortunate, the dispossessed—but without the compassionate purpose that such a project is expected to serve. Arbus's work shows people who are pathetic, pitiable, as well as horrible, repulsive, but it does not arouse any compassionate feelings. Nevertheless, despite this evident coolness of tone, the photographs have been scoring moral points all along with critics. For what might be judged as their dissociated and naïve point of view, the photographs have been praised for their candor and for an unsentimental empathy with their subjects. What is actually their aggressiveness toward the public has been turned into a moral accomplishment: that the photographs don't allow the viewer any distance from the subject.

None of the qualities of Arbus's work makes this line of praise convincing. In their acceptance of the appalling, the photographs suggest a naïveté that is both coy and sinister, for it is based entirely on distance, on privilege, on a feeling that what the viewer is asked to look at is really *other*. Buñuel, when asked once why he made movies, said that it was "to show that this is not the best of all possible worlds." Arbus took photographs to show something simpler—that there is another world.

The other world is to be found, as usual, inside this one. It explodes in photographing freaks. New York, with its drag balls and welfare hotels, was rich with freaks. And there was also a carnival in Maryland (1970), where Arbus found a human pincushion, a hermaphrodite with a dog, a tattooed man, and an albino swordswallower; nudist camps in New Jersey (1963) and in Pennsylvania (1965); Disneyland and a Hollywood set, for their "landscapes" without people; and the unidentified mental hospital where she took some of her last, and most disturbing, photographs. And then there was plain daily life, with its endless supply of oddities—if one has the eye to see them. The camera has the power to catch so-called normal people in such a way as to make them look extremely disturbed.

The camera chooses oddity, chases it, names it, elects it, frames it, develops it, titles it.

"You see someone on the street," Arbus wrote, "and essentially what you notice about them is the flaw." The insistent sameness of Arbus's work, however far she ranges from her prototypical subjects, suggests that her sensibility, armed with a camera, could insinuate anguish, kinkiness, mental illness with any subject. Two photographs are of crying babies; the babies look disturbed, crazy. Resembling or having something in common with someone else also nourished Arbus's morbid sensibility. It may be two girls (not sisters) wearing identical raincoats whom Arbus photographed together in Central Park; or the twins and triplets who appear in several pictures. Many photographs point with perverse wonder to the fact that two people form a couple. In Arbus's photographs, every couple is an odd couple: straight or gay, black or white, in an old-age home or in a junior high. People were freaky because they didn't wear clothes, like nudists; or because they did, like the waitress in the nudist camp who's wearing an apron.

20   Anybody Arbus photographed was a freak—a boy waiting to march in a pro-war parade, wearing his straw boater and his "Bomb Hanoi" button; the King and Queen of a Senior Citizens Dance; a thirtyish Westchester couple sprawled in their lawn chairs; a widow sitting alone in her cluttered bedroom. In "A Jewish giant at home with his parents in the Bronx, NY, 1970," the parents look like midgets, as freakish as their enormous son hunched over them because the living-room ceiling is too low.

The authority of Arbus's photographs comes from the contrast between their lacerating subject matter and their calm, matter-of-fact attentiveness. This quality of attention—the attention paid by the photographer, the attention paid by the subject to the act of being photographed—creates the moral theater of Arbus's straight-on, contemplative portraits. Far from spying on freaks and pariahs, catching them unawares, the photographer has gotten to know them, reassured them—so that they pose for her as calmly and stiffly as any Victorian notable sat for a studio portrait by Nadar or Julia Margaret Cameron. A large part of the mystery of Arbus's photographs lies in

what they suggest about how her subjects felt after consenting to be photographed. Do they see themselves, the viewer wonders, like *that*? Do they know how grotesque they are? It seems as if they don't.

The subject of Arbus's photographs is, to borrow the stately Hegelian label, "the unhappy consciousness." But most characters in Arbus's Grand Guignol don't know (or appear not to know) that they are ugly. Arbus photographs people in various degrees of unconscious relation to their pain, their ugliness. This necessarily limits what kinds of horrors she might have been drawn to photograph: it excludes sufferers who presumably know they are suffering, like victims of accidents, wars, famines, and political persecution. Arbus would never have taken pictures of accidents, events that break into a life; she specialized in slow-motion private smash-ups, most of which had been going on since the subject's birth.

Though most viewers are ready to imagine that these people, certainly the members of the sexual underworld as well as the genetic freaks, are unhappy, in few of the pictures do people actually show psychic distress. The photographs of deviates and real freaks don't stress their pain; rather, their detachment and autonomy. The female impersonators in their dressing rooms, the Russian midgets in a living-room on 100th Street, the Mexican dwarf in his Manhattan hotel room, and their kin are mostly shown as cheerful, self-accepting, matter-of-fact, unselfconscious. Pain is more legible in the portraits of the normals: the quarreling elderly couple on a park bench, the lady bartender in New Orleans at home with her souvenir dog, the boy clutching the toy hand grenade in Central Park.

Brassaï denounced photographers who try to trap their subjects off guard, in the erroneous belief that something special will be revealed about them.[2] In the world colonized by Arbus, subjects are always revealing themselves. There is no "privileged moment." Arbus's view that self-revelation is a continuous, evenly distributed process is another way of maintaining the Whitmanesque imperative: treat all moments as of equal consequence. Like Brassaï, Arbus wanted her subjects to be as fully conscious as possible, aware of the act in which they were participating. Instead of trying to coax the subject into a "natural" or typical position, the subject is encouraged to be awkward—that is, to pose. (Thereby, the revelation of self gets identified with what is strange, askew.) Standing or sitting stiffly makes them seem like images of themselves.

25   In most Arbus pictures, the subjects are looking straight into the camera. This often makes them look even odder, almost deranged.[3] In the normal rhetoric of the photographic portrait, facing the camera signifies solemnity, frankness. It discloses the subject's essence. That's why frontal portraits seem right for ceremonies (like weddings, graduations) but less apt for photographs used on billboards to advertise political candidates. (For politicians the three-quarter gaze is more common: not the gaze that confronts but the gaze that soars; instead of the relation to the viewer, to the present, the more ennobling abstract relation to the future.) What makes the frontal pose odd in Arbus's photographs is that her subjects are often people one would not expect to surrender themselves so amiably and ingenuously to the camera. Thus, in Arbus's photographs, frontality also implies in the most vivid way the subject's cooperation. To get these subjects to pose, the photographer has had to enter into a mysterious relation with them: has had to gain their confidence, has had to become "friends." Photographing freaks "had a terrific excitement for me," Arbus wrote. "I just used to adore them."

Perhaps the scariest moment in Tod Browning's film *Freaks* (1932) is the wedding banquet scene, when a table full of pinheads, bearded women, Siamese twins, and living torsos dance and sing their acceptance of the wicked normal-sized Cleopatra, who has just married the gullible midget hero. "One of us! One of us! One of us!" they chant as a loving cup is passed from mouth to mouth to be finally presented to the nauseated bride by an exuberant dwarf. Arbus makes some curious reflections about the charm and hypocrisy and discomfort of fraternizing with freaks. Following the elation of discovery, there is the thrill of having won their confidence, of not being afraid of them, of having mastered their terrors.

Diane Arbus's photographs were already famous to people who follow photography when she killed herself in July, 1971, at the age of forty-nine. But, as with Sylvia Plath, the attention she has gotten since her death is much larger and of another order—a kind of apotheosis. The fact of her suicide seems to guarantee that her work is sincere, not voyeuristic (like Jacopetti's Mondo Cane), that it is compassionate, not cold. It also seems to make the photographs more devastating, as if the suicide proved the photographs to have been dangerous to her.

She herself suggested the possibility. "Everything is so superb and so breathtaking," Arbus once wrote of her work. "I am creeping forward on my belly like they do in war movies." While photography is normally an omnipotent, and predatory, viewing from a distance, there is one situation when people do get killed for taking pictures: when they photograph people killing each other. Only war photography combines voyeurism and danger. Combat photographers can't avoid participating in the deadly activity they record; they even wear military uniforms, though without rank badges. To say that life is "really a melodrama" (as Arbus claimed to have discovered through taking pictures), to understand the camera as a weapon of aggression, implies there will be casualties. "I'm sure there are limits," she wrote. "God knows, when the troops start advancing on you, you do approach that stricken feeling where you perfectly well can get killed." Arbus's words in retrospect suggest a kind of combat death: having trespassed certain limits, she fell in a psychic ambush, a casualty of her own candor and curiosity.

In the old romance of the artist, any person who has the temerity to spend a season in hell risks not coming out alive or coming back psychically destroyed. The heroic avant-gardism of French literature in the late nineteenth and early twentieth centuries furnishes classic instances of artists who do not survive their trips to hell. Still, there is a huge difference between the activity of a photographer, which is always willed, and the activity of a writer, which may not be. One can be compelled to tell the story of one's own pain. One volunteers to seek out the pain of others.

30   Thus what is finally most troubling in Arbus's photographs is not their subjects at all but the cumulative impression of the photographer's consciousness: the sense that what is presented is precisely a private vision, something voluntary. Arbus was not a writer delving into her entrails to relate her own pain, but a photographer with a camera—venturing out into the world to *collect* images that are painful. When pain is sought, the Reichian explanation seems more relevant than the example of Sylvia Plath. The masochist's taste for pain does not come from a love of pain at all, Reich explains, but from the hope of procuring, by means of pain, a strong sensation; those handicapped by emotional or sensory analgesia only prefer pain to not feeling anything at all. But there is another explanation of why people seek pain, diametrically opposed to Reich's, that also seems pertinent: that they seek it not to feel more but to feel less.

In so far as looking at most of these photographs is, undeniably, an ordeal, Arbus's work is typical of the kind of art popular among sophisticated urban people right now: art that is a self-willed test of hardness. The photographs offer an occasion to demonstrate that life's horror can be faced without squeamishness. The photographer once had to say to herself, OK, I can accept that; the viewer is invited to make the same declaration.

Arbus's work is a good instance of a leading tendency of high art in capitalist countries: to suppress, or at least reduce, moral and sensory queasiness. Much of modern art is devoted to lowering the threshold of what is terrible. By getting us used to what, formerly, we could not bear to see or hear, because it was too shocking, painful, or embarrassing, art changes morals—that body of psychic custom and public sanctions that sets a vague boundary between what is emotionally and spontaneously intolerable and what is not.

The gradual suppression of queasiness does bring us closer to a rather formal truth: life is, and always was, more than the taboos constructed by art and morals would have it. But there is a stiff price to pay for the rising grotesqueness that people are able to stomach, in images (moving and still) and in print. For most people it works not as a liberation of but as a subtraction from the self; a sense of pseudo-familiarity with the horrible reinforces alienation, making people less able to react in real life. What happens to their feelings on first exposure to today's standard pornographic film product or to a televised genocide is not so different from what happens when they first look at Arbus's photographs.

The photographs make a compassionate response seem irrelevant. The point is not to be upset, to be able to confront the horrible with cheerfulness. But this look that is not compassionate is a special, modern ethical construction: not hard-hearted, certainly not cynical, but simply (or falsely) naïve. To the painful nightmarish reality "out there," Arbus applies such words as "terrific," "interesting," "incredible," "fantastic," "sensational"—the childlike wonder of the Warhol pop mentality. Arbus's breathless, deliberately naïve comments (collected from notes, letters, tapes of her lectures) which form the preface to the book are quite remarkable. Photography is a device that captures it all, that seduces people into disclosing their secrets, that broadens experience. To photograph people, Arbus writes, is necessarily "cruel," "mean." The important thing is not to blink.

35   "Photography was a license to go wherever I wanted and to do what I wanted to do," Arbus wrote. The camera is a kind of passport that annihilates moral boundaries and social inhibitions, freeing the photographer from any responsibility toward the people photographed. The whole point of photographing people is that you are not intervening in their lives—only visiting them. The photographer is supertourist, an extension of the anthropologist, visiting "natives" and bringing back news of their exotic doings and strange gear. The photographer is always trying to colonize new experiences, or find new ways to look at familiar subjects—to fight against boredom. For boredom is the reverse side of fascination: both depend on being outside rather than inside a situation, and one leads to the other. "The Chinese have a theory that you pass through boredom into fascination," Arbus once commented. Photographing an appalling underworld (and a horrible, plastic

overworld), she has no intention of entering into the horror of those images as experienced by the inhabitants of those worlds. They are to remain exotic, hence "terrific." Her view is always from the outside.

"I'm very little drawn to photographing people that are known or even subjects that are known," Arbus wrote. "They fascinate me when I've barely heard of them." However interested Arbus was in freaks or in very ugly people, it would never have occurred to her to photograph thalidomide babies or napalm victims—"public" horrors, deformities with sentimental or moral associations. Arbus was not interested in ethical journalism. She was drawn to subjects that she could believe were found, just lying about, without any values attached to them. These subjects are necessarily ahistorical: "private" rather than public pathology, secret lives rather than open ones.

For Arbus, the camera photographs the unknown. But unknown to whom? Unknown to someone who is basically protected, middle-class, who has been taught to see life in terms of moral response and prudence. Like Nathanael West, another artist who was fascinated by the deformed and the mutilated, Arbus came from a moralistic, inexorably upward-mobile, verbally skilled, compulsively well-nourished, genteel, indignation-prone, well-to-do Jewish family, where minority sexual tastes lived way below the threshold of awareness, and risk-taking was despised as another goyish craziness. "One of the things I felt I suffered from as a kid," Arbus wrote, "was that I never felt adversity. I was confined in a sense of unreality. . . And the sense of being immune was, ludicrous as it seems, a painful one." Feeling much the same discontent, West was exhilarated by his job as a nightclerk in a seedy Manhattan hotel in 1927. The camera became Arbus's way of procuring experience, and thereby acquiring a sense of reality. By experience was meant if not material adversity at least psychological adversity—the shock of immersion in experiences that cannot be beautified, the encounter with what is taboo, perverse, evil.

Arbus's interest in freaks expresses a desire to violate her own innocence, her sense of being privileged. The 1930s yield few examples of this kind of anguish, apart from West. More typically, it is the sensibility of someone educated and middle-class who came of age after 1935 and before 1955—a sensibility that was to flourish precisely in the 1960s.

The decade of Arbus's serious work coincides with, and is very much of, the 1960s. That was the decade in which freaks went public and became a safe, approved subject of art. What in the 1930s would be treated with anguish—for example, in *Miss Lonelyhearts*—would in the 1960s be treated in a perfectly deadpan way. At the beginning of the 1960s, the thriving Freak Show at Coney Island was outlawed; sometime in the 1970s the Times Square turf of drag queens and hustlers will undoubtedly be razed and replaced by skyscrapers. As the deviant underworlds are evicted from their restricted territories—banned as unseemly, a public nuisance, obscene, or just unprofitable—they increasingly come to infiltrate consciousness as the subject matter of art, acquiring a certain diffused legitimacy and metaphoric stature which creates all the more distance.

40 Who could have better appreciated the truth of freaks than someone who was, by profession, a fashion photographer—a professional fabricator of the cosmetic lie that masks the terrifying freakish world? Arbus began as a photographer doing ads for Russeks, her father's Fifth Avenue department store, in her late teens, a job she continued to hold for twenty years. Even after starting her "serious" work she went on being a fashion photographer. (As recently as a year before her death, she did twenty-four pages of vacuous photographs for a *New York Times* Sunday section on children's fashions.) Unlike Warhol, who spent many years as a commercial artist (doing such things as designing shoe ads and displays for I. Miller), Arbus did not make her serious work out of promoting and kidding the commercial aesthetic in which she had been schooled, but turned her back on it entirely.

Arbus's work is not ironic, like Warhol's, but reactive—reactive against gentility, against being protected. It was her way of saying f[***] *Vogue*, f[***] fashion, f[***] what's pretty. This challenge has two not wholly compatible strands. One is a revolt against the Jews' hyperdeveloped moral sensibility. The other revolt, itself hotly moralistic, turns against the success world. In the more militant, moralistic, subversion, life as a failure is the antidote to life as a success. In the aesthete's subversion which the Sixties was to make peculiarly its own, life as a horrorshow is the antidote to life as a bore.

Most of Arbus's work lies within the Warhol aesthetic, that is, defines itself in relation to the twin poles of boringness and freakishness; but it doesn't have the Warhol style. Arbus had neither Warhol's genius for publicity nor the self-protective shrug with which he insulates himself from the freaky nor his sentimentality. And Warhol, from a working-class background, never felt any of the ambivalence toward success which afflicted the children of the Jewish upper middle classes in the 1960s. For someone raised as a Catholic, as was Warhol (and virtually everyone in his gang), a fascination with evil comes much more genuinely than it does to someone from a Jewish background. Compared with Warhol, Arbus is more vulnerable, more innocent, and certainly more pessimistic. The Dantesque vision of the city (and the suburbs) in Arbus's photographs has no reserves of irony. Much of Arbus's material is the same as that depicted in, say, Warhol's *Chelsea Girls.* But her photographs never play with horror, milking it for laughs; they offer no opening to mockery, as do the films of Warhol and Morrissey or, more recently, John Waters's *Pink Flamingos.* She allows no possibility of finding freaks endearing, as with the character played by Holly Woodlawn in Morrissey's *Trash.*

Back in 1967, when the Museum of Modern Art first exhibited some of Arbus's photographs, some staff members hesitated, worrying about the photographs of transvestites, and particularly about showing nudity. Only five years later, such hesitation was unthinkable. Preceded (in most of the spectators' awareness) by Warholiana, gay lib, drag rock, Tod Browning revivals, the freak parades of Fellini and Alejandro Jodorowsky, R. Crumb comics, and the grotesqueries of the neighborhood porn films, Arbus's photographs are practically the art of everyday life.

The cultural distance traversed in just a few years, between 1967 and 1972, is on its way to shifting once more. Arbus's work expressed her turn against what was "public" (as she experienced it), approved, pretty, safe, reassuring—and boring—in favor of what was "private," hidden, ugly, dangerous, and fascinating. Already, by the early 1970s, these terms have changed; or become more complicated. The public is no longer "safe." Freaky is no longer "private." People who are deformed, in sexual disgrace, dispossessed, are "public" images, too. And we are still farther away from the moral soil in which Arbus's fantasies took root.

45 For the daughter of a well-off Jewish family, born in New York City in 1921, both freaks and Middle America were equally exotic. A boy marching in a pro-war parade and a Levittown housewife were as alien to Arbus as a Mexican midget or a drag queen; lower-middle-class suburbia was as remote as Times Square, Coney Island, and gay bars. But for New Yorkers born after 1945, however comfortable their family circumstances, that world could not be so fascinating. Freaks, Middle America, the sexual underground are no longer remote. They're to be seen daily on TV, in the subways. Hobbesian man roams the streets, quite visible, with glitter in his hair.

Arbus tried to stay unsophisticated when she began doing her serious work. Ignoring her forerunners in American photography, and her relation to such Europeans as Brassaï, Arbus said that she felt closest to an anti-art photographer, Weegee, the tabloid features photographer famous in the 1940s for his brutal pictures of crime and accident victims. Weegee's photographs are indeed upsetting, his sensibility is urban; but the similarity between his work and Arbus's ends there. However much she was eager to disavow sophistication, Arbus was not unsophisticated. And there is nothing journalistic about her method of photographing. What may seem journalistic (read "sensational") in Arbus's photographs places them, rather, in the main tradition of Surrealist art—with their taste for the grotesque, the proclaimed innocence with respect to their subjects, their claim that all subjects are merely *objets trouvés.*

"I would never choose a subject for what it meant to me when I think of it," Arbus wrote, a dogged exponent of the Surrealist bluff. Presumably, the viewers are not supposed to judge the people she photographs. Of course, we do. And the very range of Arbus's subjects itself constitutes a judgment. Brassaï, who photographed people like those who interested Arbus—see his "'Bijou' of Montmartre" of 1932—also did beautiful cityscapes, portraits of famous artists. Walker Evans's Chicago street portraits of 1946 are Arbus material. So are a number of photographs by Robert Frank. The difference is in the range of other subjects, other emotions, that Brassaï, Evans, and Frank also photographed. Arbus is an *auteur* in the sense in which that is most limiting, as special a case in the history of photography as is Morandi, who has spent a lifetime painting bottles, in the history of modern European painting. Arbus does not, like the great photographers, play the field of subject matter—even a little. On the contrary, all her subjects are equivalent, and it is this that constitutes the judgment at the heart of her work. Making equivalences between freaks, mad people, suburban couples, and nudists is a very powerful judgment. It is, indeed, a politics.

The photographs are hardly political in a narrow sense (being a hymn to the isolation and atomization of the individual) but they are in complicity with a particular political mood. To use a crude index: most people who like Arbus's photographs voted for McGovern. People who voted for Nixon couldn't like them. The canonization of Arbus's work since her death says a lot about where urban, educated, left-liberal Americans are in the early 1970s. They are into a certain Gothic vision of America. All Arbus's photographs are similar. They could all have been taken in one village in Lower Slobbovia. Only, as it happens, the idiot village is America. Instead of finding identity between things which are wildly and richly different (the Whitman dream), everybody looks the same.

Standing far from the Whitmanesque buoyancy is a bitter, sad embrace of experience. But the seeds of melancholy were already present even in the heyday of Whitmanesque affirmation, as represented by Stieglitz and his Photo-Secession circle. Stieglitz, pledged to redeem the world with

the camera, is still shocked by modern material civilization. He photographed New York in the 1910s, as Berenice Abbott did between 1929 and 1939, in an almost quixotic spirit—camera/lance against the windmill/skyscrapers. According to Rosenfeld, Stieglitz's work is "perpetual affirmation of a faith that there existed, somewhere, here in very New York, a spiritual America." The Whitmanesque appetites have turned pious: the photographer now patronizes reality. One needs a camera to show that "running right through the dull and marvelous opacity called the United States" are spiritual patterns.

50 Obviously, a mission as rotten with doubt about America—even at its most optimistic—was bound to get deflated fairly soon, as post-World War I America committed itself more boldly to Empire and consumerism. Photographers with less ego and magnetism than Stieglitz gradually gave up the struggle. They might continue to practice the atomistic visual stenography inspired by Whitman. But, without Whitman's delirious powers of synthesis, what they documented was discontinuity, material detritus, loneliness, greed.

Once a small tendency in photography, Surrealism has now become the dominant one. America has been discovered as the quintessential Surrealist country. Diane Arbus discovers America is freaks. Michael Lesy, making a collage of photographs that date from turn of the century Wisconsin, discovers that we are on a "death trip." Since photography cut loose from the Whitmanesque affirmation—since it has ceased to understand what it could mean for photographs to aim at being literate, authoritative, and transcendent—the best of American photography (and much else in American culture) has given itself over to Surrealism.

It is simply too easy to say that America is just a freak show—the Surrealist judgment. Arbus reflects a cut-rate pessimism, naïve and, above all, reductive. Surrealism can only deliver a reactionary judgment. It can make out of history only a garbage can, a joke, a lunatic asylum. But Americans are partial to myths of redemption and of damnation. With Whitman's dream of cultural revolution discredited, all we have left is a sharp-eyed, witty despair.

Notes

1. I suppose that Paul Strand is the greatest American photographer, as D. W. Griffith (alas!) is our greatest film director. Strand is simply the biggest, widest, most commanding talent in the history of American photography.
2. Not an error, really. There is something on people's faces when they don't know they are being observed that never appears when they are. This is the interest of Walker Evans's series of subway riders.
He rode the New York subways for hundreds of hours, standing between rush hours with the lens of his camera peering between two buttons of his top-coat, his eyes focused on the bench opposite. In these pictures it is obvious that the subway riders, although photographed close and frontally, didn't know they were being photographed; their expressions are private ones, not those they would offer to the camera.
3. And it makes them look even freakier. Compare a 1912 photograph by Lartigue of a woman in a plumed hat and veil ("Racecourse at Nice") with Arbus's "Woman With a Veil on Fifth Avenue, NYC, 1968." Apart from the characteristic ugliness of Arbus's subject (Lartigue's subject is, just as characteristically, beautiful), what makes the woman in Arbus's photograph strange is the bold unselfconsciousness of her pose. If the Lartigue woman looked back, she could be made to look almost as strange.

Reflect & Write

❑ What is the significance of the Whitman section in Sontag's piece? How does it contribute to her argument?

❑ What is Sontag's argument about photography as represented in this essay? Read carefully through this essay and then try to write a single sentence that summarizes her perspective on photography.

❑ Much of her essay relies on comparisons between Arbus and other famous photographs and artists. Why do you think she chose this strategy? How does this strategy either enhance or undermine her argument? What assumptions does Sontag seem to be making about her audience?

❑ **Write:** Look at some of Diane Arbus's work by visiting a library or viewing the images at http://www.dianearbus.net/index.htm. Select one piece and write a short essay in which you use it to support or refute Sontag's argument about Arbus's photographs and her vision of America.

■ **Katharine Mieszkowski** *has contributed articles to* All Things Considered, Slate, *the* San Francisco Chronicle, *and* Ms. Magazine. *She currently serves as the senior technology writer for Salon.com. In this article, Mieszkowski focuses on Flickr, an online service that allows users to post and share their digital photographs. She compares Flickr to Friendster (a site similar to Facebook and MySpace), an Internet community where people establish personal Websites with the goal of creating an online identity and then accumulating virtual "friends" from those people who visit their site. This article was originally published in Salon.com in December 2004.*

The Friendster of Photo Sites

Katharine Mieszkowski

Meet Josie Robson of Berkeley, Calif., who was born on Flickr, a photo-sharing site that's still in beta. Josie's two moms bought a camera phone before the birth of their first child so that they could get pictures to the new grandparents as quickly as possible. "We sent out an e-mail the night I went into labor that said, 'Here goes!'" says Conchita Robson. "Go to my link: flickr.com/photos/conchita."

In the delivery room, Conchita's wife, Ann, snapped photos on a camera phone and zipped them via e-mail to Conchita's Flickr page. Friends and family then spent hours hitting reload on their browsers, while virtually cheering on the laboring mom in the comments section below the emerging photos: "Yay! Baby is coming ... Hope she makes a quick entrance for you ... Hang in there Mom," reads one. Just after Josie was born on Sept. 28 at 3:45 p.m., in the space of an e-mail from that camera phone, her image hit the Web to a chorus of "!!!" and "Yay!" from her waiting admirers.

What will Josie and her peers be doing with their own camera phones—or whatever image machines they'll be toting around—by the time they're old enough to take digital pictures? After all, some of Josie's cohorts are already making appearances online before they're even out of the womb, judging from all the ultrasound images on Flickr.

If webcams were a voyeuristic novelty exploited by a smattering of exhibitionists to the delight of the ogling online masses, camera phones and digital cameras have reversed the equation. Now, everyone is starring in their own personal "Truman Show," sharing digital images both profound and ordinary. With every new haircut or pair of shoes that pops up on Flickr, the lines between "real" life and the mimetic are becoming ever further blurred.

5   Flickr is one of many photo-sharing sites, including, but not limited to, Fotolog, Fotothing, Zoto, Fotki, Smugmug and Pbase. Smugmug enjoyed a moment of fame in early December when the Navy launched an investigation into photos that surfaced on the site that apparently depicted Navy SEALs torturing Iraqi prisoners.

On most sites, you create your own album or page of photos, and invite your friends to look at them. But on Flickr, you can mingle all your photos with similar images, creating an endlessly beguiling cross-pollination of photos that spark a host of unique communities.

Flickr allows its more than 176,000 members to meet each other through both images and words in an ever-evolving visual playground. The onslaught of images that appear on the site range from the truly artistic to the bluntly documentary, a pool of more than 2.2 million photos that's growing at the rate of about 30,000 a day. What's unique is that 82 percent of the pictures on the site are publicly available to anyone who cares to look at them and riff off them. Members *can* keep their photos private, shared only with a specified group of intimates, but most choose not to, allowing the pictures of their cat or car to freely commingle with others.

The result is a dynamic environment, prone to all sorts of instant fads, created by members inspiring each other to go in new directions with their cameras. It makes digital photography not only instantly shareable, but immediately participatory, creating collaborative communities around everything from the secret life of toys to what grocery day looks like. The result is an only-on-the-Web conversation where text and image are intermingled in a polyglot that has all the makings of a new kind of conversation.

Since all it takes is snapping a photo and e-mailing it to the site from your camera phone, or uploading it from your digital camera, it's become easier to take and share a photo than to write an e-mail or a blog entry. Some people snap photos in the airport and upload them to the site to let friends and family know they've arrived safely in a foreign land—the digital image replacing a phone call, e-mail or text message home.

10   There's a different kind of intimacy in looking at the photos a friend took today, than even in reading a missive detailing her daily routine. "It's a perfect use of the Internet. It takes less effort to look at photos than to read somebody's blog," says photographer Eliot Shepard, whose photo blog is at slower.net. "It really is visual conversation. That's the cornerstone of the appeal of the community photo site, as opposed to the individual photo blog. It's very much like speaking to each other—making wry jokes with images but also learning about techniques, getting ideas and cross-pollination in the echo chamber."

Posting photos on Flickr "is like personal reporting," says Chad Dickerson who, like Conchita Robson, used to work at Salon. He's the roommate of new baby Josie Robson, who encouraged her moms to post their pics of the infant on Flickr. "It's a two-way conversation, because you're not just posting for someone to see them. You're posting them so they can participate in them with comments and notes." (One of the founders of Flickr, who maintains its blog, also used to work at Salon.) While comments are much like comments on a blog, notes annotate the images themselves with boxes that show text when a cursor scrolls over them, like this.

Rion Nakaya, a prolific photo blogger in New York, posts images from her Sidekick camera phone on Flickr: "It's very of the moment. I don't send anything to Flickr that I haven't taken in the last 10 or 15 minutes. I try to make it as instant as possible to feel." And she sees it becoming more mainstream: "It's now not only people in Web technology or teenagers doing their diaries online, but it's actually something that a lot of people are doing."

As members of Flickr post their photos, they attach "tags" to them. Any word or series of words smooshed together, in any language, can be a tag, like "sleeping" or "red" or "nighttime." Your tag then connects your images to any other members' photos that happen to share the same tag.

It's a phenomenon that the Internet chattering classes have dubbed a "folksonomy." Thomas Vander Wal, a self-described "information fiend," coined the term to describe the informal social categories that emerge on sites like Flickr. "In information architecture, you're always trying to marry the bottom up and the top down. The bottom up is how people normally talk about things, sort of the vernacular," he says. "If a person is trying to describe it for a group of their friends, or if they want to remember something themselves, what would they call it?" There are tags for collections and clouds, but also for satire and creepychristmas.

15   The result is a commingling of images that no team of Web designers or usability experts could dream up on their own, which produces intriguing

juxtapositions—sometimes clearly intentional, other times entirely fortuitous. On the sleeping tag, drunks sleep it off next to slumbering babies and cats. The RNC tag sports both photos of protests of the Republican National Convention last September in New York, and photos from the conference floor. The Hummer tag links up shots of the vehicle performing extraordinary feats of vehicular machismo as well as shots of Hummer-haters giving the finger to the gas-guzzling vehicle. And then there's an entire tag, fuh2, devoted to dissing the Hummer with the one-fingered salute.

If a message board or chat room is one version of online community, here the tags themselves create all kinds of cross-referencing and interlinking that brings people—and their work—together in conversation, riffing on each other's visual ideas with their own images, making comments and notes.

Yet, the most popular tags on the site are so inclusive that they can feel almost meaningless, like 2004, camera phone and photo. Though there's a check on that, as other people can come in and add another layer of detail— dog, cat, cloud, creepychristmas. So, the crowd can organize the system in ways that even the photographer might not expect or anticipate. In other words, "People in your friends group can add their own tags to it, so it makes it a bit richer," explains Vander Wal.

The end result is: "It's capturing more of what is actually human rather than a machine structure where everything is formalized," he says. And that means members using the system come together and share their visual ideas in endlessly unexpected ways. Some even hold whole conversations strictly in pictures, or turn a mere recipe for spiced banana cake or apple cake into something that looks truly new.

All this cross-pollination of ideas and images has emergent off-line social implications as well—two neighbors who meet when they see each other's images on the Calgary tag, even people who find images of themselves floating on the site, and set out to meet the person who took them. "I've taken pictures of people at conferences and put their name in the tag, and then they find the picture, and I meet them online, even though I didn't actually meet them there," says blogger Tim Bishop, who has done his own musing on the potential political implications of Flickr.

20   And, of course, the visual playground provides lots of material for social groups that already existed off-line. "It's a virtual way to be together," says Pam Wong, 30-year-old administrator for an insurance company in San Francisco, who recently posted a photo of her desk at work so her friends who live in New York who haven't been to her office could see where she spends her day. Clearly, she's not the only one who has thought to do the same.

"It's such mundane stuff, stupid little details that nobody else would care about. But it's kind of fun to share with your friends: 'What did you have for lunch today?' And you can just show them. It's definitely way more appealing than e-mailing or calling. I don't know why. Maybe it's like you're bringing them there with you." The result is nothing less dramatic than subtle changes in the way friends, family members and even strangers participate in each other's lives. "You always have your phone with you," says Wong. "That's completely different from even how you related to your friends six months or a year ago."

"A lot of my friends put little notes on each other's photos—say, looking at someone in the background. It's totally a way to goof off and make each other laugh," says Rion Nakaya, a friend of Wong's.

This is the first year that 23-year-old Bryan Partington, who lives in Toronto, won't be flying home for the holidays. But he's not missing out on the family traditions of decorating the tree. "My mom got onto Flickr to keep tabs on me," explains Partington, who is better known as "striatic" on the photo service, where he's personally posted some 692 photos and counting. Now, his mom has posted images of his Christmas ornaments. She's even done some of them, like this Deep Space Nine ornament, as squared circles, the visual craze that her son started on site.

Partington, an alpha user of the system, has 250 contacts on it, which is sort of like having a lot of friends on Friendster. He keeps up with so many different members' work that he has an RSS feed download them all, so he can stay on top of it all. "I let my computer check the RSS feed for me, and just collect the messages. So, each night, I can take my hour or two to go through what my computer has logged over the day," he says. Otherwise, there's no way he could keep up with the amount of interesting stuff he's tracking: "You have bloggers and professional photographers and people who use their cellphones all squished into one space. It's a really good incubator for all kinds of creativity. The more I see other people's work—their style—it has a ripple effect. It's almost like you're playing together, it's so social."

25   Others are amazed by what the system brings out in their own friends and family. When San Francisco Web designer Heather Champ got married in July, she and her fiancé created a group on Flickr for their 75 wedding guests. And just three days after the wedding, more than 300 photos had been uploaded. They included pictures taken with camera phones that had been posted immediately, as well as digital camera photos that people had gone home and uploaded. "The people posting back to our wedding group weren't just our tech-savvy friends with camera phones," she says. "Derek's mother, Derek's father, my sister, Derek's aunt and uncle. The barriers are coming down."

But more remarkable was the kind of running commentary from their wedding guests about their honeymoon in Amsterdam and Paris that took place on Flickr while it was still happening. "When we were wandering around we would take pictures with the camera phone, and we would post them immediately," Champ explains. "It was funny to get back and find people were having this real-time conversation about where we were. 'They're at Cafe Hugo near Place Des Vosges!' It was kind of unexpected to see all this dialogue."

And even more unexpected is the kind of strange social dynamics that can fall out from having this immediate window into your friends' lives: what they ate last night, and who they ate it with, Champ says. "There is a downside, too. Looking at your friends' photos and thinking: 'Why wasn't I invited to that party.' So many of my friends use it you can cross-reference," she explains almost apologetically: "You almost feel somewhat stalker-ish when you put two and two together, and come up with the very high-school: 'Why wasn't I invited?'"

By the time Josie Robson, the little girl born on Flickr just a few months ago, is old enough to actually be in high school, will that even seem weird to her? Maybe it will just be the new normal with everyone keeping visual tabs on their friends and family—as well as countless "contacts" they've met online—all the time.

Reflect & Write

❏ According to Mieszkowski, how does photo-sharing alter the way that we approach photography and representations of reality? How does Flickr change our understanding of the limitations and the functions of a photo album?

❏ Think about the examples that Mieszkowski uses in her article. What impressions is she creating about the Flickr community? How might she have changed that impression using different examples of photographs?

❏ What similiarities do you see between Arbus's photographs and the types of pictures that Mieszkowski discusses in her article? Would Sontag's title "America, Seen Through Photographs, Darkly" apply here? Why or why not?

❏ **Write:** Choose a key word (e.g., puppy, college, Chicago, birthday, family) and use it to search Flickr (http://www.flickr.com). Look at the first 20 photos that contain that tag and write a short reflection about how these collective images work together to define this word.

■ *In this article,* **Mike Miliard,** *a staff writer for the* Boston Phoenix, *discusses the phenomenon of video blogging—or vlogging—popularized by Internet sites such as YouTube. Vloggers use Webcameras to capture home video that they then post online for a mass audience. This article first appeared in the* Boston Phoenix *in December 2005.*

I Like to Watch: Video Blogging Is Ready for Its Close-up

Mike Miliard

A pretty artist chats silently with a toy giraffe. A guy sifts through his garage-sale junk, reminiscing about his old new-wave buttons. A man driving in his car talks to his wife about their thrilling weekend jaunt to CVS. Band nerds kill time at a high-school football game while the gridiron jocks kill each other. These are the people in your neighborhood. And they want you to see what they're up to.

Once upon a time, blogging promised anonymity. One of its big selling points was that it allowed desktop philosophers to pound out their opinions and broadcast them to the world, all while wearing their pajamas. But the

FIGURE 1. On his commute from Jamaica Plain to Allston, Ravi Jain interviews "guests" as part of his vlog *Drivetime*.

past year has seen a profusion of video blogging ("vlogging," if you prefer neologisms). People can now videotape themselves in their pajamas, and post it online with a few simple steps.

It's the next stage in blog evolution. Cheap digital cameras, free editing software, and video-hosting services have made production and publishing easy as pie. RSS aggregation technology offers the means to distribute content to loyal viewers. Broadband connections make watching it a snap. And every new iPod comes equipped with video capabilities.

Even as the iTunes music store rushes to stock up on U2 videos and episodes of *The Office,* the increasing plenitude of video blogs points to a real democratization of media. No one owns the means of distribution anymore, so more and more people are making their own shows. Some offer scattershot glances at fleeting moments. Others are meticulously edited and set to music. There are video diaries. Self-produced sitcoms. Citizen journalism. Talk shows. These real-time glimpses into strangers' lives—funny, serious, contemplative, provocative—are almost always compelling. Sure, they vary wildly in quality. So do all blogs. They're made by artists, news junkies, pop-culture addicts, high-school kids, even the politicians. And before long, they don't seem like strangers anymore.

The Vlogfather

5   If anyone can be called the father of video blogging, Steve Garfield is him. And not just because his vlog was one of the first. The forty-something Jamaica Plain resident, a freelance photographer and video producer, is one of vlogging's biggest proponents, a cornerstone in the burgeoning vlogging community. Just try doing a Google search on the subject without seeing his name or his wide-grinning mug pop up: "I want YOU to video blog!"

In late 2003, Garfield started thinking about how to integrate video with his text blog. "I'd put video on the Web before, but combining the two, I don't know if anyone had really done it," he says. "I started experimenting with different ways to do it. There weren't the services we have now to help you." His first vlog post was on January 1, 2004, in which he anticipated, hopefully, "The Year of the Video Blog." Not long afterward, he found a guy on the Internet named Jay Dedman, a New Yorker who was doing similar things. The two started a Yahoo! video-blogging group with a couple other enthusiasts. "That group of three or four grew to 30 or 40," says Garfield. "And now it's 1600 worldwide. It's amazing."

Garfield has two video blogs. *The Carol and Steve Show* is a charming episodic chronicle of his quotidian adventures with his wife—biking around Nantucket, vacationing in California wine country, eating Thanksgiving leftovers—complete with *Seinfeld*-esque theme music. *Vlog Soup* is his semi-regular round-up of the latest and greatest from across cyberspace. He's also the Boston correspondent for *Rocketboom,* arguably the Web's most popular video blog.

Spend a few hours surfing his site and looking at clips, and it's easy to surmise that Garfield is addicted to vlogging. He wants to get others hooked, too. He proselytizes, offering tips on video-hosting sites, camera angles, lighting, and editing software.

Opening his sleek Powerbook G4, Garfield shows just how easy vlogging really is. He uses a simple Canon S-400 still camera that also has video capabilities. (He takes his "muse" almost everywhere he goes.) Holding it an arm's length away, he looks into the lens. "Hi, this is Steve

Garfield, and I'm here with Mike Miliard in my living room. I've turned the tables on him. He's here to interview me, and I'm interviewing him."

10   Elapsed time from the moment Garfield picked up the camera to the moment the clip is online: about three and a half minutes. Of course, that was just a down-and-dirty demo. Usually he spends a lot more time tweaking and editing his posts, using programs like QuickTime Pro or Final Cut to get them just right.

And why shouldn't he want his posts to look as perfect as possible? A lot of people are watching. Garfield says some of his posts get as many as 4000 views a day. "Since the video iPod came out, it's been more and more. There are people all around the world who are fans of *The Carol and Steve Show.*"

Garfield isn't angling for stardom. He's just got the itch to document his life. "I don't think it's a fame thing. It's just a blogger's mentality, that urge to create and share your thoughts," he says. "The video blog just enhances my posts. If there was no video, I'd be like 'My wife and I went to wine country, and here are some pictures.' But this tells the story. And tells it in such a vibrant way."

Garfield sees himself as a collector of stories. He shares his own, and he's keenly interested in other people's. He keeps regular tabs on dozens of other vlogs, and after a while he starts to feel like their authors—people he's never met—are good friends.

There are so many uses for a video blog. The artist who wants to share his or her work with a worldwide audience. The emigrant who wants to show his or her family how life abroad is going. The citizen journalist who wants to provide a corrective to circumscribed corporate news. And it's so easy. And so cheap.

15   "At first, we were all worried, 'What if we get popular? It's gonna start costing us money,'" Garfield says. "Like, you want people to watch, but you don't because it's gonna cost you. But now, with sites like OurMedia and Blip.tv, you don't have to worry about it. Size and bandwidth issues are gone. There are no limits."

FIGURE 2. Ravi Jain conducts an interview.

The Road Ahead

Ravi Jain likes limits. They challenge him. So he conceived his vlog DriveTime with some specific restrictions in mind. It's something he learned doing graduate work at MassArt. "That's always been appealing to me. Set yourself up in some confining situation, and then figure out, within those constraints, what can you do?"

DriveTime is a talk show. One that's filmed every week entirely in Jain's car. Usually during his commute from his home in JP to his job in Allston. So it serves the dual purpose of being a way-cool conceit while allowing him the time to film regularly.

Every week Jain, 34, does an opening segment with his lovely co-host Sonia in the passenger seat. ("I'm married to you, and you drive me to work. And since I don't want to take the bus, I'm your co-host," she quips.) Then, after dropping her at work, he picks up a guest. Maybe it's James Hull of the Gallery at Green Street, or Dennis Crowley, founder of the mobile social-networking company Dodgeball. To say the least, it's a novel way to learn about the artists, musicians, scientists, and sundry other thinkers in Boston and beyond.

And it's a pleasant surprise to open my iTunes on Friday or Monday mornings and find a new DriveTime episode downloading automatically.

When I meet Ravi and Sonia on a recent morning, I'm expecting to hitch a ride in his white Audi and get interviewed for the show. But that car's old, and the roads are slick that day, so I'm picked up in a different vehicle, one sans camera. (Underscoring the closeness of the vlogging community, Ravi and Sonia bought the car from Steve Garfield.)

20   The setup in the DriveTime Audi is pretty simple. Jain stuck a clamp onto the dashboard, then affixed a basic Sony DCR-TRV11 camera to that. "It's nothing really special," he says. "I finally went out and got a wide-angle lens for a whopping $22 investment."

A couple years ago, Jain created seven eight-minute-long episodes of a Web-based sitcom called Three Abreast. But the time he put into filming and editing it was more akin to doing a feature film. "What appealed to me about video blogging," he says, "was the immediacy of it."

It's a novel medium, and Jain's is a novel approach. And even within the constraints of his automobile, he's able to offer new features from week to week. One guest called in via car phone. He's filmed during the day, on the way to work, and at night, on his way home. He's even had a musical guest. (Rather than the back-seat cello concerto he'd hoped for, he had to settle for a ukulele serenade. "Such was the power of your performance that we're completely fogged up right now," he applauded.) When it's time to read viewer mail, Sonia simply reaches into the DriveTime glove box.

There are perils. One DriveTime episode almost ended in destruction when Jain forgot to check his blind spot and was nearly side-swiped by an oncoming vehicle. But, he insists, "that near-miss was completely independent of the fact that there was a camera on the dashboard."

It's Personal

Other video blogs are more freeform. JP artist Amy Carpenter's criminally under-updated Welcome to Amyville is simply a series of funny, free-spirited slices of life. She dances with abandon to Madonna's "Vogue" in her closet. She rides a tandem bicycle with a beatific smile. In her car, she espies a mulleted dude in a white convertible in the next lane. "Look at that guy!" she gawks as the camera zooms in. "He's, like, straight out of the '80s!" She pays tribute to her soon-to-be-vacated apartment, sifting through mounds of kitschy gewgaws as she begs viewers to help her move. "Just think of all the stuff you could acquire! It would be amazing! Besides," she says, shaking a Magic-8 ball that's been altered in postproduction to read YOU WILL HELP AMY MOVE HER CRAP, "it's your destiny."

25   People—including, apparently, a sizable fan base in Germany—are watching. And they care. In one clip, Carpenter films herself sitting silent and dispirited under a brumous sky while Björk plays on the car radio. "I'm really sad looking at your last video," reads one of the post's 21 comments. "I'm so accustomed to view your wonderful smile." Amy later responds that she's okay. She hadn't slept all night, she writes; the weather corresponded with her mood, and the song happened to put her in the mind of one of those "wow, life is such a movie" moments. "I'm smiley," she reassures her fans, "but I'm not ALWAYS smiley."

Serra Shiflett, a 25-year-old grad student studying video and new media at Emerson, is another vlogger who revels in the medium's storytelling capabilities. Heads Off, the vlog she does with her boyfriend Mike MacHenry, is billed as an "exploration of our city, and our society." It does just that through its concretion of little moments.

Using a simple three-chip Cannon GL1 camera, editing her footage on her Mac with Final Cut Pro, Shiflett shoots—or allows others to shoot—things that catch her eye: carving pumpkins, making wine, getting a buzz cut on the front porch, her cat drinking from a faucet. It's like a photo album come to life, giving simple glimpses of everyday goings-on.

At first, the idea of blogging at all was absurd to her—let alone the ostensibly narcissistic impulse to document the minutiae of her daily life. "When I think of blogging, I think of LiveJournal," Shiflett says. "And I was like, 'Video blogging?' That seems so narcissistic and just, like, silly."

But then she starting watching NYC-via-JP vlogger Ryanne Hodson, who maintains one of the first and best sites around, a funny, arty, compendium of videographic self-expression. "The more I watched, the more I was like, this is just great. I realized there was so much more potential." She also thought it would be a complement to her schoolwork, a way to keep her shooting and editing skills sharp. (Heads Off hosts a prototype of her master's thesis, an interactive Flash presentation called "VideoString" that explores the shift from written language to video communication by allowing the composition of syntactical "sentences" from short video clips.)

30 Still, "I don't have any big goals," Shiflett says of the vlog. "I have about 20 to 30 people subscribed through RSS, and I'm sure if I could see who they were, I'd know 75 percent of them." Some of Heads Off's page hits have come from people searching the Web for decapitation videos. One person got there via a Google query for "Davis Square Haircut." Still, many stay and watch clip after clip, she says.

"People always want to be famous. I never wanted that, which is why I hardly ever show up on our blog. But I feel like 80 percent of the population, that's their dream come true, to be on camera. What surprises me more is that people are so interested in watching."

Left: Steve Garfield's *Vlog Soup;*
Right: Amy Carpenter's *Welcome to Amyville.*

Starting Young

A new, tech-savvy generation is keying in to the new medium early on. Phil Hamilton, a 16-year-old junior at Wellesley High, has been maintaining his own video blog, Phil Hamilton Hits the Big Time, since last March. It's a goof, in a way. Clips are seldom longer than a minute or two, and he didn't even let people know about it until August. But its adolescent sensibility is funny and smart, and its camera work is skilled. People are noticing.

"A girl just IM-ed me yesterday saying she found it on the Web somehow," Hamilton says.

So video blogging is a good way to meet chicks?

35 "Uh, no. Not really."

But who wouldn't be charmed by Phil goofily celebrating the arrival of spring in his parents' backyard? Or Phil rebuffing his mom's demand to put on his seat belt? Or Phil procrastinating a paper on David Mamet? Or Phil mugging for the camera: "Yeah, I got homework! I looove homework! Golly gee! Homework is the best!" But sometimes, this high-school junior stops being sophomoric and throws you for a loop, as when he captures the quiet beauty of the season's first snow, scoring artful shots of the softly falling flakes with choral music.

Hamilton isn't picky about what he videotapes—"just whatever, really"—but he's wary of becoming too popular. That might lead him to update more often than he ordinarily would, sacrificing quality for quantity. "I'm afraid that if everyone's watching it I'll either feel pressure or it will become too much of my own surroundings and won't be interesting to other people."

Hamilton's friend Josh Kopin has his own blog, What Is, started at Hamilton's urging. He too has had trouble with creative blockage. In one clip, posted after nearly two months without updating, he stares into the camera and—interspersed with footage of insects, Japanese cuisine, and a school play—offers hope to others with "videoblogger's block."

In the time since you saw me last, I have done a lot of things. I went back to school, and I found a cricket, and I watched miso soup settle in reverse, and I got into a musical. But I haven't had a lot of time for video blogging. Because I didn't want to make a bad video. I just pressured myself into stopping. I wanted to turn my frustration into a lesson for other video bloggers…. So for all the aspiring video bloggers out there who've hit a wall like I did, just remember that it's not really about your audience, it's about you.

40   "Some people are energized by producing for people," Kopin says. "For me, it's almost strangling to know that people might not like what I do. That day, I decided to explain why I hadn't, and to encourage people. Blogging for me is pretty personal. The fact that people watch my videos and like them is almost like a bonus."

Kopin knows that his audience, even if it only consists of his friends and other video-blogging enthusiasts, likes to watch his stuff. So he'll keep filming himself beat-boxing, or demonstrating circular breathing with a glass of water, or building a rocket powered by baking soda and vinegar. (Soundtrack: William Shatner's cover of Elton John's "Rocket Man." Of course.)

"In this world, you often feel that a lot of interactions with people are very impersonal," Kopin says. "To be able to peek into someone else's life, see what they're interested in—and show what you're interested in too—that's something different."

A Political Bonanza

Boston city councilor John Tobin recalls a tale from several years ago, when he was first running for office. An opponent's campaign had a Web site with audio capabilities. "We thought he was like a Martian," he says. But before long, Tobin found himself listening to the clips. And, lo and behold, "I thought, 'This guy's onto something!'"

Now Tobin is the trailblazer. Last spring, Steve Garfield, who's one of Tobin's constituents, showed up at his office hours. He had an idea. "I said, 'Oh, no. Somebody's pitching something that's totally crazy and I'm never going to use,'" Tobin remembers. "But after I talked to him for an hour and a half, I was sold."

45   Tobin updates his blog with video entries filmed, edited, and posted by Garfield, every other week or so—and every day in the week leading up to the last election. He goes on location to show the scourge of graffiti in Hyde Square. He checks out a sanctioned mural painted by the Mayor's Mural Crew. He visits the scene of the firebombed El Oriental de Cuba restaurant in JP, and then reports two months later from a benefit to get the place back up and running. He shows how the disused trolley tracks on Centre Street are a safety hazard, rather than just talking about it.

In this jam-packed media age, where TV forces politicians to get their message out in 15-second sound bites, and where local news channels cover City Hall and state legislature less and less, video blogging offers a cheap and substantive way for pols to communicate with their public. "People are tired of canned speeches," says Tobin. "To talk to the camera, unscripted, is a pretty unique way to get your point across." That's why he's convinced that, by the time the 2008 presidential election rolls around, every politician worth his salt will be vlogging. "It's going to be mandatory. People are going to have to do it. Voters won't accept that they don't have it."

A tireless advocate for the arts in the Hub—and co-founder of the Boston International Comedy & Movie Festival—Tobin might seem to be the pol most likely to adopt new video technology like this. But does he think some of his more hidebound council colleagues might soon be following suit? "If they were smart they would be. It just makes sense."

Perils of Popularity?

Still, the adoption of video blogging by the political establishment—and surely, soon enough, by more and more big media—is antithetical to its grassroots beginnings, in a way. As it proliferates more and more, one wonders whether vlogging might start to lose some of its populist appeal, that messy, personality—driven uniqueness that is its most salient feature, in favor of a more bland establishment imprimatur.

Phil Hamilton is wary. "I think, like, with the video iPod, it's definitely getting bigger," he says. "And I hope that it gets bigger. But I'm afraid that as it gets bigger it will just get glossed over."

Still, while we'll surely be seeing more and more sanitized and corporatized versions of the video blog as more and more companies recognize its quickness, cheapness, and ease of use, it's a safe bet it will stay a predominantly democratic medium. Look at text blogging: for every Washington Whispers or The Note, there are hundreds of independent, stridently opinionated voices out there.

When Steve Garfield looks ahead, he sees a further leveling of the playing field. And he can't wait. "People who are normally just passive consumers of video are gonna say, 'Whoa, we can create it and we can get it out there the same way the big networks are getting it out.' Everything will be equal. There are no barriers to entry, of cost or distribution. It's available to anybody. There are stories to be told. And there are a lot of stories out there."

Reflect & Write

❏ Does Miliard assume a tech-savvy or low-tech audience? How can you tell this from his different rhetorical decisions in this article?

❏ As part of his article, Miliard follows up the first section of his article with a series of examples of personal video blogs. How does this strategy enhance or undermine the strength of his argument?

❏ How do the images that accompany the article contribute to its persuasiveness? Evaluate each one as a "snapshot" representation of reality. Do they all work in the same way?

❏ Consider video blogging in relation to online photo sharing like Flickr. How do the two operate in similar ways to represent reality? How do they differ?

❏ **Write:** Visit YouTube (http://www.youtube.com) and watch three videoblogs—you may want to search using your college or university name to see if any of your classmates have video blogs. Now write a column for your school newspaper in which you provide your perspective on the new vlogging phenomenon.

COLLABORATIVE CHALLENGE

Explore an online interactive multimedia feature on BBC (http://www.bbc.co.uk), *The New York Times* (http://www.nytimes.com), MSNBC (http://www.msnbc.msn.com), or I-Reports on CNN (http://www.cnn.com). How do these Websites and news sites feature photographs of everyday people? What arguments are being made about the countries, cultures, and people represented through inevitable selectivity? Compose a hypertext photo essay or YouTube vlog with your comments on several choice examples of digitally captured identity through photo representation.

PERSPECTIVES ON THE ISSUE

1. Return to the quotation from Dorothea Lange that opened this chapter: "Photography takes an instant out of time, altering life by holding it still." Assess this quotation now in light of the readings and photographs you've examined in this chapter. Compose an argument supporting or refuting the quotation and use specific evidence from the section materials to prove your thesis.

2. What kind of writing have you encountered in this chapter? Compare the photographic review piece by Cox to the critical essay by Sontag and the more popular articles by Mieszkowski and Miliard. What are the characteristics of each in terms of the canons of rhetoric? Assess the writing itself in terms of

conventions of invention, arrangement, style or decorum, and delivery. How does each form of writing fit the expectations of the audience? Now add your own voice to the conversation by composing either a review article or a critical essay.

3. Compare the photographs of American life showcased in this chapter; what has changed over time in terms of subject matter, technique, and rhetorical elements of the image? What do such changes suggest about our changing cultural values as a society and our changing relationship with photography or the image?

4. What remains constant in looking at images of the ordinary across various media, from photographs to video blogs? What values, choice of subjects, or techniques of representing reality can you identify across media?

FROM READING TO RESEARCH

1. In an essay entitled "Photographing the Unfamous," writer Catherine Ryan asserts about the photographer Mary Ellen Mark:

   From circus performers in India to street kids in Seattle, Mary Ellen Mark photographs people on the fringes of society—the "unfamous," as she calls them—to portray aspects of the world that many people never confront. She ultimately aims to show the common threads of humanity by photographing people of varying backgrounds.

   Conduct research on this photographer to see what Ryan means about the "unfamous." Visit Mary Ellen Mark's photography through her Website at http://www.maryellenmark.com. Write up your own analysis of three images. Then compare Ryan's claim to another view on Mark's photography by reading the interview with Melissa Harris in *Aperture* (Winter 1997 n 146, p. 42–52), available in your library. Craft a Multiple Sides project (follow the directions in Chapter 3), representing the diverse views you have researched. Add your own framing perspective as editor of the collection for this research project.

2. Research the changing representations of women's roles in the media, from images in photographs you find on the news or in popular magazines (such as *People, Vogue, National Geographic, Elle*) to images on television shows (*Survivor, Extreme Makeover, American Idol*). What changes or trends do you see in representations of women? Conduct additional research into the representation of women's realities; look at the following texts for a starting point and then synthesize these views, along with your own rhetorical analysis of the images you find, in order to forge your research paper: John Berger, *Ways of Seeing;* John Tagg, *The Burden of Representation;* Marianne Hirsch, *The Familial Gaze;* and Amelia Jones, *The Feminism and Visual Culture Reader*.

3. Conduct the research project above but look at representations of masculinity, class, race, and American identity. Include additional visual representations of reality such as *Queer Eye for the Straight Guy, Everybody Loves Raymond,* and *The Jerry Springer Show*. Compose a rhetorical analysis of the texts you will study, and weave your research sources in as support for your argument. Follow the guidelines from Chapter 6 to help you draft your research paper. You might want to share it with a group of writers in class and exchange peer review feedback. When you are done, design a photo montage for the cover of your research paper. Present your work to the class.

IMAGES OF CRISIS

With the ubiquity of news coverage and global media today, we get our understanding of both local and world events from stories accompanied by powerful images. From Hurricane Katrina and the flooding of New Orleans to the 2004 tsunami disaster in Southeast Asia, we get a glimpse into the suffering of others through vivid photos, news films, blogs, and videos from those on the ground. In this way, images literally shape what it is possible for us to know about a crisis. Sometimes, looking at a particularly heart-wrenching image, we might wonder: What are the ethics involved in showing people caught in times of crisis, tragedy, pain, or suffering? Do the images accurately represent the reality of a situation or just show us one skewed view?

To begin to understand these questions, let's take the 2004 Indian Ocean tsunami as our first example. On December 26, 2004, when the natural disaster struck Southeast Asia, camera crews soon arrived to capture the devastation. Within hours, photographs of destroyed towns and coastal villages, ravaged tourist hotels, bodies of drowned victims, and grieving families swept like another tidal wave across streaming media, satellite news feeds, and newspapers worldwide. But in the wake of such media coverage emerged a tricky question of ethics—is it acceptable to use graphic representations of the affected countries and of the people who live there?

FIGURE 14.6 Two school children from Mercer Island, Washington, use images of suffering to solicit donations to raise money for victims of the 2004 tsunami in Southeast Asia.

Consider an example from the 2004 tsunami disaster in Southeast Asia. As you can see from Figure 14.6, two children use graphic photographs of the tsunami crisis to raise awareness—and money—to help the disaster victims. What do you make of the contrast between their smiling faces and the crisis-stricken people shown on their poster? The original caption for the photo, available at http://www.detnews.com/2005/lifestyle/0501/14/C06-55865.htm, seems to celebrate their actions without considering the ethics of their capitalizing on the suffering of others:

> Eight-year-old twins Themio, left, and George Pallis of Mercer Island, Wash., already have delivered $5,660 to World Vision, an aid organization that focuses on children. Since then, fellow students have donated more.

Viewed through an ironic lens, it appears that to make their work possible, the children have used such horrific images without necessarily grappling with the issue of reproducing people's pain in photos for a specific cause.

In this chapter, we will try to wrestle with the issue of representing global realities—often from times of crisis—through images. We'll ask, with Daniel Okrent, what it means to raise international awareness through visual representation, and whether we have different standards for particular countries. We'll consider Bruce Jackson's letter to the editor wondering about our limits on decency and privacy. Two views on the 1995 Oklahoma City bombing will help us explore the issue in depth, and we'll consider the significance of what Mark Glaser calls "citizen paparazzi"—people who take photos with cell phones, such as happened after the July 2005 London terrorist bombings.

We will then turn to images of crisis during wartime. In the past ten years, there has been a dramatic change in terms of the kinds of images that news journalists provide the public. From an ethical standpoint, it may be as significant as the first color images depicting the war in Vietnam or the film footage that emerged soon after, through which audiences gained unparalleled access to what was happening on the other side of the world. The most recent form of photojournalism, what the military and the media call embedded journalism, gives us a view from the front, but one that is shaped and even controlled by the military. Now photographers such as David Leeson are literally embedded or assigned to a military unit—they can't access the military field unless they travel with a military troop. But this most contemporary form of news coverage raises several compelling questions that we will explore through analyzing Leeson's photos and the interview by Dirck Halstead. Namely, are the photographers more protected from danger? Or are they able to see only part of the story? How can they represent the full reality of a situation? That is, can they offer the public a truly objective view or are they somehow now part of the military mission? And what happens when photographers stand aside in the face of true danger—when they refuse to save a life, pick up a gun, or help those who have been protecting them? At the same time, what happens when photographers do become combatants? To address these questions, we'll end our readings with analysis from PBS's *NewsHour with Jim Lehrer* of the ways in which most representations of photojournalism in wartime reflect our changing attitudes about viewing—and experiencing—images of crisis.

Reflect & Write

❏ Analyze the rhetorical properties of the photo in Figure 14.6. Look at the many complex elements: the boys' smiling faces, the grief-stricken faces of people in the newspaper photos. What are the various arguments made by each part of the image? How do the parts work together to create one comprehensive argument?

❏ Consider the context and circumstance for the photo. What can you tell about where the photo was taken and who the audience is? How does context influence an ethical interpretation of the photo?

❏ **Write:** Draft your own caption for this photo. Then write a letter to the editor explaining how your own caption offers a different perspective on the issue.

■ **Daniel Okrent** *'s article was published in* The New York Times *in the wake of the media blitz covering the 2004 tsunami tragedy. Okrent was the first public editor of* The New York Times; *he's also a baseball fan and the inventor of Rotisserie League Baseball, the best-known form of fantasy baseball.*

The Public Editor: No Picture Tells the Truth—The Best Do Better Than That

Daniel Okrent

Two Mondays ago, the scale of the Indian Ocean catastrophe was just emerging from the incomplete earlier reports (from a *Times* article the day before: a tidal wave had "killed more than 150 people in Sri Lanka"). By the 4:30 Page 1 meeting, picture editors had examined more than 900 images of devastation to find the one that would stretch across five columns and nearly half the depth of Tuesday's front page. Into a million homes came a grieving mother crouched beside the lifeless bodies of tiny children, and perhaps more horrifying, three pairs of feet extending from beneath a white sheet in an upper corner, suggesting the presence beyond the frame of row upon awful row of the tsunami's pitiless toll.

Many readers and at least a few members of The *Times*'s newsroom staff considered the picture exploitative, unduly graphic, and by its size and placement, inappropriately forced upon the paper's readers. Some felt it disrespectful of both the living and the dead. A few said *The Times* would not have published it had the children been white

Americans. Boaz Rabin of Weehawken, N.J., wrote, "Lead with letters the size of eggs, use any words you see fit, but don't put a nightmare on the front page."

I asked managing editor Jill Abramson why she chose this picture. She said in an e-mail message that after careful and difficult consideration, she decided that the photo "seemed to perfectly convey the news: the sheer enormity of the disaster, as we learned one-third of the casualties are children in a part of the world where more than 50 percent of the population is children. It is an indescribably painful photograph, but one that was in all ways commensurate to the event." When I spoke with director of photography Michele McNally, who believes the paper has the obligation "to bear witness" at moments like this, she had a question for me: "Wouldn't you want us to show pictures from Auschwitz if the gates were opened in our time?"

The surpassing power of pictures enables them to become the permanent markers of enormous events. The marines planting the flag at Iwo

Jima, the South Vietnamese general shooting his captive at point-blank range, the young John F. Kennedy Jr. saluting his father's passing coffin: each is the universal symbol for a historical moment. You don't need to see them to see them.

5 But in every case, someone needs to choose them. Photo editors (*The Times* employs 40) and their colleagues make hundreds of choices a week. Stories may whisper with nuance and headlines declaim in summary, but pictures seize the microphone, and if they're good, they don't let go. In most cases, a story gets a single picture; major stories may get more, but usually only one on the front page itself—and that becomes the picture that stands for the event.

This won't make every reader happy. From last year's mail: "The picture hardly reflects the regular Turkish population." "I have never been a particular [fan] of Richard Grasso, but *The Times* should not prejudge his lawsuit by publishing photos that portray him as a monster." "I find it appalling and disgusting that you would print an Iraqi holding up the boots of one of our dead soldiers." "Why are we shown the pictures of tragically mutilated U.S. civilian contractors but not slain Iraqi children?" One reader felt that a picture of a smiling Jesse Jackson next to George W. Bush made it appear that Jackson had endorsed the president. Another believed that a photo of a dead Palestinian child in the arms of a policeman looked staged, as if to resemble the Pietà.

Richard Avedon once said: "There is no such thing as inaccuracy in a photograph. All photographs are accurate. None of them is the truth." In this Age of Fungible Pixels, when not every publication, political campaign, or advocacy organization follows the *Times* policy prohibiting manipulation of news photographs, I'm not even sure about the accuracy part. But the untruth—or, at least, imperfect truth—of any single photograph is inescapable. Some readers object to the way a picture is cropped, arguing that evidence changing its meaning has been sliced out of the frame. But meaning is determined long before that. A photographer points the camera here, then turns three inches to the left and snaps again: different picture, maybe a different reality. A photo editor selects from the images the photographer submits (should the subject be smiling? Frowning? Animated? Distracted?). The designer wants it large (major impact) or small (lesser impact). The editor picks it for Page 1 (important) or not (not). By the time a reader sees a picture, it has been repeatedly massaged by judgment. But it's necessarily presented as fact.

Last May, for an article considering whether Brazilian President Luiz Inácio Lula da Silva had a drinking problem, editors selected a seven-month-old file photo showing the president hoisting a beer at an Oktoberfest celebration. It may have been a sensible choice; drinking was the subject, and a picture of the president standing at a lectern would have been dull and disconnected. But any ambiguity in the article was steamrolled by visual evidence that may have been factual (da Silva once had a beer), but perhaps not truthful.

Even in the coverage of an event as photographically unpromising as a guy in a suit giving a speech, pictures convey judgment. When George J. Tenet resigned as C.I.A. director in June, a front page shot showed him looking down, biting his lip, possibly near tears; according to Bruce Mansbridge of Austin, Tex., at other moments during the broadcast of Tenet's speech, "he appeared quite upbeat." When Donald H. Rumsfeld visited Abu Ghraib in May, *The Times* showed him flanked by soldiers, striding through the grounds of the prison, as if (wrote Karen Smullen of Long Island) "Karl Rove must have said, 'What we really need now is a photo of [Rumsfeld] leading soldiers and looking earnest and determined and strong.'" Did Rumsfeld pause at any point and laugh at a joke told by a colleague, or bark at a reporter who asked him a difficult question?

10   Did any of these pictures tell the whole story, or just a sliver of it?

Mix a subjective process with something as idiosyncratic as taste and you're left with a volatile compound. Add human tragedy and it becomes emotionally explosive. The day *The Times* ran the picture of the dead children, many other papers led with a photograph of a grief-racked man clutching the hand of his dead son. It, too, was a powerful picture, and it's easy to see why so many used it. But it was—this is difficult to say—a portrait of generic tragedy. The devastated man could have been in the deserts of Darfur, or in a house in Mosul, or on a sidewalk in Peoria; he could have been photographed 10 years ago, or 10 years from now. His pain was universal.

But the picture on the front page of *The Times* could only have been photographed now, and only on the devastated shores of the Indian Ocean. My colleague David House of *The Fort Worth Star-Telegram* says, "In this instance, covering life means covering death." The babies in their silent rows were as real, and as specific, as the insane act of nature that murdered them. This picture was the story of the Indian Ocean tsunami of December 2004—not the truth, but a stand-in for the truth that will not leave the thoughts of those who saw it. *The Times* was right to publish it.

Reflect & Write

❏ What do you make of the writer's decision to use "I" in this article? How might it be a persuasive and effective tool here? What rhetorical appeal is at work?

❏ Compare the many historical examples Okrent mentions in his argument. How do they work together to offer coherence and depth for his thesis? Why might he have arranged them in the order he did?

❏ Visit the *Envision In Depth* website and view the images Okrent originally included with his articles. How do these images speak to one another? What argument does each make about the conflict at hand and how do they work as a set?

❏ What are the ethical problems raised by the photos? Analyze their original captions and then the written explanations Okrent provided.

❏ **Write:** Draft your own captions for contemporary examples of ethically troubling photographs that you find for a recent conflict in the world today.

■ *In this short letter to the editor,* **Bruce Jackson** *raises a key point about the ethics of photojournalism.*

Letters to the Public Editor: "Some Words About Those Pictures"

Bruce Jackson

I agree with what you say about the impact and utility of the photograph of dead children that *The Times* used on the front page in its coverage of the tsunami. But why no similar photographs of dead and mutilated G.I.'s and civilians in Iraq, or of dead and mutilated Palestinians and Israelis?

The Times is choosing which dead are acceptable to show literally and which dead are to be shown by reference—for example, body bags or a blood-spattered vehicle or sidewalk.

Reflect & Write

❏ Not many words are needed to make a sharp and persuasive argument here. Restate the argument in your own words.

❏ What rhetorical strategies are used to make this concise yet effective argument? Consider the use of pathos, ethos, and logos.

❏ **Write:** Compose a response to both Okrent and to Jackson in which you offer a third perspective on the ethics of covering conflict in the media. Look at Chapter 3 for examples of Multiple Sides Projects that you might emulate.

Seeing Connections
Visit Chapter 2 for a refresher lesson on rhetorical strategies.

■ **Charles Porter** *is a bank clerk and an amateur photographer; he captured the defining image of the Oklahoma City bombing in April 1995. His picture won a Pulitzer Prize. The selection here is a transcription of his account of taking the photo as told to BBC News, who published it on their Website on May 9, 2005.*

Tragedy in Oklahoma

Charles Porter

I am talking about two photographs that I took on 19 April 1995 from the Oklahoma City bombing.

One being of a policeman handing an infant to a fireman and the other of a fireman gently cradling this lifeless infant.

I have these images in front of me here, looking at them now, and there are things that strike me.

One is that the fireman has taken the time to remove his gloves before receiving this infant from the policeman.

5   Anyone who knows anything about firefighters know that their gloves are very rough and abrasive and to remove these is like saying I want to make sure that I am as gentle and as compassionate as I can be with this infant that I don't know is dead or alive.

And the second image is of this fireman just cradling this infant with the utmost compassion and caring.

He is looking down at her with this longing, almost to say with his eyes: "It's going to be OK, if there's anything I can do I want to try to help you."

He doesn't know that she has already passed away.

Spring Morning

And these images are in such contrast with the day.

10   It was such a beautiful, crisp, bright spring morning. And at 0902 it was just amazing.

Our building shook and I looked out the window and saw this huge brown cloud of dust and debris and papers just flying in the air, and as I ran across towards the debris cloud, I turned this corner at the building and the street was covered with glass.

There were people on the street that were injured and bleeding, and there was a gentleman that was walking towards me who had taken his dress shirt off from the office building that he was in and had it to his head, and blood was dripping from that.

I just took my camera out and instinctively started taking pictures.

I ran to the front of the building and took some images of that, and as I ran back down the side, I noticed this ambulance where these firefighters were working on these people that were wounded and mortally wounded, and I

First frame: The police officer hands the baby to the firefighter.

noticed something out of the corner of my eye that was running across my field of vision.

15   I didn't know what it was, but I trained my camera on it and it was this police officer.

     And as this policeman handed this infant to the fireman, I took one frame and then as the fireman is cradling this infant I took the second frame and that is exactly how these images came to be on 19 April 1995.

     After I left I got my film developed and called a friend who was the head of photography at a local university.

     I called him, and he said: "If you have images that have just happened, you need to go to somebody that wants to see them, like the Associated Press or somebody like that."

     I looked the address up in the phone book, I got in my car. I drove over there. I knocked on the door and I went in and said: "Hi, I've got some images of what you're seeing on TV and wanted to know if you would like to look at them?"

Speechless

"Chills go over me just to think about the magnitude and the enormity of where that picture went"

20 Wendel Hudson, who was the AP photo editor at Oklahoma City at the time, picked them out immediately and said: "We'd like to use these." And I thought: "Wow!"

     It went out on the AP wire, and not knowing exactly what the AP wire is, I go home and I honestly went home and told my wife: "You know what, I just took some images and they might be in the *Daily Oklahoma* tomorrow."

     I go home about 1300. About 1320 I get this phone call from this lady and she says: "Hi, I am so-and-so from the *London Times* and I want to know if you are Charles Porter."

     I said: "Yes I am, but how do *you* know who I am?"

     She said: "Well I just received your image over the AP wire..."

25   And she proceeded to explain to me what the Associated Press wire was.

     I said that I didn't know how to respond and she said, "Well sir, can I ask you one question?" And this is where it hit home: "Could I get your reaction and response to what your feelings are going to be, knowing that your image is going to be over every newspaper and every magazine in the entire world tomorrow?"

     I was silent and speechless, and chills go over me just to think about the magnitude and the enormity of where that picture went and the impact that picture had at that time. It was beyond my scope of comprehension and understanding, way beyond.

■ **Joe Strupp** *is Associate Editor at* Editor & Publisher, *where this article appeared one month after the Oklahoma City bombing. Strupp writes on a number of controversial issues and has been an invited media commentator on* The O'Reilly Factor, The Fox Report, *Air America Radio, National Public Radio, Wisconsin Public Radio, Voice of America, and WPIX TV News in New York City. He has won two Jesse H. Neal Business Journalism Awards, the "Pulitzer Prize" of business journalism, and also contributes to Salon.com.*

The Photo Felt Around the World

Joe Strupp

It sparked heated debate in several newsrooms, caused one veteran newspaper editor to cry, and, for most photo editors, became the focal front-page shot of the tragic April 19 bombing in Oklahoma City.

"It was the photo that was felt around the world," said Tommy Almon, the baby's grandfather.

President Bill Clinton even mentioned it in a televised address.

Ironically, however, the dramatic photo of firefighter Chris Fields cradling the badly burned body of infant Baylee Almon in his arms—which landed on numerous front pages the next day—was shot by a local amateur, developed at a one-hour photo shop, and nearly missed being distributed by the Associated Press.

5   Charles H. Porter IV, a 25-year-old Oklahoma City bank clerk, shot the picture of Fields holding the child, just moments after the bomb blast occurred.

He then sold the photo to AP state photo editor David Longstreath, who sent it over the wires.

"It was everything that was indicative of the bombing," said Longstreath. "It was one of those rare shots that gives the entire story, but in a way that words cannot."

Once Porter took the picture, and developed it with other bomb-blast photos, he still had nowhere to publish it. He initially took the shot to Dan Smith, a photographer at the University of Central Oklahoma, who knew Longstreath.

Longstreath said Smith called him and sent the photo over to AP to be considered. But, in the chaos that followed the explosion, Longstreath almost ignored the shot.

10   "My initial reaction when he sent it was that I was too busy," said Longstreath. "I looked at the roll he shot and took that frame. He took the rest of the roll and left that afternoon."

The infant, who had turned one-year-old the day before the explosion, was pronounced dead at the scene. The baby also was the subject of another widely distributed photo, which showed the infant being handed from police Sgt. John Avera to firefighter Fields, just moments before the Porter picture was taken.

Once it reached the AP nationwide photo wire, the shot of Fields holding the young baby became the subject of debate for several major newspapers, and the main front-page photo for many others.

The *Philadelphia Inquirer,* which played the picture on Page One the following day, made it the solo front-page art, except for a mall, inside tease photo along the left column.

"That photo showed what happened better than anything I've seen," said Ashley Halsey, the *Inquirer's* national editor. "There wasn't a photo that better captured what happened there, so we decided to use it."

15   Halsey, a 27-year newspaper veteran, said he briefly discussed the decision to play up the shot with fellow editors, but believed the tragic elements were important to the story.

"When you have an event that is this absolutely horrible, you will have this kind of photo," Halsey said. "It was deeply disturbing, but it best captured the tragedy."

Halsey said the photo sparked about a dozen phone calls from concerned readers the next day, including several who opposed its publication. But, he said, most agreed it was proper.

"It touched me very deeply because I have a child that same age," Halsey said. "After we put the paper to bed, I walked out to the parking lot and cried. I have never done that before."

Other editors, such as Morton Saltzman of the *Sacramento Bee,* chose not to print the photo, deciding it was inappropriate.

20 "We had a rather lengthy discussion about which photo to use on the front page, and we decided not to use it because we believed the baby was dead," said Saltzman, the *Bee*'s assistant managing editor for news. "We viewed it as a picture of a corpse, even though there was no information about the baby's condition. It was the most dramatic photo and very compelling, but we chose to go with a photo of a live child rather than a dead one."

For other newspapers, the decision to use the Porter photo or various others involving bloody victims also included lengthy discussions and compromises.

The *San Francisco Chronicle,* for example, published the firefighter photo, but did not use it as its main art. The *Chronicle* also took the unusual step of printing a short message to readers, warning them of the brutal pictures.

"There was a lot of discussion over that baby and firefighter photo, and everyone agreed that it had to be used because there were so many children who died," said Lance Iverson, the *Chronicle*'s picture editor. "But, at the same time, we didn't want to shock or offend anyone. We just wanted to tell the story and give a visual impression; that is why we ran it."

The response from readers about the baby's condition was so great, the *Chronicle* published a short story the next day explaining how the child had died.

25 "We got close to 100 phone calls asking what happened to the baby, and we had to report it was deceased," said Iverson. "We rarely get phone calls on photos; I can't recall the last time."

At the *New York Daily News,* where the shot of Avera handing the baby to firefighter Fields made Page One, executive editor Debby Krenek said the emotion of the shot made the decision easy.

"We thought it showed the gripping feeling of the situation," said Krenek. "We didn't think it was too harsh; there were a lot of other ones that we used inside that had blood running down shirts and on faces, but this was Page One."

Still, can a newspaper go too far in portraying such a tragic, bloody event as the Oklahoma City bombing? And did the dramatic firefighter/baby photo cross that line?

For Professor Tom Goldstein, dean of graduate journalism studies at the University of California at Berkeley, the answer is no.

30 "Newspapers are supposed to reflect the world, and that's what they did," Goldstein said. "There seems to be absolutely no doubt in my mind that those riveting photos should have been used, no doubt. It's not something that you necessarily want to look at during breakfast, but they are riveting."

Abstract: Bank clerk Charles H. Porter took a picture of a firefighter cradling a burned infant in his arms right after the Oklahoma City bombing, in OK, in Apr 1995. The photograph was sold to an AP state photo editor who sent it over the wires. Different newspapers discussed how they should use such an emotionally-charged picture, and, after its publication, many readers called to ask what happened to the baby. Other readers called to protest the picture's publication. However, most newspaper officials believed that it captured the tragedy of the situation in a wordless moment. The baby died the day after the picture was taken.

Reflect & Write

❑ Both articles cover the same event—the ethical question of whether or not to publish a disturbing photo of a baby who later died as a result of the Oklahoma City bombing. What is the argument of each one? How does the first person testimony by Porter convey a different perspective than Strupp's more journalistic coverage? What rhetorical strategies are at work in each one?

❑ Porter's account ends with the offer of publication and Strupp's article takes up the debate among editors and officials about whether to publish. How does each one address a different audience? What is the *kairos* shaping each stance and the argument of each?

❑ Compare the styles of the two articles, noting differences in rhetorical appeals, language, and even formality. How do these choices influence you as a reader?

❑ **Write:** Strupp's article mentions the hundreds of calls and protests. Imagine that you are against the publication of this photo for ethical reasons. Write a letter to the editor and make your argument clear and sound.

■ **Mark Glaser** *is a freelance journalist, editor, and expert on online media and Weblogs. He currently writes a weekly column for* (Online Journalism Review), *where this article appeared on July 13, 2005, five days after the London bombing. He also writes a bi-weekly newsletter for the Online Publishers Association (www.online-publishers.org). Glaser has written essays for Harvard's* Nieman Reports *and the Website for the Yale Center for Globalization, and he has appeared on National Public Radio and Minnesota Public Radio. Glaser has also written columns on the Internet and technology for the* Los Angeles Times, *CNET, and* HotWired, *and features for* The New York Times, Conde Nast Traveler, Entertainment Weekly, *and the* San Jose Mercury News. *He was the lead writer for the* Industry Standard's *award-winning "Media Grok" daily email newsletter, and was recently named a finalist for a 2004 Online Journalism Award in the Online Commentary category. He received a Bachelor of Journalism and Bachelor of Arts in English at the University of Missouri at Columbia, and currently lives in San Francisco.*

Did London Bombings Turn Citizen Journalists into Citizen Paparazzi?

Mark Glaser

July 7, 2005, was one of the darkest days for London, as terrorists blew up three underground trains and a double-decker bus, killing scores and injuring hundreds. But out of that darkness came an unusual light, the flickering light from survivors such as Adam Stacey and Ellis Leeper as they shot the scene underground using cameraphones and videophones.

Like the tsunami disaster in Southeast Asia, the first reports came from people at the scene who had videocameras. In this case, the cameras were smaller and built into phones. But despite the day being a major breakthrough for citizen media—from Wikipedia's collective entry to group blogs such as Londonist's hour-by-hour rundown—it also brought out the worst in some bystanders.

A London blogger who identifies himself only as Justin and blogs at Pfff.co.uk, told his story of surviving the bombing on the train that exploded near Edgware Road. His harrowing account includes this scene as he finally comes out of the underground tunnel and into the fresh air: "The victims were being triaged at the station entrance by Tube staff and as I could see little more I could do so I got out of the way and left," he wrote. "As I stepped out people with cameraphones vied to try and take pictures of the worst victims. In crisis some people are cruel."

The next day, Justin reflected a bit more on the people outside who were trying to photograph the victims.

"These people were passers-by trying to look into the station," Justin wrote. "They had no access, but could have done well to clear the area rather than clog it. The people on the train weren't all trying to take pictures, we were shocked, dirty and helping each other. People were stunned, but okay. The majority of the train was okay as I walked from my carriage (the last intact one) down through the train I saw no injuries or damage to the remaining four or so carriages. Just people dirty and in shock. The other direction wasn't so pretty, but you don't need an account of this and what I saw, watching TV is enough."

While citizen media efforts became another big story, quickly picked up by the *Los Angeles Times* and *Wall Street Journal,* among many others, Justin was not so quick to exploit his story. In fact, his first impulse was not to watch any news accounts and not to give interviews to media outlets that wanted to glorify his situation.

I left a comment for him on his blog, asking him if he realized that all the people with cameraphones that day were helping to tell the story to the world. Was there a way they could tell that story in a more sensitive way?

"The news does hold a role and it's important for people to understand, comprehend and learn," Justin replied to me in another blog comment. "To ensure they're safe, systems and procedures change, that the world ultimately gets better. I don't even hold contempt really for the cameraphone people, but you must appreciate something else—were those people taking photos helping or were those people shocking the world? I've alluded to seeing [gruesome] things in the tunnel and carriage, but I've not documented them in any detail. I feel it is inappropriate and does not contribute to fact and information."

So far, gruesome images from the attacks haven't been widely distributed online or given a prominent place in Western media. That contrasts sharply with the response in the Spanish media after the Madrid train bombings on March 11,

2004, when bloody photos were on TV and in newspapers, according to a Reuters story.

The Best and Worst in All of Us

In fact, online news sources were at the top of their game on July 7 and beyond. The BBC Website experienced its most trafficked day ever on July 7 and was inundated with eyewitness accounts from readers—20,000 emails, 1,000 photos and 20 videos in 24 hours, according to editor and acting head of BBC News Interactive Pete Clifton.

"It certainly did feel like a step-change [on July 7]," Clifton told me via email. "We often get pictures from our readers, but never as many as this, and the quality was very high. And because people were on the scenes, they were obviously better than anything news agencies could offer. A picture of the bus, for example, was the main picture on our front page for much of the day."

The BBC and *Guardian* both had reporters' blogs that were updated as events unfolded, and group blogs such as BoingBoing and Londonist became instant aggregators of online information.

More surprising was the importance of alternative news sources such as Wikipedia and its useful entry created by volunteer hordes and the inundation of images on Flickr. Even across the pond, MSNBC.com experienced double its usual weekday traffic on July 7, with 10.2 million unique users, and set a record with 4.4 million users of streaming video that day.

Interestingly, both the BBC and MSNBC.com gave particular citizen journalists who survived a bit more room to tell their story on instant diaries set up for the occasion. The diarist on the BBC, a woman who would only identify herself as Rachel (previously just "R"), was not totally thrilled about becoming a media sensation herself.

"More journos phoned yesterday," Rachel wrote in one post. "I must have given my mobile to the stringer who was asking questions when I was wandering outside the hospital getting fresh air after being stitched still in shock. The *Mail* on Sunday and Metro wanted to send a photographer round! I said no way. I said I felt it was important to get witness statements out at the time as I was there and felt relatively untraumatized so I'd rather they spoke to me than shoved their mikes and cameras in the faces of those who were shell-shocked or more injured. Having done that I really do not want any more fuss. . . . I was incredibly lucky but I have no desire to become a 'Blast Survivor Girlie' one week on."

That naked impulse to tell a disaster story, glaring kleig lights and all, was once the province of mainstream and tabloid news organizations. But no longer. Now, for better and worse, our fellow citizens stand by, cameraphones in pockets, ready to photograph us in our direst times. Xeni Jardin, a freelance technology journalist and co-editor of *BoingBoing,* was aghast at the behavior of the citizen paparazzi at the scene described by Justin.

"It's like the behavior when you see with a car wreck on the highway," Jardin told me. "People stop and gawk. There's a sense that this is some sort of animal behavior that's not entirely compassionate or responsible. The difference here is that people are gawking with this intermediary device. I'm not sure if the people who did this were saying 'I've got to blog this and get it to the BBC!' But when everyone is carrying around these devices and we get used to this intuitive response of just snapping what we see that's of interest—as surreal and grotesque as that scenario sounds, I imagine we will see a lot more of that."

Jardin compared the behavior to the paparazzi that chased Princess Diana before her fatal car crash and noted that the ethical issues raised then are now applicable beyond just professional photographers.

"These are ethical issues that we once thought only applied to a certain class of people who had adopted the role of news as a profession," Jardin said. "Now that more of us have the ability to capture and disseminate evidence or documentation of history as a matter of course, as a matter of our daily lives—as a casual gesture that takes very little time, no money, not a lot of skill—those ethical issues become considerations for all of us."

Society Under Surveillance

20 Citizen paparazzi is not really a new concept, and the proliferation of cameras has continued

unabated since the first point-and-shoot 35mm cameras took off right through cheap digital cameras. But while a few amateur photos might have made it into print magazines in the past, now the Internet is awash in photos and video taken by amateurs. As the term *citizen journalist* becomes part of mainstream thought—spurred on by Big Media outlets and startups—what role do these outlets play in spurring or reining in paparazzi behavior?

Dan Gillmor, founder of citizen media site Bayosphere, wrote in his landmark book *We the Media* about the proliferation of cameras in public spaces. "We are a society of voyeurs and exhibitionists," he wrote. "We can argue whether this is repugnant, but when secrets become far more difficult to keep, something fundamental will have changed. Imagine Rodney King and Abu Ghraib times a million. . . . Everyone who works, or moves around, in a public place should consider whether they like the idea of all their movements being recorded by nosy neighbors."

When I talked to Gillmor about the citizen paparazzi at the London bombing sites, he said he hoped that societies will eventually develop a zone of privacy for people in public places—but realistically didn't think it would happen.

"The line between an obviously important public event like what happened last week and public voyeurism is unclear," Gillmor said. "It's probable that there are pictures from last week floating around that are far too gruesome for any news organization to ever go near it. . . . In the end, we're going to have to develop new cultural norms, and I hope at some level that the more we wipe out the notion of privacy in a public space, the more I hope we end up with a kind of unwritten Golden Rule about privacy in public spaces and give people some space. I doubt it, but I hope people start to think about it."

Counterbalancing that was Gillmor's journalistic instinct, which said that news is news and is fair game for citizen journalists. "In a catastrophe, that's news, and I'm not going to tell people not to take photos of historic events," he said.

25 Jeff Jarvis, outspoken blogger at Buzzmachine and former president of Advance.net, trusts that normal folks using cameras will be more polite than paparazzi.

"The more I think about it, the more I do believe that most people will be more polite than paparazzi because they aren't motivated to get the picture no one else has to make a buck," Jarvis said via e-mail. "More reporters is merely more of what we have now. And believing in the value of news and reporting openness I think we need to see this as good. Are citizen journalists rude? Are professional journalists? Same question. Same answer."

Citizen journalism efforts are slowly coming out of beta, though there's room for more maturation in the relationship between contributors and media outlets. Andrew Locke, director of product strategy at MSNBC.com, said that his site made every effort to contact citizen journalists and pulled down contributions that didn't sit right with the editorial team.

"Jeanne Rothermich, who leads our small CJ team, has put a great deal of emphasis on fostering dialogue and partnership with individual citizen reporters," Locke told me. "We not only get more accurate information, but richer, more detailed accounts that we can share with the larger audience."

The advantage of the media sites over unmediated sources such as Flickr is that they can use the wisdom of photo and editorial staff to vet contributions and filter out insensitive or invalid material. But Locke says the next step for citizen media is more than just mentoring contributors.

30   "Over time, we want to turn those passing relationships into lasting bonds [with citizen journalists]," Locke said. "Once you have a real,

ongoing relationship, then you can start sharing information and wisdom back and forth. You can develop a code of conduct that means something and can stick. It's not simply about us mentoring citizen journalists like cub reporters, it's about the community itself developing norms and standards of propriety. Yes, we'll always act as a gatekeeper, but once you're in the gate as a citizen journalist, you should be an empowered member of the storytelling community. We still have a long way to go, but for citizen journalism to grow to its full potential we have to get there."

Reflect & Write

❏   What might be Mark Glaser's purpose as a writer in linking this story to the 2004 tsunami in Southeast Asia? How does this strategy broaden the scope of his argument's significance?

❏   How do the integrated quotations work to increase the force of this argument? Consider the quotes by London Blogger Justin and the e-mail response from BBC News Interactive's Pete Clifton. Why might the writer want to include such different sources? What can you learn about the power of field research as evidence in your writing from these examples?

❏   What larger questions of privacy are coming to light with the advent of new technologies? How is our visual world transforming? Answer by building on key passages from Glaser's article.

❏   **Write:** How does Glaser raise a key issue about the ethics of everyday people—not just of photojournalists? Do you think there should be an ethical code of conduct for cell phone camera users? Draft what such a code might look like.

Photos taken by members of the public during the London subway bombings in July 2005 pose a number of important questions about the roles and responsibilities of citizen journalists.

Visual Reading: Citizen Journalists Capture Images of Crisis

FIGURE 14.7 This image, taken with a train passenger's cell phone, captures the terror and confusion of the July 2005 bombing of the London underground.

FIGURE 14.8 This image, taken minutes after the London bombings, won the first Citizen Journalism award, which was sponsored by Nokia and the UK *Press Gazette*.

Reflect & Write

❑ How do these two images—taken on the scene of the July 7, 2005 bomb attacks in London—serve as arguments for conflict in the international arena? That is, how do these images work as powerfully as words to tell a story, provide a perspective, and persuade the viewer to care?

❑ What ethical issues are involved in the taking of these photos at the scene of the conflict and in the publication of these images on the Internet?

❑ Consider the low resolution of the first image (taken from a cell phone) in comparison to the sharper images generally found in newsmagazines and newspapers. Does the context and *kairos* of that image make up for its difference in quality?

❑ Analyze the captions for the image as posted with the story at http://www.npr.org/templates/story/story.php?storyId=4733098&sourceCode=gaw

❑ **Write:** Draft new captions, reflecting on your interpretation of these images as visual arguments.

In this interview, led by **Terence Smith,** *experts in the field of media analysis, such as CBS anchor Dan Rather, and Defense Secretary Donald Rumsfeld discuss the evolution of photo-journalism and the ethics of embedded journalism in particular. The interview has been taken from the March 22, 2003, edition of* NewsHour *with Jim Lehrer.*

War, Live

March 22, 2003
Terence Smith explores how the high-tech media equipment and the "embed-ding" of some 500 journalists with U.S. military units in Iraq has changed the way wars are covered.

TERENCE SMITH: If Vietnam was the living room war on American television, and the 1991 Desert Storm was the first satellite-fed real time war, this is the high-tech 21st century version.

CORRESPONDENT PETER ARNETT, in Baghdad: This is shock and awe, Tom, for the population of Baghdad.

High-tech coverage

TERENCE SMITH: Familiar voices have been heard in the first few days such as that of veteran war correspondent Peter Arnett reporting for *National Geographic Explorer* and NBC.

His descriptions made this Operation Iraqi Freedom sound like what it is, a rerun of the first Gulf War, which he reported live from Baghdad for CNN. But this war is different.

While the military is using state-of-the art weaponry, like pilotless Predator drones, the media are employing some cutting-edge technology of their own.

On some networks, virtual view technology makes the battlefield look like a deadly version of a video game, and point of view or "tank cam" video gives viewers a sense of being aboard those armored units that rumble northward into Iraq.

Videophones made popular during the war in Afghanistan bring jerky but real-time images home.

Technology makes the coverage more current, but when the sirens warn of a possible missile-born gas attack, the reporting gets muffled.

CBS ANCHOR DAN RATHER: Hold that microphone up. That's it.

CBS CORRESPONDENT: All right.

"Embedding" Reporters with the Military

TERENCE SMITH: But technology is no protection against the very real dangers of war. An Australian journalist was killed today by a car bomb. And correspondent Terry Lloyd and a two-member crew from Independent Television News are missing after coming under fire near the southern Iraqi city of Basra.

No American journalists have been wounded so far, but there have been some close calls on air.

CNN's Walter Rodgers was traveling with U.S. troops in northern Kuwait when shells from incoming enemy fire whistled overhead.

WALTER RODGERS: We just heard an incoming. What the hell!

TERENCE SMITH: The big difference in the coverage of this war is the arrangement under which some 500 reporters are embedded or assigned to travel with specific combat units.

10 TED KOPPEL: Any potential opposition as they can. . . .

TERENCE SMITH: ABC Nightline anchor Ted Koppel has been embedded with the U.S. Army Third Infantry Division. Some of the reporters embedded with troops have not been able to report for days because of the military's concerns about compromising operational security.

CORRESPONDENT: We can't get too specific on locations.

DEFENSE SECRETARY DONALD RUMSFELD: I think we're probably watching something that is somewhat historic.

TERENCE SMITH: Defense Sec. Donald Rumsfeld acknowledged the importance of the embedding process, but cautioned that the close-up view is not always complete.

15 DONALD RUMSFELD: And what we are seeing is not the war in Iraq; what we're seeing are slices of the war in Iraq.

We're seeing that particularized perspective that that reporter or that commentator or that television camera happens to be able to see at that moment, and it is not what's taking place. What you see is taking place, to be sure, but it is one slice, and it is the totality of that that is what this war is about.

Some Pitfalls of Embedded and High-tech Coverage

20 TERENCE SMITH: Syracuse University Professor Robert Thompson sees some potential pitfalls in the embedding process.

ROBERT THOMPSON: The danger to the embedding process is that when you are part of the troops that you're going in with, these are your fellow human beings. You are being potentially shot at together, and I think there is a sense that you become part of that group in a way that a journalist doesn't necessarily want to be.

TERENCE SMITH: Prof. Thompson argues that there are advantages and disadvantages to high-tech coverage.

ROBERT THOMPSON: The tyranny of the visual, those nights where all that bombing was going on, was so spectacular, was so interesting to see that it essentially blows everything else out of your brain.

Whatever analysis, whatever background, whatever context in history might be being reported tends to be overwhelmed by the fact that you so focus on these images, the likes of which we've never seen before.

TERENCE SMITH: As long as the media connection remains intact and the lights stay on in Baghdad, officials from both sides can engage in verbal combat. The Iraqi information minister made his case directly to the American viewing audience.

IRAQI INFORMATION MINISTER MOHAMMED SAEED AL-SHAHHAF: We have destroyed two of their helicopters. We have announced that yesterday. They said no. One of them has crashed. And the American warplanes have destroyed it in order not to be in the hands of the Iraqis. Well, this is silly. This is silly.

20 TERENCE SMITH: American and Arab networks have been sharing resources as well. When the shock and awe bombing began Friday, U.S. networks broadcast a live feed from Abu Dhabi Television or al-Jazeera Television, the pan-Arab satellite channel.

But as the war continues, strains are developing that may ultimately reduce coverage.

CNN PRODUCER INGRID FORMANEK: It just got very much more difficult to work in the days during the bombing. We were not allowed to use our satellite phones.

TERENCE SMITH: After months of reporting from Baghdad CNN's correspondent Nick Robertson and his crew were expelled this weekend by Iraqi authorities.

Reflect & Write

- ❏ Analyze the vivid language and word choice of Terence Smith as he describes the current coverage provided by photojournalists. How do the words in this sentence create a striking image for the reader?: "On some networks, virtual view technology makes the battlefield look like a deadly version of a video game, and point of view or 'tank cam' video gives viewers a sense of being aboard those armored units that rumble northward into Iraq." What might be the purpose in using such visual language to set forth the scene for his listeners on this show? How does attention to his style help you as a writer decide which words might best mirror the content of your own argument?
- ❏ What is Smith's point about how technological advances have transformed the kinds of war coverage possible? Analyze more closely the argument he makes by isolating vivid passages.
- ❏ Defense Secretary Rumsfeld claims that "what we are seeing is not the war in Iraq; what we're seeing are slices of the war in Iraq." Why is this lack of what he calls "totality" a problem? Is such a totalitarian perspective ever truly possible even with the best technology?
- ❏ **Write:** What does Professor Thompson mean by "the tyranny of the visual"? Write a counterargument to his position in which you argue that high-tech coverage offers better visual access to the war than, say, embedded journalism.

COLLABORATIVE CHALLENGE

Building off the model of Terence Smith's "War, Live," roundtable on embedded journalism, collaboratively write a new interview, using research your group conducts on another historical period of war coverage. Your group might choose to research through Newseum's History of War Journalism accessible from the link below. Place your research sources as conversationalists in the interview, then enact the interview in a short skit in front of the class. Follow the example of the "Dialogue of Sources" from Chapter 5 to launch your group writing process.
www.ablongman.com/envision/242

Photographer David Leeson is well-known for his impressive fieldwork and powerful photography. A staff photographer for the Dallas Morning News *since 1984, Leeson has covered a variety of stories across the globe: from homelessness in Texas, to death row inmates across the U.S., the apartheid in South Africa, Colombia's drug wars, and the civil war in the Sudan. While on assignment in 2003, he was embedded with the Third Infantry Division in Iraq, a unit that saw a record 23 days of sustained army conflict. Leeson, along with his colleague Cheryl Diaz Meyers, was awarded a Pulitzer Prize for his work in Iraq. This interview with Leeson appeared in the* Digital Journalist *in March 2005.*

David Leeson Has Seen Hell

Dirck Halstead

David Leeson was sitting in front of his computer at his home in Dallas on a balmy spring day last year, browsing the Internet. Clicking onto *The Digital Journalist,* a Web site he had contributed to in the past, he began watching a video interview with David Douglas Duncan, in which the legendary photographer describes shooting the funeral of a Marine five decades earlier. Suddenly, Leeson started to sob. His wife happened to be watching through the window, and she ran to his side.

Different people have different names for what happened to Leeson that day: an emotional breakdown, or that all-encompassing term "exhaustion." It might also be called PTSD, or post-traumatic stress disorder, brought on by Leeson's coverage of the invasion of Iraq in 2003 for his newspaper, the *Dallas Morning News.* Embedded with the Third Infantry Division, Third Brigade Combat Team as it fought its way across the desert to Baghdad, Leeson made shattering images of American men and women in the heat of battle. The work earned him a Pulitzer Prize in 2004.

The accolades came with a price, though. According to a study by the *New England Journal of Medicine,* more than 16 percent of U.S. soldiers and Marines who served in Iraq are victims of PTSD. No one has done similar studies

Seeing Connections
For advice on composing your own interview questions and conducting interviews as part of your research project, see Chapter 5.

of the journalists who have covered the war. Recently, Leeson decided to talk about his experiences with *American Photo* contributing editor Dirck Halstead, who is also the editor of *The Digital Journalist.* Leeson hopes his story might help other photographers come to grips with their own memories. Moreover, his extraordinary account paints a vivid portrait of the life of a war photographer grown sick of the sight of war.

Tell us about your experience covering conflicts.

Well, when I started out covering conflicts I was as green as they come. I was maybe 25, 26 years old. My first conflict was Nicaragua in the 1980s. I was covering the FDN Contras—the Freedom Fighters, as President Reagan called them at the time—who were fighting a war against the communist Sandinista government. These guys were based in Honduras and would make regular forays into Nicaragua to conduct raids, then come back. So I went to Honduras and I sat around for three weeks waiting on an opportunity to get with the Contras and take off to Nicaragua. I met Jim Nachtwey at that time. I just knocked on his door. I said, "Hi, I'm David Leeson with the *Times Picayune States Item* in New Orleans. You're Jim Nachtwey, and we're here to do the same story." And it was so funny, because Jim's response was, "What story?" You see, it was a very secret type of thing that you were going to go in with the Contras—I mean, nobody spoke a word about it. And I said, "Well, the Contras." And he said, "C'mon in." And that's how we got to know one another. He was just starting his career, and I was just starting mine.

5 *How did you feel about what you were doing?*

I was intensely nervous about it. I had an attitude at that time that said that you have to be prepared to die. Over the years that changed. My attitude today is, "No, I'm prepared to come back home alive." I was so immature when I first started out that every time I went through the emotional and mental exercises of saying, "You will not come back home—you will die." And I thought, "That's what the assignment takes: You have to be okay with that. If you're not, then why are you getting on the plane?" But it's interesting, because I also took so much survival gear with me. I had learned a lot from John Hoagland, who was an early mentor of mine. And, of course, John died in 1986 in Suchitoto, El Salvador, caught in the cross fire during a fight between the leftist FMLN rebels and the Salvadoran army. But at any rate, I went really prepared. Early on, I was hiking on a mountain with all this gear, and I came back and dumped half of it. By the time I ended up with the Contras, I had almost nothing with me.

What were your goals back then?

I was just simply doing a job. I was known as the kind of photographer who would do anything. And maybe that's true. As far as why I wanted to do it, that's a lifelong question. I don't know why. I still don't know why. I want to say, "Well, because there's a story to be told and somebody needs to tell it. And it's an important story. And you have the opportunity to change lives." I think probably at the height of my career covering conflicts, I truly believed, deeply and passionately believed, that there existed a series of photographs, or a single photograph, that could end war. I wanted to find that one photo. I thought, "If that one photo could stop war, what is that photo worth? It's worth my life. It's worth anyone's life." Even today I ask people—I'm sure some people would shoot me for this—but I still ask them, "If you could find that photo, is that worth your life?" I still really believe there's a photo that's worth dying for. But can you find it? I never did. And that was probably the hardest part of it all, that I never found it.

After Nicaragua, then what?

After Nicaragua, I covered elections in El Salvador a couple of times. The first time I went there with the full intent that I would likely die. I think that's really immature and ridiculous today. I hate that I was like that at one time, but I was. I can't explain to you what it feels like when you leave your home and you say to yourself, "I will not return. If I do my job right, I will not return." But you think in terms of the search for that one image that can stop all this madness, stop this evil. And if it's worthy of your life, then it's not as crazy as it sounds, is it? I mean, would you sacrifice your life to save a busload of students careening over a bridge if there's one tiny act you could do? Would you do it for ten lives? How about five? Would you do it for one? That was my attitude. And so it may sound outrageous and crazy, but in some sense, not really. It's belief. It's desire. It's ambition. It's wanting to find that one thing that could stop all of it, to say, "No more." Maybe that's prideful to think that I could believe that I could be the one to find it. But if not me, who? Why not me?

How did that attitude affect your work?

I really gave the job my all, took risks. And because of that I had a lot of problems. I ended up held captive by the FMLN rebels in 1984 in Comalapa, El Salvador. It's right at the border near Honduras. My parents had to be notified that I was missing. My father and my mother were visiting my grandmother at the time in Gatesville, Texas, near Waco—about three hours from where I now live in Dallas. My father drove home as soon as he heard about me, and along the way somewhere a state trooper stopped him, because they had found me. I had returned safe. And these are the things that chill me, the knowledge that my father got out of the car, and my mother wondered why they were being pulled over. And she looked in the rearview mirror, and she saw my father drop to his knees because his son was safe. You know, I have to live with that for the rest of my life. When I go someplace where there's a risk—well, there's a risk for my loved ones as well.

When you were captured, did you think you'd survive?

I truly believed that I would die. They put us in front of a firing line—me and a photographer who was working for the *Washington Times* at the time, Dana Smith. Dana and I were together at that time. So, why do you do this? I don't know why anybody does it. I don't think anybody does it for money. I hope not.

10 *How many conflicts have you covered now?*

Ten or 11. It depends on whether you're talking about real wars or not. You know, once I covered the Sendero Luminosa, the Shining Path rebels in Peru, and they held me too. There wasn't a declared war there, but that was probably the most dangerous thing I ever did in my life.

Can you describe the kinds of risks and decisions you have to make as a photographer covering war?

Recently I said to someone, "If I told you that this space between you and I, 20 yards, was filled with land mines, and you really believed it, would you cross it?" And that's what news photographers face. Is it really mined? Are there really snipers there? Are you going to meet an RPG round? Once, in El Salvador, I was headed to the town of Tenancingo, and the Salvadoran army stopped me and said, "Don't go down that road, it's mined." I did it anyway. It took me two-and-a-half hours to travel 17 kilometers because I stopped at every nook and cranny investigating every tiny deformity in the road, any possible glint of anything unusual. Anyway, I didn't die, but others did in other places, like my colleague Richard Cross.

You were married previously, right?

Right.

How did your work affect your relationship?

Well, for years I denied that any of this made any difference. I mean, I knew it made a difference to me personally—you're seeing atrocities, things no man should really see—but I didn't think it would make a difference in my life as a whole. Because, you know, I'm a strong guy and I'm tough and I can take it. I mean, that's part of the whole survival aspect, isn't it? You can go through difficult circumstances in life and pull through a winner. It wasn't until a divorce came after 19 years of marriage that I stopped to reflect upon those things. It's funny, but at one point I couldn't even talk about my past and my job without stuttering. When I spoke I would be, t-t-t-like that. It was hard as hell to talk about stuff. You know, c'mon. All photojournalists know that going is the easy part. Coming home is the hard part. Come home and suddenly you're, like, the dad again, the husband again. You've got bills to pay, a yard to mow, a wife to love, a boss to make happy. There's no decompression time. There's no chance to sit back and say, "What just happened to me?" I did the best I could. I wanted to just open that closet door up and just shove the memories of what I'd seen in it and lock it as quick as I could. The best thing to do was just simply not talk about it. I don't want to talk about it. And a lot of people around me didn't want to hear about it, either. I mean, c'mon, think about it. You're at a party or you're with friends or you're having a nice dinner or you're socializing, and suddenly something reminds you of some horrible event that just occurred to you maybe a month before. Who wants to hear about it? Once, I came back from El Salvador, and a week later I was assigned to cover an Easter egg hunt in Plano, Texas. I was at the Easter egg hunt and I looked down at my watch and I realized it was 3 p.m. Well, that was the same time that a week earlier I had been photographing dead FMLN rebels, young boys. One of them couldn't have been more than 10 years old. I mean, he was shot to hell. And here I was a week later watching children at another event. I turned to a lady next to me and I said, "Wow, last week at this same time I was looking at dead rebels in El Salvador, just children." The woman took about 10 steps away from me. I mean, nobody wants to hear about that stuff in the middle of an Easter egg hunt.

When military people come back from war, unless they leave the service immediately, they are still surrounded by their colleagues, by the people who can understand what they've gone through. They can talk and they can get it out. Journalists, on the other hand, come back, and there is no way you can go to a party and start to talk about this stuff.

That's the reality of what it is to do this kind of work, especially if you work for a daily newspaper. You go and you shoot these things. And you come back and you have obligations. And you have to get back to what your life was as best you can. And that's not that easy. So, I ended up divorced after 19 years of marriage. I can't blame it all on my job. I made a lot of mistakes, a lot of bad choices. But I began to really think about what had happened to me. Because the man I had become wasn't the man that I was when I got married. I didn't have these thoughts. I didn't have these feelings. I didn't have this struggle. That's what happened. It's stupid. A kindergartner could have told me I was heading for trouble—seeing a man crushed underneath a tank is enough to change your life. Seeing starving children is enough to change your life. Seeing dead 10-year-olds in a cemetery in El Salvador is enough to change your life. But I never thought about it as doing that. And I think that cost me. What I should have done when I got home—I should have just spent a week crying.

Jump forward to 2003. What was it like when you went to Iraq for that war?

I felt more prepared than ever when I went to Iraq in 2003 to come home. I felt bad for the photographers with the embed program because so many were new, brand new to this experience. They didn't know what to expect. I knew what it would feel like, but maybe that increased awareness also made it worse in some ways for me. Because I paid attention to it for the first time, I noticed it. When I came back from Iraq, when I got off the plane in Dallas and stood on the curb waiting for my wife to pick me up, I just wanted to run. I just wanted to go back to Iraq. I mean, I wanted to see my wife, and I wanted to get back to normal, but what the hell is normal anymore? I was freaking, just standing there like that. Everything was just too much. I was really nervous—about coming home, about having to get back to my life.

15 *How do you look back on that period—the war—now?*

You know, I didn't even want to go to Iraq in the first place. I'm glad I did, and not because of a Pulitzer Prize. That's a great honor, sure, but I'm glad I went because of the people I met and the friendships I made and the experiences I had. I felt enriched by my experiences but terrified at the thought that I was going to have to come back. And not that coming back was a bad idea. I love my home. I didn't want to leave my home. I was a happy person. Prior to leaving for Iraq, I had been working for three years to get my life back in order. The last foreign assignment I'd had was covering the conflict in southern Sudan. It was typically as horrific as any other I'd been to. I just didn't want to go anywhere anymore. I wanted to be done with it. I had a new life, a new bride, and I didn't want to sacrifice another marriage. I didn't want to lose myself again, breaking down in the middle of the night. I just wanted to be like a regular guy. Like I am. Then after 9/11 the newspaper asked me to go to Afghanistan, and I was prepared to go, like every other time. I had my visa ready. And at the last minute, I just told them, I said, "I just can't do it. I just don't want to do it." So they sent someone else. And then I worried about the guys from my paper who did go. What if they die? Then it would be because of me in some way because I didn't go. I mean, I have the experience. I have the skills. I know what to expect. But I just couldn't do it, so I backed out. And then in 2003, they're giving me the phone call saying, "We'd like for you to go to Iraq." I did something unusual, for me. I actually asked to have time to speak with people and to think about it. So I said, "Give me a week." I called my parents. I called my sister, brother-in-law. Of course, I spoke with my wife, spoke with my children. I spoke with close friends and told them what was facing me. And to my surprise everyone said I should go. They had seen a young photographer grow through the years, and they knew that I had the skills to do it. They knew if anybody could go out there and tell this story, I could do it. And I knew it too, deep down. I knew that this could well be my story, because I've worked so hard to get to that place. Here it is: your chance to use all that experience, all those tough knocks you've had over the years, all those close calls, and put them to practice. It's funny, because I once heard Jay Dickman of the *Dallas Times Herald,* who won a Pulitzer for his work in El Salvador, I once heard him say that. He said that when he was doing that assignment, every single skill and experience he'd had came to play in that one story. And I would say the same is true for Iraq for me. I'd always sought for the perfect story—perfect, meaning that I didn't make a mistake, I didn't miss stuff. Although I did in Iraq, I missed something pretty big. But I got enough.

What did you miss?

I missed the death of a soldier, a U.S. soldier, during a firefight. We were in a firefight all day long on April 6, 2003. It was the most intense battle I'd ever seen in my life. I'd never seen so many things exploding and so much ammo and firepower being dished out on both sides. There were a lot of close calls. Seven soldiers were injured that day. Two of them died. It hurts because you identify with these men when you're embedded—you're experiencing the same things they are, taking as much heat as they are. I stood up at times I didn't need to stand up because I believed that I should. I mean, if they're taking fire, I should take it too. I'm here with you. My life isn't worth more— I can't sit down behind armor and hide. I mean, a 19-year-old kid dies, how do you deal with that? I'd almost rather say, "Take me, God. I'm 46. I've lived already. I've had great experiences." But a 19-year-old kid who doesn't make it home—it was really hard. I met his parents. I asked the Army if I could visit with them. I didn't know what the hell to say. The parents showed up whenever all the other soldiers were coming home, but their son wasn't coming home.

Let's talk a little bit about the regimental colors that you were awarded by the unit that you were with.

That's the greatest honor I ever received in my life. A Pulitzer Prize pales in comparison. I enjoyed getting the Pulitzer: It was my fourth time to be a finalist; I had pretty much given up on winning one. But nothing compares to the regimental colors. It was out of the blue. It was the first time in the regiment's history that a civilian received the colors—they are normally given just to commanding officers when they leave their command. As I look back and think about this honor, it symbolizes my role in Iraq. I had a role that was a greater role than being a photojournalist. It was just being a human being, being a citizen of this country. It was about caring about people. It's sort of what we do all the time. I hope we do.

Can you talk about your experience watching the interview with David Douglas Duncan on The Digital Journalist?

Well, my experiences over the years have affected me in some profound ways. I've come to realize that. And I think that's a good thing to know that, yeah, these things do affect you. But it's not as though I'm a wreck. I do have coping mechanisms. My faith in God helps me a lot. Also I simply avoid discussions about those experiences, and I avoid watching other people talk about their experiences in war. But I watched this interview with David Douglas Duncan, whom I deeply admire. And I was struck by the knowledge that those experiences are shared over the generations, that the pain is the same. It hurts as much. And I was watching it all by myself, because I have times where the memories are just too much. Well, this time I was watching and it was too much. But I didn't know my wife was watching. She came in and asked me about it. And what's disgusting is that I felt bad about that. Like I'm not supposed to show this vulnerability.

What is your advice to people who want to follow this path?

My best advice is to develop a strong sense of mission. I talked about how early on in my career I wanted to find that one image or series of images that could stop war. That is a sense of mission. If you have a strong sense of mission about who you are and what you're doing, almost nothing can stand in your path. And again, it's not popular—I could be crucified for saying it—but there are images worth dying for. That doesn't mean you should go foolishly into conflict. You should do everything you can to get home alive, safe and sound, and tell the story. You have to find that fine line between foolishness and courage.

20 *You can't screw around. . . .*

I tell young photographers to get in, get out. Know your story. Move in. Get it done. Don't dillydally around. Don't mess around. Don't ever hang out in those bad places. And never let a crowd form around you. I did that years ago. I made a lot of mistakes. And I nearly paid the ultimate price for it. In South Africa in 1985, I was shooting pictures of a riot, probably about 100 or 150 protesters coming towards me with knives and tires that they would soak in gasoline and put around the neck of victims and burn them to death. I got out and stood on top of my rental car with a lot of bravado, because I was just so confident of who I was. But I didn't pay enough attention. And I had no one watching my back, no writer, no other photographer, and I didn't see this other gang coming from behind. They grabbed me by the ankles and pulled me down. I smashed into the hood of the car. They started choking me and trying to take my cameras. I managed to get out of it. But barely. If I didn't I was going to die.

The risk can come at any time in that kind of situation.

The camera does act as a shield. When you put it in front of your face, it's not going to stop a bullet. But it does act as an emotional shield. During one of those riots I actually dropped my camera down to my waist so I could just stand there and experience that moment. And I thought, "This isn't real. This isn't real. What the hell am I doing here?" But, you know, I put the camera back up to my face and I had a sense of purpose again. In Iraq, one of my most terrifying moments had little to do with the fact that I came so close to getting killed. It had everything to do with the loss of mission. There was a mortar attack that hit within the kill zone, within 30 kilometers. I dove on the first round that hit. I dove into the back of an armored vehicle. I narrowly escaped a second round that just ripped the ground up behind me. I just barely made it. You know what was terrifying, though? As a photojournalist, we all—well, I shouldn't say we all—a lot of us have these nightmares that something big is occurring and we can't find our cameras. I was lying there with my hands over my head, because I didn't have my helmet either, and I was saying, "Oh, God, I hope it stops." And I started hearing the yells for help. And I started hearing people say, "Is everyone okay?" And there's dust everywhere. There's confusion. I grabbed for my camera and it wasn't there. I was horrified. I started screaming profanities. Later, I thought about that. I thought, "Why did that bother me more than the fact that I nearly got killed?" Because there's only one reason why I was in a place like that, and that was to take a photograph, to record this moment in history. The camera didn't leave my side after that.

Reflect & Write

❏ Analyze the interview for its rhetorical strategies. What might be the purpose in beginning with a vivid narrative? How do the questions work? Where does the interviewer turn from pathos to logos and why? Are there surprising jumps in the arrangement of questions?

❏ The interviewer claims that "his extraordinary account paints a vivid portrait of the life of a war photographer grown sick of the sight of war." Find passages that strike you as particularly vivid. What makes these passages so compelling? How might detail work as a tool of argument?

❏ When Leeson explains that he thought, "I truly believed, deeply and passionately believed, that there existed a series of photographs, or a single photograph, that could end war," he also explains that he was willing to pay the price of a life. What ethical questions does this point of view raise? What is the value of one life compared to that of many? What is the value of one life killed in war versus one life sacrificed for an image that could change the world? Do images have such power, do you think?

❏ What do you make of Leeson's statement that "some people would shoot me for" having this belief? What are the ethics of using such language in the midst of this serious issue?

❏ Leeson uses rich and vivid language, such as in his question concerning the ethics of whether one would "save a busload of students careening over a bridge"— what is the effect of such visual scenarios on you as a reader? How does this language help construct his persona as a writer? What do these examples tell us about his own life experiences?

❏ How does Leeson bring to light the ethical dilemma of the embedded journalist when he writes, "I stood up at times I didn't need to stand up because I believed that I should. I mean, if they're taking fire, I should take it too." What issues are at stake in this argument?

❏ What does Leeson mean that coming home is the hardest part? Write a short narrative explaining this perspective by creating an account of a returning photographer or soldier.

❏ **Write:** "There are images worth dying for," Leeson states. Compose two responses to this argument.

■ *The text on these pages represent photographer David Leeson's own descriptive captions for the four photos shown here.*

FIGURE 14.9 David Leeson's photo of a dead man's shoes from Iraq is titled "Body and Sole."

Visual and Verbal Reading

Photographs and Stories, David Leeson

Body and Sole, Iraq.

The shoes on the body of an Iraqi soldier killed as Army troops advanced north to Baghdad tell a story about a poorly equipped army. Almost all of the Iraqi dead—more than eight in this location—were wearing worn-out civilian-style shoes. Young soldiers came to view the bodies. A sergeant reminded them that 'this could be one of us' and that, for these war dead, 'their families will never know . . . they will just never come back home.'

Blank Stare

There was a tremendous firefight. Three soldiers died. I saw the blank stare of this wounded soldier as he passed by. I have no idea who he is. I never noticed his bandage until he filled the frame with my 200mm lens. It was his eyes I saw that day and remember.

Search Party

3rd Infantry Division soldiers from Fort Benning, Georgia, disembark from a Bradley Fighting Vehicle to surround a man who was stopped for suspicious activity somewhere in Iraq. An AK-47 automatic rifle and ammunition were found in the man's vehicle in which he traveled with another person.

FIGURE 14.10 In this photograph by Leeson, a soldier stares blankly out from a tank in Iraq.

This was my first "action" photo from Iraq. My video camera was still operational and I had to make a quick decision on which camera to grab first—my still camera or the video camera. I had made a commitment to place still photos above video in every reasonable circumstance so I made the photos as quickly as possible. As soon as I was satisfied that the still image was secured I switched to video and made very similar frames. The video from this scene became part of my documentary about the invasion.

The next day I learned that this image appeared on the front page of 43 newspapers nationwide and a video I had made the day before was aired on World News Tonight. My video camera succumbed to the dust not long after I made these final frames.

FIGURE 14.11 Leeson's photo of an American military unit arresting an Iraqi civilian appeared on the front page of 43 newspapers Leeson titled the photo "Search Party."

FIGURE 14.12 In "Taking the Plunge," Leeson captures a moment when soldiers relax through a swim in an irrigation pond in Iraq.

Taking the Plunge

(L to R) Spc. George Gillette and Spc. Robert Boucher with Task Force 2-69 Armor, 3rd Brigade Combat Team, 3rd Infantry Division from Fort Benning, Georgia, jump into an irrigation pond somewhere in Iraq. I had a goal to shoot at least one good photo each day—if possible. This image, part of the Pulitzer portfolio, was made near sunset on the drive to Baghdad. I had not made a single image all day. I was about to give up the idea that I would see anything worth shooting when I heard that soldiers were headed to some "pond" in the desert. The truth is I was very tired and was almost disappointed that I was going to have to grab my camera and follow. But, duty called and I went. Both of these soldiers stood on the side of the irrigation pond and discussed if they would get in trouble if they jumped.

I kept my mouth shut and watched. I knew if they jumped it would make a great photo but also knew that journalistic integrity meant that I could not enter into their decision-making process on whether to jump or not. Of course, they finally decided it was worth the risk and made the plunge. After making the photo—I jumped too. The water was very cold but after weeks without a bath it was a wonderful respite from the reality of war.

Reflect & Write

❏ How does each visual text—as a photographic reading—offer a specific perspective on the battle in Iraq and on war more generally? What specific rhetorical elements shape the composition of the text? Use the checklist at the end of Chapter 3 to help you answer this question.

❏ Looking closely at the first photo, "Body and Sole." How might you analyze the various visual elements, including what kind of shoe you see. How do visual signs such as shoes provide readers with *context* about persona, nationality, economic status, and history? (Look back to Chapter 3 if you are unfamiliar with any of these terms.) What kind of argument would a different set of shoes make on this Iraqi—expensive combat boots, religious slippers, or bare feet? How do the words of the photo's title shape your interpretation of the argument made by the photo?

❏ In the text for "Blank Stare," Leeson asserts that he "never noticed his bandage until he [the soldier] filled the frame with my 200mm lens." How might the camera enable the photographer to see more details in times of war? How is the camera as a tool of photojournalism a vehicle for helping us see?

❏ Analyze the images from the perspective of a soldier. What is the argument about the reality of war from this angle of vision? What kind of writing would a soldier produce to explain what these photos mean? Write out that perspective in words.

❏ Consider how David Leeson's stories operate in conjunction with the images to produce a particular perspective on the war. How do his comments reshape your interpretation of the images? How do the images suggest different meanings without out his stories about the images?

❏ **Write:** Compose your own response to David Leeson's narrative account of these images. You might even locate some images from war and create a photo essay.

■ *Best known for his work on the PBS series,* The NewsHour with Jim Lehrer, **Jim Lehrer** *has dedicated his life to the news, starting as a newspaperman in Dallas then eventually becoming an anchor on a local news show before moving into the national spotlight. CNN's Bernard Shaw has called him the "Dean of Moderators" because of his integral role in moderating more then ten debates by candidates in the last five presidential elections. Lehrer has won many awards for his work, including the 1999 presidential National Humanities Medal. The selection included here is from* The NewsHour Extra, *a special Website created to help students understand important cultural and political issues.*

Pros and Cons of Embedded Journalism

NewsHour Extra with Jim Lehrer

A partnership between the military and the media has changed the nature of war journalism.

Journalists are experiencing unprecedented access to the battlefield thanks to a partnership between the military and the media that has embedded journalists within specific military units. The embedded reporters have to follow several agreed upon rules as they live with the soldiers and report on their actions.

New rules in a new arrangement

The new arrangement was formed out of meetings between the heads of news organizations and the Defense Department officials aimed at allowing journalists to report on war with the least possible danger.

Before joining their battalions, the embedded journalists had to sign a contract restricting when and what they can report. The details of military actions can only be described in general terms and journalists agreed not to write at all about possible future missions or about classified weapons and information they might find.

5   In addition, the commander of an embedded journalist's unit can declare a "blackout," meaning the reporter is prohibited from filing stories via satellite connection. The blackouts are called for security reasons, as a satellite communication could tip off a unit's location to enemy forces, the Pentagon explains.

Seeing a slice of the war

At the beginning of the experiment, U.S. Secretary of Defense Donald Rumsfeld called the embedding of journalists "historic," but cautioned that the close-up view is not always complete.

"What we are seeing is not the war in Iraq; what we're seeing are slices of the war in Iraq," he said.

"We're seeing that particularized perspective that that reporter or that commentator or that television camera happens to be able to see at that moment, and it is not what's taking place. What you see is taking place, to be sure, but it is one slice, and it is the totality of that that is what this war is about."

Thus far, editors of many large papers are pleased with the quality of journalism coming from embedded journalists, according to *Editor and Publisher* magazine. Susan Stevenson of *The Atlanta Journal-Constitution* said the embedded reporters give a "sense of immediacy and humanity" that make the stories very real. "From what a blinding sandstorm feels like to reporting how one of our embeds broke his unit's coffee pot, we're giving readers a better sense of the field."

How embedding can distort

10 However there have been instances when the embedded reporters transmitted inaccurate information. On Wednesday, embedded correspondents for several news organizations reported seeing a convoy of up to 120 Iraqi tanks leaving the southern city of Basra, and most news outlets reported a large troop movement.

The next day, a spokesman for the British military said the "massive movement" was really just 14 tanks.

Additionally, some journalism professors have warned that the embedding process can distort war coverage. Syracuse University Professor Robert Thompson warns, "When you are part of the troops that you're going in with, these are your fellow human beings. You are being potentially shot at together, and I think there is a sense that you become part of that group in a way that a journalist doesn't necessarily want to be."

Final results unknown

The results of the embedding experiment will not be known for some time. Bob Steele, from the Poynter Institute, an organization for journalists, says the access "has allowed reporters and photographers to get closer to understanding (the complexities of war), to tell the stories of fear and competence, to tell the stories of skill and confusion. I think that's healthy."

But, Steele cautioned that while "closeness can breed understanding," journalists must remain objective and not write about "we" or "our," but about "they."

15 "There's nothing wrong with having respect in our hearts for the men and women who are fighting this war, or respect for the men and women who are marching in the anti-war protests. The key is to make sure those beliefs don't color reporting," Steele said.

Reflect & Write

❏ How do the "new rules" set the contested parameters for a new form of photojournalism in war? That is, while this article might seem straightforward and informative, how does it actually offer a particular argument—the official version—on the proper form of photography for America's military engagements today?

❏ Looking closely at how the article uses both subheads and quotations, assess the writing in terms of both arrangement, or structure, and research depth. Use your reading of Chapter 3 and Chapter 5 to help you assess the writing of this piece.

Why do you think the author made these particular rhetorical choices? What is the effect of these choices on you as a reader?

❏ For the closing line of this article, the author relies upon a quotation by Bob Steele from the Poynter Institute, in which the ideal of objectivity is advanced: "The key is to make sure those beliefs don't color reporting." How does the quotation use visual discourse? What visual choices might a reporter make in presenting "colored" reporting? What does this mean? And how does the last subtitle destabilize the finality of that closing quotation?

❏ **Write:** Draft your own response to the article. First, identify the central arguments made by each authority, and then compose two alternative perspectives on each argument. You might consult Chapter 3, on the Multiple Sides Project, as you write your responses. Include images that offer arguments for each of your own written texts, so that the visual and the verbal work in conjunction to convey your point of view for each response.

COLLABORATIVE CHALLENGE

Together with two or three classmates, compose a blog post in which you respond to several of the articles here; you might post your own code of conduct for photojournalists in the new century, or draft a set of guidelines for cell phone camera users. Include the photos that moved you most from this chapter and write new captions to show your understanding of the complex issues at stake in covering conflict.

PERSPECTIVES ON THE ISSUE

1. The articles in this chapter offer various contemporary perspectives on the question of whether or not—and how—to publish disturbing photographs of people who are dying, dead, or suffering. How do these debates differ from the controversy discussed by Nora Ephon in her article, "The Boston Photographs," reproduced in Chapter 3? What has changed since the 1970s? What remains constant despite decades of social change, an increasingly global media coverage, and seemingly greater sensitivity to suffering and death?

2. Mark Glaser raises crucial questions about privacy and human nature as he reflects on the many photos taken with camera phones in the wake of the 2005 London bombings. How is the question of privacy a key issue in each of the articles in this chapter, even if the writers don't mention it overtly? Pick three articles to discuss in formulating your answer. Draft your own position on privacy in an age of technological innovation.

3. The conflicts covered range from domestic tragedies—such as the New Orleans hurricane disaster and the Oklahoma City bombing—to international crises—such as the 2004 tsunami and the London bombings. How do media sources show a contextual bias depending on the given audience, the location of the writer, and the purpose of the article? What issues of cross-cultural rhetoric emerge from cross-cultural coverage of these events in both words and images?

4. Discussing "Search Party," Leeson explores the different kinds of photographs possible with different technological tools—the still camera and the video. How do still photos versus videos capture different aspects of an experience such as that in "Search Party"? In other words, are we shown only part of the story? How might more photos, or a video, shape a reader's opinion differently?

5. Compare Leeson's description of his own actions photographing the soldier's "blank stare" to photographer Stanley Forman's account of capturing a young woman falling off a fire escape as recounted in Nora Ephron's article (see Chapter 3). What is the relationship between the photographer as visual writer of moments in crisis and the visual text as one of many possible snapshots? How do the words of the photographers shape our own understanding of these texts as persuasive images and representations of reality?

FROM READING TO RESEARCH

1. Read Professor Paul Lester's book, *Photojournalism: An Ethical Approach,* from the library or online at http://commfaculty.fullerton.edu/lester/writings/pjethics.html and famous critic Susan Sontag's article, "Regarding the Torture of Others" at http://www.southerncrossreview.org/35/sontag.htm. What arguments are shared between the writers? How might each one contribute to your understanding of the issues involved in photo ethics, both nationally and internationally? Using these sources as a starting point, compose a research-based argument in which you provide your own perspective on these questions. You might format your argument as a feature article modeled after Daniel Okrent's piece. Refer to Chapter 1 for strategies on developing a thesis, and to Chapter 3 for a lesson on synthesizing sources.

2. Locate photos from the Abu Ghraib torture and prisoner abuse scandal and conduct research into international human rights treaties in order to determine if the photos can be used as evidence grave abuses. Read the coverage of the scandal—and the subsequent military trials—in order to shape your own research argument about photo ethics in times of war or military morals in an age of digital photography. For historical context, go to the *Envision* Website and read Dan Kennedy's article, "Witness to an Execution" (the *Boston Phoenix,* 13-20 June, 2002; http://www.bostonphoenix.com/boston/news_features/dont_quote_me/multi-page/documents/02309509.htm). In this provocative article, Kennedy tackles the complex issue of photojournalistic ethics, looking at cases from World War II to recent years.

3. Based on your reading of the articles in this chapter, how might you argue that the mode of photojournalism has changed over the years through developments in writing and communication technologies? Specifically, how do new technologies of writing and visual communication—such as blogs, video footage, multimedia reports, photo essays, and email—transform our understanding of the issues involved in combat reporting? How do independent photographers attempt to offer an alternative perspective on war by relying on new writing technologies such as blogs and digital photo essays? Conduct research on this topic and compose a photo essay to post online.

CHAPTER 15

Globalization

Today, as countries across the globe become more closely connected by economic trade and technology, so too do cultures become more intertwined. There is now a Starbucks inside the once inaccessible Forbidden City of Beijing, China; there are McDonald's restaurants all over India selling not burgers but vegetarian items such as the McAloo Tikki Burger; there is a rage for Japanese anime in small town America; and we hear East Asian influences on African-American hip-hop bands such as the Wu-Tang Clan. The term used with reference to the economic practices that spurs such global influence and cultural exchange is "globalization."

While "globalization" as a term has existed since 1944, it was a landmark 1983 essay entitled "Globalization of Markets" by Harvard professor and economist Theodore Levitt that brought the term into popular use. In recent years, the complex nature of globalization has caused a polarization of opinion into two camps: those against globalization who see it as a new form of Western domination and a destructive practice that takes advantage of developing counties, and those who see globalization as bringing progress and financial help to improve living conditions and human life across the world.

FIGURE 15.1 This image of the world as embraced or constricted by international corporate monopolies reveals two different perspectives on Globalization.

One way to understand the debate is to consider the op-ad in Figure 15.1, in which corporate ads encircle the earth. As you look at this image, you might begin to see the two opinions about globalization. On the one hand, you might see these corporate logos as connecting diverse nations and bringing economic prosperity to developing countries. On the other hand, you could see the corporations as literally choking the earth. The image of the United States, visually located under the CNN label, could be seen either as one of leadership and guidance (with CNN informing the world through the news) or instead as the source of so many companies that seek to make profits from developing nations across the globe. Your visual analysis of this image might lead you to see globalization as a positive force, or what Thomas Friedman calls "a new milestone in human progress and a great opportunity for the world." Alternatively, you might begin to side with Naomi Klein's perspective that outsourcing equates with sending American workers to steal good jobs from people in struggling countries.

Throughout the rest of this chapter, we'll study the issues and the debates surrounding globalization as a phenomenon. We'll start with one of the most contentious issues: the increasing prevalence of big corporations, such as McDonald's, that conduct business in countries where such practices might change local customs, cultures, and values—even the very look of a country's national identity. We'll also question how long such corporations can last in a constantly changing world—and we'll consider Mark Rice-Oxley's question whether Disney, Nike, and McDonald's can endure as icons of wealthy Western society.

Next, we'll look at globalization from another angle of vision. Specifically, what happens when East meets West? The second section will explore how Eastern cultural icons—from Hello Kitty to anime, Buddhist religion to India's Bollywood cinema—have in turn shaped Western practices, pastimes, and fashions. As writer and photographer David Wells argues, India in particular is one developing country that now "sees itself as equally important as Russia, China and the U.S., believing it has much to offer the rest of the world." We'll look at how globalization moves in both directions, with all countries influencing each other both economically and culturally.

Finally, we'll tackle some of the more economic and political questions in the globalization debate, and we'll read articles about the growing connectedness of world communities through trade, commerce, technology, and travel. We'll explore perspectives, from Brian Behlendorf's claim that outsourcing can help bring about world peace to Naomi Klein's assertion that "free-trade policies are a highly efficient engine of dispossession." As you delve into the complex issue of globalization presented from many vantage points throughout this chapter, you can begin to shape your own perspective about our changing world.

MCDONALDIZATION

FIGURE 15.2 Protesters revise the word "McDonaldization" into "McDomination," a term that reflects a common perception of the impact of American franchises abroad.

In many ways, McDonald's and the golden arches have become symbols for globalization because they are such visible signs of the export of U.S. culture and business. As the American-based fast-food chain McDonald's has continued to expand into new markets across the globe, it has been met with both voracious criticism and supportive praise. The image in Figure 15.2, for instance, captures a demonstration where the restaurant name has been transformed from "McDonald's" to "McDomination." You can see the famous golden arches, but the word above it—"RESIST"—turns the symbol from a sign for a fast-food store into a sign of what the protesters see as global oppression or "McDomination."

What's at stake, is that McDonald's sells more than food; it creates what blog columnist Paul Feine calls "McCulture" or a way of life that it imports to various countries around the world (http://www.aworldconnected.org/Stories/id.113/story_detail.asp). This is often very good for the nation, Feine argues, in terms of bringing hygiene, nutrition, and entertainment for children, among other benefits. But critics of McDonald's, such as George Ritzer, see McCulture as a threat to human creativity. As we'll learn, Ritzer contends that McDonald's sells a "false image" of world unity through shared food preferences. Ritzer coined the term *McDonaldization* to mean "the process by which the principles of the fast-food restaurant are coming to dominate more and more sectors of American society as well as the rest of the world" (*The McDonaldization of Society* by George Ritzer, p.1).

This, perhaps, is the crux of the debate: when another restaurant opens across the globe with the golden arches on top, do we see McDonald's as the example of an American company exporting Western looks, values, poor eating habits, and economic practices including heavy consumerism and use of natural resources? Or do we see a model of international development that shows respect for local cultures, customs, and practices? We'll address these questions in the pages that follow.

We'll also look at how McDonald's as a corporation works hard to design visual rhetoric for its restaurants, its ad campaigns on billboards, and even its Internet identity.

The McDonald's Website in China, for instance, shown in Figure 15.3, uses the hip image of a young Asian musician who holds his hands up in a rap gesture and is surrounded by pop-up buttons that evoke trends in Chinese youth culture from music to games. As the screen shot of the Website reveals, McDonald's marketing campaigns employ rhetorical strategies effectively to entice the Chinese youth audience with careful attention to color, layout, emotional appeals, shared values, and the nation's own goals.

By contrast, the Website for McDonald's in Sweden, seen in Figure 15.4, represents a different identity for the company. Notice the traditional setting of the library filled with dusty books, the plastic magnetic letters on a black board, and the old-fashioned feel to the Website. Instead of one hip youth in a game-like atmosphere, the Swedish Website suggests tradition, home-schooling, and very young children learning to eat from McDonald's. The visual design of this site suggests a company that has embraced Sweden's traditional values and love of family, using food and education to perpetuate those values.

FIGURE 15.3 Bright colors and a busy layout entice visitors to McDonald's Chinese Website.

FIGURE 15.4 The McDonalds' Website for Sweden portrays traditional values of education and childcare in order to appeal to consumers.

Reflect & Write

❏ Look closely at the Chinese Website and the Swedish Website in Figures 15.3–15.4. Why do you think there is more coverage of people actually eating the food in one versus the other?

❏ How are American cultural values, fashions, and musical trends reproduced in Web design ads such as those shown here?

Student Writing

Dexian Cai, Student essay on McDonald's "I'm Lovin' It" commercials in Singapore: "West Meets East: The Evolution of McDonald's Marketing in East Asia"

www.ablongman.com/envision/243

❏ Based on the pattern of visual arguments you find here, what types of Web marketing would you expect for other countries? What do you make of representing a country in this way and trying to win audiences through this visual rhetoric?

❏ Comparing the images in Figures 15.3–15.4, do you find a standard McDonald's look or do you find variation that attends to cultural differences? How are individual countries represented differently? Go online to the McDonald's homepage, select another country from the pulldown menu, and analyze the visual rhetoric strategies you find there.

❏ **Write:** Draft a letter to McDonald's explaining your response to their international ad campaign. Use specific visual evidence from one or all of the three Websites you've examined above.

COLLABORATIVE CHALLENGE

Together in a group of three or four, surf the McDonald's Website for any country that interests you and discover what argument each specific ad strategy or restaurant design makes about both McDonald's and the home country. Take several screen shots and then, in groups of two or three, compose captions for each of these visual texts; the captions you write should indicate your interpretation of the meaning of the image. Present your visual rhetoric analysis and your collaborative writing to the class.

Mark Rice-Oxley *is a correspondent for the* Christian Science Monitor, *where this article appeared on January 15, 2004. He has written stories on British manners and the "Gross National Happiness Index"; most recently, he performed the role of* David Copperfield *at the West Yorkshire Playhouse.*

In 2,000 Years, Will the World Remember Disney or Plato?

Mark Rice-Oxley

Down in the mall, between the fast-food joint and the bagel shop, a group of young people huddles in a flurry of baggy combat pants, skateboards, and slang. They size up a woman teetering past wearing DKNY, carrying *Time* magazine in one hand and a latte in the other.

She brushes past a guy in a Yankees' baseball cap who is talking on his Motorola cellphone about the Martin Scorsese film he saw last night. It's a standard American scene—only this isn't America, it's Britain. US culture is so pervasive, the scene could be

played out in any one of dozens of cities. Budapest or Berlin, if not Bogota or Bordeaux. Even Manila or Moscow.

As the unrivaled global superpower, America exports its culture on an unprecedented scale. From music to media, film to fast food, language to literature and sport, the American idea is spreading inexorably, not unlike the influence of empires that preceded it. The difference is that today's technology flings culture to every corner of the globe with blinding speed. If it took two millenniums for Plato's "Republic" to reach North America, the latest hit from Justin Timberlake can be found in Greek (and Japanese) stores within days. Sometimes, US ideals get transmitted—such as individual rights, freedom of speech, and respect for women—and local cultures are enriched. At other times, materialism or worse becomes the message and local traditions get crushed. "The US has become the most powerful, significant world force in terms of cultural imperialism [and] expansion," says Ian Ralston, American studies director at Liverpool John Moores University. "The areas that particularly spring to mind are Hollywood, popular music, and even literature." But what some call "McDomination" has created a backlash in certain cultures. And it's not clear whether fast food, Disney, or rock 'n' roll will change the world the way Homer or Shakespeare has.

Cricket or basketball?

Stick a pin in a map and there you'll find an example of US influence. Hollywood rules the global movie market, with up to 90 percent of audiences in some European countries. Even in Africa, 2 of 3 films shown are American. Few countries have yet to be touched by McDonald's and Coca-Cola. Starbucks recently opened up a new front in South America, and everyone's got a Hard Rock Café T-shirt from somewhere exotic. West Indian sports enthusiasts increasingly watch basketball, not cricket. Baseball has long since taken root in Asia and Cuba. And Chinese young people are becoming more captivated by American football and basketball, some even daubing the names of NBA stars on their school sweatsuits. The NFL plans to roll out a Chinese version of its website this month. Rupert Murdoch's satellites, with their heavy traffic of US audiovisual content, saturate the Asian subcontinent. American English is the language of choice for would-be pop stars in Europe, software programmers in India, and Internet surfers everywhere.

America's preeminence is hardly surprising. Superpowers have throughout the ages sought to perpetuate their way of life: from the philosophy and mythology of the ancient Greeks to the law and language of the Romans; from the art and architecture of the Tang Dynasty and Renaissance Italy to the sports and systems of government of the British. "Most empires think their own point of view is the only correct point of view," says Robert Young, an expert in postcolonial cultural theory at Oxford University. "It's the certainty they get because of the power they have, and they expect to impose it on everyone else."

5 Detractors of cultural imperialism argue, however, that cultural domination poses a totalitarian threat to diversity. In the American case, "McDomination" poses several dangers.

First, local industries are truly at risk of extinction because of US oligopolies, such as Hollywood. For instance in 2000, the European Union handed out 1 billion euros to subsidize Europe's film industry. Even the relatively successful British movie industry has no control over distribution, which is almost entirely in the hands of the Hollywood majors.

Second, political cultures are being transformed by the personality-driven American model in countries as far-reaching as Japan and the Philippines.

Finally, US domination of technologies such as the Internet and satellite TV means that, increasingly, America monopolizes the view people get of the world. According to a recent report for the UN Conference on Trade and Development, 13 of the top 14 Internet firms are American. No. 14 is British. "You have to know English if you want to use the Internet," says Andre Kaspi, a professor at the Sorbonne in Paris.

A main problem is that culture is no longer a protected species, but subject to the inexorable drive for free trade, says Joost Smiers, a political science professor at the Utrecht School of the Arts. This means that it is increasingly difficult for countries to protect their own industries. France tries to do so with subsidies, while South Korea has tried quotas. Such "protectionist" tactics meet with considerable US muscle, Dr. Smiers says. "America's aggressive cultural policy . . . hinders national states from regulating their own cultural markets," he says. "We should take culture out of the WTO."

10   Another danger, detractors say, is the consolidation of the communications industry into a few conglomerates such as AOL-TimeWarner, Disney, and News Corporation, which means that the "infotainment" generated for global consumption nearly always comes from an Anglophone perspective. "You can't go on with just three music companies organizing and distributing 85 percent of the music in the world," says Smiers. "It's against all principles of democracy. Every emotion, every feeling, every image can be copyrighted into the hands of a few owners."

American, with a twist

A backlash is being felt in certain places. In Japan, locals have taken US ideas like hip-hop and fast food, and given them a Japanese twist, says Dominic al-Badri, editor of *Kansai Time Out.* In Germany, there is still strong resistance to aspects of US pop culture, though there is an appetite for its intellectual culture, says Gary Smith, director of the American Academy in Berlin. In France, resistance is growing partly because of frustra-

tions over the Iraq war—but partly because Americanization is already so advanced in the country, says Mr. Kaspi.

He notes one interesting anecdotal sign of US influence—and the futility of resistance. France has repeatedly tried to mandate the use of French language in official capacities to check the advance of English. "But most of the time, the law is impossible to apply, because if you want to be understood around the world you have to speak English," Kaspi says.

In the Philippines, even the best US ideals have caused complications. "The pervasive American influence has saddled us with two legacies," notes respected local commentator Antonio C. Abaya. "American-style elections, which require the commitment of massive financial resources, which have to be recouped and rolled over many times, which is the main source of corruption in government; and American-style free press in which media feel free to attack and criticize everything that the government does or says, which adds to disunity and loss of confidence in government."

Meanwhile, for all the strength of the US movie industry, sometimes a foreign film resonates more with a local audience than a Hollywood production—and outperforms it. For instance, Japan's "Spirited Away" (2001) remains the top-grossing film in that country, surpassing global Hollywood hits like

"Titanic." In addition, British TV has influenced and served up competition to US shows, spawning such hits as "Who Wants to Be a Millionaire?", "The Weakest Link," and "American Idol."

1,000 years from now

15   So how much good does American culture bring to the world? And how long will it last? Ian Ralston cautions against sweeping dismissals of US pop culture. British television may be saturated with American sitcoms and movies, but while some are poor, others are quite good, he says. "British culture has always been enriched by foreign influences. In some ways American culture and media have added to that enrichment." Others note that it is not all one-way traffic. America may feast largely on a diet of homegrown culture, but it imports modestly as well: soccer, international cuisine, Italian fashion, and, increasingly, British television.

As to the question of durability, some experts believe US domination of communication channels makes it inevitable that its messages will become far more entrenched than those of previous empires. "The main difference now in favor of American culture is the importance of technology—telephone, Internet, films, all that did not exist in ancient Greece or the Mongol empire," Kaspi says. "American influence is growing, it's so easy to get access to US culture; there are no barriers. "Disney is known worldwide now," he adds. "Plato is more and more unknown, even in Greece."

But not everyone thinks American culture will stand the test of time. "It remains to be seen whether the Monkees and Bee Gees are as durable as Plato," says Professor Young, with a dab of irony. "Let's have another look in 4,000 years' time."

Reflect & Write

❏ How does this article immediately engage your interest as a reader with two particularly vivid opening paragraphs? Discuss the detailed names in the opening and how they relate both to globalization and to what Mark Rice-Oxley calls "McDomination"?

❏ How does the writer both construct an audience and create a unique persona through word choice? What word choices make this article targeted at a specific demographic?

❏ How does the article integrate quotations as research and as appeals to authority? What is the effect of this rhetorical strategy on you as a reader? What is the effect of this on the writing as a text?

❏ What structure of arrangement does this article employ? Return to Chapter 6 to understand and refresh on strategies of Arrangement.

❏ How does this article itemize its arguments logically? Map out the strategies of rebuttal, concession, and qualification.

❏ Notice the writer's careful analysis of trends in globalization. Locate your own examples and conduct your own analysis of these instances.

❏ **Write:** Compose a narrative about visual rhetoric of globalization in the world around you. What instances of globalized culture strike you as having "staying power"?

■   *This article appeared in the June 1, 2004, edition of the* China Daily, *an English-language newspaper published in China. Sometimes called the "Window to China," the* China Daily *and its Website (chinadaily.com.cn) are dedicated to providing the world with information about China and its role in the international community.*

KFC and McDonald's: A Model of Blended Culture

Qui Jianghong

CEOs of America Tricon Global Restaurants, the group that owns KFC and Pizza Hut, promotes Traditional Peking Chicken Roll at a KFC restaurant in Shanghai.

At present, there are more than 1,000 KFC restaurants in China, and they are increasing at annual rate of 200. A new KFC restaurant opens every other day. Western counterpart McDonald's also continues to expand its premises.

Having arrived on the mainland in the early 1990s, McDonald's has more than 600 restaurants in nearly 100 cities. Although there have been fewer golden arches in America, its native country, in the past two years, China's McDonald's have grown at a rate of 100 restaurants per year.

The total income of fast food restaurants in China now stands at 180 billion yuan RMB, and KFC and McDonald's account for eight percent. What kind of magic has brought them such success in China? How do they sustain growth rates? Their standardized business operation apart, the key is excellent inter-cultural management.

Western Fast Food Chinese Style

5 Alluring the captious customers is a hurdle every foreign fast food restaurant must clear. The novelty of these fast food restaurants initially won many customers. Although cheap and commonplace in America, at the time the Chinese government's opening-up policy was newly enacted, fast food was exotically foreign enough to whet Chinese people's curiosity about the outside world. Managers took advantage of this by charging the relatively high prices of 10 yuan for a hamburger, and 5 yuan for a Coke.

By the mid-1990s, there were 100 fast food restaurants around Beijing; the convenience, efficient service, comfortable environment, pleasing music and jovial atmosphere garnered fans. Office workers enjoyed grabbing a quick bite on their way to work, and friends enjoyed relaxing over a Coke. However, certain eagle-eyed managers noticed that some people never dropped in when they passed by. Some customers complained that fast food was not as good as their Chinese cuisine, and that it lacked variety. McDonald's and KFC restaurants were almost empty during the traditional celebrations of Spring Festival and Mid-autumn Festival, while Chinese restaurants were heaved and bustled.

The reason? Cultural differences. Fast food restaurants like KFC and McDonald's are distinct American brands. Differences between China and US politics, economics, social development and ideology became obstacles to international enterprises operating in China. Corporate culture could not be understood or accepted here, especially in the restaurant field, where culture plays a crucial role.

So the solution was to adapt: when in Rome, do as the Romans. Deep-rooted in the Chinese consciousness is the traditional culture of food and drink that features color, fragrance, flavor and variety. Fast food simply does not compare. Now that curiosity had faded, people returned to their own more extensive cuisine. Under such circumstances, the only way out was to combine the two different cultures. Fast food restaurants have been learning to absorb elements of Chinese culture.

10 Since the summer of 2001, KFC has introduced many Chinese items onto their menus. Preserved Sichuan Pickle and Shredded Pork Soup was one of the first. Consumers felt their traditions were being respected when they could taste Chinese cuisine at a foreign restaurant. The soup proved a success, and Mushroom Rice, Tomato and Egg Soup, and Traditional Peking Chicken Roll were soon added to the menu. KFC also serves packets of Happy French Fry Shakes that contain beef, orange and Uygur barbecue spices.

Not content to lag behind, McDonald's Vegetable and Seafood Soup and Corn Soup were introduced, and the company worked to modify the restaurants' design. During the 2004 Spring Festival, McDonald's on Beijing's Wangfujing Street attracted many people with a traditional Chinese look, decorating their interiors with paper-cuts of the Chinese character Fu (Happiness), magpies and twin fishes, all auspicious symbols.

Inter-cultural Management Mode

KFC and McDonald's have absorbed the Chinese cultural elements of showing respect, recognition, understanding, assimilation and amalgamation, while maintaining the substance of the Western culture of efficiency, freedom, democracy, equality and humanity. This inter-cultural management mode, with American business culture at the core, supplemented by Chinese traditional culture, provides reference for international enterprises which need to adjust, enrich and reconstruct their corporate culture to enhance local market flexibility.

There are, however, certain conditions essential to inter-cultural management mode. On the objective side, there must be similarities in environment in order for the two cultures to connect and synchronize. KFC and McDonald's embody an accommodation of the fast tempo of modern life: a product of development and a market economy. Their resultant speed and efficiency are only meaningful in countries with a market economy. China's rapid economic development offered the environmental conditions corre-

sponding to fast food culture. Services offered by fast food chains express their full respect for freedom, an American value, as well as the psychological statement of Chinese open-mindedness that yearns to understand and experience the Western lifestyle. Two cultures

proactively crashed, connected, and assimilated. KFC and McDonald's use the localization strategy to re-express American business culture, with profound traditional Chinese cultural emblems, catering to local customs on the basis of standardized management.

Reflect & Write

❑ Notice the heavy reliance on logos in this article. What might be the reason for using so many statistics, facts, and dates in presenting this argument about the integration of McDonald's into Chinese culture?

❑ Summarize the argument of this essay. What side of the globalization debate is represented here?

❑ Who is the audience for this essay? What details and descriptions suggest this to you? What aspects of the writing would need to change in order to address a different audience?

❑ **Write:** Copy down the menu of a fast food restaurant in your college town, one that is very different from the food in your home town. How do menus create a visual representation of the cultural community?

The two pieces that follow appeared in Rutgers University's newspaper, the Daily Targum, *in October 2002. The* Targum *ran the first piece, written by 2001 Rutgers graduate* **Joseph Davicsin,** *in its October 16th edition; "Globalization or McDonaldization?" appeared in response the following day. Its author,* **Jeremy Sklarsky,** *was a first-year student at Rutgers at the time.*

The Daily Targum: Two Opinions on McDonaldization

Corporations Leave Small Business Behind
Joseph Davicsin

Three months ago, a coffee shop opened on Church Street—where the used CD store "Tunes" was—called Basic Elements. This shop offered homemade beverages and food at prices comparable to similar chain stores. I say "offered" because, as of recently, the place has flown the coop like so many boiler room scams. I later saw the proprietors at Starbucks doing espresso shots and mumbling Wicca chants

Globalization or McDonaldization?
Jeremy Sklarsky

I am writing in response to Joseph Davicsin's commentary about international corporations conquering the world and eliminating "mom and pop" establishments. Davicsin's comments exemplify some of the most commonly held misperceptions about globalization and corporations.

Globalization is not an enemy. It is an international, socioeconomic-political system. Due to advances in information technology, the rise at the Cranium board game. Basic Elements deserved a hell of a lot more than it was given—a crappy side street with little visibility, despite being right near the Court Tavern (which I know for a fact that you frequent because I can never get a square foot of space to stand on when I'm in there), irregular hours—which is understandable in a quality place run by two people (you can't expect Walmart)—and most of all, our apathy.

Our apathy is linked largely to globalization, which is trying to unite the planet in blanket sameness so that you can experience a thrill at the notion of shopping at a Gap in Prague and eating at a McDonalds in India. Now, something in your mind should tell you there's something wrong with going to a McDonalds in India. The idea of going abroad is to experience new things outside your microcosm. But alas, the success of these businesses in pandering their crack all over the world has gotten people comfortable with this sameness. We stick to the chains because they're familiar, convenient and plowed into our faces on a regular basis. When you get that taste of mocha, you're hooked and nothing else seems to matter.

Of course, if it were simply laziness and chemical brainwashing causing the underdogs to fail, it would be easier to rectify, but life is never that simple. There's also the notion of capital to think of. Corporations like Starbucks have enough money to keep their prices relatively the same no matter where you go, so there's not only uniformed coverage, but also uniformed prices. The same cannot be said of the localized stores because they have less coverage and really need the extra money to stay alive, forcing them to increase their prices to compete. This delegates them to the "fine arts" category in which only the wealthy can indulge, resulting in an even split between cheap and prevalent and expensive and exclusive, with the midways—i.e. the moderately priced Basic Elements—getting squished in the ever-shrinking gap. Our culture becomes the following: Either you go to McSystem for victuals or spend exorbitant amounts of cash on the trendier French fry.

5　　Then, of course, there's the small matter of demand, and that's when convenience takes prece-

of a postindustrial economy and the collapse of the bipolar Cold War world, a system has arisen in which the interests of individuals and governments around the world are intertwined. The overlap of people's interests has led to increased global cooperation. It can even be argued that the motivation for acts of international terrorism like Sept. 11 is actually a categorical rejection of the globalization system. The young men who crashed airplanes into the World Trade Center were born and raised in some of the countries that are the least globalized.

Globalization is not trying to "unite the planet in blanket sameness." Actually, quite the contrary is true. Take McDonald's, a notorious symbol of globalization, for example. McDonald's was not introduced into foreign countries in order to push American cultural hegemony over the rest of the world. McDonald's was mostly imported into foreign countries by nationals of those countries that wanted to make some profit—not as a part of a master plan to make everyone American. McDonald's is just a company that wants to make money. It isn't part of a "conspiracy of American corporations to take over the world."

Furthermore, a quick trip to the McDonald's Web site will put to rest anyone's fears that Ronald and friends are trying to undermine the culture of a local population. In Italy, McDonald's serves Mediterranean salads. Japanese customers can get teriyaki burgers. In Israel there are several kosher McDonald's restaurants, and in Mexico burritos are served. These are just a few examples of when McDonald's has actually changed itself to fit into the local culture. In India, the country that Davicsin used in his column as an example, consumers can get McDonald's sandwiches made with mutton and chicken instead of beef, as McDonald's recognizes the importance of the dietary laws in Indian religions and cultures. McDonald's has also initiated many community service programs. In Saudi Arabia, it was the first chain restaurant to sponsor a campaign to increase seatbelt awareness.

5　　A McDonald's in every country? Sounds good to me. Thomas Friedman, columnist for *The New York Times,* recently put forth a theory—which has been proven—that states that dence. Anyone who still reads out there will have little hope of finding a Recto & Verso when the majority only cares about getting textbooks and spirit clothing. The alternative is Barnes and Noble. If you want a real alternative you have to walk the world over to Pyramid Books in Highland Park, which, judging by the abundance of romance novels infesting their shelves, leads me to believe that they too are trying desperately to stay afloat.

Countless fables tell of local pizza places rejecting the system, but are they really? Or are they just biding their time before Burger King offers pizza for breakfast? They too seem to be getting increasingly gimmicky (check out King's Pizza and the ultimate tax write-off that is their widescreen TV) and streamlined (toppings ranging from tortellini to ecstasy). There are still a few locales, like Noodle Gourmet, that do solid business on their own two legs, but it's not enough. What we need to do is alternate our habits a little. Back to coffee—like Café 52? I know you do because I see you bastards flood it every Monday night for the free music, then try West End on alternate nights. Spread out! Balance the pros and cons of each place and try to find a niche in one when the other doesn't meet your needs. But above all, give newer places your undivided attention because they may not be around long enough without you. Show the smaller places that there's a need for them and that quality need not mean pricey. And don't let companies know where you're going, lest they turn that into a trend as well. Be as random as a chaos pendulum.

no two countries with a McDonald's has gone to war with each other since McDonald's arrived in their countries. In Friedman's own words, people in countries that have developed an economy at the level needed for McDonald's to be successful would rather "wait in line for burgers instead of in line for gas masks."

Davicsin refers to corporations as though they are some supernatural enemy imposed upon us by some external forces. Where did they get all of their money? And why are they so successful? A chain like McDonald's or Starbucks Coffee has had so much success for one simple reason: They are just better than the "corner shop." But chances are, if a local store can make a lower-priced product of higher quality, it will thrive. Take another corporation—Pizza Hut. Pizza Hut just isn't that good. Result? There are hundreds of individually owned pizza parlors around America. We shouldn't, however, support every local pizza place just for the sake of fighting corporations—that's just silly.

I'm not suggesting globalization or corporations are perfect—they are far from it. Many Third World countries would probably be better off if the World Bank or IMF behaved better. And corporations could probably afford to pollute a little less and pay their workers a little bit more. But that's really not the issue. The point is that globalization is not a choice. The real question is how everyone is going to act in order to benefit from its existence. If local coffee shops wish to thrive in the globalization system, they'd better be damned good, otherwise Starbucks will run them out of business—and for good reason. Consumers deserve to consume good products. If the only reason to go to a local burger joint is to prevent the domination of McDonald's, then I'll have another Big Mac.

Reflect & Write

❏ Map out the points of each argument. How does each writer use concrete examples and structure his perspective through carefully chosen rhetorical appeals?

❏ Davicsin emphasizes the necessity of what he calls "visibility" and small establishments. How does his language create a favorable image for local

stores in contrast to his disparagment of "blanket sameness" across
the globe?

❏ How does Sklarsky structure his rebuttal? What points does he choose to refute
and do you follow the logic of his conclusion? Which piece is more persuasive to
you, and why?

❏ **Write:** Draft a response to both pieces, synthesizing and advancing beyond the debate between Joseph Davicsin and Jeremy Sklarsky. Be certain to quote passages
from both in your own article. Where might you publish your composition?

Professor of Sociology at the University of Maryland, **George Ritzer** *has published extensively but
is best known for his "McDonaldization thesis." He has published numerous books, including*
The McDonaldization of Society *(1993) and* The Globalization of Nothing *(2004). This interview was conducted by One-Off Productions in February 1997.*

Interview with George Ritzer

One-Off Productions

*You have described the McDonaldised society as a system of "iron cages" in
which all institutions come to be dominated by the same principle. So what
sort of world would you like us to be living in ?*

Well, obviously (laughter) . . . a far less caged one. I mean the fundamental
problem with McDonaldised systems is that it's other people in the system structuring our lives for us, rather than us structuring our lives for ourselves. I mean,
that's really what McDonald's is all about. You don't want a creative person clerk
at the counter—that's why they are scripted. You don't want a creative hamburger cook—you want somebody who simply follows routines or follows
scripts. So you take all creativity out of all activities and turn them into a series of
routinised kinds of procedures that are imposed by some external force. So that's
the reason why it is dehumanising. Humanity is essentially creative and if you develop these systems that are constraining and controlling people they can't be
creative, they can't be human. The idea is to turn humans into human robots.
The next logical step is to replace human robots with mechanical robots. And I
think we will see McDonaldised systems where it is economically feasible and
technologically possible to replace human robots with non-human robots. I'd
like to see a society in which people are freed to be creative, rather than having
their creativity constrained or eliminated.

*To what extent do you think McDonald's threats of lawsuits and censorship are
an attempt to control their public image?*

Well, I think they are certainly not the first or alone in trying to control the public
image that they have, and of course their public image has been very important

to them. I suppose it could be related to the control idea, you are accustomed to controlling everything else so why not try to control that public image.

How important is McDonald's image?

Well, the fact is of course that they are producing what everybody else produces—there is very little to distinguish the McDonald's hamburger from anybody else's hamburger, except maybe the special sauce or something like that. Basically they have to manufacture a sense of difference and a lot of that manufacture has to do with the fun and the colours, the clowns and the toys, and the squeaky clean image.

How much duplicity do you think there is going on here in terms of the image McDonald's presents?

I think there is a duplicitousness about McDonald's in the sense that it wants to portray an image of children and happy employees and one big joyous happy family and everyone having a good time. I think that American corporations in various ways try to create a duplicitous image, a false image. I mean that's what, in a sense, successful capitalism is about it's "WE ARE THE WORLD" and a number of major companies have tried to do essentially the same thing.

5   *You say very rightly that it's not just McDonald's—but why do you think that you, and Helen and Dave, and other people keep choosing McDonald's as the one to pick on?*

They are the icon and McDonald's is chosen by critics because it stands for a variety of things. I mean, from my point of view, it stands for efficiency and predictability. For other people it stands for America and America's influence throughout the world, so it gets picked up as a positive model. Although all of these things are virtues, the problem is that they are taken to such extraordinary lengths by McDonald's that they end up producing all kinds of irrational consequences so that the irrationalities outweigh the rationalities.

Do you go as far as to say that McDonald's represents capitalism?

Well it's a funny kind of capitalism that McDonald's represents because after all capitalism—American capitalism—for generations was the symbol of the huge smoke-stack industry, steel and automobiles . . . but it is not the automobile industry that represents America around the world now it is McDonald's and Disney and Coca Cola.

Do you think going into McDonald's, particularly in other countries, is more like entering the Western Dream than just buying a product?

It's not just that you are buying a product—you are buying into a system. In the 1940s there was a big flap in France over what was called a Coca Colonisation. The French were very upset about the coming of Coca Cola to France. They felt it threatened the French wine industry, it threatened the French way of life. But that was just the influx of an American product—what we have here is the influx of an American way of life, which is to trivialise eating, to make it something that is fast, make it something that's to get done and over with.

But it's striking to me that the last time I was in Paris the Parisians appeared to have embraced this kind of fast food phenomenon . You have developments of fast food croissanteries where this model French way of life—the croissanterie— has been reduced to fast food. French bread is more and more treated on a fast basis rather than lots of local bakeries baking their own distinctive kind, so if the French succumb to this in the realm of food then it strikes me that there is little that is safe from the expansion of this process.

The significance here is not buying the big Mac, it's buying the system, buying the whole package and being part of America, that's the key.

Do you think this process is ever going to be reversed?

Well the caged imagery suggests that there is an inevitability to it. Clearly, all the trends are in the direction of the greater spread of McDonald's or greater spread of the process of McDonaldisation. And there is certainly plenty of room for it to expand into other cultures, and there are still many cultures which are completely or relatively completely unaffected.

But there are also always counter-reactions, there are also always all sorts of things that are coming up from the people that represent innovations and creations. I mean you are not going to get innovations and creations from McDonaldised systems. Those innovations and creations—those non-McDonaldised ways of doing things—are going to well up from the people. But what makes me most pessimistic is that anything that's any good, anything not successful, some entrepreneur or organisation is going to come along and make great to rationalise it, make great to McDonaldise it, trivialise it, they are going to turn it into a system—a cash counter—and generate money. There is nothing that seems to be immune to this process, no aspect of life that seems to be immune to it. It's difficult to think of things that can avoid the process.

Does it mean that it is appealing to some fundamental call of human nature?

Well, sociologists don't believe in human nature. You never say human nature to a sociologist because if it was human nature that really mattered, then sociologists would be out of business. I think that there are a variety of things that people need at some level, like some degree of efficiency in their lives and some degree of predictability. What McDonald's has done is pick up on those and transform them into a system. I don't think people need the level of efficiency that McDonald's provides for them or want that level of efficiency . . . it's not something that is innate.

Another sort of pessimistic aspect to this is that you have children born into this McDonaldised world, you have people being trained, being lured into the system by the commercials and the toys and the clowns and the bright lights.

They are trained that this is the way you eat, this is the way a hamburger should taste, this is how a French fry should taste, salty-sweet. These are the standards and so you if try to say to people of this generation "well look, this is not really how a hamburger should be, here is a home cooked hamburger" they will likely turn their nose up and say "well, that doesn't taste like. . . "

There are really, it seems to me, only two groups that historically have been critics of the process of McDonaldisation. They are the people who were born before the process and knew a different way of life and then were stunned by the development of McDonaldisation, or people from non-McDonaldised cultures who see this influx and are able to react. But once that generation that was born before McDonaldisation dies off, and once all these other cultures are McDonaldised, well where is the opposition going to come from . . . from children who have been trained by McDonald's or gone to McDonald's schools and done everything that they had to do from one McDONALD'S SYSTEM AFTER ANOTHER?

Obviously McDonalds and related corporations are spending billions of dollars to socialise children into this system so that this becomes their standard.

One of the basic premises of McDonald's is to focus on quantity, low price (or what appears to be low price) and large quantities of things and inevitably what suffers when you emphasise quantity is quality so they are serving what is at best mediocre food.

10 *But why do you think that Dave and Helen are able to criticise the process?*

You see I don't think that England is as McDonaldised as the U.S.A. In Europe you have some degree of McDonaldisation but nothing to the degree that this process has proceeded in the U.S. So there would be examples of people in other cultures who, because of the nature of that culture and the large number of non-McDonaldised aspects of that culture, would be sensitised to it. I think fewer and fewer Americans are sensitised to it, question it. I mean they don't know anything else, you are going to go and eat you go to fast food restaurant and eat. You mentioned the French cuisine and I think one of the trends in the future of Mc-Donaldisation is the McDonaldisation of higher-up restaurants, of haute cuisine. You already see sort of middle range restaurants and restaurant chains in the U.S. now. Red Lobster or a chain like that is selling fairly upscale food but you now see signs that some elegant restaurants are trying to move in the direction of developing chains. So the challenge is going to be how do you McDonaldise a system by retaining quality because all McDonaldised systems have sacrificed quality. It's the process that's the problem here.

Do you think that the issue should be broadened to include more than just the specific case of McDonald's?

Yeah, see for me it's that they've set in motion something which is so much bigger than they are, that this process is so much broader than what they are. In fact, McDonald's could disappear tomorrow, or could go out of business tomorrow and this process would continue on. You might have to give it a

Seeing Connections
For instructions on how
to conduct your own
interviews as part of your
field research process,
see Chapter 5.

different name but the process would continue, I mean the process has a history long before McDonald's. In Weber's theory of rationalisation and in Weber's model was the bureaucracy, the German bureaucracy, and we're living in an extension, a massive extension of that process with a new model in the fast food restaurant. The fast food restaurant, or McDonald's could disappear but that process will be transformed into some new form.

Is there a 1984/Brave New World kind of element to this?

The Brave New World/1984 image is one of centralised control. What McDonaldisation means for me is kinds of microsystems of control or whole systems of microsystems of control. Actually Michel Foucault, the French post-structural theorist, talked about these micropolitics of control, micromechanisms of control and I think that what's being set in place here is not an iron cage, but innumerable mini iron cages and there are so many of them and they're so widely spaced throughout society that the iron cages envisioned here is one where you simply have your choice of which cage to enter but there's nothing but cages to go to.

What effects does a McDonaldised society have its people?

I think that McDonald's has a profound effect on the way people do a lot of things I mean it leads people to want everything fast, to have, you know, a limited attention span so that kind of thing spills over onto, let's say, television viewing or newspaper reading, and so you have a short attention span, you want everything fast, so you don't have patience to read the *New York Times* and so you read McPaper, you read *USA Today*. You don't have patience to watch a lengthy newscast on a particular issue so you watch CNN News and their little news McNugget kinds of things so it creates a kind of mindset which seeks the same kind of thing in one setting after another. I see it in education where you have, in a sense, a generation of students who've been raised in a McDonaldised society, they want things fast, they want idealic nuggets from Professors, they don't want sort of slow build up of ideas, you gotta keep them amused, you gotta come in with the Ronald McDonald costume and quip a series of brilliant theoretical points or else they're going to turn you off. It's quite amazing what they've done, what they've undertaken here.

What do you think of what Helen and Dave are doing?

I think that clearly, from very small beginnings, they've created a worldwide movement here, worldwide attention, and have laid the basis for a real potential threat to McDonald's and the process of McDonaldisation. We talked about this earlier, the possibility of bringing together these disparate groups and I think that McDonald's has got to devote, I mean if they want to prevent this from occurring, they've got to devote some attention to how to diffuse and strategically keep apart these oppositional forces that seem likely to come together, to focus on it as a negative force. I mean if there really comes to be a time where McDonald's is viewed as this evil force in the world by a significant number of people, then that becomes a real threat to the organisation. But again I want to point out that even if McDonald's disappeared tomorrow, even if they closed their doors because of the McLibel trial the process would continue apace.

15 *Do you eat at McDonald's?*

Only when I'm in the iron cage and it's the only alternative. I mean, you do find yourself in the United States in a situation especially when you're on the highways now where there is no place to go other than a fast food restaurant. One of the big developments on American highways is that virtually all of the rest stops have been taken over by the fast food chains and so if you're driving on the highway and you wanna eat you're gonna eat in a fast food restaurant.

There is no alternative unless you get off the highway and then all of the restaurants that are immediately off the highway are going to be fast food restaurants too, so you've got to search quite a bit to avoid eating in a fast food restaurant. So occasionally you just find yourself now in the States where that's your only alternative and of course again that's the ultimate iron cage. I mean, when the whole society's like that, where you just cannot find any kind of alternative, you just throw up your hands and say "ok, I'm gonna eat this way, I'm gonna do things this way".

Reflect & Write

❏ How does George Ritzer introduce quite an innovative angle into the debate over McDonald's with his opening points on "dehumanizing" robot conditions? Does he make this argument successfully?

❏ Ritzer's focus on McDonald's "public image" takes into account the toys, the Website, and the commercials. What do you learn about the power of visual rhetoric from this interview?

❏ What argument is Ritzer making about historical shifts? How different is the "automobile industry that represent[ed] America around the world" compared to "McDonald's and Disney and Coca Cola"? What's at stake in terms of cultural values?

❏ When Ritzer brings in foundation texts—such as Weber's model and Foucault— what happens to the depth of his argument? How do such references transform his ethos as a writer?

❏ How does Ritzer make use of the cage image in this piece? How does he apply his focus on McDonald's to the news and society more broadly? Do you find these applications effective?

❏ **Write:** Compose your assessment of the conclusion. What other questions would you like to ask this author?

COLLABORATIVE CHALLENGE

Gather with two or three classmates at a shared computer space. Visit the Comprehensive Activist Website, McSpotlight, available through the *Envision* Website. Conduct a rhetorical analysis of the online features. Spend some time at the Special Page for Family Fun, Subverted Billboards, and Animation. Watch the 30-second Quicktime ad for Peter Heller's *Jungleburger,* a documentary that focuses on the Costa Rican cattle raising and meat export business and investigates how the fast food industry affects third world countries. Then compare Peter Heller's *Jungle burger* to the McDonald's commercial found at http://www.mcdonalds.com/usa/fun/tv.html. What argument is each text making? How is the image of McDonald's constructed in each one? As a group, write a review of each one, then storyboard your own film in response to these two texts.

www.ablongman.com/envision/244

PERSPECTIVES ON THE ISSUE

1. What type of writing or persuasion do you find most compelling? Mark Rice-Oxley's researched article? The competing *Daily Targum* pieces? The interview with George Ritzer? How do the visual and written texts both contribute positions on the issue of McDonald's in the world theater?

2. Compare the different texts in this unit. What is the persona, audience, stance, and argument of each one? What logical appeals are used to construct an argument? (See Chapter 2 to refresh your understanding of logical appeals.) How does each text use strategies of visual persuasion, whether through embedding images as evidence in the text or through evoking visual aspects of culture? When you are done discussing each text, pick two of the articles that seem most rich to you and write a rhetorical analysis comparing them.

3. Compose an opinion essay or blog in response to one of the conversations about McDonald's you have encountered here. Send your short article to the campus newspaper or post it on a blog site.

4. Look at Mark Rice-Oxley's article and analyze the visual descriptions of culture in its opening paragraph. How do visual details construct an argument about the way in which culture has changed as a result of globalization? How does this visual rhetoric narrative establish the premise of the argument? What details are particularly American forms of visual culture and which seem to have become more international? Now compose your own visual rhetoric narrative about the elements of contemporary culture that have changed your town or community.

5. In what ways are sports a means of transnational communication and connection? Do you agree with Rice-Oxley's implied argument that the infiltration of American sports, such as baseball, football, and basketball indicates America's imposition of power on other countries? Compose an argument in response. Include images from transnational sports intersections, such as a still shot from the Visa Check Card commercial showcasing Yao Ming in an American Chinatown with Yogi Berra, or the Nike ad depicting LeBron James in China.

FROM READING TO RESEARCH

1. Conduct a Google search to locate more images of McDonald's abroad in order to create a research-based photo essay. You might want to include images of protests against McDonaldization, depictions of deforestation, or images of families enjoying time together in the restaurant. Your selection of images will necessarily shape your group's argument on the issue. Together with your team members, organize these images into a slide show to convey your argument about McDonald's abroad. You might record quotes from the articles above and use them as evidence or research sources in your slideshow.

2. Use your research skills from Chapters 5 and 6 to locate articles on the debate over EuroDisney. How, according to your research, does seemingly innocuous visual culture in the form of cartoons, magic castles, family rides, and popcorn potentially threaten national languages and traditions? Applying your skills in visual production from Chapter 8, design an op-ad to convey your research-based argument about Disney's influence internationally.

EAST MEETS WEST

To many, globalization has become synonymous with the expansion of American culture and American businesses across the globe. As we hear of another Kentucky Fried Chicken restaurant opening in Southeast Asia, or we see signs of American fashion in Tokyo, we might wonder whether the world is becoming homogenized into one giant America. Yet cultural influences work in both directions. This chapter will focus on the increasing prevalence of Eastern culture upon American soil.

We see evidence of such cross-cultural fertilization everywhere, from the popularity of Anime cartoons on children's television programs in the United States to the rise in participation in martial arts and meditation. East is meeting West on home turf here in America, bringing powerful new ideas in the design of toys to the look of fashion, in ads for sports and the visual elements of film production. We can see it in Figure 15.5 a movie poster for the 2004 film *Bride & Prejudice*. With its tagline "Bollywood meets Hollywood," this film represents a cross-over moment between cultures: filmed in English, Hindi, and Punjabi, it adapted Jane Austen's traditional British courtship novel to accommodate a young Indian couple's much more modern dating experience. The poster clearly captures the tension between East (represented with a traditional Indian scene on the right) and the West (symbolized through the iconic Hollywood sign on the left), culminating in a moment of cross-cultural celebration.

FIGURE 15.5 The movie poster for *Bride and Prejudice* visually represents its caption: "Bollywood meets Hollywood."

This meeting of East and West happens across many areas, not just in film. From sports figures such as Yao Ming and Ichiro Suzuki, to children's toys such as Hello Kitty or Pokemon, or to the growing popularity of henna tattooing, yoga, and Tae Bo, we can see the growing interrelationship of Eastern and Western cultural practices. In this chapter, we invite you to explore many such examples of the way in which cross-cultural rhetoric reflects the changing shape of our mutually interdependent globe. We invite you to read, respond, and participate in this change.

Visual Reading: A Cross-Cultural Moment of East Meets West

FIGURE 15.6 A young Buddhist monk plays pool in the Chinese province of Yunnan.

Reflect & Write

❏ What rhetorical elements suggest a merging of eastern and western cultures in the photograph shown in Figure 15.6?

❏ What other examples of culture fusion are you familiar with in your own community?

❏ **Write:** Compose a blog entry in which you comment on cross-cultural experiences in your life, your school, or your town. Take photos of visual evidence, such as students reading anime, playing Japanese video games, learning martial arts, watching Bollywood film, or wearing traditional dress. Post your photos along with the writing in your blog to make an argument about the everyday experience of globalization in America.

Visual Reading: Muslim Barbie

FIGURE 15.7 First introduced in the Middle East in 2003, the Fulla doll is known as Muslim Barbie, although the manufacturers have no affiliation with Mattel.

Reflect & Write

❏ As you look at the photographs above, what elements in the images (dress, skin color, headdress, expression) symbolize the individual cultures? Do the images suggest that the influence operates in one direction (for instance, the West influencing the East), or is there a possibility for counter-influence as well?

❏ What effect do you think this doll might have on young girls of the Muslim faith? Comment on the power of visual models as examples—for ways of living, for an understanding of culture and identity, for statements about how accepted a practice is in a particular community.

❏ **Write:** Think about other dolls you have encountered in America and how they represent cultural identit.y Now, select one or two examples to serve as the starting point for a hypothetical research paper on dolls and cross-cultural identity.

■ **David Wells,** *a freelance photographer from Providence, RI, won the Alicia Patterson Foundation fellowship for journalists. This article and photo essay was published on the* APF Reporter, *Vol. 21, #1, as the culmination of his project.*

Gateways of India's Globalization

David H. Wells

Globalization is hardly a new force affecting India. To think so is to ignore a diverse and pluralistic long-standing civilization that was shaped by a long list of "invading" (globalizing) cultures that became what we now know as India. The previous globalizers of India include the Aryans, Hindus, Dravidians, Greeks, Buddhists, Turks, Afghans, Scythians, Muslims and most recently, the Europeans, Portuguese, French, Dutch and finally the English. One has to understand that as India has been globalized it has also been a globalizer too, with millennia of colonialism across Southeast Asia, with temples like Angkor Wat left behind as a reminders of India's one time presence.

Long viewed by the West, as "poor and impoverished," to its neighbors such as Sri Lanka, Bangladesh and Pakistan, India is wealthy and powerful. To these smaller neighbors, India is a great power, a globalizer of its own, which expects deference from them and is sometimes angered when those nations downplay their Indian lineage. They prefer to play up their own local cultures, which are frequently hybrids of the larger Indian culture and their own indigenous ones.

India, knowing its past as a globalizer, sees itself as one of the great nations of the world. But today, India has yet to build on the onetime greatness of its civilization to earn international influence and respect. India sees itself as equally important as Russia, China and the U.S., believing it has much to offer the rest of the world. Historically this has a basis since important aspects of trigonometry were developed in India, as was the decimal system, which, was later taken from India by Arab mathematicians, and on to Europe in the 10th century, only to come back to India through books from the West. Similarly, at the start of the 18th century,

India was a major economic power with 23 percent of the world's GDP according to some economic historians and over 25 percent share of the global trade in textiles. By 1995, this had declined to less than 5 percent of world income and less than half a percent of world trade.

The most recent wave of globalization affecting India came with the British who were important to Indian development, in positive and negative ways. The British consolidated a land of many separate regions and kingdoms into what we know of as modern India. While the British exploited India's population, economy and resources as colonial rulers, they also left India, after two centuries of rule in 1948, with democracy, laws, a judiciary, and a free press, 40,000 miles of railroad track, canals, and harbors. English as the language of Indian business and the English language schools are arguably some of the most important remnants of the British, giving India a linguistic global gateway not found in former French, Spanish or Dutch speaking colonies.

5   Another British relic is cricket, which has largely displaced local games in rural areas, in both Nepal, a land not known for interest in cricket, and in India. The place of cricket in Indian life exemplifies a unique aspect of "Indian-ness," the ability to absorb outside influences and to transform them through a peculiar Indian magic into something else that becomes a natural part of India.

The experience of McDonald's, one of the ultimate globalizers, illustrates the idea of Indian adaptation to globalization. While McDonald's can boast of selling billions of hamburgers worldwide, they have not done nearly as well among the one billion Indians. In deference to local religious sensibilities—and finicky taste—the burger giant has radically revised its lineup. Since Hindus avoid beef and practicing Muslims do not eat pork, only mutton satisfies religious restrictions and thus the Maharaja Mac was born. It is considered too bland for the taste buds of some consumers in the land of hot curry and sharp Cardamom. McDonald's struggle in India makes it one of a number of fast food companies that despite such troubles, has an appeal as foreign food, conferring status on the flush with cash Indian middle-class.

The former globalizers that came with invading armies have increasingly been replaced by less violent but equally powerful globalizers. Television is arguably the most dominant gateway of globalization affecting India today. While TV was launched in India in the late 1950s it only became widespread in the 1980s, after the governments ended their monopoly as the only broadcaster. Satellite TV arrived in 1991, bringing with it Indian versions of MTV and later "Who Wants to Be a Millionaire?" Because of the abrupt end of the monopoly of the state channels, the instantaneous arrival of satellite TV has been more disruptive and far reaching in India than elsewhere in the world. According to reports, traditional dress is increasingly displaced by Western dress seen on TV. In the southern state of Kerala, a study showed that teenage abortions rose by 20 per cent in a year, as teenagers feel pressure to have sex, purportedly due to the explosion of sexually explicit imagery from sources like MTV and the Indian equivalent channels.

Another example of TV's globalization in India can be seen in how India globalizes neighboring nation's media markets. While English may be perceived as the dominant language of TV, in South Asia, India's Hindi is TV's dominant language, transforming neighboring countries into little more than passive recipients of Indian Hindi TV and displacing local languages like Bangla in Bangladesh and Nepali in Nepal. Increasingly, local languages, inside India and across South Asia fade under attack from Hindi as Indian film and sports stars are made as familiar to Bangladeshis and Pakistanis as they are to Indians.

The other way TV globalizes is in how it helps keep NRIs (Non Resident Indians) in

contact with their culture of origin. These people, who are of Indian origin (and are also derided as Not Really Indian) make up the great Indian Diaspora, an estimated 15 to 21 million people spread across the world who are often better educated than the dominant populations they live amongst. NRIs are the third largest direct foreign investors in India after the U.S. and Britain. They stay in touch with India by viewing regional language in their homes across the world. Subhash Chandra, founder of the most famous of these channels, India's Zee Television, offers the popular Indian cable channel in many parts of the world. Similar globalization occurs through the spiritual gurus, whose discourses are available to the Western and Indian global community through cable TV and the Internet. Similarly, Indi-pop music is the fusion of Indian popular music with Western rhythms that first emerged among Indian youth in England and then successfully traveled back to India.

Likewise, Westerners and NRIs have rediscovered classical Indian music, which went global a generation ago at the time of the Beatles, with Ravi Shankar and Ali Akbar Khan. Today is has become big business as some classical musicians devote a third of their time to overseas concerts. With globalization's economic and communications revolution, Indians abroad (and increasingly their Western friends and neighbors) feel closer to India than ever before with a growing appetite for things Indian. The explosion of interest in Indian cinema, known as Bollywood film, is prominent particularly in the U.S. and the U.K. The thousands who similarly come to India to study Yoga, Buddhism and other important under-appreciated aspects of Indian culture highlight the fact globalization is more of a two way street than most people realize.

To understand the NRI community in America, note that Indian immigration to the United States has been particularly related to the high-tech sectors. Until recently, about 25% of the graduates of India's four most prestigious technology institutes immigrated to the U.S. This has lead to a situation where more Indian technological talent is in the U.S. rather than India. *Business Week* reported that an extraordinarily large number of enterprises in Silicon

Valley—more than 30 percent—were started by Asians, with the overwhelming number being Indian. Some argue that the globalization of this migration was a way for talent to find opportunities. The argument goes that some Indians were already more ambitious and hardworking than their compatriots back home, but they often saw their efforts being obstructed or under valued in India.

Though even this is changing as NRIs, in some ways the ultimate globalizers, who alter India when they return with western goods, values and spouses, are returning to India to run for election there, starting on local levels, promising to apply the expertise they learned in the West. The prominence of NRIs in America and the West is growing rapidly as seen when Pulitzer prizes, Nobel prizes and other important awards are increasingly bestowed upon Indians, in India, the US and across the world.

While India clearly has access to important gateways of globalization, such as well-established channels of media and commerce, it also has its own unique, large NRI community, a large and potentially important gateway of globalization. The ultimate question is whether these gateways of globalization will bring real progress and modernity to India. While India has some characteristics of modernism one can not yet call India modern. Modernity is not just Westernization, with Japan being a modern country that has its on values at its core rather than Western values.

In classical social theory, modernity increases the credence given to status of education or other merit based achievements while it reduces the credence given to birth status. The psychological concept of intersubjectivity, the ability to empathize with and share in another's plight and fate, is at the heart of modernity and lacking it, many argue modernity in a society degenerates to crass commercialism. Likewise, if consumer items remain in the hands of the few rather than being disseminated among the many, such a society has the visible signs of modernism but not the ideological underpinnings. Some ask if the caste system, which came to India through previous invaders, the Aryans, will continue to keep the different classes divided or will modernism's system of meritocracy finally tear caste's walls down? Only time

will tell if India's gateways of globalization will spread ideology and not just consumption throughout the Indian subcontinent.

Movies as a Two Way Street

15 Movie posters try to grab the attention of consumers on the streets of the South Indian City of Madurai. Despite the growth of TV in India, the cinema continues to be the Indian great passion. Hindi films are exported to more than 100 countries across the world meaning that overseas bookings and video rights account for as much as 30% of a film's potential revenue. India has the largest cinema industry in the world, producing over 800 films a year, often with similar scripts/topics for the various languages while American film Industry produces about 400 major films a year. Five billion theater tickets are sold annually. Five rip-off versions of the American action film, "Rambo," were made in India. Film and TV viewing is not always passive as Indians adapt and adopt messages of personal improvement, gender equity and self-confidence. For women, this can conflict with the caricature of the good (read "subordinate") Indian woman, replacing her with a bolder and more self-directed female myth. The rarity of Indian men active in housework and child rearing continues to wane, as ideals of equitable sharing in the media will shift India away from its historical imbalance, which left such work to women.

Reflect & Write

❑ How does Wells overturn common perceptions by beginning with the argument that India, long seen as "poor and impoverished," is actually wealthy and powerful? Why might he begin the article with this rhetorical strategy?

❑ How does Wells expand our understanding of "East meets West" with his research and attention to detail? Map the develop of his argument in terms of points of analysis.

❑ What, according to Wells, is the difference in strategy between McDonald's and television as a globalizing force in India? How are images from television transforming Indian culture?

❑ What argument does the photograph make about "Movies as a Two Way Street"? Look at the dress of the figures in front of the movie poster; compare the women's clothing to the dress of the actress in the poster. Look at the man holding a gun in one of the posters and how the man on the street pauses, engaged by this image. What might be the writer's point in capturing this moment of encounter? What rhetorical choices did he make in choosing this composition and contrast of elements? How do such choices shape the argument of the photo?

❑ **Write:** Review the other photos and short articles available through the web essay at http://www.aliciapatterson.org/APF2101/Wells/Wells.html—how does each one offer greater insight into and support for the main argument Wells makes above? Write your analysis of one or two case studies available on the Website. What have you learned from this focused look at India?

COLLABORATIVE CHALLENGE

Together in a group of three or four, construct a map of globalizing influences across the major countries discussed in David Wells's article: India, China, Russia, and the U.S. Locate images to depict key moments in historical rise to power for each country. You might want to compose a Webpage for your map and link it to additional articles you find about the current dynamic shift in power from America to Asia. Present your work to the rest of the class.

Seeing Connections
Compare David Wells's argument about women in Indian film with Allison Woo's argument about Asian women in American film, from Chapter 6.

■ **Sapna Samant** *specializes in issues related to the representations of Asians in the mainstream media. As founding trustee of the Asia New Zealand Film Foundation trust, she plays a key role in organizing the Asia Film Festival Aotearoa and the AsiaNZ Short Film contest. A freelance radio producer, Samant also writes articles and film scripts. She published this article in the Summer 2005 issue of* Metro Magazine, *an Australian journal focused on film and media.*

Appropriating Bombay Cinema: Why the Western World Gets Bollywood So Wrong

Sapna Samant

I can't keep it inside of me any more! All this preaching by the Western media about what I should appreciate from my own popular culture. One *Bride and Prejudice* (Gurinder Chadha, 2004) comes along aimed at ignorant white audiences, and they lap it up because everything Indian is the flavour of the season.

Dahling Bollywood is so much fun! Love those songs and dances! Your weddings are so musical! India is so exotic! A few academic scholars apart, there was a time when film analysts, the Western media and the Western world in general rejected Bombay cinema as trite. Not because it actually was, but because they could not comprehend it. Over-the-top melodrama, songs, multiple changes of clothes and locations in one song, no kissing or sex, corny dialogue, cheesy moments . . . How could this be serious? The films were too long and too ridiculous for Westerners. No one cared to know about any talent from Bombay cinema. The vision of Bimal Roy, the sophistication of Vijay Anand, the sensitivity of Guru Dutt, the grandeur of Nasir Hussain, the deliberate illogic of Manmohan Desai and the genius of Kishore Kumar were alien to the West. No one drooled over the ethereal, timeless beauty of Madhubala or the serenity of Waheeda Rehman. These were—and are—strange names to Western ears. It is unlikely many Western film critics have seen *Mother India* (Mehboob Khan, 1957), the first Indian movie to be nominated for an Oscar (Best Foreign Language Film, 1958).

The main principle of capitalism is that anything that makes money is legitimate, and the drawing power of Bombay cinema now suddenly has everyone jumping on the bandwagon. Every Geeta, Gina and Gurinder wants to make snazzy musicals that the Weinstein brothers' machinery endorses. Now that India is a consuming giant, multi-national cosmetic companies have Indian actresses as brand ambassadors and the most whitelooking Indian actress is put on the cover of *Time Asia* with a photoshopped tan. No wonder Western analysts now have the time for serious critiques of all the kitsch of Bombay cinema. I am now lectured on my own film culture! This present-day love affair of the West with anything Indian, especially pop culture, is annoying because no attempt is made to understand where the pop culture comes from, or how it works for Indians. That is why they can't even make out that so-called Bollywood musicals like *Bride and Prejudice* are fake. The film did not even run for even two weeks in India. Diaspora Indians gave it the cold shoulder too. That is a unanimous rejection

from one billion, twenty million inhabitants of this earth. Know why? We can smell an imposter miles away. A few songs and dances and a wedding or two combined with inane situations, foreign locations and eye candy does not a Bollywood film make. Even involving the best technicians from the Bombay film industry, as *Bride and Prejudice* did with composer Anu Mallik and choreographer Farah Khan, will not make it authentic. Hardcore Bombay cinema has several ingredients that only those immersed in this form can replicate, understand and enjoy. It comes from the heart and the audience willingly accepts it as such. I want to share these ingredients after seeing audiences fooled by bogus wannabes.

A primary necessity: Bombay cinema is emotionally engaging and highly manipulative. Bombay cinema is at the very core of Indian popular culture. The form, content and aftereffects are in the Indian bloodstream. And it works in strange ways. You know it when you see audiences remove their footwear before entering the theatre to see the screen avatar of the Goddess Santoshi in *Jai Santoshi Maa* (Vijay Sharma, 1975); when they fling coins at the screen as Bhagwan Dada boogies to the songs in *Albela* (Deepak Sareen, 2001); when a nation stops to fast and pray for days as Amitabh Bachchan hovers between life and death after being injured while shooting *Coolie* (Manmohan Desai, 1983), and then goes to see 'that' shot when the film is released. (Which was frozen and captioned by the director.) Emotional engagement is when the entire theatre mouths word-for-word, pause-for-pause, and style-for-style the dialogue of all the characters in *Sholay* (Ramesh Sippy, 1975) over and over again. Emotional engagement is when you happily buy tickets for seats in the fourth row of the lower stalls and watch *Lagaan* (Ashutosh Gowariker, 2001) with your neck extended the entire time, while the rest of the audience in the house-full, cavernous theatre roars and claps as if at a real cricket match. You know you are being manipulated when, in spite of your cynicism, you feel a prick of tears as Kajol pines for Shahrukh Khan while getting dressed for her engagement with Salman Khan in *Kuch Kuch Hota Hai* (Karan Johar, 1998), when Jaya Bachchan tells her husband Amitabh that she wants her exiled son back in *Kabhi Khushi Kabhi Gham* (Karan Johar, 2001), or when a handcuffed Arvind Swamy rolls over the Indian flag, in slow motion, to stop it from burning in *Roja* (Mani Ratnam, 1992). I could go on and on and on. Is there one scene or a single moment in *Bride and Prejudice* that touches the soul like this?

5   A recent survey by Indian magazine *Outlook* showed that seventy-seven per cent of males in the all India sample had cried at least once when watching a Hindi film. (1)

I don't even know of any girl whose heart went aflutter over that block of wood who played Darcy in *Bride and Prejudice*. Not many Indians are aware of the book *Pride and Prejudice,* so it was not as if they knew what was going to happen. Yet no one fretted over the fate of the Bakshi girls or even cared whether they got married or suffered a spinster's existence. Forget replicating Jane Austen's delicious irony—even the banter between Lalita and Darcy is not sexually charged. (*Bride and Prejudice*'s star Aishwarya Rai, by the way, is notorious for her lack of screen chemistry with not only her co-stars but even her boyfriend.) I won't get into the bad script and bad acting, the stereotypes, or the fact that Jalandhar girls don't float around the beaches of Goa in bikini tops and sarongs. It feels like the Punjab of Southall, not the Punjab of Bombay cinema. How else could a random backpacker live in the same house as young, unmarried, Indian virgins? In a small town, too? Tsk tsk! Where does the modernity begin and the traditionalism end here? It is well-delineated in hardcore Hindi films, and the cause of many conflicts that don't get resolved between one garbs (it was actually a dandia raas) and another song sequence. (Both of which were poorly done, too.)

Which brings us to the second important ingredient of Bombay cinema: the music and song picturisation. Picturisation, a term unique to Bombay cinema, encapsulates the visual aspect of the mood and dynamics of a particular song. So song situations are not just spaces in which the romantic lead gets to indulge in activities that are otherwise not socially sanctioned. They punctuate the narrative, carry it forward, abbreviate it, take it into another dimension—and they are all picturised accordingly. It takes vision and talent to integrate and picturise songs, and yet make each one different from the other. The creation and use of these spaces has changed somewhat after economic liberalization and in a post-globalized India. Karan Johar and Farah Khan, the current gurus of the craft, understand this very well. But do we see it in *Bride and Prejudice*? If the film is set in today's India, then the song picturisation is obsolete and unimaginative. The wedding songs are pink and dull, the sad songs are blue and boring. 'No Life Without Wife' is neither funny nor ironic, and the romantic song is asexual—imagine, a Bollywood love song with no signs of foreplay! Then there is the legacy of the songs. Hindi film songs are played at weddings, festivals, clubs, discos, public celebrations and every possible occasion year after year and decades after the film fades away. Not one song from *Bride and Prejudice* has been replayed in public memory so far. Not one song—either in Hindi or in English.

The third necessary ingredient to make Bombay cinema is repeat value. Hardcore Bombay cinema has repeat value. Either a film works in its entirety, or there is one aspect that pulls in the crowds again and again. Repeat value is when your paisa is vasool (full return for your money), when after buying an expensive ticket and seeing a film you book another ticket for another session of the same film. Farah Khan's *Main Hoon Naa,* the biggest hit of 2004, had the perfect mixture of corn, cheese and masala: great music, superb picturisation, the very sexy Sushmita Sen in sarees and Shahrukh Khan espousing Indo-Pak peace. It was emotionally engaging, highly manipulative and very enjoyable, with immense repeat value. Repeat value is why a backward-looking film like *Dilwale Dulhania Le Jayenge* (Aditya

Chopra, 1995) completes an uninterrupted run of 500 weeks at the Maratha Mandir theatre in Bombay. It's why the re-minted, re-released *Mughal-e-Azam* (K. Asif, 1960) makes a profit twenty-five years after the public first saw it. Repeat value is when you watch Amitabh Bachchan in *Don* (Chandra Barot, 1978), *AmarAkbarAnthony* (Manmohan Desai, 1977), *Trishul* (Mash Chopra 1978) and *Deewar* (Milan Luthria, 2004). Repeat value is when the public goes to Govinda's films just to be able to copy his dhinchak dance moves. Does *Bride and Prejudice* make anyone feel like doing that? Where are the goosebumps, the tingling and the dramatic dialogue? It is as bland as the most detached, stiff-upper-lip Westerner could wish it.

Bombay cinema is more than a hundred years old. The Lumiere brothers' cameraman brought the first film to Bombay. When the British banned public meetings and marches, the patriotic songs came via Bombay cinema. Nehru's socialist vision, Mahatma Gandhi's philosophies, the BJP's form of nationalism and anti-Pakistan sentiments, the slums, the old middle class, the new middle class, the new materialism, non-resident Indians and much more are shown in Bombay cinema. There was even an attempt to tackle the Emergency imposed by Indira Gandhi. Brad Pitt, Tom Cruise or Gael Garcia Bernal cannot dance like Shahid Kapur and Hrithik Roshan. Neither can they cause hysteria like Amitabh Bachchan and Shahrukh Khan. Not a single actress anywhere in the world can match Madhuri Dixit's bosom-heaving. Bombay cinema has many failings. It is regressive, patriarchal, stereotypical and treats women like sex objects. It is the behemoth that has chewed up regional cinema and suppresses any new non-Bollywood styles. But Bombay cinema is my cinema. I know what it is all about, where it comes from, and hopefully where it is heading. I don't like those Johnny-come-latelys,

ignorant Westerners and media people advising me about it. Hence this rant. Don't be fooled by 'Bollywood' films made by Gurinder Chadha-types and marketed by Miramax know-it-alls. Don't waste reams over someone who has borrowed indiscriminately from a whole peoples' psyche without bothering to get to the root of it. Thank you very much.

Reflect & Write

❏ According to Samant, how is an assessment of the rhetorical situation for the film *Bride and Prejudice* important for understanding its composition and how it factors into the Bollywood tradition?

❏ Consider Samant's voice in the essay. What type of persona does she create? Is it a consistent persona? Point to actual sentences or word choice to support your opinion. How does her voice either contribute to or undermine her persuasiveness?

❏ In this essay, Samant uses two terms to refer to the films she is discussing: Bollywood and Bombay Cinema. Does she use these terms in different ways? How? How does her decision to use these different terms underscore her argument? How would the essay have been different if she had simply used the popular term Bollywood to describe the films in question?

❏ Note how Samant introduces the term "picturisation." How does her use and definition of this concept serve as an ethos appeal? What relationship does she assume in relation to her audience by using this definition strategy?

❏ Samant ends with the line "Thank you very much." What is the effect of including this as the parting line for the article? Does this line fit in with the prevailing tone of the article? Again, use reference to specific lines or techniques to support your opinion.

❏ **Write:** Watch *Bride and Prejudice* and write your own review of the film for an American movie magazine.

■ *In this article,* L.A. Times *reporter* **Michael Jarvis** *interviews Stuart Levy, chief executive officer and chief compliance officer of Tokyopop, a company that specializes in manga creation. Levy's efforts in bringing manga to U.S. audiences is recognized as being responsible for shaping contemporary cross-cultural teen culture. This article originally appeared in the* L.A. Times *in October 2003.*

The Godzilla-Sized Appeal of Japan's Pop Culture

Michael Jarvis

When Stuart Levy started Tokyopop Inc. in 1997, he had a tough time convincing venture capitalists that Japanese comic books could be popular in America. But "comic books" doesn't adequately describe the mass appeal of full-length black-and-white graphic novels spanning every genre from hard-boiled action-adventure sages to sci-fi and fantasy. Today L.A.–based Tokyopop has a projected revenue of $35 million for 2003 and brings to the U.S. about 40 English-language *manga* titles a month in addition to producing spin-offs in formats such as *anime,* soundtracks and CD-Roms. Levy, 36, has a degree in economics from UCLA and a law degree from Georgetown University. He first visited Japan at 21 on a student program, returning for a year after law school to immerse himself in the language. After his Northridge apartment was destroyed in the 1994 earthquake, the self-described "digital guy" went back to Japan, read his first *manga* and promptly put his multimedia and legal chops to work unleashing Japan's graphic operatics on the U.S.

We went to Levy for some East-West synergy.

Why manga?

I didn't grow up reading comic books. I grew up a music and film fan. When I was living in Japan, a graphic designer handed me a *manga.* I read it and thought, "This is like a Hollywood film." This was in 1995. The whole [Japanese] video game thing was happening, but *manga* was very nichey and it wasn't on my radar. I thought, "Wow, the design style is so aesthetically arresting." It was just incredible pop culture that [finally] hit me.

Anime and manga had cult status here in the U.S. for years. Is there a crossover into mass popularity underway?

There was a buddy of ours in high school and everybody thought he was kind of freaky because he had this huge collection of laser discs of Japanese animation. Five or six years after that I'm getting into this with my job. He was like an "early, early, early adapter" guy. I didn't know

about cult status. I only saw it as something with potential. It's timing. These [Japanese] kids who are creators have been influenced by thousands of years of their own artistic upbringing as well as our Hollywood entertainment mentality. They've come up with some really great stuff. Whoever says the Japanese are not creative is [wrong].

How do anime and manga differ from American cartoons and comics?

It's a stylistic thing. You look at [Disney's animated feature] "Treasure Planet," and how it did not do well. DreamWorks came out with one that bombed too, "Sinbad: Legend of the Seven Seas." I just look at the ads and say, "Gawd, that's never going to do well." The design style is not poppy enough; it's a little too rendered. Kids today are into more of a simple, funky, pop-art style look. [Also], content in *manga* is just so broad. You do your taxes and the pamphlet that comes with it has a little *manga* explaining how you do it on the form prepared by the government. It's brilliant

5   Female characters in Japanese pop culture often have "little-girl" voices and clothing, yet frequently play heroic action roles.

The typical Japanese view on female attractiveness tends to be more on the side of "cute," whereas in America it's more on the side of voluptuous. The cutesy voice and cutesy little look they call *buriko*. It's a kind of a female personality. She acts a little ditzy, a little airheadish, kind of childish to make a guy think she's irresistible. Kind of like Marilyn Monroe.

How do anime voice-overs transfer to the U.S.?

The Japanese have a different perspective on silence, whether it's in music, in speech or even in a meeting. Silence can be just as important and can say as much as sound. There can be something really loud happening and then all of a sudden dead silence, but to an American that's weird. In [an anime film] we'll do what's called sweetening and add in different sound effects, different music and different lines to fill the silence for America.

Japan once emulated American culture, but that seems to be reversing.

I'm not a big history guy, but Japan has been a country that has gone from saying, "We don't want any outside influences, we're going to figure it out ourselves," to "We welcome outside influences," and then tweaking them into their own style. They've sort of gone back and forth on that for millennia. *Manga* was based on a combination of Japanese woodblock drawings plus the original Disney stuff. A lot of the older Japanese guys now talk about growing up and reading "Blondie" and those kinds of American comics. That's what's amazing about Japan. I really think that mentality is perfect for the digital generation because everything is about remixing—using existing tools and turning it into something aesthetically more pleasing than existed before.

Are you a manga devotee yourself?

I'm what the Japanese call a casual user. I dabble in everything. I love karaoke even though I can't sing.

Reflect & Write

❏ Look at the title of the article. Why do you think that Jarvis chose it? Was it a smart rhetorical choice? Why or why not?
❏ In his remarks, Levy draws a comparison at least twice to Disney's films and products. Why do you think he chose that example? As a reader, how does this comparison affect the persuasiveness of his argument?
❏ At the end, when Levy is asked if he's a manga devotee, he replies that he is a "casual user." Does this relatively conservative response influence his ethos in this piece? How would it have changed your assessment of his argument if he had admitted to being a true manga fan?
❏ **Write:** During the interview, Levy mentions that in Japan "[y]ou do your taxes and the pamphlet that comes with it has a little manga explaining how you do it on the form prepared by the government." Identify a task that could use explanation: for instance, enrolling online for courses; programming your DVD player; changing a tire; replacing a fuse. Look at some examples of manga and sketch out a manga to help explain how to accomplish this task. Share your drawing with the class.

Images of Media Globalization

FIGURE 15.8 Dark Yugi from the Yu-Gi-Oh series is a popular figure both for the television series and its trading cards.

FIGURE 15.9 The American craze over the Japanese import, Pokemon, has moved from television to toys, trading cards, and, shown here, video games.

Reflect & Write

❏ Both these images are from products targeted at a youth market. Analyze the visual elements of these products. How do they represent Japanese culture? How do they target American youth culture?
❏ How do these product sell themselves as fads or collectibles to their audience? Which elements of the picture feed directly into a culture of consumption in this way?
❏ **Write:** Compose a blog entry analyzing these images. Locate another visual rhetoric example of media globalization and post it on the blog. What trends do you see across the images?

■ *This selection is taken from the first chapter of* **Susan Jolliffe Napier's** *2001 book,* Anime from Akira to Princess Mononoke, *in which she explores the influence of Japanese anime film across cultures. Napier is the Mitsubishi Professor of Japanese Studies in the Department of Asian Studies at the University of Texas at Austin and specializes in Japanese literature; her interest in manga and anime was kindled after a student loaned her a copy of* Akira, *a popular 1980s manga. Her work,* Anime, *is in its 4th edition and has been published in both Japanese and Korean.*

Why Anime?

Susan Jolliffe Napier

There are many answers to the question that titles this chapter, as the rest of this introduction will demonstrate, but for now it is worth exploring the question itself. Japanese animation, or "amine," as it is now usually referred to in both Japan and the West, is a phenomenon or popular culture. This means that much (some would argue most) of its products are short-lived, rising and falling due to popular taste and the demands of the hungry market place. Can or even should anime be taken as seriously as the extraordinary range of high cultural artifacts, from woodblock prints to haiku, that Japanese culture is famous for? Can or should anime be seen as an "art," or should it only be analyzed as a sociological phenomenon, a key to understanding some of the current concerns abounding in present-day Japanese society?

These are legitimate questions. As John Treat, one of die major scholars in this area, notes in his ground-breaking introduction to *Contemporary Japan and Popular Culture:*

> To worry about the relation of the popular to high or official culture is to think about the perennial problem of value: perennial first because value is so exasperatingly mercurial. . . and second because its determination only deflects us from understanding how cultures high, low and in-between exist in discursive and material relations of exchange, negotiation and conflict with each other."

The "culture" to which anime belongs is at present a "popular" or "mass" culture in Japan, and in America it exists as a "sub" culture. However, as Treat's point about the mercuriality of value suggests, this situation may well change. Indeed, in Japan over the last decade, anime has been increasingly seen as an intellectually challenging art form, as the number of scholarly writings on the subject attest.

Furthermore, anime is a popular cultural form that clearly builds on previous high cultural traditions. Not only does the medium show influences from such Japanese traditional arts as Kabuki and the woodblock print (originally popular culture phenomena themselves), but it also makes use of worldwide artistic traditions of twentieth-century cinema and photography. Finally, the issues it explores, often in surprisingly complex ways, are ones familiar to readers of contemporary "high culture" literature (both inside and outside Japan) and viewers of contemporary art cinema. Anime texts entertain audiences around the world on the most basic level, but, equally importantly, they also move and provoke viewers on other levels as well, stimulating audiences to work through certain contemporary issues in ways that older art forms cannot. Moreover, precisely because of their popular reach they affect a wider variety of audiences in more ways than some less accessible types of high cultural exchange have been able to do. In other words, anime clearly appears to be a cultural phenomenon worthy of being taken seriously, both sociologically and aesthetically.

The following anecdote illustrates the often surprising ways anime affects its audience. In 1993 the Japanese critic Ueno Toshiya made a visit to the city of Sarajevo in war-torn Serbia. Wandering through the bombed-out city, he encountered an unexpected sight. In the middle of the old city was a crumbling wall with three panels. On the first was drawn a picture of Mao Zedong with Mickey Mouse ears; the second had a slogan for the Chiappas liberation group, the Zapatistas, emblazoned on it. But when he came to the third he was "at a loss for words. Incredibly, it was a large panel of a scene from Otomo Katsuhiro's *Akira.* Against the crumbling walls of the collapsing group of buildings, that 'mighty juvenile delinquent' Kaneda was saying 'So its begun!"

5 Ueno's story is a thought-provoking one. Unquestionably a masterpiece of technical animation, *Akira* is also a complex and challenging work of art

that provoked, bewildered, and occasionally inspired Western audiences when it first appeared outside Japan in 1990. However, it is not a work whose image might have been expected to appear on a wall in Sarajevo three years later as an icon of political resistance. At the time of *Akira's* first appearance in the West, animation was generally regarded as a minor art, something for children, or, perhaps, the occasional abstract, art-house film. Animation from Japan was marginalized even further. If audiences took note of it at all, it was to fondly remember watching *Speed Racer* after school on television, often without realizing its Japanese origin. The notion that a sophisticated Japanese animated film could cross international borders to become a political statement in a war-wracked European country would have been deemed bizarre at best and most likely absurd.

Things have changed. Whereas Japan has been known for such "high cultural" products as haiku, Zen, and the martial arts, the Japan of the 1990s began to develop a new export, animated films and videos—anime, a Japanese abbreviation of the English word "animation." Anime has now entered the American vocabulary as well, to the extent that it has appeared in recent years in a New *York Times* crossword puzzle.

Through anime Japan has become an increasingly significant player in the global cultural economy. Indeed, one scholar has gone so far as to label anime Japans "chief cultural export." As a 1997 cover story in the Japanese version of *Newsweek* makes clear, amine's reach extends around the world. Its products are popular in countries such as Korea and Taiwan, and also in Southeast Asia, where the children's animated series *Doraemon* became a big hit in Thailand in the early 1990s. Anime has also penetrated Europe, from the United Kingdom, where *Akira* was a top-selling video in the year after its release, to France, a country not known for its generosity to non-native cultural products, which in the mid 1990s carried over 30 hours a week of Japanese cartoons. In America as well, anime's popularity has grown enormously in the last decade. While even a few years ago it was known only to small subgroups among science fiction fans, anime is increasingly moving to at least a marginal niche in the mainstream. Whether it will ever be totally integrated into Western pop culture is still debatable. Indeed, a strong part of its appeal, as will be seen, is its difference from the Western mainstream.

Despite (or thanks to) this difference, anime clubs continue to attract growing numbers of members. Anime is shown on the Sci-Fi Channel, is available at such mainstream video venues as Blockbuster Video, and has a whole section devoted to it at Virgin Megastore in London. Anime's influence also extends beyond Japanese exports of actual tapes and videodiscs to include everything from the *Pokemon* toy give-away in 1999 at Kentucky Fried Chicken (a product tie-in with the extremely popular children's animated television show) to American museums where anime-inspired artists such as Yanobe Kenji have received favorable critical comment. Perhaps anime's "greatest" moment of transcultural recognition so far was a cover story about *Pokemon* in *Time* (November 22, 1999) that included a special section on anime in general.

What exactly is anime? To define anime simply as "Japanese cartoons" gives no sense of the depth and variety that make up the medium. Many definitions in the West attempt to explain anime by comparison to American animation, specifically Disney. Thus, the *Time* article attempts to answer the question by suggesting that in comparison to Disney "anime is all kinds of differents . . . Anime is kids' cartoons: *Pokemon* yes, and *Sailor Moon*. . . But it's also post-doomsday fantasies (*Akira*), schizo-psycho thrill machines (*Perfect Blue*), sex and samurai sagas—the works." If anything. *Time's* focus on the more extreme visions of anime actually minimizes the variety of the form, since anime also includes everything from animations of children's classics such as *Heidi* to romantic comedies such as *No Need for Tenchi.* Nor do the insistent comparisons with Disney permit the appreciation of the fact that anime does not deal only with what American viewers would regard as cartoon situations. Essentially anime works include everything that Western audiences are accustomed to seeing in live-action films—romance, comedy, tragedy, adventure, even psychological probing of a kind seldom attempted in recent mass-culture Western film or television.

10 It is not surprising, therefore, that animated works are a major part of the output of Japanese studios. Japanese television studios produce around 50 animated series a year and a comparable number of OVAs (Original Video Animation). Animated films are also far more important in Japan than in the West, amounting to "about half the tickets sold for movies." In fact, in 1997 *Princess Mononoke* broke all box office records to become, briefly, the highest-grossing film of all time In Japan, and it remains to this day the highest-grossing Japanese film ever.

Unlike cartoons in the West, anime in Japan is truly a mainstream pop cultural phenomenon. While rabidly fanatical fans of anime are called by the pejorative term *otaku* and looked down upon by conservative Japanese society, anime is simply accepted by virtually all the younger generation of Japanese as a cultural staple. Viewers range from little children watching *Pokemon* and other child-oriented fantasies, to college students or young adults enjoying the harder-edged science fiction of films like *Akira* and its many descendants, such as the bleak *Evangelion* series. Sometimes, as was the case with *Princess Mononoke* and other films by its director, Miyazaki Hayao, anime cuts across generational lines to be embraced by everyone from children to grandparents.

Images from anime and its related medium of manga (graphic novels) are omnipresent throughout Japan. Japan is a country that is traditionally more pictocentric than the cultures of the West, as is exemplified in its use of characters or ideograms, and anime and manga fit easily into a contemporary culture of the visual. They are used for education (one manga explains the Japanese economy), adornment (numerous shirts are emblazoned with popular manga and anime personages), and, of course, commercial enterprise. When the bit television and manga series *Sailor Moon* was at its most popular in the mid 1990s, pictures of its heroine Serena (*Usagi* in the Japanese version) peered down ubiquitously from billboards, while *Sailor Moon*-related paraphernalia—everything from "moon prism power wands" to bath towels—were snapped up by devoted fans of the series, largely young girls who were attracted by the characters' unique combination of cuteness and fantastic powers.

On a more ominous note, Japanese society has on occasion convulsed into what the sociologist Sharon Kinsella has described as a "moral panic" regarding the *otaku* culture, as it determined anime and manga to be socially unhealthy. The first time this occurred was in the 1980s when a young man accused of murdering four little girls was found to be an avid watcher of violent pornographic anime. More recently, the Japanese media, indulging in an orgy of blame-finding for the disastrous sarin gas subway attack in 1995 by the cult group Aum Shinrikyo, claimed that many of Aum's "best and brightest" followers were also avid fans of apocalyptic science fiction anime.

Reasons to study anime within its Japanese context should by now be obvious. For those interested in Japanese culture, it is a richly fascinating contemporary Japanese art form with a distinctive narrative and visual aesthetic that both harks back to traditional Japanese culture and moves forward to the cutting edge of art and media. Furthermore, anime, with its enormous breadth of subject material, is also a useful mirror on contemporary Japanese society, offering an array of insights into the significant issues, dreams, and nightmares of the day.

15   But anime is worth investigating for other reasons as well, perhaps the most important being the fact that it is also a genuinely global phenomenon, both as a commercial and a cultural force. Commercially, it is beginning to play a significant role in the transnational entertainment economy, not only as an important part of the Japanese export market, but also as a small but growing part of the non-Japanese commercial world, in terms of the increasing number of non-Japanese enterprises that deal with anime. These range from small video rental operations in big cities throughout the world to mail order houses up to and including such behemoths as Amazon.com (which has a special anime section) and most famously the mammoth Walt Disney Enterprises, which, in 1996, made a deal with Studio Ghibli, Japan's most well-known animation studio, to distribute its products in America and Canada. To be sure, its international commercial impact is still small compared to the global returns on a successful Hollywood blockbuster, but anime and its related products are increasingly drawing attention from marketers around die world.

Investigating anime as a cultural force is even more fascinating than inquiring into its commercial aspects, as it brings insight into the wider issue of the relationship between global and local cultures at the beginning of the twenty-first century. In a world where American domination of mass culture is often taken for granted and local culture is frequently seen as either at odds with or about to be subsumed into hegemonic globalism, anime stands out as a site of implicit cultural resistance. It is a unique artistic product, a local form of popular culture that shows clear indications or its Japanese roots but at the same time exerts an increasingly wide influence beyond its native shores.

Westerners raised on a culture of children's cartoons may find anime's global popularity surprising. Noted scholar Arjun Appadurai has suggested that "the most valuable feature of the concept of culture is the concept of difference," and certainly one salient aspect of anime, as *Time's* disquisition makes clear, is its insistent difference from dominant American popular culture. As Susan Pointon astutely comments, "[W]hat is perhaps most striking about anime, compared to other imported media that have been modified for the American market, is the lack of compromise in making these narratives palatable." This is not only true in regards to the many specifically Japanese references within the narratives, but also in regards 10 narrative style, pacing, imagery, and humor, not to mention emotions and psychology, which usually run a far wider gamut and often show greater depth than do American animated texts.

Anime is uncompromising in other ways as well. Its complex story lines challenge the viewer used to the predictability of Disney (or of much of Hollywood fare overall, for that matter) while its often dark tone and content may surprise audiences who like to think of "cartoons" as "childish" or "innocent." Indeed, what appears to be the single most-asked question about anime in America, "why is anime so full of sex and violence?," is an inquiry that, while betraying an ignorance or the complexity and variety of the art form, is still significant in that it reveals the bewilderment of Western audiences in confronting so-called adult themes within the animated medium.

Given its apparently uncompromising "otherness," why has anime succeeded so remarkably as a cross-cultural export? The short answer to this, called from many interviews with anime fans in America, Europe, and Canada, would have to do with the fact that the medium is both different in a way that is appealing to a Western audience satiated on the predictabilities of American popular culture and also remarkably approachable in its universal themes and images. The distinctive aspects of anime—ranging from narrative and characterization to genre and visual styles—are the elements that initially capture Western viewers' attention (and for some viewers these may be the main keys of attraction), but for others it is the engrossing stories that keep them coming back for more.

20   Up to this point, much of the academic discourse about anime has centered on its visual properties; understandably so, given that this is what most obviously differentiates animation from live-action cinema. It is also important to emphasize how the visual style of anime is significantly different from mass-audience American cartoons. As anime critics Trish Ledoux and Doug Ranney point out, even early 1970s Japanese animated television series "absolutely overflow with tracking shots, long-view establishing shots, fancy pans, unusual point-of-view 'camera angles' and extreme close-ups . . . [i]n contrast [to] most American-produced TV animation [which] tends to thrive in an action-obsessed middle-distance."

However, Japanese animation merits serious consideration as a narrative art form, and not simply for its arresting visual style. Anime is a medium in which distinctive visual elements combine with an array of generic, thematic, and philosophical structures to produce a unique aesthetic world. Often this world is more provocative, more tragic, and more highly sexualized (even in lighthearted romantic comedies) and contains far more complicated story lines than would be the case in equivalent American popular cultural offerings.

Much of this book will be an investigation into the themes, imagery, and ideas of some of the more memorable anime created over the last two decades, the period of the so-called anime boom, in an attempt to understand what makes anime the distinctive art form that it is. It should be stressed that not all of the texts to be considered are masterpieces (as with any entertainment medium, much that is produced is simply commercial fodder), but each work that I have chosen to discuss will ideally help to reveal some of the more fascinating and distinctive features of the anime world and ultimately illuminate the reasons behind its increasingly global appeal. This is an appeal that is strongly related to the increased importance of such contemporary issues as technological development, gender identity and relations between the sexes, and the problematic role of history in contemporary culture.

It may be that animation in general—and perhaps anime in particular—is the ideal artistic vehicle for expressing the hopes and nightmares of our uneasy contemporary world. Even more than live-action cinema, animation is a fusion of technology and art, both suggesting in its content and embodying in its form new interfaces between the two. It is perhaps no accident that two of anime's most popular genres, the cyberpunk and the so-called *mecha* genres, are within science fiction. Cyberpunk, well known from such Western science fiction classics as William Gibson's *Neuromancer* (a major influence on Japanese science fiction in general), is a genre focusing on dystopian futures in which humans struggle in an overpoweringly technological world where the difference between human and machine is increasingly amorphous. *Mecha* (a shortening of the English word "mechanical") privileges a favorite form from Japanese popular culture, the robot. Although in such classics as Tezuka Osamu's *Astro Boy* the robot is drawn in a positive light, more recent *mecha* often feature humanoid machines in a more ominous mode.

Both these genres are particularly appropriate ones for our increasingly high-tech world. As J. P Telotte says of Western science fiction film:

> In a near fixation on the artificial, technologized body—the robot, cyborg, android—the [science fiction] genre has tried to examine our ambivalent feelings about technology, our growing anxieties about our own nature in an increasingly technological environment and a kind of evolutionary fear that these artificial selves may presage our own disappearance or termination.

25 It is not only anime's references to technology that make it such an appropriate art form for the turn of the millennium. In its fascination with gender roles and gender transgression—seen in lighthearted terms in romantic comedies or *shoho* (young girl) narratives and more bleakly in occult pornography—anime encapsulates both the increasing fluidity of gender identity in contemporary popular culture and the tensions between the sexes that characterize a world in which women's roles are drastically transforming. Perhaps many of anime's most important characters are female because it is so often the female subject who most clearly emblematizes the dizzying changes occurring in modem society. Anime texts also explore (sometimes implicitly and sometimes explicitly) the meaning of history in contemporary society. These works usually involve a specifically Japanese context, such as the period of samurai warfare, but even the most specific texts, like *Grave of the Fireflies,* set in the waning days of World War II, implicitly suggest larger issues, including the political nature of historical memory. Most recently Miyazaki's historical epic *Princess Mononoke* problematized the nature of historical identity in relation to the modern world through its complex mixture of fantasy and fact.

Indeed, anime may be the perfect medium to capture what is perhaps the overriding issue of our day, the shifting nature of identity in a constantly changing society. With its rapid shifts or narrative pace and its constantly transforming imagery, the animated medium is superbly positioned to illustrate the atmosphere of change permeating not only Japanese society but also all industrialized or industrializing societies. Moving at rapid—sometimes breakneck—pace and predicated upon the instability of form, animation is both a symptom and a metaphor for a society obsessed with change and spectacle. In particular, animation's emphasis on metamorphosis can be seen as the ideal artistic vehicle for expressing the postmodern obsession with fluctuating identity. What animation scholar Paul Wells describes as "the primacy of the image and its ability to *metamorphose* into a completely different image," is a function of animation that has powerful resonances with contemporary society and culture.

Such a protean art form as anime is impossible to completely sum up in a single book and I shall not attempt to do so. Rather, I intend to look at a variety of anime in terms of three major expressive modes that I have termed the apocalyptic, the festival, and the elegiac. The next chapter will discuss how these modes fit into Japanese cultural norms, but they also exist in more autonomous terms. The apocalyptic is perhaps the most obvious mode, since a vision of worldwide destruction seems to be a staple across all cultures. It is certainly a major part of American film culture, ranging from the alien invasion cinema of the 1950s to the late 1990s spate of end-of-the-world films such as *Armageddon* or *End of Days*. As will be seen, however, the apocalyptic can range beyond material catastrophe (although this is well represented in an enormous number of Japanese anime), to include more intimate forms of apocalypse, such as spiritual or even pathological ones. The flexible visuals available to animation make apocalypse a natural subject for the medium, but it is in the interplay of character that amine offers its most distinctive visions of apocalypse.

Perhaps equally important in anime is the mode of the festival. "Festival" here is used as a direct translation of the Japanese term *"matsuri"* but the term "carnival" as theorized by Mikhail Bakhtin has very similar connotations. According to Bakhtin the "carnival sense of the world" is one predicated on *"the pathos of shifts and changes, of death and renewal."* This privileging of change is at the heart of animation, but animation's narrative structure and themes can also be carnivalesque. In Bakhtin's view carnival is a liminal period of topsyturvy that expresses "the *joyful relativity* of all structure and order, of all authority and all (hierarchical) position." For a brief moment norms are transgressed or actually inverted. The weak hold power, sexual and gender rules are broken or reversed, and a state of manic intensity replaces conventional restraint. Comedies are usually the most obvious sites of the carnival/festival mode, and it may be suggested that sex-reversal comedies such as *Some Like It Hot* in America or *Ranma 1/2* in Japan are particularly carnivalesque in their implicitly transgressive antics. Again, the visual flexibility of animation, with its intense palette of colors and ability to transform figures, shapes, and even space itself, also makes the medium peculiarly suited to the extreme and sometimes grotesque mode of the festival.

The elegiac mode, with its implications of loss, grief, and absence, may at first seem a less obvious mode to Western viewers, who are used to emotions being painted with broad brush in animation. Even in live-action films the elegiac may not be so wide a category in the West, although movies like *The Way We Were,* with its mourning for a more innocent romantic time, or even *Blade Runner,* with its privileging of genuine emotional response in reaction to growing dehumanization, might be considered candidates. In Japan, the elegiac—in terms of a lyrical sense or mourning often connected with an acute consciousness of a waning traditional culture—is an important element in both anime and live-action cinema. Although it is important to acknowledge the immense range of anime—its fascinating variety of genres, its mixture of traditional and modern elements, and its disparate assemblage of subjectivities—it is also rewarding to see how the modes of apocalypse, festival, and elegy continually appear, reworking and recombining themselves across the broad tapestry of contemporary animation.

30   To return once more to the question asked at the beginning of this chapter, "Why anime?," there now should be enough evidence to show me value in studying this complex and fascinating medium. As a form of popular culture, anime is important for its growing global popularity but it is also a cultural form whose themes and modes reach across arbitrary aesthetic boundaries to strike significant artistic and psychological chords. Furthermore, the three modes used to examine anime are ones that go beyond any distinction between "high" and "low" culture or beyond any nation-specific site to illuminate in a timely fashion some of the major issues of global society at the turn of the millennium.

Reflect & Write

❑ Consider the anecdote from Serbia that Napier shares in her fourth paragraph. What point is she making with this example? How does this example strategically contribute to her argument?

❑ Where does Napier put her definition of anime? Is this an effective choice? Why or why not? What assumptions does she seem to make about her audience based on where she places this definition?

❑ Throughout the first few pages of this selection, Napier is implicitly arguing for the relevance of manga as both a cultural form and as an object worthy of academic study. How could she have made this point more effectively?

❑ How does Napier transition from arguing that studying manga is important because it is a vital part of Japanese culture to arguing that we should study it as an example of global culture? Is this an effective transition?

❑ **Write:** Considering Napier's arguments, write a reflection or blog post about the way in which you see Japanese anime or manga influencing American popular culture. Be sure to consider whether you feel it is as powerful a cross-cultural force as she contends. Some examples that you might reflect on include Sailor Moon, Akira, Pokeman, or Yu-Gi-Oh.

COLLABORATIVE CHALLENGE

Working with several peers from class, locate images of cross-cultural influence in your own community. Compose a blog with your group's stance about the way traditional values are transformed—cosmetically or deeply—through exposure to other cultures, images, and practices. Include photos, video clips, posters, screen shots, and other evidence to document your group's position.

PERSPECTIVES ON THE ISSUE

1. This chapter provides many examples of what is called "media globalization," namely the way in which visual media such as film and video games serve as a primary site of globalization. What other media examples can you think of that function in a similar manner? Conversely, what other examples of cross-cultural influence can you think of that might not rely principally on visual media? How do these factor into your overall understanding of globalization?

2. Compare Fulla, featured at the beginning of the chapter, to Mattel's nearest equivalent, Moroccan Barbie (http://www.barbiecollector.com/showcase/product.aspx?id=150469&t=modern&y=t150095 &sort=name). Why do you think one doll was more popular than the other? How might you evaluate this success in rhetorical terms—considering issues of ethos, *kairos,* and the rhetorical situation?

3. In the title of her article, Samant uses the term "Appropriating"—referring to the concept of "appropriation" which indicates how one culture takes over and reshapes elements of another culture to suit its own needs. The term itself is more negative than one such as "adoption." Choose an example such as yoga, martial arts, or zen gardens, and write an opinion entitled either "The Adoption of X in Western Culture" or the "The Appropriation of X by Western Culture." If you argue for appropriation, be sure to follow Samant's lead in arguing the difference between the way the practice is conceived in its original culture and the way it has been transformed as it moved across the globe.

FROM READING TO RESEARCH

1. Watch *Bride and Prejudice* and another film that Samant mentions in her article. Now, drawing on her article and at least three reviews from the films (which you can find through sites such as http://www.brns.com/bollywood/pages1/bollyrevs.html and http://www.planetbollywood.com/ index.php), write a short source-based argument in which you argue a position about Bollywood film and cross-cultural rhetoric or globalization.

2. Read the article entitled "What Is This Thing Called Hello Kitty?" found at http://www.popcultmag.com/ criticalmass/books/kitty/hellokitty1.html. Now develop a PowerPoint presentation in which you explain to your audience how Hello Kitty reflects a global marketplace and the extent to which she was adapted for her different audiences. Frame this talk in terms of an understanding of globalization, and be sure to use images, quotations from the article, and material from other sources that you find through an Internet search.

OUTSOURCING AND GLOBAL COMMUNITIES

From McDonald's in Bombay to crime in America, one consequence of globalization has been the cross-fertilization of cultural values, practices, and corporate structures across borders. But such consequences have not gone unexamined by social critics and economists. As the cartoon in Figure 15.10. indicates, the complex issue of globalization becomes even more loaded when we consider how it impacts employment practices and local economies across the globe.

If we all really are living in the new Global Village, how do we feel about competing with our international neighbors for jobs? Is outsourcing completely negative both for the American economy and for the countries practicing this manifestation of globalization? The texts in this chapter explore the complex nature of the global economy and the delicate balance between fostering community and outsourcing employment across national borders.

FIGURE 15.10 Igor Aleshin's cartoon uses nationalist symbols for its commentary on software outsourcing.

We'll be looking at texts from editorial cartoons to economic analysis articles to get a sense of different arguments on the value and consequences of living in a global economy. From the effects on local communities to questions of outsourcing workers, these varied texts each provide insight into how new global networks are transforming how people think, live, and work.

In the political cartoon shown in Figure 15.10, for instance, two young boys wearing hats with American and Chinese flags are shown to be playing instruments to lure out a snake. But note how the snake is drawn to look like an Indian person. Does this visual argument suggest that the current superpowers are in charge of India's population? Are they literally making Indian workers move the way they wish? Or are they working with India through playing their song? Many issues involved in the debate over outsourcing are shown in this cartoon.

FIGURE 15.11 This cartoon offers a cynical perspective on the issue of American outsourcing.

Similarly, the controversy over what might happen to American workers finds visual representation in the argument in Figure 15.1. Here a white middle-class father pauses in his reading of the evening paper to tell his child, "No, you may NOT outsource your homework to India." Notice the child's angry expression, denoted by the black mark and crossed arms. Notice, too, how the father seems in possession of great knowledge as suggested by the stack of books and the newspaper. How does the cartoon then make the argument that our children and our country will become less educated, skilled, and self-reliant if we outsource more and more tasks to other countries?

These editorial cartoons are only two of the hundreds that speak to us today about the complex issue of outsourcing as a practice of globalization. You might consider how the argument made here is also made in written letters to the editor, articles in news magazines, and scholarly treatments of our highly interconnected economy. As you prepare to participate in this world, what contribution will you make?

Reflect & Write

❑ Comparing the images above, can you synthesize the arguments surrounding outsourcing? What are they key issues and problems, as suggested by these visual arguments? Who are the key players in this global situation? Answer by citing concrete visual detail from these images.

❑ Visit Daryl Cagle's Professional Cartoonists Index website at http://www.cagle.com/ and locate additional cartoons on this topic. How does audience and author shape the argument made in the cartoon?

❑ **Write:** Story board your own initial perspective about outsourcing and global communities. After completing the readings in this chapter, you can return to this story board and compose a comparative analysis about what how your thinking has changed.

■ **Brian Behlendorf** *is one of the most prominent figures in the international open-source software movement. He is perhaps most well-known for his role in developing the Apache Web server, the most popular Web server software available on the Internet. He currently serves at the chief technology officer at a company he co-founded to advance the development of open-source software. He published this article in the July 8, 2003, edition of* Salon.

How Outsourcing Will Save the World: The Growth of White-Collar Jobs in Developing Nations Is Essential to Global Peace and Prosperity

Brian Behlendorf

One of the biggest challenges facing the globe is the gap that exists in the wealth and standards of living enjoyed by the world's nations. Foreign trade and communication are the best tools for addressing this, when combined with trade agreements that limit exploitation by setting minimum wages, work environment standards, environmental standards, and so on. Foreign trade is not a replacement for foreign aid, of course, but foreign aid to a country that doesn't also engage in significant amounts of foreign trade is more likely to end up in the pockets of dictators and cronies.

There is no better form of trade a developing nation can engage in than to sell services provided by an educated population. Compare it to anything else a developing nation can sell—natural resources like oil or minerals or agribusiness, hard labor in manufacturing, for instance—and you'd probably find that white-collar jobs would be the most sustainable and most eco-friendly of any of them.

Those concerned about solving the world's problems should be falling over themselves to encourage developing nations to build a white-collar workforce, and to open that workforce to the world. Nations like India and China understood the importance of this generations ago and invested heavily in educational institutions rivaling the best of those in Europe and North America. Over the last generation the white-collar workforce has made itself more portable, more communications-oriented, more automated, and all these factors mean that where you are geographically is even less important in performing your job.

What still matters in the white-collar world are relationships between people. Often relationship building requires face-to-face communication, face-to-face collaboration, and shared experiences and challenges. That's why the outsourcing of white-collar work to remote locations isn't an all-or-nothing decision. Software engineering will not disappear from the developed-nation markets the same way steel production did, for example.

5   India in particular is facing its own talent crunch—Indian Institute of Technology and other top technical schools crank out a huge number of engineers, for example, more than the U.S. universities, but right now even they are being swamped with demand. Salaries are getting more competitive and growing even faster than U.S. engineers' salaries grew during the boom. The best and brightest can command salaries not far from the same salary they'd get today in the U.S. At the same time, tech jobs are also one of the few ways in which those born outside the middle or upper classes can elevate their own lot in life. The amount of good this is doing within India cannot be underestimated, and we should hope this pattern can be repeated in other nations. What could possibly be more positive than a child deciding that a technical education is the key to his or her future?

Engineers in the developed world should be arguing not for protectionism but for trade agreements that seek to establish rules that result in a real rise in living standards. This will ensure that outsourcing is a positive force in the developing nation's economy and not an exploitative one.

Interestingly, middle-class white-collar workers often become the ones most convinced of the importance of traditional liberal values of freedom of speech, freedom from tyranny, and transparency within and access to government, and they tend to care most about global issues such as the environment. Strong middle-class white-collar economies create stable, liberal societies.

There is no doubt that this kind of change exacts a toll on people who are often least able to adjust. It's a shame we elected a government in the U.S. whose economic policies leave little room for "bleeding-heart, big-government" programs like job retraining or technical public works projects. Nations do have a role to play in assisting their citizens through painful periods of readjustment, in addition to playing a strong role in setting work standards in trade agreements. Perhaps that's the kind of change those hit hard by these changes should seek.

Seeing Connections
To refresh your understanding of political cartoons as arguments, see Chapter 1. You can also work through the thesis writing activity in Chapter 1 to help you sharpen the point of your cartoon.

Reflect & Write

❑ How does the title of this article provide a clear indication of the writer's stance? Where do you find echoes of that title in the article itself?

❑ Look at how style helps shape the argument. What do you make of passages such as "be falling over themselves" and "it's a shame"—how does this kind of writing suggest the audience of the piece?

❑ The article paints a vivid picture of our global word today. What words help construct a visual representation of Brian Behlendorf's view of outsourcing?

❑ Assess the writer's elaboration of one central point, that "What still matters in the white-collar world are relationships between people." In what ways does the writer develop this point? Are there any logical fallacies in the rest of his argument?

❑ **Write:** Write a response to this piece, quoting lines to show your analysis of the argument. What would be your take on the claim that outsourcing can "save the world" and "is essential to global peace and prosperity"?

COLLABORATIVE CHALLENGE

As a group, create your own series of political cartoons to reflect your new perspective on globalization. You might base your cartoons on the reading you have done in this chapter so far, or draw the cartoon as a visual argument in response to the ones you have examined here. Use color, composition, arrangement, and carefully selected words in creating your cartoon. Share your work with the rest of the class.

Published as part of the "In the News Column" of Software IEEE *20.3 (May–June 2003), this article by* **Laurianne McLaughlin** *sets up the stakes that will be debated in the following pieces by Thomas Friedman, Naomi Klein, and others.*

An Eye on India: Outsourcing Debate Continues

Laurianne McLaughlin

"Anything you can do I can do better, and cheaper."

In this economy, that's a pitch that businesses don't ignore. Indian software-application-developer firms have learned.

US companies increasingly began outsourcing software development work to countries such as India, which touts low personnel costs and plentiful technical expertise, during the dot-com shakeout. Today, the trend shows no sign of stopping. It has changed the landscape for US software professionals, reshaping how companies plan projects and choose employees.

US software developers won't be going the way of the dinosaurs, analysts say. But they will need to cleverly manage their careers and thoroughly understand the new environment. At the same time, businesses are learning more about offshore outsourcing's challenges. And the debate about its merits grows.

Behind the Numbers

5 Just how big a trend is afoot? Forrester Research reports that 27,121 computer and mathematical jobs moved off US shores in 2000. The company predicts that 108,991 of these jobs will leave the US by 2005, rising to 276,954 by 2010 and 472,632 by 2015. That's US$6,549,539,142 in computer-job-related wages moving outside the country by 2005, Forrester predicts.

"For people in the United States who do heads-down, baseline development, the demand is only going down over the next 10 years," says John McCarthy, Forrester's group director for research. "The skills in hot demand in the future are project management and program management."

Industry analysts estimate that hiring programmers outside the US in locales such as India saves about 30 percent in salary costs. That's one reason India's outsourcing leaders, Infosys Technologies and Wipro, based in Bangalore, and Tata Consultancy Services in Bombay, are flourishing. From April to December 2002, software and services exports from India generated revenues of $6.9 billion, up from $5.6 billion in the corresponding 2001 period, according to Indian trade group Nasscom (National Association of Software and Service Companies).

But does this mean most developer jobs are rapidly leaving the US? It's not that simple, claims Stephen Hendrick, group vice president for application development at market research firm International Data Corporation.

IDC estimates that 2.335 million people in the US had software developer jobs in 2000, and that figure dropped slightly to 2.317 million in 2001 before rising back up to 2.429 million in 2002. The firm projects 2.574 million such jobs in 2003.

10 In North America in 2002, one in every 133 people was a software developer, Hendrick says. "We're reaching a point of saturation. That's one reason (developer job) growth has capped in the United States."

"I'm not entirely convinced there will be a huge loss of jobs. My experience is there's still a lot of complexity in outsourcing," he adds.

The Quality Question

No doubt, any outsourcing project can backfire if a business fails to thoroughly examine the pros and cons. What's the biggest pro? Quality—a concern for many industries considering offshore outsourcing—has become a selling point for the Indian software houses, says Jeffrey Tarter, a veteran software industry analyst and editor of the *Softletter* newsletter.

"What offshore forces a company to do is write a very detailed spec for a product," Tarter says. "That form of discipline is incredibly valuable. It forces people to consider every screen, the flow of the product, and which features are necessary. This turns out to be why the Indian firms have been successful."

Indeed, Forrester's clients report higher satisfaction with the quality and the timeliness of work from offshore firms than with US development teams. As for cultural barriers, the thorny problems relate to the US client's ability to manage the project, specify the work, and develop metrics that hold the software developers accountable, Forrester's McCarthy says.

15 Tarter believes in-house developer groups are used to working in an environment where it's acceptable to change features or delay solving bugs until quite late—a classic development problem. Outsourcers tend to make fewer false steps.

The detailed spec is the key to success. US teams can turn work around fast, given the same project framework, Tarter adds.

Recognizing a Bad Fit

While quality and timeliness won't be huge concerns, plenty of potential problems remain. Software outsourcing works most simply for routine maintenance or upgrade work, and it creates the biggest savings on large projects, analysts claim. Owing to the required management time and costs, outsourcing proves impractical for many small projects.

A company with a fast-moving rival might also find outsourcing an unwise choice. "If you have a product that really has to evolve in response to competitive situations, the complete-spec approach may be overly rigid," Tarter says.

Even with internal corporate applications, a business must carefully consider whether requirements might change, say as a department changes its mission or as new technology standards arrive.

20 "If you keep rewriting the spec, you're going to increase costs and create delays," Tarter says.

The training necessary to work with particular technologies and with clients can also knock outsourcing out of the running, says Jim Welch, CEO of MetroWerks, a software development tools and services firm. This Austin, Texas-based Motorola subsidiary with 600 employees worldwide has a team of about 30 developers in India. This lets the company find quality talent, even when the US hiring situation is competitive, and utilize people working in multiple time zones, Welch says. But outsourcing makes sense for his firm only in limited cases, he adds.

"Our product is very technical in nature," Welch says. "We need our developer centers to become experts in our technology. Sometimes when you outsource, you may not get the same people back next time."

Product design and strategy jobs, meanwhile, won't be leaving the US anytime soon, predicts Amy Wohl, president of consulting firm Wohl Associates, which advises technology companies on issues including outsourcing.

"Designing interfaces is a cultural issue," Wohl says. "Doing it offshore is tough."

25 In the long run, outsourcing of customer support positions might prove more important to US companies, Wohl believes. English speakers in locales from India to Ireland let US companies offer 24/7 support at manageable costs, she says. "Think about the number of people coding, compared to the number of people who support a product over its lifetime."

Cheaper Software?

As for consumer reaction to outsourcing's promises, some might hope that increased efficiency could lead to lower software prices, but that looks unlikely. It's more a matter of companies maximizing profit margins and keeping up with competitors.

Remember, research and development costs run only about 15 to 20 percent of a software product's cost, Tarter says, while marketing and sales costs can gobble upwards of 50 percent for enterprise software.

However, the outsourcing trend could increase the variety of software titles available. A company will more likely put out a new version of a not-so-hot seller if the development cost is low.

For example, consider what has happened to the market for Macintosh versions of Windows applications in the past few years, owing partly to one company—Software MacKiev. It made a business out of low-cost Mac ports of Windows products.

30 With a US headquarters in Cupertino, California, the company employs highly trained programmers in Kiev, Ukraine. "They changed the economics of producing Mac versions dramatically," Tarter says. "It didn't take many sales to make up the development cost. Suddenly there were many more ports on the market."

MacKiev has become the industry leader among development houses doing Mac ports, with big-name clients such as IBM and Electronic Arts.

Will an Indian company similarly help shake up a particular software market? Perhaps. Today's software giants are certainly spending time and money to encourage Indian programmers to use their respective technologies.

Microsoft CEO Bill Gates visited Bangalore in November 2002 to pledge $400 million in investment in the next three years, supporting IT education and a "Partnering with India" program. It's designed to increase developer skills for Microsoft's .NET Web services architecture and to encourage Indian companies to develop and sell .NET products and services. Sun Microsystems similarly promotes its rival SunONE Web services architecture in India.

Job Hunters Feel a Pinch

In the US, software professionals have become keenly aware of this attention on India.

35   "It's a soft market" for job hunters, says Joe Kumiszcza, executive director of MESDA, Maine's Software & Information Technology Industry Association. "The trend has been a down market for about 18 months here."

Although hiring budgets seem to be loosening now, group members do notice offshore outsourcing's effects, he says. In response, he encourages group members to network more extensively and to expand their skill sets—for example, by taking open source technology classes and learning more about their companies' business and marketing sides.

"While the core coding can happen offshore, America still has skill sets around marketing and project management that aren't duplicated overseas," Kumiszcza says. "Those are our ultimate strengths. Those people who are well rounded in that regard are well protected at times like this."

In the Austin area, long a hot spot for developers, the total number of developer jobs has fallen since 2000, but the future trend looks encouraging. The number of area software companies rose between 2000 and 2002, according to the Texas Workforce Commission.

Companies are trying to leverage the talents of Austin's software veterans, says Carolyn Stark, the executive director of the Austin Technology Council, an industry association for software companies and developers. But to win a developer job now, you must bring more to an interview than technology prowess, Stark cautions. "You can't afford these days to have employees who don't understand the business as a whole," she says.

40   You should be able to articulate the business hurdles you have helped previous employers leap, says Michael Cation, chairman of the Austin Technology Council Board of Directors and CEO of Austin-based Novus, a security technology firm.

"In my own company, we're trying to hire developers that understand they're trying to solve business problems," Cation says. "If you can distinguish yourself that way, there's a ton of opportunities."

"Offshore, you can't have the tight engagement with a customer necessary to solve a problem," he adds.

Outsourced and offshore teams also create a management opportunity for US technology veterans, claims MetroWerks' Welch. "We're looking for people with solid management skills who can manage geographically dispersed teams," he says.

Politics Checks In

Of course, as in any discussion involving US jobs, politics can play a part, and sometimes cool down a trend.

45   For example, after a company hired by New Jersey for a state contract utilized call center employees in Bombay, state senator Shirley Turner introduced a bill in late 2002 to keep such contracts fulfilled by US employees if possible.

Lawmakers in several other states have called for similar measures. In response, the Indian trade group Nasscom has hired a New York public relations firm to promote offshore outsourcing and to lobby against such legislation.

Laid-off technology workers don't share Nasscom's viewpoint on offshore outsourcing. Grassroots lobbying efforts have popped up online. One group, NYSLA (New York Software Industry Association), launched a "Buy NY" campaign to encourage companies to utilize technology workers, products, and services in the New York area before looking overseas. (For details, see www.nysia.org/buyny.)

The political impact is hard to predict. But besides the cost efficiencies of outsourcing, there's one related upside for the US economy, IDC's Hendrick says. The outsourcing market's growth has made India one of the few bright spots for US technology sales—including a PC sales opportunity that IDC estimates will grow to $4.2 billion by 2006.

Where does this leave US software workers today? Hopefully, not chained to their desks, says Jeff Tarter. "A lot of the direct interfacing with clients, product design, upgrade design jobs, will stay here," he predicts. "But the fact is, some programmers hate talking to customers. And the ones that are working in isolation are probably the first ones to get replaced."

Reflect & Write

❏ How does the writer engage the reader's attention with a funny saying from childhood? How does this set the tone and mood?

❏ Assess the writer's use of data and statistics in this piece. How convincing are the use of these figures?

❏ What is the benefit of focusing the outsourcing debate on one case study, such as software, as this writer has done?

❏ Determine the writer's ultimate stance on the issue. Do you agree with it?

❏ **Write:** Compose a reverse outline of this article to map out its main points. Now draft a counterpoint or a supporting argument. Share your work with the class.

Thomas L. Friedman *is a foreign affairs columnist for* The New York Times, *where this article was published on April 3, 2005. He has won three Pulitzer Prizes, the most recent one for Commentary in 2002. He has authored several books, including* From Beirut to Jerusalem *(winner of the 1989 National Book Award for non-fiction),* The Lexus and the Olive Tree *(the winner of the 2000 Overseas Press Club award for best nonfiction book on foreign policy), and* The World Is Flat *(2005), his exploration of the international effects of globalization.*

It's a Flat World, After All

Thomas L. Friedman

In 1492 Christopher Columbus set sail for India, going west. He had the Nina, the Pinta and the Santa Maria. He never did find India, but he called the people he met "Indians" and came home and reported to his king and queen: "The world is round." I set off for India 512 years later. I knew just which direction I was going. I went east. I had Lufthansa business class, and I came home and reported only to my wife and only in a whisper: "The world is flat."

And therein lies a tale of technology and geoeconomics that is fundamentally reshaping our lives—much, much more quickly than many people realize. It all happened while we were sleeping, or rather while we were focused on 9/11, the dot-com bust and Enron—which even prompted some to wonder whether globalization was over. Actually, just the opposite was true, which is why it's time to wake up and prepare ourselves for this flat world, because others already are, and there is no time to waste.

I wish I could say I saw it all coming. Alas, I encountered the flattening of the world quite by accident. It was in late February of last year, and I was visiting the Indian high-tech capital, Bangalore, working on a documentary for the Discovery Times channel about outsourcing. In short order, I interviewed Indian entrepreneurs who wanted to prepare my taxes from Bangalore, read my X-rays from Bangalore, trace my lost luggage from Bangalore and write my new software from Bangalore. The longer I was there, the more upset I became—upset at the realization that while I had been off covering the 9/11 wars, globalization had entered a whole new phase, and I had missed it. I guess the eureka moment came on a visit to the campus of Infosys Technologies, one of the crown jewels of the Indian outsourcing and software industry.

Nandan Nilekani, the Infosys C.E.O., was showing me his global video-conference room, pointing with pride to a wall-size flat-screen TV, which he said was the biggest in Asia. Infosys, he explained, could hold a virtual meeting of the key players from its entire global supply chain for any project at any time on that supersize screen. So its American designers could be on the screen speaking with their Indian software writers and their Asian manufacturers all at once. That's what globalization is all about today, Nilekani said. Above the screen there were eight clocks that pretty well summed up the Infosys workday: 24/7/365. The clocks were labeled U.S. West, U.S. East, G.M.T., India, Singapore, Hong Kong, Japan, Australia.

"Outsourcing is just one dimension of a much more fundamental thing happening today in the world," Nilekani explained. "What happened over the last years is that there was a massive investment in technology, especially in the bubble era, when hundreds of millions of dollars were invested in putting broadband connectivity around the world, undersea cables, all those things." At the same time, he added, computers became cheaper and dispersed all over the world, and there was an explosion of e-mail software, search engines like Google and proprietary software that can chop up any piece of work and send one part to Boston, one part to Bangalore and one part to Beijing, making it easy

for anyone to do remote development. When all of these things suddenly came together around 2000, Nilekani said, they "created a platform where intellectual work, intellectual capital, could be delivered from anywhere. It could be disaggregated, delivered, distributed, produced and put back together again—and this gave a whole new degree of freedom to the way we do work, especially work of an intellectual nature. And what you are seeing in Bangalore today is really the culmination of all these things coming together."

5   At one point, summing up the implications of all this, Nilekani uttered a phrase that rang in my ear. He said to me, "Tom, the playing field is being leveled." He meant that countries like India were now able to compete equally for global knowledge work as never before—and that America had better get ready for this. As I left the Infosys campus that evening and bounced along the potholed road back to Bangalore, I kept chewing on that phrase: "The playing field is being leveled."

"What Nandan is saying," I thought, "is that the playing field is being flattened. Flattened? Flattened? My God, he's telling me the world is flat!"

Here I was in Bangalore—more than 500 years after Columbus sailed over the horizon, looking for a shorter route to India using the rudimentary navigational technologies of his day, and returned safely to

prove definitively that the world was round—and one of India's smartest engineers, trained at his country's top technical institute and backed by the most modern technologies of his day, was telling me that the world was flat, as flat as that screen on which he can host a meeting of his whole global supply chain. Even more interesting, he was citing this development as a new milestone in human progress and a great opportunity for India and the world—the fact that we had made our world flat!

This has been building for a long time. Globalization 1.0 (1492 to 1800) shrank the world from a size large to a size medium, and the dynamic force in that era was countries globalizing for resources and imperial conquest. Globalization 2.0 (1800 to 2000) shrank the world from a size medium to a size small, and it was spearheaded by companies globalizing for markets and labor. Globalization 3.0 (which started around 2000) is shrinking the world from a size small to a size tiny and flattening the playing field at the same time. And while the dynamic force in Globalization 1.0 was countries globalizing and the dynamic force in Globalization 2.0 was companies globalizing, the dynamic force in Globalization 3.0—the thing that gives it its unique character—is individuals and small groups globalizing. Individuals must, and can, now ask: where do I fit into the global competition and opportunities of the day, and how can I, on my own, collaborate with others globally? But Globalization 3.0 not only differs from the previous eras in how it is shrinking and flattening the world and in how it is empowering individuals. It is also different in that Globalization 1.0 and 2.0 were driven primarily by European and American companies and countries. But going forward, this will be less and less true. Globalization 3.0 is not only going to be driven more by individuals but also by a much more diverse—non-Western, nonwhite—group of individuals. In Globalization 3.0, you are going to see every color of the human rainbow take part.

"Today, the most profound thing to me is the fact that a 14-year-old in Romania or Bangalore or the Soviet Union or Vietnam has all the information, all the tools, all the software easily available to apply knowledge however they want," said Marc Andreessen, a co-founder of Netscape and creator of the first commercial Internet browser. "That is why I am sure the next Napster is going to come out of left field. As bioscience becomes more computational and less about wet labs and as all the genomic data becomes easily available on the Internet, at some point you will be able to design vaccines on your laptop."

10   Andreessen is touching on the most exciting part of Globalization 3.0 and the flattening of the world: the fact that we are now in the process of connecting all the knowledge pools in the world together. We've tasted some of the downsides of that in the way that Osama bin Laden has connected terrorist knowledge pools together through his Al Qaeda network, not to mention the work of teenage hackers spinning off more and more lethal computer viruses that affect us all. But the upside is that by connecting all these knowledge pools we are on the cusp of an incredible new era of innovation, an era that will be driven from left field and right field, from West and East and from North and South. Only 30 years ago, if you had a choice of being born a B student in Boston or a genius in Bangalore or Beijing, you probably would have chosen Boston, because a genius in Beijing or Bangalore could not really take advantage of his or her talent. They could not plug and play globally. Not anymore. Not when the world is flat, and anyone with smarts, access to Google and a cheap wireless laptop can join the innovation fray.

When the world is flat, you can innovate without having to emigrate. This is going to get interesting. We are about to see creative destruction on steroids.

How did the world get flattened, and how did it happen so fast?

It was a result of 10 events and forces that all came together during the 1990's and converged right around the year 2000. Let me go through them briefly. The first event was 11/9. That's right—not 9/11, but 11/9. Nov. 9, 1989, is the day the Berlin Wall came down, which was critically important because it allowed us to think of the world as a single space. "The Berlin Wall was not only a symbol of keeping people inside Germany; it was a way of preventing a kind of global view of our future," the Nobel Prize-winning economist Amartya Sen said. And the wall went down just as the windows went up—the breakthrough Microsoft Windows 3.0 operating system, which helped to flatten the playing field even more by creating a global computer interface, shipped six months after the wall fell.

The second key date was 8/9. Aug. 9, 1995, is the day Netscape went public, which did two important things. First, it brought the Internet alive by giving us the browser to display images and data stored on Web sites. Second, the Netscape stock offering triggered the dot-com boom, which triggered the dot-com bubble, which triggered the massive overinvestment of billions of dollars in fiber-optic telecommunications cable. That overinvestment, by companies like Global Crossing, resulted in the willy-nilly creation of a global undersea-underground fiber network, which in turn drove down the cost of transmitting voices, data and images to practically zero, which in turn accidentally made Boston, Bangalore and Beijing next-door neighbors overnight. In sum, what the Netscape revolution did was bring people-to-people connectivity to a whole new level. Suddenly more people could connect with more other people from more different places in more different ways than ever before.

15   No country accidentally benefited more from the Netscape moment than India. "India had no resources and no infrastructure," said Dinakar Singh, one of the most respected hedge-fund managers on Wall Street, whose parents earned doctoral degrees in biochemistry from the University of Delhi before emigrating to America. "It produced people with quality and by quantity. But many of them rotted on the docks of India like vegetables. Only a relative few could get on ships and get out. Not anymore, because we built this ocean crosser, called fiber-optic cable. For decades you had to leave India to be a professional. Now you can plug into the world from India. You don't have to go to Yale and go to work for Goldman Sachs." India could never have afforded to pay for the bandwidth to connect brainy India with high-tech America, so American shareholders paid for it. Yes, crazy overinvestment can be good. The overinvestment in railroads turned out to be a great boon for the American economy. "But the railroad overinvestment was confined to your own country and so, too, were the benefits," Singh said. In the case of the digital railroads, "it was the foreigners who benefited." India got a free ride.

The first time this became apparent was when thousands of Indian engineers were enlisted to fix the Y2K—the year 2000—computer bugs for companies from all over the world. (Y2K should be a national holiday in India. Call it "Indian Interdependence Day," says Michael Mandelbaum, a foreign-policy analyst at Johns Hopkins.) The fact that the Y2K work could be outsourced to Indians was made possible by the first two flatteners, along with a third, which I call "workflow." Workflow is shorthand for all the software applications, standards and electronic transmission pipes, like middleware, that connected all those computers and fiber-optic cable. To put it another way, if the Netscape moment connected people to people like never before, what the workflow revolution did was connect applications to applications so that people all over the world could work together in manipulating and shaping words, data and images on computers like never before.

Indeed, this breakthrough in people-to-people and application-to-application connectivity produced, in short order, six more flatteners—six new ways in which individuals and companies could collaborate on work and share knowledge. One was "outsourcing." When my software applications could connect seamlessly with all of your applications, it meant that all kinds of work—from accounting to software-writing—could be digitized, disaggregated and shifted to any place in the world where it could be done better and cheaper. The second was "offshoring." I send my whole factory from Canton, Ohio, to Canton, China. The third was "opensourcing." I write the next operating system, Linux, using engineers collaborating together online and working for free. The fourth was "insourcing." I let a company like UPS come inside my company and take over my whole logistics operation—everything from filling my orders online to delivering my goods to repairing them for customers when they break. (People have no idea what UPS really does today. You'd be amazed!). The fifth was "supply-chaining." This is Wal-Mart's specialty. I create a global supply chain down to the last atom of efficiency so that if I sell an item in Arkansas, another is immediately made in China. (If Wal-Mart were a country, it would be China's eighth-largest trading partner.) The last new form of collaboration I call "informing"—this is Google, Yahoo and MSN Search, which now allow anyone to collaborate with, and mine, unlimited data all by themselves.

So the first three flatteners created the new platform for collaboration, and the next six are the new forms of collaboration that flattened the world even more. The 10th flattener I call "the steroids," and these are wireless access and voice over Internet protocol (VoIP). What the steroids do is turbocharge all these new forms of collaboration, so you can now do any one of them, from anywhere, with any device.

The world got flat when all 10 of these flatteners converged around the year 2000. This created a global, Web-enabled playing field that allows for multiple forms of collaboration on research and work in real time, without regard to geography, distance or, in the near future, even language. "It is the creation of this platform, with these unique attributes, that is the truly important sustainable breakthrough that made what you call the flattening of the world possible," said Craig Mundie, the chief technical officer of Microsoft.

20 No, not everyone has access yet to this platform, but it is open now to more people in more places on more days in more ways than anything like it in history. Wherever you look today—whether it is the world of journalism, with bloggers bringing down Dan Rather; the world of software, with the Linux code writers working in online forums for free to challenge Microsoft; or the world of business, where Indian and Chinese innovators are competing against and working with some of the most advanced Western multinationals—hierarchies are being flattened and value is being created less and less within vertical silos and more and more through horizontal collaboration within companies, between companies and among individuals.

Do you recall "the IT revolution" that the business press has been pushing for the last 20 years? Sorry to tell you this, but that was just the pro-

logue. The last 20 years were about forging, sharpening and distributing all the new tools to collaborate and connect. Now the real information revolution is about to begin as all the complementarities among these collaborative tools start to converge. One of those who first called this moment by its real name was Carly Fiorina, the former Hewlett-Packard C.E.O., who in 2004 began to declare in her public speeches that the dot-com boom and bust were just "the end of the beginning." The last 25 years in technology, Fiorina said, have just been "the warm-up act." Now we are going into the main event, she said, "and by the main event, I mean an era in which technology will truly transform every aspect of business, of government, of society, of life."

As if this flattening wasn't enough, another convergence coincidentally occurred during the 1990's that was equally important. Some three billion people who were out of the game walked, and often ran, onto the playing field. I am talking about the people of China, India, Russia, Eastern Europe, Latin America and Central Asia. Their economies and political systems all opened up during the course of the 1990's so that their people were increasingly free to join the free market. And when did these three billion people converge with the new playing field and the new business processes? Right when it was being flattened, right when millions of them could com-

pete and collaborate more equally, more horizontally and with cheaper and more readily available tools. Indeed, thanks to the flattening of the world, many of these new entrants didn't even have to leave home to participate. Thanks to the 10 flatteners, the playing field came to them!

It is this convergence—of new players, on a new playing field, developing new processes for horizontal collaboration— that I believe is the most important force shaping global economics and politics in the early 21st century. Sure, not all three billion can collaborate and compete. In fact, for most people the world is not yet flat at all. But even if we're talking about only 10 percent, that's 300 million people— about twice the size of the American work force. And be advised: the Indians and Chinese are not racing us to the bottom. They are racing us to the top. What China's leaders really want is that the next generation of underwear and airplane wings not just be "made in China" but also be "designed in China." And that is where things are heading. So in 30 years we will have gone from "sold in China" to "made in China" to "designed in China" to "dreamed up in China"—or from China as collaborator with the worldwide manufacturers on nothing to China as a low-cost, high-quality, hyperefficient collaborator with worldwide manufacturers on everything. Ditto India. Said Craig Barrett, the C.E.O. of Intel, "You don't bring three billion people into the world economy overnight without huge consequences, especially from three societies"—like India, China and Russia—"with rich educational heritages."

That is why there is nothing that guarantees that Americans or Western Europeans will continue leading the way. These new players are stepping onto the playing field legacy free, meaning that many of them were so far behind that they can leap right into the new technologies without having to worry about all the sunken costs of old systems. It means that they can move very fast to adopt new, state-of-the-art technologies, which is why there are already more cell phones in use in China today than there are people in America.

25   If you want to appreciate the sort of challenge we are facing, let me share with you two conversations. One was with some of the Microsoft officials who were involved in setting up Microsoft's research center in Beijing, Microsoft Research Asia, which opened in 1998—after Microsoft sent teams to Chinese universities to administer I.Q. tests in order to recruit the best brains from China's 1.3 billion people. Out of the 2,000 top Chinese engineering and science students tested, Microsoft hired 20. They have a saying at Microsoft about their Asia center, which captures the intensity of competition it takes to win a job there and ex-

plains why it is already the most productive research team at Microsoft: "Remember, in China, when you are one in a million, there are 1,300 other people just like you."

The other is a conversation I had with Rajesh Rao, a young Indian entrepreneur who started an electronic-game company from Bangalore, which today owns the rights to Charlie Chaplin's image for mobile computer games. "We can't relax," Rao said. "I think in the case of the United States that is what happened a bit. Please look at me: I am from India. We have been at a very different level before in terms of technology and business. But once we saw we had an infrastructure that made the world a small place, we promptly tried to make the best use of it. We saw there were so many things we could do. We went ahead, and today what we are seeing is a result of that. There is no time to rest. That is gone. There are dozens of people who are doing the same thing you are doing, and they are trying to do it better. It is like water in a tray: you shake it, and it will find the path of least resistance. That is what is going to happen to so many jobs—they will go to that corner of the world where there is the least resistance and the most opportunity. If there is a skilled person in Timbuktu, he will get work if he knows how to access the rest of the world, which is quite easy today. You

can make a Web site and have an e-mail address and you are up and running. And if you are able to demonstrate your work, using the same infrastructure, and if people are comfortable giving work to you and if you are diligent and clean in your transactions, then you are in business."

Instead of complaining about outsourcing, Rao said, Americans and Western Europeans would "be better off thinking about how you can raise your bar and raise yourselves into doing something better. Americans have consistently led in innovation over the last century. Americans whining—we have never seen that before."

Rao is right. And it is time we got focused. As a person who grew up during the cold war, I'll always remember driving down the highway and listening to the radio, when suddenly the music would stop and a grim-voiced announcer would come on the air and say: "This is a test. This station is conducting a test of the Emergency Broadcast System." And then there would be a 20-second high-pitched siren sound. Fortunately, we never had to live through a moment in the cold war when the announcer came on and said, "This is a not a test."

That, however, is exactly what I want to say here: "This is not a test."

30   The long-term opportunities and challenges that the flattening of the world puts before the United States are

profound. Therefore, our ability to get by doing things the way we've been doing them—which is to say not always enriching our secret sauce—will not suffice any more. "For a country as wealthy we are, it is amazing how little we are doing to enhance our natural competitiveness," says Dinakar Singh, the Indian-American hedge-fund manager. "We are in a world that has a system that now allows convergence among many billions of people, and we had better step back and figure out what it means. It would be a nice coincidence if all the things that were true before were still true now, but there are quite a few things you actually need to do differently. You need to have a much more thoughtful national discussion."

If this moment has any parallel in recent American history, it is the height of the cold war, around 1957, when the Soviet Union leapt ahead of America in the space race by putting up the Sputnik satellite. The main challenge then came from those who wanted to put up walls; the main challenge to America today comes from the fact that all the walls are being taken down and many other people can now compete and collaborate with us much more directly. The main challenge in that world was from those practicing extreme Communism, namely Russia, China and North Korea. The main challenge to America today is from those practicing extreme capitalism, namely China, India and South Korea. The main

objective in that era was building a strong state, and the main objective in this era is building strong individuals.

Meeting the challenges of flatism requires as comprehensive, energetic and focused a response as did meeting the challenge of Communism. It requires a president who can summon the nation to work harder, get smarter, attract more young women and men to science and engineering and build the broadband infrastructure, portable pensions and health care that will help every American become more employable in an age in which no one can guarantee you lifetime employment.

We have been slow to rise to the challenge of flatism, in contrast to Communism, may be because flatism doesn't involve ICBM missiles aimed at our cities. Indeed, the hot line, which used to connect the Kremlin with the White House, has been replaced by the help line, which connects everyone in America to call centers in Bangalore. While the other end of the hot line might have had Leonid Brezhnev threatening nuclear war, the other end of the help line just has a soft voice eager to help you sort out your AOL bill or collaborate with you on a new piece of software. No, that voice has none of the menace of Nikita Khrushchev pounding a shoe on the table at the United Nations, and it has none of the sinister snarl of the bad guys in "From Russia With Love." No, that voice on the help line just has a

friendly Indian lilt that masks any sense of threat or challenge. It simply says: "Hello, my name is Rajiv. Can I help you?"

No, Rajiv, actually you can't. When it comes to responding to the challenges of the flat world, there is no help line we can call. We have to dig into ourselves. We in America have all the basic economic and educational tools to do that. But we have not been improving those tools as much as we should. That is why we are in what Shirley Ann Jackson, the 2004 president of the American Association for the Advancement of Science and president of Rensselaer Polytechnic Institute, calls a "quiet crisis"—one that is slowly eating away at America's scientific and engineering base.

35 "If left unchecked," said Jackson, the first African-American woman to earn a Ph.D. in physics from M.I.T., "this could challenge our preeminence and capacity to innovate." And it is our ability to constantly innovate new products, services and companies that has been the source of America's horn of plenty and steadily widening middle class for the last two centuries. This quiet crisis is a product of three gaps now plaguing American society. The first is an "ambition gap." Compared with the young, energetic Indians and Chinese, too many Americans have gotten too lazy. As David Rothkopf, a former official in the Clinton Commerce Department, puts it, "The real

entitlement we need to get rid of is our sense of entitlement." Second, we have a serious numbers gap building. We are not producing enough engineers and scientists. We used to make up for that by importing them from India and China, but in a flat world, where people can now stay home and compete with us, and in a post-9/11 world, where we are insanely keeping out many of the first-round intellectual draft choices in the world for exaggerated security reasons, we can no longer cover the gap. That's a key reason companies are looking abroad. The numbers are not here. And finally we are developing an education gap. Here is the dirty little secret that no C.E.O. wants to tell you: they are not just outsourcing to save on salary. They are doing it because they can often get better-skilled and more productive people than their American workers.

These are some of the reasons that Bill Gates, the Microsoft chairman, warned the governors' conference in a Feb. 26 speech that American high-school education is "obsolete." As Gates put it: "When I compare our high schools to what I see when I'm traveling abroad, I am terrified for our workforce of tomorrow. In math and science, our fourth graders are among the top students in the world. By eighth grade, they're in the middle of the pack. By 12th grade, U.S. students are scoring near the bottom of all industrialized nations. . . . The percentage of a population with a college degree is important, but so are sheer numbers. In 2001, India graduated almost a million more students from college than the United States did. China graduates twice as many students with bachelor's degrees as the U.S., and they have six times as many graduates majoring in engineering. In the international competition to have the biggest and best supply of knowledge workers, America is falling behind."

We need to get going immediately. It takes 15 years to train a good engineer, because, ladies and gentlemen, this really is rocket science. So parents, throw away the Game Boy, turn off the television and get your kids to work. There is no sugar-coating this: in a flat world, every individual is going to have to run a little faster if he or she wants to advance his or her standard of living. When I was growing up, my parents used to say to me, "Tom, finish your dinner — people in China are starving." But after sailing to the edges of the flat world for a year, I am now telling my own daughters, "Girls, finish your homework—people in China and India are starving for your jobs."

I repeat, this is not a test. This is the beginning of a crisis that won't remain quiet for long. And as the Stanford economist Paul Romer so rightly says, "A crisis is a terrible thing to waste."

Reflect & Write

❏ How does the writer, Thomas Friedman, make use of "I" in this essay? Why is it acceptable for him to write in first person? What does he mean by the claim, "I became upset at the realization that while I had been off covering the 9/11 wars, globalization had entered a whole new phase, and I had missed it"?

❏ Notice the vivid details in this article. How does Friedman's narrative work as a unifying structure? How does it rely on details?

❏ Map the different definitions of globalization provided here. How do these terms provide what we call "historicizing," or the construction of a particular historical account that complicates the topic. Why is this move to "historicize" a valuable act to make in your writing?

❏ One of the strengths of this writing is its reliance on concrete examples; what purpose do these instances serve? Answer with regard to Friedman's point about the ripple effects and implications of Netscape going public.

❏ Who is the audience? How do you know this from analyzing a line such as, "Some three billion people who were out of the game walked, and often ran, onto the playing field. I am talking about the people of China, India, Russia, Eastern Europe, Latin America and Central Asia."

❏ **Write:** Do you think this article is ultimately a call to arms? What does the writer mean by quoting Rajesh Rao, a young Indian entrepreneur: "Americans whining— we have never seen that before"? Write your answer as a letter to your own family member, modeled after Friedman's writing strategy of communicating his ideas with his wife, parents, or daughters. You might even begin your writing by responding to the line, "So parents, throw away the Game Boy, turn off the television and get your kids to work."

■ *Canadian* **Naomi Klein** *is an award-winning journalist and author of the international best-seller* No Logo: Taking Aim at the Brand Bullies, *which was translated into 25 languages. This article appeared in the March 4, 2004, issue of* The Nation; *Klein also publishes in Canada's* Globe and Mail, *Britain's* The Guardian, *as well as in* The New Statesman, Newsweek International, The New York Times, *the* Village Voice, *and* Ms. Magazine. *She published* Fences and Windows: Dispatches from the Front Lines of the Globalization Debate *in 2002.*

Outsourcing the Friedman

Naomi Klein

Thomas Friedman hasn't been this worked up about free trade since the anti-World Trade Organization protests in Seattle. Back then, he told *New York Times* readers that the work environment in a Sri Lankan Victoria's Secret factory was so terrific "that, in terms of conditions, I would let my own daughters work" there.

He never did update readers on how the girls enjoyed their stint stitching undergarments, but Friedman has since moved on—now to the joys of call-center work in Bangalore. These jobs, he wrote on February 29, are giving young people "self-confidence, dignity and optimism"—and that's not just good for Indians, but for Americans as well. Why? Because happy workers paid to help US tourists locate the luggage they've lost on Delta flights are less inclined to strap on dynamite and blow up those same planes.

Confused? Friedman explains the connection: "Listening to these Indian young people, I had a déjà vu. Five months ago, I was in Ramal-

lah, on the West Bank, talking to three young Palestinian men, also in their 20's. . . . They talked of having no hope, no jobs and no dignity, and they each nodded when one of them said they were all 'suicide bombers in waiting.'" From this he concludes that outsourcing fights terrorism: By moving "low-wage, low-prestige" jobs to "places like India or Pakistan. . . we make not only a more prosperous world, but a safer world for our own 20-year-olds."

Where to begin with such an argument? India has not been linked to a major international terrorist incident since the Air India bombing in 1985 (the suspected bombers were mostly Indian-born Canadian citizens).

Neither is the 81 percent Hindu country an Al Qaeda hotbed; in fact, India has been named by the terrorist network as "an enemy of Islam." But never mind the details. In Friedmanworld, call centers are the front lines of World War III: The Fight for Modernity, bravely keeping

5

brown-skinned young people out of the clutches of Hamas and Al Qaeda.

But are these jobs—many of which demand that workers disguise their nationality, adopt fake Midwestern accents and work all night—actually the self-esteem boosters Friedman claims? Not for Lubna Baloch, a Pakistani woman subcontracted to transcribe medical files dictated by doctors at the University of California San Francisco Medical Center. The hospital pays transcribers in the United States 18 cents a line, but Baloch was paid only one-sixth that. Even so, her US employer—a contractor's subcontractor's subcontractor—couldn't manage to make payroll, and Baloch claimed she was owed hundreds of dollars in back wages.

In October, frustrated that her boss wouldn't respond to her e-mails, Baloch contacted UCSF Medical Center and threatened to "expose all the voice files and patient records. . . on the Internet." She later retracted the threat, explaining, "I feel violated, helpless. . . the most unluckiest person in this world." So much for "self-confidence, dignity and optimism"—it seems that not all outsourced tech jobs are insurance against acts of desperation.

Friedman is right to acknowledge, finally, that there is a clear connection between fighting poverty and fighting terrorism (a step up from his usual practice of blaming suicide bombing on "collective madness"). He is wrong, of course, to argue that free-trade policies will alleviate that poverty: In fact, they are a highly efficient engine of dispossession, pushing small farmers off their land and laying off public-sector workers, making the need all the more desperate for those Victoria's Secret and Delta call center jobs.

But even if Friedman genuinely believes that low-wage export jobs are the key to economic development, holding them up as the cure for hopelessness in Ramallah verges on obscene. Every credible study on the economy in the occupied territories has concluded that the single greatest cause of Palestinian unemployment—now at over 50 percent—is the occupation itself. Israel's brutal system of sealing off Palestinian towns and villages—through checkpoints, roadblocks, curfews, fences and now the vile "security" wall—has "all but destroyed the Palestinian economy," states a September 2003 Amnesty International Report. "Closures and curfews have prevented Palestinians from reaching their places of work. . . . Factories and farms have been driven out of business."

10   In other words, economic development will not come to Palestine via call centers but through liberation. Friedman's argument is equally absurd when applied to the country where terrorism is rising most rapidly: Iraq. As in Palestine, Iraq is facing an unemployment crisis, one fueled by occupation. And no wonder: Paul Bremer's first move as chief US envoy was to lay off 400,000 soldiers and other state workers. His second was to fling open Iraq's borders to cheap imports, predictably putting hundreds of local companies out of business.

Laid-off workers looking to land a job rebuilding their shattered country were mostly out of luck: The reconstruction of Iraq is a vast job-creation program for Americans, with Halliburton et al. importing US workers not only as engineers but also as cooks, truck drivers and hairdressers. Second-tier jobs go to migrants from Asia, and Iraqis pick up the trash. It seems worth noting that John Kerry and John Edwards, while eager to condemn the loss of American jobs to "offshoring," have had nothing to say about this massive outsourcing of desperately needed Iraqi jobs by US corporations.

Yet these policies, maybe more than any others, have fueled the violence that now threatens to push Iraq into civil war. The men Bremer laid off are "the water tap that keeps the insurgency going. It's alternative employment," Iraqi entrepreneur Hussain Kubba told *Asia Times*. It's a view supported by Hassam Kadhim, a 27-year-old resident of Sadr City, who told *the New York Times* he is so desperate for work that "if someone comes with $50 and asks me to toss a grenade at the Americans, I'll do it with pleasure."

Friedman's bright idea of fighting terrorism with outsourced American jobs seems overly complicated. A better plan would be to end the occupation and stop sending American workers to steal Iraqi jobs.

Reflect & Write

❏ How does Klein take on Thomas Friedman from the very first paragraph? Assess her own use of "I" in this essay and map the trajectory of her argument.

❏ Notice the strong language in this essay. How does this work as an appeal to pathos? What response do you have to the following line: "But even if Friedman genuinely believes that low-wage export jobs are the key to economic development, holding them up as the cure for hopelessness in Ramallah verges on obscene."

❏ Visit http://www.nologo.org and read additional articles Klein has written. How do you get a picture of her political and research interests based on your synthesis of her writing subjects?

❏ **Write:** Draft your own response to both articles, quoting lines in emulation of Klein's techniques.

■ **Cliff Barney** *specializes in issues surrounding technology and has written articles on the subject for over 40 years. He published this piece in the April 14, 2004, issue of Salon.com. He currently resides in Ashland, Oregon, as well as Yelapa, Mexico, which is the setting for this story.*

Think Locally, Act Globally

Cliff Barney

Computer class at Yelapa telesecundaria

Yelapa, Mexico—More than seven years ago, Ric Hunt, a wandering computer jock from Iowa, proposed to an astonished Pedro Gómez, the principal of Yelapa's telesecundaria school (for kids in seventh to ninth grades) that they start a computer lab in the jungle. At that time Yelapa, an indigenous community down the Bay of Banderas coast from Puerto Vallarta, had no grid-based electricity; Gómez was still struggling with the satellite technology that brought lessons to the school daily from Mexico City.

But the Honda-powered satellite was precisely the point for Hunt; he had somehow stranded himself in one of the few places on earth where he couldn't plug in easily. That was important to him, since he wanted to become a registered Microsoft technician and travel through Central America wiring up hotels. He needed to use a computer to study for the Microsoft exams, and his elegant solution to this problem was to invent the jungle computer school in exchange for the right to use A.C. power at the telesecundaria.

The story of how the jungle computer school has struggled into existence, despite the differing motives and understanding of its founders, provides some perspective on how the technological frontier advances—by chance as much as design. From its almost accidental beginning, a computer school has taken root, with a dozen Pentium 5 machines, some of them networked to a printer, and classes not only for the secondary school kids but also for students in the new preparatorio (the equivalent of high school), which shares the space.

Hunt jump-started the school with a donation of two old computers, one with an AMD 586 processor and the other with an Intel 386, plus a scanner and a laser printer. Just getting this hardware to Yelapa was a logistical triumph, since there were no roads to the place and everything had to come in by boat. But he and Gómez quickly ran into difficulty with each other, partly because of the language barrier, partly because the school considered Hunt's Microsoft activities to be using too much generator time when gas was getting expensive, and partly because Hunt's plans, which included a satellite network connecting all the schools in the district, were far too grand for Yelapa's simple needs and Gómez didn't understand them. The teacher was totally baffled, for instance, when Hunt showed him how he had gotten the machines to boot in any one of three operating systems—DOS, Windows 95, or Unix. Gómez had only a vague idea of what any operating system did. (A map of the satellite network, which Hunt is still promoting, may be found on his Web site).

5   I met Hunt in 1998 and took part in many meetings between him and Gómez. With other North American residents, I helped translate for the computer school, structure a program, write proposals, and make contacts, all the while suspecting, as most of us did, that Hunt could never pull it off. What he proposed to do was technically feasible, but it was far beyond the Yelapa kids' needs or the school's ability to manage.

Yelapa has electricity now, and eventually, says Gómez, the school would have thought about computers. It eventually got equipment for its current lab through the Jalisco Department of Education and COBAEJ, a public organization that helps direct state funds for education, as well as software from Microsoft (partly due to Hunt's efforts). But, Gómez adds, "This [the computer lab] is the future of Yelapa. And Ric got it going."

By doing so he helped give the town a toehold on the network frontier. With local resources now accessible from anywhere in the world, the environment here is essentially defenseless. Local agencies have to meet pressures that result from decisions they have no control over and that they have few resources to counter. Considering the changes wrought by what he sees as a new social form, the "network society," sociologist Manuel Castells suggests that the old '60s slogan has to be flipped over; people must think locally and act globally. "If you don't act globally in a system in which the powers are global, you make no difference in the power system," Castells says.

It is hard to see how a hamlet like Yelapa can have much of a global impact, though it is already acting globally through the various Web sites that advertise tourist residences in town. None of these, however, are run by Yelapans. In time, the computer school will generate a cadre of local youths who understand something of global technology. COBAEJ requires schools to maintain a strict curriculum, with classes in computer science as well as math, chemistry, physics and English. Students in the prepa are getting instructions in theoretical "informatics" from Alex Urrutia, a Yelapa native who left town at an early age and wound up as a Microsoft techie in Montreal before returning to the village on a self-generated sabbatical two years ago. The secondary school kids are learning Word and Excel, and looking things up in Encarta, just as Microsoft had hoped.

There is still no Internet connection. Urrutia wants to teach a second-year class on the needs of businesses and the use of the Internet, but can't go online. The original appropriation to get the prepa going included Internet money, he says, but Gómez vetoed it, partly because he wanted to spend the funds elsewhere. Yelapa is so remote that it had never had a high school before; it could not justify spending the money on importing teachers to live there. (The telesecundaria gets its lessons by satellite for the same reason.) The first two years of prepa operation have been carried out with pickup teaching staffs; last month, in fact, the school lost its English teacher, a North American, when he abruptly left town with no notice.

10   There will be plenty of time for the Internet, Gómez told me, when the students have a firmer grasp of the basics and when the school's enrollment reaches three full classes. (It started with only a sophomore class, adding a junior class this year as the first students advanced; only next year will there be a full complement.) Nevertheless, the indefatigable Hunt, who now lives in Mexico City, has scared up a small private donation to cover initial ISP costs and is working with UNETE, a business group that supports public schools, to provide more equipment and network connections. Meanwhile Urrutia says that some of his students e-mail him from their homes. Some Yelapa families have computers, and there is one locally run cybercafe, a single machine in a local restaurant, Mimi's.

Mimi herself is part of another movement to bring Yelapa's young people into the mainstream; she is on the all-Yelapan board of a project to start a youth center in town that will offer art, music, dance, martial arts and computer classes for kids, using both local and expatriate talent for instruction. Before opening its doors, the school received donations of four laptops and promises of five more desktop computers this year. The center grew out of a bequest from a longtime American resident, Sam Harrison, who died in Yelapa and left $5,000 to be spent for the benefit of the local youth.

Aware that their $5,000 would melt very quickly, the project leaders went looking for official backing, an effort that succeeded beyond anyone's expectations; the youth center dovetailed neatly with the plans of the Mexican government for the development of Yelapa. The municipio of Cabo Corrientes, of which Yelapa is a part, wants to create a cultural center in the town. On receiving a presentation about the youth project, the municipio promptly made its board the lead agency for formation of the cultural center, with the municipio's ecology officer, Yelapa resident Luis Enrique Morales, as liaison. (It bothered no one that these goals and responsibilities are significantly out of sync; everyone in Yelapa expects to multitask.)

The presence of Morales, the establishment of a municipio office in Yelapa, the appearance of actual police here, plus Yelapa's increasing Internet presence, all attest to the new influence of the outside world on the town. Whether it has the political skill, and influence, to keep local control is questionable. The community leaders are well aware of the effects of development on other Mexican locales that have become tourist centers. Their control of the land and their traditional political autonomy, as part of an indigenous community, give the locals some protection. Nevertheless, Yelapa politicians have frequently been bought in the past, and the land has become very valuable. In addition, the indigenous Chacala community that Yelapa belongs to is in debt to the federal government for unpaid taxes on the land it leases to tourist developers. Urrutia thinks that the combination of fiscal mismanagement and rising crime and drug problems may create a wedge for outsiders to gain control of community land.

As this issue is being decided, Yelapa's people will go on wiring up as fast as they can, and more tourists will be attracted to it from all over the globe. Already, its new commercial villas promise all the comforts of home, rather than jungle romance in a thatched hut. It is hard to say what the impact of the first neon sign will be. Given Yelapa's small size and skimpy economy, the coming of electricity and digital technology may cause very fast growth and make it a frontier boomtown. At the same time, projects like the computer school and the youth center, and the town's new political sophistication in dealing with Mexican governments, rather than relying on its weakening protection as an indigenous community, offer Yelapa some way of interacting with the network that has annexed it to the global economy.

Reflect & Write

❏ How does the image for the story both provide an illustrative preview for the content and offer an independent argument that shapes the reader's expectations of what is to follow?

❏ Why might Cliff Barney use the term "the jungle computer school" to depict this classroom in Mexico?

❏ What new perspective does this article provide on the issue of globalization and outsourcing? How is the economy here transforming? Why might the writer include so many physical details about the school in this piece?

❏ **Write:** Using photos of your own classroom, create a short article about computer use at your school. Include the images at the beginning of your own piece, and follow it by a written argument.

COLLABORATIVE CHALLENGE

Together with two classmates, compose a dialogue of sources with the articles in this chapter in order to delve deeper into the arguments presented here about outsourcing and globalization. Follow the guidelines from Chapter 5 to help you structure the dialogue. Be sure to add your own voices as well. You might decide to enact the dialogue in a brief skit before your class or to film it and create a multimedia argument about outsourcing and globalization.

1. The perspectives on outsourcing that you've encountered in this chapter are quite polarized and heated. Compare the titles of the pieces to capture, from a bird's-eye view, the different stances of the writers. Look again, for instance, at Brian Behlendorf's title—"How Outsourcing Will Save the World: The Growth of White-Collar Jobs in Developing Nations Is Essential to Global Peace and Prosperity" and Laurianne McLaughlin's "An Eye on India: Outsourcing Debate Continues." How does a rereading of titles give you insight into the major issues and positions? What title would you compose for your own contribution to this debate?

2. Notice how several writers, including Thomas Friedman, Naomi Klein, and Cliff Barney rely on vivid, compelling narratives filled with rich visual detail to make their arguments. Compare the structure, message, and use of evidence in two of these articles. What writing strategies do you find most effective and why?

3. How does the case study of Yelapa provide a solid material example (versus just theory) for this case study on outsourcing? What other geographic locations, mentioned in the articles above, moved you? Which ones made you rethink your own conclusions concerning globalized economies and global communities?

FROM READING TO RESEARCH

1. Pursue the themes of this chapter through field research and then write a report on your findings. Get started by conducting a series of interviews with people in your university, community, and town concerning economics and the globalization of jobs. What are the opinions and perspectives of your own location? Use the recordings to create a research argument in response to the texts you've encountered in this chapter.

2. Conduct a library search using the key terms "outsourcing" and "globalization." You might locate several books and articles to synthesize in constructing your own research argument. A good place to begin would be with the following sources: Andrew Ross, *Fast Boat to China: Corporate Flight and the Consequences of Free Trade* (N.Y.: Pantheon Books, 2006), William Marling, *How "American" is Globalization?* (Baltimore: Johns Hopkins University Press, 2006), and "The Next Wave of Offshoring" by Robyn Meredith in the *Far Eastern Economic Review* (March 2005). See also the article, "The Muddles over Outsourcing," by Jagdish Bhagwati, Arvind Panagariya, and T. N. Srinivasan in the *Journal of Economic Perspectives* 18.4 (Fall 2004): 93–114.

Works Cited

CHAPTER 1

Aristotle. "Rhetoric." *The History and Theory of Rhetoric.* By James A. Herrick. Boston: Allyn & Bacon, 1998.

Blakesley, David, and Collin Brooke. "Introduction: Notes on Visual Rhetoric." *Enculturation* 3.2 (2001): Node 4. <http://enculturation.gmu.edu/3_2/introduction.html>.

Diamond, Matthew. "No Laughing Matter: Post-September 11 Political Cartoons in Arab/Muslim Newspapers." *Political Communication* 19 (2002): 251–72.

Gellis, Mark. "Six Ways of Thinking about Rhetoric." The Rhetoric Page at Kettering University. Par. 1. <http://www.gmi.edu/~mgellis/HANDT001.HTM>.

Holkins, Jerry. "The Hipness Threshold." Penny Arcade Blog. 12 Mar. 2004. 22 June 2006. <http://www.penny-arcade.com/comic/2004/03/12>.

Horn, Robert. *Visual Language: Global Communication for the 21st Century.* MacRovu Inc., 1999.

Huntington, Samuel P. "'Under God': Michael Newdow is right. Atheists *are* outsiders in America." *Wall Street Journal* 16 June 2004.

Lehrer, Jim. "Illustrated Men." *Online Focus.* Transcript. 31 Oct. 1996. <http://www.pbs.org/newshour/bb/election/october96/cartoonists_10-31.html>.

Marlette, Doug. "I Was a Tool of Satan." *Columbia Journalism Review* Nov./Dec. 2003: 52. <http://www.cjr.org/issues/2003/6/satan-marlette.asp>.

McCloud, Scott. *Understanding Comics.* New York: HarperPerennial, 1993.

Melandri, Lisa. "Drawing the Line." Philadelphia, PA. 18 Mar. 2003. <http://thegalleriesatmoore.org/publications/cartoons/politicalcartoons.shtml>.

Mitchell, J. T. "The Pictorial Turn." *Picture Theory.* Chicago: U of Chicago P, 1994.

Moore, Art. "'What Would Muhammad Drive?': Pulitzer-winner's cartoon terrorist spurs death threats from Muslims." WorldNetDaily.com. 28 Dec. 2002. 18 Mar. 2003 <http://www.worldnetdaily.com/news/article.asp?ARTICLE_ID530197>.

Plato. *Gorgias.* Trans. Robin Waterfield. New York: Oxford UP, 1994. 21. Villanueva, Victor Jr. *Bootstraps: From an American Academic of Color.* Urbana, IL: National Council of Teachers of English, 1993.

Watterson, Bill. *Calvin and Hobbes Sunday Pages 1985–1995.* Kansas City, MO: Andrews McMeel Publishing, 2001.

CHAPTER 2

Bowen, Laurence, and Jill Schmid. "Minority Presence and Portrayal in Mainstream Magazine Advertising: An Update." *Journalism and Mass Communications Quarterly* 74.1 (2004): 134–46.

Burgin, Victor. "Art, Common Sense, and Photography." *Visual Culture: The Reader.* Eds. Jessica Evans and Stuart Hall. London: Sage Publications, 1999. 41–50.

Caputi, Jane. "Seeing Elephants: The Myths of Phallotechnology." *Feminist Studies* 14.3 (1988).

Hacker, Andrea. *New York Times* 14 June 1984.

Kinneavy, James. "Kairos in Classical and Modern Rhetorical Theory." *Rhetoric and Kairos: Essays in History, Theory and Praxis.* Eds. Phillip Sipiora, James Baumlin, and Carolyn Miller. Albany: State U of New York P, 2002. 58–76.

"Merchants of Cool." *Frontline.* Dir. Barak Goodman. PBS. 27 Feb. 2001. <http://www.pbs.org/wgbh/pages/frontline/shows/cool/>.

Messaris, Paul. *Visual Persuasion: The Role of Images in Advertising.* Thousand Oaks, CA: Sage Publications, 1997.

Stevenson, Seth. "You and Your Shadow." Slate.com. 4 Mar. 2004. <http://www.slate.com/id/2096459/>.

Twitchell, James B. *Adcult USA.* New York: Columbia UP, 1996.

—. "Listerine: Gerard Lambert and Selling the Need." *Twenty Ads That Shook the World.* New York: Three Rivers Press, 2000. 60–69.

Williams, Roy H. "The Wizard of Advertising." *Secret Formulas of the Wizard of Ads.* Bard Press, 1999.

CHAPTER 3

Boese, Alex. *Museum of Hoaxes.* <http://museumofhoaxes.com>. Cicero. *De Inventione.* Trans. H. M. Hubbell. Cambridge, MA: Loeb Classical Library, 1949.

Curtis, James. "Dorothea Lange, Migrant Mother, and the Culture of the Great Depression." *Winterthur Portfolio: A Journal of American Material Culture* 21 (Spring 1986) 1–20.

Dunn, Geoffrey. "Photographic License." *San Louis Obispo Times.* 17 Jan. 2002. <http://www.newtimes-slo.com/archives/cov_stories_2002/cov_01172002.html>.

Gottesman, Jane. *Game Face.* New York: Random House, 2001.

Harris, Christopher, and Paul Martin Lester. *Visual Journalism.* Boston: Allyn & Bacon, 2002.

Sontag, Susan. "Looking at War: Photography's View of Devastation and Death." *The New Yorker* 9 Dec. 2002: 82–98.

CHAPTER 4

Bizzell, Patricia, and Bruce Herzberg. "Research as a Social Act." *Background Readings for Instructors Using The Bedford Handbook.* 6th ed. Ed. Glenn Blalock. Boston: Bedford/St. Martin's, 2002. 321–26.

Booth, Wayne. *Craft of Research.* Chicago: U of Chicago P, 1995.

Drew, Elizabeth. *Poetry: A Modern Guide.* New York: Dell Publishing, 1959.

Gorgias. "Encomium of Helen." *The Older Sophists: A Complete Translation by Several Hands of the Fragments.* Ed. Rosamond Kent Sprague. Columbia: U of South Carolina P, 1972. 50–54. 7 Apr. 2003. <http://www.phil.vt.edu/mgifford/phil2115/Helen.htm>.

Hunt, Douglas. *The Riverside Guide to Writing.* Boston: Houghton Mifflin, 1991.

CHAPTER 5

Ballenger, Bruce. *The Curious Researcher.* 4th ed. New York: Longman, 2004.

Bowen, Catherine Drinker. *Adventures of a Biographer.* Boston: Little, Brown, 1959.

"Bush vs. Bush." *The Daily Show with Jon Stewart.* <http://www.comedycentral.com/tv_shows/ds/videos_corr.jhtml?startIndex513&p5stewart>.

Clark, Jocalyn. "Babes and Boob? Analysis of JAMA Cover Art." *British Medical Journal* (18 Dec. 1999): 1603.

Gonser, Sarah. "Revising the Cover Story." *Folio: The Magazine for Magazine Management* 1 Mar. 2003.

Huff, Darrell. *How to Lie with Statistics.* New York: Norton, 1993.

Rea, Alan, and Doug White. "The Changing Nature of Writing: Prose or Code in the Classroom." *Background Readings for Instructors Using The Bedford Handbook.* 6th ed. Ed. Glan Blalock. Boston: Bedford/St. Martin's, 2002. 217–30.

"Statistical Significance." Creative Research Systems, 2000. <http://www.surveysystem.com/signif.htm>.

"Stem Cells, Regenerative Medicine and Cancer." The Beckman Symposium. 14–15 Apr. 2003. <http://beckman.stanford.edu/events/symp_videos.html>.

Stewart, John. *America.* New York: Warner Books, 2004.

Vogel, Gretchen. "Can Old Cells Learn New Tricks?" *Science* 25 Feb. 2000: 1418–19.

Zimbardo, Philip G., Ann L. Weber, and Robert L. Johnson. *Psychology: Core Concepts.* 4th ed. Boston: Allyn & Bacon, 2003.

CHAPTER 6

Adamson, Eric. "Malleability, Misrepresentation, Manipulation: The Rhetoric of Images in Economic Forecasting." Boothe Prize Essay, Winter 2003. Program in Writing and Rhetoric, Stanford University. <http://pwr.stanford.edu/publications/>.

Antohin, Anatoly. "Storyboard." <http://afronord.tripod.com/film/storyboard.html>.

Blast, Joseph. "Gorgeous Propaganda, Frightening Truth." *Heartland Perspectives.* June 2006. <http://www.heartland.org/Article.cfm?artId519239>.

Burke, Kenneth. "Rhetoric—Old and New." *New Rhetorics.* Ed. Martin Steinmann. New York: Scribner, 1967. 59–76.

Collier, John, Greg Daniels, and Paul Lieberstein. "Homer, Hank & the American Dream: Social & Political Satire on American Television." The Program in American Studies. Stanford University, Stanford, CA 7 Nov. 2003.

Gibaldi, Joseph. *MLA Handbook for the Writers of Research Papers.* 6th ed. New York: Modern Language Association, 2003.

Goodwin, Doris Kearns. "How I Caused That Story." 27 Jan. 2002. <http://www.time.com/time/nation/article/0,8599,197614,00.html>.

Hilligoss, Susan. *Visual Communication.* 2nd ed. New York: Longman, 2002.

Kaplan, Deborah. "Mass Marketing Jane Austen: Men, Women and Courtship in Two Film Adaptations." *Jane Austen in Hollywood*. Eds. Linda Troost and Sayre Greenfield: U of Kentucky P, 1998. 177–87.

Lamott, Anne. *Bird by Bird: Some Instructions on Writing and Life*. New York: Anchor, 1995.

"Merchants of Cool." *Frontline*. Dir. Barak Goodman. PBS. 27 Feb. 2001. <http://http://www.pbs.org/wgbh/pages/frontline/shows/cool/>.

Moore, Michael. *Fahrenheit 9/11*. Sony Pictures, 2004.

Morgan, Peter W., and Glenn H. Reynolds. "A Plague of Originality." *The Idler*. <http://www.the-idler.com/IDLER-02/1-23.html>.

Paton, Alan. *National Observer* 8 Nov. 1965.

Phillips, William H. *Film: An Introduction*. 2nd ed. Boston: Bedford/St. Martins, 2002.

Rasch, David. "How I Write Interview." Stanford Writing Center. Stanford University. 17 Nov. 2003.

CHAPTER 7

Adbusters: Culturejammers. <http://www.adbusters.org>.

Agee, James. Foreword. *Let Us Now Praise Famous Men*. Boston: Houghton Mifflin, 1969.

Burton, Gideon. *Silva Rhetoricae: The Forest of Rhetoric*. <http://humanities.byu.edu/rhetoric/silva.htm>.

Cody, Anthony. "Teaching Practices: Digital Photoessays." Apple Learning Exchange. <http://ali.apple.com/ali_sites/ali/neccexhibits/1000308/The_Lesson.html>.

Crowley, Sharon, and Debra Hawhee. *Ancient Rhetorics for Contemporary Students*. New York: Longman, 1999.

George, Diana. "From Analysis to Design: Visual Communication in the Teaching of Writing." *CCC* 54.1 (2002): 11–39.

Greenfield, Laura. *Girl Culture*. San Francisco, CA: Chronicle Books, 2002.

Levy, Matthew. "A Rescue Worker's Chronicle." <http://www.umbc.edu/window/levy.html>.

Lanham, Richard. *The Electronic Word: Democracy, Technology, and the Arts*. Chicago: U of Chicago P, 1993.

Landow, George. *Hypertext*. Baltimore: Johns Hopkins UP, 1992.

Nielsen, Jakob, and Marie Tahir. *Homepage Usability: 50 Websites Deconstructed*. Indianapolis: New Riders Publishing, 2002.

Sammons, Martha. *The Internet Writer's Handbook*. New York: Longman, 2004.

Stephenson, Sam, ed. *Dream Street: W. Eugene Smith's Pittsburgh Project*. New York: Norton, 2001.

CHAPTER 8

Burton, Gideon. *Silva Rhetoricae: The Forest of Rhetoric*. <http://humanities.byu.edu/rhetoric/silva.htm>.

Byrne, David. "Learning to Love PowerPoint." *Wired Magazine* Sept. 2003. <http://http://www.wired.com/wired/archive/11.09/ppt1.html>.

Covino, William, and David Jolliffe. *Rhetoric: Concepts, Definitions, Boundaries*. Boston: Allyn & Bacon, 1995.

Hocks, Mary. "Understanding Visual Rhetoric in Digital Writing Environments." *CCC* 54.4 (June 2003): 629–56.

Ingleman, Kelly. "Delivery." Rhetoric Resources at Tech. Georgia Institute of Technology. <http://www.lcc.gatech.edu/gallery/rhetoric/terms/delivery.html>.

Kilbourne, Jean. *Slim Hopes: Advertising and the Obsession with Thinness*. Dir. Sut Jhally. Northampton, MA: Media Education Foundation, 1995.

Parker, Ian. "Absolute PowerPoint." *The New Yorker* 28 May 2001: 76–87.

Shugart, Stephen. "Beyond PowerPoint." *Educator's Voice* 15 Aug. 2001. <http://www.title3.net/TechTips/misusingpp.html>.

Tufte, Edward. "PowerPoint Is Evil: Power Corrupts. PowerPoint Corrupts Absolutely." *Wired Magazine* Sept. 2003. <http://www.wired.com/wired/archive/11.09/ppt2.html>.

CHAPTER 9

Chicago Manual of Style. 15th ed. Chicago: U of Chicago P, 2003.

The Concise Rules of APA Style. APA, 2005.

Cone, Justin. "Building on the Past." <http://justincone.com/main.html>.

Gibaldi, Joseph. *MLA Handbook for the Writers of Research Papers.* 6th ed. New York: Modern Language Association, 2003.

Goodwin, Doris Kearns. "How I Caused That Story." *Time* 27 January 2002. *Publication Manual of the American Psychological Association.* 5th ed. APA, 2001. *Scientific Style and Format.* 7th ed. Reston, VA: Council of Science Editors, 2006.

CHAPTER 10

Atkinson, Michael. *Tattooed: The Sociogenesis of a Body Art.* Toronto: U of Toronto P, 2003.

Atlas, Charles. "The Insult That Made a Man Out of 'Mac.'" <http://www.charlesatlas.com/classicads5.htm>.

"Cultural Differences Seen in Male Perceptions of Body Image," *All Things Considered.* National Public Radio, March 15, 2005.

DeMello, Margo. "'Not Just for Bikers Anymore': Popular Representations of American Tattooing" Journal of Popular Culture." *The Journal of Popular Culture.* 29.3 (Winter 1995): 37–52.

Franke-Folstad, Kim. "G.I. Joe's Big Biceps Are Not a Big Deal." *Rocky Mountain News.* May 24, 1999.

Ganahl, Jane. "Curves, Confidence, and Style." *San Francisco Chronicle* April 3, 2005. M2.

LaFerla, Ruth. "Wearing Their Beliefs on Their Chests." The *New York Times* March 29, 2005. 7.

McClelland, Susan. "Distorted Images: Western Cultures Are Exporting Their Dangerous Obsession with Thinness." *Maclean's* Aug. 14, 2000. 41–46.

Mitchell, Paul. "Faith and Fashion." *BreakPoint,* June 1, 2005.

Orbach, Susie. "Fat Is an Advertising Issue." *Campaign,* June 17, 2005.

PETA, "Think Ink, Not Mink" <http://www.petacatalog.org/prodinfo.asp?number=SKN172&variation=&aitem=2&mit>.

Pope, Harrison Jr., Robert Olivardia, Amanda Gruber, and John Borowieki, "Evolving Ideals of Male Body Image as Seen through Action Toys" *International Journal of Eating Disorders* 26 (1999): 65–72.

Riviello, John. "What If Barbie Was an Actual Person?" <http://www.johnriviello.com/bodyimage/barbie.html>.

Satrapi, Marjane. *Persepolis: The Story of A Childhood.* NY: Random House, 2003.

Stetz, Michael. "Overpowered." *The San Diego Union-Tribune.* March 19, 2005. E1.

Udovitch, Mim. "A Secret Society of the Starving" *The New York Times* September 8, 2002. 14.

CHAPTER 11

Boyd, Todd. *Young, Black, Rich and Famous.* NY: Doubleday, 2003.

Brkic, Courtney Angela. "Group Therapy: A Nation Is Born." *National Geographic.* <http://www7.nationalgeographic.com/ngm/0606/feature1/#croatia>.

Dreifus, Claudia. "Olympian Talent, and a Little Artificial Help: A Conversation with Thomas H. Murray." *The New York Times* August 3, 2004.

Jones, Thomas. "Ode to Maradona: Falklands' Revenge." *National Geographic.* <http://www7.nationalgeographic.com/ngm/0606/feature1/#argentina>.

Juffer, Jane. "Who's the Man? Sammy Sosa, Latinos, and Televisual Redefinitions of the 'American' Pastime." *Journal of Sport & Social Issues.* 26.4 (2002) 337–359.

Leonard, David. "Yo Yao! What Does the 'Ming Dynasty' Tell Us about Race and Transnational Diplomacy in the NBA?" *Colorlines Magazine.* Summer 2003.

Mumford, Thad. "The New Minstrel Show: Black Vaudeville with Statistics." *New York Times.* May 23, 2004. 11.

Shapin, Steven. "Clean Up Hitters: The Steroid Wars and the Nature of What's Natural." *The New Yorker.* April 18, 2005.

Sokolove, Mike. "Drug in Sport: The Shape to Come." *Observer.* Feb 8, 2004. 50.

Tilin, Andrew. "Ready, Set, Mutate!" *Wired* September 2000.

Wensing, Emma. "Olympics in an Age of Global Broadcasting." *Yale Global.* August 10, 2004.

CHAPTER 12

Aoki, Keith, James Boyle, and Jennifer Jenkins. *Bound by Law?* Center for the Study of the Public Domain. 2006. <http://www.law.duke.edu/cspd/comics/digital.php>.

Creative Commons, "Licenses Explained." <http://creativecommons.org/about/licenses/comics1/>.

Dawson, Bret. "The Privatization of Our Culture." Shift.com <http://shift.com/content/10.1/50/1.html>.
Eisner, Michael. "Address Before Members of the United States Congress." <http://www.mpaa.org/copyright/>.
Forsythe, Todd. "Food Chain Barbie" <http://www.illegal-art.org/print/popups/forsythe.html>.
Frere-Jones, Sasha. "The New Math of Mashups." *The New Yorker*. January 10 2005.
Grossman, Lev. "It's All Free! Music! Movies! TV Shows!" *Time Magazine*. May 5 2003.
Healey, John and Richard Cromelin, "When Copyright Law Meets the 'Mash-up.'" *LA Times*. March 21 2004. <http://www.soundcommons.org/Members/CindyBernard/documents/LAT.3.21.html>.
Lessig, Lawrence. "Free Culture." Keynote. OSCON 2002. <http://www.oreillynet.com/pub/a/policy/2002/08/15/lessig.html?page=1>.
Mann, Charles C. "Who Will Own Your Next Great Idea?" *The Atlantic* September 1998.
Matthews, Scott. "Copying Isn't Cool." Salon.com. September 12, 2003. <http://www.salon.com/tech/feature/2003/09/12/file_sharing_one/print.html>.
Schultz, Jason. "File Sharing Must Be Made Legal." Salon.com. September 12, 2003. <http://www.salon.com/tech/feature/2003/09/12/file_sharing_two/print.html>.
Terrell, Kenneth and Seth Rosen. "A Nation of Pirates." *US News & World Report*. July 14 2003: 40–42.
Werde, Bill. "Hijacking Harry Potter, Quidditch Broom and All." *New York Times* June 7 2004.

CHAPTER 13

Cassell, Justine and Henry Jenkins, Eds. "An Interview with Nancie S. Martin (Mattel)" *From Barbie to Mortal Combat*. MA: MIT Press, 1998.
Cobbett, Richard. "Writing a 'Girls in Gaming' Article." http://www.richardcobbett.co.uk/codex/articlelibrary/filingcabinet/writing_a_girls_in_games_article/.
Downing, Jim. "Army to Potential Recruits: Wanna Play?" *Seattle Times*. December 7 2004. A1.
Fazzone, Amanda. "Game Over." *The New Republic*. July 2 2001.
Flower, Zoe. "Getting the Girl; The Myths, Misconceptions, and Misdemeanors of Females in Games." Gamespy.com. January 1 2005.
Foster, Andrea. "Video Games with a Political Message." *The Chronicle of Higher Education* October 29 2004.
Frasca, Gonzalo. "Ideological Videogames: Press Left Button to Dissent." Digital Games Research Association. November 2003. <http://www.igda.org/columns/ivorytower/ivory_Nov03.php>.
—. "Playing for the White House." *Interact* 11. <http://www.interact.com.pt/11/int11int-GFrasca.htm>.
Jones, Gerard. "Violent Media is Good for Kids." *Mother Jones* June 28 2000.
Kennedy, Helen W. "Lara Croft: Feminist Icon or Cyberbimbo?" *Game Studies* December 2002. <http://www.gamestudies.org/0202/kennedy/>.
Laber, Emily. "Men are From Quake, Women are from Ultima." *The New York Times*. January 11 2001.
Provenzo, Eugene F., Jr. Testimony before the Senate Commerce Committee Hearing on the "Impact of Interactive Violence on Children." <http://commerce.senate.gov/hearings/0321pro.pdf>.
Ratan, Suneel. "Game Makers Aren't Chasing Women." Wired.com July 15, 2003. <http://www.wired.com/news/games/0,2101,59620,00.html>.
Ray, Sheri Graner. *Gender Inclusive Game Design - Expanding the Market*. Charles River Media, 2003.
Reichhardt, Tony. "Video Violence: Playing with fire?" *Nature* July 2003.
Ruberg, Bonnie. "Games for Girls." *Planet Gamecube*. February 10 2005.
Ryan, Joan. "Army's War Game Recruits Kids." *San Francisco Chronicle*. September 23 2004.
Schleiner, Anne-Marie. "Velvet-Strike: War Times and Reality Games." OpenSourcery.net. <http://www.opensorcery.net/velvet-strike/about.html>.
Taylor, T.L. *Play Between Worlds: Exploring Online Game Culture*. MA: MIT Press, 2006.
Thompson, Clive. "The Making of an X Box Warrior." *The New York Times* August 22 2004.
Terdiman, Daniel. "Playing Games with a Conscience." *Wired* April 22 2004.

CHAPTER 14

Cox, Patrick. "*America 24/7*: A Family Photograph Album." *The Digital Journalist*. November 2003.
Fleetwood, Nicole. "Carrie Mae Weems Brings Love to Harlem." *Black Renaissance/Renaissance Noire* Summer 2003.
Glaser, Mark. "Did London Bombings Turn Citizen Journalists into Citizen Paparazzi?" Online Journalism Review. July 13 2005. <http://www.ojr.org/ojr/stories/050712glaser/>.

Halstead, Dirck. "David Leeson Has Seen Hell" *The Digital Journalist* March 2005 <http://www.digitaljournalist.org/issue0503/halstead_leeson.html>.

Lester, Paul Martin. "The Merger of Photojournalism and Ethics" *Photojournalism: An Ethical Approach* NJ: Lawrence Erlbaum Associates, 1991.

Mieszkowski, Katharine. "The Friendster of Photo Sites." Salon.com December 2004.

Miliard, Mike. "I Like to Watch: Video Blogging Is Ready for Its Close up." *The Boston Phoenix* December 2005.

Okrent, Daniel. "No Picture Tells the Truth. The Best Do Better Than That." *New York Times* January 9, 2005: 2.S.

Porter, Charles. "Tragedy in Oklahoma" BBC News May 9 2005. <http://news.bbc.co.uk/go/pr/fr/-/1/hi/world/americas/4529389.stm>.

Ryan, Catherine. "Photographing the Unfamous" In.Flux 2004, an online magazine featuring articles produced by students at the University of Oregon School of Journalism & Communication. http://influx.uoregon.edu/2004/html/mem.html.

Skenazy, Lenore. "Don't Smile for the Camera." *The Daily News.* January 25 2003.

Smith, Terence. "War, Live" News Hour Extra. March 27 2003.

Sontag, Susan. "America, Seen Through Photographs, Darkly." *New York Review of Books* November 15 1973.

Strupp, Joe. "The Photo Felt around the World" *Editor & Publisher,* May 13, 1995: 12.

CHAPTER 15

Barney, Cliff. "Think Locally, Act Globally." Salon.com April 14, 2004.

Behlendorf, Brian. "How Outsourcing Will Save the World." *Salon* July 8, 2003.

Davicsin, Joseph. "Corporations Leave Small Business Behind" *The Daily Targum*, Rutgers University, October 16, 2002.

Dobbs, Lou. "Exporting America: False Choices." CNNMoney.com March 2004. <http://money.cnn.com/2004/03/09/commentary/dobbs/dobbs/>.

Elliot, Michael. "What Globalization Has Done for You Lately." *Time Magazine* August 13, 2001. <http://www.time.com/time/columnist/elliott/article/0,9565,170970,00.html>.

Feine, Paul. "McBastards: McDonald's and Globalization" A World Connected <http://www.aworldconnected.org/Stories/id.113/story_detail.asp>.

Friedman, Thomas L. "It's a Flat World, After All." *The New York Times* April 3 2005.

Interview with George Ritzer. One-Off Productions. February 1997. <http://www.mcspotlight.org/people/interviews/ritzer_george.html>.

Jarvis, Michael. "The Godzilla-Sized Appeal of Japan's Pop Culture." *LA Times* October 2003.

Klein, Naomi. "Outsourcing the Friedman." *The Nation* March 4, 2004.

"KFC and McDonald's: A Model of Blended Culture." *The China Daily* June 1 2004.

McLaughlin, Laurianne. "An eye on India: outsourcing debate continues." *Software IEEE* 20.3 (May–June 2003): 114–117.

Napier, Susan Jolliffe. *Anime: From Akira to Princess Mononoke.* Palgrave Macmillan, 2001.

Rice-Oxley, Mark. "In 2,000 Years, Will the World Remember Disney or Plato?" *Christian Science Monitor.* January 15, 2004.

Samant, Sapna. "Appropriating Bombay Cinema" *Metro Magazine* 145 (summer 2005): 82(5).

Sklarsky, Jeremy. "Globalization or McDonaldization?" *The Daily Targum*, Rutgers University, October 17, 2002.

Wells, David H. "Gateways of India's Globalization." *APF Reporter* (21.1) <http://www.aliciapatterson.org/APF2101/Wells/Wells.html>.

Credits

IMAGES

Page v: Copyright 2004 Nick Anderson. All rights reserved. Reprinted with permission of Nick Anderson in conjunction with Washington Post Writers Group and the Cartoonist Group.
Page 1: Abed Omar Qusini/Reuters.
Figure 2.1: Photograph by Alyssa J. O'Brien.
Figure 2.2: Courtesy of RUSK PROFESSIONAL HAIRCARE.
Figure 2.4: © Chevron Corporation and used with permission.
Figure 2.5: ©The Procter & Gamble Company. Used by permission.
Figure 2.6: Courtesy of Volkswagen of America, Inc.
Figure 2.7: Photograph by Alyssa J. O'Brien.
Figure 2.9: Photograph by Alyssa J. O'Brien.
Figure 2.10: General Motors Corp. Used with permission. GM Media Archives.
Figure 2.11: Courtesy of Ford Motor Company.
Figure 2.12: © The American Legacy Foundation.
Figure 2.13: Image courtesy of The Advertising Archives.
Figure 3.1 and page vi: AP Images/Eric Gay.
Figure 3.2: Margaret Bourke-White/Time & Life Pictures/Getty Images.
Figure 3.3: Todd Heisler/Polaris Images.
Figure 3.4: Library of Congress.
Figure 3.5: Library of Congress.
Figure 3.6: Bettmann/CORBIS.
Figure 3.7: "Triathlon Start," Harvey's Lake, Pa., 1994. © Mark Cohen.
Figure 3.8: "By a Nose" Philadelphia, Pa., 1980. Photograph Copyright NORMON Y. LONO.
Figure 3.9: "Girl on a Swing" Pitt Street, NYC, 1938. Photograph by Walter Rosenblum.
Figure 3.10: Cordell Hauglie.
Figure 3.12: Courtesy of Deseret Morning News Archives.
Page 69: AP Images/Laurent Rebours.
Figure 3.13: Abed Omar Qusini/Reuters.
Figure 3.14: Courtesy *Boston Herald*.
Page 83: Miramax/Photofest.
Figure 4.1 and page vi: Patrick Broderick/ModernHumorist.com.
Figure 4.2: Hoover Institution Archives Poster Collection.
Figure 4.4: Courtesy National Archives, 513533.
Figure 4.5: Courtesy National Archives, 516102.
Figure 4.6: Courtesy National Archives, 514597.
Figure 4.7: Library of Congress.
Figure 4.8: The Art Archive / Musée des 2 Guerres Mondiales Paris/ Dagli Orti.
Figure 4.9: Library of Congress.
Figure 4.10: Image courtesy of The Advertising Archives.
Figure 4.14: Courtesy of Micah Ian Wright & AntiWarPosters.com.
Figure 4.15: © 2003—WHITEHOUSE.ORG.
Figure 4.16: Courtesy of Steve Horn.
Figure 4.17: Courtesy of Micah Ian Wright & AntiWarPosters.com.
Page 105: Courtesy National Archives, 513533.
Figure 5.1 and page vii: ArcticNet—NCE/Time & Life Pictures/ Getty Images.
Figure 5.2: Cover text only from SCIENCE Vol. 311, No. 5768 (24 March 2006). Reprinted with permission from AAAS. Photo: Nevada Wier/CORBIS.
Figure 5.3: Time & Life Pictures/Getty Images.
Figure 5.4: Steve Bronstein/The Image Bank/Getty Images.
Figure 5.5: *Rocket Blitz from the Moon* by Chesley Bonestell. Bonestell Space Art.
Figure 5.6: Time & Life Pictures/Getty Images.
Figure 5.12: *Stem Cells*, March 2006 cover © AlphaMed Press.
Figure 5.13: Courtesy of the Yale Scientific Magazine.
Figure 5.18: Still courtesy of COMEDY CENTRAL.
Figure 6.1 and page vii: Courtesy of Universal Studios Licensing LLLP.
Figure 6.4: Miramax/Photofest.
Figure 6.5: Lions Gate/Photofest.
Page 182: Warner Bros./Photofest.
Page 183 (left): Danjaq/Eon/UA/The Kobal Collection/Keith Hamshere.
Page 183 (right): Paramount/Icon/The Kobal Collection/Andrew Cooper.
Figure 7.8: Reproduced with the kind permission of The Body Shop International, plc.
Figure 7.9: Courtesy www.adbusters.org.
Figure 8.1 and page ix: AP Images.
Page 208 (left): AP Images/Vince Bucci/Pool.
Page 208 (center): Paramount Classics/Photofest.
Page 208 (right): AP Images/Jason Reed/Pool.
Figure 8.2: © Die Höge, 1999. Photo by Monika Beyer.
Figure 8.3: AP Images/Paul Sakuma.
Figure 8.17: Bettmann/CORBIS.
Figure 8.18: Topham/The Image Works.
Figure 9.1 and page ix: *Building on the Past* by Justin Cone.
Figure 10.1 and page x: WireImageStock/Masterfile Corporation.
Figure 10.2: Brand X Pictures/Fotosearch.
Figure 10.8: Image courtesy of The Advertising Archives.
Figure 10.9: Fernanda Calfat/Getty Images.
Figure 10.10: Kate Brooks/Polaris Images.
Figure 10.11: Courtesy of PETA.
Figure 10.12: Courtesy of Scott Veldhoen.
Figure 10.13: Amessé Photography, amessephoto.com.
Figure 10.16: Arely D. Castillo/The News-Star.
Figure 11.1 and page xi: Time & Life Pictures/Getty Images.
Figure 11.7: Courtesy of Speedo.
Figure 11.8: Steven Harris/Newsmakers/Getty Images.
Figure 11.9: Gideon Mendel/CORBIS.
Figure 11.10: AP Images/Themba Hadebe.
Figure 11.11: © 2005 NBA Entertainment/Courtesy Everett Collection.
Figure 11.12: Mark Fredrickson/Sports Illustrated.
Figure 11.13: TK.
Figure 11.14: Walter Iooss, Jr./Sports Illustrated.
Figure 11.15: AP Images/Sports Illustrated.
Figure 11.16: John Biever/Sports Illustrated.
Figure 12.18: Courtesy of Justin Hampton.
Figure 12.20: Courtesy of Panic Struck Productions, Original Artwork by Sonia Hillios.
Figure 13.1 and page xiii: Courtesy of Electronic Arts.
Figure 13.2: Courtesy of Eidos.
Figure 13.5: Copyright ©2005 Majesco Entertainment Corp. All Rights Reserved. The BloodRayne logo, characters and artwork are trademarks of Majesco Entertainment Corp.
Figure 13.6: Red Ninja: End of Honor and the Red Ninja: End of Honor logo are registereed trademarks of Vivendi Games, Inc., and are used with the permission of Vivendi Games, Inc.
Figure 13.8: Jon Haddock/whitelead.com.Figure.
Figure 13.11: Courtesy of Kuma Games.
Figure 13.12: Created by Ian Bogost for Videogames with an Agenda Exhibition, 2004.
Figure 14.1 and page xiv: Michael Ainsworth/The Dallas Morning News.
Figure 14.2: Karl Maasdam Photography.
Figure 14.4: Courtesy of Marc-Yves Regis I.
Figure 14.3: Courtesy of Rich Addicks.

Figure 14.5: Peggie Peattie/The San Diego Union-Tribune/ZUMA Press.

Page 553: Geoffrey Kula/KULAFOTO.com.

Page 554: Courtesy of Ravi Jain.

Page 556 (left): Steve Garfield, SteveGarfield.com.

Page 556 (right): Image courtesy of Amy Carpenter. http://welcometoamyville.blogspot.com/.

Figure 14.6: AP Images/Elaine Thompson.

Page 565 (both): Charles Porter/ZUMA Press.

Figure 14.7: Image taken by Adam Stacey, This work is licenced under a Creative Commons Licence.

Figure 14.8: Scoopt.com.

Figure 14.9: David Leeson/The Dallas Morning News.

Figure 14.10: David Leeson/The Dallas Morning News.

Figure 14.11: David Leeson/The Dallas Morning News.

Figure 14.12: David Leeson/The Dallas Morning News.

Figure 15.1 and page xv: Courtesy of Axel Feuerberg.

Figure 15.3: Used with permission from McDonald's Corporation.

Figure 15.4: Used with permission from McDonald's Corporation.

Figure 15.5: Miramax/Photofest.

Figure 15.7: Jerome Kramer/Getty Images.

Page 616: David H. Wells /www.DavidHWells.com /Alicia Patterson Foundation.

Figure 15.8: Courtesy of Warner Bros/Bureau L.A. Collection/CORBIS.

Figure 15.9: Michael Newman/PhotoEdit Inc.

Page 650: Photo by Cliff Barney, first published in Salon, http://www.Salon.com.

TEXT

AAAS. Screen shot of AAAS Science & policy web page http://www.aaas.org/spp/sfrl/projects/stem/index.shtml. Reprinted with permission from AAAS.

"American Alphabet" by Heidi Cody, 2000. http://www.heidicody.com. Reprinted by permission of Heidi Cody.

"And Now, a Game from Our Sponsor," *The Economist*, June 9, 2005. © 2005 The Economist Newspaper Ltd. All rights reserved. Reprinted with permission. Further reproduction prohibited. www.economist.com.

Aoki, Keith, James Boyle, Jennifer Jenkins. Reprinted from Bound By Law, available online at http://www.law.duke.edu/cspd/comics/, by Keith Aoki, James Boyle, and Jennifer Jenkins, copyright © 2006. By permission.

Barney, Cliff. "Think Locally, Act Globally." This article first appeared in *Salon.com*, April 14, 2004, at http://www.Salon.com. An online version remains in the Salon archives. Reprinted with permission.

Behlendorf, Brian. "How Outsourcing Will Save the World," *Salon.com*, July 8, 2003.

Bodarky, George. "Tattooing Their Grief." WFUV FM radio transcript aired September 2002. http://www.wfuv.org. Reprinted by permission of George Bodarky, WFUV FM, Bronx, NY.

Bowen, Laurence and Jill Schmid. "Minority Presence and Portrayal in Mainstream Magazine Advertising: An Update," *Journal and Mass Communication Quarterly*, 74:1, 134–146.

Boyd, Todd. "Doin Me" from *Young, Black, Rich & Famous: The Rise of the NBA, The Hip Hop Invasion and the Transformation of American Culture* by Todd Boyd. Copyright © 2003 by Todd Boyd. Used by permission of Doubleday, a division of Random House, Inc.

Brkic, Courtney Angela. "Group Therapy: A Nation Is Born" as appeared in National Geographic June 2006, excerpted from "Croatia," pp. 96–100 from *The Thinking Fan's Guide to the World Cup*, edited by Matt Weiland and Sean Wilsey. Copyright © 2006 by Trim Tables LLC. Reprinted by permission of HarperCollins Publishers.

CNN.com. Screen shot CNN.com "The Stem Cell Debate" from http://www.cnn.com/SPECIALS/2001/stemcell/. ©2003 Cable News Network LP, LLLP. All rights reserved. Reprinted with permission.

Cobbett, Richard. "Writing a 'Girls in Gaming' Article." Originally written in Richard Cobbett's online journal. http://www.richardcobbett.co.uk. Reprinted by permission of the author.

Cox, Patrick. "America 24/7: A Family Photograph Album," *The Digital Journalist*, November 2003. Reprinted by permission of the author.

Cromelin, Richard. And Healcy, John. "When Copyright Law Meets the 'Mash-Up'" from *The Los Angeles Times*, March 21, 2004. Copyright © 2004 The Los Angeles Times. Reprinted by permission.

Curtis, James. "Dorothea Lange, Migrant Mother, and the Culture of the Great Depression," *Winterthur Portfolio*, 1986, 21. 1:2.

Davicsin, Joseph. "Corporations Leave Small Business Behind," *The Daily Targum*, October 16, 2002. By permission of The Daily Targum.

Dawson, Brett. "The Privatization of Our Culture" from *Shift* (2002). Reprinted by permission of the author.

DeMello, Marge. "'Not Just for Bikers Anymore': Popular Representations of American Tattooing," *Journal of Popular Culture*, 29 (3) 1995: 37–53. Reprinted by permission of the publisher, Blackwell Publishing Ltd.

"Do No Harm" screen shot from http://www.stemcellresearch.org/. Reprinted by permission from Do No Harm: The Coalition of Americasns for Research Ethics.

Downing, Jim. "Army to Potential Recruits: Wanna Play?" from *The Seattle Times*, December 7, 2004. Copyright 2004, Seattle Times Company. Used with permission.

Dreifus, Claudia. "Olympian Talent, and a Little Artificial Help: A Conversation with Thomas H. Murray," *The New York Times*, August 3, 2004. Copyright © 2004 by The New York Times Co. Reprinted with permission.

Dunn, Geoffrey. From "Documentary Photography from the Outside In: Dorothea Lange and Migrant Mother," *Deconstructing Documentary: theory and Practice in Documentary Film and Photography*, a dissertation submitted in partial satisfaction of the requirements for the degree of *Doctor of Philosophy in Sociology*, September 2004, pp. 106–11. Reprinted by permission of the author.

Eisner, Michael. Address before U.S. Congress, June 7, 2000.

Ephron, Nora. "The Boston Photographs," from *Scribble, Scribble: Notes on the Media*. Copyright © 1978 by Nora Ephron. Reprinted by permission of International Creative Management, Inc.

Fazzone, Amanda. "Game Over," *The New Republic*, July 2, 2001. Reprinted by permission of The New Republic, © 2001, The New Republic LLC.

Flower, Zoe. "Getting the Girl, The Myths, Misconceptions, and Misdemeanors of Females in Games." Reprinted from http://www.1up.com, January 2005, with permission. Copyright © 2005 Ziff Davis Publishing Holdings Inc. All rights reserved.

Frag Dolls. © 2007 Ubisoft Entertainment. All rights reserved. Frag Dolls, Ubisoft, Ubi.com and the Ubisoft logo are trademarks of Ubisoft Entertainment in the US and/or other countries. Used by permission.

Franke-Folstad, Kim. "G.I. Joe's Big Biceps Are Not a Big Deal," *Rocky Mountain News*, May 24, 1999. Reprinted by permission of Rocky Mountain News.

Frasca, Gonzalo. "Ideological Videogames: Press Left Button to Dissent." Published in the "Ivory Tower" column of the International Game Developers Association, November 2003. Copyright © Gonzalo Frasca. Reprinted by permission of the author.

Frere-Jones, Sasha. "The New Math of Mashups" from *The New Yorker*, January 10, 2005. Reprinted by permission of the author.

Friedman, Thomas L. "It's a Flat World, After All" appeared in The New York Times Magazine, April 3, 2005 and was adapted by the author from his book, *The World Is Flat: A Brief History of the Twenty-First Century* by Thomas L. Friedman. Copyright © 2005 by Thomas L. Friedman. Reprinted by permission of Farrar, Straus and Giroux, LLC.

Ganahl, "Curves, Confidence, and Style," *San Francisco Chronicle*, April 3, 2005. Copyright 2005 by San Francisco Chronicle. Reproduced with permission of San Francisco Chronicle in the format Textbook via Copyright Clearance Center.

Glaser, Mark. "Did London Bombings Turn Citizen Journalists into Citizen Paparazzi?" from *Online Journalism Review*, July 13, 2005.

Goodwin, Doris Kearns. "How I Caused That Story," *Time*, January 27, 2002. © 2002 Time, Inc. Reprinted by permission.

Gottesman, Jane. Screen shots from the online version of *Game Face*, found at http://washingtonpost.com/wp-srv.photo.onassignment.gameFace/. Reprinted by permission of Game Face Productions.

Graner Ray, Sheri. "But What If the Player is Female?" from *Gender Inclusive Game Design: Expanding the Market*, 1st edition by Graner Ray. © 2004. Reprinted with permission of Delmar learning, a division of Thomson Learning: http://www.thomsonrights.com Fax 800-730-2215.

Grossman, Lev. "It's All Free! Music! Movies! TV Shows!" from *Time*, May 5, 2003. © 2003 Time Inc. Reprinted by permission. TIME is a registered trademark of Time Inc. All rights reserved.

Halstead, Dirck. "David Leeson Has Seen Hell," *The Digital Journalist*, March 2005. Reprinted by permission of the author.

Holkins, Jerry. Blog entry for "The Hipness Threshold," from *Penny Arcade*, March 12, 2004. Reprinted by permission.

Huntington, Samuel P. Excerpt from "Under God." Reprinted from *The Wall Street Journal*, June 16, 2004. © 2004 Dow Jones & Company. All rights reserved. By permission of The Wall Street Journal and the author.

"Interview with George Ritzer," February 1997, from the documentary "McLibel." Reprinted by permission of Spanner Films Ltd, http://www.spannerfilms.net.

Jackson, Bruce. "Other Voices: Some Words About Those Pictures." Sent by Bruce Jackson, Buffalo, January 9, 2005. Published January 16, 2005 in *The New York Times*. Reprinted by permission of Professor Bruce Jackson.

Jarvis, Michael T. "The Godzilla-Sized Appeal of Japan's Pop Culture," *Los Angeles Times Magazine*, 10/26/03. Reprinted by permission of the author.

Jianghong, Qiu. "KFC and McDonald's: A Model of Blended Culture," *China Today*, June 1, 2004. http://www.chinatoday.com. Reprinted by permission of China Today.

Jolliffe Napier, Susan. From *Anime from Akira to Princess Mononoke: Experiencing Contemporary Japanese Animation*. Copyright © Susan J. Napier 2001. Published by Palgrave. Reproduced with permission of PalgraveMacmillan.

Jones, Gerard. "Violent Media Is Good for Kids." Reprinted with permission from MotherJones.com, where it was originally published on June 28, 2000. © 2000, Foundation for National Progress.

Jones, Thomas. "Ode to Maradona: Falkland's Revenge" as appeared in *National Geographic* June 2006, excerpted from "Argentina," pp. 50–55 from The Thinking Fan's Guide to the World Cup, edited by Matt Weiland and Sean Wilsey. Copyright © 2006 by Trim Tables LLC. Reprinted by permission of HarperCollins Publishers.

Juffer, Jane. Excerpt from "Who's the Man? Sammy Sosa, Latinos, and Televisual Redefinitions of the 'American Pastime,'" *Journal of Sport & Social Issues* 26 (4) 2002: 337–342. Copyright © 2002. Reprinted by permission of Sage Publications, Inc.

Kennedy, Helen W. "Lara Croft: Feminist Icon or Cyberbimbo?" from *Game Studies*, December 2002. Reprinted by permission of the author.

Klein, Naomi. "Outsourcing the Friedman." Copyright © 2004 by Naomi Klein. Reprinted by permission of Klein Lewis Productions Ltd.

LaFerla, Ruth. "Wearing Their Beliefs on Their Heads," *The New York Times*, March 29, 2005. Copyright © 2005 by The New York Times Co. Reprinted with permission.

Lehrer, Jim. "Pros and Cons of Embedded Journalism" by Jim Lehrer, NewsHour Extra, March 27, 2003. Copyright © 2003 Mac-Neil-Lehrer Productions. All rights reserved. Reprinted with permission.

Leonard, David. "Yo Yao! What Does the 'Ming Dynasty' Tell Us about Race and Transitional Diplomacy in the NBA" from *ColorLines* 6.2 (2003) 34–36. Reprinted by permission of *ColorLines Magazine*, http://www.colorlines.com.

Lessig, Lawrence. "Free Culture," speech delivered at the July 2002 Open Source Convention. Reprinted by permission of Lawrence Lessig.

"Licenses Explained," 3 images from Creative Commons web site http://creativecommons.org. Reprinted with permission.

Mann, Charles C. from "Who Will Own Your Next Good Idea." © 1998 Charles C. Mann, first published in The Atlantic Monthly, September 1998. Reprinted by permission of the author.

Marlette, Doug. "I Was a Tool of Satan." Reprinted from *Columbia Journalism Review*, November/December 2003. © 2003 by Columbia Journalism Review. Reprinted by permission of the publisher and the author.

Marlette, Doug. "What Would Mohammed Drive?" Cartoon courtesy of Doug Marlette.

Matthews, Scott. "Copying Isn't Cool." This article first appeared in *Salon.com*, September 12, 2003, at http://www.Salon.com. An online version remains in the Salon archives. Reprinted with permission.

McClelland, Susan, "Distorted Images: Western Cultures Are Exporting Their Dangerous Obsession with Thinness," *Maclean's Magazine*, February 22, 1999. Reprinted by permission of Maclean's.

McLaughlin, Laurianne. "An Eye on India: Outsourcing Debate Continues." © 2003 IEEE. Reprinted, with permission, from *IEEE Software*, May/June, 2003.

Mieszkowski, Katharine. "The Friendster of Photo Sites." This article first appeared in *Salon.com*, December 20, 2004, at http://www.Salon.com. An online version remains in the Salon archives. Reprinted with permission.

Miliard, Mike. "I Like to Watch: Video Blogging Is Ready for Its Close Up," *The Boston Phoenix*, December 2005. © Boston Phoenix, Inc. Reprinted by permission.

Mitchell, Paul. "Faith and Fashion." From *BreakPoint*, June 1, 2005. Reprinted with permission of Prison Fellowship, http://www.breakpoint.org.

Mumford, Thad. "The New Minstrel Show: Black Vaudeville with Statistics," *The New York Times*, May 23, 2004. Copyright © 2004, The New York Times Co. Reprinted with permission.

National Eating Disorders Association. Ad used with permission from the National Eating Disorders Association. Copyright © National Eating Disorders Association. All Rights Reserved. http://www.NationalEatingDisorders.org. Toll-free Helpline 1-800-931-2237.

National Public Radio. *All Things Considered*: Transcript "Cultural Differences Seen in Male Perceptions of Body Image," March 15, 2005. © 2006, National Public Radio, Inc. Reprinted with permission.

Okrent, Daniel. "The Public Editor; No Picture Tells the Truth. The Best Do Better Than That," *The New York Times*, January 9, 2005. Copyright © 2005, The New York Times Co. Reprinted with permission.

"Olympic Drug Testing." Graphic from CBSNews.com "Dope & Glory," http://www.cbsnews.com. Reprinted by permission of CBS News, a Division of CBS Inc.

Orbach, Susie, "Fat Is an Advertising Issue," *Campaign*, June 17, 2005. Reproduced from *Campaign* magazine with the permission of the copyright owner, Haymarket Business Publications Limited.

Playing Unfair. Transcript of documentary film *Playing Unfair* (2002) with Mary Jo Kane, Pat Griffin, and Michael Messner, produced by the Media Education Foundation, from http://www.mediaed.org. Reprinted with permission.

Pope, Harrison Jr. et al. "Evolving Ideals of Male Body Image As Seen Through Action Toys," *International Journal of Eating Disorders*, July

1999, Vol. 26, No. 1, pp. 65–72. Reprinted by permission of John Wiley & Sons, Inc.

Porter, Charles. "Picture Power: Tragedy in Oklahoma," *BBC News Online*, May 9, 2005. Reprinted by permission of the author.

Provenzo, Eugene F. Testimony before the U.S. Senate, March 21, 2000.

Ratan, Suneel. "Game Makers Aren't Chasing Women," *Wired News*, July 15, 2003. Copyright © 2006 Condé Nast Publications. All rights reserved. Originally published in *Wired News* Online. Reprinted by permission.

Rice-Oxley, Mark. "In 2000 Years, Will the World Remember Disney or Plato?" Reproduced with permission from the January 15, 2004 issue of The Christian Science Monitor (http://www.csmonitor.com). © 2004 The Christian Science Monitor. All rights reserved.

Riviello, John. "More Than Just Dolls" from *What If Barbie Was an Actual Person?* A flash movie by John Riviello. Reprinted with permission. http://www.johnriviello.com/bodyimage/barbie.html.

Ruberg, Bonnie. "Games for Girls," *Planet GameCube* (now known as *Nintendo World Report*), February 10, 2005, http://www.nintendoworldreport.com. Reprinted by permission of Nintendo World Report.

Samant, Sapna. "Appropriating Bombay Cinema: Why the Western World Gets Bollywood So Wrong," *Metro Magazine* 145 (Summer 2005): 82. Reprinted by permission of Metro Magazine, http://www.metromagazine.com.au.

Schleiner, Anne-Marie. "Velvet-Strike: War Times and Reality Games" (2002). http://www.opensorcery.net/velvet-strike/about.html. Reprinted by permission of Anne-Marie Schleiner.

Schultz, Jason. "File Sharing Must Be Made Legal," *Salon.com*, September 12, 2003. Reprinted by permission of the author.

Shapin, Steven. "Clean Up Hitters: The Steroid Wars and the Nature of What's Natural," *The New Yorker*, April 18, 2005. Reprinted by permission of the author.

Skenazy, Lenore. "Don't Smile for the Camera," *New York Daily News*, January 5, 2005. © New York Daily News, L.P. Reprinted with permission.

Sklarsky, Jeremy. "Globalization or McDonaldization," *The Daily Targum*, October 17, 2002. By permission of the Daily Targum.

Sokolove, Michael. "The Shape to Come" from *The Observer Sports Magazine*, adapted from "In Pursuit of Doped Excellence: The Lab Animal," *The New York Times Magazine*, January 18, 2004. Copyright © 2004 by Michael Sokolove. Reprinted by permission of The New York Times Syndication Sales Corp.

Sontag, Susan. "America, Seen through Photographs, Darkly," from *On Photography* by Susan Sontag. Copyright © 1977 by Susan Sontag. Reprinted by permission of Farrar, Straus and Giroux, LLC.

"Spectrum of Rights" image from Creative Commons web site http://creativecommons.org. Reprinted with permission.

Stem Cell Research Foundation. Screen shot from http://www.stemcellresearchfoundation.org. Image appears courtesy of the Stem Cell Research Foundation.

Stetz, Michael. "Overpowered" from *The San Diego Union-Tribune*, March 19, 2005. By permission of The San Diego Union-Tribune.

Stevenson, Seth. "You and Your Shadow," *Slate.com*, March 2, 2004. Slate.com and Washingtonpost. Newsweek Interactive. All rights reserved. Reprinted by permission of United Media.

Strupp, Joe. "The Photo Felt Around the World," *Editor & Publisher*, May 1995. © Nielsen Business Media, Inc. Reprinted by permission of Nielsen Business Media.

Terdiman, Daniel. "Playing Games with a Conscience," *Wired News*, April 22, 2004. Copyright © 2006 Condé Net, a division of Condé Nast Publications. All rights reserved. Originally published in *Wired News* Online. Reprinted by permission.

TheTruth.com. "Crazyworld," screen shot from http://www.thetruth.com. Reprinted by permission of the American Legacy Foundation.

Thompson, Clive. "The Making of an Xbox Warrior," *The New York Times Magazine*, August 22, 2004. Reprinted by permission of Featurewell.com.

Tilin, Andrew. "Ready, Set, Mutate" from *Wired* 8.09, September 2000. Reprinted by permission of the author.

"Tired of Being Treated Like a Criminal for Sharing Music Online?" from http://www.eff.org/IP/P2P/music-to-our-ears.php. Included courtesy of the Electronic Frontier Foundation.

Udovitch, Mim, "A Secret Society of the Starving," *The New York Times Magazine*, September 8, 2002. Reprinted by permission of the author.

U.S. Army Office of Global Communication. "Friendship," leaflet air-dropped in Afghanistan, n.d.

Velvet-Strike. Screen shots of sprays from the Velvet-Strike website, http://www.opensorcery.net/velvet-strike/sprays.html. Reprinted by permission of Anne-Marie Schleiner.

"Velvet-Strike Intervention Recipes" from the Velvet-Strike website, http://www.opensorcery.net/velvet-strike/recipes.html. Reprinted by permission of Anne-Marie Schleiner.

Vogel, Gretchen. "Can Old Cells Learn New Tricks?" Reprinted with permission from *Science* 287: 1418-19, 25 February 2000. Copyright 2000 AAAS.

"War, Live," an interview led by Terence Smith from the March 22, 2003 edition of *NewsHour with Jim Lehrer*. Copyright © 2003 MacNeil-Lehrer Productions. All rights reserved. Reprinted with permission.

Wells, David H. "Gateways to India's Globalization," APF Reporter (2003), Vol. 21, No. 1, including photograph "Movies As a Two-Way Street." © 2003 David H. Wells. Reprinted by permission of David H. Wells.

Wensing, Emma. "Olympics in an Age of Global Broadcasting," *YaleGlobal*, August 10, 2004. Reprinted with permission from *YaleGlobal Online*, (http://yaleglobal.yale.edu) a publication of the Yale Center for the Study of Globalization. Copyright © 2004 Yale Center for the Study of Globalization.

Werde, Bill. "Hijacking Harry Potter, Quidditch Broom and All," *The New York Times*, June 7, 2004. Copyright © 2004, The New York Times Co. Reprinted with permission.

"What's Wrong with the Body Shop?" Referenced version from the "Beyond McDonald's" pages at http://www.mcspotlight.org. Original (unreferenced) version from London Greenpeace leaflet.

"You Can Click, But You Can't Hide." Copyright © 2004 Motion Picture Association of America, Inc. Reprinted by permission.

Index